The Trinity

The Trinity
Global Perspectives

Veli-Matti Kärkkäinen

Westminster John Knox Press
LOUISVILLE • LONDON

Scripture quotations from the New Revised Standard Version of the Bible are copyright © 1989 by the Division of Christian Education of the National Council of the Churches of Christ in the U.S.A. and are used by permission.

Scripture quotations from *The Holy Bible, New International Version* are copyright © 1973, 1978, 1984 International Bible Society. Used by permission of Zondervan Bible Publishers.

Book design by Sharon Adams
Cover design by Lisa Buckley
Cover art: Red Trees, *2002 Sue Jamieson/Bridgeman Art Library/Gettyimages*

First edition
Published by Westminster John Knox Press
Louisville, Kentucky

This book is printed on acid-free paper that meets the American National Standards Institute Z39.48 standard. ♾

PRINTED IN THE UNITED STATES OF AMERICA

07 08 09 10 11 12 13 14 15 — 10 9 8 7 6 5 4 3 2 1

Library of Congress Cataloging-in-Publication Data is on file at the Library of Congress, Washington, D.C.

ISBN-13: 978-0-664-22890-3
ISBN-10: 0-664-22890-9

Contents

Preface

If it can be said that "publishing a system of theology is an irremediably hubris-
tic enterprise," quoting the world-renowned Lutheran systematician Robert W.
Jenson,[1] I fear that writing a globally representative critical analysis of Trinitarian theologies including their biblical and historical developments is an enterprise beyond hubris. Some would say it is totally impossible—and more than
once, to be honest, I have told myself that and repented of ever contracting this
book project!

Each time as I thought I was approaching the end of the tunnel, I was either
reminded of a lack of interaction with another major (re)source or discovered
a publication that had just seen the light of day or found out yet another lacuna
in my learning and forced myself back to the library. At some point, however,
I had to finish the project and humbly confess what Jenson did when completing his earlier major monograph on the Trinity: "Finally, the very great historical and reflective range that I have tried to cover means that I know less than

---

1. Robert W. Jenson, *Systematic Theology*, vol. 1, *The Triune God* (Oxford: Oxford University
Press, 1997), vii.

I need to at some places; without spending my life on this book, that could not be fully rectified."[2]

Yet with all its challenges and moments of despair, walking with the masters of Trinitarian theology, both past and contemporary, has been an exceptionally fruitful and fulfilling experience. Though a longer—and more windy—journey than anticipated, it has also provided many more opportunities for growth and again and again called for patient listening as well as sharpening of intellectual skills. How well—or poorly—I have achieved my goals in all of that, I will of course leave to the judgment of the reader.

While finishing the book, I had the opportunity to lead a doctoral seminar on the topic of contemporary perspectives on the Trinity at Fuller Theological Seminary. With the students, I studied again the main works of some leading theologians, including those on which I had already finished writing the chapter. Against my own wishes, the review of their writings as well as the inspiring class presentations and discussions and students' pointed questions made me revise a number of places in my manuscript. While I take responsibility for all mistakes and limitations, I also dedicate this study with gratefulness to that special class of students. They are (in alphabetical order): Maria Doerfler (Austria), Naoki Inoue (Japan), Young-Chun Kim (South Korea), Quentin Kinnison (U.S.A.), Getachew Kiros (Ethiopia and Sweden), Lisa Lamb (U.S.A.), Kirsten Oh (U.S.A. and South Korea), Jennifer Rosner (U.S.A.), Hongxia Song (China), William Whitney (U.S.A.), and Gideon Yohannes (Ethiopia). The current Director of Fuller's Center for Advanced Theological Studies, Dr. Eugen Matei (Romania; now U.S.A.), who recently finished his PhD dissertation comparing the Reformed Jürgen Moltmann's and the Romanian Orthodox Dimitru Stăniloae's views of the Trinity in relation to community, was kind enough to sit in on the seminar with the students. During the preparation of the manuscript I was also well served by two Fuller research assistants, Tim Howerzyl, who compiled an annotated bibliography of almost eighty pages for me, and Quentin Kinnison, who checked footnotes. Two of my students, Dr. Eve Tibbs, who finished her dissertation comparing John Zizioulas's Trinitarian theology with that of Colin Gunton, and Lewis Winkler, whose doctoral dissertation topic relates to Wolfhart Pannenberg's Trinitarian theology in dialogue with contemporary Moslem theology, visited the seminar and gave superb presentations on their topics. Yet another Fuller PhD, Rob Muthiah, whose dissertation was on the implications of the doctrine of the Trinity for the priesthood of all believers in our postmodern context, shared his research with the class. To all these students, soon-to-be theological colleagues, I dedicate my book.

Another significant note of thanks goes to Susan Carlson Wood, in Fuller Seminary's School of Theology Faculty Publications Services. I have been relying

2. Robert W. Jenson, *The Triune Identity: God according to the Gospel* (Philadelphia: Fortress, 1982), xiii.

on her competent, incisive editorial work for the past six years; this is now the eighth manuscript on which she has transformed my "Finnish English" into proper written English.

This book is also special to me because this is my first publishing effort with Westminster John Knox Press. The fatherly care of Donald K. McKim, Academic and Reference Editor, has been a constant source of encouragement. When writing this book I have had an earlier WJKP title constantly open at my desk, namely, Ted Peters's *God as Trinity* (1993). While my own book falls far short of the expertise and lucidity of that work, I also feel honored to pick up more than a decade later the Trinitarian conversation so ably carried on by this leading American Lutheran theologian. Another title that has provided a number of insights and inspiration, by the late evangelical theologian Stanley J. Grenz, is *Rediscovering the Triune God* (Fortress, 2004).

From the very beginning idea of this project, many years agb, I have kept at hand the wise counsel from the bishop of Hippo, Augustine, who in the first part of his fifteen-volume *De Trinitate* makes this incisive remark:

> Thus let us enter together on the path of charity in search of whom it is said: "Seek his face evermore." This is the sacred and safe compact into which I, in the presence of the Lord our God, shall enter with those who read what I am writing, in all my writings, and especially in the present one where we are investigating the unity of the Trinity, of the Father, the Son, and the Holy Spirit. For nowhere else is the error more dangerous, the search more laborious, and the results more rewarding. (1.3.5)

Introduction

The Significance of the Doctrine of the Trinity for Theology and Christian Life

Why Study the Trinity?

"What do we think of when we hear the name of the Triune God? What ideas do we associate with the Trinity? What do we experience in the fellowship of the Father, the Son and the Holy Spirit?" These are the opening sentences in the magnum opus on the Trinity of a leading systematic theologian in our times, Jürgen Moltmann.[1] He asks further: "Why are most Christians in the West, whether they be Catholics or Protestants, really only 'monotheists' where the experience and practice of their faith is concerned? Whether God is one or triune evidently makes as little difference to the doctrine of faith as it does to ethics."[2] Moltmann echoes here the sentiments of many, for example, the Roman Catholic Karl Rahner, who once remarked, "We must be willing to admit that, should the doctrine of the Trinity have to be dropped as false, the major part of religious literature could well remain virtually unchanged."[3] A number of other contemporary theologians have expressed the same concern: the perceived lack of meaning of the

---

1. Jürgen Moltmann, *The Trinity and the Kingdom: The Doctrine of God*, trans. Margaret Kohl (San Francisco: Harper & Row / London: SCM Press, 1981), 1.

2. Ibid., 1.

3. Karl Rahner, *The Trinity*, trans. Joseph Donceel (New York: Herder & Herder, 1970), 10–11.

Trinity among some theologians and especially among the laity. What Stanley J. Grenz says of himself is so true: "For as long as I can remember I have been a Trinitarian." Yet he admits—having been raised a typical Western Christian—his approach to God was from the perspective of the oneness rather than threeness.[4] Western Christians have been called "practical modalists."[5]

Unlike some other theological topics such as, say, the doctrine of the church and its ministry, the importance of studying the Trinity is not self-evident to all. Well-known are the deprecatory words of the great Enlightenment philosopher Immanuel Kant: "The doctrine of the Trinity, taken literally, has *no practical relevance at all*, even if we think we understand it; and it is even more clearly irrelevant if we realize that it transcends all our concepts. Whether we are to worship three or ten persons in the Deity makes no difference."[6] Others have joined in.[7]

Up until the present, theological treatises on the Trinity have begun with a preface in the mood of an apology. Reservations about and objections to the relevance of the doctrine are registered, and then the author advances a massive defense of the importance of the topic, somewhat similar to what used to be the case when introducing studies in pneumatology, the doctrine of the Spirit.[8] An apology, however, is no longer needed. The Trinity has so well established itself as a viable and vibrant topic that it is not uncommon to hear statements such as "the rebirth of Trinitarian theology must be presented as one of the most far-reaching theological developments of the century."[9]

Testimonies to the indispensability of the Trinity are easy to find in contemporary theology across the ecumenical spectrum: from the Eastern Orthodox John Zizioulas—"Trinitarian theology has profound existential consequences"[10]—to the (United) Reformed Colin Gunton, who says, "[m]uch, indeed everything depends on the way that that particular doctrine [of the Trinity] is articulated,"[11] to mention a couple of leading theologians. The Baptist Millard J. Erickson, in his preface to a major study on the Trinity, presents no less than

4. Stanley J. Grenz, *Rediscovering the Triune God: The Trinity in Contemporary Theology* (Minneapolis: Fortress, 2004), ix–x.

5. Robert Letham, *The Holy Trinity: In Scripture, History, Theology, and Worship* (Phillipsburg, NJ: P&R Publishing, 2004), 5.

6. Immanuel Kant, "The Conflict of the Faculties," in *Religion and Rational Theology*, trans. and ed. Allen W. Wood and George di Giovanni, The Cambridge Edition of the Works of Immanuel Kant (Cambridge: Cambridge University Press, 1996), 264.

7. Friedrich D. E. Schleiermacher, *The Christian Faith*, trans. H. R. Mackintosh and J. S. Stewart (Edinburgh: T & T Clark, 1928), 741.

8. See further Veli-Matti Kärkkäinen, *Pneumatology: The Holy Spirit in Ecumenical, International, and Contextual Perspective* (Grand Rapids: Baker Academic, 2002), 16–19.

9. Grenz, *Rediscovering the Triune God*, 1.

10. John Zizioulas, "The Doctrine of God the Trinity Today: Suggestions for an Ecumenical Study," in *The Forgotten Trinity*, vol. 3, *A Selection of Papers Presented to the British Council of Churches Study Commission on Trinitarian Doctrine Today*, ed. Alasdair I. C. Heron (London: British Council of Churches / CCBI, 1991), 19.

11. Colin E. Gunton, *The One, the Three and the Many: God, Creation and the Culture of Modernity*, Bampton Lectures, 1992 (Cambridge: Cambridge University Press, 1993), 149.

thirteen reasons for the importance of this doctrine, including historical priority, current attention, importance for Christian uniqueness, and its implication
for practice and piety.[12]

Affirming the importance of the doctrine of the Trinity for laypersons, however, may take more effort. It is true that

> [t]his doctrine in many ways presents strange paradoxes. It is very widely
> held. It is not simply the special view of a particular denomination or sect.
> It is part of the faith of the universal church. Yet it is a widely disputed doc-
> trine, which has provoked discussion throughout all the centuries of the
> church's existence. It is held by many with great vehemence and vigor. These
> advocates are certain they believe the doctrine, and consider it crucial to the
> Christian faith. Yet many are unsure of the exact meaning of their belief. It
> was the very first doctrine dealt with systematically by the church, yet it is
> still one of the most misunderstood and disputed doctrines."[13]

While for most Christians Trinity may be "the guilt-producing doctrine"—a
doctrine that is hard to understand even though its indispensability is affirmed[14]—
there are many to whom the Trinity seems more of a *mysterium logicum* (logical
mystery) than a *mysterium salutis* (mystery of salvation).[15] As a consequence, the
Trinity "has been reduced to a curiosity rather than being a reality that matters to
us because it sheds light on our own existence."[16] Yet a *mystery* is different from a
contradiction. Mystery is "an apparent contradiction which there is good reason to
believe." It is rational to believe in mystery when there is sufficient reason to believe
that its alleged contradictory nature is just that—alleged—not real; even more so
when there are compelling theological reasons to believe that mysterious doctrine.[17]

The Doctrine of the Trinity as a Continuing
Theological Task for the Church

Few Christians would dispute the claim that the Trinity is an indispensable doctrine among all Christian churches. Amid differing interpretations of the way the
doctrine is best formulated, there is a consensus that Trinity is a distinguishing mark
of the religion that is currently the largest in the world.[18] This consensus, however,
does not mean that the Trinity is a finished doctrine. Rather, "'The doctrine of the
Trinity' is less a homogenous body of propositions than it is a task: that of the

---

12. Millard J. Erickson, *God in Three Persons: A Contemporary Interpretation of the Trinity* (Grand
Rapids: Baker Books, 1995), 11–29.
    13. Ibid., 11–12.
    14. Timothy F. Lull, "The Trinity in Recent Theological Literature," *Word & World* 2 (Winter
1992): 61.
    15. Leonardo Boff, *Trinity and Society*, trans. Paul Burns (Maryknoll, NY: Orbis Books, 1998), 111.
    16. Ibid., 19.
    17. See further Stephen T. Davis, *Logic and the Nature of God* (Grand Rapids: Eerdmans, 1983),
141–43.
    18. Stanley J. Grenz, *Theology for the Community of God* (Grand Rapids: Eerdmans, 1994), 53.

church's continuing effort to recognize and adhere to the biblical God's hypostatic being. This has been done in more than one way."[19] As such it is a task for the whole church. Indeed, the only way to come to a fuller understanding of this cardinal doctrine is to continue working toward an ecumenical, thus catholic, understanding. What Jenson says of theology in general, namely, that "theology is the church's enterprise of thought, and the only church conceivably in question is the unique and unitary church of the creeds,"[20] can be applied to the Trinity as well.

The early history and emergence of this *doctrine* testifies to the struggle the Christian church underwent in trying to grasp in a more explicit way the content and form of its confession of faith. As Leonard Hodgson remarked decades ago, "Christianity began as a Trinitarian religion with a Unitarian theology. The question at issue in the age of the Fathers was whether the religion should transform the theology or the theology stifle the religion."[21] Religion—or to be more precise, the salvation history as revealed in the Scriptures—came to shape theology, and rightly so.

True, the *doctrine* of the Trinity as such cannot be found in the Bible, yet "it is a theological doctrine which defends the central faith of the Bible and of the Church."[22] Theologians' continuing struggle with and debate about the formulation of the doctrine is but another way of responding to the call of the church to both understand and express the faith revealed in the Bible and tradition for each new generation. This continuing dialogue among various, at times diverse, even contrasting voices is the fertile soil out of which real spiritual fruit grows.[23]

Learning the Grammar of the Trinity

The difficulty with the doctrine of Trinity has much to do with the limitations and scarcity of human language to capture the meaning of this ancient doctrine. For many, Trinity is a logical problem[24] or nothing more than a "mathematical conundrum, full of imposing philosophical jargon."[25] Augustine observed this difficulty: "When it is asked three what, then the great poverty from which our language suffers becomes apparent. But the formula three persons has been coined, not in order to give a complete explanation by means of it, but in order that we might not be obliged to remain silent."[26]

---

19. Jenson, *Systematic Theology*, 1:90.
20. Ibid., 1:vii.
21. Leonard Hodgson, *The Doctrine of the Trinity* (New York: Scribner's Sons, 1944), 103.
22. Emil Brunner, *The Christian Doctrine of God*, trans. Olive Wyon (Philadelphia: Westminster Press, 1950), 206. See also Moltmann, *Trinity and the Kingdom*, 16.
23. For the importance of dialogue as the way to shape the doctrine of the Trinity, see Moltmann, *Trinity and the Kingdom*, xiii–xiv.
24. For example, Michael Durrant, *Theology and Intelligibility* (Boston: Routledge & Kegan Paul, 1973), 172, claims that "no intelligible account can be offered of the doctrine of the Trinity." For a helpful discussion of logical ramifications of the doctrine of the Trinity, see William L. Power, "Symbolic Logic and the Doctrine of the Trinity," *Illiff Review* 32, no. 1 (1975): 35–43.
25. Letham, *Holy Trinity*, 1.
26. Augustine, *On the Trinity* 5.9.10.

Only think of some of the technical apparatus by which the church has attempted to be more precise in its confession of faith in the Father, Son, and Spirit, such as *homoousios, hypostasis,* or *substance.* Obviously these are not part of our everyday vocabulary. Some may also remind us that these terms do not appear in the Bible, which is true. Are they then necessary? The ensuing discussion, beginning with biblical and historical developments, attempts to address that issue among others.[27] After all, saying something is better than submitting to silence. Speaking of God, even in less than perfect ways, is a calling for human beings.

While at the intellectual level we often sense the difficulty of the topic, deep in the Christian existence there is a conviction that the Trinity is essential to our faith. The "sense of faith" tells us that "the mystery of the Trinity should be the deepest source, closest inspiration and brightest illumination of the meaning of life that we can imagine." The challenge to those who teach and preach about the Trinity is thus immense: "There has to be a way of presenting it that will not hide these riches but bring them out in an adequate manner."[28]

A crucial part of that task is to learn the grammar of Trinity. Again, while human terminology is wanting, utilizing the tools at our disposal is far more beneficial than surrendering the whole enterprise. The liberationist Leonardo Boff reminds us:

> Every science has its technical terms for expressing exactly what it wants to say. Theology has a mass of key words to express what is thought in faith. Words are more important in theology than in any other science, since no one can see or experience God empirically, as the realities of the world are experienced. Technical terms in theology established the consensus reached after many trials, errors and insights through generation after generation of Christian thinkers.[29]

In the midst of all intellectual, philosophical, and linguistic challenges, in the final analysis the Trinity has everything to do with Christian life and piety at the levels of the individual and society as well as the world. Again, Leonardo Boff states,

> We need to go beyond the understanding of Trinity as logical mystery and see it as saving mystery. The Trinity has to do with the lives of each of us, our daily experiences, our struggles to follow our conscience, our love and joy, our bearing the sufferings of the world and the tragedies of human existence; it also has to do with the struggle against social injustice, with efforts at building a more human form of society, with the sacrifices and martyrdom that these endeavours so often bring. If we fail to include the Trinity

27. For helpful remarks, see further Justo L. González, *Mañana: Christian Theology from a Hispanic Perspective* (Nashville: Abingdon Press, 1990), 102.

28. Boff, *Trinity and Society,* 111. Another Roman Catholic theologian, Gerald O'Collins, speaks of the "Trinitarian sense" among Christians; even when doctrinal formulations are still in the making, there is a need and inclination to think in terms of biblical salvation history, which is Trinitarian, speaking of Father, Son, and Spirit. Gerald O'Collins, *The Tripersonal God: Understanding and Interpreting the Trinity* (Mahwah, NJ: Paulist Press, 1999), 4–5. There is a parallel in the work of the philosopher of science Michael Polanyi, *The Tacit Dimension* (Chicago: University of Chicago Press, 1958).

29. Boff, *Trinity and Society,* 58.

in our personal and social odyssey, we shall have failed to show the saving mystery, failed in evangelization.[30]

Similarly, the advice from Philipp Melanchthon is sound: "We adore the mysteries of the Godhead. That is better than to investigate them."[31] Knowing *about* the doctrine of the Trinity is not the same as knowing the Triune God. As Moltmann reminds us, for the church fathers, knowing meant "knowing in *wonder*. By knowing or perceiving one participates in the life of the other."[32] This is doxological knowledge, knowing God by the way of worshiping the Triune God—Father, Son, and Spirit. This is true Trinitarian grammar! I am reminded of Colin Gunton's wish that the Western church would be like the church of the Christian East, with an ability to "think trinitarianly without, so to speak, having to think about it."[33]

Trinitarian grammar discusses practical implications of the doctrine of the Trinity, a topic that has been advanced by a number of contemporary theologians, as will be evident in the ensuing discussion.[34]

Trinitarian Renaissance

One of the most exciting developments in contemporary theology at the ecumenical and international level is the rise to prominence of the doctrine of the Trinity. This tendency defies any theological restrictions; the evidence of renewed interest ranges from Eastern Orthodox to Roman Catholic to mainline Protestant to conservative evangelicalism. It also resists geographical restrictions; not only are European and North American theologians producing new studies and reflections on the Trinity, but also African, Asian, and Latin American thinkers are joining the ranks, as the discussion that follows will show. The renewed interest has caught the attention of both male and female theologians.

Since the Trinity relates to Christian life and praxis as well as doctrine, it is no wonder that a number of studies have related the Trinity with topics such as the critique of sexism and affirmation of equality,[35] ecclesiology,[36] mission,[37] pastoral theology and ministry,[38] political theology,[39] and economics.[40] Even theologies

30. Ibid., 157.
31. Quoted in Moltmann, *Trinity and the Kingdom*, 1.
32. Ibid., 9 (italics in original).
33. Colin Gunton, *Father, Son and Holy Spirit: Essays towards a Trinitarian Theology* (Edinburgh: T & T Clark, 2003), 4.
34. For starters, see Letham, *Holy Trinity*, 7–13.
35. Alvin F. Kimel Jr., ed., *This Is My Name Forever: The Trinity and Gender Language for God* (Downers Grove, IL: InterVarsity Press, 2001).
36. Miroslav Volf, *After Our Likeness: The Church as the Image of the Trinity* (Grand Rapids: Eerdmans, 1998).
37. Lesslie Newbigin, *The Open Secret*, rev. ed. (Grand Rapids: Eerdmans, 1995).
38. Paul Fiddes, *Participating in God: A Pastoral Doctrine of the Trinity* (Louisville, KY: Westminster John Knox Press, 2001).
39. Miroslav Volf, *Exclusion and Embrace: A Theological Exploration of Identity, Otherness, and Reconciliation* (Nashville: Abingdon Press, 1966).
40. M. Douglas Meeks, *God the Economist: The Doctrine of God and Political Economy (Searching for a New Framework)* (Minneapolis: Augsburg Fortress, 1989).

such as process theology, often considered oblivious to the concept of the Trinity, are showing interest in the topic,[41] and now postmodernist contributions to the Trinity are emerging.[42]

Some theologians claim that the reason for the rise of atheism may lie in the neglect of the Trinity in Christian faith.[43] Theologians such as the late Colin Gunton contended that the intellectual incoherence and ethical confusion of modern Western society can be attributed theologically to a Trinitarian anemia.[44]

In the widely acclaimed British Council of Churches study *The Forgotten Trinity*, this doctrine is placed in the widest possible context: "We seek to find in Trinitarian doctrine, in our beliefs about the very being of God, the foundation for the unity of humankind."[45] Likewise, the Trinity has been related to other religions such as Buddhism[46] and Islam,[47] as well as to various aspects of the theology of religions in general.[48] This is in keeping with the claim that the Trinity is the most distinctive feature of Christian faith. At the same time, being a relational and dynamic concept, it can also help Christians relate to the religious Other.[49]

Trinitarian Theology in Dialogue

No theology is done in a vacuum. All theology, then, is contextual, meaning that we learn and interpret the texts (of the Bible and tradition) in a con-text. Being contextual, all theology is also limited by a particular location. Unlike too many theologians, Moltmann in his *Trinity and the Kingdom* freely "recognizes the conditions and limitations of his own position, and the relativity of his own particular environment."[50] This acknowledgment, however, is an asset rather than an

---

41. Joseph Bracken, *The Triune Symbol: Persons, Process, and Community* (Lanham, MD: University Press of America, 1985).

42. David S. Cunningham, "The Trinity," in *The Cambridge Companion to Postmodern Theology*, ed. Kevin J. Vanhoozer (Cambridge: Cambridge University Press, 2003), 186–202.

43. Michael J. Buckley, *At the Origins of Modern Atheism* (New Haven, CT: Yale University Press, 1987).

44. See especially Colin Gunton, *The Promise of Trinitarian Theology* (Edinburgh: T & T Clark, 1991); Gunton, *One, the Three and the Many*.

45. British Council of Churches, *The Forgotten Trinity*, vol. 1, *The Report of the B.C.C. Study Commission on Trinitarian Doctrine Today* (London: British Council of Churches/CCBI, 1989), 40.

46. Roger Corless and Paul F. Knitter, eds., *Buddhist Emptiness and Christian Trinity: Essays and Explorations* (New York: Paulist Press, 1990).

47. Risto Jukko, *Trinitarian Theology in Christian-Muslim Encounters: Theological Foundations of the Work of the French Roman Catholic Church's Secretariat for Relations with Islam Trinitarian Theology in Christian-Muslim Encounters* (Helsinki: Luther-Agricola-Society, 2001).

48. S. Mark Heim, *The Depth of the Riches: A Trinitarian Theology of Religious Ends* (Grand Rapids: Eerdmans, 2001). Gavin D'Costa, *The Meeting of Religions and the Trinity* (Maryknoll, NY: Orbis Books, 2000); Raimundo Panikkar, *The Trinity and the Religious Experience of Man: Icon-Person-Mystery* (Maryknoll, NY: Orbis Books/London: Darton, Longman & Todd, 1973); the book is also titled *The Trinity and the World Religions*. For a critical dialogue with these and similar proposals, see Veli-Matti Kärkkäinen, *Trinity and Religious Pluralism: The Doctrine of the Trinity in Christian Theology of Religions* (Aldershot, UK: Ashgate, 2004).

49. See further Marjorie Hewitt Suchocki, *Divinity and Diversity: A Christian Affirmation of Religious Pluralism* (Nashville: Abingdon Press, 2003).

50. Moltmann, *Trinity and the Kingdom*, xii.

obstacle for doing a more inclusive theology. Speaking of himself in the third person, Moltmann remarks: "For him this means a critical dissolution of naïve, self-centered thinking. Of course he is a European, but European theology no longer has to be Euro*centric*. Of course he is a man, but theology no longer has to be *androcentric*. Of course he is living in the 'first world,' but the theology which he is developing does not have to reflect the ideas of the dominating nations."[51]

Acknowledging the situatedness and particularity of one's own approach to doing theology, in this case Trinitarian theology, frees the theologian to enter a dialogue. Moltmann, thus, claims that

> truth is to be found in unhindered dialogue. Fellowship and freedom are the human components for knowledge of the truth, the truth of God. And the fellowship I mean here is the fellowship of mutual participation and unifying sympathy. . . . This free community of men and women, without privilege and without discrimination, may be termed the earthly body of truth. . . . [I]t is only in free dialogue that truth can be accepted for the only right and proper reason—namely, that it illuminates and convinces *as* truth. Truth brings assent, it brings about change without exerting compulsion. In dialogue the truth frees men and women for their own conceptions and their own ideas. . . . Christian theology would wither and die if it did not continually stand in a dialogue like this, and if it were not bound up with a fellowship that seeks this dialogue, needs it and continually pursues it.[52]

Doing theology from a global perspective is in vogue at the beginning of the third millennium. It is widely acknowledged as the only proper way to advance the quest of Christian truth and as such a necessary enterprise. Doing *Trinitarian* theology from a global perspective, however, may call for some explanation. What has the Trinity—an ancient doctrine of the church—to do with *global* perspectives? Aren't there topics more pertinent and "practical"? In other words, is it relevant? Only a careful discussion and dialogue with emerging theologies from various contexts of our globe can address that question. Addressing that question is one of the main tasks of this work.

Dialogue in a global perspective also highlights the importance of *ecumenical* dialogue in the pursuit of Christian truth. There is a healthy dynamic here, though:

> The theological testimonies of the Christian faith can be viewed in the light of their *particularity*. Then there are Orthodox, Catholic, Anglican, Lutheran and many other theological testimonies. But they can also be investigated and interpreted in the light of their *universality*. Then they can be seen as the testimonies of the one church of Christ, and we can interpret them as contributions to the theology of this one church of Christ. Then, whatever denominational stamp a text may have, the important thing is simply its contribution to the truth to which all together are subject. Truth is universal. Only the lie is particularist.[53]

51. Ibid. (italics in the original).
52. Ibid., xiii (italics in original).
53. Ibid., xv (italics mine).

Doing theology in the beginning of this new millennium is not only global and ecumenical but also entails dialogue with history.[54] While contemporary theology cannot satisfy itself with dogmatically repeating the formulae of old, it would be foolish and detrimental to the faith to be oblivious to the rich and diverse traditions of the past. Even when going beyond the questions set by tradition or correcting the perceived misconceptions of earlier theologians, true dialogical theology never dares dismiss the achievements of the Fathers and subsequent Christian theologians.

The Goal and Plan of This Book

These three dimensions of a dialogical approach to doing theology in the contemporary world have guided me in preparing of this book. Let me briefly set forth my purpose. I attempt to offer a critical theological dialogue and assessment of the state of Trinitarian theology in the beginning of the third millennium in light of biblical and historical tradition and the ever-expanding global theologizing enterprise. Part of the expanding worldwide dialogue about the Trinity is the introduction of ideas from other religions and exploring Christianity's relation to them. Unlike other books available, this book offers several views into the theology of religions discourse through the lens of the Trinity.

Not giving precedence or privilege to any area of the world, I have selected a few leading theologians, both men and women, to speak to Trinitarian theology. I will engage the conversation as a critical partner and will draw other theological voices into the conversation.

In the first part of the book, I will take a careful look at biblical and historical traditions. While doing constructive theology means going beyond the answers—and questions—of the tradition, it would be foolish to ignore tradition. One of the reasons so-called contextual theologies are sometimes received with cynicism is that they tend to overlook the importance of dialogue with the views of our forebears. I do not intend to offer a typical history of Trinitarian traditions; on the contrary, I will look at key developments, movements, as well as challenges, during the history of Trinitarian doctrine to ascertain the defining issues, how they were resolved, and implications and tasks for our own time.

Following the discussion of tradition, I offer both exposition of and critical dialogue with Trinitarian theologies from five contexts. With each theologian, I will first attempt a fair and balanced exposition of the Trinitarian doctrine in light of tradition and contemporary discussion as well as its relation to the particular context of that theologian and his or her specific agenda. This is based, of course, on primary sources. The second part of the discussion consists of my critical reflections. While I incorporate a number of critical comments from other theologians, nowhere do I attempt an exhaustive literature coverage. I take into

---

54. See further ibid. xiii–xiv.

consideration secondary literature to the extent that it helps my argument and the dialogue and is representative of responses to that particular theologian.

There are two main goals in the critical part of the study. On the one hand, I try to honor the specific task and framework underlying that particular Trinitarian doctrine. On the other hand, wherever relevant, I also pay attention to key themes and challenges that emerge. Those themes will be first presented in summary form at the end of the European section. They make sense only as they arise from the discussion and dialogue. In my discussion, both exposition and critical analysis, I also attempt to model a proper theological methodology that I believe is helpful for younger theologians. Much of theological work is not only learning the language and content but also the skill of thinking theologically and carrying on with careful, patient theological analysis, both critical and constructive.

I begin with European contributions, not only because chronologically that is a justified decision but also because much of the emerging global theology is a response to and development of those views, not to mention that until recently the European academia has been the locus of much of theological education and served as the pacesetter. From a number of European theologians I have selected only five, with two criteria in mind: first, their theological and ecumenical diversity—Orthodox, Roman Catholic, and Protestant voices, both Lutheran and Reformed—and second, their continuing influence on the worldwide discourse. The two Karls, Barth and Rahner, are hailed as the originators of the contemporary worldwide Trinitarian renaissance. They have also shaped much of the agenda of the contemporary discussion. The input of the Orthodox John Zizioulas to communion theology is unsurpassed. The two leading systematic theologians at the worldwide and ecumenical level, Wolfhart Pannenberg and Jürgen Moltmann, gather all the main developments from tradition and contemporary conversation and thus provide the most creative constructive proposals currently being discussed everywhere. I have allotted space accordingly: Pannenberg and Moltmann get about twice as much space as the rest of the theologians in any category. This is to do justice to their superb place on the current theological scene. A number of other Trinitarian theologians from Europe could have been included: the Reformed theologians Thomas F. Torrance[55] and Colin Gunton,[56] the Lutheran Eberhard Jüngel,[57] the Roman Catholic Walter Kasper,[58] to name the most obvious ones.

---

55. Thomas F. Torrance, *The Trinitarian Faith: The Evangelical Theology of the Ancient Catholic Church* (Edinburgh: T & T Clark, 1988); *The Christian Doctrine of God, One Being Three Persons* (Edinburgh: T & T Clark, 1996); *Trinitarian Perspectives: Toward Doctrinal Agreement* (Edinburgh: T & T Clark, 1994).

56. Gunton is United Reformed. Gunton, *Promise of Trinitarian Theology*.

57. Eberhard Jüngel, *The Doctrine of the Trinity: God's Being Is in His Becoming* (Edinburgh: T & T Clark, 1976); *God as the Mystery of the World: On the Foundation of the Theology of the Crucified One in the Dispute between Theism and Atheism*, trans. Darrell L. Guder (Grand Rapids: Eerdmans, 1983).

58. Walter Kasper, *The God of Jesus Christ*, trans. Matthew J. O'Connell (New York: Crossroad, 1984), especially part 3, "The Trinitarian Mystery of God."

Much of the energy of North American Trinitarian reflection, especially in its first phase, comes in reaction to European views. The quite different context and milieu both challenges and enriches the European discourse. To highlight these differences, in the beginning of the North American section (as well as those on Africa, Asia, and Latin America), I include a reflection on the distinguishing features of that particular context for doing Trinitarian theology. Theologians selected as representatives for North American Trinitarian theology represent widely the theological and ecclesiastical diversity so prevalent on the New Continent. A fitting bridge between the theologies of the Old and New Continents is the senior Lutheran scholar Robert W. Jenson, Wolfhart Pannenberg's student. The late Roman Catholic Catherine Mowry LaCugna, a student and dialogue partner of Rahner, is one of the few female theologians, not only in North America but also at the global level, ever to produce a full-scale monograph on the Trinity. Another female theologian represented in this section is Roman Catholic Elizabeth Johnson, whose primary agenda is feminist. As the representative of the so-called evangelical movement, whose theological contributions are almost nonexistent in the older continent, I will discuss the Trinitarian theology of Millard J. Erickson, who gleans especially from Moltmann, Pannenberg, and Zizioulas. On Christianity's relation to other religions and religious pluralism, among several North American theologians who have attempted to place Trinity at the center of this theological reflection, the leading American constructive theologian is S. Mark Heim, another Protestant. A pair of theologians writing together and approaching the Trinity from the perspective of religious studies and insights from other religions is the Anglican Ninian Smart and his Eastern Orthodox student Steven Konstantine.

Because of the limitations of space, I have had to exclude several other candidates, such as the Lutheran Ted Peters, who has worked hard in relating the Trinity not only to history but also to time,[59] and the leading evangelical theologian from Canada, Clark Pinnock, with his distinctively pneumatological orientation.[60] Reluctantly I also decided to leave out process theologies even though I included a critical survey of some of their contributions in the introductory chapter on North America. Three other key theological voices from North America will appear in the Latin American and Asian sections, namely, the Asian/Asian Americans Raimundo Panikkar and Jung Young Lee, as well as the Hispanic/Latin American Justo González, since their theologies offer a unique synthesis of the new in-between genre of theological reflection bridging the East and West, North and South. Thus, I have included in the North American section two Roman Catholics, two mainline Protestants, an Anglican, and an evangelical; two women and four men. The wider selection of North American than European voices is

---

59. Ted Peters, *God as Trinity: Relationality and Temporality in Divine Life* (Louisville, KY: Westminster John Knox Press, 1993).

60. Clark Pinnock, *Flame of Love: A Theology of the Holy Spirit* (Downers Grove, IL: Inter-Varsity Press, 1996).

based on two considerations. This reflects the shift of the theological center from the Old to the New Continent. And it reflects the diversity and plurality found on that side of the Atlantic.

For Asia, Africa, and Latin America, I have selected two representative theologians each in addition to a separate chapter on the distinctive features of Trinitarian reflection from those particular contexts. Am I thus unfair? Not necessarily. This division of labor also illustrates quite well the contemporary state of the emerging global dialogue. It is true that Europe and North America, with their vast resources and personnel, still dominate the worldwide theological academia and production of literature.

Asia is represented by Jung Young Lee, originally North Korean and now residing in the United States, who builds his vision of the Trinity on the Asian Confucian and Taoist principle of *yin-yang,* and by the Indian (from India)/American Raimundo Panikkar, whose view of the Trinity rests on a Hindu-based "cosmotheandric" vision. Lee is Protestant (United Methodist) and Panikkar is Roman Catholic. While they both reside in the United States, they can be regarded as the leading Asian representatives in constructive Trinitarian theology. Both of them explicitly build their reflections on Asian sources.

From the Latin American and Hispanic perspective, I have selected Leonardo Boff, a former Franciscan priest from Brazil, and Justo L. González, a Methodist theologian born in Cuba, now based in the United States. Having two theologians, a Roman Catholic from South America and a Protestant from the United States, speak from Hispanic perspectives is an attempt to illustrate a unique feature of theological reflection among Latin Americans: the origin of Latino Christianity both in terms of two locations and two main Christian traditions.

The African context is represented by the Roman Catholic Charles Nyamiti, whose Trinitarian theology is based on the veneration of ancestors, and the Methodist A. O. Ogbonnaya, who attempts to retrieve the meaning of the first North African Trinitarian theologian Tertullian's Trinitarian doctrine. Representing Roman Catholic and Protestant traditions, these two theologians give a fair picture of African ecumenical and theological diversity.

PART ONE
THE BIBLICAL ROOTS
OF THE DOCTRINE
OF THE TRINITY

Chapter 1

Old Testament Monotheism and the Idea of Plurality in God

Two givens guide us as we approach the question of the biblical roots, particularly in the Old Testament, of the Christian doctrine of the Trinity: the uncompromising monotheism of the faith of Israel and the indispensable nature of the Old Testament as the source for anything the New Testament says of God. The monotheistic faith is best illustrated in the famous Shema, Israel's "confession of faith": "Hear, O Israel: The LORD our God, the LORD is one" (Deut. 6:4 NIV). Any appeal to other gods was considered blasphemy; however, the "OT contains, in anticipation, categories used to express and elaborate the doctrine of the Trinity." Therefore, "a theology of the Trinity that ignores or plays down the OT can only be radically deficient."[1]

In the Old Testament, the one God is known under various names, the most

---

1. Gerald O'Collins, *The Tripersonal God: Understanding and Interpreting the Trinity* (New York/Mahwah, NJ: Paulist Press, 1999), 11. Oddly enough, the recent compilation of essays on the biblical, historical, and contemporary systematic perspectives on the Trinity by leading international scholars does not have any discussion of the role of the Old Testament; Stephen T. Davis, Daniel Kendall, and Gerald O'Collins, eds., *The Trinity: An Interdisciplinary Symposium on the Trinity* (Oxford: Oxford University Press, 1999).

peculiar being *Yahweh,* going back to the significant self-revelation of God in Exodus 3:14.[2] Yahweh demands unreserved loyalty vis-à-vis the constant tendency of the people to succumb to the worship of the pantheon of gods and goddesses in their environment. How can this strict monotheism be reconciled with and seen as the background for the emerging Christian view of God as triune?

Older Christian exegesis and theology tried to reconcile this apparent tension by either referring to the yet underdeveloped nature of Old Testament faith before the coming of the Messiah or working hard to find any kind of clues to the alleged plurality in the Israelite concept of God. These proof texts included familiar references such as Genesis 1:26 ("Let *us* make . . ."), which current exegesis regards as an example of plurality of majesty (not unlike the pronouncements of royal individuals in the form of "We declare . . ."); the famous Isaianic threefold "Holy, holy, holy" exclamation (6:3); and the interpretation of the theophanies of the "Angel of Yahweh" (for example, Gen. 18) as preincarnation appearances of the second person of the Trinity. Contemporary scholarship has seen here insurmountable obstacles and does not find such "evidence" well taken. At their best, these kinds of proof texts may give an indication of the idea of plurality in God, but certainly not a view of the Triune God: Why not a binitarian or quadritarian view of God? It is also very problematic to consider the Old Testament view of God as infantile since the New Testament does not do so.[3]

The contribution of these passages as well as the yet undeveloped idea in the Old Testament of God as Father to the emerging New Testament view of God as triune lies in the idea of plurality and relationality, both key aspects of the Christian doctrine of God developed later. Take Genesis 1 as an example: Even though contemporary exegesis cannot read the idea of the Trinity into 1:26 ("Let us make . . .") any more than into the presence of God (*Elohim*), God's Spirit (*ruach*), and God's Word (*dabar*) in the narrative, these are foundational ways of pointing to both plurality and relationality in the one God.[4]

Contemporary theology has taken a different approach from the old prooftext method to account for the legitimacy of the emergence of faith in the Triune God in early Christian theology in the New Testament and beyond. This approach attempts to do full justice to the teachings of the Old Testament on

2. For discussion concerning the meaning and origins of the term, see, e.g., Veli-Matti Kärkkäinen, *The Doctrine of God: A Global Introduction* (Grand Rapids: Baker Academic, 2004), 15–35, with relevant bibliographical guidance.

3. For a classic study, see Arthur W. Wainwright, *The Trinity in the New Testament* (London: SPCK, 1962).

4. For the idea of relationality in this context, see further Ben Witherington III and Laura M. Ice, *The Shadow of the Almighty: Father, Son, and Spirit in Biblical Perspective* (Grand Rapids/Cambridge, UK: Eerdmans, 2002), 17; Robert Letham, *The Holy Trinity: In Scripture, History, Theology, and Worship* (Phillipsburg, NJ: P&R Publishing, 2004), 19–22. For an important discussion between OT creation stories and Trinity/relationality, see Herman Bavinck, *In the Beginning: Foundations of Creation Theology,* ed. John Bolt, trans. John Vriend (Grand Rapids: Baker Books, 1999), 39–45 especially.

their own terms, before "baptizing" them into a New Testament understanding.[5] The question could be put like this: What is there, if anything, in the Old Testament understanding of monotheism that allowed the early Christian theology to conceive of God in plural, especially triune, terms? It is the consensus of much of contemporary scholarship that the incipient plurality in the one God is expressed in terms of "Wisdom," "Word," and "Spirit," which seem to serve as (semi-)personified agents of divine activity.[6] In other words, the existence of personified agents, pointing to the idea of plurality in the one God, was not seen as a threat to monotheism.[7]

There is no need to go into a detailed biblical exposition here concerning these three "agents." Suffice it to say here that *khokmah*, Wisdom, occurs more than three hundred times in the Old Testament literature, especially in the Wisdom literature. According to the famous passage of Proverbs 8:22–31, Wisdom was "begotten" or "created" "long ago" as God's "firstborn." In the beginning of the book, Wisdom, in the form of a sophisticated Lady, invites people to the sources of true wisdom. Word, beginning from the first creation account (Gen. 1:1–2:4a) appears as the agent of God; it was through the Word (and Spirit) that creation was accomplished (Ps. 33:8–9), and the Word is able to accomplish its God-given purposes (Isa. 55:10–11). Spirit (with more than four hundred occurrences in the OT[8]), sometimes coupled with either Word (Ps. 33:8–9) or Wisdom (Deut. 34:9; Job 32:8–9; Isa. 11:2), brings about and sustains life (Gen. 1:2), sustaining all life (Gen. 1:2; Ps. 104:29–30).

In addition to these three semi-personified agents of the one God, the Jewish Bible knows others, such as the name of Yahweh, especially in the Deuteronomic theology. The name of Yahweh dwells in the temple (Deut. 12:5, 11, etc.), while God is in heaven (26:15). Another example is the glory of God that acts as an agent separately from, yet sent by, Yahweh; the book of Ezekiel is the prime example here (43:4, 7 being a telling example).[9]

An intriguing recent proposal by Richard Bauckham, who is both exegete and theologian, maintains that the early Jewish definition of God could include the person of the Son without a violation of monotheism.[10] What distinguished Yahwistic faith from polytheistic faiths was not so much the desire

5. This is not to deny the need for Christians to read the First Testament in light of the coming of Christ. What this means is that in order to do it in a proper way, one needs to first listen to the First Testament's own testimony in its own setting.

6. For details, see further O'Collins, *Tripersonal God*, 23–34; my exposition here is greatly dependent on his lucid exposition.

7. Ibid., 23. See also Letham, *Holy Trinity*, 28–31.

8. For details, see Veli-Matti Kärkkäinen, *Pneumatology: The Holy Spirit in Ecumenical, International, and Contextual Perspectives* (Grand Rapids: Baker Academic, 2002), 23–27.

9. See further Wolfhart Pannenberg, *Systematic Theology*, vol. 1, trans. Geoffrey W. Bromiley (Grand Rapids: Eerdmans, 1991), 276.

10. Richard Bauckham, *God Crucified: Monotheism and Christology in the New Testament* (Grand Rapids: Eerdmans, 1998), 1ff. Bauckham has thus challenged the older scholarly consensus according to which predication of a divine nature to Jesus (and thus equality to God) came from

to place Yahweh at the summit of a hierarchy of divinity, but rather to place Yahweh "in an absolutely unique category, beyond comparison with anything else."[11] In other words, even the highest angels or heavenly powers, which were so highly appreciated in the apocalyptic literature especially, while participating in God's rule over the earth, did not share God's essence. However, as will be evident in what follows, distinctions within one Godhead, such as between God's Spirit and God's Word, were not necessarily understood as compromising divine unity. Consequently, Bauckham concludes—and this is highly significant for a New Testament incipient Trinitarian outlook: "The Second Temple Jewish understanding of the divine uniqueness . . . does not make distinctions within the divine identity inconceivable."[12] Whatever is the verdict of biblical scholarship on the details of Bauckham's proposal, it seems to be in line with the idea that plurality as such was not necessarily considered a threat in the Jewish faith.[13]

So, when the New Testament writers' encounter with the risen Christ and the Holy Spirit forced them to develop a theology that could account for the plurality in unity, they could build on these incipient foundations in the Israelite faith. Wolfhart Pannenberg makes a brilliant comment here: "Christian statements about the Son and Spirit take up questions which had already occupied Jewish thought concerning the essential transcendent reality of the one God and the modes of his manifestation."[14] Yes, they went beyond the Old Testament faith, no doubt, but not against it, and they could hold on to the Shema of Israel while talking about Father, Son, and Spirit as one God.[15] As O'Collins succinctly summarizes it,

> The vivid personifications of Wisdom/Word and Spirit, inasmuch as they were *both* identified with God and the divine activity *and* distinguished from God, opened up the way toward recognizing God to be tripersonal. The leap from mere personifications to distinct persons is always, to be sure, a giant one. Nevertheless, without these OT personifications (and the Father/Son language applied to God), the acknowledgment of the Trinity would not have been so well and providentially prepared—by foreshadowings and by an already existing terminology.[16]

---

the Hellenistic culture rather than from the Jewish heritage. See further Witherington and Ice, *Shadow of the Almighty,* 67–68.

11. Bauckham, *God Crucified,* 15.

12. Ibid., 22.

13. In addition to the sources given above, see also the helpful discussion on the plurality in unity in Peter Toon, *Our Triune God: A Biblical Portrayal of the Trinity* (Wheaton, IL: Victor/SP Publications, 1996), 95–112.

14. Pannenberg, *Systematic Theology,* 1:276–77. So also O'Collins, *Tripersonal God,* 89.

15. See Roger E. Olson and Christopher A. Hall, *The Trinity,* Guides to Theology (Grand Rapids: Eerdmans, 2002), 10; Pannenberg, *Systematic Theology,* 1:277.

16. O'Collins, *Tripersonal God,* 34 (italics in the original).

While the New Testament builds on the foundations laid by the First Testament, it also is true that it focuses clearly on Jesus, the Son.[17] As C. Seitz expresses it, "In the older testament things are seen from the Father's point of view, whereas the Father is largely viewed from the Son's point of view in the New Testament."[18]

17. See the important comment by Thomas F. Torrance, *The Christian Doctrine of God, One Being Three Persons* (Edinburgh: T & T Clark, 1996), 46.
18. Christopher R. Seitz, *Word without End: The Old Testament as Abiding Theological Witness* (Grand Rapids: Eerdmans, 1998), 258.

Chapter 2

The Rise of the Trinitarian Understanding of God in the New Testament

THE GOD OF THE OLD TESTAMENT IS THE FATHER OF JESUS CHRIST

It was no less a figure of Christian theology than Karl Barth who set forth the statement that the "doctrine of the Trinity is what basically distinguishes the Christian doctrine of God as Christian, and therefore what already distinguishes the Christian concept of revelation as Christian, in contrast to all other possible doctrines of God or concepts of revelation."[1] Therefore, if the Old Testament did not yet have a view of God as triune, certainly the New Testament, the book of the Christian church, does have such a view, most Christians assume.

The issue is not quite that simple. The following comment in a recent textbook needs to be taken seriously: "There is no mention of the word 'Trinity' in the New Testament. What we do discover from the New Testament writers, though, is a

---

1. Karl Barth, *Church Dogmatics*, vol. I/1, ed. G. W. Bromiley and T. F. Torrance (Edinburgh: T & T Clark, 1956), 301. Likewise, A. W. Argyle notes that God is not specifically "named" in the NT; A. W. Argyle, *God in the New Testament* (Philadelphia: Lippincott, 1965), 9.

consistent argument for the filial uniqueness of Jesus Christ in relationship to the Father of the old covenant."[2] Why so? For the simple reason that the God of the New Testament is that of the Old Testament. In Wolfhart Pannenberg's words, the "God of Jesus is none other than the God of Jewish faith. . . . He is the God of Abraham, Isaac, and Jacob (Matt 12:26–27), the God whom Israel confesses in the *shema* of Deut. 6:4 (Mark 12:29)."[3] Whatever we think of the New Testament basis of the doctrine of the Trinity, we need to acknowledge not only that the roots of the New Testament doctrine of God are to be looked for in the Old Testament, but also that the New Testament presupposes the teaching about God as explicated in the Old Testament.

Whence then the emergence of the doctrine of the Trinity? Stanley J. Grenz succinctly states:

> The initial impetus in the direction of what became the church's teaching about God as triune was spawned by the theological puzzle posed by the early church's confession of the lordship of Jesus and the experience of the indwelling Holy Spirit, both of which developments emerged within the context of the nonnegotiable commitment to the one God of the Old Testament that the early believers inherited from Israel.[4]

That development, however, took centuries and was a matter of much debate. In hindsight one may ask, If the New Testament does not contain a doctrine of the Trinity, how can we then justify the later Christian doctrine as legitimate?[5] The answer to this question is that rather than looking for proof texts or a *doctrine* of the Trinity in the New Testament, we need to look at how the first Christians came to understand salvation history, namely, what the God of Israel was doing through his Son in the power of the Spirit. The doctrine of the Trinity was a later, second-order, interpretation of the happenings of salvation history. It began more or less as a binitarian understanding of God: Father and Son, soon to be complemented by the crucial role of the Spirit, distinct, yet integrally related to both.

Clearly, the way the New Testament introduces its incipient Trinitarianism is through the coming of the person of Jesus Christ, who, the early Christians claimed, shares in the divinity of the Father God. The Synoptic Gospels and the Gospel of John present the understanding of the history and claims of Jesus that for the early Christians pointed to the plurality-in-unity, and more specifically, trinity in the Godhead.

2 Roger E. Olson and Christopher A. Hall, *The Trinity,* Guides to Theology (Grand Rapids: Eerdmans, 2002), 6.

3. Wolfhart Pannenberg, *Systematic Theology,* vol. 1, trans. Geoffrey W. Bromiley (Grand Rapids: Eerdmans, 1991), 260.

4. Stanley J. Grenz, *Rediscovering the Triune God: The Trinity in Contemporary Theology* (Minneapolis: Fortress, 2004), 7.

5. Cf. the comment of Argyle, an exegete of the previous generation: "Broadly speaking, we may say that the God of the New Testament is the God of the Old Testament reinterpreted and more fully revealed in the light of the Person and Work of Jesus Christ." Argyle, *God in the New Testament,* 10.

In that sense, the emerging revelations of God in both testaments are not so different, even though it is only in the light of the New Testament salvation history that we achieve a fuller understanding of the triune nature of God.[6] For the New Testament writers, Jesus is the way to know God. But the God of Jesus is none other than the God of the Jewish faith, as mentioned above. The God of the Old Testament is the God whom Jesus said to love wholeheartedly as the first great commandment (Matt. 22:37). The self-distinction of Jesus from his Father on the one hand and their unity on the other hand is the foundation of the New Testament orientations to the Trinity.[7]

THE DISTINCTION AND UNITY BETWEEN FATHER AND SON[8]

As O'Collins puts it, there is a "trinitarian face" to the history of Jesus.[9] This becomes evident as we read the New Testament Gospels and beyond. In the beginning of his Gospel, Luke tells us that the conception of Jesus was an act of God in the power of the Spirit (Luke 1:35). Matthew's way of connecting the coming of Jesus to a Trinitarian understanding is to name Jesus, the Son, as Emmanuel, the presence of God, the Yahweh of Israel, with his people (Matt. 1:23).[10] The Gospel of John goes back to the Old Testament idea of the Word as God's agent and names the Word, Logos, as God (John 1:1). Exegetical disputes aside, these are indications of the fact that the coming of Jesus from the "beginning" was understood by the Gospel writers as linked to God and his Spirit, yet distinct from it, giving a form for the idea of a Trinitarian understanding of God.

The Gospel of John builds on the Synoptic witnesses and at the same time offers a distinctive perspective. During his life, Jesus claimed to have been sent by God (John 5:37), and more important, to have been given the authority to give life

---

6. Ibid., 11–12.

7. For a careful analysis, see Pannenberg, *Systematic Theology*, 1:263–64. The self-distinction of Jesus from the Father is also a key to the emerging NT Christology.

8. In focusing on the theme of the sonship of Jesus in relation to the emerging doctrine of the Trinity, I will limit my considerations strictly to the title "Son" as counterpart to the Father. Thus, I exclude consideration of the most frequent self-description of Jesus, namely, "Son of Man." A helpful discussion in relation to the doctrine of the Trinity can be found in Craig A. Evans, "Jesus' Self-Designation 'The Son of Man' and the Recognition of His Divinity," in *The Trinity: An Interdisciplinary Symposium on the Trinity*, ed. Stephen T. Davis, Daniel Kendall, and Gerald O'Collins (New York: Oxford University Press, 1999), 29–47. For a helpful discussion of various other titles such as God, Lord, Son of Man, Son of God, Immanuel, Divine Son, Logos, I am, Alpha and Omega, see Ben Witherington III and Laura M. Ice, *The Shadow of the Almighty: Father, Son, and Spirit in Biblical Perspective* (Grand Rapids/Cambridge, UK: Eerdmans, 2002), 71–97.

9. Gerald O'Collins, *The Tripersonal God: Understanding and Interpreting the Trinity* (New York/Mahwah, NJ: Paulist Press, 1999), 35 (chapter title: "The History of Jesus and Its Trinitarian Face").

10. As a way of inclusion, Matthew picks up the theme of "presence" at the end of the Gospel in that the resurrected Lord promises to be with his own to the end of the ages (28:20).

(5:21) and to execute judgment as his Father does (5:22). Indeed, Jesus claimed that whoever does not honor the Son does not honor the Father (5:23). The same Gospel puts forward these bold statements by Jesus:

> No one has ever seen God, but God the Only Begotten, who is at the Father's side, has made him known. (John 1:18 NIV alternative reading)

> I am the way, and the truth, and the life. No one comes to the Father except through me. (14:6 NRSV)

> Anyone who has seen me has seen the Father. (14:9 NIV)

In the New Testament witness, before his cross and resurrection, Jesus claimed to have the authority and approval of his Father. And when, as Romans 1:3–4 maintains, Jesus was raised from the dead by his Father, the early Christians interpreted that as divine confirmation.[11] This is crucial for the emergence of the conviction of the deity of Jesus, a claim that was of course hotly contested during Jesus' lifetime by his Jewish opponents; they accused him of blasphemy (John 5:18).[12] Resurrection from the dead was seen by early Christian theology as suggesting that "the Son of God was also at the side of God from all eternity" even though the "church's later view of the full deity of the Son did not have to be related to the idea of pre-existence."[13] At first, the concept of the Son's preexistence was fluid, moving between the preexistence of an idea (in the mind of God) and a "real" preexistence.[14] Another route, however, also led to the affirmation of full deity of the Son, the critical stage in the emerging Trinitarian faith (albeit often in its binitarian form), namely, the applying of the title *Kyrios* to the risen and exalted Son. This is the title *Lord* reserved for the God in the Old Testament (Septuagint, the Greek translation). The *Kyrios*, Son, could be invoked in prayer (a possible interpretation of 2 Cor. 12:8). Pannenberg sums up this key contribution to the incipient Trinitarian history in the New Testament:

---

11. See the important article by Richard Bauckham, "The Sonship of the Historical Jesus in Christology," *Scottish Journal of Theology* 31, no. 3 (1978): 245–60.

12. Olson and Hall, *Trinity,* 8. See also Pannenberg, *Systematic Theology,* 1:264–65.

13. See further Pannenberg, *Systematic Theology,* 1:264–65.

14. Ibid., 1:265. The whole question of whether—or in what sense—the belief in Christ's preexistence was a gradual development or a stratum of the earliest traditions is a highly disputed question in New Testament (NT) theology. J. D. G. Dunn, for example, has been very skeptical of the older view according to which the idea of preexistence goes back to Paul and thus to earlier traditions. On the other hand, NT scholars such as Seyoon Kim (and perhaps Ralph P. Martin) have argued that preexistence was affirmed by Paul. For basic sources in the debate, see, e.g., L. W. Hurtado, "Pre-Existence," in *Dictionary of Paul and His Letters,* ed. Gerald F. Hawthorne and Ralph P. Martin (Downers Grove, IL: InterVarsity Press, 1993), 743–46; for a brief consideration, see Robert Letham, *The Holy Trinity: In Scripture, History, Theology, and Worship* (Phillipsburg, NJ: P&R Publishing, 2004), 48–49.

The title Kyrios implies the full deity of the Son. In the confession of Thomas in John 20:28 the titles God and Lord are expressly set alongside one another. Yet the Son is not Kyrios in competition with the Father but in honor of the Father (Phil. 2:11). The confession of Jesus Christ as the one and only Kyrios in no way weakens the confession of the one God. The former confession is so related to the latter that all things proceed from the one God, the Father, but all are mediated through the one Kyrios (1 Cor. 8:6).[15]

The foundation for the emerging New Testament Trinitarian faith was laid by the two ideas we have explicated above: the shared identity of the Yahweh of the Old Testament and the God of Jesus Christ of the New Testament as well as the self-distinction, and yet unbroken unity between the Jesus and his Father.[16] In order to see the significance of these ideas, we must pay close attention to the distinctive ways the New Testament develops the motif of the fatherhood of God. Here we come to the crux of the Trinitarian faith in the New Testament. Following that consideration, the course from binitarian (Father-Son) to Trinitarian (Father-Son-Spirit) will be in focus.

THE FATHER OF JESUS CHRIST

The idea of the fatherhood of God is not unknown to the Old Testament, but neither is it a major theme.[17] After surveying in detail the occurrences of the term and the idea of the fatherhood of God in the Old Testament, O'Collins summarizes his findings in this way:

Naming God *Father* expressed his deep involvement in the story of Israel, its kingly leaders, and its righteous ones. . . . The use of the Father metaphor centered on God's free and creative choice of the people. This name conveyed the steadfast commitment and compassionate love of God in protecting, cherishing, and nourishing a people whose infidelity could also call for discipline.[18]

Therefore, as O'Collins further notes, while the name of the Father "cannot be called frequent in the OT, . . . it will become the favored name in the NT."[19] This comes into focus in Jesus' way of addressing the God of Israel as centered on God as the Father.[20] At the heart of the message of Jesus was the announcement

---

15. See further Pannenberg, *Systematic Theology*, 1:266.

16. Ibid., 1:263–64.

17. Witherington and Ice, *Shadow of the Almighty*, 1; for possible reasons behind this scarcity of father imagery in the OT, see further pp. 4–6.

18. O'Collins, *Tripersonal God*, 23 (italics in the original); see also pp. 12–22.

19. Ibid. See also Boris Bobrinskoy, *The Mystery of the Trinity: Trinitarian Experience and Vision in the Biblical and Patristic Tradition*, trans. Anthony P. Gythiel (Crestwood, NY: St. Vladimir's Seminary Press, 1999), 64.

20. For the various meanings of the term "Father" in the NT, see Marianne Meye Thompson, *The Promise of the Father* (Louisville, KY: Westminster John Knox Press, 2000), 39.

of the nearness of the kingdom of God;[21] this God was none else than the Heavenly Father whose reign was near:[22]

> God shows himself to be Father by caring for his creatures (Matt 6:26; cf. Luke 12:30). He causes his sun to shine and his rain to fall on the bad as well as the good (Matt 5:45). He is a model of the love for enemies which Jesus taught (5:44–45). He is ready to forgive those who turn to him (Luke 15:7, 10, 11ff.), ask for his forgiveness (11:4), and forgive others (Matt 11:25; cf. 6:14–15; 18:23–35). He lets himself be invoked as Father, and like earthly fathers, and even more than they, he grants good things to his children when they ask (Matt 7:11). Thus the prayer to the Father which Jesus taught his disciples combines the prayer for daily bread, the sum of all earthly needs, with the prayer for forgiveness, which is connected with a readiness to forgive (Luke 11:3–4). This prayer also shows that Jesus' proclamation of God's fatherly goodness is related to his eschatological message of the nearness of the divine rule. For the prayer begins with three petitions that are oriented to the coming of the lordship of the Father God.[23]

Much has been written about the use of *abba* as the unique way of addressing the Father by Jesus. Jesus not only addressed God as *abba,* but also taught his disciples to address God as "our Father." It is the basic contention of the classic study by Joachim Jeremias, *The Prayers of Jesus,*[24] that while Jesus' view of God was not completely new, his mode of address to God was novel because his relationship with God was unique.[25] While the older scholarship—as well as popular teaching even today—maintained that the significance of the address *abba* lies in its daddy-like nature, as in the language of small children, biblical scholars tell us that the term indicates rather an intimate relationship between an adult son and father.[26] "The term *abba* is clearly enough an intimate way of addressing God using family language, whether by a child or an adult, and as such is less formal than addressing God simply as God or Lord . . . [The] main point is that Jesus' choice of this term reveals Jesus' awareness of his special relationship with God."[27] This is further

---

21. For a helpful, balanced study see Robert Hamerton-Kelly, *God the Father: Theology and Patriarchy in the Teaching of Jesus* (Philadelphia: Fortress Press, 1979), 70–81.

22. For the integral linking between the kingdom of God and Father in Jesus' ministry and life, especially when it comes to the awaited eschatological coming of God's rule, see George E. Ladd, *A Theology of the New Testament,* rev. ed., ed. Donald A. Hagner (Grand Rapids: Eerdmans, 1993), 83.

23. Pannenberg, *Systematic Theology,* 1:259. In all of the Gospels, the theme of God's fatherhood is evident, but a curious development can be seen: Mark, the earliest Gospel, records only 4 occurrences; Matthew has many more, 30 altogether; whereas the Gospel of John, written a few decades later, has no less than 120!

24. Joachim Jeremias, *The Prayers of Jesus* (Philadelphia: Fortress Press, 1978).

25. Joachim Jeremias, *New Testament Theology: The Proclamation of Jesus* (New York: Scribner's Sons, 1971), 67.

26. For a critique of the older view, see especially James Barr, "Abba Isn't 'Daddy,'" *Journal of Theological Studies* 39, no. 1 (1988): 28–47. For the role of *abba* as a way of expressing the intimacy, union, and obedience of the Son to the Father, see D. R. Bauer, "Son of God," in *Dictionary of Jesus and the Gospels,* ed. Joel B. Green (Downers Grove, IL: InterVarsity Press, 1992), 769–75.

27. Witherington and Ice, *Shadow of the Almighty,* 22. For several distinctive features in the usage of *abba* by Jesus, see also pp. 23–24.

confirmed by the striking scarcity of its usage by Paul and other early Christians, who used this expression very sparingly.[28]

FROM BINITARIANISM TO AN EMERGING TRINITARIAN FAITH

The critical stage in moving from a binitarian to a Trinitarian understanding of God had to do with the growing insistence on the Spirit as the "medium of the communion of Jesus with the Father and the mediator of the participation of believers in Christ."[29] According to the Pauline testimony, Jesus Christ was raised from the dead by the power of the Spirit (Rom. 1:4). The God who raised the Son from the dead by the power of the Spirit will raise believers from the dead as well (8:11). Jesus' Spirit indwelling the believers is the guarantee. The Spirit cries *"Abba"* in the hearts of believers, echoing the prayer of Jesus in relation to his Father (8:15–16).

In the "Spirit-Christologies"[30] of the Synoptic Gospels, Jesus is anointed by the Spirit at his baptism and receives a confirmation from the Father, "You are my beloved Son" (Mark 1:11 par.). In Mark's narrative, the Spirit comes down in the form of a dove, and the Father's voice is heard from above to confirm the sonship of Jesus. The Gospels also link Jesus' ministry and the Spirit. Mark views the miracles of Jesus as the work of the Spirit (3:20–30), Matthew attributes exorcism to the same Spirit (12:28), and Luke depicts Jesus as filled with the Spirit (4:1, 14, and so on).[31]

While the integral unity between Son and Spirit is easier to affirm in the New Testament, the same has to be said also of the relation between Father and Spirit in order to affirm a genuine Trinitarian foundation. If the ministry and life of Jesus in the Gospels is an expression of the presence of the Spirit of God, as described above, it means then that there is no separation between God and Spirit. "In the working of the Spirit[,] God himself is present."[32] This means that the inclusion of believers in the filial relationship between Father and Son is also mediated by the Spirit, similarly to the mediation of God's presence by the Spirit in all creation. "The Spirit is thus given to believers, and by receiving the Spirit they have a share in the divine sonship of Jesus."[33] In sum:

---

28. See Thompson, *Promise of the Father*, 65.

29. Pannenberg, *Systematic Theology*, 1:266.

30. Quotation marks indicate here that one does not have to subscribe to any particular kind of Spirit Christology (as developed in contemporary systematic theology) to say so much.

31. See further Eduard Schweizer, *The Holy Spirit* (Minneapolis: Fortress Press, 1980), 50–52 especially; Veli-Matti Kärkkäinen, *Pneumatology: The Holy Spirit in Ecumenical, International, and Contextual Perspectives* (Grand Rapids: Baker Academic, 2002), 29–30.

32. Pannenberg, *Systematic Theology*, 1:267.

33. Ibid. Thus it is understandable that the baptismal formula became Trinitarian, even though binitarian forms were also in use earlier.

The involvement of the Spirit in God's presence in the work of Jesus and in the fellowship of the Son with the Father is the basis of the fact that the Christian understanding of God found its developed and definitive form in the doctrine of the Trinity and not in a biunity of the Father and the Son. . . . The NT statements do not clarify the interrelations of the three but they clearly emphasize the fact that they are interrelated.[34]

While the basic outline of the emergence of the Spirit as the third in the triad of Father, Son, and Spirit seems quite unambiguous, it is debated how much of the Trinitarian language is explicitly invoked in the New Testament. This issue has been labeled "explicit binitarianism and implicit trinitarianism."[35] Even a cursory look at the New Testament shows that there are a number of binitarian passages about Father and Son[36] and well as triadic ones in various forms, either in statements where the Spirit is mentioned alongside Father and Son[37] or in a wider triadic pattern such as the implicitly Trinitarian structure of Ephesians 1:3–4, based on the salvation history of Father, Son, and Spirit.[38] It has been rightly suggested that even in binitarian passages, there is already a basic Trinitarian consciousness even when the Spirit is not explicitly mentioned.[39]

These are the contours of the emergence of the Trinitarian consciousness and outlook based on the salvation history in the New Testament. Without this, no later Trinitarian doctrine would have arisen. At the same time, one has to acknowledge that that the New Testament basically leaves us here, and it is here that early postbiblical theology picks up the task of clarifying the concepts. A number of questions are left open, and at best some definitive pointers are provided by New Testament authors. In what follows, we will take a theological look at the various ways that first the Fathers and then later Christian theologies attempted to take up these challenges and further clarify the complex set of issues.

34. Ibid., 1:268–69.

35. Letham, *Holy Trinity*, 52 (section heading title).

36. Rom. 1:1; 1 Cor. 1:1–3; Gal. 1:1–5; 1 Tim. 1:1–2; Phlm. 3, etc. For a detailed discussion, see Larry W. Hurtado, *One God, One Lord: Early Christian Devotion and Ancient Jewish Monotheism* (Philadelphia: Fortress Press, 1988).

37. Rom. 15:30; 1 Cor. 12:4–6; 2 Thess. 2:13–14; Titus 3:4–7, etc. See further Letham, *Holy Trinity*, 56–63.

38. Gal. 4:4–6 is another familiar example of a triadic pattern. See further Letham, *Holy Trinity*, 63–69.

39. So Peter Toon, *Our Triune God: A Biblical Perspective of the Trinity* (Wheaton, IL: Victor Books, 1996), 117.

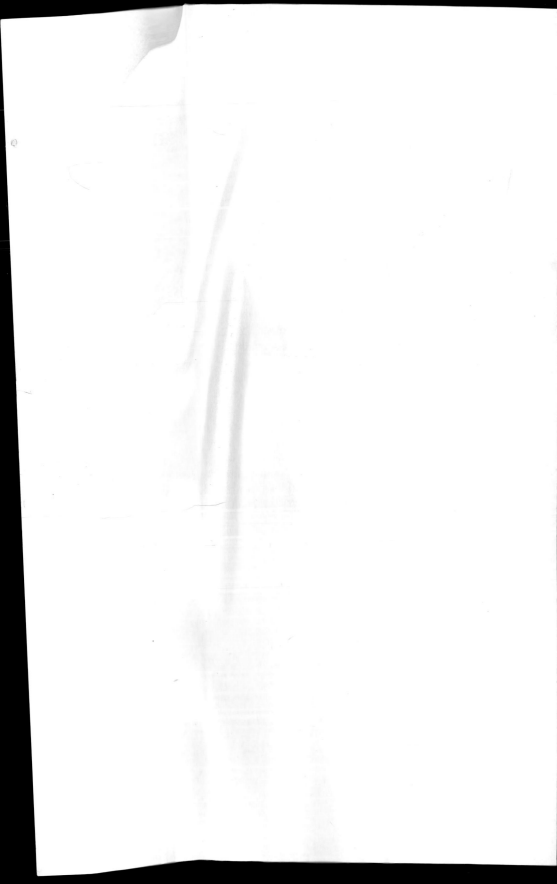

PART TWO
THE HISTORICAL
GROWTH OF TRINITARIAN
TRADITIONS

Chapter 3

The Emergence of Trinitarian Canons in Early Christian Theology

TASKS FOR THE DEVELOPING CHRISTIAN
UNDERSTANDING OF THE TRINITY

A number of accessible, lucid expositions of the history of Trinitarian traditions are available, especially in English.[1] The goal of this presentation is not to add to that genre. My purpose in this section is to continue the story started by the biblical canon and try to discern the main turns taken by subsequent Trinitarian traditions in terms of trying to both resolve the many problems and give at least a tentative answer to urgent questions. While this is best done by roughly follow-ing the chronological order, no attempt is made here to try to be in any way comprehensive or fill in any details unrelated to the development of the argu-mentation. At times the chronological order is replaced by thematic concerns. Informed selectivity is the key here; references for further study will be provided in the footnotes.

---

1. For a helpful up-to-date bibliographic guide, see Roger E. Olson and Christopher A. Hall, *The Trinity*, Guides to Theology (Grand Rapids: Eerdmans, 2002), part 2: Annotated Bibliography, 119–50.

The goal is to set forth a theological reading of Trinitarian traditions in terms of its main moves, key issues, and critical issues. In no way is this an effort to suppress the rich variety and diversity within what can be considered to be the orthodox tradition (in contrast to those deemed heretical). On the contrary, while sensitive to the plurality of approaches taken, the theological reading makes every effort to comprehend in a sound and critical manner the mosaic of developments during the first two millennia of Christian theology.

The focus of the present book is to offer a theological assessment of Trinitarian reflection in contemporary theology at the global level. Why then delve into the history of the ancient church, which for the most part is the history of Western thought, even when the contributions of the Christian East are recognized? The reason is simple: this is the mother of contemporary theology not only in the West or the Christian East but also of all Christian churches in Asia, Africa, Latin America, among men and women, those in power and those underprivileged, colored or white, and so on.

It is valid to remind ourselves of the truism that we need to know history in order to understand the present. The deeper one goes into the rich tapestry of local Trinitarian theologies in the postmodern global village, the better we can read the Trinitarian history of the past and more urgently acknowledge the need to know the origins. Knowing the history of the developments is important in light of the fact that all or most non-Western theologians are trained in these traditions, and in their contemporary work they try to respond to the challenges that have long occupied the best minds of the church. It is also essential for appreciating the shared unity of our Christian faith—to which the ecumenical work of the churches relentlessly testifies—amid growing plurality and diversity. Trinitarian faith, anchored in the biblical witness, ancient creeds, liturgical life, and devotion of the people of God, is confessed by all Christians at all times everywhere. Trinitarian faith is the prime example of the principle of *catholicity* cherished by Christian theologians since the time of Boethius (the fifth century) up to the present.

A good place to begin is to ask, What were the urgent tasks facing the earliest Christian theology in the postbiblical period? It is helpful to list them here even though many of them have already been alluded to in the biblical section:[2]

1. As long as the Spirit was not differentiated from the Son as a separate hypostatic[3] entity, it was difficult to say if the Spirit was the power or influence of the Father (filling or empowering the Son) or something else less than a person. In other words, how do we distinguish Son and

2. See further Wolfhart Pannenberg, *Systematic Theology*, vol. 1, trans. Geoffrey W. Bromiley (Grand Rapids: Eerdmans, 1991), 269–70; Gerald O'Collins, *The Tripersonal God: Understanding and Interpreting the Trinity* (New York/Mahwah, NJ: Paulist Press, 1999), 85–87, among others.
3. From the Greek term *hypostasis*, the basic meaning of which here is "personal" or "something with identity." This term has a checkered history in early Christian theology, as noted in what follows.

Spirit without separating them in a way that would threaten to truncate the Trinitarian doctrine? This distinction was quite unclear in the theologies of the second and third centuries.[4]

2. As long as the distinction between the Son and Spirit was ambiguous and, subsequently, the hypostatic nature of both in the process of being more precisely defined, the relation to *Logos*/Word and Wisdom was confusing. To take an example, what is the relation of the Son to the preexistent Wisdom of Proverbs 8:22–23? Or should we ask, as some early theologians did, what is the relation of the Spirit to Wisdom?

3. While affirming the deity of the Son (and later the deity of the Spirit), early theologians also brought about the major problem in relation to the monotheism of Jewish-Christian faith.

4. Having gradually affirmed the deity of both Son and Spirit, the major challenge to Christian theology was to negotiate between two extremes, tritheism, the belief in Father, Son, and Spirit as "separate gods" on the one hand, and modalism, the idea of lack of personal distinctions in the one Godhead, on the other hand. Modalism, which may take more than one form, insists on the unity of the Godhead to the point where the names Father, Son, and Spirit are just that, names. They denote various manifestations or modes of being of the one and the same Godhead.[5]

5. Often resolution of this question was attempted by resorting to subordinationism, the subjecting of the Son and Spirit under the Father. Again, this can happen in more than one way, for example by treating the Father as the "source" (*archē*) of the two. Early heresies, especially Arianism (according to which Christ was a creature rather than an uncreated deity) and various types of monarchianist views (both modalistic and dynamic versions), were efforts to reconcile the seemingly impossible equation between strict monotheism and the idea of three equal divine beings sharing one Godhead.

6. From early on the Christian East and West developed not only distinctive approaches to spirituality and theology in general but also encountered severe linguistic problems directly related to a key issue in the Trinitarian (and christological) doctrine, namely, the meaning of *hypostasis*

---

4. See further Maurice Wiles, "Reflections on the Origins of the Doctrine of the Trinity," in *Working Papers in Doctrine* (London: SCM Press, 1976), 10. An interesting way to account for the lack of distinction between Son and Spirit both in the history of theology and in contemporary theology is the view of the one God as the Spirit who works in/through Jesus Christ and by whom Christ is present to believers. While it is true that Paul in a few places seemingly comes close to equating the risen Lord and the Spirit, as in 1 Cor. 15:45, which speaks of the risen Christ as "life-giving Spirit," these statements need to be read in light of distinctions made elsewhere in the Pauline corpus; see G. W. H. Lampe, *God as Spirit* (Oxford: Oxford University Press, 1977).

5. A classic introduction to these early heresies (plus two others, Apollinarism and Eutychianism, related mainly to christological debates) is provided by J. W. C. Wand, *The Four Great Heresies* (London: Mowbray, 1955). While outdated in some respects, the main outline is still reliable and highly accessible to readers with limited theological training.

("person[hood]"). Not only did it take time for both Eastern and Western theologians to begin to understand what the other meant with key concepts, but more so, to agree on a common meaning, somewhat independently from purely linguistic and etymological meanings. Any field of inquiry entails an established, often technical terminology; the doctrine of the Trinity is no exception. Often, however, it takes time for this terminology to be developed in a way that would clarify the discourse.

All of these issues will be taken up in what follows, using a few examples from representative theologians with a view to how these questions were resolved and if not resolved, what were the further tasks. The first task, then, is to discern the early developments till the Councils of Nicaea (325) and Constantinople (381), the first definitive ecumenical attempts by the church catholic to come to a consensus or at least a common understanding.

SON OF THE FATHER

Reflecting the development in the New Testament from a binitarian toward a Trinitarian understanding, early Christian theology struggled first with relating the Son to the Father. One key development here is the so-called *Logos* theology in which the idea of Jesus as Word/*Logos* was related to God as Father. This was the occupation of the second-century Apologists Justin Martyr, Theophilus of Antioch, Tatian, and others. The idea of the *Logos*—going back to philosophical schools, the Jewish philosopher Philo, the Old Testament idea of the *dabar*, and Johannine theology—seemed to be well-suited to account for the defense of monotheism on the one hand and the distinction in some way or another between Father and Son. The emphasis, however, was in the idea of unity. "As pre-existent, Christ was the Father's thought or mind . . . as manifested in creation and revelation, . . . its extrapolation or expression."[6] To insist on the Son's eternal oneness with the Father (God's Word is always in the life of God) and his appearance in human history was exactly what John the Evangelist seemed to be saying (1:1; 1:14). The idea of derivation from the Father, in the analogy of human reason and its expression in speech, also implied the shared substance between Father and Son. Other metaphors were used, especially those from nature like sun and its rays or fire kindling fire. Insisting on the unity of the Godhead—and thus anticipating the question of "consubstantiality" much debated in later theology—the Apologists were careful not to read the idea of separation or difference in the Father-Son relationship. Justin put it pointedly: the begetting of the Son does not mean an "abscission, as if the essence of the Father were divided."[7]

---

6. J. N. D Kelly, *Early Christian Doctrines* (New York: Harper Press, 1958), 95.
7. Justin Martyr, *Dialogue with Trypho, A Jew* 128, in *The Ante-Nicene Fathers: Translations of the Writings of the Fathers Down to A.D. 325* (reprint, Grand Rapids: Eerdmans, 1981), 1:264; I am indebted to O'Collins, *Tripersonal God*, 89, for this reference.

With all these benefits, *Logos* theology of course encounters serious challenges when pressed. This is not to say that we have to deem the theological efforts of the Apologists as worthless; that would mean requiring of them answers to the questions raised by later generations.[8] However, in the theological reading of emerging Trinitarian traditions in hindsight, it is appropriate to point to further tasks. These have to do with establishing the distinction between Word/Son and Father beyond the obvious, namely, coming to existence in creation. A corollary challenge has to do with the lack of personality in the Word. Furthermore, again not unrelated to these concerns is the implied subordinationism: that which is derived is obviously lower than the source of the derivation. In other words, the kind of mutuality of relations emphasized in contemporary Trinitarian theology is absent here. Finally, there is of course the question of the role of the Spirit in all of this.[9]

The Father-Son relationship continued to challenge patristic theology until Constantinople (381) and beyond, and we will reflect on those developments. In tandem with that question arose the challenge of relating Son and Spirit to each other and then again, both of them to the Father.

HOW TO ACCOUNT FOR THE DISTINCTION BETWEEN THE SON AND SPIRIT

While the triadic pattern was deeply implanted in the minds of the earliest theologians[10] there was not a little confusion about what that triad is. Until the end of the third century or so, confusion remained about the mutual relationship and distinction between the Son and Spirit for the simple reason that the New Testament does not make it clear. Another reason is that the Old Testament seems to take Word and Spirit as parallel and virtually interchangeable entities in the service of Yahweh.[11]

In the earliest postbiblical writings such as the second-century *2 Clement*, it is not uncommon to find a blurring of the distinction between Son and Spirit.[12] Speaking of those who abuse flesh, it says that "such a person will not receive

---

8. See the wise counsel of Kelly, *Early Christian Doctrines*, 100–101.

9. For the last challenge, see ibid., 101–4.

10. For examples in early creedal statements and liturgy, see O'Collins, *Tripersonal God*, 95. By the time of Irenaeus, the rule of faith (*regula fidei*) was explicitly Trinitarian in structure: "The Church, though dispersed throughout the whole world, even to the ends of the earth, has received from the apostles and their disciples this faith: [She believes] in one God, the Father Almighty, Maker of heaven, and earth, and the sea, and all things that are in them; and in one Christ Jesus, the Son of God, who became incarnate for our salvation; and in the Holy Spirit, who proclaimed through the prophets the dispensations of God . . ." Irenaeus, *Against Heresies* 1.10.1, in *Ante-Nicene Fathers* 1:330.

11. O'Collins, *Tripersonal God*, 23–34, 91.

12. For such examples in Justin Martyr, see J. N. D. Kelly, *Early Christian Creeds*, 3rd ed. (London: Longman, 1972), 148.

the Spirit, which is Christ" (14:4). Another telling early example of the lack of Trinitarian canons is *The Shepherd of Hermas*, a highly influential writing of the second century that

> struggled to make sense of the Son and Spirit. Indeed, Hermas appears to fall into a number of errors also repeated by later theologians. For example, it is not clear whether Hermas considered the Son to be an angel or more ancient than the angels. Occasionally he blurs the distinction between Son and Spirit, and in one instance seemingly unites them, writing that "the Spirit is the Son of God" (Parable 9.1.78). . . . Although we find support for the unity of God in Hermas' writing, his struggle to define plurality of God was characteristic of his time.[13]

Even in later second-century theologians such as Theophilus of Antioch and Irenaeus, the Trinitarian pattern is still in the making. Both of them define the triad in terms of God, Word, and Wisdom.[14] To make things more complicated, Theophilus equated the Spirit with Word while Irenaeus with Wisdom, illustrating also the difficulties related to the development of a defined pneumatological doctrine in early theology.[15] Soon the equation of the Son with the Word, *Logos,* on the basis of Proverbs 8:22–23, became the standard view.[16]

Behind *Logos* theology, apart from its biblical contours, is the Apologists' desire to defend the transcendence of Father. *Logos* as intermediary (and at times the Spirit as well) fits this purpose very well. As O'Collins puts it helpfully: "Justin developed the theme of the intermediary roles of the Son, who is 'another' or 'second' God. As Logos, he mediates and is present in all creation."[17] When pressed, this idea of course leans toward subordinationism and prepares the way for the later Arianist ideas of the different "substance" of deity between Father and Son.

An aspect in the developing understanding concerning the role of the Son and Spirit in the Trinity was the discussion of the spheres of activities assigned to both as well as to the Father. Take for example the inspiration of the prophecy of the Old Testament and the birth of the Messiah. They could be assigned to both Spirit and Son (to the latter because of the link to *Logos*). The creation of the world provides another illustration. Irenaeus had considered creation the result

13. Olson and Hall, *Trinity*, 18.
14. Theophilus of Antioch, *Theophilus to Autolycus: Book II*, 2.15, in *Ante-Nicene Fathers* 2:101, among others; Irenaeus, *Against Heresies* 4.20.1ff. (pp. 487ff.).
15. For the early history of the doctrine of the Spirit, see further Veli-Matti Kärkkäinen, *Pneumatology: The Holy Spirit in Ecumenical, International, and Contextual Perspectives* (Grand Rapids: Baker Academic, 2002), 37–46 especially.
16. So Justin Martyr, *Dialogue* 61.1.ff. (pp. 227ff.), and Tertullian, *Against Praxeas* 6–7/8, in *Ante-Nicene Fathers* 3:601–3, among others. See further Pannenberg, *Systematic Theology*, 1:270. For some references in what follows I am indebted to the careful and detailed discussion in von Georg Kretschmar, *Studien zur frühchristlichen Trinitätstheologie* (Tübingen: Mohr, 1956), 27–61.
17. O'Collins, *Tripersonal God*, 94. Another favorite christological image in Justin, namely, Angel (of the Lord), was also helpful in highlighting the mediatory role of Christ, as in OT theophanies. Ibid., 88–89, 94.

of the "two hands of God," Son and Spirit.[18] Origen's idea of the differentiation of the three members of the Godhead based on their distinctive operations is famous. According to him, while the Father works in all things, the Son works only in rational creatures and the Spirit only in the church.[19]

What is to be said theologically of these attempts to establish distinctions based on different roles in relation to the works of the Trinity? While the distinction of works may function as a way of illustration, it can hardly establish the distinct identities of each Trinitarian member.[20] This was grasped quite soon, and attempts to account for the distinct nature of Son and Spirit as well as their relation to the Father took a different route.

The great Eastern Trinitarian thinkers, the Cappadocians (Gregory of Nyssa and of Nazianzen [sometimes also Nazianzus] as well as Basil) and Athanasius, differently from tradition, insisted that instead of separation there should be rather an emphasis on the common participation of all Trinitarian members in the works in the world. The unity of works is both a condition and consequence of the unity of essence.[21] While a valid criticism of the earlier view that tried to build distinctions on different roles in the world, the Eastern view is also subject to criticism. One can hardly argue that the common activity is constitutive for the persons or their distinctions. In other words, with the emphasis on the unity of works, whence then the basis for distinction?[22] It seems that in general the Cappadocians could only resort to church tradition, Scripture, and the baptismal formula as the basis of distinction,[23] reasons that hardly settle the case for contemporary theology but which should not be taken too lightly since all those elements have been formative in the growth of theology.

There were more promising clues provided by earlier theologians even though in the midst of the existing confusion they were not grasped and valued as they should have been. This other way to find the basis for the distinction among Father, Son, and Spirit makes reference to the inner relations of the Son, Father, and Spirit. Based on the Paraclete passages in John 14, Tertullian suggested that the Son distinguished both the Father and Spirit from himself.[24] Origen similarly

18. Irenaeus, *Against Heresies* 4.20.1 (pp. 487–88). So also Theophilus, *Theophilus to Autolycus* 2.18 (pp. 101–2). At times Irenaeus was more analytic in attributing revelation of the Spirit to prophecy, revelation of the Son to incarnation, and revelation of the Father to the eschatological consummation. Irenaeus, *Against Heresies* 4.20.5 (pp. 488–89). See also Pannenberg, *Systematic Theology*, 1:270–71.

19. Origen, *On First Principles* 1.3.5–8, in *Ante-Nicene Fathers* 4:253–56. Also Pannenberg, *Systematic Theology*, 1:271.

20. For that see incisive comments by Pannenberg, *Systematic Theology*, 1:278–79.

21. Wiles, "Reflections on the Origins," 11ff.; Pannenberg, *Systematic Theology*, 1:271.

22. See Pannenberg, *Systematic Theology*, 1:278. In this respect I have to be critical of the comment by Michel René Barnes on Augustine, that "the unity of the trinity is found in its inseparable activities or operations." See Michel René Barnes, "Rereading Augustine's Theology of the Trinity," in *The Trinity: An Interdisciplinary Symposium on Trinity*, ed. Stephen T. Davis, Daniel Kendall, SJ, and Gerald O'Collins, SJ (Oxford: Oxford University Press, 1999), 145–76.

23. Wiles, "Reflections on the Origins," 14.

24. Tertullian, *Against Praxeas* 9 (pp. 603–4), quoting John 14:28 and 14:16.

had affirmed that Jesus' referring to the Father and the Paraclete as distinct from himself implies the existence of three persons and one shared substance or entity.[25] This, Pannenberg suggests, and I agree, means that the "self-differentiation of the Son from the Father on the one side and the Spirit on the other forms a basis for the thesis that there is a threefold distinction in the deity."[26]

While not yet fully satisfactory, the simple, yet profound idea of Athanasius according to which the Father would not be Father without the Son and that therefore the Father never was without the Son, points in the same direction.[27] The abiding contribution of the Athanasian rule is the implication of relationality as the way to defining the distinction as well as the unity. The shortcoming, however, is obvious: the idea of fatherhood may include more than only one son. Furthermore—but this was not obviously in Athanasius's mind and therefore should not be taken as a major criticism—the Son-Father relationality hardly helps us much in thinking of the role of the Spirit in relation to the two. The only way to focus and limit the Athanasian rule is to tie it strictly to the unfolding of the biblical salvation history in the coming of Jesus as the Son sent by the Father. That safeguards the incipient idea against losing its contours. Even then, at best, the Athanasian idea of the mutuality of the Father-Son relationship could account only for the distinction-in-unity between the two; it does not give much help in considering the role of the Spirit.[28]

In sum, early patristic theology was unable to resolve the question of the basis for establishing the identities of Son and Spirit, their mutual distinction and unity. However, eventually there was an agreement on the deity of both the Son and the Spirit. Scriptural passages deemed implicitly Trinitarian were the final basis for affirming their divinity. While contemporary exegesis basically disqualifies those attempts, their value is not to be dismissed because they show that early theologians were convinced that the Trinity was a datum of revelation.[29] With

---

25. Origen, *Homilies on Numbers* 12.1, referenced in Pannenberg, *Systematic Theology*, 1:272 n. 48.

26. Pannenberg, *Systematic Theology*, 1:272; see also 278–79.

27. Athanasius, *Four Discourses against the Arians* 1.29, in *Nicene and Post-Nicene Fathers of the Christian Church*, Series 2 (reprint, Grand Rapids: Eerdmans, 1994), 4:323. Athanasius was not the first to express this idea. Origen had already taught it earlier in his *First Principles* 1.2.9–10 (pp. 249–51); see further Peter Widdicombe, *The Fatherhood of God from Origen to Athanasius* (New York: Oxford University Press, 1994), 69–70. However, Athanasius made it a theological theme in Trinitarian deliberations.

28. In his letters to Serapion, Athanasius made some efforts to transfer the argument from the Father-Son relation to considering the Spirit-Father-Son web of relations; those attempts are hardly convincing since it is very difficult to discern the compelling logic behind it. See further Pannenberg, *Systematic Theology*, 1:279.

29. According to Pannenberg, there is also a deeper truth to the attempts to prove the deity of the Son and Spirit with the help of implicitly Trinitarian passages: "To modern historico-critical exegesis this procedure seems to be mistaken from some angles. Yet it stands in relation to the history of the exposition of such texts in Jewish thinking. This connection is important. It shows that the Christian view of the Son as a preexistent hypostasis alongside the Father, and similar views concerning the Spirit that developed in the course of the formation of the doctrine of the Trinity, were not from the very outset opposed to Judaism and its belief in one God." Pannenberg, *Systematic Theology*, 1:275.

affirmation of the deity of Son and Spirit, there began to emerge a consensus about the need to affirm the distinct personalities of the three without compromising their unity. From these experiments we learn that the basis can be found neither in the different spheres of operation nor in Christian tradition or liturgy itself (as much as they helped establish the doctrinal developments) nor in the generic idea of fatherhood. The father-son idea, implying both plurality and relationality, however, is a major advancement.

As soon as distinct identities are affirmed, regardless of the underlying basis, an inevitable question arises as to how this plurality can be reconciled with the uncompromising monotheism of the First Testament.

NEGOTIATING THE DIVINITY OF SON AND SPIRIT IN RELATION TO BELIEF IN ONE GOD

The question of how to negotiate monotheism with the idea of the plurality of the divine persons has of course occupied Christian minds from the beginning and has taken various turns.[30] This concern either caused or helped bring about several theological challenges, some of them deemed heretical, such as Monarchianist views, subordinationistic views of various sorts, and Arianism. The continuing struggle between tritheism (belief in three deities) and modalism (the idea that replaces the real distinctions among Father, Son, and Spirit for "modes" of being) are the two extreme contours that have guided Christian theology in this endeavor. "Where tritheism sacrificed the vital identity of Father, Son, and Holy Spirit to their multiplicity, the opposite heresy of modalism took monotheism so rigidly that it sacrificed the multiplicity of the divine persons to their unity."[31]

A tempting way to negotiate the tension between monotheism and the need to affirm the deity of the Son alongside the Father is to resort to the *subordination* of Son and Spirit to the "higher" status of the Father. Justin Martyr's idea of the Son being "second" and Spirit being "in the third place" in the Godhead is a classic example of a subordinationist view.[32] The Irenaean idea of the Spirit and Son as two hands of the Father is of course another one.[33] The motif behind Irenaean subordinationism was his concern to uphold the uniqueness and transcendence of the Father, the Creator, a concern going back to earlier theology, as noted above.[34]

30. See further Kelly, *Early Christian Doctrines*, 83, 87.
31. O'Collins, *Tripersonal God*, 86. See also the helpful discussion in Robert Letham, *The Holy Trinity: In Scripture, History, Theology, and Worship* (Phillipsburg, NJ: P&R Publishing, 2004), 97.
32. Justin Martyr, *The First Apology* 13, in *Ante-Nicene Fathers* 1:166–67. For helpful comments on this passage and similar passages in Justin, see O'Collins, *Tripersonal God*, 90–91.
33. Irenaeus, *Against Heresies* 4.20.1 (p. 487): "In carrying out his intended work of creation, God did not need any help from angels, as if he did not have his own hands. For he has always at his side his Word and Wisdom, the Son and the Spirit. Through them and in them he created all things of his own free will. And to them he says, 'Let us make human beings in our image and likeness.'"
34. For details, see Kelly, *Early Christian Doctrines*, 86–89.

Quite fittingly, Irenaeus's view, however, has been named "orthodox subordination-ism."[35] This highlights the theological sophistication and candor of his view: it is a very fine-tuned subordinationism. For Irenaeus, Son (as Word) has always been with the Father[36] and is the one who makes the Father known.[37] In anticipation of later debates, Irenaeus taught that the Son "did not then begin to exist, being with the Father from the beginning."[38] While taking his clue from the Apologists' *Logos*-theology, Irenaeus also develops their view by insisting on the unity between Rea-son/Intelligence (Father) and Speech/Word (Son).[39] The apparent weakness of Irenaeus's idea of the Son and Spirit as two hands, though, is the lack of clarity regarding the mutual relationship between the "two hands." Perhaps this is too much to expect of a metaphor; however, it is another indication of the supreme dif-ficulties early theologians faced in establishing the mutuality of Trinitarian relation-ships in a way that would prevent the idea of Tri-unity from becoming merely an auxiliary idea.

Another early theologian, Tertullian,[40] to whom we owe the launching of key concepts such as *trinitas, persona,* and *ousia* into the Trinitarian vocabulary, strug-gled with the challenge of subordinationism among other issues. Tertullian was fighting on several fronts, Gnosticism being one of them.[41] Gnostics compro-mised the unity of the Godhead, which Tertullian vehemently rejected.[42] His main opponents, whose teaching gleaned from the subordinationism of Irenaeus and others, he described as *Monarchians* (from Greek *monē archē,* "sole sover-eignty").[43] Noetus and Praxeas in the second century and Sabellius in the third are the principal names associated with this heresy.[44] For Tertullian, these heretics were unable to reconcile the monarchy, "sole sovereignty," of the Father with the participation of Son and Spirit in the lordship of the Father. Monarchians found the *Logos* theology problematic for this very reason: the idea of the preex-istent *Logos* seemed to imply two gods.[45] The monarchical view not only subor-

35. Catherine Mowry LaCugna, *God for Us: The Trinity and Christian Life* (San Francisco: Harper-SanFrancisco, 1991), 24–30.
36. Irenaeus, *Against Heresies* 2.30.9; 4.20.3 (pp. 406; 488).
37. Ibid., 4.20.6; 4.6.7 (pp. 489, 469).
38. Ibid., 3.18.1 (p. 446). In book 4 he says: "We have shown at length that the Word, that is the Son, was always with the Father." In this same passage, while unfortunately confusing Wisdom and Spirit, Irenaeus extends the idea of consubtantiality to the third member of the Trinity as well: "And that Wisdom, which is the Spirit, was present with Him, anterior to all creation." Ibid., 4.20.3 (p. 488).
39. See Kelly, *Early Christian Doctrines,* 105.
40. A classic study is Benjamin B. Warfield, "Tertullian and the Doctrine of the Trinity," in *Studies in Tertullian and Augustine* (New York: Oxford University Press, 1930), 1–109. As always, a reliable short guide to basic issues is Kelly, *Early Christian Doctrines,* 110–15. Letham, *Holy Trinity,* 97–101, offers a balanced, helpful overall assessment of Tertullian's role in the development of Trinitarian traditions.
41. For a basic statement on the complicated issue of Gnosticism, see Veli-Matti Kärkkäinen, *The Doctrine of God: A Global Introduction* (Grand Rapids: Baker Academic, 2004), 63.
42. Tertullian, *Against Marcion* 1.3: "If God is not one, then there is no God" (*Ante-Nicene Fathers* 3:273).
43. Tertullian, *Against Praxeas,* 10 (p. 604).
44. For Monarchianism, see further Kärkkäinen, *Doctrine of God,* 71–72.
45. Tertullian, *Against Praxeas,* 13 (pp. 607–9).

dinated the Son to the Father but also blurred the personal distinctions between Father and Son; by extension, Sabellianism included the Spirit in the scheme. Those names are just that, names expressing transient manifestations in salvation history. In other words, "Father," "Son," and "Spirit" are but *modes* of the one and undifferentiated Godhead—thus the nomenclature "modalism." A heresy by the name *patripassianism* is one corollary of the lack of distinctions: God the Father (*patēr*) suffered and died in the coming of the Son.[46]

This was consequently the challenge given to the North African Tertullian: how to reconcile the divinity of the Son with rigid monotheism without on the one hand ending up affirming modalism or on the other hand becoming polytheist. His argument is based on two foundational convictions: that the monarchy of the Father does not necessarily preclude sharing it with an equal, and that God is three in one or one in three with real distinctions, yet with no separation. With regard to the first part of his thesis, Tertullian argued forcefully that the threeness of deity as revealed to us in the economy of salvation is in no way incompatible with the unity of the Godhead. To cite Kelly, "He argued that, though three, the Persons were severally manifestations of a single indivisible power, noting that on the analogy of the imperial government one and the same sovereignty could be exercised by coordinate agencies."[47] Concerning the latter part of his thesis, in line with the Apologists and Christian tradition, he maintained that the distinction between Father, Son, and Spirit did not imply separation or division; technically put, it was a matter of *distinctio* rather than *separation*.[48] Illustrations from nature such as the unity of the root and shoot or the source and river, and perhaps more importantly, sun and light, made this case.[49] In carefully drafted seminal statements, again anticipating later debates concerning consubstantiality, the North African theologian surmised that the Johannine Jesus' saying "I and the Father are one" means that Father and Son are of "one substance";[50] it is a mater of identity of substance rather than numerical unity.[51] By extension, Son and Spirit are of the same substance with Father.[52] Thus, we can speak of God's one "substance" and three distinct yet undivided "persons."[53] This is the emergence of the Western church's semi-canonized way of expressing its faith in the Trinity, coined by Tertullian: "one substance in three persons" (*una substantia, tres personae*). Tertullian

46. Ibid., 2 (p. 589).
47. Kelly, *Early Christian Doctrines*, 113.
48. Tertullian, *Against Praxeas* 12 (pp. 606–7).
49. Ibid., 8 (pp. 602–3).
50. Ibid., 2 (p. 598).
51. Ibid., 25 (p. 621).
52. Ibid., 3 (pp. 598–99). Even then, Tertullian's thinking was still tied to the derivationist tendency of the Apologist tradition in that he regarded Father as the "whole substance" and Son as derivation from the whole. See further Kelly, *Early Christian Doctrines*, 114.
53. Tertullian, *Against Praxeas* 2 (p. 598). Father, Son, and Spirit are three "not in condition, but in degree; not in substance, but in form; not in power, but in aspect; yet of one substance, and of one condition, and of one power, inasmuch as he is one God." Ibid.

is said to be the first to apply *persona* and *Trinitas*[54] to the Christian God. "Where *substance* stood for the common fundamental reality shared by Father, Son, and Holy Spirit, Tertullian understood *person* as the principle of operative individuality."[55] Clearly, then, Tertullian helped avoid the modalistic heresy with his insistence on real distinctions in the united Godhead. His weakness, however, lies in his incapability to fully avoid the persistent subordinationism. In line with the Apologists (Justin Martyr), Tertullian taught that there is an ordering of persons in the Godhead (Father being the first, Son the second, and Spirit the third).

Much has been written about the history of the term *persona* and its applicability to Trinitarian language. The contours of the term are both obscure and wide. In its original sense it has the meaning of "mask" as worn by an actor in a play, thus denoting something that is not "real" for the human being behind the mask. The other extreme, the modern one, is to regard the *persona* as not only something "real" about the human being but also highly individualistic. Tertullian probably meant something like a concrete individual.[56] Understandably, neither the etymology of the term nor its highly individualized modern meaning captures the principles of distinction-in-unity meant by those who first applied it to describe the Christian God. In several places in our subsequent discussion, therefore, this concept will emerge when we study various ways later theologians have tried to express their Trinitarian faith.

By looking back at this juncture, we may gather that significant advances in early Christian Trinitarian theology had been reached in several respects, two of which stand out for the purposes of this discussion. The distinction between Spirit and Son was affirmed even though the doctrine of the Spirit was still very much in the making.[57] Furthermore, there was a growing consensus on the necessity and possibility of affirming both the deity of the Three and belief in one God; this question, while far from being resolved yet, was not so great as to necessar-

---

54. Ibid., 8 (pp. 602–3).

55. O'Collins, *Tripersonal God*, 105. The term "substance" rather than "essence" (from Latin *essentia*) was adopted by the Westerners to speak of the undivided unity of the Godhead, corresponding to the Eastern Christians' Greek term *ousia*. To the terminological obscurities and challenges we will come later.

56. George L. Prestige, *Fathers and Heretics* (London: SPCK, 1940), 84. See also the careful discussion in Roy Kearsley, *Tertullian's Theology of Divine Power* (Carlisle, UK: Paternoster, 1998), 135–38. Tertullian also had a hard time with the other key term in the formula, namely, *substantia*: Owing to his Stoic leanings, Tertullian had difficulty in describing essence apart from any kind of bodily ramifications, as the following citation from *Against Praxeas* 7 clearly illustrates: "For who will deny that God is a body, although 'God is spirit?' For Spirit has a bodily substance of its own kind, in its own form." While scholars have debated what it is that Tertullian affirms here and what are the implications for his understanding of the Spirit, the statement at face value of course reflects highly "materializing" language. See further O'Collins, *Tripersonal God*, 105; for a short statement on Stoicism, see Kärkkäinen, *Doctrine of God*, 62.

57. I will leave aside the study of the development of the doctrine of the Spirit except where it is necessary for the development of the argumentation. For the growth of pneumatological traditions in the Bible and history, see Kärkkäinen, *Pneumatology*, 23–65.

ily lead to an impasse. Subordinationism, however, was not yet overcome either in the West or East, even when the monarchical type of subordinationism was rejected. The fledgling Trinitarian doctrine continued struggling with the question of how to best *express* the conviction that the deity of the Son (and Spirit) can be compatible with monotheism. That was the question known in the history of theology as the Arian(ist) controversy.

THE CONTINUING STRUGGLE TO RELATE THE DIVINITY OF THE SON TO THE DEITY OF THE FATHER

A significant milestone on the way to the Arianist challenge to Trinitarian formulation was the contribution of the Eastern Father Origen. His lasting legacy, gleaned from Irenaeus and others,[58] was the attempt to establish the eternal Trinity in the Godhead with the help of an insistence on the eternal begetting of the Son.[59] While Origen's views are open to more than one interpretation,[60] this was a major step on the way to relating Son and Spirit to Father. For Origen, there was no time when *Logos* was not.[61] Father and Son share a unity of nature and substance; there is no unlikeness between them.[62] Yet another way to affirm the eternal generation of the Son was to use the expression "light from light" that found its way into the creeds.[63] Affirmations such as these anticipated the Arians' rejection of the coeternality of Son and Spirit.

At the same time, Origen was not able to fully overcome subordinationism in more than one way—although in a more subtle manner. He continued supporting the idea of gradations in the Godhead with Father being the "highest" one.[64] Furthermore, only God/Father is *autotheos*, self-subsistent, without origins,[65] Son

58. Letham, *Holy Trinity*, 93.
59. Origen, *First Principles* 1.2.4 (p. 247). See further Widdicombe, *Fatherhood*, 90–92.
60. For a helpful discussion of the ambiguity, see Olson and Hall, *Trinity*, 24–26.
61. Origen, *First Principles* 1.2.9; 2.11; 4.1.2.; 4.1.4 (pp. 249, 251, 350–51, 352). Origen makes every intellectual effort to make the point that the Son never had a beginning: "Wherefore we have always held that God is the Father of his only-begotten Son, who was born indeed of him, and derives from him what he is, but without any beginning, not only such as may be measured by any divisions of time, but even that which the mind alone can contemplate within itself. . . . Therefore we must believe that Wisdom was generated before any beginning that can be either comprehended or expressed." Ibid., 1.2.2 (p. 246).
62. Ibid., 1.2.6.; 1.2.12 (pp. 247–48, 251). For a helpful discussion, see Letham, *Holy Trinity*, 102–4.
63. Origen, *First Principles* 1.2.7 (p. 248).
64. E.g., in Origen, *Commentary on the Gospel according to John*, trans. Ronald E. Heine (Washington, DC: Catholic University of America Press, 1989), 13.25, Origen affirms that there are gradations of being, Father being the highest. Pannenberg goes so far as to say that for Origen the son was in Pannenberg's view a "creature." Pannenberg, *Systematic Theology*, 1:275. I am not quite sure what he means here.
65. Origen, *First Principles* 1.2.13 (p. 251); Origen, *Against Celsus* 5.39, in *Ante-Nicene Fathers* 4:561.

and Spirit by derivation from the Father.[66] This idea was picked up by Arians even though Origen of course rejects the Arian idea according to which there was a time when the Son was not. Origen's legacy is thus ambiguous, "occasioned by his propensity to think on his feet," as Letham succinctly puts it: "Stress on the subordination of the Son and Spirit would lead to the denial of their deity (by the Arians and the *pneumatomachoi*[67]), while the assertion of their deity in that context would foster allegations of tritheism (which Gregory of Nyssa would rebut)."[68] Ironically, then, Origen with all his superb achievements indirectly contributed to Arianism.

Arianism, one of the "The Four Great Heresies," to cite the title of a classic study,[69] picked up the pressing theme in the third and fourth centuries, namely, how to reconcile the unity of God with the deity of Jesus Christ. Arius,[70] a Presbyter in Alexandria, inherited the teaching of Origen concerning Father, Son, and Spirit sharing the one divine nature yet the Father being the source, thus implying in some way or another the inferior role of the Son and Spirit.[71] Arius pushed the idea of the inferiority of the Son to the point where only Father is without origins and without birth, transcendent, beyond. The Father does not share absolute deity with any creatures, not even with the Son. Arius is attributed with teaching that there was a time when the Son was not, that the Son was made out of nothing, and that the Son had an origin similar to other creatures.[72]

O'Collins compares Arianism with an early heresy that also struggled with the challenge of reconciling the deity of the Son with that of the Father:

> Like the modalist monarchians (e.g., Sabellius), Arius and his followers wanted to preserve an absolute "mon-archy" of God, but unlike the Sabel-

66. While it has been said in Origen's defense that he did not necessarily equate derivation of substance with inferiority (see Letham, *Holy Trinity*, 107), I have a hard time seeing the point: after all, it became the received view in the Christian East to insist on the Father as the source of the Godhead.

67. *Pneumatomachoi* (Pneumatomachians), literally "Spirit fighters," were fourth-century heretics who denied the deity of the Holy Spirit.

68. Letham, *Holy Trinity*, 107.

69. J. W. C. Wand, *The Four Great Heresies* (New York: Morehouse-Gorham, 1955), 38–62, discusses Arianism. A highly regarded contemporary study on various aspects of Arianism is R. P. C. Hanson, *The Search for the Christian Doctrine of God: The Arian Controversy 318–381* (Edinburg: T & T Clark, 1988). A reliable guide is also Rowan Williams, *Arius: Heresy and Tradition* (Grand Rapids: Eerdmans, 2002).

70. For the checkered historiography behind Arius, the alleged architect of Arianism, see M. R. Barnes and Daniel H. Williams, eds., *Arianism after Arius: Essays on the Development of the Fourth Century Trinitarian Conflicts* (Edinburgh: T & T Clark, 1993). As is well known, historians debate whether Arius is to be attributed with the teaching carrying his name or whether Arianism is a more generic heresy defined by Arius's opponents rather than himself. For (alleged) views of Arius, we are totally dependent on his orthodox opponent Athanasius's writings and his quotations from Arius's *Thalia*. According to M. R. Barnes's introduction, "Arius himself . . . had only a minor role in the theological debates which were reputed to be a conflict over his views and which eventually bore his name." Barnes, *Arianism after Arius*, xv.

71. For differences between Arius and Origen, see the helpful discussion in Letham, *Holy Trinity*, 114–15.

72. Key ideas can be found conveniently in Athanasius, *Against the Arians* 308–309. A helpful summary and explanation of Arian claims can be found in Letham, *Holy Trinity*, 111–14; and in Kelly, *Early Christian Doctrines*, 226–31.

lians and other modalist monarchians, they held onto the real difference of identity between the Father and the Son. . . . Where Sabellianism asserted a strict unity of the divine essence without any real distinction of subjects, Arianism distinguished the subjects while denying their unity of essence.[73]

To understand the significance of the challenge of Arianism to developing Trinitarian orthodoxy we have to acknowledge that it was not only about christological[74] and Trinitarian debates; it also had everything to do with our salvation. Arius's logic seems quite well taken. For him, because the Son was a creature just as we are, there opens a way for humans to imitate the Savior in conforming their will to the will of the Father as the obedient Son did. Like the Son, who was adopted into sonship, we can be adopted, too. Both the monarchy of the Father and the role of the Son as "assistant to the Father, operating under orders,"[75] were affirmed.[76] While there is no reason to deny the importance of ontological considerations of deity, the significance of the soteriological agenda should be reckoned with. While Arian soteriology makes sense, for his opponents, especially those coming from the Christian East, it also raises insurmountable problems. These soteriological problems can be summed up in this main difficulty: How can a creature-Savior help us be elevated into the divine life of God?[77] Only God is able to save; no creature possesses soteriological resources. Yet at the same time the "Arian hermeneutic cannot be misconstrued: what is predicated of the redeemer must be predicated of the redeemed."[78]

What came to be the orthodox position was affirmed at the Council of Nicaea and vehemently defended by Athanasius. When looking at those responses, we need to keep in mind that we can speak of an orthodox consensus only in hindsight. During the time of Arius, the Trinitarian canons were still in the making in all camps, and therefore to imply that Arius was attacking a stronghold of orthodoxy with his deviant views is historically not accurate at all. Furthermore, while Athanasius deserves great credit in helping formulate the orthodox position, he was by no means the sole defender of the majority view.[79]

73. O'Collins, *Tripersonal God*, 112.
74. Arius was conspicuously silent about the Spirit.
75. Letham, *Holy Trinity*, 112.
76. Robert C. Gregg and Dennis E. Groh, in an important study fittingly titled *Early Arianism: A View of Salvation* ([Philadelphia: Fortress Press, 1981], x), put it well: "Early Arianism is most intelligible when viewed as a scheme of salvation. Soteriological concerns dominate the text and inform every major aspect of the controversy. At the center of the Arian soteriology was a redeemer, obedient to his Creator's will, whose life of virtue modeled perfect creaturehood and hence the path of salvation for all Christians."
77. In the Christian East, salvation is understood in terms of *theōsis*, deification, divinization.
78. Gregg and Groh, *Early Arianism*, 50. See further Ted Peters, *God as Trinity: Relationality and Temporality in Divine Life* (Louisville, KY: Westminster John Knox Press, 1993), 60–62.
79. Athanasius and Arius, as far as we know, did not have a personal encounter, Arius probably having died before Athanasius as a young man started opposing his views. For an interesting study, see C. Kannengiesser, *Arius and Athanasius: Two Alexandrian Theologians* (Aldershot, UK: Variorum, 1991).

A death blow to the views of Arius was offered by the First Council of Nicaea (AD 325)[80] by its insistence on the consubstantiality of the Son with the Father.[81] The key term here is *homoousios*, a debated term. Against Arians it affirms the unity of the Son with the Father. Its danger of course lies in its modalistic tones.[82] Therefore, many preferred the slightly different form *homoiousios*, "of similar substance," which, while it avoids the danger of modalism, also opens to an Arian type of lack of identity, consubstantiality.[83] Consubstantiality was also argued with the saying "from the substance (*ousia*) of the Father." With all the difficulties of terminology (which we explore further), there is no denying that Nicaea's "main achievement was to place on record once and for all that the being of the Son is identical to the being of the Father, dealing a mortal blow to subordinationism."[84] At the same time, we have to acknowledge that Nicaea was hardly able to resolve the issues of Trinity, nor was it regarded as a major milestone in its own time. It is of course only in hindsight that Nicaea can be accorded the significance it now has.[85]

Athanasius both prepared and built on Nicaean foundations and offered a more nuanced reasoning for the rejection of Arianism:[86]

First, he argued that Arianism undermined the Christian doctrine of God by presupposing that the divine Triad is not eternal and by virtually reintroducing polytheism.[87] Second, it made nonsense of the established liturgical customs of baptizing in the Son's name as well as the Father's, and of addressing prayers to the Son.[88] Third, and perhaps most importantly, it undermined the Christian idea of redemption in Christ, since only if the Mediator was himself divine could people hope to reestablish fellowship with God.[89]

Athanasius's theological response confirms the earlier judgment that the fight

---

80. For a definitive analysis and discussion, see Kelly, *Early Christian Doctrines*, 223–51. What we know today as the Nicene Creed is not the product of the 325 council but rather of the Council of Constantinople of 381; of course Constantinople is largely based on the earlier council.

81. The key argument of Nicaea for our purposes reads: "We believe . . . in one Lord Jesus Christ, the Son of God, begotten from the Father, only-begotten, that is, from the substance of the Father, God from God, light from light, true God from true God, begotten not made, of one substance with the Father." Translation in Kelly, *Early Christian Doctrines*, 232.

82. A number of reasons made *homoousios* a highly suspect term for many Nicene theologians: it was not a biblical term; it had a checkered history, having at times been condemned; and because it could be applied to material substances it could be used as a way to reinforce the once-used but now rejected "material" analogies of deity. See O'Collins, *Tripersonal God*, 119.

83. For a careful discussion of these terms, their background, and various nuances, see Kelly, *Early Christian Doctrines*, 233–37.

84. Letham, *Holy Trinity*, 117.

85. While it clarified the relation of the Son to Father in a foundational way, it also brought about Anti-Nicene parties; for an accessible account, see Kelly, *Early Christian Doctrines*, 247–51, and Letham, *Holy Trinity*, 122–26.

86. Kelly, *Early Christian Doctrines*, 233. The following three references to Athanasius are provided by Kelly in the cited text.

87. E.g., Athanasius, *Against the Arians* 1.17–18; 1.20; 3.15–16 (pp. 316ff., 318, 402ff.).

88. Ibid., 2.41–42 (pp. 370ff.).

89. Ibid., 2.67; 2.70 (pp. 384–85, 386–87).

over Arianism had as much to do with salvation as ontology, as well as spirituality, according to the ancient rule *lex orandi lex credendi*: the law of prayer is the law of belief. Trinitarian doctrine, like other key Christian doctrines, was hammered out, not in sterile study, but rather in the midst of lived spirituality, prayer, and the worship life of the church.

Against Arian charges that the Son is a creature, Athanasius presented the counterargument that since the Father is not a creature, neither is the Son; whatever is in the Father is in the Son.[90] This is also the meaning of his famous saying that the Son is "whole God" (*holos theou*).[91] "He who looks at the Son, he says, sees the Father. In turn, the Father's Godhead is in the Son and is seen in the Son. The Father is in the Son."[92] One way to express this mutuality for Athanasius is to use the ancient term *perichōrēsis* (literally, "dancing around").[93] It was not only in the East that Arianism was opposed. Latin writers such as Ambrose, bishop of Milan at the end of the fourth century, accumulated a number of biblical passages against the Arian claim of the creaturehood of the Son.[94]

THE CONSUBSTANTIALITY OF THE SPIRIT

Above I discussed the early attempts, including those of Athanasius and the Cappadocians, to affirm the distinctions among Father, Son, and Spirit. Having rejected the idea of Origen concerning different spheres of operation in the outward works of the Trinity, the Cappadocians focused on the unity of works *ad extra*. As noted, the weakness of this approach is that it still falls short of the establishment of distinctions among the Trinitarian persons in general and the role of the Spirit in particular. Probably aware of these challenges, building on the Athanasian principle of relationality ("Father cannot be Father without the Son"), the Cappadocians argued that relations define the distinctions.[95] While that was a valuable suggestion and one that has been followed by later tradition, it still leaves open the question of the Spirit's inclusion in the Trinity; Athanasius's

90. Athanasius, *On Luke 10:22 (Matthew 11:27)* 4–6, in *Nicene and Post-Nicene Fathers*[2] 4:89–90. For other examples in Athanasius, see Thomas F. Torrance, *Trinitarian Perspectives: Toward Doctrinal Agreement* (Edinburgh: T & T Clark, 1994), 8–10.
91. Athanasius, *Against the Arians* 3.6 (pp. 396–97).
92. Letham, *Holy Trinity*, 137.
93. For examples, see Widdicombe, *Fatherhood*, 206–7; Letham, *Holy Trinity*, 140. According to Letham, "Although the precise word *perichōrēsis* was not used for some time yet, the truth it signifies was already widely accepted." Ibid., 178.
94. "God is One, neither dividing His Son from Him, as do the heathen, nor denying, with the Jews, that He was begotten of the Father before all worlds." Ambrose, *Of the Christian Faith* 1.1.6, in *Nicene and Post-Nicene Fathers*[2] 10:202. Another key Latin thinker of the fourth century is Hilary of Poitiers, whose *The Trinity* is a landmark Western contribution. Hilary of Poitiers, *The Trinity* in *Fathers of the Church*, vol. 25, trans. Stephen McKenna (Washington, DC: Catholic University of America Press, 2002).
95. Basil of Caesarea, *Letters* 38.7, in *Nicene and Post-Nicene Fathers*[2] 8:202; Gregory of Nazianzus, *Orations* 29.16, in *Nicene and Post-Nicene Fathers*[2] 7:306–7; also *Orations* 31.9 (pp. 320–21).

attempt to transfer to Spirit the argument from the Father-Son relationality and as a consequence of the deity of the Son is hardly convincing.[96] Furthermore, the Cappadocians followed the rule in the East to make the Father the source and principle of deity.[97] This idea, however, is subordinationist since it makes Spirit and Son dependent on the Father but not vice versa. While not an Arian idea itself, it can be used by Arians and other subordinationists to defend the monarchy of the Father and thus compromise a genuine mutuality.[98]

The role of the Spirit in the Trinity was being clarified and the Spirit "elevated" to the same status as the Son (even when the two still tended to be regarded in some way or another as "inferior" to the Father as the source) through the slow growth of pneumatological doctrine and its insistence on the deity of the Spirit. This happened with reference to biblical passages, even though, as is well known, a number of biblical references to the Spirit can be read in a more generic way rather than as specific references to the Spirit as "divine person"; to the liturgical tradition of *epiclesis,* the prayer for the descent of the Spirit at the eucharistic table; and to the Trinitarian baptismal practice, to name the most obvious bases.

Key to the development of pneumatological doctrine were the Eastern theologians. Against *tropicii* (Tropici), a group that was not willing to give the same divine status to the Spirit as to the Son, Athanasius wrote his *Letters to Serapion on the Holy Spirit* (355–360). This work as well as Basil the Great's *On the Holy Spirit* (376, directed against the *Pneumatomachoi*) are landmark works in affirming the Spirit's deity and thus equality with the Son. Other Cappadocians affirmed the same.[99] Athanasius insisted that the Spirit is in Christ as the Son is in the Father.[100] Kelly summarizes Athanasius's contribution. In response to Arians and others who denied the deity of the Spirit,[101] Athanasius's teaching

---

96. Athanasius did this in his letter on the Holy Spirit to Serapion. See further Pannenberg, *Systematic Theology,* 1:279.

97. Basil of Caesarea, *Against Eunomius* 2.17; *Letters* 38.7 (pp. 140–41); Gregory of Nazianzus, *Orations* 2.36–38 (pp. 212–13); 29.2 (p. 301); Gregory of Nyssa, *Against Macedonius* 13; Gregory of Nyssa, *Against Eunomius* 17, in *Nicene and Post-Nicene Fathers*² 5:54–55. For some references in this note and the previous one, I am indebted to Pannenberg, *Systematic Theology,* 1:279 nn. 68, 69.

98. Pannenberg's evaluation of the Cappadocians' view, while quite critical, is worth hearing: "The idea of the Father as the source and origin of deity so fused the person of the Father and the substance of the Godhead that the divine substance is originally proper to the Father alone, being received from Him by the Son and Spirit. In distinction from Athanasius this means a relapse into subordinationism, since the idea of the mutual defining of the distinctiveness of the persons does not lead to the thought of an equally mutual ontological constitution of their personhood but is interpreted in terms of relations of origin, of which it can be said that strictly they are constitutive only for the personhood of the Son and Spirit if the Father is the source and origin of deity." Pannenberg, *Systematic Theology,* 1:280.

99. For a helpful discussion, see Kelly, *Early Christian Doctrines,* 258–63; and Letham, *Holy Trinity,* 149–51. Important contributions to emerging pneumatological doctrine came also from Gregory of Nazianzus, who in his *Orations* (esp. 29, 30, and 31) discusses widely the deity of the Spirit and the Spirit in relation to Father and Son. For a helpful discussion, see Letham, *Holy Trinity,* 159–64.

100. Athanasius, *Epistola 1 ad Serapionem* 1.14, in *Patrologiae cursus completus: Series graeca,* vol. 26 (1857; reprint, Turnholti, Belguim: Typographi Brepols Editores Pontificii, 1975), 564–65. For the Spirit's role in the Trinity in Athanasian theology, see Letham, *Holy Trinity,* 141–44.

101. Kelly, *Early Christian Doctrine,* 257. The four following references to Athanasius are provided by Kelly.

is that the Spirit is fully divine, consubstantial with the Father and the Son . . . [T]he Spirit "belongs to and is one with the Godhead Which is the Triad."[102] . . . [T]he Spirit comes from God, bestows sanctification and life, and is immutable, omnipresent and unique.[103] . . . [T]he Triad is eternal, homogenous and indivisible, and . . . since the Spirit is a member of it He must therefore be consubstantial with Father and Son.[104] . . . He belongs in essence to the Son exactly as the Son does to the Father.[105]

In the Nicene Creed of Constantinople I (381) the consubstantiality of the Spirit was officially confirmed: the Holy Spirit is to be "worshiped and glorified together with the Father and the Son."[106]

THE SHARED TRINITARIAN FAITH: ONE GOD WITH THREE PERSONS

Toward the end of the fourth century after Nicaea (325) and on the eve of the Council of Constantinople (381), a growing convergence was emerging, the confession of Trinitarian faith in terms of one God with three persons, Father, Son, and Spirit. Above we noticed that in the Christian West, it was expressed with the formula: "one substance in three persons" (*una substantia, tres personae*). In the Christian East, the way Athanasius[107] and the Cappadocians[108] came to express the orthodox doctrine was *mia ousia, treis hypostaseis*.[109] God is one being (*ousia*) with three persons (*hypostaseis*).[110]

Terminological confusion, however, was a major challenge among Christians, not only between the Christian East and West—the Greek-speaking Eastern theologians and Latin-speaking Westerners had a hard time understanding the key terms, let alone agreeing on a shared meaning[111]—but also in the same language

102. Athanasius, *Serapion* 1.21.
103. Ibid., 1.22–27.
104. Ibid., 1.2; 1.20; 3.7.
105. Ibid., 1.25; 3.2.
106. The Nicene Creed as translated in Hanson, *Search for the Christian Doctrine of God*, 815–16.
107. For a careful discussion of Athanasius's Trinitarian theology, see Letham, *Holy Trinity*, 127–45.
108. For a careful discussion of the Cappadocians' Trinitarian theology, see Letham, *Holy Trinity*, 146–66; and Kelly, *Early Christian Doctrines*, 263–69.
109. This is often called the "Cappadocian settlement." So, e.g., George L. Prestige, *God in Patristic Thought* (London, Toronto: Heinemann, 1936), 233–34. This is of course only a scholarly construct, a conclusion from the emerging theology of the Cappadocians, and as such it needs to be handled with care. For words of warning, see Joseph T. Lienhard, SJ, "*Ousia* and *Hypostasis*: The Cappadocian Settlement and the Theology of 'One *Hypostasis*,'" in Davis, Kendall, and O'Collins, *Trinity*, 99–103.
110. See the important note by Torrance, *Trinitarian Perspectives*, 15. For the contribution of the Cappadocians to the establishment of patristic Trinitarian doctrine, see Stanley J. Grenz, *Theology for the Community of God* (Grand Rapids: Eerdmans, 2000), 60–61; and Letham, *Holy Trinity*, 164–66.
111. See further Hanson, *Search for the Christian Doctrine of God*, 181: "People holding different views were using the same words as those who opposed them, but, unawares, giving them different

domain, there was uncertainty about the exact meaning of the terms used. A key term was *hypostasis*.[112] The Greek fathers had used *hypostasis* and *ousia* more or less synonymously.[113] To add to the confusion, in the Christian West from the time of Tertullian onward, *hypostasis* was considered to be the equivalent of the Latin term *substantia* (essence).[114] Therefore, the Eastern suggestion of one *ousia* with three *hypostaseis* for Latin speakers meant of course tritheism. As long as *hypostasis* and *ousia* were considered to have more or less the same meaning, the *homoousios* statement of Nicaea could be understood in a modalistic way (i.e., that Father and Son [as well as Spirit by derivation] do not denote real distinctions).[115]

Leaving behind the continuing terminological confusion, theologically it is a commonplace to maintain that for Eastern theologians "it was natural that they should make the three hypostases, rather than the one divine substance, their starting point."[116] This means that "while the formula which expresses their position is 'one *ousia* in three *hypostaseis*,' their emphasis often seems to be on the latter term, connoting the separate subsistence of Father, Son and Holy Spirit, rather than on the former, which stood for the one indivisible Godhead common to Them."[117] At the same time, however, both Athanasius[118] and the Cappadocians were also strong defenders of the *homoousion* formula of Nicaea and later the consubstantiality of the Spirit as well. Basil the Great's formulation illustrates:

> For all things that are the Father's are beheld in the Son, and all things that are the Son's are the Father's; because the whole Son is in the Father and has all the Father in Himself. Thus the hypostasis of the Son becomes as it were form and face of the knowledge of the Father, and the hypostasis of the

meanings from those applied to them by their opponents." And even more: "Tertullian may well have supplied the West with its Trinitarian vocabulary; he certainly did not supply the East with its Trinitarian theology," 184. I am indebted to Letham, *Holy Trinity*, 118–20, for finding these two references in Hanson's monumental work.

112. For the history behind this term, see O'Collins, *Tripersonal God*, 117–18.

113. Christopher Stead, *Divine Substance* (Oxford: Clarendon Press, 1977), 160–61. For a careful discussion, see Lienhard, "*Ousia* and *Hypostasis*," 99–121.

114. Even Augustine hesitated calling the persons hypostases because *hypostasis* and *substantia* were considered to be synonyms. Augustine, *On the Trinity* 7.5–6, in *Nicene and Post-Nicene Fathers*, Series 1 (reprint, Grand Rapids: Eerdmans, 2001), 3:111–14.

115. See further O'Collins, *Tripersonal God*, 118. Basil the Great framed the contours in a pointed way: "As he who fails to confess the community of the essence or substance falls into polytheism, so he who refuses to grant the distinction of the hypostases is carried away into . . . Sabellius." Basil of Caesarea, *Letters* 210.5 (p. 251). Other terms in need of clarification were those describing the idea of birth and coming into existence as long as they were applied to Trinitarian members: *genetos/agenetos* (created/uncreated, that which has never existed before but rather is eternal) and *gennetos/agennetos* (begotten, generated/unbegotten, ingenerate). In earliest Christian theology before Origen there was little distinction between the idea of being created and being generated. Orthodox doctrine had it that the Son was *gennetos non genetos*, begotten of the Father but not created, while Arians taught that the Son is *genetos*. See further Prestige, *God in Patristic Thought*, 37–53.

116. Kelly, *Early Christian Doctrines*, 264.

117. Ibid.

118. Athanasius had a hard time in adopting the term *homoousios* for its alleged modalistic tones and checkered history; yet his theology is consubstantialist.

Father is known in the form of the Son, while the proper quality which is contemplated therein remains for the plain distinction of the hypostases.[119]

By derivation, this principle of mutuality and coinherence (perichoresis) can also be applied to the Spirit. Catherine LaCugna is on to something when she suggests that in the Cappadocian theology each person "is the divine *ousia;* the divine *ousia* exists hypostatically, and there is no *ousia* apart from the *hypostaseis.* To exist as God is to be the Father who begets the Son and breathes forth the Spirit."[120] Therefore, Trinitarian persons cannot be thought of as disconnected from each other; in other words, "*It is impossible to think of the divine essence in itself or by itself.*"[121] If LaCugna's interpretation is correct, it means that a major achievement has been reached in the development of Trinitarian theology regarding the question of how to relate the unity to distinctions. Unlike some Western views in which the unity of the Godhead almost appears to be understood in terms of something "separate behind" the three-ness (as if there were Father, Son, and Spirit plus one Godhead),[122] here the "per-sons" (*hypostasis*) and "being/essence" (*ousia*) are related to each other in a mutual, perichoretic way. Out of this grows the contemporary emphasis on communion the-ology in which the only way to think of one God is to think of one God as existing as Father, Son, and Spirit.[123] O'Collin's observation is important: "At the heart of God, the Cappadocians saw an interpersonal communion or *koinōnia,* with com-munion as the function of all three divine persons and not simply of the Holy Spirit. For this interpersonal model of the Trinity, God's inner being is relational, with each of the three persons totally related to the other two in 'reciprocal delight'—to bor-row an Athanasian expression."[124] At the same time, as mentioned earlier, the Cap-padocians were not yet able to avoid subordinationism regarding the Father as the source.[125] However, their insight concerning perichoresis and mutual relationality is extremely valuable and in hindsight can be developed into the understanding that even Father cannot be conceived of as "Father" apart from the web of the mutual relations of the Three.

---

119. Basil of Caesarea, *Letters* 38.8 (p. 141). (It is not certain if Basil or Gregory of Nyssa is the author; in any case, this quotation nicely reflects the view of the Cappadocians.)

120. LaCugna, *God for Us,* 69.

121. Ibid., 70. I am indebted to Letham, *Holy Trinity,* 165, for turning my attention to this passage in LaCugna.

122. I do not claim that any seriously respected Western theology ever taught this; I am using this merely as an illustration of the *danger* behind some Western approaches to Trinity.

123. Human language of course fails us here. Gregory of Nazianzen tried to express this in a some-what paradoxical way: God exists "undivided . . . in separate Persons." Of course this statement can be misinterpreted to imply tritheism if the term "separate" is pressed; the only purpose of that somewhat unfortunate expression is to insist on real distinctions among Father, Son, and Spirit. Gregory of Nazianzen, *Orations* 31.14 (p. 322).

124. O'Collins, *Tripersonal God,* 131–32.

125. O'Collins's comment is nuanced here. When speaking of the Cappadocians' insistence on the Father as the source, and thus of the Father's monarchy, he says: "This 'mon-archy' of the Father could be seen, however, to favor a descending view of the Trinity and even an unacceptable subordination of the Son and Spirit to the Father, the sole unoriginated fountainhead of divinity. But, properly under-stood, the 'mon-archy' of the Father does not mean superiority (let alone any exclusive superiority) or

The Cappadocians' emphasis on the threeness as the way to understand one God is sometimes too cheaply charged with "tritheism." Aware of these suspicions, Gregory of Nyssa wrote a study titled *On "Not Three Gods" to Ablabius*. Gregory considers the possibility of illustrating the Trinity by comparing it to three men sharing a common nature yet distinct personalities. At the end of the day he acknowledges the obvious limitations of the illustration (such as the fact that there are of course more than three human beings, but only three divine persons) even though he with other Cappadocians was fond of the analogy of universals and its particulars with the application to three men.[126]

In the Nicene[-Constantinopolitan] Creed produced by the Council of Constantinople in 381,[127] the early Trinitarian canons were hammered out. This creed is highly significant since it is confessed even today by both Eastern and Western churches. Although there would be later disputes about the Trinity, the Nicene-Constantinopolitan Creed represents the shared consensus.[128] It affirms the Council of Nicaea's incipient doctrine and expands on key issues. Its main omission is the phrase "from the substance (*ousia*) of the Father." The exact reason for the omission is unclear.[129] The theology of the Nicene-Constantinopolitan Creed is fully consubstantial; it maintains the *homoousion* phrase ("consubstantial with the Father"). While the creedal statement from Nicaea lacked details about the deity of the Spirit, Constantinople has it more fully: "And in the Holy Spirit, the Lord and life-giver, who proceeds from the Father, who is worshipped and glorified together with the Father and Son, who spoke by the prophets."[130] The application of the term *kyrios* to the Spirit makes a strong statement of the deity of the Spirit, as is of course the inclusion of the Spirit in the worship of the Triune God. This is all the more telling when we keep in mind the fact that even at the end of the fourth century many orthodox Christians felt reserved about calling the Spirit "God."[131] Unlike the later *filioque* clause, accord-

---

a false subordination, but both unity and distinction." O'Collins, *Tripersonal God*, 132–33. Pannenberg's assessment of the Cappadocians (and Athanasius) in this respect is much more reserved when it comes to subordinationism. Pannenberg, *Systematic Theology*, 1:280. Letham makes the less than convincing claim that Gregory of Nazianzus clearly and determinatively leaves behind subordinationism by applying "monarchy" to other Trinitarian persons, too, including the Spirit. Letham, *Holy Trinity*, 159.

126. See further Kelly, *Early Christian Doctrines*, 267; Letham, *Holy Trinity*, 156–57.

127. As mentioned earlier, the Nicene Creed as we know it today comes from Constantinople rather than the Council of Nicaea in 325, even though the Creed of course is based on the Nicene Council. For a careful and insightful comparison between the creedal statement of Nicaea and the Nicene Creed, see O'Collins, *Tripersonal God*, 121–26; see also 114–21.

128. I leave aside the thorny historical question of whether Constantinople (381) even produced that creed. Whoever or whatever produced it, it is an ecumenical theological landmark, still authoritative for the Christian church in the East and the West. For those interested in historical details, a good source is Kelly, *Early Christian Creeds*, 305–12.

129. See further Hanson, *Search for the Christian Doctrine of God*, 817–18.

130. Here and in the rest of the chapter, the Nicene Creed as translated in Hanson, *Search for the Christian Doctrine of God*, 815–16.

131. To Gregory of Nazianzen we owe the classic statement about the slow development of the idea of the deity of the Spirit in Christian theology: "The Old Testament proclaimed the Father openly, and

ing to which the Spirit proceeds from both the Father and Son, this creed makes
the Father the source.[132] What is missing in the Nicene-Constantinopolitan
Creed are the explicit statements about the perichoretic relational mutuality
advanced by the Cappadocians and Athanasius. There is conspicuously little
about relationality as such.

In a very helpful way, Robert Letham outlines the "implications of the Trinitarian settlement"[133] based on Constantinople and the tradition so far, especially
that of the Eastern theologians. First, the concept of one being with three persons is the guiding principle. "It could be said either that God is one being who
exists as three persons (this proved to be the preferred route in the West) or, alter-
natively, that he is three persons who are simultaneously one undivided being
(which tended to be the approach favored in the East)."[134] Second, consubstantiality is strongly affirmed even when the very term *homoousion* is not applied to
the Spirit. "There is only one essence or being of God, which all three persons
share completely. Furthermore, each person is God in himself."[135] Third, while
not present explicitly in the Nicene-Constantinopolitan Creed itself, there is the
growing tradition of perichoresis advocated by the Eastern theologians. Later
Eastern theologian John of Damascus picks up this insight and makes it a major
theme for the Trinitarian theology of the Christian East.[136] Fourth, there is the
order of the persons, the divine *taxis*:

> *from the Father through the Son by the Holy Spirit.* These relations cannot
> be reversed—the Son does not beget the Father, nor does the Father pro-
> ceed from the Holy Spirit. . . . Thus, the Father is the Father of the Son,
> and the Son is the Son of the Father. The Father begets the Son, and the
> Son is begotten by Father. This relation is not interchangeable, nor can it
> be reversed—it is eternal and unchangeable. *Mutatis mutandis,* the Holy
> Spirit proceeds from the Father . . . while the Father spirates the Spirit.
> Again this is never reversed."[137]

---

the Son more obscurely. The New [Testament] manifested the Son, and suggested the deity of the Spirit.
Now the Spirit Himself dwells among us, and supplies us with a clearer demonstration of Himself. For
it was not safe, when the Godhead of the Father was not yet acknowledged, plainly to proclaim the Son;
nor when that of the Son was not yet received to burden us further . . . with the Holy Ghost." Gregory
of Nazianzen, *Orations* 31.26 (p. 326).

132. O'Collins makes the important point that the approach of Constantinople as well as of Nicaea
is "genetic," meaning that the divinity streams from the Father to the Son and to the Spirit rather than
with the idea of one divine substance that would subsist in three persons. The Father is the source of
the unity. O'Collins, *Tripersonal God*, 122. In this regard, Letham's statement that in the Nicene Creed
"[t]here is nothing . . . to suggest that the Son or the Holy Spirit derives his deity from the Father" is
not well taken. Letham, *Holy Trinity*, 177. Maybe I have misunderstood his point since in what follows
he freely speaks of the "order of persons," thus making Father the "first" (pp. 189–81).

133. Subheading for the section in Letham, *Holy Trinity*, 175–81.

134. Ibid., 176. For further exposition, Letham refers here to Thomas F. Torrance, *The Christian Doctrine of God, One Being Three Persons* (Edinburgh: T & T Clark, 1996), 112–67.

135. Letham, *Holy Trinity*, 177.

136. See further ibid., 178–79.

137. Ibid., 179–80 (italics in the original).

Early Christian theology made significant advances during the first four centuries, the more significant since it was only about this same time that the canon of the New Testament was finally ratified (even though, of course, the basic list of writings deemed to be canonical was already quite fixed by the end of the second century). The development of the Trinitarian canons constantly went back to the writings of the New Testament canon and, with the help of existing philosophical and cultural devices, attempted to clarify the incipient biblical Trinitarianism.

Several challenges and developments were yet to come. Much theological work still awaited further clarification; to these we turn next.

Chapter 4

The Role of Trinitarian
Doctrine in the Developing
Christian Tradition

CONTINUING TASKS FOR POSTPATRISTIC
TRINITARIAN BELIEF

The importance of patristic developments cannot be overstated. The first four centuries represent not only the earliest tradition but also the tradition of the undivided church. The term "undivided" church is not meant to imply a naive belief that there were no divisions or differences, but rather the fact that enough common basis was found to keep the unity of the church unbroken.

To help structure the following discussion—which is not meant to offer a systematic or chronological account of the development of Trinitarian faith after the patristic era but rather a theological reading of the main challenges and attempted resolutions—it may be helpful to list the main issues facing the church in the aftermath of Constantinople:

1. The question of the theological and ecumenical significance of the difference between the Christian East and West has occupied the minds of theologians until our days. Terminological confusion is part

of the question, but only part.[1] The question can be put this way: Are Eastern and Western Christians confessing the same Trinitarian faith? A corollary question is then: Is the difference a matter of expression or of belief?

2. How do we best understand the Spirit in the Trinity? If the Spirit is Love shared by Father and Son, how does it relate to the biblical teaching of God as Love?

3. Both of these points culminate in the famous *filioque* debate about the derivation of the Spirit. This issue became the "official" reason for the split of the church in the beginning of the second millennium.

4. What is the place and role of the doctrine of the Trinity in Christian theology? For the West, the key challenge was the establishment of the role and status of the Trinity in the doctrine of God. In the West the Trinity could easily become an appendix because the order of theological discussion moved from one God to threeness. When pressed, the question could be put like this: Why bother with Trinity if Christian faith is monotheistic to the point that it can be first presented in the form of one God and only then, in the second movement, introduce the threeness?

5. The rise of communion theology going back to Richard of St. Victor.

DO EAST AND WEST CONFESS THE SAME TRINITARIAN FAITH?

According to conventional theological wisdom, "in general, Greek theology [of the Christian East] emphasizes the divine hypostases (persons), whereas Latin theology [of the Christian West] emphasizes the divine nature."[2] In other words, it is claimed that the East begins with the threeness of the Trinity, the West with the oneness or unity.[3] While not without grounds, this kind of description is also a caricature.[4] In order to address the question put forth in the subheading, I will take a closer look at key postpatristic developments in the West. The reason for this choice is the common understanding that begin-

1. A helpful discussion of the cultural, linguistic, and theological influences and differences can be found in J. N. D Kelly, *Early Christian Doctrines* (New York: Harper Press, 1958), 3–28.

2. Catherine Mowry LaCugna, "The Trinitarian Mystery of God," in *Systematic Theology: Roman Catholic Perspectives*, ed. Francis Schüssler Fiorenza and John P. Galvin, vol. 1 (Minneapolis: Fortress, 1991), 170. LaCugna calls the Eastern view emanationist in terms of descending order from Father to Son to Spirit and finally to the world, whereas the Western can be depicted as a circle enclosing all Trinitarian members in which the whole Trinity relates to the world. Ibid., 170–71.

3. The classic work contrasting Eastern and Western views is Théodore de Régnon, *Études de théologie positive sur la sainte Trinité*, 3 vols. (Paris: Retaux, 1892–98); see also Yves Congar, *I Believe in the Holy Spirit*, trans. David Smith, 3 vols. (New York: Seabury Press, 1983), 3:xv–xxi.

4. Gerald O'Collins, *The Tripersonal God: Understanding and Interpreting the Trinity* (New York and Mahwah, NJ: Paulist Press, 1999), 140.

ning with Augustine, theological work in general and Trinitarian reflection in particular has its center in the Latin-speaking church. Furthermore, early Eastern contributions have already been mentioned extensively.

What is the legacy of Augustine's Trinitarian thinking?[5] And how does it relate to the question in the subheading: Do East and West confess the same Trinitarian faith? At the moment it is challenging to discern scholarly consensus in the interpretation of Augustine's view of the Trinity.[6] The older consensus is that because of his Neoplatonic leanings, Augustine put stress on the unity of the divine essence and had a hard time in accounting for distinctions. That would of course mean that his approach would be diametrically opposed to the Eastern view.[7] One of the most vocal contemporary critics of Augustine along this line, Colin Gunton, has argued Augustine did not correctly understand the tradition, certainly not the teaching of the Cappadocians, and ended up viewing the divine substance "behind" relations. For the Cappadocians, so this critic says, on the contrary, relations are "ontological" whereas for the Bishop of Hippo only "logical."[8] Thomas Marsh joins in and accuses Augustine of replacing the earlier Latin emphasis on the divine monarchy of the Father with "divine substance or nature which *then* is verified in Father, Son and Holy Spirit."[9] All of this has even caused some to speak of a "theological crisis of the west"![10]

Not all are convinced that this is a fair reading of Augustine.[11] Two foundational problems are found in the older interpretation of Augustine, the correction of which may change our picture of the view of the Trinity held by this most influential early Western theologian. First, it is doubtful whether the Cappadocians had as developed a social doctrine of the Trinity as is assumed, and second, it is unclear whether Augustine really started with the unity of the divine essence

---

5. "It is impossible to do contemporary Trinitarian theology and not have a judgment on Augustine." Michel René Barnes, "Rereading Augustine's Theology of the Trinity," in *The Trinity: An Interdisciplinary Symposium on Trinity*, ed. Stephen T. Davis, Daniel Kendall, SJ, and Gerald O'Collins, SJ (Oxford: Oxford University Press, 1999), 145.

6. Rightly, Barnes laments that too much of Augustine's interpretation goes without actually reading Augustine! Barnes proposes to offer a new reading of the Bishop of Hippo based on reading everything he wrote on the topic of the Trinity; however, while fresh, Barnes's reading is also somewhat idiosyncratic since he focuses so much on the earlier writings. Ibid., 145–46.

7. So, e.g., George L. Prestige, *God in Patristic Thought* (London and Toronto: Heinemann, 1936), 237; and Bertrand de Margerie, *The Christian Trinity in History*, trans. Edmund J. Fordman (Petersham, MA: St. Bede's Publications, 1982), 110–21.

8. Colin Gunton, *The Promise of Trinitarian Theology*, 2nd ed. (Edinburgh: T & T Clark, 1997), 38–43 especially.

9. Thomas Marsh, *The Triune God: A Biblical, Historical, and Theological Study* (Mystic, CT: Twenty-Third Publications, 1994), 132.

10. Colin Gunton, "Augustine, the Trinity, and the Theological Crisis of the West," *Scottish Journal of Theology* 43 (1990): 33–58.

11. The most vocal critic of the alleged Neoplatonic influence on Augustine is Barnes, "Rereading Augustine's Theology of the Trinity." A careful, cautious interpretation, quite critical of the old consensus, is offered by Basil Studer, *Trinity and Incarnation: The Faith of the Early Church*, trans. Matthias Westerhoff, ed. Andrew Louth (Collegeville, MN: Liturgical Press, 1993), 167–85.

rather than with the distinctiveness of persons. Rather, it has been suggested, Augustine could have built on the Cappadocians' view: "Augustine begins where the Cappadocians leave off: accepting their answer to the question 'Why not three gods?' he proceeds to ask 'Three what?'"[12] The best way to look at this debate is to discern key ideas in Augustine's Trinitarian teaching.[13]

Augustine of course affirms the tradition concerning consubstantiality as well as distinctions of the Son and Spirit.[14] Furthermore, somewhat similarly to Eastern theologians, Augustine depicts the Father as the *principium,* primary or beginning of the Deity.[15]

Well-known are the reflections of Augustine on the Spirit in the Trinity. He conceives of the Spirit as communion (of the Father and the Son),[16] their shared love,[17] and a gift.[18] In book 8 of *On the Trinity,* he develops his thought on the Trinity with the help of the idea of interpersonal love in terms of filiation and paternity. The Father is Lover, the Son the Beloved, and the Spirit the mutual Love that connects the two. Here of course the obvious question arises whether this depersonalizes the Spirit: shared love can hardly be a "person."[19]

For Augustine, incarnation is a major Trinitarian event, and it shapes his view of the Trinity more fully than is often acknowledged by his interpreters.[20] He takes pains to convince his readers that incarnation is a unique event. For example, in expositing the Gospel story about Jesus' baptism, Augustine argues that while the manifestation of the Spirit in the form of a dove and the Father's voice

---

12. Philip Cary, "Historical Perspectives on Trinitarian Doctrine," *Religious and Theological Studies Fellowship Bulletin,* November–December 1995, 9. A helpful summary of views pro and con can be found in Roger E. Olson and Christopher A. Hall, *The Trinity,* Guides to Theology (Grand Rapids: Eerdmans, 2002), 44–45.

13. Main sources for Augustine's Trinitarian teaching besides the fifteen-volume *On the Trinity,* written between 400 and 420, are *The City of God, Confessions, Tractates on the Gospel of John,* Letter 169 to Bishop Evodius, Letter 11 to Nebridius, *On the Spirit and the Letter, On the Soul and Its Origins,* and *Sermons on Selected Lessons of the New Testament.* Olson and Hall contains a comprehensive listing of Augustine's writings on the Trinity (*The Trinity,* 46 n. 97).

14. E.g., Augustine, *Letters* 169 in *The Nicene and Post-Nicene Fathers of the Christian Church,* Series 1 (reprint, Grand Rapids: Eerdmans, 2001), 1:540: "The Son is not the Father, the Father is not the Son, and neither the Father nor the Son is the Holy Spirit . . . These are equal and co-eternal, and absolutely of one nature, . . . an inseparable trinity." For the consubstantiality of the Son with the Father, see, e.g., Augustine, *On the Trinity* 1.6.9 (pp. 21–22); and for the Spirit with the Father and Son, see, e.g., ibid., 1.6.13 (pp. 23–24); 7.3.6 (pp. 108–9).

15. Augustine, *On the Trinity* 4.20.28–29 (pp. 84–85). See further Basil Studer, *The Grace of Christ and the Grace of God in Augustine of Hippo: Christocentrism or Theocentrism?* (Collegeville, MN: Liturgical Press, 1997), 104–5.

16. Augustine, *On the Trinity* 5.11.12 (p. 93); 15.27.50 (pp. 226–27). See further Joseph Ratzinger, "The Holy Spirit as *Communio*: Concerning the Relationship of Pneumatology and Spirituality in Augustine," *Communio* 25 (1998): 325–39.

17. Augustine, *On the Trinity* 15.17.27 (p. 215); Augustine, *[Homilies] Tractates on the Gospel of St. John* 105.7.3, in *Nicene and Post-Nicene Fathers,* 7:396.

18. Augustine, *On the Trinity* 5.12.13 (pp. 93–94); 5.15.16 (p. 95).

19. Bernd Jochen Hilberath, "Pneumatologie," in *Handbuch der Dogmatik,* ed. Theodor Schneider, et al., vol.1 (Dusseldorf: Patmos, 1992), 446–47.

20. See further Barnes, "Rereading," 154–68; Studer, *Trinity and Incarnation,* 168–85 especially.

from above were temporary and symbolic, the incarnation is a permanent assumption of humanity in a real union of two natures.[21]

Pannenberg, who otherwise is somewhat critical of the Augustinian legacy,[22] has shown convincingly that "Augustine took over the relational definition of the Trinitarian distinctions which the Cappadocians, following Athanasius, had developed. He made the point that the distinctions of the persons are conditioned by their mutual relations."[23] For Augustine the relations are eternal.[24] The Eastern idea of perichoresis, mutual interpenetration, is no stranger to his views.[25] At the same time, Augustine was also building on the Cappadocians' idea mentioned above of the unity of the three persons in their outward works, the consequence of which is that from the creaturely works we may know the divine unity.[26]

It is often claimed that the psychological analogies are key to the Trinitarian teaching in Augustine. It is true that the latter part of his *On the Trinity*[27] employs images such as *mens/notitia/amor*—mind, mind's knowledge of itself, and the mind's love for itself—an illustration of Father as Being, Son as Consciousness, and Spirit as Love.[28] His logic is compelling: if the human mind knows love in itself, it knows God, since God is love. These illustrations are of course biblically sustainable, based on the idea of humanity as *imago Dei* (Gen. 1:26–27). However, it is important to note that

> Augustine did not try to derive the Trinitarian distinctions from the divine unity. The psychological analogies that he suggested and developed in his

---

21. Augustine, *Letters* 169.2.5–9, in *Nicene and Post-Nicene Fathers*[1], 1:540–41.

22. Pannenberg is critical of the entire Western tradition up until Barth, which employs a mental or psychological analogy of the Trinity, which in Pannenberg's view leads to the primacy of a divine single mind rather than the idea of divine unity in terms of relationality. Pannenberg calls this approach a "pre-trinitarian, theistic idea of God." Wolfhart Pannenberg, "Father, Son, Spirit: Problems of a Trinitarian Doctrine of God," *Dialog* 26, no. 4 (August 1987): 251.

23. Pannenberg here refers to Augustine, *On the Trinity* 8.1; Wolfhart Pannenberg, *Systematic Theology*, vol. 1, trans. Geoffrey W. Bromiley (Grand Rapids: Eerdmans, 1991), 284. In his *Sermon on Matthew 3:13*, Augustine speaks of a distinction of persons, and an inseparableness of operation. Augustine, *Sermon on New Testament Lessons: Matthew 3:13*, 2.1–23, especially 2.15, in *Nicene and Post-Nicene Fathers*[1], 6:259–66 (262). See also Augustine, *On the Trinity* 5.11.12 (p. 93) for an important statement about relationality in Trinity.

24. Pannenberg, *Systematic Theology*, 1:284.

25. Augustine in *On the Trinity* says it strongly: "In that highest Trinity one is as much as the three together, nor are two anything more than one. And They are infinite in themselves. So both each are in each, and all in each, and each in all, and all in all, and all are one." Augustine, *On the Trinity* 6.10.12 (p. 103).

26. Ibid., 1.4.7 (p. 20); 4.21.30 (p. 85); see further Pannenberg, *Systematic Theology*, 1:283–84.

27. In addition to *On the Trinity* 8–15 (pp. 166–228), analogies are also discussed in *[Homilies] Tractates on the Gospel of St. John* 23 (pp. 150–57), as well as in *Letters* 11 (pp. 228–30) and 169 (pp. 539–43), among others.

28. Augustine, *On the Trinity* 8.10.14 (p. 124); 9.2.2 (pp. 126–27). The idea of mind, of course, has its legacy in early Christian theology beginning with the Apologists, who taught that as the Word the Son is the Father's thought/idea. Augustine also developed further the idea of the "vestiges of the Trinity" with the help of the tripartite constitution of the human soul, *memoria/intelligentia/voluntas*: memory, intelligence, and willing. Augustine, *On the Trinity* 9.8 (p. 131); 10.10.14–16 (pp. 141–42); 11.10–11.17–18 (pp. 153–54).

work on the Trinity were simply meant to offer a very general way of linking the unity and trinity and thus creating some plausibility for trinitarian statements.[29]

Furthermore, the bishop of Hippo was aware of the limitation of the images.[30] The potential weakness of this analogy of self-presence, self-knowledge, and self-love—widely used in subsequent tradition—is that it leans toward a "monopersonal, modalistic view of God."[31] This is interesting in that in principle Augustine's analogies grow out of an interpersonal, thus communal and relational, context, especially when it comes to love. Richard of St. Victor in the medieval era picks up the relational aspect of Augustine's emphasis on love and develops it into a communion theology.

He considers the origin of the Spirit in a nuanced way. The Spirit proceeds "originally" from the Father and also in common from both the Father and Son, as something given by the Father.[32] In other words, Augustine is careful in safeguarding the Father as the primary source of the Spirit.[33] And even when the Son is included in the act of procession of the Spirit, it is not from two sources but rather from a single source in order to protect divine unity.[34] I think it is important to notice here that again Augustine's legacy is somewhat ambiguous. On the one hand, there is no denying that Augustine's idea of the Spirit as the shared love between Father and Son and his teaching about the double procession of the Spirit helped the Christian West to ratify the *filioque* clause. On the other hand, had the West been more sensitive to the shared tradition and to the sensibilities of the East, Augustine's idea of the procession of the Spirit from the Father through the Son, and thus in a secondary way, possibly could have helped avoid the conflict between East and West. Eastern theologians are not necessarily against the idea of the Spirit proceeding from the Father (who is the source after all) through the Son. And for Augustine, unlike so much of later Western tradition, the Spirit's derivation also from the Son did not necessarily mean inferiority in status any more than the Son's generation from the Father does (this was of course the affirmation against the Arians).[35]

Now, in light of key ideas of Augustinian teaching, we are in a place to try to address at least tentatively the question of the subheading, namely, do East and West confess the same Trinitarian faith? I think it very important to make the distinction between Augustine's own ideas and his legacy as carried on by later (Western) tradition.[36] Looking at Augustine's own writings, "[i]t hardly appears

29. Pannenberg, *Systematic Theology*, 1:284; see also 287: "Augustine's psychological analogies should not be used to derive the trinity from the unity but to simply illustrate the Trinity in whom one already believes."
30. Augustine, *On the Trinity* 15.23.43 (p. 222).
31. O'Collins, *Tripersonal God*, 137.
32. Augustine, *On the Trinity* 15.26.47 (p. 225).
33. See ibid., 4.20.29 (pp. 84–85).
34. Ibid., 5.14 (pp. 94–96).
35. See further O'Collins, *Tripersonal God*, 139.
36. For a balanced judgment, see Robert Letham, *The Holy Trinity: In Scripture, History, Theology, and Worship* (Phillipsburg, NJ: P&R Publishing, 2004), 198–200.

that Augustine had little interest in the distinctions of the persons, or that he was averse to the full import of the Incarnation."[37] Nor is it true that Augustine developed his Trinitarian theology abstractly based on analogies; he did not. He is thoroughly biblical, as a quick look, for example, in the first half of *De Trinitate* clearly shows, let alone his biblical expositions. Nor is it right to say that—in contrast to the Cappadocians and Athanasius—Augustine neglected spirituality and salvation.[38] His focus on incarnation alone would counterargue this charge.

In light of these considerations, a more nuanced and sophisticated way of looking at the differences between the Christian East and West is in order.[39] I think it is best done by trying to discern the key characteristics and unique features in each without trying to artificially reconcile those or make them more dramatic than they are.[40] Almost every one agrees that for Eastern theologians the significance of the *hypostatic* distinctions among Father, Son, and Spirit has often been a key concern. The East has wanted to speak of the "concrete particularity of Father, Son, and Spirit."[41] Furthermore, as noted several times, they have emphasized the Father as the source of the Deity. Son and Spirit proceed from the Father from eternity. In the West, there has often been more emphasis on the divine being/substance/essence from which the personal distinctions derive. Consequently, there has been emphasis on the joint working of the three in the world.[42] Whatever the difference between the Christian East and West, each of them has faced its own challenges: for the East, it was the danger of tritheism because of the emphasis on three different *hypostaseis* and subordinationism because of the idea of the Father as the source of divinity. Westerners have tended to be more modalistic. Moreover, Eastern theological traditions in general and Trinitarian ones in particular have been more pneumatologically oriented, whereas in the West Christology has often played the key role. This again brings us to the question of the *filioque,* to be discussed in what follows.

Having said all this, one also has to acknowledge that there are several aspects of the Augustinian tradition that were picked up by later Western tradition that led to the eclipse of the Trinitarian doctrine so evident in the judgment of contemporary theologians. First, with all his stress on relationality, there is no denying

37. Ibid., 195. So also O'Collins, *Tripersonal God,* 135.
38. This is one of the theses of Catherine Mowry LaCugna's *God for Us: The Trinity and Christian Life* (San Francisco: HarperSanFrancisco, 1991), 81–104.
39. Overstatements abound and need to be corrected: "We must acknowledge that the doctrine of the trinity in the East is an integral part of its total theological understanding. The same cannot be said for the Western formulation stemming chiefly from Augustine. Here, the doctrine is an unneeded appendage to theology." John B. Cobb Jr., "The Relativization of the Trinity," in *Trinity in Process: A Relational Theology of God,* ed. Joseph A. Bracken and Marjorie Hewitt Suchocki (New York: Continuum, 1997), 5.
40. Letham's *Holy Trinity* includes a quite helpful chart of the key features of both East and West even when it tends to be quite categorical (250–51).
41. Stanley J. Grenz, *Rediscovering the Triune God: The Trinity in Contemporary Theology* (Minneapolis: Fortress, 2004), 8. See also Gunton, *Promise of Trinitarian Theology,* 39.
42. This is the so-called Augustinian rule: the works of the Trinity *ad extra* are indivisible.

that Augustine also emphasizes the divine unity and substance.[43] Therefore, there is some truth in the insistence that whereas for the Christian East distinctions of persons (*hypostaseis*) are the key to Trinity, for Augustine substance is, though not to the neglect of relations. Second, Augustine's idea of the Spirit as shared love between Father and Son is problematic ecumenically and biblically. In the Bible, God is love rather than Spirit. Furthermore, Augustine's idea feeds the idea of *filioque*. And last but not least, this analogy can hardly argue for any distinct personality of the Spirit. Third, while Augustine seemed to handle analogies of the Trinity with care and was aware of their limitations, many of his followers elevated them to a role that easily leads away from the concrete biblical salvation history into abstract speculations. While valid in itself—based on the idea that humanity is created in the image of the Triune God—it can end up being a Trinitarian theology "from below." There are not only similarities but also differences between the Trinity and humanity.[44]

A helpful way to continue reflecting on the developments and key challenges of Trinitarian traditions in Christian history is on the one hand to try to discern the place and role of the Trinity in theology and on the other hand to see the development of the East-West divide in terms of the *filioque* debate. After that the rise of Social Trinitarianism will be studied. The rise of the social analogy, to which I turn in what follows, was an attempt to rediscover the Eastern tradition and at the same time to highlight and develop those ideas in the Augustinian and Western tradition that were in danger of being undermined.

THE PLACE AND ROLE OF THE TRINITY
IN CHRISTIAN THEOLOGY

Thomas Aquinas is the one who both ratified the Augustinian heritage and clarified many of the key issues. Aquinas builds on Augustine, including the order of discussion: he begins with the unity and then discusses triunity.[45] He develops Augustinian ideas by refining significantly the nature of relations in the divine nature. For the Angelic Doctor there are four—and only four—relations, namely,

---

43. LaCugna's comment is an overstatement, yet contains a kernel of truth: "[Augustine's] focus on the individual apart from its personal and social relations flows directly from the ontology that begins from substance rather than person." LaCugna, *God for Us*, 102. LaCugna, however, qualifies this by saying that was not Augustine's intention, yet it was picked up by his followers.

44. See further Miroslav Volf, "'The Trinity Is Our Social Program': The Doctrine of the Trinity and the Shape of Social Engagement," *Modern Theology* 14, no. 3 (July 1998): 403–23.

45. Aquinas discusses Trinity first in his *Summa contra Gentiles*, trans. Charles J. O'Neil (Notre Dame: University of Notre Dame Press, 1975), 4.1–26 (pp. 35–146). His approach is more apologetic in relation to Muslims, Jews, and some heretical views; it is noteworthy that he had already discussed widely the unity in book 1. The main systematic discussion can of course be found in Thomas Aquinas, *Summa theologiae*, Latin text and English trans. (London: Blackfriars/New York: McGraw-Hill, 1964), 1a.27–43 (part 1a, questions 27–43). Again, prior to discussing trinity, Aquinas deals widely with unity in articles 1–26.

fatherhood and sonship as well as procession and spiration. The significant and lasting contribution of Aquinas is that the relations rising out of the divine processions must be real.[46] This means that these relations (such as Father-Son) are identical with the divine nature. However there are distinctions since relations as defined by Aquinas here refer to relative oppositions. In other words, while fatherhood and sonship are identical with divine nature, they also imply real distinctions: one is Father, one is Son.[47]

Whereas Augustine focused much of his attention on Love as the proper biblical category for developing the idea of the Triune God, for Aquinas intellect and will are the key actions in the spiritual world.[48] As mentioned, the Son's proceeding is generation; the procession of the Word reproduces the likeness of its originator, the Son.[49] This can be compared to the father-son relationship and even more—since it is "likeness in the nature of the same species."[50] An illustration from the likeness of the word to the human intellect in the act of self-knowledge is a way to put it. Being similar, the Word can be named the Son of God. The "spiration" of the Spirit, unlike the generation of the Son, is more subtle; it is from the will, which for Aquinas means "an urge or motion toward something." Therefore, as David Coffey describes Aquinas here, "'what proceeds from the will in God is not generated as a son, but rather proceeds as a spirit, a vital motion or impulse. This is the case when someone is moved by love to accomplish something,' and in God, what comes forth from the divine will is none other than the Holy Spirit."[51] Following Augustine, Aquinas teaches that the Holy Spirit proceeds from both the Father and the Son and is their mutual love. The way he defends the dual procession is interesting: if not from the Son, too, the distinction between Son and Spirit would be blurred.[52]

In addition to advancing significantly the meaning of the relations in the divine nature, yet another lasting contribution of Aquinas has to do with the concept of "person." Building on Boethius's classic definition from the fifth century, according to which *person* is "an individual substance of rational nature,"[53] Aquinas argued that individual beings, including God, with a rational nature are called persons. Since the word *person* refers to something most perfect in the world, it is appropriate to apply it to God even though of course

46. Being real means that they are not "accidental." In line with Aristotelian-medieval ontology, "accident" is something that is not permanent or essential to the nature of the thing.

47. Aquinas, *Summa theologiae* 1a.28.1–4 (part 1a, question 28, articles 1–4). A very helpful brief exposition can be found in William J. La Due, *The Trinity Guide to the Trinity* (Harrisburg, PA: Trinity Press International, 2003), 71–72.

48. See further O'Collins, *Tripersonal God*, 144–45.

49. Aquinas, *Summa theologiae* 1a.27.1–2.

50. As put by David Coffey, *Deus Trinitas* (New York: Oxford University Press, 1999), 29.

51. Ibid.

52. Both proceedings are explained in Aquinas, *Summa theologiae* 1a.27.3–5. I have gleaned from La Due, *Trinity Guide to the Trinity*, 73.

53. Boethius, *Contra Eutychen et Nestorium* (also known as *Liber de persona et duabus naturis Christi*), #3.

only analogically.[54] A corollary development of Aquinas is that relations as defined above are persons when speaking of the Triune God. Because of real relations (Father-Son most importantly), there are several subsistent persons in the Deity, to be more precise, three. Fatherhood and sonship belong to Father and Son; spiration—because of the dual procession of the Spirit—belongs to both Father and Son. In sum, then, there are three relations, that is, three persons, Father, Son, and Spirit. "Person" is common to all three.[55] Finally, Aquinas affirms both the eternal equality of divine persons as well as their perichoresis: The Father is in the Son, the Son in the Father; the same can be predicated of the Spirit because of the unity of the divine essence.[56] O'Collins's summary is worth hearing:

> Thomas along with other medieval theologians endorsed the radical, loving interconnectedness (circumincessio) of the three divine persons, something better expressed in Greek as their perichōrēsis, or reciprocal presence and interpenetration. Their innermost life is infinitely close relationship with one another in the utter reciprocity of love.[57]

Thomas's achievements are significant. While beginning with divine unity in line with received tradition in the West, he also works hard in accounting for the distinctions and thus relations.[58] His decision to equate "persons" with relations is both an advantage and problematic. It is advantage in that it argues for the reality of distinctions. Its problem lies in its modalistic leanings even though, I think, making Aquinas a "closet" modalist is a mistaken judgment.[59] While building on the tradition, he advances the quest for a better theological understanding of relationality and mutuality in the divine nature.[60] The challenges to Aquinas's thinking are obvious. While the idea of perceiving the divine nature in terms of intellect (and will) is not totally foreign to the Bible, it is hardly the best approach. In that regard, the Augustinian emphasis on love with corollary relational and communal implications does more justice to biblical material.[61] Aquinas's view

54. Aquinas, *Summa theologiae* 1a.29.1–4.
55. Ibid., 1a.30.1–4. See also La Due, *The Trinity Guide to the Trinity*, 73. La Due gives reference here to Bernard Lonergan, "Christology Today: Methodological Reflections," in *A Third Collection*, ed. Frederic E. Crowe (New York: Paulist Press, 1985), 99.
56. Aquinas, *Summa theologiae* 1a. 42.
57. O'Collins, *Tripersonal God*, 147.
58. Edmund J. Fortman is excited about the contribution of Aquinas here: "For the first time in Trinitarian history there is a clear-cut differentiation of divine generation and divine procession in terms of the intimate life of the Triune God." Edmund J. Fortman, *The Triune God: A Historical Study of the Doctrine of the Trinity* (Philadelphia: Westminster Press, 1972), 206.
59. Olson and Hall, *Trinity*, 64, agree with this judgment.
60. Olson and Hall make an important comment here by claiming that Aquinas's view of the Trinity "centered around his subtle, creative synthesis of the traditional Augustinian psychological model and the communal-social model of Richard of St. Victor" [whose ideas will be studied in what follows]. Ibid.
61. However, Aquinas develops the idea of an intellectual nature toward relationality, combining it with love and will: "An intellectual nature requires some degree of multiplicity, as does love—which God is, as well as intellect. The intellectual love of the Father gives rise to the eternal begetting of the

of the Spirit shares the weaknesses of tradition in endorsing the dual procession (*filioque*), and its idea of "passive" spiration and thus lack of distinct personality helps further blur the role and personality of the Spirit in the Trinity.

The main weakness of Aquinas's Trinitarian view, however, lies in its one-sided emphasis on the oneness prior to trinity.[62] Here we come to the concern set forth in this section's subheading, namely, the role and place of the Trinity in Christian theology. This issue is not raised simply out of historical interest or for the purpose of discussing theological method per se.[63] I believe most any theologian currently agrees on this thesis at least in principle: If it can be shown that the Christian doctrine of God is best expressed in the form of one God, then Trinity is a secondary addition, at best a helpful appendix to the doctrine but not necessary for presenting the God of the Bible.[64] While few if any Christian theologians have ever argued for that kind of "monotheism," the way the doctrine of the Trinity evolved in the post-Augustinian tradition in the West *implied* that the oneness of God is the defining issue while the Trinity may or may not be integral to the doctrine.[65] Technically put, it meant that in the presentation of Christian theology the order was from one God to God Triune. It became an established procedure by the time of Thomas Aquinas.[66] Reformation theology followed the same order.[67]

The influence of Neoplatonism and its stress on the unity of the divine essence certainly played a role here. Its significance for Augustine's own views is debated, as mentioned above. In post-Augustinian theology, however, it has had a definite effect in moving the Trinity from the center to the margins.[68]

Son who is distinct from the Father. . . . The love between the Father and Son gives rise to the eternal procession of the Holy Spirit." Olson and Hall, *Trinity*, 64.

62. In that respect, Grenz's judgment of the legacy of Aquinas seems to be warranted: "Regardless of the extent to which we might want to laud Aquinas's greatness as a theological mind, his proposal not only stood at the apex of medieval Trinitarian theology, but it also became the precursor of its demise." Grenz, *Rediscovering the Triune God*, 13.

63. An extremely helpful, detailed study is offered by Pannenberg under the title "The Place of the Doctrine of the Trinity in the Dogmatic Structure and the Problem of Finding a Basis for Trinitarian Statements." Pannenberg, *Systematic Theology*, 1:280–99.

64. "The moment it appears that the one God can be better understood without rather than with the doctrine of the Trinity, the latter seems to be a superfluous addition to the concept of the one God even though it is reverently treated as a mystery of revelation. Even worse, it necessarily seems to be incompatible with the divine unity." Ibid., 291.

65. Pannenberg states that Peter Lombard of the early Middle Ages is an exception. In his *Sentences*, book I, Lombard started with Trinity and then moved to consider Trinity and unity. Ibid., 282.

66. As noted above, in *Summa contra Gentiles*, Aquinas discusses one God in book 1 and delays the discussion of Triune God until book 4. The same applies to *Summa theologiae*, part 1a, where unity again precedes Trinity. Commenting on this, Pannenberg has this to say: "In the presentation of the Christian Doctrine of God, High Scholasticism established the procedure of beginning with the question of the existence of the one God, then dealing with the nature and attributes of this God, and only then handling the doctrine of the Trinity." Pannenberg, *Systematic Theology*, 1:280–81. A similar judgment is that of Karl Rahner, *The Trinity*, trans. Joseph Donceel (New York: Herder & Herder, 1970), 15–16.

67. Pannenberg, *Systematic Theology*, 1:281, with examples from Melanchthon and Calvin.

68. Pannenberg cites examples of this in Pseudo-Dionysius the Areopagite, who made an effort to derive the Trinity from the unity of the divine essence, and in Anselm of Canterbury. Ibid., 285–86.

While some Protestant theologians such as A. Calov argued that Trinity is indispensable for the presentation of the Christian doctrine of God,

> There was a feeling, nevertheless, that the OT justifies a prior presentation of God as the Supreme Being (Ex. 3:14) and also of his attributes. . . . The doctrine of the Trinity was then added to the existing idea of the one God as the specifically Christian revelation. It could thus act as an appendix to the general doctrine of God.[69]

Behind the choice of beginning either with Trinity or unity is the complicated question of the relation between unity and Trinity. Can unity be derived from trinity, or vice versa?[70] As our discussion has shown, the usual way of resolving this issue is to insist on the unity of the divine substance prior to Trinitarian distinctions. This has not only been the approach of Augustine and his legacy but also in a sense that of the Cappadocians in their insistence on the unity of the Trinitarian persons in their outward works.

Part of the problem is the debate about the role of revelation and faith in relation to Trinity. The question is simply this, and no unanimity was established in tradition: Is Trinity a matter of faith and revelation alone, or can Trinity be inferred with the help of human reason? Gilbert de la Porrée regarded Trinity as a matter of faith (for him, any attempt to derive Trinity from unity smacked of modalism). The Augustinian solution was that even when there are vestiges of Trinity in the human soul, one cannot rationally demonstrate Trinity in any conclusive way; Aquinas agreed with that.[71] Yet Aquinas—no more than some earlier Western thinkers such as the highly speculative Anselm of Canterbury[72]—was not consistent. In his *Summa* Aquinas indeed derives the Trinitarian statements from the concept of one God. How can this be explained? He puts this question to himself and responds that indeed revelation is needed but that human reason can argue from and elaborate on the basis of what it already presupposed from revelation.[73] It was only in Reformation theology that the conviction emerged that Trinity is known only by revelation; Scripture alone teaches it to us, even though the generic concept of God, one God, can be to a significant extent derived from nature and natural revelation.[74] The insistence on Trinity as a datum of revelation, ironically, led to the counterthesis by Antitrinitarians at the time of the Reformation; they argued that the only thing we can say of the Trinity has to do with economy, and there is no going back to the inner life of God.[75] This is basically the same claim made by contemporary economic Trinitarians, such as Oneness Pentecostals:

69. Ibid., 281–82.
70. See ibid., 283.
71. Ibid., 282 with references to original works.
72. For Anselm's highly rationalistic attempt to "prove" Trinity, see Olson and Hall, *Trinity*, 55–57; Letham, *Holy Trinity*, 221–25.
73. Thomas Aquinas, *Summa theologiae* 1.32.1. ad 2.
74. Pannenberg, *Systematic Theology*, 1:289–90.
75. Ibid., 290–91. For Faustus Socinus, see further Olson and Hall, *Trinity*, 77–79.

while freely speaking of Father, Son, and Spirit, they refuse to speculate beyond the economic language, as they see it, of the New Testament.[76] So here we have a full circle.

Summa summarum: The end result of the medieval and Reformation developments regarding the Trinity and its place in Christian theology was this:

> By thus distinguishing and arranging the presentation of the one God and that of the Trinity Thomas gave the structure of the doctrine of God its classical form for the age that followed. Basic to this structure is the derivation of the trinity of persons from the concept of the unity of substance.[77]

Curiously enough, later Eastern theology was not totally immune to this tendency even though more nuanced. The eighth-century John of Damascus's *Orthodox Faith* first briefly discusses the topic of one God and his incomprehensible nature and only then launches into the Trinity. Yet the difference from Aquinas is noteworthy in that unlike the Angelic Doctor, the Damascene names Trinity as the overall topic of the first two chapters of *Orthodox Faith*, and his treatment of one God is minimally brief when compared to the Western counterpart.[78]

In modern Western theology the marginalization of the doctrine of the Trinity came to its zenith. As is routinely noted, Schleiermacher's *The Christian Faith*, a monumental 800-page book, devoted only a little more than ten pages to the topic, discussing it under "Conclusion."[79] Kant's chiding remark was that the

---

76. See further "Oneness Pentecostalism," in *The New International Dictionary of Pentecostal and Charismatic Movements*, ed. Stanley M. Burgess (Grand Rapids: Zondervan, 2002), 936–43.

77. Pannenberg, *Systematic Theology*, 1:288; so also agree Rahner, *Trinity*, 16–17; and LaCugna, *God for Us*, 145; as well as Grenz, *Rediscovering the Triune God*, 13. In defense of Aquinas, see David Cunningham, *These Three Are One: The Practice of Trinitarian Theology* (Cambridge, MA: Blackwell, 1998), 32–33.

78. The judgment of Letham about a dramatic difference between John and Aquinas is an overstatement. However, where Letham is right is that already in the first part of his work, the Damascene speaks of the distinctions of Trinitarian persons and their perichoretic relations. Letham, *Holy Trinity*, 237. See further John of Damascus, *Exposition of the Orthodox Faith* 1.6–7, in *Nicene and Post-Nicene Fathers* Series 2 (reprint, Grand Rapids, Eerdmans, 1994), 9:4 (pagination in this volume restarts from the beginning with this work of John). Pannenberg's judgment is balanced and convincing: "If we look at the basic structure of his [John of Damascus's] argument, we are forced to say that there, as in Gregory of Nyssa, we can see a trace of the derivation of the Trinitarian distinctions from the divine unity, i.e., from the divine spirituality ([*The Orthodox Faith*]1.6–7), but the point is that this trace does not determine the systematic treatment of the doctrine of God as it would later do in the Latin theology of the Middle Ages." Pannenberg, *Systematic Theology*, 1:289.

79. Friedrich Schleiermacher, *The Christian Faith*, ed. H. R. Mackintosh and J. S. Stewart (Philadelphia: Fortress Press, 1928), 738–51. Claude Welch claims that the reason for the dismissal was that for the Father of Modern Theology, Trinity was nothing more than an "unnecessary and unwarranted addition to the faith." Claude Welch, *In This Name: The Doctrine of the Trinity in Contemporary Theology* (New York: Scribner's Sons, 1952), 5. More recent theological research, however, has reconsidered Schleiermacher's understanding of the Trinity and suggested that perhaps he made a more significant contribution to the doctrine than is believed. See Grenz, *Rediscovering the Triune God*, 17–24.

doctrine has "no practical relevance at all, even if we think we understand it," and we do not, since "it transcends all our concepts."[80]

One reason for the marginalization of the Trinity had to do with the theological method that began to change over the course of time. Unlike earlier theology, which discerned Trinity in the salvation history recorded in the biblical testimonies, later theology became more interested in the "inner" life of God instead of the "economy" of salvation, making Trinity an abstract speculation rather than reading it from the works of God.[81] George W. Hegel's philosophical, idealistic approach to Trinity is the hallmark of this tradition.[82] Here the approach of the Reformers is refreshing. Both Martin Luther and especially John Calvin eschewed abstract philosophical speculation[83] and initiated a call back to the biblical exposition while not leaving behind creedal and patristic tradition.[84]

Since the Enlightenment, the waning of the doctrine of the Trinity also has had to do with the rise of biblical and dogmatic critique. Whereas for even older Protestant theology, the Bible offered proofs of the Trinity, biblical criticism of the Enlightenment destroyed that approach.[85]

Two tasks lie ahead before closing these historical considerations, namely, another look at the role of the Spirit in the Trinity through the lens of the famous *filioque* debate, and consideration of the significance of the rise of the social analogy.

IS THE ORIGIN OF THE SPIRIT STILL A THEOLOGICAL IMPASSE?

The consideration of the earliest Christian Trinitarian traditions showed clearly that the Bible does not clarify the interrelations of Father, Son, and Spirit. A classic example, with reverberations still felt, is the question of the procession

---

80. Immanuel Kant, *The Conflict of the Faculties*, trans. Mary J. Grefor (New York: Abaris Books, 1979), 65.

81. For a contemporary critique of this development, see Rahner, *Trinity*, 14–21 especially.

82. For a fine exposition and assessment, see Grenz, *Rediscovering the Triune God*, 24–32. Hegel, of course, made a massive major effort to develop Trinity from his idea of the Absolute Spirit. For Pannenberg's incisive dialogue with and critique of Hegel and other idealists such as Lessing, who attempted to derive Trinity from self-consciousness, see Pannenberg, *Systematic Theology*, 1:292–98.

83. A good example here is Luther's right hand, Philipp Melanchthon: "There is no reason why we should spend much labour over those supreme topics of God, His Unity and Trinity. . . . I ask you what the scholastic theologians have achieved in so many ages by occupying themselves with these questions alone." Philipp Melanchthon, introduction to his first edition of *Loci theologici* (1521).

84. For Luther's approach to Trinity, see John R. Loeschen, *Divine Community: Trinity, Church, and Ethics in Reformation Theologies* (Kirksville, MO: Sixteenth Century Journal, 1981), 17–18. For a fine exposition of Calvin's biblically based exposition in the first part of his *Institutes* (final edition of 1559), see Letham, *Holy Trinity*, 252–68. With some overstatement, Letham says that "from . . . *Institutes* we gather that the Trinity *is* his doctrine of God. It contains nothing expressly on God other than a section on the Trinity. Here is a major departure from Aquinas's separation of his discussion of the one God from his discussion of the Trinity." Ibid., 253; see also 267–68: "Clearly, he breaks significantly from the late medieval scholastic approach and restores a thoroughly biblical exposition. He eschews speculation."

85. See further Pannenberg, *Systematic Theology*, 1:301–2.

of the Spirit. On the one hand, Jesus says that he himself will send the Spirit (John 16:7) or that he will send the Spirit (called *paraklētos* here) who proceeds from the Father (15:26). On the other hand, Jesus prays to the Father for him to send the Spirit (14:16), and the Father will send the Spirit in Jesus' name (14:26).[86] Because of the lack of clarity in the biblical record as well as the rise to prominence of the Augustinian idea of the Spirit as shared love (another idea which of course has its basis in the biblical idea of the Spirit as *koinōnia*), the Christian West added the Spirit's dual procession, *filioque* (Latin: "and [from] the Son") to the Nicene Creed, which originally said that the Holy Spirit "proceeds from the Father." While some historical details are debated,[87] it is clear that in the first major breach of the Christian church in 1054 the *filioque* phrase played a major role with political, ecclesiastical, and cultural issues. The Christian East objected vigorously to this addition, claiming that it was a one-sided addition without ecumenical consultation,[88] that it compromises the monarchy of the Father as the source of divinity,[89] and that it subordinates the Spirit to Jesus with theological corollaries in ecclesiology, the doctrine of salvation, and so on.[90] While the details of the origin of the *filioque* addition in the West are not fully known, besides the Augustinian idea of the Spirit as the mutual

86. In terms of biblical scholarship, speculation into the "immanent" and "economic" sendings is quite problematic. See, e.g., Letham, *Holy Trinity*, 203. Those distinctions have to do with postbiblical historical and systematic constructions.

87. The standard view is that this addition was first accepted by the Council of Toledo in 589 and ratified by the 809 Aachen Synod. It was incorporated into later creeds such as that of the Fourth Lateran in 1215 and Council of Lyons in 1274. See, e.g., Justo L. González, *The Story of Christianity*, vol. 1, *The Early Church to the Dawn of the Reformation* (San Francisco: Harper & Row, 1984), 264–65; Kenneth Scott Latourette, *A History of Christianity* (New York: Harper & Row, 1953), 304, 360. A standard full-scale study on the theology and history of *filioque* is Bernd Oberdorfer, *Filioque: Geschichte und Theologie eines Ökumenischen Problems* (Göttingen: Vandenhoeck & Ruprecht, 2001).

88. "Can a clause deriving from one theological tradition simply be inserted in a creed deriving from another theological tradition without council?" Theodore G. Stylianopoulos and S. Mark Heim, eds., *Spirit of Truth: Ecumenical Perspectives on the Holy Spirit* (Brookline, MA: Holy Cross Orthodox Press, 1986), 32.

89. Kallistos Ware, *The Orthodox Church* (New York: Penguin Books, 1993), 210–14, defends the Father's monarchy as the reason for opposing *filioque*. Ware critiques the Western idea of Father and Son as two independent sources of the Spirit. Ware, however, does not take into consideration the quite nuanced view of Augustine according to which the Father is the principal source while the Son is the source of the Spirit in a derivative sense, Augustine, *On the Trinity* 15.17.27.

90. Vladimir Lossky has most dramatically articulated the charge of "Christomonism" against Western theology. According to him, Christianity in the West is seen as unilaterally referring to Christ, the Spirit being an addition to the church, to its ministries and sacraments. Vladimir Lossky, "The Procession of the Holy Spirit in Orthodox Trinitarian Doctrine," in *In the Image and Likeness of God*, ed. John H. Erickson and Thomas E. Bird (Crestwood, NY: St. Vladimir's Seminary Press, 1985), chap. 4. See also Nikos A. Nissiotis, "The Main Ecclesiological Problem of the Second Vatican Council and Position of the Non-Roman Churches Facing It," *Journal of Ecumenical Studies* 6 (1965): 31–62. All of these three objections, namely, that it was a unilateral act, it subordinates the Son to the Spirit, and it compromises the Father's monarchy were already presented by the most vocal critic in history, the ninth-century patriarch of Constantinople, Photius, in his *On the Mystagogy of the Holy Spirit* (Astoria, NY: Studien Publications, 1983), 51–52, 71–72 especially.

love, it is believed that the addition also served a function in opposing Arianism. Mentioning the Son alongside the Father as the origin of the Spirit was seen as a way to defend consubstantiality.[91]

With all its exaggerations,[92] the Eastern critique of the *filioque* is important both ecumenically and theologically and should not be dismissed.[93] The West did not have the right to unilaterally add *filioque*.[94]

In my judgment, *filioque* is not heretical even though ecumenically and theologically it is unacceptable and therefore should be removed.[95] Ecumenically and theologically it would be important for the East to be able to acknowledge the non-heretical nature of the addition. Furthermore, the Christian East should keep in mind the fact that with all its problems, at first *filioque*, as mentioned above, was used in the West in support of consubstantiality, an idea shared by both traditions.[96]

While there are those who for some reason or another support the *filioque* phrase,[97] there is a growing consensus among Western theologians, both Roman Catholic and Protestant, about the need to delete the addition and thus return to the original form of the creed.[98] J. Moltmann for years has appealed for the

91. Against the standard view, Richard Haugh surmises that the addition happened just by way of transposition and without any conscious theological reason. Richard Haugh, *Photius and the Carolingians: The Trinitarian Controversy* (Belmont, MA: Norland, 1975), 160–61.

92. Photius insisted that the Holy Spirit proceeds from the Father *alone*, the Son having no part to play. The intention of this polemical statement was not of course to argue the total exclusion of the Son from the Spirit but to defend vigorously the monarchy of the Father as the source of the deity of both Spirit and Son. See further Letham, *Holy Trinity*, 205.

93. For an important Orthodox statement, see Nick Needham, "The Filioque Clause: East or West?" *Scottish Bulletin of Evangelical Theology* 15 (1997): 142–62.

94. Peters puts it bluntly: "The insertion of *filioque* in the Western version of the Nicene Creed was an act of unwarranted authority and certainly not done in the interest of church unity." Ted Peters, *God as Trinity: Relationality and Temporality in Divine Life* (Louisville, KY: Westminster John Knox Press, 1993), 65.

95. Pannenberg, *Systematic Theology*, 1:319 concurs. Peters makes the brilliant point that in principle there is nothing against adding to the creeds as long as it is done in concert. Theology is an ongoing reflection, elaboration, and processing of tradition. No creed as such has to be the final word. Peters, *God as Trinity*, 66.

96. See further Letham, *Holy Trinity*, 213.

97. Well-known is the defense of *filioque* by Karl Barth, who feared that dismissing it would mean ignoring the biblical insistence on the Spirit being the Spirit of the Son. See Karl Barth, *Church Dogmatics*, ed. G. W. Bromiley and T. F. Torrance (Edinburgh: T & T Clark, 1956), I/1:480. Gerald Bray defends the addition with reference to the doctrine of salvation. In his opinion, the Eastern doctrine of *theōsis* with its focus on pneumatology severs the relationship between Son (atonement) and Spirit. Gerald Bray, "The *Filioque* Clause in History and Theology," *Tyndale Bulletin* 34 (1983): 142–43. While I disagree with Bray, I also commend his relating the question of the *filioque* to the Spirit, which is indeed at the heart of Eastern theology. For this, see further the comment by Theodore Stylianopoulos ("The Biblical Background of the Article on the Holy Spirit in the Constantinopolitan Creed," in *Le IIe Concile Oecuménique*, Études théologiques 2 [Chambésy-Genève: Centre Orthodoxe du Patriarcat Oecuménique, 1982], 171): "At stake was not an abstract question but the truth of Christian salvation." For this quotation, I am indebted to Letham, *Holy Trinity*, 203.

98. For a helpful discussion, see *Spirit of God, Spirit of Christ: Ecumenical Reflections on the Filioque Controversy*, ed. Lukas Vischer (London: SPCK, 1981). For Roman Catholic support of the removal of the *filioque* clause, see Congar, *I Believe in the Holy Spirit*, 3:72ff. In addition to Moltmann and Pannenberg, to be discussed in what follows, a strong defender of the Eastern view has been the Reformed Thomas F. Torrance, who was instrumental in the Reformed-Orthodox dialogue. For the dialogue, see

removal of the addition and has suggested a more conciliar way of putting it, namely, that the Spirit proceeds "from the Father of the Son." He wants to emphasize the biblical idea of reciprocity of Spirit and Son.[99] An alternative to *filioque,* "from the Father through the Son," would be also acceptable to the Christian East. It would defend the monarchy of the Father (and in that sense, some kind of subordination of the Son to Father, an idea not foreign to the East) and still be ambiguous enough.[100]

I agree with Pannenberg that beyond *filioque* there is a weakness that plagues both traditions, namely, the understanding of relations mainly in terms of origins. Both East and West share that view, though in their own distinctive way, the East by insisting on the role of the Father as the source and the West by making the Father primary in the Deity with the idea of the proceeding of the Son from the Father and then the Spirit from both.[101] This blurs the key idea of Athanasius—the importance of which he himself hardly noticed—that relations are based on mutuality rather than origin.

The Lutheran Ted Peters, who supports the removal of the *filioque* clause, however remarks that the idea of the Spirit proceeding from both the Son and the Father also points to something valuable. It highlights relationality and communality, the Spirit being the shared love between Father and Son (and by extension, between the Triune God and the world). Furthermore, on this side of Pentecost, it reminds us of the importance of resurrection and ascension: the risen Christ in Spirit is the presence of Christ. "In this work of transcending and applying the historical event of Jesus Christ to our personal lives, we must think of the Spirit as proceeding from Jesus Christ."[102] Finally, Peters notes, within the divine life the Spirit indeed is the principle of relationship and unity. "The separation that takes place between Father and Son—the separation that defines Father as Father and the Son as Son—is healed by the Spirit. It is the Spirit that maintains unity in difference."[103]

THE RISE OF SOCIAL TRINITARIANISM

The changing understanding of the term *person,* as mentioned several times, has played a role in the shaping of Trinitarian traditions. After the patristic period, intellectual and individualistic tones began to emerge and take over in the yet

---

Thomas F. Torrance, ed., *Theological Dialogue between Orthodox and Reformed Churches,* vol. 2 (Edinburgh: Scottish Academic Press, 1993), 219–32. For his own views in this respect, see Thomas F. Torrance, *Trinitarian Perspectives: Toward Doctrinal Agreement* (Edinburgh: T & T Clark, 1994), 110–43. For these references to Torrance, I am indebted to Letham, *Holy Trinity,* 218 n. 66.

99. Jürgen Moltmann, *The Trinity and the Kingdom: The Doctrine of God* (London: SCM Press, 1981), 178–79, 185–87.

100. Boris Bobrinskoy, *The Mystery of the Trinity: Trinitarian Experience and Vision in the Biblical and Patristic Tradition,* trans. Anthony P. Gythiel (Crestwood, NY: St. Vladimir's Seminary Press, 1999), 302–3. Again, my appreciation for bringing this source to my attention goes to Letham, *Holy Trinity,* 217 n. 64. For incisive comments, see also O'Collins, *Tripersonal God,* 139.

101. Pannenberg, *Systematic Theology,* 1:319.

102. Peters, *God as Trinity,* 66.

103. Ibid.

undefined understanding of the Latin term *persona*, as the definition of Boethius illustrates: "an individual substance of rational nature."[104] The implications were significant to Trinitarian understanding: "This influential account of *person* highlighted the individuality and rationality of the reality that is the center of action and attribution. It had nothing as such to say about the freedom, history and interrelatedness of persons, let alone about the way *person* functions analogically."[105] Reason becomes a key way to define the Deity whereas the biblical idea of love and thus relationality become obscured.

In earlier traditions, both biblical and patristic, however, there were resources to help Christian theology be more appreciative of personal, relational, and communal aspects. In the New Testament, one way to describe God is to use *koinōnia* language. It speaks of communion, koinonia between Father and Son or among the three Trinitarian persons, as well as koinonia between the Triune God and the people of God. While the Holy Spirit at times is connected with koinonia in the New Testament, the Spirit is not described as love. God is love.[106]

Athanasius and the Cappadocians, while certainly not yet "Social Trinitarians," offered seed thought to the later emergence of the social analogy by focusing, on the one hand, on three distinct persons (*hypostaseis*) and their plurality in unity and on the other hand, by speaking of mutuality (the Athanasian rule) and perichoresis.[107] While none of these ideas, as noted above, was a stranger to the Western tradition, they were not fully appreciated in the development of Trinitarian theology. Augustine had developed the theology of Trinity in terms of the Spirit as the mutual love between Father and Son. This is of course a relational, personalistic, and communal approach. Again, during the course of the development of traditions it was not made a theological theme with many implications to be drawn out, and instead was often developed in ways other than communal and personalistic.

The Augustinian lead was picked up and significantly recast by the medieval developer of social Trinitarianism Richard of St. Victor in his highly acclaimed *De Trinitate* (never fully translated into modern English).[108] While he was tutored by Hugh of St. Victor,[109] a spiritual and mystical theologian, and was fascinated by the personalistic approach to Trinity in terms of love, Richard was at

104. Boethius, *Against Eutyches and Nestorius* 3.
105. O'Collins, *Tripersonal God*, 143.
106. Cf. Colin Brown's comment that in contemporary theology the majority of those who advocate social Trinitarianism are philosophers and systematic theologians while biblical theologians opt for "monotheism." Colin Brown, "Trinity and Incarnation: In Search of Contemporary Orthodoxy," *Ex auditu* 7 (1991): 87.
107. See further Cornelius Plantinga Jr., "Gregory of Nyssa and the Social Analogy of the Trinity," *The Thomist* 50 (1986): 325–52.
108. A helpful discussion and theological assessment of St. Victor's Trinitarian teaching can be found in Congar, *I Believe in the Holy Spirit*, 3:103–8. See also the important discussion of the influence of St. Victor on contemporary theology in Gary D. Badcock, "Richard of St. Victor," in *The Dictionary of Historical Theology*, ed. Trevor A. Hart (Grand Rapids: Eerdmans, 2000), 488–89.
109. For a brief introduction of Hugh of St. Victor, see Veli-Matti Kärkkäinen, *The Doctrine of God: A Global Introduction* (Grand Rapids: Baker Academic, 2004), 98.

the same time, like any mainline medieval theologian, a sharp rational thinker. His interest in developing a love-based social analogy did not emerge because of any lack of analytic and intellectual efforts—as is sometimes implied in uninformed expositions. On the contrary, Richard attempted to provide necessary reasons for a better understanding of the Trinity.[110]

In arguing for the plurality of persons in God, Richard's logic is compelling even though not without challenges. His point of departure is God as supreme goodness (*summum bonus*), which includes love. Self-love however is not highest love; therefore, for the love to be able to turn to another, there needs to be another person, the one who receives the love. Love given and received is mutual love. However, Richard reasons, by having just two to share love still implies some kind of selfishness in that while giving love one may expect a return. But essentially he reasoned that love between two is less perfect than three. For the love to be perfect, totally free from selfishness, yet another person needs to be added to the circle. In other words, there is a movement from self-love (Father) to mutual love (Father-Son) to shared love (Father-Son-Spirit).[111]

There is of course a serious challenge to Victor's thinking, routinely noticed by most commentators, namely, "Why stop with three persons?" Wouldn't four or twenty or more be an illustration of even higher love? I don't think Victor was unaware of this challenge. He was bound to the biblical text that spoke of God—Father, Son, and Spirit—as love. His goal was to elucidate the necessity of plurality in the one God revealed in the biblical canon.

In contemporary theology, there is a tendency to make Richard of St. Victor's theology quite dramatically different from Augustine's, with the assumption that Richard disavowed his predecessor's psychological analogy because of personalistic orientation[112] and also to read this medieval suggestion of Trinity as a full-blown "social Trinity." The same applies sometimes to the assessment of the Cappadocians' theology, as mentioned above.[113] Yet, Richard's contributions are significant and help shape later tradition.[114] His effort to think of Trinity in terms of love has the advantage of approaching Trinity in terms of personal encounter, a highly biblical idea. Another key implication and a significant corrective to the traditional idea of Spirit as love is Richard's way of seeing love as the essence of the divine being, again, a thoroughly

110. See Grover A. Zinn, "Introduction," in *Richard of St. Victor*, ed. Grover A. Zinn, The Classics of Western Spirituality (New York: Paulist Press, 1979), 46.

111. Richard of St. Victor, *The Trinity* 3.2–3, 14–15, in *Richard of St. Victor*, 374–76, 387–89. Congar summarizes well: "This special way of existing which characterizes the divine Persons consists in the manner of living and realizing Love. That Love is either pure grace or it is received and giving, or it is purely received and due." Congar, *I Believe in the Holy Spirit*, 3:105.

112. Gunton, *Promise of Trinitarian Theology*, 92, clearly makes the case.

113. For a balanced judgment, see John Zizioulas, "The Doctrine of the Holy Trinity: The Significance of the Cappadocian Contribution," in *Trinitarian Theology Today: Essays on Divine Being and Act*, ed. Christoph Schwöbel (Edinburgh: T & T Clark, 1995).

114. For the importance of Victor, see Fortman, *Triune God*, 191.

biblical concept. Therefore, even though the Trinitarian tradition had to wait for few centuries before these ideas came to the center of theological reflection, Richard's Trinitarian contribution helped theology understand in a more proper way the significance of the personality of Trinitarian persons and their communion.[115]

How did the subsequent tradition utilize and reshape this emerging social model? Much of our answer depends of course on the definition of the social analogy, an unsettled issue in contemporary theology. Thomas Thompson has offered a definition often referred to. For him Social Trinitarianism is a view in which God "is conceived of most fundamentally neither as one divine person . . . nor as three persons in some weak, highly equivocal sense, whose individualism is finally dubious. . . . Rather, God is conceived of quite unequivocally as three divine persons who coexist as one God in a unity sublimely unique, but best likened to that of a family, or a community, or a society, for example the Church."[116] The advantage of this definition is that it is open-ended enough to give space for various kinds of social approaches; at the moment, one can hardly present too tight a definition: suggestions as to who are the "real" Social Trinitarians vary in literature.

Eugen Matei, who has recently written a major study on Social Trinitarianism, claims, "Practically no significant development can be qualified as social in the history of the Trinitarian Doctrine from the twelfth to the nineteenth century."[117] While earlier names have been suggested as candidates,[118] after Richard of St. Victor one needs to jump to the nineteenth-century idealists to continue the story.

Imbued with many ideas quite foreign to orthodox Christianity, British idealism of the nineteenth century[119] advocated the idea that everything is interconnected and that relations between things imply a universal mind. The Anglican (formerly Unitarian) founder of the Christian Socialist movement in England, Frederick Denison Maurice, proposed a view significant to this story; his "social theory seems to be the first consistent attempt to contextualize social theory within a Trinitarian view of God."[120]

---

115. For insightful comments, see Pannenberg, *Systematic Theology*, 1:286–87.

116. Thomas Robert Thompson, "*Imitatio Trinitatis*: The Trinity as Social Model in the Theologies of Jürgen Moltmann and Leonardo Boff" (PhD diss., Princeton Theological Seminary, 1996), 26.

117. Eugen Matei, "The Practice of Community in Social Trinitarianism: A Theological Evaluation with Reference to Dumitru Stăniloae and Jürgen Moltmann" (PhD diss., Fuller Theological Seminary, School of Theology, 2004), 75. In what follows in this section I am indebted to this work.

118. The eighteenth-century name most often mentioned is the German Pietist Nikolaus Ludwig von Zinzendorf, famous for naming the Holy Spirit as "mother," who was fond of the ancient concept of perichoresis as the way to speak of the relationships among the persons for the Trinity. The American Jonathan Edwards is another standard candidate in this category, who is known for some Trinitarian formulations similar to those of Cappadocians. See further Gary Steven Kinkel, *Our Dear Mother the Spirit: An Investigation of Count Zinzendorf's Theology and Praxis* (Lanham, MD: University Press of America, 1990): 79–131 especially; Clarence Henry Faust and Thomas Herberet Johnson, *Jonathan Edwards: Representative Selections with Introduction, Bibliography and Notes*, American Writers Series (New York: American Book Co., 1935), 373–81.

119. Represented mainly by Thomas Hill Green, Edward Caird, and Francis Herbert Bradley.

120. Matei, "Practice of Community," 79. See further Guy H. Ranson, "The Trinity and Society: A Unique Dimension of F. D. Maurice's Theology," *Religion in Life* 26 (1959): 64–74.

These developments and others[121] pressed toward a relational theory of personality, and thus understanding of the Trinity as well, among several theologians at the turn of the nineteenth century.[122] A full-blown social Trinitarianism can be found in Leonard Hodgson in the first part of the twentieth century.[123] In his desire to make his case, he finds a number of social Trinitarians in Christian history, not only the Cappadocians but also Augustine, Aquinas, and Calvin, among others.[124] This again shows how fluid are the contours of definition. From the tradition Hodgson picks up the idea of love as central to viewing the Trinity and emphasizes the personal and interpersonal implications.[125] He blames Christian traditions, including creeds, for replacing the (biblical) organic concept of unity with the mathematical one, ending up elevating the concept of the unity to some kind of mystical sphere.[126]

At the end of this brief survey it is appropriate to revisit the question of the meaning of social Trinitarianism using the perspective of our own time.[127] Whatever else social Trinitarianism may mean—and it might be better to speak of a family of social analogies in Trinitarian theology[128]—there is a consensus on the need to define *person* in terms of relationality.[129] Based on the biblical idea of God as love and the cultural resources of the twentieth century evident in fields as diverse as psychology, philosophy, and linguistics, among others, the idea of communion/community is the defining criterion for speaking of the Trinity. Therefore, "'person' has more to do with relationality than with substantiality and . . . the term stands closer to the idea of communion or community than to the conception of the individual in isolation or abstracted from

121. For example, the emergence of personalist philosophies such as that of Martin Buber can be mentioned here. For a brief comment, see O'Collins, *Tripersonal God*, 158–59; for a more thorough discussion, see Stanley J. Grenz, *The Social God and Relational Self: A Trinitarian Theology of the Imago Dei* (Louisville, KY: Westminster John Knox Press, 2001), 1–14.

122. The leading theologians who developed these ideas at the turn of the century were Wilfred Richmond, John Richardson Illingworth, Charles Frederick D'Arcy, Robert C. Moberley, and in the U.S.A. Francis J. Hall. Hall's *The Trinity* (New York: Green, 1910) is a landmark work.

123. Leonard Hodgson, *The Doctrine of the Trinity* (New York: Charles Scribner's Sons, 1944).

124. Criticism was voiced especially concerning the inclusion of Augustine and Aquinas in the list by Claude Welch. See Welch, *In This Name*, 295–302.

125. "The New Testament presents us with a God in whose eternal being the Son gives himself in mutually responsive love to the Father through the Spirit, the Spirit being equally personal with the Father and the Son in every sense in which the word is used of them." Hodgson, *Doctrine of the Trinity*, 84.

126. See especially ibid., 96.

127. A massive recent study is offered by Grenz, who offers a brilliant summary of the implications of the move "From the One Subject to the Three Persons" (title of chap. 1). Grenz, *Social God*, 23–57.

128. A representative list of contemporary theologians and their works across the theological and ecumenical borders who have adopted the relational understanding of personhood and of Trinity is given in ibid., 4–9.

129. This is not to say that social Trinitarianism as such is universally embraced by theologians. There are also critical voices concerning, e.g., the appropriateness of applying human language of "personality" to God, among other things. See further John L. Gresham Jr., "The Social Model of the Trinity and Its Critics," *Scottish Journal of Theology* 46, no. 3 (1993): 325–43.

communal embeddedness."[130] Theologically, the best-known advocate of this move is the Orthodox John Zizioulas with his highly acclaimed work *Being as Communion*.[131] Its basic thesis is simple and profound: personhood—divine and human—only exists in communion, in relationship; any other kind of existence is that of "individuality." God does not "first" exist as One and "then" Three; rather, the Christian God exists as the communion of Father, Son, and Spirit.

Relationality, unity-in-diversity, and communion, at the heart of social Trinitarian approaches, are currently widely employed in a number of theological works focusing on topics such as ecclesiology,[132] theology of religions,[133] political theology,[134] feminist theology,[135] and process theology,[136] to name a few of the most obvious ones.

---

130. Grenz, *Social God*, 4. So also, e.g., Peters: "God must be reconceived in terms of relationality" (*God as Trinity*, 34). And also, "The idea of person-in-relationship seems to be nearly universally assumed" (ibid., 37).

131. John Zizioulas, *Being as Communion: Studies in Personhood and Communion* (Crestwood, NY: St. Vladimir's Seminary Press, 1985). An excellent, concise introduction to the question of the appropriateness of the use of "person" in contemporary Trinitarian theology is offered by Patricia A. Fox, *God as Communion: John Zizioulas, Elizabeth Johnson, and the Retrieval of the Symbol of the Triune God* (Collegeville, MN: Liturgical Press, 2001), 25–32.

132. Miroslav Volf, *After Our Likeness: The Church as the Image of the Trinity* (Grand Rapids: Eerdmans, 1998).

133. S. Mark Heim, *The Depth of the Riches: A Trinitarian Theology of Religious Ends* (Grand Rapids: Eerdmans, 2001).

134. Leonardo Boff, *Trinity and Society*, trans. Paul Burns (Maryknoll, NY: Orbis Books, 1988); Miroslav Volf, *Exclusion and Embrace: A Theological Exploration of Identity, Otherness, and Reconciliation* (Nashville: Abingdon Press, 1966).

135. Elizabeth Johnson, *She Who Is: The Mystery of God in Feminist Theological Discourse* (New York: Crossroad, 1992); Anne Carr, *The Transforming Grace: Christian Tradition and Women's Experience* (San Francisco: Harper & Row, 1988).

136. Joseph Bracken, *The Triune Symbol: Persons, Process, and Community* (Lanham, MD: University Press of America, 1985).

PART THREE
CONTEMPORARY
TRINITARIAN VIEWS:
WESTERN THEOLOGIES
A. European Traditions

Chapter 5

Karl Barth
The Uniqueness of the Trinitarian God

According to Robert W. Jenson, a renowned Barth expert, it is from this Swiss theologian, hailed as the "church father" of our era, that "twentieth-century theology has learned that the doctrine of the Trinity has explanatory and interpretative use for the whole of theology."[1] Outlining the major points of Barth's doctrine of the Trinity, however, is a quite daunting task, for several reasons. Barth, as is well known, produced his theology in the form of the multivolume *Church Dogmatics* over three decades, thus subjecting his theology to constant revision. Also, as Donald W. Dayton pointedly notes, often in his writings Barth "takes away with one hand [what] he gives back with the other"![2] Furthermore, the often polemical and reactionary way of doing theology—so

---

1. Robert W. Jenson, "Karl Barth," *The Modern Theologians: An Introduction to Christian Theology in the Twentieth Century*, ed. David F. Ford, vol. 1 (Oxford, UK/Cambridge, MA: Blackwell, 1989), 42. Others have echoed this judgment; see, e.g., Ted Peters, *God as Trinity: Relationality and Temporality in Divine Life* (Louisville, KY: Westminster John Knox Press, 1993), 82; and Stanley J. Grenz, *The Social God and the Relational Self: A Trinitarian Theology of the Imago Dei* (Louisville, KY: Westminster John Knox Press, 2001), 33–34.

2. Donald W. Dayton, "Karl Barth and Wider Ecumenism," in *Christianity and the Wider Ecumenism*, ed. Peter Phan (New York: Paragon House, 1990), 184.

characteristic of a "dialectical" theology, responding to the misgivings of classical liberalism—often ends up highlighting the counterposition to the point and leaves later readership, distanced from the debates of the past, to hear a one-sided argumentation.

In my understanding, the judgment of Alar Laats, based on a careful recent study of Barth's Trinitarian doctrine (in correlation with the leading Eastern Orthodox theologian of the past generation, Vladimir Lossky), that Barth constructed his doctrine of the Trinity in two movements,[3] is a helpful methodological starting point. According to Laats, the first phase is based on the first volume of *Church Dogmatics*, in which Barth lays out his view of revelation. Here Barth explicitly constructs his doctrine of the Trinity. The second phase, quite independent from the first, takes place in later volumes as part of the unfolding of the doctrine of election and redemption. Key Trinitarian considerations are discussed but now subsumed under soteriological and christological topics. Most theologians probably agree with my assumption that Barth did not pay due attention to reconciling these two movements of this Trinitarian construction.[4]

Before delving into Barth's Trinitarian doctrine, a couple of questions beg for consideration. How can the human being know God in any way? Doesn't that make God an object, like other objects to be observed? Barth's response is a qualified yes. This means that God is an "object" only to the extent that he gives himself to us to be known. God "gives Himself to man in His Word as a real object" (II/1:10).[5] God is object by his own grace, from his own initiative, in his sovereign freedom. A related question is, If so, could human words ever reach to the level of speaking about God? Here again, Barth gives a qualified yes. Human words can only be used to speak of the transcendent God to the extent God "elevates" our words to their proper use, thus "giving them truth" (II/1:230).

REVELATIONAL TRINITARIANISM

Quite appropriately, Stanley J. Grenz calls Barth's view of the Trinity "revelational trinitarianism."[6] This means two things. On the one hand, Barth argued that the way we come to know the Triune God is through God's self-revelation in Christ—and nowhere else. On the other hand, revelational Trinitarianism also places the discussion of the Trinity in systematic theology in a particular location, namely, as part of the doctrine of revelation. To be more specific, we even have

---

3. Alar Laats, *Doctrines of the Trinity in Eastern and Western Theologies: A Study with Special Reference to K. Barth and V. Lossky*, Studien zur Interkulturelen Geschichte des Christentums 114 (Frankfurt am Main: Peter Lang, 1999), 68 and elsewhere.
4. See, e.g., ibid., 43.
5. References in the main text following this format refer to Karl Barth, *Church Dogmatics* [*CD*], trans. and ed. Geoffrey W. Bromiley and Thomas F. Torrance (Edinburgh: T & T Clark, 1956–1975). The first (Roman) numeral denotes volume; the second (Arabic) number indicates the part; and the third, the page (thus: II/1:230 means second volume, first part, page 230).
6. Grenz, *Social God*, 34.

to say that not only is the doctrine of the Trinity in Barth's dogmatics placed in the beginning of the theological system, as a prolegomenon, but that it also serves as the major structuring principle of theological discussion.

For Barth, as is well known, the Word of God subsists in three interrelated forms: as preached (proclamation of the church), written (the Bible), and revealed (Christ); revelation in Christ is the basis for the other two forms. This takes us to the foundational Trinitarian formula in Barth: "God reveals himself. He reveals himself through himself. He reveals himself" (I/1:340). Barth could also say that God's self-revelation, namely, that "God reveals Himself as the Lord," is what can be called "'The root of the doctrine of the Trinity'" (I/1:353). Trinitarian doctrine is nothing more and nothing less than an analysis of this statement, based on the biblical revelation (I/1:354). While we come to know the immanent Trinity proceeding from the economic, these two cannot be separated. We can say that the "Trinity is antecedently in itself what it is in revelation."[7]

In other words, God for Barth is Revealer, Revelation, and Revealeadness (I/1:344). As Laats summarizes it,

> The modes of being of God "evolve" from one another in the same way as the three different moments of the one event of revelation. The Son proceeds from the Father as revelation proceeds from the revealer and the Holy Spirit proceeds from the Son, and therefore also from the Father, as the revealedness proceeds from revelation and through that from the revealer. . . . And the unity of the Trinity is the unity of the single event of revelation.[8]

Building his doctrine on the basis of revelation,[9] Barth also wants to insist on the close connection between the being-in-himself-of-God ("immanent" Trinity) and being-in-relation-to-us-of-God ("economic" Trinity). There is no other God "behind" the God of the Bible revealed to us in Christ Jesus (e.g., I/1:548). The God known in revelation is the God in himself from eternity. In other words, "God, the Revealer, is identical with His Act in revelation" (I/1:340).[10] Laats succinctly summarizes the meaning of this theological principle:

> According to Barth God reveals himself as God our Father because as the Father of God the Son he is so antecedently in himself. He reveals himself as the Son come to us, or the Word spoken to us, because he is so antecedently in himself, as the Son or the Word of God the Father. And also he reveals himself as the Holy Spirit, by receiving whom we become the children of God, because, as the Spirit of the love of God the Father and God the Son, he is so antecedently in himself.[11]

7. Laats, *Doctrines of the Trinity*, 32.
8. Ibid., 25.
9. For the significance of this starting point to the ancient dualism between the *ordo essendi* (should we bring our inquiry into the Triune God based on the "order of being"?) and *ordo cognoscendi* (or on the "order of knowing"?), see Alan Torrance, "Trinity," in *The Cambridge Companion to Karl Barth*, ed. John Webster (Cambridge, UK: Cambridge University Press, 2000), 73–74.
10. See further ibid., 76.
11. Laats, *Doctrines of the Trinity*, 35. In n. 120, Laats gives the following references in *CD* I/1:441, 457, 513.

When we speak of the close relationship between the immanent and economic Trinity, we also need to acknowledge the fact that, unlike many later theologians such as Moltmann, Barth is careful in not identifying these two to the point of subsuming the immanent into the economic. God exists as Father, Son, and Spirit, that is, God-in-himself, even without reference to us since the Triune God exists in his freedom and love.[12] Barth explicitly says this (I/1:426): "He remains free, in operating, in giving Himself. On this freedom of His rests the distinction between the essence as such and His essence as the Operator, the Self-manifesting." In other words, there is a close correspondence between the immanent and economic Trinity, but no identity if identity means lack of distinction.

WORD AND SPIRIT IN THE TRINITY

Taking its source in revelation, Barth's doctrine of the Trinity is of course integrally related to Christ, the Word. "He is the eternal Word of the Father who speaks from all eternity, or the eternal thought of the Father who thinks from all eternity, the Word in which God thinks Himself, or expresses Himself by Himself" (I/1:499). Thus, Barth says of God that "he is antecedently in himself his speech to himself and then his speech in his revelation to us."[13]

Jesus Christ as the self-revelation of God is identical with God: "The reality of Jesus Christ is that God Himself in person is actively present in the flesh. God Himself in person is the Subject of a real human being, and acting."[14] Otherwise, Jesus Christ, could not of course be God's *self*-revelation.[15]

What about the role of the Spirit in Barth's Trinitarian doctrine?[16] Is the Spirit as "important" as Father and Son? First of all, Barth affirms that the Holy Spirit is not only the Spirit of the Father and of the Son "in his operation *outwardly* and upon us, but that He is to all eternity . . . none other than the Spirit of the Father and of the Son" (I/1:549, emphases mine). The way for Barth to introduce the Spirit is to insist on the Spirit being the Spirit of Christ. The Spirit about whom the Scripture speaks "does not come from any place but only from Christ" (I/2:250). This was the reason why in Barth's estimation the inclusion of the *filioque* phrase into the ancient creeds is justified: "Its intention was to recognize the fact that in God's revelation the Holy Spirit is the Spirit of Jesus Christ, that he cannot be separated from him, that He is only the Spirit of Jesus Christ" (I/2:250).

The way Barth tries to tie the Spirit and Christ together in revelation is to

---

12. See *CD*, II/1:257ff.; IV/2:756ff., 777ff. For these references, I am indebted to Laats, *Doctrines of the Trinity*, 34 n. 114.

13. Laats, *Doctrines of the Trinity*, 28.

14. Claude Welch, *In This Name: The Doctrine of the Trinity in Contemporary Theology* (New York: Scribner's Sons, 1952), 165.

15. Grenz, *Social God*, 37.

16. In this paragraph, my exposition is heavily indebted to Laats, *Doctrines of the Trinity*, 28–29.

speak of them as subjective and objective realities of God's revelation, respectively. The incarnation of the Son is an objective reality and in this sense independent from its appropriation by human beings. The subjective reality is the reception by humans of the revelation in Christ. For Barth, revelation in Christ cannot be acknowledged or embraced by humans without the intervention of the Holy Spirit, and therefore, "the inevitable precondition of the effective activity of the Holy Spirit is the existence of the objective revelation in Jesus Christ."[17] Yet in my understanding, Christ takes the upper hand, as it were, since Christ represents the objective reality of revelation. Could that be one reason why Barth hesitated about assigning any kind of "personhood" to the Spirit? (He of course, expressed reservations about calling Father and Son "persons"; yet, in his later theology, as noticed, he came close to affirming the personality of not only the one God [or Godhead] but also Father and Son.) Barth seemed to be aware of the danger of subordinationism—relegating the Spirit to an inferior state.[18]

PERSONHOOD AND THE "MODES OF BEING"

One of the unique turns that Barth takes in his development of the Trinitarian doctrine is that rather than utilizing the typical "personhood" terminology in referring to Father, Son, and Spirit, he prefers the German term *Seinsweise* (literally "ways of being/existence"), very difficult to translate into English. Usually the term "modes of being" is used as the English equivalent, but that may be misleading because of its close connection with the term "modalism." (The question of whether Barth is modalist I will address in what follows.) Why this move? Barth believes that referring to God in terms of "persons," as a threefold subject, would lead to tritheism (II/1:297). For him, rather, "Father, Son, and Holy Spirit are the divine ways of being that eternally subsist within God in absolute unity, yet whose distinctions form the precondition for God's revelation in Jesus Christ."[19]

Now that Barth chooses not to refer to Father, Son, and Holy Spirit as persons, is he still willing to apply personhood language to the one divine subject? The question can be put in this form for Barth: Is the divine subject Father (as the first "mode of being") or the one divine essence? The judgments of Barth's interpreters are not unanimous here,[20] and I think we have to leave the question open. Yet the idea that personhood in Barth refers primarily to the one divine subject seems to be the most commendable view.

17. Ibid., 29.
18. See, e.g., *CD* I/2:208: "Any subordination [of the Spirit] in principle would indirectly call in question the *homoousia* of the Holy Spirit, compared with the Father and the Son."
19. Grenz, *Social God*, 37.
20. See further Grenz (ibid., 37) and Laats (*Trinitarian Doctrines*, 37). See also Jürgen Moltmann, *The Trinity and the Kingdom* (London: SPCK, 1981), 143.

TRINITY AND HISTORY IN THE LATER
THEOLOGY OF BARTH

So far we have looked at the shape of Barth's Trinitarian doctrine in light of the first part of *Church Dogmatics* where Barth actually constructs his doctrine. What happens in the later parts of his systematics when he ventures into the areas of redemption and salvation? Thomas Torrance's comment about the role of the Trinity for the rest of Barth's theology seems warranted: "Far from being one doctrine among others, the doctrine of the Holy Trinity occupies a central authoritative place in the foundation of all true knowledge of God."[21] Later volumes of his *Church Dogmatics* expand—and to some extent transform—the Barthian view of the Trinity in two main ways.

The first one has to do with the idea of God as love. As such, there is both the inner-Trinitarian love and the desire of the Triune God to create fellowship with humans.[22] To exist as love and to be able to love entails relationality; this again means that there needs to be on the one hand diversity and difference, and on the other hand, "proximity and remoteness in irresolvable unity" (II/1:462). This simply means that Barth introduces here the idea of distinctions and differences into the triune Godhead, an idea that pushes his "modalistically" oriented doctrine toward a social or relational view as well as toward the threeness of the Godhead. As Laats succinctly puts it, when discussing Barth's understanding of the love relationship between Father and Son: "The mutual love and fellowship demand the existence of two separate personalities."[23]

Barth's doctrine of election illustrates not only this principle but also the second new development that has to do with the introduction of history into the divine Godhead, a clue picked up by so many contemporary theologians such as Pannenberg, Moltmann, and LaCugna. The way Barth introduces history into the being of God comes to focus in the last volume (IV/1) of *Church Dogmatics*. He describes the incarnation as the Son of God's journey into a far land. Acting as the prodigal son of Luke 15, the Son of God effects reconciliation since the journey is that of God himself revealed in the Son. "Barth brought the immanent and economic Trinities together by positing that the Son's journey is God's own journey and that the Son's self-humiliation in birth, life, and death is an expression of God's transcendence. God is exalted in the humility of the Son."[24] The basis for this is the eternal act of the covenant of grace. It is God's self-

---

21. Thomas Torrance, *Karl Barth, Biblical and Evangelical Theologian* (Edinburgh: T & T Clark, 1990), 120.
22. These two are brought together most clearly in *CD* II/1:285. According to Barth, God is "capable of fellowship—capable of fellowship on the basis of His own power and act, capable of fellowship of achieving fellowship in Himself and without the need of this other, but at the same time capable of fellowship and capable of achieving fellowship with reference to the other."
23. Laats, *Doctrines of the Trinity*, 45; see further his careful discussion of this topic on pp. 43–46.
24. Roger E. Olson and Christopher A. Hall, *The Trinity*, Guides to Theology (Grand Rapids: Eerdmans, 2002), 97.

determination "to be God, from everlasting to everlasting, in a covenantal relationship with human beings and to be God in no other way."[25] God makes the choice in Jesus Christ to love and show mercy for human beings; as a result, Christ subjects himself to the human experience of death on the cross.[26] The cry from the cross, "My God, my God, why has thou forsaken me?" (IV/1:185) means the death of Jesus Christ "in God-abandonment, precisely as a human experience" is nothing other than "an event in God's own life."[27]

In other words, not only are the roles of the Father and Son different in the sphere of election and reconciliation, but history is also being incorporated into the divine being. Thus McCormack fittingly titles his chapter on Barth in *The Cambridge Companion* as "Grace and Being," meaning that this self-distinction in election and reconciliation has ontological significance to the being of God.[28]

CRITICAL REFLECTIONS

The contributions of Barth's doctrine of the Trinity are many and far-reaching. We can summarize them here in four statements. First, Barth helps save discussion of the Trinity from the snares of abstract, speculative approaches, so typical of much of earlier theologies; in this he anticipates and prepares for the work of Rahner. Even if the way he bases the doctrine on Scripture is not fully satisfactory (as will be discussed in what follows), his method in principle is one that deserves praise. Second, by introducing history into the Godhead, he helps contemporary theology negotiate the transcendence-immanence dialectic in a more helpful way, and he directs our attention to the importance of salvation history in our understanding of God. Third, Barth makes Trinity a structuring principle of theology. By doing so, he is not only offering a needed corrective to classical liberalism, for which to "speak about God meant to speak about humanity,"[29] but also helping theological discourse to answer the question, Who is this God who has revealed himself in Christ?[30] Indeed, this is something Barth saw clearly himself. Fourth, for him, Trinity is the basic criterion for distinguishing the Christian God: "It is the doctrine of the Trinity which fundamentally distinguishes the Christian doctrine of God as Christian—it is it, therefore, also, which marks off the Christian concept of revelation as Christian, in face of all other possible

---

25. Bruce McCormack, "Grace and Being," in *The Cambridge Companion to Karl Barth*, ed. John Webster (Cambridge, UK: Cambridge University Press, 2000), 98.

26. For this, see *CD* IV/1:222.

27. McCormack, "Grace and Being," 98.

28. Ibid.

29. Karl Barth, "The Humanity of God," in *Karl Barth: Theologian of Freedom*, ed. Clifford Green (London: Collins, 1989), 48.

30. Wolfhart Pannenberg, *Systematic Theology*, trans. Geoffrey W. Bromiley, vol. 1 (Grand Rapids: Eerdmans, 1991), 300.

doctrines of God and concepts of revelation" (I/1:346). This is a viewpoint fully developed by the American Robert W. Jenson and picked up by many theologians, as will be seen in what follows.[31]

Barth's proposal, as influential it has been for the rest of the twentieth-century theology of the Trinity, also has raised some serious questions. One has to do with his method. Is Barth indeed anchoring his Trinitarian doctrine on the witness of Scripture? So he claims, but as many critics have noted, he was not able to redeem that promise. Rather than building on biblical revelation, he constructs his Trinitarian doctrine on logical analysis; in other words, Barth derives his doctrine from the formal concept of revelation and its logical analysis (namely, that of revealer, revelation, and revealedness). Pannenberg has been a most vocal critic here,[32] and it is hard to contest this observation. Yet, at the same time, one may miss Barth's helpful insight that—against the older tradition which tended to look for isolated proof texts in the Bible in support of the doctrine—one should rather look at the whole sweep of the biblical record. So the principle of what Barth attempts is commendable even though his way of doing it needs refinement. Pannenberg's own approach, as will be observed later, seems to be a more viable way, namely, to begin with the unfolding of salvation history as evident in the coming of Jesus to serve his Father's kingdom.

Another methodological question has to do with the placement of the doctrine of the Trinity in dogmatics. While theologically the Trinitarian doctrine should function as the structuring principle of theology, it is less than evident that the place of the doctrine is in the context of the discussion of revelation; its place rather is in the discussion of God.[33]

The most frequent complaint against Barth is that his theology is modalistic.[34] Modalism, as explained in the historical section, refers to the early heresy according to which Father, Son, and Spirit are not "persons" but names— "modes"—of one and the same being. Is this accusation valid in light of Barth's larger theological framework? In the first phase, based on a formal analysis of revelation, this charge carries a lot of weight. While Barth acknowledges the danger, he does not offer convincing counterarguments.[35] However, when we move to the second phase of Barth's view of the Trinity, in which history (of Jesus especially) is introduced into the Trinity, the modalistic charge loses much of its weight. Based on the discussion above in which the inclusion of history—

---

31. See further Veli-Matti Kärkkäinen, *Trinity and Religious Pluralism: The Doctrine of the Trinity in the Christian Theology of Religions* (Aldershot, UK: Ashgate, 2004), chap. 2.

32. Pannenberg, *Systematic Theology*, 1:296, 303–4.

33. See ibid., 1:300. See also Torrance, "Trinity," 76–78.

34. The most vocal critic here is Wolfhart Pannenberg, *Grundfragen systematischer Theologie*, 2 vols. (Göttingen: Vandenhoeck & Ruprecht, 1980), 2:96–11.

35. See Torrance, "Trinity," 81, for references to several critics of Barth. Torrance himself denies that Barth's view is modalistic, but in my understanding Torrance does not make the needed distinction (as I will do in what follows) between the two major phases of the development of Barth's Trinitarian doctrine.

especially the history of Jesus Christ—comes into the picture, Barth can hardly be deemed a modalist.

Yet there are related challenges I would like to raise here. The first has to do with the fact that while (the later) Barth was not a modalist, he still advocated a view of the Trinity that begins from the unity and only then, in the subsequent moment, begins to speak of the threeness. A number of contemporary theologians, while welcoming Barth's turn to revelation and history, level strong criticism against the "monotheistic" tendency. Moltmann has the been the sharpest critic, as will become evident later; others have joined in, such as Pannenberg and LaCugna.

Another critical remark has to do with Barth's reluctance to employ the term "person." In his own time, the reasons for eschewing personalistic language made more sense, namely, his fear of tritheism because of the highly individualistic understanding of personality. In light of both historical antecedents such as the legacy of the Cappadocians (with all its ambiguity) and especially in light of contemporary advances toward a relational, communal, nonindividualistic understanding of personhood, those fears can be addressed. The communion theology of John Zizioulas, to be studied in chapter 7, which has been enthusiastically followed by most contemporary Trinitarian theologians and is a needed corrective to Barth's one-sided unity-based approach, avoids the danger of tritheism, but does that at the expense of failing to appreciate threeness as it should. In sum, while Barth's reservations about personhood talk make sense in light of his own argumentation, there is no compelling reason why theology cannot establish a more satisfying way of understanding personhood.[36]

The other pioneer of twentieth-century Trinitarian thought was the Catholic Karl Rahner, who built on the groundbreaking idea of the close relationship between the immanent and economic Trinity and made it the most distinctive feature of his theology.

---

36. Torrance, "Trinity," 79–80, disagrees with this view, but I do not find his argument convincing.

Chapter 6

Karl Rahner

The Immanent and Economic Trinity

AGAINST THE "ANTI-TRINITARIAN TIMIDITY"

What Karl Barth is for Protestant theology, Karl Rahner is for Roman Catholic theology. If Barth initiated the Trinitarian renaissance in the twentieth century, it was Karl Rahner who established the canons of later Trinitarian language with his insistence on the identity of the economic and immanent Trinity.

Rahner opposed what he considered to be not only underdeveloped Trinitarianism but even more, an attitude of "anti-trinitarian timidity."[1] "[D]espite their orthodox confession of the Trinity, Christians are, in their practical life, almost mere 'monotheists,'" he wrote.[2] Even worse, he said, "[S]hould the doctrine of the Trinity have to be dropped as false, the major part of religious literature could well remain virtually unchanged."[3] As true as this statement must have been at the time of its writing, the complaint hardly does justice to the situation in the beginning of a new millennium.

1. Karl Rahner, *The Trinity*, trans. Joseph Donceel (New York: Herder & Herder, 1970), 13.
2. Ibid., 10.
3. Ibid., 10–11.

Rahner's complaints against traditional Trinitarian treatments focus on three interrelated issues. First, he laments the typical structure of the doctrine of God in terms of having the treatise "On the One God" precede that of "On the Triune God" as if the latter were more or less an appendix. While this separation established itself no earlier than Thomas Aquinas, subsequently it has become a norm.[4] The implication of this methodological choice is that it "looks as if everything which matters for us in God has already been said"[5] in the first treatise. In other words, the unity of God has taken the upper hand over the threeness.[6] Rahner traces the reason to the differences between West and East (Augustine and the Cappadocians, respectively); whether this analysis is accurate we discussed in the historical section. One of the corollaries of this separation is that Christian theology has not been able to incorporate the Trinity as an integral topic; instead, it typically "occupies a rather isolated position."[7]

Rahner's second target of critique against the older theological approach is that the Augustinian rule of the indivisibility of the works of the Triune God *ad extra* (in relation to the world and us) has helped theologians lose sight of the peculiarity of each Trinitarian person. It has become customary to speculate whether, for example, any of the three divine members could have become incarnate. Rather than emphasizing that it was the Son, Logos, who became human, theology textbooks routinely assign incarnation to "God" (in the generic sense) in assuming humanity. Consequently, Trinitarian theology becomes abstract and lacks specificity when speaking of divine hypostases.[8]

The third lament, consequently, has to do with the separation of the Trinity from salvation history. According to Rahner, the doctrine "becomes quite philosophical and abstract and refers hardly at all to salvation history."[9] This is in opposition to the way the biblical canon speaks of salvation history:

> For should one make use of salvation history, it would soon become apparent that one speaks always of him whom Scripture and Jesus himself calls the Father, *Jesus'* Father, who sends the Son and gives himself to us in the Spirit, in his Spirit.[10]

Therefore, for Rahner the only legitimate way to approach the Trinity is to take salvation history, the mystery of salvation, as the starting point. In other words, "the Trinity is for us a mystery of salvation"[11] rather than an abstract

---

4. Ibid., 15–17.
5. Ibid., 17.
6. For a helpful discussion of this, see Stanley J. Grenz, *The Social God and the Relational Self: A Trinitarian Theology of the Imago Dei* (Louisville, KY: Westminster John Knox Press, 2001), 39.
7. Rahner, *Trinity*, 14.
8. Ibid., 11–12.
9. Ibid., 17.
10. Ibid., 18–19 (italics in the original).
11. Ibid., 21.

speculation into the Godhead apart from the world. This takes us to the best-known contribution of Rahner, namely, the identity of the economic and immanent Trinity.

THE UNITY OF THE ECONOMIC AND IMMANENT TRINITY

What has been dubbed "Rahner's Rule"[12] states simply the following: "*The 'economic' Trinity is the 'immanent' Trinity and the 'immanent' Trinity is the 'economic' Trinity.*"[13] What is the meaning and significance of this oft-quoted formula?

> Rahner was concerned that too much focus on the inner life of God and especially on God's unity of being ("simplicity") led the church into a neglect of the Trinity and of the intrinsic link between it and the doctrine of salvation. He wanted to make the Trinity more practical by demonstrating its connection with salvation. His goal was to forbid or discourage all speculation about the immanent Trinity that was not relevant to salvation (including Christian life). He was convinced that the only purpose of speaking of God's immanent triune being is to guard against dissolving God into history and to protect God's transcendence and the graciousness of salvation.[14]

In other words, Rahner's rule means that God is in himself the same God we meet in salvation history. We can trust that the way God appears to us in his dealings with us is the way God exists in his own inner life. This is the meaning of Rahner's quite robust statement: "No adequate distinction can be made between the doctrine of the Trinity and the doctrine of the economy of salvation."[15]

As mentioned before, one of the targets of Rahner's criticism is an abstract way of talking about the Triune God, as if God as a whole would meet us in salvation history. Not so for Rahner. "Jesus is not simply God in general, but the Son. The second divine person, God's Logos, is man, and only he is man." Consequently, there is something about the economic Trinity's existence in the world that can only be said of the Son, in this case the mission of the Son. As Rahner puts it concretely, "Here something occurs 'outside' the intra-divine life in the world itself." That the whole Trinity "causes," as it were, incarnation—this is as far as Rahner seems to be ready to go with the Augustinian rule mentioned above—does not contradict the idea that there "has occurred in salvation history something which can be predicated only of one divine person."[16]

But why does Rahner bother to dwell on this theme? Because if we assume

---

12. Ted Peters, *God as Trinity: Relationality and Temporality in Divine Life* (Louisville, KY: Westminster John Knox Press, 1993), 96ff.
13. Rahner, *Trinity*, 22 (italics in the text).
14. Roger E. Olson and Christopher A. Hall, *The Trinity*, Guides to Theology (Grand Rapids: Eerdmans, 2002), 98.
15. Rahner, *Trinity*, 24.
16. Ibid., 23.

that every divine person could be incarnated, then it would mean that incarnation would not reveal anything specific or peculiar about the Son but only of the Godhead in general.[17] It is only this threefold relation of God to us that makes it possible that "each one of the three divine persons communicates himself to man in gratuitous grace in his own personal particularity and diversity."[18] Yet in order to avoid the absurd notion of tritheism, Rahner also reminds us of the fact these three self-communications are the self-communications of the one God in three interrelated ways. Rahner puts it succinctly:

> God relates to us in a threefold manner, and this threefold, free, and gratuitous relation to us *is* not merely a copy or analogy of the inner Trinity, but this Trinity itself, albeit as freely and gratuitously communicated. That which is communicated is precisely the triune personal God.[19]

CAN AN IMMUTABLE GOD CHANGE?

It does not take much reflection to notice that an inevitable question arises out of Rahner's equation of the immanent Trinity with the economic, and it has to do with the notion of change. If what happens in the world (economic Trinity) is a faithful revelation of God, it means that incarnation, cross, and resurrection bring about something "new" in God's own life. They are not mere "acts" in terms of a play but acts that have implications for God's own existence. How would this be reconciled with classical theism's insistence on the immutability of God? Unlike many of his contemporaries, Rahner was not willing to give up the notion of the unchanging nature of the Godhead.

Rahner, of course, was too good a theologian to dismiss the question even though, curiously enough, in his main treatise on *The Trinity* he does not really devote due attention to it. He attends to it elsewhere.[20] Rahner makes a twofold claim here. First, with all his insistence on the unchanging nature of God, he also insists on the reality of the "becoming flesh" of God by arguing that, in that event, history (in the world) becomes the history of God:

> But after all this is said it still remains true that the *Logos became* man, that the history of the becoming of this human reality became *his own* history, that our time became the time of the eternal One, that our death became the death of the immortal God himself.[21]

17. For this see further ibid., 28 especially.
18. Ibid., 34–35. For Rahner (in contrast to his neo-scholastic teachers) "grace" means the presence of God; grace is a real communication of God's own presence in the depths of the human person.
19. Rahner, *Trinity*, 35–36 (italics in the original).
20. Karl Rahner, *Foundations of Christian Faith: An Introduction to the Idea of Christianity*, trans. William V. Dych (New York: Crossroad, 1982), 212–24, especially 219–23; and idem, "On the Theology of the Incarnation," in *Theological Investigations*, vol. 4, trans. Kevin Smith (New York: Crossroad, 1982), 105–20.
21. Rahner, *Foundations of Christian Faith*, 220 (italics in the text).

In other words, the real question for Rahner is how to understand the truth that the assertion of God's immutability need not make us lose sight of the fact that what took place in Jesus as becoming and as history here in our midst, in our space, in our time and world, in our process of becoming, in our evolution and in our history, that this is precisely the history of the Word of God himself, *his own* becoming.[22]

So it means there appears to be change in the Godhead. Yet—and this is the second part of his argumentation—Rahner posits that indeed it is possible to speak of change in an immutable God if that change is relegated to something that is not internal to the Deity. In his typically technical way, he expresses this truth: "He who is not subject to change in himself can *himself* be subject to change in *something else*."[23] In other words, there is a distinction between inner and outer change in the Triune God, and he argues we "may not regard this process by which one changes in something else as a contradiction to God's immutability."[24] For Rahner, the idea of a change in something else makes the idea of the immutability a "dialectical assertion" not unlike the idea of the Trinity vis-à-vis unity, but not a contradictory idea.[25] And in light of the fact that the human creature, created by God and created in God's image, has been established as the *"grammar of God's possible self-expression,"* one can argue (as Rahner does) that the human creature is a most fitting vehicle for God's self-expression. In other words, not only is the coming-to-flesh of the Son of God a proper self-expression of God, but the self-expression can only happen to the *Logos* rather than to the undifferentiated Godhead: "If this God expresses his very own self into the *emptiness* of what is not God, then this expression is the outward expression of his immanent Word, and not something arbitrary which could also be proper to another divine person."[26]

One last question to deal with concerns the terminology Rahner chooses to use. For him—as for Barth—this choice goes beyond mere terminology and is involved with foundational theological issues.

HOW TO NAME THE TRIUNE GOD

One would expect Rahner to welcome Barth's rejection of the term "person" and instead go with the term "mode of being." While Rahner in general agrees with Barth's criticism of the term "person," his own solution differs from that of his Protestant counterpart.[27] Rahner notes that the typical danger in the Trinitarian

---

22. Ibid. (italics in the text).
23. Ibid. (italics in the text).
24. Ibid., 221.
25. Ibid.
26. Ibid. 223. Rahner, as is well known, speaks of the human person as the "cipher of God" (see pp. 224–27).
27. Rahner, *Trinity*, 44, states this explicitly.

discourse is not modalism but rather tritheism, and this is because of the usage of the term "person" that for any contemporary person means about the same as "individual," thus implying a distinct consciousness and center of activity. Even more do we see the danger when, as Rahner further notes, theologians are apt to note that the term "person" has undergone significant changes from "mask" to individual. Any talk about three persons in the Godhead subjects itself to misunderstanding. Yet with all these reservations, Rahner quite practically notes that the term "person" has survived now for more than fifteen hundred years and commends itself to theological use, even if the dangers mentioned above need to be acknowledged.[28] At the same time, Rahner makes another practical note, namely, that no amount of theological caution may be able to stop the secular usage of the term from taking its own course.[29]

However, the issue is not yet settled for Rahner. In case the theological guild decides to look for potential candidates other than "person," his own suggestion would be "distinct manner of subsistence." What is its intended meaning? In order to avoid tritheism, this term is supposed to underline the idea that in the Godhead "there are not three consciousnesses; rather, the one consciousness subsists in a threefold way. There is only one real consciousness in God, which is shared by Father, Son, and Spirit, each in his own proper way."[30] In other words, Rahner wants on the one hand to avoid modalism, by speaking of *distinct* manner of subsistence, and on the other, to avoid tritheism, by speaking of *subsistence,* which is not "as personal" as *person.*

CRITICAL REFLECTIONS

Rightly, Rahner's rule has been called a "decisive watershed in twentieth-century trinitarian thinking."[31] With Barth, he has been an originator of the current Trinitarian renaissance by showing the centrality of the Trinity to Christian life and doctrine. Yet there is a peculiar irony here routinely ignored by his critics. The irony is simply this: while this Austrian theologian dealt with the topic of the Trinity in various parts of his collected essays known as *Theological Investigations,* even a cursory look at his theological summa, titled *Foundations of Christian Faith,* convinces one that in Rahner's own systematic theology the Trinity did not play any significant role. In fact, the marginality of the Trinity in that massive book, which claims to summarize his distinctive theology, is staggering.[32]

28. Ibid., 42–45; see also 104–6.
29. Ibid., 56–57.
30. Ibid., 107; see further pp. 109–13.
31. Peters, *God as Trinity,* 102.
32. Rahner's *Foundations of Christian Faith* includes a brief consideration of Trinity on pp. 133–37, summarizing some key ideas of *The Trinity,* and there are scattered references to the Trinity, especially in the context of christological discussion. Yet no separate treatment is given to the topic to any significant extent.

For me, it is amazing how rarely Rahner's interpreters make note of this lacuna or inquire into possible reasons behind it (that would make a fruitful topic for a doctoral student in systematic theology!).

This lacuna notwithstanding, there is no doubt that Rahner's rule and its implications mark the watershed of contemporary Trinitarian theology, namely, the incorporation of salvation history into the divine life (even if relegated to the status of "external" change by Rahner himself) and the trustworthiness of revelation and salvation history as the "gateways to the knowledge of God." Although theologians routinely add qualifiers to Rahner's rule, those working in his wake are conscious of the essential connection between the doctrine of God and soteriology. Moreover, Trinitarian thinkers since Rahner seek to give utmost seriousness to the epistemological link between the economic Trinity and the immanent Trinity.[33] Ted Peters summarizes the significance of Rahner's advancement:

> It says something decisively important about relationality in God—namely, God's relationship to the world is internal to the divine life. God's relation to the world in redemption and consummation is not merely external, not merely an add-on to a God whose being is already intact. . . . Rather, God's involvement in the course of the world affairs is so intimate that the character of divinity itself is shaped by it. The trinitarian understanding of God is that God's full self-investment in the incarnation redefines divinity to include humanity, the humanity of the historical Jesus. God's full self-investment in the Holy Spirit binds believers to Christ, so that in faith they are at one with Christ and, hence, at one with God.[34]

Peters's assessment is also helpful in that it points to the direction later interpreters of Rahner have pushed Rahner's rule: the freedom to speak of "change" in the divine life even more than Rahner felt appropriate. The discussion of Moltmann's and Pannenberg's views especially illustrate this tendency.

Along with the praise, Rahner has elicited criticism by theologians from across the ecumenical spectrum. Going back to Grenz's comment above, what type of "qualifiers" are being added to Rahner's conception? What are the challenges? On the one hand, there have been those who feel uneasy about too-strict an identity between the economic and immanent Trinity. That could potentially lead to the compromising of divine freedom. The immanent-economic distinction protects the freedom of God. There is the legitimate concern as to whether "the total collapse of the immanent Trinity into the economic Trinity result[s] in a finite God who is dependent for divine definition upon the world."[35] The other challenge to the principle of the identity between the economic and immanent Trinity is the question of the "newness" of the revelation of God—or better, lack thereof.

---

33. Grenz, *Social God*, 41.
34. Ted Peters, *God—The World's Future: Systematic Theology for a Postmodern Era* (Minneapolis: Fortress, 1992), 108.
35. Ibid.

What I mean is this: if God's self-revelation in Christ in terms of God becoming human does not introduce anything "new" to the world and the divine life, wouldn't that strip the incarnation of its profound meaning? However one speaks of the change in or immutability of God, one has to agree that after the incarnation, the cross, and resurrection, in one way or another God "exists in a different way." This is of course the point of Rahner's struggle with the idea of change: even though he is not willing to give up the idea of immutability, he also does not want to water down the significance of the incarnation as something "new" (even though not as something arbitrary or external to God).

Yet, insisting on the distinction between the immanent and economic Trinity too strongly raises another problem—that of "subordinationism"—the idea of the economic Trinity only being "a temporal image of a much more real and hence much more important eternal and unrelated Trinity."[36] In other words, what happens in the world is a kind of superficial "act" as in a play, more or less distinct from the absolutely unmoved deity of the eternity.[37] Rahner's rule is of course presented to combat this error, which is not foreign to older theology in its insistence on the immutability of the Deity.

How to negotiate this tension between, on the one hand, not fully equating the two forms of the Trinity and, on the other hand, neither separating them? Catherine Mowry LaCugna, the ablest student of Rahner (whose radical recasting of Rahner's rule will be studied in what follows) is to the point when she notes that amid a number of differing responses to Rahner, the bottom line has to do with the question of method. She argues that what Rahner was up to in the formulation of his rule had to with the methodological insight that relates to "the order of theological knowledge [that] must adhere to the historical form of God's self-communication in Christ and the Spirit."[38] If understood *epistemologically* rather than *ontologically*, the rule is simply saying that no gap exists between the way God exists in himself and the way God relates to the world and to us. While a few commentators have wondered if Rahner is going beyond the epistemological principle (order of knowing) to affirming an ontological identity (order of being) of the economic and immanent Trinity that would of course lead to compromising God's freedom,[39] it seems clear to me that Rahner only wanted his rule to be read in terms of connecting divine life with salvation history and assuring us that it is a faithful way to the knowledge of God.[40] A fellow Catholic theologian, Edmund Hill—having made the obvious, yet needed,

36. Ibid., 107.

37. See further Peters, *God as Trinity*, 102, with reference to Walter Kasper, *The God of Jesus Christ*, trans. Matthew J. O'Connell (New York: Crossroad, 1984), 275–76.

38. Catherine Mowry LaCugna, introduction to Karl Rahner, *The Trinity*, trans. Joseph Donceel (New York: Seabury Press, 1997), xv. I am indebted to Grenz, *Social God* (p. 38 n. 76) for turning my attention to this edition of Rahner's work.

39. That is the concern of John Thompson, *Modern Trinitarian Perspectives* (New York: Oxford University Press, 1994), 28.

40. So also, e.g., Stanley J. Grenz, *Rediscovering the Triune God: The Trinity in Contemporary Theology* (Minneapolis: Fortress, 2004), 69–70.

note that the talk about the economic and the immanent Trinities should not be understood in terms of two Trinities—calls Rahner's rule a "theological shorthand": "'The Trinity of the economy of salvation' means the mystery of the Trinity as revealed in, and as studied through, the economy of salvation." Consequently, the "Trinity of the economy of salvation" means "the Trinity revealed in and then approached through such saving events and realities as the incarnation, Pentecost, the Church."[41]

What raises questions about Rahner going beyond the epistemological principle is his talk about "self-expression" and "self-possession." Borrowing from Hegel, Rahner surmises that it is in the Son, the "other" (who however is of the same essence with him) that the Father expresses himself in order to possess the Spirit in himself.[42] That dialectic idea, however, has the potential of introducing necessity to divine life: it takes incarnation (and of course creation)—that is, salvation historical events—to make God's self-expression and self-possession happen. As his fellow Catholic theologian DiNoia says, "Rahner's trinitarian theology risked a pattern of explanation in which the free actions of creation, incarnation, and grace could be seen as necessary extensions of God's inner self-expression and self-possession."[43] However, I agree with Stanley J. Grenz that "although his critics may have put their collective finger on an unfortunate implication of Rahner's rule, Rahner himself clearly did not move in this direction, at least not fully or intentionally."[44] This is because Rahner grounded the external self-expression in a prior act in the inner life of God, in eternity: "It is because God 'must' 'express' himself inwardly that he can also utter himself outwardly; the finite, created utterance *ad extra* is a continuation of the immanent constitution of 'image and likeness'—a free continuation."[45]

Several Roman Catholic theologians,[46] while affirming Rahner's rule in principle, have also wanted to qualify it to make room for the kind of asymmetry between the economic and immanent Trinity that preserves God's freedom. Yves Congar says that while there is only one Trinity, "'this [self-communication] takes place in a mode that is not connatural with the being of the divine Persons.' The mode of the economy is condescension, *kenōsis*. Thus there remains a certain degree of disparity between what God is *in se*, and what God is able to be *ad extra*."[47] As a result LaCugna puts forth a rule that is in keeping with Rahner's intentions: "The incomprehensible and ineffable mystery of God is not dimin-

---

41. Edmund Hill, *The Mystery of the Trinity* (London: Geoffrey Chapman, 1985), 45.

42. See Rahner, "The Theology of the Symbols," in *Theological Investigations*, vol. 4, trans. Kevin Smith (New York: Crossroad, 1982), 236.

43. J. A. DiNoia, "Karl Rahner," in *The Modern Theologians: An Introduction to Christian Theology in the Twentieth Century*, ed. David F. Ford, 2 vols. (New York: Blackwell, 1989), 1:198.

44. Grenz, *Rediscovering the Triune God*, 69.

45. Rahner, "Theology of the Symbol," 236–37. Catherine Mowry LaCugna's *God for Us: The Trinity and Christian Life* (San Francisco: HarperSanFrancisco, 1991), 213, agrees with this interpretation.

46. Piet Schoonenberg, Walter Kasper, and Yves Congar.

47. As paraphrased by LaCugna, *God for Us*, 219, quotation within the quotation from Yves Congar, *I Believe in the Holy Spirit*, trans. David Smith, 3 vols. (New York: Seabury Press, 1983), 3:15.

ished by God's self-expression in the history of salvation. Nonetheless, because of the unity of *theologia* and *oikonomia*, the specific details of God's self-revelation in Christ and the Spirit reveal God's nature."[48]

The way Grenz puts Rahner's rule in the context of successive Trinitarian theology is instructive:

> It seems, then, that Rahner—like Barth—retained the classical belief that God's eternal being is ultimately independent of historical events. If this is the case, then the question that lies at the heart of Rahner's Rule is, to cite LaCugna's characterization, "Can we affirm that God as God is altogether present in the economy of salvation history, and at the same time that God also exceeds and outstrips the human capacity to receive or explain this self-communication?"[49]

Many successors of Rahner, both Roman Catholic (LaCugna as the prime example) and Protestant (especially Moltmann) have gone beyond the epistemological principle and affirmed an ontological identity between the economic and immanent Trinity. They have also negotiated in more than one way the unity of the economic and immanent Trinity with reference to eschatology. Theologians such as Moltmann and Pannenberg on the Continent and Robert W. Jenson and LaCugna in the United States have all contributed significantly to this eschatological orientation, as the ensuing discussion will show.

As a representative voice of those who have radically revised Rahner's rule, let me take here the Lutheran Ted Peters. While not denying that methodologically Rahner's rule applies also to the order of our knowledge of God, he also insists that we should think of the distinction between the immanent and economic Trinity as eschatological. In order to do so, however, one needs to posit a specific understanding of time and eternity (the details of which will be worked out in the contexts of discussing Jenson's Trinitarian doctrine). For Peters (and Jenson), eternity does not mean timelessness,[50] but rather "everlastingness that takes up into itself the course of temporal history." Thus what "happens in time contributes to the content of what is eternal."[51] On the one hand, eternity is related to history; on the other hand, God's Trinitarian activity is not divorced from the eternity of the Triune God. Clearly, Peters is not satisfied to take Rahner's rule only as an epistemological rule but wants to inquire into the ontology of the Triune God.

---

48. LaCugna, *God for Us*, 221.

49. Grenz, *Rediscovering the Triune God*, 70; citation from LaCugna, *God for Us*, 217.

50. From Augustine on, one way of understanding time/eternity is to argue that since God is the creator of everything, even time is a created entity, and thus God—in his eternity—exists outside of the time.

51. Peters, *God—the World's Future*, 109; see also chap. 4, "The Temporal and Eternal Trinity," in Peters, *God as Trinity* (pp. 146–87). Robert Jenson says the same when he argues that the "'economic Trinity' is *eschatologically* God 'himself,' an 'immanent' Trinity." Robert Jenson, *The Triune Identity: God According to the Gospel* (Philadelphia: Fortress, 1982), 141.

While I find Peters's argument for eternity as everlastingness quite persuasive, I still wonder why we should—even in terms of the eschaton—make too much of ontology. I could take his proposal as a pious, perhaps well-taken hypothesis, but I don't see how I could possibly go further to an affirmation. Biblically that is neither possible nor desirable. Theologically and philosophically, I am less certain than Peters that this is a superb way of fully asserting God's freedom in terms "openness to the future" as radically different from the traditional notion of "the spurious freedom of unaffectedness."[52] (The other question in my mind is whether it is fair to label the view of classical theology in those terms.) In the context of discussing Moltmann's theology, I will revisit the issue and raise some more critical questions concerning his version of an eschatological solution. At this point, let me say this much in terms of my own tentative reflections on this issue. In my understanding, taking Rahner's rule as epistemological (thus methodological) is a helpful choice when thinking of the distinction between the immanent and economic Trinity on this side of eternity. While there is absolutely no reason to doubt the integrity of God in his self-revelation, neither can a mortal human being claim too much knowledge of the inner life of God. While appeal to the "mysterious" nature of the immanent Trinity can also be misused in a way noted earlier, the assumption concerning the identity of God-in-himself with the God-for-us cannot be used as a pretext for claiming to know too much of God. Let us be more humble and say that whatever God—in his absolute freedom and love—has decided to reveal of himself faithfully reflects who God is. Yet, at least on this side of eternity, one can say that the economic Trinity is the immanent Trinity but should be careful to not turn the equation too hastily the other way.

I find Peters's comments on Rahner's struggle with change in God quite convincing. I agree with him that by introducing the idea of two kinds of changes Rahner hardly clarifies the issue. One has to ask, naturally, what is the relationship between the internal and external change? If the external change is really "external" to the divine life (even though, as Rahner says, not arbitrary), how can it relate to the inner life of the Trinity? Peters raises the obvious question: Why continue to insist on the immutability of God?[53] Contemporary theology seems to allow talk about the faithfulness of God—and isn't that in the keeping with the biblical teaching?—without taking the Greek metaphysical notion of "immutability" as an absolute rule. For example, the debate within the North American evangelical movement about "open theism" has encouraged even the more traditional theology to take up more seriously the biblical insistence on God being related to the world in a real sense.[54] Rahner's struggle against immutabil-

52. Peters, God—the World's Future, 109, quoting from Robert W. Jenson, "The Triune God," in Christian Dogmatics, ed. Carl E. Braaten and R. W. Jenson, 2 vols. (Philadelphia: Fortress, 1984), 1:155–56.
53. Peters, God as Trinity, 101.
54. When we discuss Clark Pinnock's Trinitarian doctrine, we will take a more in-depth look at some aspects of this debate.

ity at the time of writing *The Trinity* is understandable, but its urgency is felt much less now, a couple of decades later.

I think one reason for the struggle in Rahner's theology is that he fears too much the application of the Augustinian rule—according to which the *ad extra* works of the Trinity are indistinguishable (whereas inner-Trinitarian works, of course, are distinguishable, otherwise any talk about the Trinity would not make any sense at all!). True, that rule can be abused in a way that is not helpful, for example by speculating about the possibility of any of the Trinitarian persons becoming human. Yet that has little to do with the theological value of the rule (whatever Augustine's original motivation for affirming the rule), which is to protect the unity of (the works of) the Triune God in God's going out of his own life, an idea opposed by hardly anyone.

A number of theologians, especially Jürgen Moltmann and Wolfhart Pannenberg, both in their own distinctive ways, have taken up and further developed the proposal by Rahner. We will look at their ideas in chapters 8 and 9.

Chapter 7

John Zizioulas
Trinity as Communion

THE LEGACY OF THE CHRISTIAN EAST

John Zizioulas, the bishop of Pergamon, Greece, is undoubtedly the best-known and most influential contemporary spokesperson for the mystical, apophatic tradition of Eastern Orthodoxy. What is interesting about the work of this Orthodox theologian, who has previously taught theology in England and engaged widely in ecumenical work, is that he has never produced a Trinitarian treatise per se. His magnum opus, fittingly titled *Being as Communion* (1985), is about ecclesiology, the nature of the church as communion, and how it relates to the notion of personhood (thus, the subtitle, *Studies in Personhood and Communion*).[1]

---

1. John Zizioulas, *Being as Communion: Studies in Personhood and Communion* (Crestwood, NY: St. Vladimir's Seminary Press, 1985). In addition to this book, which is in fact a collection of essays published elsewhere (thus making it less than accessible to the beginning student), a brief introduction to the main ideas of his Trinitarian thinking can be found in John Zizioulas, "Human Capacity and Human Incapacity: A Theological Exploration of Personhood," *Scottish Journal of Theology* 28, no. 5 (October 1975): 401–48. An accessible introduction to the theology of Zizioulas is offered by Miroslav Volf, *After Our Likeness: The Church as the Image of the Trinity* (Grand Rapids: Eerdmans, 1998), 73–123.

Zizioulas literally stands between the West and the East,[2] not only because he—with Bishop Kallistos Ware—is a widely acclaimed spokesperson for Eastern Orthodoxy in the West, but also because his theology builds critically and creatively on his own Eastern tradition, while reaching out to and in some significant ways building on the contemporary Western renaissance of Trinitarian theology. The Cappadocian Fathers of the East are his main theological resources.[3] Occasionally he revisits the ideas of more contemporary Eastern forebears, especially Vladimir Lossky, yet he also reserves the right to critique him and other Easterners.

The most influential Eastern Trinitarian theologians of the twentieth century are Sergius Bulgakov and V. Lossky, originally from Russia, as well as Dumitru Staniloe of Romania. Bulgakov gleaned from various sources such as the personalist Russian thinker Vladimir Solovyov (or Solovyev, Soloviev), the mystical philosopher Nikolai Berdiaved, as well as several Russian theologians. In keeping with these influences, Bulgakov approached the Trinity from the perspective of the analysis of personhood and communion, an idea going back all the way to Richard of St. Victor, as noted in the historical section. Terms such as "personalism," "love," and "perichoresis" became crucial to Bulgakov's Trinitarian theology.[4]

Vladimir Lossky, the most important dialogue partner to Zizioulas, has taught the Christian West the importance of mystical and apophatic approaches to theology. Thus the title of one of his main books: *The Mystical Theology of the Eastern Church.*[5] In the negative way of the East, the knowledge of God is not really knowledge but rather total ignorance. Rather than intellectual knowledge, it is a mystical ecstasy.[6] God is not inaccessible to us, however; in his "energies," in contrast to his inaccessible essence, God is present to us.[7] A leading theme in Lossky's Trinitarian theology is insistence on the simultaneous and equal coexistence of one nature and three persons, "a primordial antinomy of absolute identity and no less absolute diversity."[8] In other words, Lossky does not want to go with either textbook approach: the Eastern starting point with threeness or the Western starting point with unity. He wants to have them both. In keeping with

---

2. For a helpful study of the differences between the East and West, see Duncan Reid, *Energies of the Spirit* (Atlanta: Scholars Press, 1997).

3. For a helpful discussion of the Trinitarian traditions in the East, see Boris Bobrinskoy, *The Mystery of the Trinity: Trinitarian Experience and Vision in the Biblical and Patristic Tradition*, trans. Anthony P. Gythiel (Crestwood, NY: St. Vladimir's Seminary Press, 1999).

4. For a full study, see Michael Aksionov Meerson, *The Trinity of Love in Modern Russian Theology: The Love Paradigm and the Retrieval of Western Medieval Love Mysticism in Modern Russian Trinitarian Thought (from Solovyov to Bulgakov)* (Quincy, IL: Franciscan Press, 1998). For a helpful brief discussion, see Robert E. Letham, *The Holy Trinity: In Scripture, History, Theology, and Worship* (Phillipsburg, NJ: P&R Publishing, 2004), 323–38, especially 327.

5. Vladimir Lossky, *The Mystical Theology of the Eastern Church* (London: James Clarke, 1957).

6. See further ibid., 7–22.

7. Letham (*Holy Trinity*, 346) reflects a typical Western misunderstanding of the Eastern position by claiming that "right at the heart of Lossky's theology is total agnosticism."

8. Lossky, *Mystical Theology of the Eastern Church*, 88.

Eastern tradition, Lossky affirms the monarchy of the Father. This is the way for the East to establish a *personal* origin of Trinity, against what they consider the fallacy of the West, namely, the impersonal divine essence as the source.[9]

Dumitru Staniloe, writing from the particular context of the Roman Orthodox Church, was a neopatristic scholar whose approach to the Trinity was unique by both Eastern and Western standards.[10] On the one hand, in line with typical Western dogmatic manuals—as well as that of *The Orthodox Faith* of John Damascene—he begins his Orthodox dogmatic theology with questions about the existence of God, followed by the attributes of God, and only then treatment of the topic of the Trinitarian God.[11] Yet, on the other hand, his theology is more nuanced than that might indicate. Somewhat similarly to Barth, he touches on the question of the Trinity early, in the introductory chapter on revelation. The reason is that there are two movements in his logic of the doctrine of the Trinity. Stăniloae believes that natural revelation already gives us some knowledge, albeit inadequate, of the plurality in the Godhead. Special revelation gives the full knowledge of the Triune God, especially through the work of salvation in Jesus Christ.[12] While affirming the apophatic approach of his church, Stăniloae also affirms the need for a cataphatic approach as a complement.[13] Echoing the approach of his own tradition, Stăniloae's view of the Triune God is fully communal, based on the idea of God as love.[14] In keeping with the approach of John of Damascus, Stăniloae both affirms the unity of God and the idea of perichoresis, the mutual interpenetration.[15]

THE ONTOLOGY OF COMMUNION

The main thesis of Zizioulas's theology is simple and profound: there is no true being without communion; nothing exists as an "individual" in itself. Therefore, to be a "person" in contrast to an "individual," there needs to be communion, relation, and opening to the Other, or as he often calls it, an *ekstasis* ("going out" of one's self). Human existence, including the existence of the church communion, thus reflects the communal, relational being of God.

By being a member of the church, a human being becomes an "image of God,"

9. Ibid., 58ff.

10. The main source for his theology is Dumitru Stăniloae, *The Experience of God*, 2 vols., trans. Robert Barringer and Ioan Ioaniță (Brookline, MA: Holy Cross Orthodox Press, 1994; reprint, 1998). The original Romanian edition has three volumes.

11. See comments by Wolfhart Pannenberg, *Systematic Theology*, trans. Geoffrey W. Bromiley, vol. 1 (Grand Rapids: Eerdmans, 1991), 281 n. 72.

12. Eugene Matei, "The Practice of Community in Social Trinitarianism: A Theological Evaluation with Reference to Dumitru Stăniloae and Jürgen Moltmann" (PhD diss., Fuller Theological Seminary, School of Theology, 2004), 144.

13. See Letham, *Holy Trinity*, 349.

14. See further Stăniloae, *Experience of God*, 1:204, among others.

15. Ibid., 1:258–64 especially.

existing as God Himself exists; he or she takes on God's "way of being." "This way of being . . . is a way of *relationship* with the world, with other people and with God, an event of *communion,* and that is why it cannot be realized as the achievement of an *individual,* but only as an *ecclesial* fact."[16]

This means nothing less than that communion is an ontological category; even God exists in communion. In Zizioulas's estimation, this groundbreaking insight was first developed in the Christian East by the Cappadocians. Theirs was the construction of a specific ontology—one that contrasted with the ancient Greek ontology, which looked at the "person" as an individual.[17] No individual apart from others can ever be a "person" since personhood is not "an adjunct to a being, a category that we add to" a person,[18] but rather, personhood is itself the essence of being. (Here Zizioulas's use of *essence* takes up the ancient Trinitarian and christological language of *hypostasis,* from the Greek term meaning "essence" or "substance.") Zizioulas expresses the relational nature of his ontology by using the term *ecstasy.* A person is *ecstatic* in terms of being "a movement toward communion," toward self-transcendence. It is only in *"communion* that this being is *itself* and thus *is at all"* rather than "in its 'self-existence.'"[19]

Greek ontology was fundamentally monistic: the being of the world and the being of God formed an unbreakable unity. The Platonic conception of the creator God did not satisfy the Fathers precisely because the doctrine of creation from preexisting matter limited divine freedom. So it was necessary to find an ontology that avoided monism as the gulf between God and the world. In the Greek patristic view, communion becomes an ontological concept. Nothing in existence is conceivable in itself, as for instance posited by Aristotle.[20] Zizioulas insists that communion is not just another way of describing being, whether individual or ecclesial, but it belongs to the ontology of being, and thus we should rather speak of an actual "ontology of communion."

With his ontology of communion, Zizioulas wants to propose a new understanding of personhood, an "ontology of personhood" over against the Greek "non-personal" view.[21] The Greek term for "person" originally referred to the mask of an actor in the theater. Then it gained the meaning of something added to a being, implying that the "person" is not one's true "hypostasis" (essence). In that view, personhood does not have any ontological content.[22] It was out of the desire among the Fathers to give ontological expression to its faith in the Trinity that a new kind of understanding of personhood as communion emerged. In

---

16. Zizioulas, *Being as Communion,* 15 (italics in original).
17. Ibid., 16.
18. Ibid., 39.
19. Zizioulas, "Human Capacity," 408 (italics in original).
20. Zizioulas, *Being as Communion,* 16–18. Here Zizioulas draws on the work of his theological teacher, the Russian-born theologian Georges Florovsky, "Patristic Age and Eschatology," in *Collected Works,* vol. 4 (Belmont, MA: Nordland, 1975), 63–78.
21. Zizioulas, *Being as Communion,* 27; the subheading uses this term.
22. Ibid., 32–33 especially, but see all of chap. 1.

other words, the Fathers wanted to address the question, "what does it mean to say that God is Father, Son and Spirit without ceasing to be one God?" The revolutionary insight of the Cappadocians was the identification of the "hypostasis" (essence) with the "person." Tertullian's formula, *una substantia, tres personae* (one substance/essence, three persons) did not meet this requirement, since the term "person" here lacked ontological content.[23]

TRINITY AS COMMUNION

On the basis of their ontology of communion, the Cappadocians criticized the ancient Greek ontology in which God first is God (his substance), and then exists as Trinity, as three persons, the way Christian theology has approached God.[24]According to Zizioulas, the "Holy Trinity is a *primordial* ontological concept and not a notion which is added to the divine substance or rather which follows it, as is the case in the dogmatic manuals of the West and, alas, in those of the East in modern times." In other words, the substance of God, "God," has no ontological content, no "true being, apart from communion," a mutual relationship of love.[25] God's being coincides with God's personhood, which cannot be construed apart from communion.[26] Biblically that is expressed by the idea of God as love:

> Love is not an emanation or "property" of the substance of God . . . but is *constitutive* of His substance, i.e., it is that which makes God what He is, the one God. Thus love ceases to be a qualifying—i.e., secondary—property of being and becomes *the supreme ontological predicate*. Love as God's mode of existence "hypostasizes" God, *constitutes* His being.[27]

God cannot be known as "God," only as Trinitarian persons in communion: "man can approach God only through the Son and in the Holy Spirit."[28] Zizioulas insists that the way God exists as person is the community of three persons. Outside the Trinity there is no God. In other words, God's being coincides with God's communal personhood. For Zizioulas, then, "the being of God could be known only through personal relationships and personal love. Being means life, and life means *communion*."[29]

23. Ibid., 36–37; quotation 36 (emphasis in original).
24. The basic philosophical and theological orientation is given in chap. 2.
25. Ibid., 17.
26. John Zizioulas, "The Teaching of the Second Ecumenical Council on the Holy Spirit in the Historical and Ecumenical Perspective," in *Credo in Spiritum Sanctum: Atti del congresso teologico internationale di pneumalogia* (Vatican: Liberia Editrice Vaticana, 1983), 37.
27. Zizioulas, *Being as Communion*, 46 (italics in the original); see also Zizioulas, "Human Capacity," 410.
28. Zizioulas, *Being as Communion*, 19.
29. Ibid., 16 (italics in original).

The same applies to the other persons of the Trinity. Zizioulas's Christology is communion Christology. Christ is the person par excellence. Christ is not merely an individual, but rather a person, since his identity is constituted by a twofold relation, namely, his relationship as Son to the Father and as head to his body.[30]

THE HYPOSTATIC AND ECSTATIC NATURE OF PERSONHOOD

As mentioned, to Zizioulas a key distinction is that between an "individual" and a "person." Critical of Western tradition in which rational individuality (Boethius, Aquinas) and psychological consciousness (Augustine) have shaped the idea of personhood, Zizioulas harks back to what he believes to be the Cappadocian notion of dynamic rather than static, relational rather than individualistic, and ecstatic rather than self-centered personhood. The result of this reshaped notion of personhood is freedom (to which I return in what follows).[31]

Zizioulas summarizes the constitution of personhood with two terms he uses liberally in his writings: *ekstasis* and *hypostasis*. The ecstatic principle means "a movement toward communion which leads to transcendence of the boundaries of the 'self' and thus to freedom." Freedom, in its turn, means that each person, ecstatically constituted, is also unique and irreplaceable; the person can never be "'contained' or 'divided,' . . . [and] its existence, *hypostasis*, is absolutely unique and unrepeatable."[32]

The ecstatic and hypostatic constitution of personhood is not only a theological-anthropological principle based on Trinitarian theology, but also the principle of salvation. In line with the soteriology of the Christian East, Zizioulas maintains that divinization (*theōsis*) of the human being by the grace of God means "participation not in the nature or substance of God, but in His personal existence."[33]

If personhood is based on a movement toward others in the freedom of uniqueness, it also means, Zizioulas argues, that difference no longer implies division but rather communion, unity-in-diversity. In his presentation fittingly titled "Communion and Otherness," he claims that this Trinitarian communion theology

---

30. See further Volf, *After Our Likeness,* 84–88.
31. Zizioulas, "Human Capacity," 405–8.
32. Ibid., 408.
33. Zizioulas, *Being as Communion,* 50. Therefore, for Zizioulas "salvation is identified with the realization of personhood." Ibid. Since the present study's concern is neither in theological anthropology nor in soteriology, I leave it to others to inquire into the possibility of being a human person in the full sense of the term for those who are not part of the communion of the church and God. In my reading, Zizioulas has not been able to address this issue in a satisfactory way, and I see it as a question in need of more elaboration. See further Patricia A. Fox, *God as Communion: John Zizioulas, Elizabeth Johnson, and the Retrieval of the Symbol of the Triune God* (Collegeville, MN: Liturgical Press, 2001), 44–45.

helps us to embrace rather than distance ourselves out of a pathological fear of difference. The reason for this radical reorientation is that "otherness is constitutive of unity, and not consequent upon it" because "God is not first one and then three, but simultaneously One and Three. . . . Each Person in the Holy Trinity is different not by way of difference of qualities but by way of simple affirmation of being who He is."[34]

THE PERSON OF THE FATHER
AS THE SOURCE OF THE DEITY

Zizioulas is an Orthodox theologian, and as such he subscribes to the typical view of the Eastern Church according to which the source (*aitia*) of the Trinity is the Father. Zizioulas believes that this is what the Cappadocians taught; rather than the *ousia* (essence) of God, the *hypostasis* (person) of the Father is the source of deity. "Thus God as person—as the hypostasis of the Father—makes the one divine substance to be that which it is: the one God."[35] In other words, the Trinitarian communion is "hypostasized" through the ecstatic character of the Father. The Father's monarchy comes to expression in that the Father is the source of the Son and Spirit, and so also of the Trinitarian communion.[36] Perhaps surprisingly, this also means that according to Zizioulas (and in line with the Eastern view), the concept of hierarchy belongs to the idea of person.[37]

In this hierarchy, there is reciprocity if not symmetry. Reciprocity means that the Spirit and Son are the presupposition of the Father's identity: "The identity even of God depends on the relation of the Father with the persons other than himself. There is no 'one' whose identity is not conditioned by the 'many.'"[38] Similarly, the Son and Spirit exist only through the Father; Father is the "ground" of God's being.[39] Yet the lack of symmetry means that this reciprocity is not equal:

> The communion is always *constituted and internally structured by an asymmetrical-reciprocal relationship between the one and the many*. The reciprocity consists in the many [Son and Spirit] being unable to live as communion without

---

34. Zizioulas, "Communion and Otherness," *St. Vladimir's Theological Quarterly* 38, no. 4 (1994): 353. "The Father, the Son and the Spirit are absolutely different [*diaphora*], none of them being subject to confusion with the other two"; see also *Being as Communion*, 106.

35. Zizioulas, *Being as Communion*, 41; see also Zizioulas, "On Being a Person: Towards an Ontology of Personhood," in *Persons, Divine and Human*, ed. C. Shwöbel and C. Gunton (Edinburgh: T & T Clark, 1991), 41.

36. Zizioulas, *Being as Communion*, 44, 46.

37. John Zizioulas, "Die pneumatologische Dimension der Kirche," *Internationale Katholische Zeitschrift "Communio"* 2 (1973): 141.

38. John D. Zizioulas, "La Mystère de l'Église dans la tradition orthodoxe," *Irénikon* 60 (1987): 330. Quoted in Volf, *After Our Likeness*, 78 n. 33.

39. Zizioulas, *Being as Communion*, 89.

the one [Father], and in the one being unable to exist without the many. The asymmetry, however, consists in the many being constituted by the one, whereas the one is only conditioned on the many; although he cannot exist without them, they are not his cause, but rather he theirs.[40]

The reason Zizioulas posits the monarchy of the Father—and thus the asymmetry among the Trinitarian members—is that for him the only other option would be going back to the "ontology of substance."[41] Regarding the Father as the origin of the Trinity means the precedence of "person" over substance.[42] This relates to a highly important corollary in Zizioulas's thinking: the establishment of the principle of freedom based on the idea of Father as person being the source. If the "nature" of God were the source, that would mean necessity and lack of freedom. However, when "person"—which for Zizioulas can only be constituted in-relation-to-other, that is, *ecstatically* ("standing out [of one's self]")—is the source, freedom follows. In the Bible that reaching out by God, that will to communion, is defined in terms of love: "Love is a relationship, . . . free[ly] coming out of oneself." Love makes the other—us as God's creatures—unique and irreplaceable. We can be persons, free.[43]

CRITICAL REFLECTIONS

While Zizioulas is well aware of the shift in contemporary philosophical and psychological thought toward relationality in defining personhood,[44] and he emphasizes that Trinitarian theology has "profound existential consequences,"[45] the prime motive for the bishop's communion theology lies not in the existential implications for ecclesiology and anthropology but rather in his theological method "from above." "Zizioulas begins his Trinitarian theology from above from what God has revealed about Godself through encounters with the Chosen People."[46] The fact that at the same time Zizioulas's Trinitarian theology emerges out

40. Volf, *After Our Likeness*, 78–79 (italics in the original; text in brackets added).
41. Zizioulas, "Teaching of the Second Ecumenical Council on the Holy Spirit," 45 n. 18.
42. For a helpful discussion, see further Volf, *After Our Likeness*, 79.
43. John Zizioulas, "The Contribution of Cappadocia to Christian Thought," in *Sinasos in Cappadocia*, ed. Frosso Pimenides and Stelios Roïdes (Athens: National Trust for Greece, Agra Publication, 1986), 34.
44. Zizioulas "Human Capacity," 408, mentions a number of contemporary thinkers who advocate the idea of relationality being the principle of personhood, such as Martin Buber.
45. John D. Zizioulas, "The Doctrine of God the Trinity Today: Suggestions for an Ecumenical Study," in *The Forgotten Trinity*, vol. 3, *A Selection of Papers Presented to the British Council of Churches Study Commission on Trinitarian Doctrine Today*, ed. Alasdair I. C. Heron (London: British Council of Churches/CCBI, 1991), 19. Some of the implications have to do with"personhood, freedom, community and the world's survival" (p. 29).
46. Fox, *God as Communion*, 187. Fox offers an excellent discussion of Zizioulas's theological method in a critical dialogue with the "theology from below" of the feminist theologian Elizabeth Johnson (pp. 186–94).

of the eucharistic[47] and soteriological contexts does not mean his starting point is salvation history (as in "theology from below") but rather that Trinitarian theology is a doxological response to the Triune God. He states this explicitly: "The safest theology is that which draws not only from the Economy, but also, and perhaps mainly, from the vision of God as He appears in worship."[48] As mentioned, this method from above does not mean downplaying the existential implications of the doctrine of the Trinity.

The contribution of Zizioulas to contemporary Trinitarian discourse is unsurpassed.[49] The way he has highlighted the centrality of communion in defining personhood has been enthusiastically adopted by all theologians. As such, this move reflects—even though probably independently—the turn taken in philosophical, anthropological, and psychological discussions on the notion of "person." Person in this newer understanding has less to do with substance and individualism and more with relationality and community.[50] It is not an overstatement to say that the main thesis of his *Being as Communion* "has become almost a methodological axiom of the order of Rahner's Rule."[51] Rahner's idea of the identity of the immanent and economic Trinity and Zizioulas's contention that the person—whether divine or human—can only exist as communion, have tutored the lively Trinitarian discussion at the end of the second millennium and brought about a new paradigm, the reverberations of which are felt in so many other theological loci.

By building his Trinitarian theology on the concept of "person," "the most dear and precious good" of humanity,[52] Zizioulas dismisses those contemporary voices that speak against the appropriateness of that category in relation to God[53] and so represents the growing consensus in ecumenical and international theol-

---

47. For the significance of the Eucharist as a source for Trinitarian theology and spirituality, see Zizioulas, *Being as Communion*, 16–17. An Orthodox theologian, Zizioulas of course subscribes to a eucharistic ecclesiology according to which the church life and liturgy not only focuses on the celebration of the Eucharist but more important, the ecclesiality of the church is received from the Eucharist. Thus, the theological principle: "The Church makes the Eucharist—the Eucharist makes the Church." For the relationship between Trinity, Communion, and church in Zizioulas, see Veli-Matti Kärkkäinen, *An Introduction to Ecclesiology: Ecumenical, Historical and Global Perspectives* (Downers Grove, IL: InterVarsity Press, 2002), 96–98.

48. Zizioulas, "Teaching of the Second Ecumenical Council on the Holy Spirit," 40. Again, Zizioulas appeals to the Cappadocians here.

49. Stanley J. Grenz, *Rediscovering the Triune God: The Trinity in Contemporary Theology* (Minneapolis: Fortress, 2004), 135, suggests a neologism, "the Zizioulas Dictum."

50. For a very helpful, concise discussion with appropriate sources, see Stanley J. Grenz, *The Social God and the Relational Self: A Trinitarian Theology of the Imago Dei* (Louisville, KY: Westminster John Knox Press, 2001), 3–14 especially.

51. Ibid., 51.

52. Zizioulas, *Being as Communion*, 65.

53. As noted above, Barth replaced the concept of person with modes of being, and Rahner used it only reluctantly and in a qualified sense. More recently a vocal opponent of the application of the term *person* to God has been Nicholas Lash, *Believing Three Ways in One God* (London: SCM Press, 1992), 31–32. Similarly Elizabeth Johnson, "Trinity: To Let the Symbol Sing Again," *Theology Today* 34, no. 3 (1997): 304–5.

ogy. A number of contemporary theologians have joined in emphasizing the relational and communal understanding of *person* in both Trinitarian theology[54] and theological anthropology.[55] Almost every commentator agrees that Zizioulas's communion ontology and doctrine of the Trinity has not only been immensely influential for the doctrine of God during the last two decades, but still continues to shape the landscape.

His proposal, however, is not without challenges. A serious critical question has been raised recently having to do with the very foundation of Zizioulas's thinking, namely, his interpretation of the work of the Greek Fathers, especially of the Cappadocians. With recent developments in the study of the Greek Fathers and their philosophical presuppositions, serious question marks have been placed on the propriety of Zizioulas's reading of their theology.[56] Even Orthodox critics have noted that the foundational idea of Zizioulas, the distinction between "individual" and "person," cannot be read back to the Cappadocians.[57] Critics have also seriously questioned whether the Cappadocians advocated the kind of idea of the primacy of the person of the Father so central to Zizioulas's argument.[58] However, while for some this appears to be a decisive blow against the validity of Zizioulas's theology as such, I would rather go with the balanced judgment of Miroslav Volf, who contends that Zizioulas's doctrine of the Trinity (and ecclesiology) can stand on its own feet even if his treatment of the historical materials can be shown to be flawed.[59]

Regarding his *theological* proposal, my main question relates to Zizioulas's contention of the monarchy of the Father and asymmetrical reciprocity among the Trinitarian members. Should we maintain the idea of asymmetry? Volf explicates the problem here:

54. Catherine Mowry LaCugna, *God for Us: The Trinity and Christian Life* (New York: HarperSanFrancisco, 1991); William Hill, *The Three-Personed God: Trinity as a Mystery of Salvation* (Washington, DC: Catholic University of America Press, 1982), 222–34 especially; Walter Kasper, *The God of Jesus Christ*, trans. Matthew J. O'Connell (New York: Crossroad, 1991), 154–56; Anthony Kelly, *The Trinity of Love* (Wilmington, DE: Michael Glazier, 1989), 185; Lawrence B. Porter, "On Keeping 'Persons' in the Trinity: A Linguistic Approach to Trinitarian Thought," *Theological Studies* 41 (1968): 530–48; Christopher Kiesling, "On Relating to the Persons of the Trinity," *Theological Studies* 47 (1986): 599–616.

55. Grenz's *Social God* is a full-scale contemporary project to develop the implications of a Trinitarian theology of the *imago Dei*.

56. The most vocal critics of Zizioulas's reading of the Cappadocians (to whose company Zizioulas adds the less-known Amphilochius of Iconium) have been André de Halleux, "Personalisme ou essentialisme trinitaire chez les Pères cappadociens? Une mauvaise controverse," *Revue théologique de Louvain* 17 (1986): 129–55, 265–92; and Gaëtan Baillargeon, *Perspective Orthodoxes sur L'Église Communion: L'œvre de Jean Zizioulas,* Brèches théologiques 6 (Paris: Médias Paul, 1989).

57. Lucian Turescu, "'Person' Versus 'Individual,' and Other Modern Misreadings of Gregory of Nyssa," *Modern Theology* 18, no. 4 (October 2002): 536.

58. Most important, John G. F. Wilks, "The Trinitarian Ontology of John Zizioulas," *Vox evangelica* 25 (1995): 77. Wilks's basic contention is opposite to that of Zizioulas, namely, that it was the *ousia* of the Father rather than *hypostasis* that served as the locus of unity for the Cappadocians (pp. 78, 82).

59. Volf, *After Our Likeness*, 75: "The critical inquiries which I do introduce during the course of my presentations refer exclusively to the theological plausibility of *his* thinking" (italics in the original).

Zizioulas distinguishes between being *constituted* (the Son and Spirit through the Father) and being *conditioned* (the Father by the Son and Spirit). If one presumes that the Father alone is the constitutive entity within God, then . . . it is difficult not to ascribe priority to the person before the communion. If, on the other hand, one takes seriously the notion that the Father is conditioned, then the differences between the persons risk being leveled. If the Father is conditioned by the Son and Spirit, then he is constituted by them. That is, he is God *only as Father.* As soon as one allows innertrinitarian reciprocity, the innertrinitarian asymmetry seems to vanish, unless one distinguishes between the level of constitution at which the Father as cause is first, and the level of relations at which all three are equal and mutually conditioned by one another.[60]

The conclusion is that Zizioulas's distinction between the constitution and conditioning is less than convincing.[61] The asymmetrical relation sounds not only subordinationist but also may compromise the free *hypostatic* freedom of Son and Spirit as persons alongside the Father.[62]

We are also tempted to ask the question, If God is love—an idea Zizioulas enthusiastically affirms—why is it that we need to postulate the Father as the source to preserve the unity of God? It seems to me Zizioulas fails to give reasons for that.[63] A related question has to do with the idea of hierarchy in the Triune God, based on the monarchy of the Father. If there is hierarchy, how then can the Trinity—again, an idea Zizioulas champions—serve as a paradigm for the communion of persons who love each other? What are the implications for the church's communion? Inevitably, it leads to an asymmetrical relationship between the one and many: in Eastern theology, the bishop and church members. I wonder if the idea of a symmetrical relationship between the one and many—along the lines drawn by Volf—would be a more natural way for Zizioulas to develop the idea of community as fellowship of persons.

In the beginning of this section I mentioned that Zizioulas's method is one from above. With all its merits, that method applied by the bishop also raises questions, the most poignant of which has to do with suffering. Unlike many contemporary theologians, Zizioulas is reluctant to attribute suffering to God

---

60. Ibid., 80 (italics in the original). Similarly Grenz, *Rediscovering the Triune God,* 145.

61. For important insights, see Paul Fiddes, *Participating in God: A Pastoral Doctrine of the Trinity* (Louisville, KY: Westminster John Knox Press, 2001), 79–80. He corrects Zizioulas's view by highlighting the importance of perichoresis and thus mutual conditioning. See also Colin Gunton, *The Promise of Trinitarian Theology* (Edinburgh: T & T Clark, 1991), 165–67.

62. See further Nonna Verna Harrison, "Zizioulas on Communion and Otherness," *St. Vladimir's Theological Quarterly* 42, nos. 3–4 (1998): 279.

63. See also Volf, *After Our Likeness,* 79. While I find Alan Torrance's charge against Zizioulas—that he not only advocates surbordinationism (which is of course true) but also makes the Father "the exclusively primordial reality"—somewhat exaggerated for the simple reason that Zizioulas is not advocating a "monistic" understanding of deity, in this case the Father, but an ecstatic view that makes communion with others constitutive element, it is still worth hearing. Alan J. Torrance, *Persons in Communion: An Essay on Trinitarian Description and Human Participation* (Edinburgh: T & T Clark, 1996), 292–93.

existing as God Himself exists; he or she takes on God's "way of being." "This way of being . . . is a way of *relationship* with the world, with other people and with God, an event of *communion,* and that is why it cannot be realized as the achievement of an *individual,* but only as an *ecclesial* fact."[16]

This means nothing less than that communion is an ontological category; even God exists in communion. In Zizioulas's estimation, this groundbreaking insight was first developed in the Christian East by the Cappadocians. Theirs was the construction of a specific ontology—one that contrasted with the ancient Greek ontology, which looked at the "person" as an individual.[17] No individual apart from others can ever be a "person" since personhood is not "an adjunct to a being, a category that we add to" a person,[18] but rather, personhood is itself the essence of being. (Here Zizioulas's use of *essence* takes up the ancient Trinitarian and christological language of *hypostasis,* from the Greek term meaning "essence" or "substance.") Zizioulas expresses the relational nature of his ontology by using the term *ecstasy.* A person is *ecstatic* in terms of being "a movement toward communion," toward self-transcendence. It is only in *"communion* that this being is *itself* and thus *is at all"* rather than "in its 'self-existence.'"[19]

Greek ontology was fundamentally monistic: the being of the world and the being of God formed an unbreakable unity. The Platonic conception of the creator God did not satisfy the Fathers precisely because the doctrine of creation from preexisting matter limited divine freedom. So it was necessary to find an ontology that avoided monism as the gulf between God and the world. In the Greek patristic view, communion becomes an ontological concept. Nothing in existence is conceivable in itself, as for instance posited by Aristotle.[20] Zizioulas insists that communion is not just another way of describing being, whether individual or ecclesial, but it belongs to the ontology of being, and thus we should rather speak of an actual "ontology of communion."

With his ontology of communion, Zizioulas wants to propose a new understanding of personhood, an "ontology of personhood" over against the Greek "non-personal" view.[21] The Greek term for "person" originally referred to the mask of an actor in the theater. Then it gained the meaning of something added to a being, implying that the "person" is not one's true "hypostasis" (essence). In that view, personhood does not have any ontological content.[22] It was out of the desire among the Fathers to give ontological expression to its faith in the Trinity that a new kind of understanding of personhood as communion emerged. In

---

16. Zizioulas, *Being as Communion,* 15 (italics in original).

17. Ibid., 16.

18. Ibid., 39.

19. Zizioulas, "Human Capacity," 408 (italics in original).

20. Zizioulas, *Being as Communion,* 16–18. Here Zizioulas draws on the work of his theological teacher, the Russian-born theologian Georges Florovsky, "Patristic Age and Eschatology," in *Collected Works,* vol. 4 (Belmont, MA: Nordland, 1975), 63–78.

21. Zizioulas, *Being as Communion,* 27; the subheading uses this term.

22. Ibid., 32–33 especially, but see all of chap. 1.

other words, the Fathers wanted to address the question, "what does it mean to say that God is Father, Son and Spirit without ceasing to be one God?" The revolutionary insight of the Cappadocians was the identification of the "hypostasis" (essence) with the "person." Tertullian's formula, *una substantia, tres personae* (one substance/essence, three persons) did not meet this requirement, since the term "person" here lacked ontological content.[23]

TRINITY AS COMMUNION

On the basis of their ontology of communion, the Cappadocians criticized the ancient Greek ontology in which God first is God (his substance), and then exists as Trinity, as three persons, the way Christian theology has approached God.[24]According to Zizioulas, the "Holy Trinity is a *primordial* ontological concept and not a notion which is added to the divine substance or rather which follows it, as is the case in the dogmatic manuals of the West and, alas, in those of the East in modern times." In other words, the substance of God, "God," has no ontological content, no "true being, apart from communion," a mutual relationship of love.[25] God's being coincides with God's personhood, which cannot be construed apart from communion.[26] Biblically that is expressed by the idea of God as love:

> Love is not an emanation or "property" of the substance of God . . . but is *constitutive* of His substance, i.e., it is that which makes God what He is, the one God. Thus love ceases to be a qualifying—i.e., secondary—property of being and becomes *the supreme ontological predicate*. Love as God's mode of existence "hypostasizes" God, *constitutes* His being.[27]

God cannot be known as "God," only as Trinitarian persons in communion: "man can approach God only through the Son and in the Holy Spirit."[28] Zizioulas insists that the way God exists as person is the community of three persons. Outside the Trinity there is no God. In other words, God's being coincides with God's communal personhood. For Zizioulas, then, "the being of God could be known only through personal relationships and personal love. Being means life, and life means *communion*."[29]

---

23. Ibid., 36–37; quotation 36 (emphasis in original).

24. The basic philosophical and theological orientation is given in chap. 2.

25. Ibid., 17.

26. John Zizioulas, "The Teaching of the Second Ecumenical Council on the Holy Spirit in the Historical and Ecumenical Perspective," in *Credo in Spiritum Sanctum: Atti del congresso teologico internationale di pneumalogia* (Vatican: Liberia Editrice Vaticana, 1983), 37.

27. Zizioulas, *Being as Communion*, 46 (italics in the original); see also Zizioulas, "Human Capacity," 410.

28. Zizioulas, *Being as Communion*, 19.

29. Ibid., 16 (italics in original).

because he believes that doing so would end up denying that the immanent Trinity is more than the economic Trinity; in other words, God's transcendence would be compromised.[64] Behind this reluctance is the understanding—in Zizioulas's estimation apparent in much of contemporary theology, Moltmann being an example—of too close a relationship between the being of God and of the world.[65] I do not see Zizioulas's critique of assigning suffering to God convincing. I think his fear is misguided, especially when he says that speaking of the suffering of God means that "the Incarnation is projected into God's eternal being; he becomes suffering by nature."[66] For me, that is what much of classical theology has always insisted: the assumption of humanity by God, the Son, means that human capacity to suffer is not foreign to the being of God. How else could one speak of God as love, an argument Moltmann makes convincingly and which for me seems to be a thoroughly biblical idea? Furthermore, as Pannenberg, among others, has insisted, having created the world in his absolute freedom, God cannot be unrelated to the world and its suffering. This does not mean denying God's ontological freedom but rather highlighting the theme of the ecstatic nature of God's love—the very theme of Zizioulas's communion theology: It is more biblical to think of God as passionate love, the Father who chooses to engage the suffering of the world created by him, than as a Transcendent One whose separation from the world's suffering guards his freedom.

---

64. Fox, *God as Communion*, 226. In order to defend the freedom of God, Zizioulas highlights the significance of the doctrine of creation ex nihilo. See, e.g., *Being as Communion*, 65.

65. Zizioulas, "The Doctrine of God," 23–24. He regards contemporary theology's desire to connect suffering to God's nature "nothing but a return to the classical monistic view of existence according to which the being of God and the being of the world are inseparably linked up in some kind of affinity" (p.23). For Zizioulas, this is an unwarranted post-Enlightenment accommodation of the doctrine of God to be "relevant."

66. Ibid., 24.

Chapter 8

Jürgen Moltmann

Trinitarian Panentheism

A DISTINCTIVELY *CHRISTIAN* UNDERSTANDING
OF GOD, GOD AS TRINITY

Even though Jürgen Moltmann may well be the best-known and most distinguished systematic theologian of our times, unlike Barth and Wolfhart Pannenberg, he has produced no systematic theology[1] per se but rather "contributions" to theology as well as a number of other monographs. While currently he is known as one of the major architects of the renewed doctrine of the Trinity, it took almost two decades for him to produce a separate work on the topic, the widely acclaimed *The Trinity and the Kingdom of God* (1981). Yet in his earlier works,

---

1. Moltmann's reason for not producing a "dogmatics" is that "every theological system lays claim to totality, perfect organization, and entire competence for the whole area under survey." In contrast, the term "contributions" for him "recognizes the conditions and limitations of his own position, and the relativity of his own particular environment." Jürgen Moltmann, *The Trinity and the Kingdom: The Doctrine of God,* trans. Margaret Kohl (San Francisco: Harper & Row/London: SCM Press, 1981), xi–xii. For Moltmann, truth is found in dialogue rather than dogmatic statements (ibid., xiii). Theological statements or, as Moltmann calls them, "testimonies of Christian faith" can be best viewed in the light of their particularity (ibid., xv).

especially *The Crucified God*[2] and his first major book, *Theology of Hope* (original German edition in 1964),[3] he had already started incorporating Trinitarian insights into his theology. After the publication of *The Trinity and the Kingdom of God*, he has had opportunities to continue fine-tuning and expanding his Trinitarian view, especially toward a panentheism.[4]

Moltmann laments the neglect of the doctrine of the Trinity in theology and ethics,[5] and he thinks there are several reasons for this state of affairs. One has to do with the incapacity of "experience" to mediate the knowledge of God; for Schleiermacher and the subsequent classical liberal tradition, religion and faith of course were a function of "experience." The other main obstacle to the doctrine of the Trinity had to do with the perceived lack of practicability, routinely mentioned by many before Moltmann, such as Immanuel Kant.[6]

Over against two traditional approaches to God in Christian theology—in Moltmann's estimation mistaken traditions—namely, the idea of God as supreme substance and God as absolute subject, both of which build on a monotheistic and thus non-Trinitarian conception of God, Moltmann advocates the understanding of God as "triunity, the three-in-one."[7] Trinity means nothing less than "the Christianization of the concept of God."[8] To accomplish this, the Trinity has to be constructed from its christological basis.[9] Trinity presupposes Christology and Christology presupposes Trinity. The basis for the Trinitarian view of God is the history of Jesus, which cannot be understood apart from the history of Father and Spirit.[10]

Methodologically and theologically, then, for Moltmann the threeness of God is a given: "We are beginning with the trinity of the Persons and shall then go on to ask about the unity. What then emerges is a concept of the divine unity as the union of tri-unity, a concept which is differentiated and is therefore capable of being thought first of all." As a result, a "social doctrine of the Trinity" emerges. Rather than on one divine substance, it focuses on "relationships and communities."[11] With his leaning toward a social doctrine and relationality,

2. Jürgen Moltmann, *The Crucified God: The Cross of Christ as the Foundation and Criticism of Christian Theology* (London: SCM Press, 1974; original German edition, 1972).

3. Jürgen Moltmann, *Theology of Hope: On the Ground and the Implications of a Christian Eschatology* (London: SCM Press, 1967).

4. Stanley J. Grenz labels Moltmann's view "Trinitarian eschatological panentheism" (and traces the label back to Richard Bauckham, *The Theology of Jürgen Moltmann* [Edinburgh: T & T Clark, 1995], 17). See Stanley J. Grenz, *The Social God and the Relational Self: A Trinitarian Theology of the Imago Dei* (Louisville, KY: Westminster John Knox Press, 2001), 41.

5. "Why are most Christians in the West, whether they be Catholics or Protestants, really only 'monotheists' where the experience and practice of their faith is concerned? Whether God is one or triune evidently makes as little difference to the doctrine of faith as it does to ethics." Moltmann, *Trinity and the Kingdom*, 1.

6. Ibid., 5–9.

7. Ibid., 10–16 (10).

8. Ibid., 132.

9. Ibid., 97, 129 among others.

10. Ibid., 16, 131–32.

11. Ibid., 19.

Moltmann acknowledges he is echoing a more general turn from "subject" to relationality and relativistic theories about the world.[12]

As a creative theologian, Moltmann employs a number of resources, some of which are quite unknown in contemporary systematic theology, such as panentheistic ideas from the Jewish and Christian traditions as well as resources that help make the doctrine ecologically relevant.[13] A key concern, related to the christological starting point, is the rejection of the immutability doctrine of classical theism, which in Moltmann's mind leads to dismissal of the key biblical idea of God as love.

Regarding the theological and methodological locus of Moltmann's Trinitarian proposal, it is obvious that he builds on the tradition of Barth and Rahner, yet both develops and critically alters them. His main concern with both Barth and Rahner—as the main representatives of contemporary Trinitarian theology—is on the one hand modalism and on the other hand the priority given to the unity at the expense of the Trinity.[14] One of the key issues—if not *the* issue—in contemporary Trinitarian reflection has to do with the way the eternal God could be related to the temporal, historical life of ours and the world.[15] Stanley J. Grenz asks a hypothetical question that helps to locate Moltmann at the center of this inquiry: "What would happen, however, if this classical assumption were cast aside? What would emerge if theologians were—to cite Peters' description—'to reconceive the relationship between time and eternity so that what happens in the history of salvation becomes constitutive of the content of eternal life?'"[16] This would mean nothing less than the "historicizing of Barth's suggestion that the Christ event is constitutive for the divine life in all eternity"[17] and the taking up of Rahner's insistence on the identity of the economic and immanent Trinity to its eventual eschatological union when God will be "all in all." These twin themes set forth the overall framework for Moltmann's search for an authentically Christian understanding of the Trinity over against any monotheistic notion (tritheism he doesn't consider a real problem; he claims that has never been a real problem for Christian theology).

Some commentators have posited a two-stage development in Moltmann's doctrine of the Trinity, the first phase being the publications prior to the 1981 Trinity monograph.[18] While that scheme might be helpful pedagogically, one could also make the case—and I think the ensuing discussion of key topics such as the suffering of God and the creation of the world will clearly indicate—that

12. Ibid.

13. Ibid.

14. For his dialogue with Barth and Rahner, see ibid., 139–48. See also Jayne H. Davis, "Opening Dialogue: Jürgen Moltmann's Interaction with the Thought of Karl Barth," *Review and Expositor* 100, no. 4 (Fall 2003): 695–711.

15. Ted Peters, *God as Trinity: Relationality and Temporality in Divine Life* (Louisville, KY: Westminster John Knox Press, 1993), 102.

16. Grenz, *Social God*, 41, quoting from Peters, *God as Trinity*, 102.

17. Grenz, *Social God*, 41.

18. So ibid., 41–46.

while there is certainly development in Moltmann's thought, it is rather in terms of expanding and elaborating of ideas already presented in earlier publications. Two key developments are being noticed by many. First, in *The Trinity and the Kingdom*, he widens the scope of the history of Jesus from the cross to resurrection as part of the Trinitarian history as well as highlights in a new way the role of the Spirit in the Trinitarian history. Second, Moltmann envisions an eschatological unity of the Trinitarian persons, Father, Son, and Spirit, which also has implications for creation in that the Triune God will come to indwell his creation.

THE CROSS OF JESUS CHRIST AND THE TRINITY

Christology is the starting point of the Trinitarian doctrine for Moltmann. As a result, "the cross of the Son stands from eternity in the centre of the Trinity."[19] While *The Crucified God* is the first major contribution to the incipient Trinitarian doctrine of this German theologian, who already in his *Theology of Hope* was in critical dialogue with atheistic philosophers (such as Ernst Bloch), Moltmann highlighted the importance of the future of Jesus Christ, as confirmed by the resurrection from the dead by the power of the Spirit, to a specifically Christian understanding of God. The God who raised Jesus from the dead, and so showed his faithfulness, is the God with "future as the essence of his being" (a designation borrowed from Bloch). The God of the Bible is different from the God of the philosophers; this is the God declared first to the Jewish people as the God of the promise.[20] This God has given "*the promise of life as a result of the resurrection* from the dead, and *the promise of the kingdom of God* in a new totality of being."[21] This God of the future is the powerful one who overcomes death, remoteness from God.

In *The Crucified God*, as the name pointedly illustrates, Moltmann focuses on not only the suffering *of* God but even more the suffering *in* God. Whereas *Theology of Hope* lives by the anticipation of the future, *The Crucified God* lives by the memory of Christ's death.[22] In his Trinitarian monograph Moltmann deepens the theological significance of the idea of the suffering God. Borrowing from Luther's theology of the cross, Moltmann takes a critical look at the established doctrine of divine impassibility, the "apathy axiom."[23] "How can Christian faith understand Christ's passion as being the revelation of God, if the deity cannot suffer?"[24] As a

---

19. Moltmann, *Trinity and the Kingdom*, xvi; so also, e.g., 78.
20. Moltmann, *Theology of Hope*, 141.
21. Ibid., 203 (italics in original).
22. See further Geiko Müller-Fahrenholz, *The Kingdom and the Power: The Theology of Jürgen Moltmann* (Minneapolis: Fortress, 2001), 63.
23. Moltmann, *Trinity and the Kingdom*, 22; chap. 2 in that book, "The Passion of God," is dedicated to the topic. In opposing the impassibility doctrine, he gleans widely from various sources such as the Jewish theologian Abraham Heschel, nineteenth- and twentieth-century English theology, the Spanish mystic Miguel de Unamuno, and the Russian thinker Nikolay Berdyayev. A helpful discussion can be found in chap. 3 of Bauckham, *Theology of Jürgen Moltmann*, 47–69.
24. Moltmann, *Trinity and the Kingdom*, 21.

result, Moltmann advocates the doctrine of *theopathy*.[25] Echoing the Lutheran Reformer, Moltmann argues that the God of the Bible is revealed in the suffering and shame of the cross. The cross distinguishes God from other gods. This God is different from the passionless God of Greek metaphysical notions, Moltmann argues.[26] This means that God is only revealed as "God" in his opposite: godlessness and abandonment by God. In concrete terms, God is revealed in the cross of Christ, who was abandoned by God.[27] Moltmann thus turns the tables and, rather than trying to defend the doctrine of impassibility, instead makes the "axiom of God's passion" the starting point.[28] This passion can be called an "active passion," since it is voluntary identification with the suffering of the world and is based on love.[29]

The God of the dying Son, Jesus Christ, does not shy away from the suffering of either his Son or of the world, but rather makes it his own and so overcomes it and brings about hope. All suffering becomes God's so that God may overcome it.[30] This brings us again to the cross of Christ. Moltmann takes the words of Psalm 22, "My God, my God, why have you forsaken me?" on the lips of the dying Jesus, not only as an expression of the utmost suffering and anguish of the innocent victim,[31] but also as a cry of the Father who deserts his Son: "The grief of the Father is here as important as the death of the Son."[32] In other words, the Son suffers the pain of being cut off from the life of the Father, and the Father suffers the pain of giving up his Son. By doing so, God "also accepts and adopts it [suffering] in himself, making it part of his own eternal life."[33] Therefore, the cross is not an event only between God and humanity. For this theologian "what happened on the cross was an event between God and God. It was a deep division in God himself, in so far as God abandoned God and contradicted himself, and at the same time a unity in God, in so far as God was at one with God and corresponded to himself."[34] Thus, the cross belongs to the inner life of God, not only occurring between God and estranged humanity.[35] "God's being is in suffering and suffering in God's being itself," because God is love.[36] In other words, at the cross, which speaks of the "death of Jesus for God himself, one must enter into the inner-Trinitarian tensions and relationships of God" and thus move "from the exterior of the mystery which is called 'God' to the interior, which is Trinitarian."[37]

25. Ibid., 25.
26. Ibid., 22 especially.
27. Moltmann, *Crucified God,* 27.
28. Moltmann, *Trinity and the Kingdom,* 22; see also p. 47.
29. Ibid., 23.
30. Moltmann, *Crucified God,* 246.
31. Ibid., 146–47.
32. Ibid., 243.
33. Moltmann, *Trinity and the Kingdom,* 119.
34. Moltmann, *Crucified God,* 244.
35. Ibid., 249.
36. Ibid., 72; see further Müller-Fahrenholz, *Kingdom and the Power,* 72–73.
37. Moltmann, *Crucified God,* 204. In speaking of the Son suffering death in forsakenness and the Father suffering the death of the Son, Moltmann concludes: "Here the innermost life of the Trinity is at stake." Moltmann, *Trinity and the Kingdom,* 81.

If the cross belongs to the inner life of God, certainly the incarnation does. Incarnation for Moltmann is not primarily an "outward" event regarding the Triune God but an event based on divine love's intention to reach out to the Other and as such belongs to the inner life of God. Of course, humanity and the world are in need of redemption, but this need is only the occasion rather than the reason for incarnation.[38]

GOD'S LOVE AND FREEDOM

It is the biblical notion of love that in the final analysis becomes the catalyst for Moltmann's idea of God as sufferer. Rather than being a neutral observer of world events, God is "pathetic" in that "he suffers from the love which is the superabundance and overflowing of his being."[39] The main fault Moltmann finds in the tradition's love talk is that it almost ends up denying reciprocity. God cannot be affected by the objects of his love. For Moltmann, however, God's love is twofold: it is not just activity on others but involvement with others in which one is moved and affected.[40] Therefore, in his pointed style, Moltmann says, "A God who cannot suffer is poorer than any man. For a God who is incapable of suffering is a being who cannot be involved. Suffering and injustice do not affect him. . . . But the one who cannot suffer cannot love either. So he is also a loveless being."[41]

What about God's freedom? One of the reasons tradition has been slow to speak of God's suffering is the fear—as Moltmann acknowledges it—of God's becoming "a prisoner of his own history."[42] Tradition has thus affirmed God's independence from the world: God does not need us.[43] For Moltmann all speculations into whether God could or could not be without the world are just that, speculations, and as such are foreign to theology. He reasons, on the contrary, that for God to be who he says he is, "God's freedom can never contradict the truth which he himself is," namely, love. Love can never exist alone; love shares; love gives.[44] The concept of "freedom" that posits a solitary God is a concept based on the idea of lordship and domination. For Moltmann, the biblical idea of God as love is based on the concept of freedom related to community and fellowship: "The triune God reveals himself as love in the fellowship of the Father, the Son and the Holy Spirit. His freedom therefore lies in the

38. Moltmann, *Trinity and the Kingdom*, 115.

39. Ibid., 23. Among the Fathers, most of whom were occupied in defending the immutability doctrine, Moltmann attributes to Origen the acknowledgment of God as suffering love (pp. 23–25).

40. See further Bauckham, *Theology of Jürgen Moltmann*, 49–50.

41. Moltmann, *Crucified God*, 222.

42. Moltmann, *Trinity and the Kingdom*, 52.

43. Moltmann gives references to Barth who in contemporary theology has been a vocal advocate of God's freedom and independence from the world. Ibid., 52–55.

44. Ibid., 53, 99, among others.

friendship which he offers men and women, and through which he makes them his friends."[45] In this sense Moltmann is ready to say that "God 'needs' the world and man. If God is love, then he neither will nor can be without the one who is his beloved."[46]

Here we come to Moltmann's doctrine of creation, which he casts in a Trinitarian framework, while continuing the program of incorporating history into the divine life, but now extending it to creation as a whole. While Moltmann's full-fledged doctrine of creation evolved later in his career, as shown in his 1985 monograph *God in Creation*, the Trinity monograph already offered the basic idea of what appropriately is being called "Trinitarian panentheism."[47]

In terms of the Trinitarian doctrine, the genesis of the world, creation, is a result of God's love: the same love with which the Father loves the Son from eternity brings about the world.[48] Moltmann maintains that the world is created by God's free will. Unlike Barth, who sees freedom and love as complementary ("the One who loves in freedom") and implies that God could have chosen not to create the world if he so wished, since God is self-sufficient in himself, for Moltmann creation "out of freedom" means "out of love."[49] God's freedom is the freedom of love; love and freedom are virtually synonymous.[50] Yes, God could choose not to create, but that was not what he did, since God chooses only that "which corresponds to his essential goodness, in order to communicate the goodness as his creation and in his creation."[51] This brings us to the starting point of Christian panentheism, which starts from the divine essence:

> Creation is a fruit of God's longing for his Other and for that Other's free response to the divine love. That is why the idea of the world is inherent in the nature of God himself from eternity. . . . And if God's eternal being is love, then the divine love is also more blessed in giving than in receiving. God cannot find bliss in eternal self-love if selflessness is part of love's very nature. God is in all eternity self-communicating love.[52]

In other words, there is a reciprocal relationship between the world and God.[53] Having stated this, Moltmann asks the logical question: What does it take for God to "make space" for the Other, for the creation separate from him? This is the matter of God's self-humiliation: "With the creation of a world, which is not

45. Ibid., 56 (italics in original)
46. Ibid., 58.
47. So called by Bauckham, *Theology of Jürgen Moltmann*, 17. Moltmann presents "Christian panentheism" as an alternative to classical theism and pantheism. See Moltmann, *Trinity and the Kingdom*, 105–8.
48. Moltmann, *Trinity and the Kingdom*, 58–59, 106–08, 111–12.
49. Jürgen Moltmann, *God in Creation: An Ecological Doctrine of Creation* (London: SCM Press, 1985), 75.
50. Ibid., 130.
51. Ibid., 76.
52. Moltmann, *Trinity and the Kingdom*, 138.
53. Ibid., 98, among others.

God, but which none the less corresponds to him, *God's self-humiliation* begins—the self-limitation of the One who is omnipresent, and the suffering of the eternal love."[54] In his *God in Creation,* Moltmann further develops this idea with the help of the Jewish kabbalistic notion of *zimzum* ("self-limitation").[55] Moltmann posits a "self-limitation of the infinite, omnipresent God." In other words, "before God issues creatively out of himself, he acts inwardly on himself, resolving for himself, committing himself, determining himself."[56] In order to create something "'outside' himself, the infinite God must have made room for this finitude beforehand, 'in himself.'"[57] This is a creative recasting of the classical view of *creatio ex nihilo:* through the self-withdrawal of the omnipotent "within God-self," the *nihil* comes into being.[58] An important conclusion from this type of "Trinitarian creation"[59] is not only that the idea of the world is already inherent in the love of the Father to the Son, but also that "the process of creating the world is . . . identified with the inner-trinitarian life."[60]

THE CONSTITUTION OF THE TRINITY

Beginning from three persons rather than one divine subject, Moltmann considers a presupposition in keeping with the biblical record: "The New Testament talks about God by proclaiming in narrative the relationships of the Father, the Son and the Spirit, which are relationships of fellowship and are open to the world."[61] In the historical and eschatological history of Jesus, the Son, we can thus perceive "the differences, the relationships and the unity of the Father, Son and the Spirit."[62] Moltmann works hard in trying to follow this methodological guide as he outlines the constitution of the Trinity, the relationships among Father, Son, and Spirit.

The cross, as mentioned, belongs to the inner-Trinitarian life and thus is constitutive of the persons of the Trinity in unity-in-diversity, or presence-in-absence. According to Moltmann, in forsaking his Son to death the Father loses his fatherhood, corresponding to the Son's losing his sonship in subjecting himself to being abandoned by his Father. Yet paradoxically, in this forsakenness the Son "is still

---

54. Ibid., 59 (italics in the original). For a lengthier discussion, see pp. 108–111.

55. Moltmann, *God in Creation,* 86–87.

56. Ibid., 86.

57. Moltmann, *Trinity and the Kingdom,* 109.

58. Ibid.; Moltmann, *God in Creation,* 86ff.

59. Subheading in Moltmann, *Trinity and the Kingdom,* 111.

60. Ibid., 107–8 (107).

61. Ibid., 64 (in the original, the whole text is in italics). For the importance of "openness" in the Trinity, see also Jürgen Moltmann, *The Church in the Power of the Spirit: A Contribution to Messianic Ecclesiology,* trans. Margaret Kohl (Minneapolis: Fortress, 1993), 60; Moltmann, *Crucified God,* 249.

62. Moltmann, *Trinity and the Kingdom,* 65. In keeping with his more inclusive view of the history of Jesus (as mentioned above), Moltmann discusses in detail various "stages" in the history of Jesus from his baptism and call to the cross, resurrection, and raising to exaltation, and finally to the eschatological future (pp. 65–96).

the Son," and in the act of forsaking "the Father is still present."[63] This paradox becomes more understandable in light of Moltmann's idea that the oneness of Father and Son extends to the point that they "represent a single surrendering movement."[64] Furthermore, the cross is also the way to connect the Spirit to Father and Son. The Spirit proceeds "from this event [of the cross] between the Father and the Son" and thus is the "boundless love which proceeds from the grief of the Father and the dying of the Son" and reaches out to humanity.[65] The Spirit also opens up the Trinity to creation. In the sending of the Spirit the Trinity is an open Trinity; in this act the Trinitarian history of God becomes open to the world as well as the future. Men and women are thus integrated into the history of the Trinity.[66]

Having established the threeness of the Christian God, two major tasks face Moltmann, namely, the question of the mutuality of the three persons and the problem of unity. Let me first concentrate on the ways Moltmann attempts to defend the idea of the Trinitarian members as mutually "dependent" on each other for their personhood. Subsequently I will inquire into the question of the oneness of God. It seems to me Moltmann employs two kinds of tactics to insure the mutuality. One is the eschatological movement and the second—in keeping with his social analogy—the emphasis on the social and thus relational nature of the concept of personhood, an idea warmly embraced by most contemporary writers.

Moltmann believes mutuality can be established, first, with reference to the eschatological "movement" of the kingdom from one Trinitarian person to another. Quite similarly to Pannenberg, Moltmann argues for the mutual constitution of the three Trinitarian members. Speaking of the eschatological history of the Son, Moltmann says:

> Here we must particularly note the mutual workings of the Father and the Son: the Father subjects everything to the Son, the Son subjects himself to the Father. Through "the power of the resurrection" the Son destroys all other powers and death itself, then transferring the consummated kingdom of life and the love that is free of violence, to the Father. The kingdom of God is therefore transferred from one divine subject to the other; and its form is changed in the process. So *God's triunity precedes the divine lordship.*[67]

In other words, no one person (Father, Son, Spirit) thus is the "source"; all three "depend" on each other in the dynamic process of the shifting of the kingdom from one divine person to the other.

63. Ibid., 80; see also Moltmann, *Crucified God,* 244.
64. Moltmann, *Trinity and the Kingdom,* 82. So also Moltmann, *Crucified God,* 244.
65. Moltmann, *Crucified God,* 245.
66. Moltmann, *Trinity and the Kingdom,* 89–90.
67. Ibid., 92–93 (italics in the original); see also Wolfhart Pannenberg, *Systematic Theology,* trans. Geoffrey W. Bromiley, 3 vols. (Grand Rapids: Eerdmans, 1991–98), 1:313 especially.

The second way Moltmann advocates the idea of mutuality has to do with the understanding of "person" in the context of relationships: "The three divine Persons exist in their particular, unique natures as Father, Son and Spirit in their relationships to one another, and are determined through these relationships. It is in these relationships that they are persons. Being a person in this respect means existing-in-relationship."[68] While the relation "constitutes the persons," there is also a genuine reciprocal relationship between "person" and "relation": there "are no persons without relations, but there are no relations without persons either."[69] If "person" were reduced to "relation," that would of course mean modalism. Going back to Richard of St. Victor and his followers (but also owing to Augustine's relational understanding as noted in the historical section), Moltmann says that in this social reciprocal framework, persons "ex-ist totally in the other: the Father ex-ists by virtue of his love, as himself entirely in the Son; the Son, by virtue of his self-surrender, ex-ists as himself totally in the Father; and so on." Indeed, "each Person receives the fullness of eternal life from the other."[70] This is of course a tribute to Hegel's idea of the person giving himself to the counterpart and thus receiving one's personhood from the Other, an idea employed also by Pannenberg.[71]

Putting together these two ideas—the eschatological shifting of the kingdom from one divine person to the other as well as the social constitution of the persons—Moltmann believes he has succeeded in reaching a major goal of his Trinitarian theology, which he summarizes in this way: "Only when we are capable of thinking of Persons, relations, and changes in the relations *together* does the idea of the Trinity lose its usual static, rigid quality. Then not only does the eternal life of the triune God become conceivable; its eternal *vitality* becomes conceivable too."[72]

There is a surprising move, however, in Moltmann's thinking that to me seems to run counter to the effort to establish mutuality: he desires to lift up the Father as the "source" of the divinity, yet differently from the typical Eastern Orthodox way. Taking his clue from the way the Apostles' Creed names God the "Father," Moltmann surmises that God is the Father of his only begotten Son, our elder brother. Rather than being "the Father of the Universe," an idea that supports a hierarchical and oppressive view of God,[73] Father is exclusively "the Father of the Son," Jesus Christ. No patriarchal connotations can be found in this Father of the Son.[74] Now, the Son and Spirit proceed eternally from

68. Moltmann, *Trinity and the Kingdom*, 145, among others.
69. Ibid., 172.
70. Ibid., 173–74; for the Augustinian reference, see 172.
71. Ibid., 174.
72. Ibid. (first italics in original, second mine).
73. Moltmann notes that the Creed names God "Father" twice. The first time, which Moltmann finds mistaken, has to do with God being "the Father Almighty" and thus the highest authority in the universe. That, in his view, leads to a hierarchical view not appropriate to his understanding of the Christian God. Ibid., 162–63.
74. Ibid., 163.

the Father. While the Father has no origin, Father is constituted through him-self.[75] Acknowledging the implications of this idea for his insistence on their mutuality, Moltmann makes the distinction between the inner-Trinitarian and economic constitution of the Trinity, claiming that the "monarchy of the Father" thus defined only applies to the immanent Trinity.

Before inquiring into the ways Moltmann attempts to combat the tendencies of tritheism so prevalent in this social analogy, let me first register how Moltmann highlights the role of the Spirit in the Trinity. It is especially the pneumatologi-cal part of the Trinitarian doctrine that the 1981 monograph on the Trinity devel-ops in a new way.[76] The role of the Spirit as "person" or "subject" comes to the fore in that the Spirit glorifies (with the Son) the Father on the way to the escha-tological unity of God and world. Moltmann criticizes Barth among others for failing to affirm a real personhood of the Spirit.[77] Over against fears that the Spirit be reduced to mere divine energy or a nonpersonal entity, Moltmann speaks of the Spirit as "subject."[78] Moltmann argues that

> the glorifying of the Son and the Father by the Spirit is the personal act which most decisively expresses the subjectivity of the Spirit over against the other two persons, and above all that we must regard this doxological activ-ity of the Spirit as an intratrinitarian relation because it is not directed out-ward but to the Son and the Father.[79]

UNITY AS PERICHORESIS

Critical of the tradition's ways of establishing the unity of God, either based on the unity of divine substance or one divine subject,[80] Moltmann represents a rad-ical social Trinitarianism that begins with three persons and works from that toward unity rather than vice versa. The Tübingen theologian seeks to establish the unity "neither as homogenous substance nor as identical subject." Rather, unity is considered in light of the Trinitarian history and is developed in Trini-tarian terms.[81] Claiming to start from the biblical history, Moltmann makes the

75. Ibid., 165. "He [Father], being himself without origin, is the origin of the divine Persons of the Son and the Spirit" (ibid.). So also 177.
76. For helpful comments, see Stanley J. Grenz, *Rediscovering the Triune God: The Trinity in Con-temporary Theology* (Minneapolis: Fortress, 2004), 80–81; see also the comments in Douglas Meeks, "Trinitarian Theology: A Review Article," *Theology Today* 38, no. 4 (January 1982): 477.
77. Moltmann, *Trinity and the Kingdom*, 143.
78. Subtitle in ibid., 125; see 125–26.
79. Pannenberg, *Systematic Theology*, 1:330, with reference to Moltmann, *The Trinity and the Kingdom*, 126–27.
80. The first approach in early creeds is represented by the Nicene Creed with its emphasis on homoousios, the latter one by the Athanasian Creed's idea of *unus Dei* (one God). Moltmann, *Trin-ity and the Kingdom*, 149.
81. Ibid., 19.

unity of the three persons the problem rather than vice versa.[82] For Moltmann the "concept of divine unity" is "the union of the tri-unity."[83]

The eschatological consummation is the key to both the unity of the Trinity as well as the way to reconcile the relationship between the economic and immanent Trinity. There is an eschatological movement to the unity. Unity is a dynamic concept, a process as it were: "The unity of the Father, the Son and the Spirit is then the eschatological question about the consummation of the trinitarian history of God."[84]

Since the Trinitarian members as "three divine subjects are co-active in this history," there is no way to define the unity in terms of "monadic unity." The unity spoken of here rather "lies in the *union* of the Father, the Son and the Spirit. . . . It lies in their *fellowship*."[85] Being a dynamic concept, it is also "*communicable* unity and . . . an *open, inviting unity, capable of interaction*" over against the traditional exclusive ways that build on the ideas of the oneness of the substance or the sameness of the absolute subject.[86]

Moltmann utilizes the ancient concept of perichoresis to elaborate on his view: it is the mutual indwelling of Trinitarian persons in each other, "the unitedness, the at-oneness of the three Persons with one another, or: the unitedness, the at-oneness of the triune God." This unity "must be perceived in the perichoresis of the divine Persons."[87]

> We have understood the unity of the divine trinitarian history as the open, unifying at-oneness of the three divine Persons in their relationships to one another. If this uniting at-oneness of the triune God is the quintessence of salvation, then its "transcendent primordial ground" cannot be seen to lie in the one, single, homogenous divine essence (*substantia*), or in the one, single, absolute subject. It then lies in the eternal perichoresis of the Father, the Son and the Spirit.[88]

In the social notion of "personhood" Moltmann sees the way to affirm both the distinction and unity of Father, Son, and Spirit: as persons, "they are just as much united with one another and in one another, since personal character and social character are only two aspects of the same thing. The concept of person must therefore in itself contain the concept of unitedness or at-oneness."[89]

Moltmann wants to combat the charge that the perichoresis spoken of here is a second movement where "three different individuals . . . only subsequently

---

82. Ibid., 149.
83. Ibid., 19.
84. Ibid., 149.
85. Ibid., 95 (italics in the original); see also 96.
86. Ibid., 149–50 (quotation from 149; italics in the original).
87. Ibid., 150.
88. Ibid., 157.
89. Ibid., 150.

enter into relationship with another." This is the danger of tritheism. Nor is the perichoresis to be understood in terms of modalism in which (like Barth in Moltmann's estimation) Father, Son, and Spirit are only "three repetitions of the One God." There is no reducing the threeness to the unity, nor dissolving the unity in the threeness. Moltmann contends: "The unity of the triunity lies in the eternal perichoresis of the trinitarian persons. Interpreted perichoretically, the trinitarian persons form their own unity by themselves in the circulation of the divine life."[90]

As mentioned, this perichoresis will be consummated in the eschaton in the coming union of God and of God and the world in the eschaton. This again goes back to the Trinitarian history of Son, Spirit, and Father. Because of the fact that "glorifying by the Spirit effects the union of the Son with the Father as well as our own union with and in God (John 17:21)," Moltmann can then "link the consummation of salvation history in eschatology with the consummation of the trinitarian life of God in itself."[91] This finally takes us to the culmination of Moltmann's theological vision and is the way he reconciles the economic-immanent Trinity distinction: "The economic Trinity completes and perfects itself to immanent Trinity when the history and experience of salvation are completed and perfected. When everything is 'in God' and 'God is in all,' then the economic Trinity is raised into and transcended in the immanent Trinity."[92] This is the way for God to "indwell" his creation eternally, a desire that is already present in the act of creation when God, in his love, reaches out to the Other. This is the eschatological perichoresis, "mutual indwelling." Divine unity exists as a result: "the trinitarian persons form their unity by themselves in the circulation of the divine life."[93] Here we come to the divine unity to which the Trinitarian history is the prelude and in which Son, Spirit, and Father mutually indwell each other, in eternal union (based on the promise of 1 Cor 15:28).[94] This is the theme of his (second, after *Theology of Hope*) major book on eschatology, *The Coming of God* (1996), and it is also applied to the unity between God and the created order. In that vision, "God desires to come to his 'dwelling' in his creation, the home of his identity in the world, and in it to his 'rest,' his perfected, eternal joy."[95] In this eschatological Shekinah the whole creation will be new. The eschatological indwelling of God is the presence of God in the space of his created beings.[96] When God comes to inhabit creation, it means that the "Cre-

---

90. Ibid., 175; for the idea of the perichoresis denoting the "circulatory character of the eternal divine life," an eternal life process in the triune God through the "exchange of energies," see also 174.

91. Pannenberg, *Systematic Theology,* 1:330, with reference to Moltmann, *Trinity and the Kingdom,* 126 especially.

92. Moltmann, *Trinity and the Kingdom,* 161.

93. Ibid., 175.

94. Jürgen Moltmann, *The Coming of God: A Christian Eschatology* (Minneapolis: Fortress, 1996), 307.

95. Ibid., xiii.

96. Ibid., 265.

ator becomes the God who can be inhabited. God as living space of the world is a feminine metaphor."[97]

Is there any place then for the distinction between the immanent and economic Trinity? Fully aware of the reasons why the distinction has been held in Christian theology—most prominently, as the way to safeguard the freedom of God and the grace of God—he is also critical of it. For a concept of God as love that resists the speculative and artificial distinction between freedom and necessity—as if God could exist alone without the Other with whom to share love—the distinction seems to be both arbitrary and self-contradictory. Therefore, for Moltmann, the distinction cannot be maintained; the immanent and economic Trinities rather "form a continuity and merge into one another."[98]

The only legitimate way of continuing the distinction is to relegate it to doxology, the human response to the experience of salvation and anticipation of the coming kingdom.[99] Doxological response means participation in and transformation into God rather than an attempt to know God *in se*: "Then to know God means to participate in the fullness of the divine life." Doxological knowledge, therefore, can be rightly called *theologia* in distinction from *oikonomia*, the economy of salvation.[100] The way to doxological knowledge, of course, is the way of economy. Nothing can be assumed of God that contradicts the history of salvation; conversely, nothing can be assumed in the experience of salvation which does not correspond with God. "There is only one, single, divine Trinity and one, single, divine history of salvation."[101]

THE FUNCTION OF THE DOCTRINE OF THE TRINITY: THE KINGDOM OF FREEDOM

One of Moltmann's major contributions to contemporary Trinitarian theology is the way he utilizes trinity as a critical theological-social-political criterion.[102] His thesis is simple and bold: human societies, including the church, should reflect the principle of egalitarianism and mutual "indwelling" evident in the Trinity.

As explained above, Moltmann is critical of all notions of hierarchy and dominion in the Triune God. God's fatherhood does not mean exercising power but being the Father of the Son, our elder brother. Even more, in light of the Son proceeding from the Father, there is an idea of begetting and birth related to the

---

97. Ibid., 299.
98. Moltmann, *Trinity and the Kingdom*, 152.
99. Ibid., 152, 161.
100. Ibid., 152.
101. Ibid., 153; see also p. 154.
102. While a profound thinker, Moltmann declares that the practical implications of theology are high on his agenda. See further Moltmann, "An Autobiographical Note," in A. J. Conyers, *God, Hope, and History: Jürgen Moltmann and the Christian Concept of History* (Macon, GA: Mercer University Press, 1988), 204.

Deity, which inspires Moltmann to speak of "motherly Father" and "fatherly Mother."[103] Rejecting both monotheism, the religion of the patriarchy, as well as pantheism, the religion of matriarchy, Moltmann advocates the concept of the Triune God that leads to an equal fellowship of men and women.[104]

Moltmann wants to set the record straight: "monotheism is monarchism"[105] whether it manifests itself in politics[106] or church life.[107] In his view this means that non-Trinitarian "monotheism" supports domination and abuse of power. For him, monotheism and monarchism are virtually synonyms.[108] In other words, Moltmann sees a reciprocal conditioning between religion and politics, faith and power.[109] From early on, Christian theology has taken a mistaken route by affirming a kind of monotheism in which the universe itself has a monarchial structure: one God—one Logos—one cosmos. This leads to the hierarchical view of reality and communities. The way to combat this is to speak of the Trinitarian God as a "community of equals, vulnerable and open to the human suffering, who experiences this suffering in himself."[110] Trinity is not a hierarchical entity, but rather a fellowship of persons: "We understand the scriptures as the testimony to the history of the Trinity's relations of fellowship, which are open to men and women, and open to the world."[111] God's kingdom is about fatherly and motherly compassion rather than about domination and subjection.[112]

This view of course carries over to the nature of the church community. His view of the church is "a fellowship of equal persons" patterned according to the Trinity.[113] Trinity in the New Testament means "relationships of fellowship" that are "open to the world."[114] Notions of hierarchy, subordination, and subjugation are foreign to his social vision. This is an antidote to what he calls "clerical monotheism" based on the early practice in the Christian church of a monarchial episcopate: the bishop as a representative of Christ over the people of God, which of course culminated in the idea of the papacy.[115] The biblical vision of John 17:20–21 is different: "Here the unity of the Christian community is a trinitarian unity. It corresponds to the indwelling of the Father in the Son, and of the Son in

103. Moltmann gives reference to the saying from the Council of Toledo (675) about the Son having been begotten out of the Father's womb. Moltmann, *Trinity and the Kingdom*, 165.
104. Ibid., 164–65.
105. Ibid., 191.
106. Ibid., 192–200.
107. Ibid., 200–202.
108. Ibid., 130.
109. Ibid., 193.
110. Eugen Matei, "The Practice of Community in Social Trinitarianism: A Theological Evaluation with Reference to Dumitru Stăniloae and Jürgen Moltmann" (PhD diss., Fuller Theological Seminary, School of Theology, 2004), 213.
111. Moltmann, *Trinity and the Kingdom*, 19; see also pp. 17–18 and 191–92.
112. Ibid., 71.
113. Moltmann, *Church in the Power of the Spirit*, 57 (cf. 114–121, 314–17); idem, *Trinity and the Kingdom*, 157–58. See further Veli-Matti Kärkkäinen, *An Introduction to Ecclesiology: Ecumenical, Historical and Global Perspectives* (Downers Grove, IL: InterVarsity Press, 2002), 128–29.
114. Moltmann, *Trinity and the Kingdom*, 64,
115. Ibid., 201.

the Father. It *participates* in the divine triunity, since the community of believers is not only fellowship *with* God, but *in* God too."[116]

Matei helpfully summarizes the two aspects that guide Moltmann's view of community in the Social Trinitarian understanding. On the one hand, creation and history are seen as part of a Trinitarian process that "takes place in and with a God in whom there is no structure of domination, only a structure of equalitarian love." On the other hand, "the perichoretical relationships of love present in the Holy Trinity are the archetype for all relationships between different parts of the created reality including between human beings themselves."[117]

One of the ways Moltmann supports his critique of inequality is to refer to his eschatological vision of perichoresis, according to which there will be "a harmonious fellowship of liberated nature and humans with God"[118] rather than a lordship by God. In that vision humans will not be "servants" nor "children" but "friends."[119]

CRITICAL REFLECTIONS

Undoubtedly, Moltmann (with Pannenberg) has not only been an important agent in the most recent revival of the Trinitarian doctrine but has also shaped the discussion in a definitive way.[120] A number of theologians from a wide variety of ecumenical and theological persuasions such as feminist (Elizabeth Johnson), liberationist (Leonardo Boff), and even evangelical (Millard J. Ericksson) have picked up key ideas from him. Stanley J. Grenz's comment that "[t]he reception of Moltmann's trinitarian theology . . . has been nothing short of phenomenal" well illustrates his significance.[121] At the same time, Moltmann has elicited a number of critical responses; his Trinitarian proposal is probably the one most widely debated currently.

One frequent question to Moltmann and other social Trinitarians is whether they have ended up affirming tritheism in their fear of "monotheism." Scholars from a wide variety of theological orientations have expressed strong concerns about tritheism;[122] some even leveled the charge of tritheism.[123] I think Ted

---

116. Ibid., 202.

117. Matei, "Practice of Community," 214.

118. Grenz, *Social God*, 45.

119. Moltmann, *Trinity and the Kingdom*, 221.

120. So, e.g., Stanley J. Grenz and Roger E. Olson, *Twentieth Century Theology: God and the World in a Transitional Age* (Downers Grove, IL: InterVarsity Press, 1992), 185: "Moltmann has done more than anyone since Karl Barth to revitalize the doctrine of the Trinity in contemporary theology."

121. Grenz, *Rediscovering the Triune God*, 84; for a good survey of praises given to Moltmann in this respect, see pp. 73–75, 84–85.

122. Thomas F. Torrance, *The Christian Doctrine of God, One Being Three Persons* (Edinburgh: T & T Clark, 1996), 247 n. 39; Gerald O'Collins, *The Tripersonal God: Understanding and Interpreting the Trinity* (Mahwah, NJ: Paulist Press, 1999), 158 among others. Regarding the same issue in Moltmann's *Crucified God*, see the comment by George Hunsinger, "The Crucified God and the Political Theology of Violence," *Heythrop Journal* 4 (1973): 278.

123. Paul D. Molnar, *Divine Freedom and the Doctrine of the Immanent Trinity: In Dialogue with Karl Barth and Contemporary Theology* (Edinburgh: T & T Clark, 2002), 201–2, with references to

Peters's remark is both fair and enlightening. He says that Moltmann's social doctrine of the Trinity

> may unnecessarily take him too far toward sacrificing divine unity. His emphasis on the three separate subjects or centers of action risks a final plurality. Moltmann does not want to posit the existence of three gods, of course. He is no polytheist. . . . Nevertheless, his continued emphasis on three discrete subjects or centers of activity makes it difficult to conceive of a principle of unity that is comparable to that of the plurality. It appears that we end up with a divine nominalism.[124]

Yet Peters also helpfully notes that Moltmann's own response to this charge would probably go along with the new developments in the understanding of the person, which focuses on the principle of relationality. Even so, Peters wonders if Moltmann's overall Trinitarian orientation still suffers from the lack of the unity.[125] Moltmann's key concept is the perichoresis. I have two kinds of remarks about the use of this concept in his theology.[126] On the one hand, I applaud his untiring effort to combat the charge of tritheism, which, after all, he doesn't think has been a real problem in Christian theology. He makes every effort to insist on mutuality, mutual dependence; he refers to the circulation of divine energy, and he also notes that eventually it is a matter of eschatological development. All of this is good. On the other hand, the fear still lurks that the resort to perichoresis is more a matter of *insistence* than a carefully worked out theological *rationale*. What makes me further question is the fact that contemporary theology—not only Moltmann for that matter, but others too, such as the evangelical Millard J. Erickson, whose views will be discussed later—claims the heritage of this ancient concept going back to John of Damascus and others, and believes it was always used as a means of defending unity. That is not necessarily the case; for John a perichoresis is not the means of affirming unity, but rather unity is the presupposition for perichoresis. Unity for John is established by the idea of Father as the source of Spirit and Son.[127] The Damascene, and perhaps others who followed him, took the unity as their first premise and, having established that, elaborated the unity-in-threeness and threeness-in-unity with the help of this idea. This is not

---

many others; Robert E. Letham, *The Holy Trinity: In Scripture, History, Theology, and Worship* (Phillipsburg, NJ: P&R Publishing, 2004), 307–9.

124. Peters, *God as Trinity*, 109.

125. Ibid.

126. A helpful discussion is to be found in Randall E. Otto, "The Use and Abuse of Perichoresis in Recent Theology," *Scottish Journal of Theology* 54, no. 3 (2001): 366–84. My discussion here, however, goes in somewhat different directions from that of Otto.

127. Pannenberg, *Systematic Theology*, 1:334; this is argued in more detail in Michael L. Chiavone, "The Unity of God as Understood by Four Twentieth-Century Trinitarian Theologians: Karl Rahner, Millard Erickson, John Zizioulas, and Wolfhart Pannenberg" (PhD diss., Southeastern Baptist Theological Seminary, Wake Forest, NC, 2005), 125–27. The structure of John's discussion confirms this judgment. He begins the discussion of the Trinity with the oneness of God and proceeds from there to considering Trinity, thus—ironically—anticipating the standard Western tradition.

necessarily a charge against the use of perichoresis as a means of establishing unity; it is an idea that may stand on its own feet. However, what concerns me is that those who use it most enthusiastically, such as Moltmann, Leonardo Boff, and M. Erickson, do not discuss the different task this ancient concept plays in their theology. The most that can be said about the unity of the Triune God in Moltmann's theology is that he has not successfully satisfied even the most moderate critics. From another perspective, this issue is of course ironic in light of the fact that Moltmann, unlike most contemporary theologians, struggles hard to reconcile the doctrine of the Trinity with the monotheism of Judaism.[128]

A corollary question is whether Moltmann is rejecting the distinction between the economic and immanent Trinity. Many commentators believe Moltmann has taken Rahner's rule to its logical end, finally conflating the immanent Trinity into the economic.[129] Indeed, there are many reasons to raise this question; rightly it has been called the Achilles' heel of his theology.[130] Speaking of the theology of cross as his methodological starting point, Moltmann says bluntly: "In order to grasp the death of the Son in its significance for God himself, I found myself bound to surrender the traditional distinction between the immanent and the economic Trinity, according to which the cross comes to stand only in the economy of salvation, but not within the immanent Trinity."[131] Furthermore, Moltmann argues that the economic Trinity not only reveals the immanent Trinity but that it also has a retroactive effect on the immanent Trinity. "The pain of the cross determines the inner life of the triune God from eternity to eternity" similarly to the responsive love in glorification through the Spirit.[132] Therefore, if it is the case that the histories of Jesus and the Spirit "not only belong to but actually constitute the history of the triune God," meaning that the *history* (economic Trinity) of God constitutes the *being* (immanent Trinity) of God, it means subsuming the immanent into the economic.[133] Pannenberg's word of warning, thus, is appropriate here. He says the danger in "the equation of the two means the absorption of the immanent Trinity in the economic Trinity. This steals from the Trinity of salvation history all sense and significance. For this Trinity has sense and significance only if God is the same in salvation history as he is from eternity."[134]

128. See the important comments by Richard John Neuhaus, "Moltmann vs. Monotheism," *Dialog* 20, no. 3 (Summer 1981): 241. For a helpful discussion, see Müller-Fahrenholz, *Kingdom and the Power*, 138–40.

129. Even the most sympathetic and moderate critics have expressed this opinion, such as Richard Bauckham, "Jürgen Moltmann," in *The Modern Theologians: An Introduction to Christian Theology in the Twentieth Century*, ed. David F. Ford, 2 vols. (New York: Blackwell, 1989), 1:304; Samuel Powell, *The Trinity in German Thought* (Cambridge: Cambridge University Press, 2000), 201–2.

130. Grenz, *Rediscovering the Triune God*, 85. I find Grenz's handling of this issue (pp. 85–87) one of the most careful and theologically informed treatments.

131. Moltmann, *Trinity and the Kingdom*, 160.

132. Ibid., 160–61 (quotation from 161). See also Roger Olson, "Trinity and Eschatology: The Historical Being of God in Jürgen Moltmann and Wolfhart Pannenberg," *Scottish Journal of Theology* 36 (1983): 217–18.

133. Grenz, *Rediscovering the Triune God*, 86.

134. Pannenberg, *Systematic Theology*, 1:331.

This, however, is not the whole picture of Moltmann's somewhat more nuanced—and undoubtedly more ambiguous—view of the economic-immanent distinction. In *The Trinity and the Kingdom* he acknowledges himself having surrendered the traditional distinction in his earlier book, *The Crucified God*, in order to safeguard the inclusion of the cross in the inner life of God.[135] Another reason for the hesitancy to acknowledge the distinction is the implication that there are *two* Trinities rather than one.[136] Yet, as the previous discussion has shown, there is a way in which Moltmann still holds on to the distinction at least in some qualified sense, and that is in reference to doxology. In the order of knowing, the economic of course takes precedence; in the order of being, Moltmann still seems to be imagining some kind of "transcendent ground" for the Godhead, in other words, God *in se*. Remarking that while doxology is based on and derives from the experience of salvation, it also "grow[s] up out of the conclusion drawn from this experience about the *transcendent conditions which make the experience possible,*" which leads to "that experience's *transcendent ground.*"[137] Grenz finds yet another reason for arguing that Moltmann does not totally conflate the immanent into the economic with his emphasis on eschatological ontology: "In the end Moltmann elevates the God who is all-in-all in the eschatological horizon and who thereby stands in some sense as judge over the world and the historical process."[138] Many others, myself among them, are far less confident about this argument: it seem to me that Moltmann's reference to the future, "God is all in all" (to which Grenz also refers as the basis for his view), is rather a statement of the subsuming of the immanent into the economic Trinity. Therefore, my final assessment—somewhat similar to the problem of the unity of the Triune God—is that in his Trinitarian magnum opus Moltmann is aware of the tendency of his theology to erase the distinction, and while there are many reasons for him to do so, in the end he tries to preserve the distinction in some way. As a result, the question is not totally resolved and ambiguity results.[139]

The centrality of the cross in Moltmann's Trinitarian theology also raises a

---

135. Moltmann, *Trinity and the Kingdom,* 160. Warren McWilliams agrees that while in his earlier work Moltmann rejected the distinction, in his later work he is much more nuanced. Warren McWilliams, "Trinitarian Doxology: Jürgen Moltmann on the Relation of the Economic and Immanent Trinity," *Perspectives in Religious Studies* 23, no. 1 (1996): 26.

136. Moltmann, *Trinity and the Kingdom,* 151.

137. Ibid., 153 (italics mine). Grenz (*Rediscovering the Triune God,* 87) agrees with this interpretation. Introducing doxology as the way to speak of the immanent Trinity is of course open to the difficult question of the epistemological status of doxological statements. Moltmann doesn't address this issue at any length. This prompts Peters (*God as Trinity,* 107–8) to call Moltmann's description of the immanent Trinity "the product of pious imagination, an abstraction from the concrete economy of the divine life that is actualized in history." See also McWilliams, "Trinitarian Doxology," 32–33, 37–38.

138. Grenz, *Rediscovering the Triune God,* 87.

139. Similarly, ibid. I don't know how helpful is the nomenclature "neo-economic trinitarianism" (applied to not only Moltmann but also Pannenberg, Gordon Kaufman, and Piet Schoonenberg) coined by William J. Hill, *The Three-Personal God: The Trinity as a Mystery of Salvation* (Washington, DC: Catholic University Press of America, 1982), 149–84.

number of questions.[140] First, how "literally" should we speak of the "death" of God? Second, does this make Deity too much dependent on the world and its happening? Third, is Moltmann's idea of the suffering and dying God in keeping with the biblical and theological view of God as the one who overcomes suffering and death? Let me look at each question.

First, is Moltmann advocating an idea of a dying God, and if he is, what should we think of that theologically? How literally should we take the title *The Crucified God*? It is difficult to say. Eugen Matei in his recent dissertation on Moltmann's Trinitarian doctrine argues that this is what happens:

> The cross, therefore, where God *himself* was in Christ (2 Cor. 5:19), is the place where God represents and reveals himself, and even more than that, it is the place where he identifies and defines himself. To take this thought to its logical conclusion means to accept that on the cross God himself suffered in Jesus and that God himself dies in Jesus for us. The suffering and dying of Jesus are works of God towards himself, and therefore, they are passions of God. In the cross, God passes the judgment on human sin upon himself, and this means that the cross of the Son of God reveals a change in God.[141]

While it is important to avoid making the cross an event external to the Deity—"an event which concerned only the human nature that the divine Logos assumed, as though it did not affect in any way the eternal placidity of the trinitarian life of God"[142]—it is not correct to speak of the death of God. I agree with Pannenberg that we need to speak of the death of the *Son* of God, or to be more precise to say that "the Son of God, though he suffered and died himself, did so according to his human nature."[143]

Second, with his inclusion of the cross and resurrection in the divine life, is Moltmann making the Deity too much dependent on the world and its happenings? The Roman Catholic Gerald O'Collins expresses concern that many have voiced: "Many fear that Moltmann's insistence on the crucifixion and resurrection as an inner-trinitarian event (with a rupture in the divine life and the Father 'ceasing' to be the Father) may be confusing the intradivine life with the story of human salvation even to the point of 'imprisoning' God in the world's becoming."[144]

Here we come to the wider question of Moltmann's Trinitarian panentheism. The question is, of course, this: Has he correlated God and world such that

---

140. For an important discussion, see further Dennis W. Jowers, "The Theology of the Cross as Theology of the Trinity: A Critique of Jürgen Moltmann's Staurocentric Trinitarianism," *Tyndale Bulletin* 52, no. 2 (2001): 245–66. With his focus on the cross in Trinitarian doctrine, Moltmann reflects many key ideas of Eberhard Jüngel, *God as the Mystery of the Universe*, trans. Darrell L. Guder (Grand Rapids: Eerdmans, 1983), 368–73 especially.

141. Matei, "Practice of Community," 186.

142. Pannenberg, *Systematic Theology*, 1:314.

143. Ibid.

144. O'Collins, *Tripersonal God*, 158. Similarly, John Thompson, *Modern Trinitarian Perspectives* (New York: Oxford University Press, 1994), 51.

God's freedom is qualified to the point that pantheism lurks on the horizon?[145] What does it mean to say, as he does, that in some sense God "needs" the world, being Love who cannot exist except as sharing and giving? It is one thing to say, as Pannenberg does, that having created the world, God cannot exist without reference to the world. Yet God is fully God without creation.[146] It is another thing to say, as Moltmann does, that bringing about the world is a necessary event. But doesn't that make God a solitary monad? Not necessarily. Trinitarian relations between Father, Son, and Spirit can be described as themselves actions, as Christian theology has done.[147] In this respect it is interesting that both Moltmann and Pannenberg utilize some Hegelian concepts, yet it is Moltmann who tends to follow the lead of Hegel in making world history the arena in which God realizes himself.[148]

Third, what about Moltmann's insistence on God as one who not only is capable of suffering but also takes the place of the fellow-sufferer alongside humans. As Bauckham puts it: "The cross does not solve the problem of suffering, but meets it with the voluntary suffering of love."[149] This prompted Barth to ask Moltmann a chiding question: "If you will pardon me, your God seems to me to be rather a pauper."[150] Robert Letham rightly notes that the main reason for Moltmann's view of God as sympathetic fellow sufferer rather than the God who overcomes evil has to do with his refusal to acknowledge the lordship of God in any authoritative or power-laden sense.[151] While there is no denying that the view of God as the Almighty God has been misused and mispresented in Christian theology and piety, it is also one-sided and against Christian tradition to eliminate any notion of the power and authority of God. This is not only somewhat naive,[152] but it also leads to inconsistencies in Moltmann's own thinking: how could Christ subdue all opposition to the kingdom, as he claims Christ is doing, when handing back the kingdom to the Father? If it is true, as some harsher critics claim about Moltmann's view, that it leads to the kind of compassionate God who cannot overcome evil, hope grounded in real history can hardly be everlasting hope.[153] Recently Thomas Weinandy has mounted a massive critique against Moltmann's view of the suffering God at the mercy of hostile forces in creation.[154] While Weinandy's view is not fully convincing, it is welcome as a needed check and balance to Moltmann.

---

145. Again, the harshest critique comes from Molnar, *Divine Freedom*, 62.

146. Pannenberg, *Systematic Theology*, 2:1.

147. Ibid.

148. So Bauckham, *Theology of Jürgen Moltmann*, 25.

149. Ibid., 12.

150. Letter dated November 17, 1964, in Karl Barth, *Letters 1961–1968*, trans. and ed. Jürgen Fangemeier and Geoffrey W. Bromiley (Grand Rapids: Eerdmans, 1981), 176.

151. See also Letham, *Holy Trinity*, 309–10.

152. So rightly ibid., 310.

153. As he often does, Molnar (*Divine Freedom*, 203) puts it quite categorically, yet his concern that Moltmann's God is not able to deal with evil should be registered.

154. Thomas Weinandy, *Does God Suffer?* (Notre Dame, IN: University of Notre Dame Press, 2000).

My final comment on the implications of the cross for Moltmann's theology may sound surprising, if not contradictory, in light of the foregoing discussion that has focused on the danger of tritheism. I wonder with some others whether the charge of modalism lurks behind his program in the form of patripassianism.[155] When the Son suffered and died on the cross, the Father did so with him. Moltmann is aware of patripassianist leanings and, against Christian tradition, does not necessarily consider it heretical.[156]

Moltmann's relentless critique of "monotheism" also raises critical questions.[157] First of all, I wonder if the exaggerated fear of utilizing any kind of lordship language is in keeping with the biblical testimony where that kind of language is used deliberately—yet often qualified to make it distinct from abusive or egoistic power language. The biblical talk about the Triune God hardly supports the kind of abuse of power Moltmann wants to combat with his fear of monotheism. Second, with Ted Peters we need to ask what Moltmann really means by the idea of monotheism being equated with monarchism. This statement has to be regarded as either false or true; if the latter, then it seems to be trivial. Moltmann cannot possibly maintain (in the strong sense of the term) that only monotheistic societies are monarchist since a number of polytheistic ones are too. Then what he must mean is the weak sense of the term, namely, that monotheism can be put to a monarchist use, which of course is true—but also trivial; anything can be used for abusive power purposes. Third—similarly to the question of the unity of God—there is again this irony of on the one hand desiring to connect with the Jewish faith (of monotheism) and on the other hand, rejecting the whole talk about monotheism in a very unqualified and naive way.[158]

Over against Moltmann's rejection of hierarchical structures and "monotheism" as well as his efforts to defend the mutuality of the three persons in the Trinity, I find surprising and theologically misguided his idea of the Father as "origin" and "monarch" of the Deity. He argues for this on the basis of the distinction between the economic and inner-Trinitarian constitution of the Trinity. But how viable is this route? Doesn't that finally lead to the breaking of the basic rule of Rahner's that Moltmann claims to follow? If God in his inner life is different from what appears in the economy, can we then trust any knowledge of God? Furthermore, doesn't this represent subordinationism, an idea Moltmann claims to refute with his idea of perichoresis?[159] Moltmann has not been able to address this issue in a satisfactory way, other than by contending that the idea of the

---

155. Most forcefully argued by Paul D. Molnar, "The Function of the Trinity in Moltmann's Ecological Doctrine of the Trinity," *Theological Studies* 51, no. 4 (1990): 689–93.

156. Moltmann, *Trinity and the Kingdom*, 32–33; Moltmann, *Crucified God*, 241–42 especially. See also Letham, *Holy Trinity*, 309.

157. For a rebuttal of Moltmann's emphasis on monotheism, see Otto Randall, "Moltmann and the Anti-Monotheism Movement," *International Journal of Systematic Theology* 3, no. 3 (2001): 298–308.

158. Peters, *God as Trinity*, 40–42.

159. Moltmann, *Trinity and the Kingdom*, 175.

eternal origin of the Godhead of the Father "has no validity within the eternal circulation of the divine life, and none in the perichoretic unity of the Trinity. Here the three Persons are equal."[160] This is confusing, to say the least: How can an *eternal* constitution be differentiated from the *eternal* life of the Trinity! To add to the confusion, Moltmann also surmises that we should indeed lay aside all "metaphysical thinking in terms of origin . . . in the doctrine of the inner-trinitarian processions" as has happened in the tradition because its starting point lies in cosmology rather than in God. Against this line of thinking, Moltmann contends, we "have to adhere to the equally primordial character of the trinitarian Persons" in spite of the origin of the other two in the Father, lest Trinity be dissolved in monotheism.[161] But by positing the Father as the eternal origin, isn't Moltmann not only contradicting the idea of mutuality but also exercising "metaphysical" thinking in terms of origin? That it is not necessarily related to cosmology, in my view, is not the issue (that has to do with Moltmann's rejection of any talk about the Father as the origin of the world in any other way than in the Father's role first as the Father of the Son[162]).

My final question has to do with the overall method of Moltmann's Trinitarian theology. It seems to me there is an inherent irony in his effort throughout his theological career on the one hand to resist the temptation of abstract theology of tradition in in his insistence on the importance of anchoring theology in concrete history, and on the other hand to construct his Trinitarian doctrine in a highly speculative way. Many commentators have remarked along this line; Letham calls it "unbridled speculation."[163] This is especially true of the way he constructs his Trinitarian understanding of creation or his vision of eschatology as the "homecoming" of the Triune God.

---

160. Ibid., 176.
161. Ibid., 165–66.
162. See Ibid., 163.
163. Letham, *Holy Trinity*, 306. See also Bauckham, *Theology of Jürgen Moltmann*, 167.

Chapter 9

Wolfhart Pannenberg

Trinity as "Public Theology"

"THE TRIUNE GOD AS THE TRUTH OF HISTORY"[1]

The way Wolfhart Pannenberg titles the first chapter of the first volume of his *Systematic Theology* reveals the basic agenda of all of his theology: "The Truth of Christian Doctrine as the Theme of Systematic Theology."[2] Against all the forces of modernity and postmodernism, Pannenberg boldly sets up a coherent, logical presentation of Christian doctrine in defense of truth. The task of systematic theology is the exposition of Christian doctrine in a way that leads to a coherent presentation in correlation with what we know of God and reality as a whole.[3] He strongly opposes the widespread privatization and subjectivization of

1. The heading above is from Stanley J. Grenz, *Rediscovering the Triune God: The Trinity in Contemporary Theology* (Minneapolis: Fortress, 2004), 88.
2. Wolfhart Pannenberg, *Systematic Theology,* trans. Geoffrey W. Bromiley, 3 vols. (Grand Rapids: Eerdmans, 1991–98), 1:1. For a succinct discussion of Pannenberg's method in light of his overall theology, see Stanley J. Grenz, *Reason for Hope: The Systematic Theology of Wolfhart Pannenberg* (New York/Oxford: Oxford University Press, 1990), chap. 1.
3. For his definition of theology along these lines, see Pannenberg, *Systematic Theology,* 1:59–60.

theology[4] and argues for theology as a public discipline, the purpose of which is to give a "rational account of the truth of faith."[5] There is a universal orientation in truth claims; truth that is truth to one person only cannot be universal truth.[6] In that sense, theological claims are by nature hypotheses to be tested and, if possible, confirmed.[7] The truth of Christian claims cannot be presupposed, but rather is the goal of argumentation.[8]

No other theologian on the contemporary scene has labored so untiringly to establish the intellectual credibility of Christian theology, nor shown a wider intellectual breadth in dialogue not only with biblical, historical, and contemporary Christian views, but also with philosophy, science,[9] history of religions, and cultural disciplines.[10] This is in keeping with his advocacy of a coherent theory of truth. Everything is to be related to the whole.[11]

Pannenberg sees his approach as a necessary task given to Christian theology, especially systematic theology,[12] now that—as a result of the decay of the Scripture principle which assumed Christian truth rather than argued for it[13]—the word *God* no longer has factual content in modern Western culture's public consciousness. In radical contrast to the past, when the term *God* implied something "real," for modern (and especially "postmodern") secular culture "the existence of God has not only become doubtful, but the content of the concept of God has also become unclear." Ironically, Christian theology has contributed to this plague by relegating God-talk to religious experience and the subjective realm. Therefore, in the public arena the truthfulness of statements about God are not even discussed, let alone confirmed.[14] Against

---

4. Wolfhart Pannenberg, *The Idea of God and Human Freedom*, trans. R. A. Wilson (Philadelphia: Westminster Press, 1973), 87ff. In reference to privatization in pneumatology, see also idem, "The Doctrine of the Spirit and the Task of a Theology of Nature," *Theology* 75, no. 1 (1972): 10.

5. Wolfhart Pannenberg, *Basic Questions in Theology*, trans. George H. Kehm, 2 vols. (Philadelphia: Fortress, 1971), 2:52–53. For a full-scale study, see Mark William Worthing, *Foundations and Functions of Theology as a Universal Science: Theological Method and Apologetic Praxis in Wolfhart Pannenberg and Karl Rahner* (Frankfurt am Main: Peter Lang, 1996).

6. Wolfhart Pannenberg, *Anthropology in Theological Perspective* (Philadelphia: Westminster Press, 1985), p. 15.

7. Pannenberg, *Systematic Theology*, 1:50, 56–58; "The Nature of a Theological Statement," *Zygon* 7, no. 1 (March 1972): 8–9. See also Mark C. Mattes, "Pannenberg's Achievement: An Analysis and Assessment of His *Systematic Theology*," *Currents in Theology and Mission* 26, no. 1 (February 1999): 52.

8. Pannenberg, *Systematic Theology*, 1:52.

9. See further Joel Haugen, "Introduction: Pannenberg's Vision of Theology and Science," in *Beginning with the End: God, Science, and Wolfhart Pannenberg*, ed. Carol Rausch Albright and Joel Haugen (Chicago: Open Court, 1997), 1–8.

10. For many praises to this effect, see Grenz, *Rediscovering the Triune God*, 88.

11. Wolfhart Pannenberg, *An Introduction to Systematic Theology* (Grand Rapids: Eerdmans, 1991), 8; so also Pannenberg, *Systematic Theology*, 1:21–22 especially.

12. For the distinct role of systematic theology in the theological curriculum in this perspective, see Pannenberg, *Systematic Theology*, chap. 1, especially p. 8.

13. See "The Crisis of the Scripture Principle," in Pannenberg, *Basic Questions in Theology*, 1:1–14.

14. Pannenberg, *Systematic Theology*, 1:63–65, quote on 64. Christian philosophy and theology have also contributed to the loss of the factual content of the term *God* by their reluctance to connect the God of the Bible with the "god of the philosophers." According to Pannenberg, Christian theology has

the mind-set of timidity, Pannenberg wants to rehabilitate the role of metaphysical talk in the theological enterprise.

THE DOCTRINE OF GOD AGAINST THE HISTORICAL, ANTHROPOLOGICAL, AND ESCHATOLOGICAL HORIZONS

While for Pannenberg there is no way after the advent of the Enlightenment to offer undisputed proof for God's existence, Christian theology should make every effort to win the anthropological starting point by arguing for the intelligibility of God-talk in a post-Enlightenment culture. In defense of that, Pannenberg sets forth the bold thesis that humanity is "incurably" religious."[15] Therefore, faith in God/god(s) is not something external imposed upon the human. Rather, religiosity is inherent to humanity. In his view, religion is an essential dimension of human life; it belongs to the nature of humanity to be open to God and search for meaning and truth.[16] Pannenberg arrives at this fundamental conclusion by way of arguing with Descartes (and Schleiermacher) that the only way to posit the finite is to assume the infinite as the necessary horizon.[17] Of course, anthropological reasoning can never guarantee the truth of theological claims, let alone the existence of a particular god. Rather, it is a necessary but not satisfactory evidence for arguing for the truthfulness of theological talk about God.[18]

One of the salient features of Pannenberg's theological method is the idea of revelation happening in (universal) history.[19] "History is the most comprehensive horizon of Christian theology"[20] is a methodological canon hammered out early in Pannenberg's theological career. As a result, "of the three voices [in addition to him, Moltmann, and Robert W. Jenson] who took seriously the move to history that Barth and Rahner bequeathed to trinitarian theology, Pannenberg

---

missed the fact that in the Bible the term *god* serves not only as a proper name but also as a general designation. In the Bible, we find both Yahweh (proper name) and Elohim (a generic term for God). Proper names, Pannenberg notes, only make sense in connection with terms for species. Therefore, to make God-talk intelligible, Christian theology had better not cut off this general term as the background for talking about the particular God Yahweh, the Father of Jesus Christ. The Christian mission, if it continues to issue truth claims in its proclamation of the revelation of the one God in Jesus Christ, needs to affirm the concept of God in philosophical theology. Otherwise, it is "involuntarily regressing to a situation of a plurality of gods in which Christian talk about God has reference to the specific biblical God as one God among others." Ibid., 1:69.

15. Ibid., 1:157.

16. For a short statement, see ibid., 1:154–57 especially. For a full-scale treatment, see his *Anthropology in Theological Perspective* (Philadelphia: Westminster Press, 1985), which in fact is an attempt to fight against the opponents of religion on their own field, namely, psychology, anthropology, sociology, and history.

17. Pannenberg, *Systematic Theology*, 1:113–18, 136–41 especially.

18. Ibid., 1:93.

19. For a full discussion of "Revelation as History (and the Word of God)" by the mature Pannenberg (with self-critical notes to the groundbreaking *Offenbarung als Geschichte* [1961] project), see chap. 4 of *Systematic Theology*, vol. 1.

20. Pannenberg, *Basic Questions in Theology*, 1:15.

has offered the most sustained systematic and philosophically oriented development of the idea that the Trinity is the fullness of the historical process."[21] Therefore, in tandem with the anthropological argumentation, Pannenberg also turns to the history of religions to advance the quest for the credibility of God-talk and the truthfulness of *Christian* claims about the God of the Bible. Against Barth, Pannenberg has restored religion to the central place in theology.[22]

Perhaps surprisingly, his point of departure for assessing the value of religions is the phenomenology of religions,[23] but in terms of a *theological* interpretation and "critical appropriation" of religions.[24] The history of religions represents this endless search for universal truth. Even though Pannenberg believes that God can only be known as God reveals Godself,[25] he also acknowledges the fact that the only way to examine divine revelation is through human religion.[26] For Pannenberg, the significant development in the Jewish view of God, subsequently adopted by Christian theology, was the emergence of monotheism, which against rival ancient religions was able to provide believers with the concept of the unity of the culture. For ancient people, gods were looked upon as the providers of this unity.[27] Consequently, in Israel Yahweh came to be regarded as the one God, who was in control of all spheres of life.[28]

On the basis of monotheism, thus, the one God was also looked upon as the ground of the world as a whole as well as of human life. Consequently, the dispute concerning religious claims finds its resolution in the sphere of the experience of the world, since the world shows that it is determined by God.[29] History and world experience, rather than mythical orientation of religions,[30] becomes

---

21. Grenz, *Rediscovering the Triune God*, 89. Fittingly, Grenz titles chap. 3, which discusses Pannenberg, Moltmann, and Jenson, "The Trinity as the Fullness of History." Ibid., 72.

22. A comprehensive treatment of the topic can be found in Pannenberg, *Systematic Theology,* 1:119–36; see also Wolfhart Pannenberg, *Theology and the Philosophy of Science* (London: Darton, Longman & Todd, 1976), 31.

23. Pannenberg, "Toward a Theology of the History of Religions," in *Basic Questions in Theology,* 2:72.

24. Pannenberg, *Anthropology in Theological Perspective*, p. 18.

25. See especially Pannenberg, *Systematic Theology,* 1:189. Here Pannenberg of course agrees with Barth, even though his approach to revelation is markedly different from his predecessor.

26. The main focus of Pannenberg's treatment of the topic "The Reality of God and the Gods in the Experience of the Religions" is a dialogue between Christianity and ancient religions (rather than Christianity and contemporary religions). Pannenberg, *Systematic Theology,* 1:119–87; the basic ideas are already present in one of his first essays, "Toward a Theology of the History of Religions," in *Basic Questions in Theology,* 2:65–118.

27. Pannenberg, *Systematic Theology,* 1:53; see also Pannenberg, *The Idea of God and Human Freedom*, 130; *Theology and the Philosophy of Science*, pp. 311ff. especially. A full-scale study is Cornelius A. Buller, *The Unity of Nature and History in Pannenberg's Theology* (Lanham, MD: Littlefield Adams, 1996).

28. It is against this background that the exclusive claim to worship only Yahweh can be understood. Pannenberg, *Systematic Theology,* 1:148 especially.

29. See further Pannenberg, *Theology and Philosophy of Science*, 300–303.

30. By saying this, I am not ignoring the fact that Pannenberg also creatively recasts the "myth" in Israelite religion for use in this historical outlook. See Pannenberg, *Systematic Theology*, 1:184–85 especially.

the focal point of the doctrine of God, and thus of the Trinity. "Thus there emerges a coherent scheme of interpreting the reality of the world and of human history in terms of a trinitarian theology."[31]

Yet it is only with reference to eschatology that the final confirmation—or lack thereof—can be waited for.[32] This brings us to the ontology of the future, another salient feature of Pannenberg's view of God. In the 1960s, Pannenberg came to be known, with Moltmann, as a "theologian of hope" (even though the theological pilgrimage of these two theologians, once colleagues, has taken them in different directions). In the theology of hope, God's transcendence was defined less spatially and more in relation to time: God "comes to us from the future." This plays into Pannenberg's understanding of truth.

The truth of Christian claims about God—and thus of theological claims—awaits its final confirmation (or lack thereof) until the end of times.[33] It is only at the End that the deity of the one God is undisputed and evident to all eyes.[34] The unfolding of history, in other words, is "a self-demonstration of God's existence."[35] Truth is thus historical and eschatological.[36] What about in the meantime? Is there any way for us to have at least some kind of certainty before the End? According to Pannenberg, the "[d]ecision regarding their [truth claims] rests with God himself. It will be finally made with the fulfillment of the kingdom of God in God's creation. It is provisionally made in human hearts by the convicting ministry of the Spirit of God."[37] Decisive here is Christ's resurrection from death, a divine confirmation of Christ's claim to be the Son of God and thus the agent to usher in the final victory of God in his kingdom.[38]

In light of all this, it is understandable that for Pannenberg God is the "power on which all finite reality depends"[39] or "the power of the future" determining the future of all that is present.[40] In keeping with this view, the whole of systematic theology is essentially the doctrine of God.[41] Consequently, if the idea of God must be able to illumine not only human life, but also our experience of the

---

31. Pannenberg, *Introduction to Systematic Theology*, 67.

32. Pannenberg, *Systematic Theology*, 1:54–55, 208–13; idem, *Metaphysics and the Idea of God*, trans. Philip Clayton (Grand Rapids: Eerdmans, 1990), 109. Very accurately, then, Pannenberg's turn to history has been described as "a decisive *turn* toward an eschatological theology of history." E. Frank Tupper, *The Theology of Wolfhart Pannenberg* (Philadelphia: Westminster Press, 1973), 20 (italics in original).

33. Pannenberg, *Systematic Theology*, 1:54.

34. Among others, "On Historical and Theological Hermeneutics" and "What Is a Dogmatic Statement," in Pannenberg, *Basic Questions in Theology*, 1:137–210.

35. Pannenberg, *Introduction to Systematic Theology*, 12.

36. Among others, see "What Is Truth?" in Pannenberg, *Basic Questions in Theology*, 2:1–27.

37. Pannenberg, *Systematic Theology*, 1:56.

38. Wolfhart Pannenberg, *Jesus—God and Man*, trans. Lewis L. Wilkins and Duane A. Priebe, 2nd ed. (Philadelphia: Westminster Press, 1977), 67–69.

39. Pannenberg, *Introduction to Systematic Theology*, 8.

40. Pannenberg, *Theology and the Kingdom of God*, ed. Richard John Neuhaus (Philadelphia: Westminster Press, 1969), 55–56.

41. Pannenberg, *Systematic Theology*, 1:59–61; idem, *Introduction to Systematic Theology*, 8, 13; idem, *Basic Questions in Theology*, 2:1–27.

world,[42] then theology should also.[43] Decisive here is whether "the idea of God corresponds to an actual reality . . . [and is] able to illumine human existence, as well as our experience of the world as a whole."[44]

Now, in light of his overall approach to systematic theology and theological method, what is the shape and content of the doctrine of the Trinity in Pannenberg? Let me first highlight his method and then delve into an exposition of key features before coming to critical reflections.

REVISING THE TRINITARIAN CANONS

Probably because of the late appearance in his long theological career of the three-volume *Systematic Theology* (in German, 1988–93; ET, 1991–98), the doctrine of the Trinity was not at the forefront of Pannenberg's production.[45] Before the appearance of that magnum opus, however, Pannenberg announced his desire to produce a dogmatic presentation "more thoroughly Trinitarian than any example I know of."[46] As a result, there emerged a systematic theology fully centered and built on the doctrine of the Trinity. For Pannenberg, all systematic theology is but an expansion of the doctrine of God, and therefore it is only with the consummation of the world from creation to redemption to the eschatological coming of the kingdom that the doctrine of God finally comes to its final goal.[47] Therefore, Trinity is not just *a* topic in the Christian dogmatics, nor an appendix to the discussion of the one God. Rather, the only way to give an account of the Christian God is to speak of Father, Son, and Spirit.

> The moment it appears that the one God can be better understood without rather than with the doctrine of the Trinity, the latter seems to be a super-fluous addition to the concept of the one God even though it is reverently treated as a mystery of revelation. Even worse, it necessarily seems to be incompatible with the divine unity.[48]

In keeping with this basic methodological choice, Pannenberg reverses the order of traditional systematic treatment in beginning with the doctrine of the

---

42. Pannenberg, *Systematic Theology,* 1:92–93 especially.

43. Pannenberg "What Is Truth?" in *Basic Questions in Theology,* 2:1.

44. L. Miller and Stanley J. Grenz, eds., *Fortress Introduction to Contemporary Theologies* (Minneapolis: Fortress, 1998), 132.

45. Cf. Ronald J. Feenstra and Cornelius Plantinga Jr., eds., *Trinity, Incarnation, and Atonement: Philosophical and Theological Essays,* Library of Religious Philosophy 1 (Notre Dame, IN: University of Notre Dame Press, 1989), 3.

46. W. Pannenberg, "God's Presence in History," *Christian Century* 11 (March 1981): 263. Many commentators have acknowledged this: Roger E. Olson, "Wolfhart Pannenberg's Doctrine of the Trinity," *Scottish Journal of Theology* 43, no. 2 (1990): 175–76; Grenz, *Reason for Hope,* 44.

47. Pannenberg, *Systematic Theology,* 1:447–48; see also pp. 59–61, 335.

48. Ibid., 1:291.

Trinity and only after that moving to the question of the unity and attributes of God.[49] Whereas Barth and Rahner can be challenged because of their tendency to elevate the oneness of God at the expense of threeness, and Moltmann and Catherine Mowry LaCugna (to be studied in the North American section) for emphasizing the threeness to the point of threatening the oneness, Pannenberg wants to carefully negotiate both extremes. He begins with the threeness but never loses sight of the oneness of God; indeed, he regards the Trinity as "concrete monotheism."[50] In keeping with this effort, a commentator helpfully titles the two-part discussion of the doctrine of God in Pannenberg "The Threeness of the One God of Revelation" and the "Unity of the Triune God."[51]

Why this approach? Why begin with threeness when speaking of one God? Pannenberg sees the order and content of his Trinitarian doctrine built on revelation.[52] Anchoring Trinitarian theology to revelation means of course following Barth, yet with significant departure from what Pannenberg sees as the main weakness of his predecessor, namely, basing the doctrine on a *formal* principle rather than concrete salvation history as it is unfolding in Scripture.[53] The place of the Trinitarian discussion in the first volume of *Systematic Theology* is methodologically appropriate: it follows the chapter on revelation and precedes the chapter on the unity and attributes of God.[54] By taking his departure from revelation, Pannenberg is also following Rahner. Rather than basing the doctrine on abstract speculation of God's life *in se,* the starting point is the concrete salvation history, *oikonomia.* It is a faithful gateway to the knowledge of the Father, Son, and Spirit as one God.

Because Pannenberg wants to go beyond the formal, logical principle drawn from scriptural teaching, he more specifically takes as his point of departure for the doctrine of the Trinity the coming of Jesus as the announcer and inaugurator of his Father's kingdom. Submission to his heavenly Father as "Son" forms the concrete basis for the Trinitarian self-distinction;[55] this is of course also the beginning point for early Christology, and it will also involve the self-distinction of the Spirit from and unity with Father and Son.[56] Beginning with the coming and self-distinction of Jesus as Son means also—in keeping with contemporary Trinitarian canons—tying the doctrine to (salvation) history.

49. Chap. 5 in *Systematic Theology*, vol. 1, is titled "The Trinitarian God," and chap. 6, "The Unity and Attributes of the Divine Essence."

50. Pannenberg, *Systematic Theology*, 1:335.

51. Grenz, *Reason for Hope*, 46, 54, respectively. I have adopted the first heading here.

52. Pannenberg, *Systematic Theology*, 1:299; see also p. 304, among others.

53. On criticism of Barth in this respect, see Pannenberg, *Systematic Theology*, 1:296, 303, and the discussion in critical reflections on Barth above.

54. Chap. 4 on Revelation, chap. 5 on Trinity, and chap. 6 on Unity and Attributes, in Pannenberg, *Systematic Theology*, vol. 1.

55. The first section in chap. 5, "The Trinitarian God," is appropriately titled "The God of Jesus and the Beginning of the Doctrine of the Trinity," in Pannenberg, *Systematic Theology*, 1:259.

56. See especially Pannenberg, *Systematic Theology*, 1:263.

Yet another methodological remark is in order. In that Pannenberg's under-standing of truth is historical, it comes as no surprise that his discussion of the doctrine of the Trinity (as well as any other major locus in theology) is embed-ded in a careful, critical tracing of the history of developments. It means that this German theologian, practically speaking, travels through the whole history of the doctrine and, unlike most theologians, is not content to dialogue only with patristic contributions; he goes all the way through the medieval and Reforma-tion periods to modernity and finally to the twentieth century. Even when depart-ing from tradition—beginning from the radical departure in the order of discussion—he puts in practice the conviction that truth is something that evolves in the course of history.

THE THREENESS OF THE ONE GOD OF REVELATION

The genesis of the Trinitarian doctrine, as mentioned, is the coming of Jesus and his relation to his heavenly Father, whose rule was dawning.[57] As Son, Jesus dis-tinguished himself from the Father in submitting himself to his Father and the service of the coming of the kingdom;[58] he "also realized that he was very closely linked to the Father in his work. . . . [S]ince he proclaimed that the Father's king-dom is not only imminent but also dawning in his own work, no room is left for any future talk about God which will replace his [own talk]."[59] That the Son is the eternal counterpart of the Father was only seen in light of the resurrection, which serves as the divine confirmation of Jesus' claim to sonship.[60] In Pannen-berg's estimation, the church's emerging view of the deity of the Son was not nec-essarily related to the idea of preexistence (even though that idea established itself quite soon);[61] rather, the decisive factor in the establishment of the divinity was the application of the term *Kyrios* to Jesus.[62]

The third member of the Trinity, the Spirit, is understood from the beginning as the medium of the communion of Jesus with the Father as well as the medium of our participation in Christ.[63] Pannenberg summarizes the starting point of the rise of the Trinitarian understanding:

> The involvement of the Spirit in God's presence in the work of Jesus and in the fellowship of the Son with the Father is the basis of the fact that the Chris-tian understanding of God found its developed and definitive form in the doctrine of the Trinity and not in a biunity of the Father and the Son. . . .

---

57. Ibid., 1:259ff.
58. Ibid., 1:263; so also p. 309, among others.
59. Ibid., 1:263–64.
60. Ibid., 1:264–65.
61. See further ibid., 1:265.
62. Ibid., 1:265–66.
63. Ibid., 1:266–67.

The N[ew] T[estament] statements do not clarify the interrelations of the three but they clearly emphasize the fact that they are interrelated.[64]

The deity of the Spirit came to be established because of the Spirit's role as the medium of the fellowship; otherwise, "the Christian doctrine of the deity of the Spirit would be a purely external addition to the confession of the relation of the Son to the deity of the Father."[65]

Starting with the concrete salvation history as revealed in Scripture and building on the idea of self-distinction and relationality, Pannenberg is offering an alternative to traditional ways of deriving the Trinitarian persons from the concept of God as one being. In keeping with tradition's habit of beginning with one God and only then considering the threeness, the plurality of persons had been considered to derive from the idea of God as either love (beginning with Augustine and refined by Richard of St. Victor, among others) or spirit (Hegel and German idealism). This, however, cannot establish threeness. These attempts, including Barth's with all his desire to build on revelation, end up with an idea of the "one divine subjectivity" that does not leave room for a genuine plurality of persons in the one God.[66] Pannenberg clarifies and sharpens the effort to establish the threeness by a careful systematic-philosophical construction by borrowing the idea of "self-distinction" from Hegel.[67] According to this idea "person" is a relational, correlative term: one gains one's personality by giving oneself to one's counterpart; thus identity is gained in separation from, yet also in dependence on, the other. Self-distinction and mutual dependency are the key ideas Pannenberg takes from this, and he makes them leading themes in the way he further develops the distinctness of persons in unity. Fittingly enough, that section of Trinitarian discussion is titled "The Reciprocal Self-Distinction of Father, Son, and Spirit as the Concrete Form of Trinitarian Relations."[68]

SELF-DISTINCTION AND MUTUAL DEPENDENCY IN THE TRINITY

By subjecting himself as creature to his heavenly Father, Jesus shows himself to be the Son, and so at one with the Father from eternity, as the Father's counterpart: "The eternal God cannot be directly thought of as from eternity related

64. Ibid., 1:268–69.
65. Ibid., 1:268; so also pp. 304–5.
66. Ibid., 1:296, 298. Pannenberg, though, acknowledges the fact that starting from the idea of love is closer to the Christian concept of God than the approach of German idealism, which takes divine self-consciousness as the basis for Trinity (p. 298). An extended discussion of the role of the Trinity in theology, including the order of discussion, can be found in ibid., 1:280–99.
67. As discussed in his christological work *Jesus—God and Man*, 181–83, 340. See also W. Pannenberg, *Grundfragen systematischer Theologie: Gesammelte Aufsätze*, vol. 2 (Göttingen: Vandenhoeck & Ruprecht, 1980), 109.
68. Pannenberg, *Systematic Theology*, 1:308.

to a temporal and creaturely reality unless this is itself eternal, as a correlate of the eternal God."[69] In other words, this self-distinction (which of course is not opposite to but another side of the unity) is the basis for affirming the sonship of Jesus in relation to the Father. What about the Father's relation to the Son? Could something similar be said of that? And furthermore: How is the idea of self-distinction to be applied to the Spirit's relation to the Father and Son and vice versa?

Unlike tradition, which assigns the Father the status of being without origin (and conversely, the origin of the deity of Son and Spirit), Pannenberg argues for a genuine mutuality, appropriately labeled by Ted Peters as the principle of "dependent divinity."[70] While the relations between the Father and Son are irreversible (Father is not begotten by Son), the Father's fatherhood is dependent on the Son. As the holder of lordship and position of rule (Matt. 11:27; 28:18; Luke 10:22; Phil. 2:9ff.) given to him by the Father, the Son destroys "every rule and every authority and power," and he "must reign until he has put all his enemies under his feet" (1 Cor. 15:24–25) and finally hands the kingdom back to the Father in the eschatological consummation. In keeping with Rahner's rule (while not mentioned here), the intra-Trinitarian relations can be inferred from the mutual relations between the historical person of Jesus and the Father.[71]

> In the handing over of lordship from the Father to the Son, and its handing back from the Son to the Father, we see *a mutuality in their relationship* that we do not see in the begetting. By handing over lordship to the Son the Father makes his kingship *dependent* on whether the Son glorifies him and fulfils his lordship by fulfilling his mission. The self-distinction of the Father from the Son is not just that he begets the Son but that he hands over all things to him, so that his kingdom and his own deity are now *dependent* upon the Son. The rule of the kingdom of the Father is not so external to his deity that he might be God without his kingdom.[72]

As the last sentence indicates, Pannenberg makes the kingdom, the rule of God, an integral part of the Father's person. "The deity of God is his rule" is a claim he has presented in various places during his career.[73] Unlike Moltmann but in agreement with Barth, he sees creation as not necessary to the Deity because inner-

---

69. Ibid., 1:311. Here we see also the differentiation between the human, creaturely, and divine reality, expressed in classical Christology in terms of two natures. While Pannenberg basically affirms that idea, he doesn't find the terminology of two natures the best possible way of expressing it. Ibid.

70. Ted Peters, *God as Trinity: Relationality and Temporality in Divine Life* (Louisville, KY: Westminster John Knox Press, 1993), 135.

71. Pannenberg, *Systematic Theology,* 1:312–13 (the biblical passage is quoted on p. 312).

72. Ibid., 1:313 (italics mine).

73. Wolfhart Pannenberg, *Theology and the Kingdom of God,* ed. Richard John Neuhaus (Philadelphia: Westminster Press, 1969), 55–56; Pannenberg, *Basic Questions in Theology,* 2:240–42. This has been labeled "Pannenberg's Principle" by Roger Olson, "Pannenberg's Doctrine of the Trinity," 199. Karl Barth expressed this kind of idea in his *Church Dogmatics,* I/1, *The Doctrine of the Word of God,* trans. G. W. Bromiley (Edinburgh: T & T Clark, 1975), 349.

Trinitarian relations can be understood as actions.[74] Since God created the world, its existence is not compatible with his deity apart from his lordship.[75]

Here is the place to look at the meaning of the cross for inner-Trinitarian relations. Going in the same direction as Moltmann but not quite as far, Pannenberg agrees with his German colleague that "in the death of Jesus the deity of his God and Father was at issue," and that therefore it is an event that does "affect eternal placidity of the Trinitarian life of God." Yet to speak of the "death of God" or even "directly of the death of God in the Son" is not acceptable. Rather, the ultimate humiliation and acceptance of death is the ultimate consequence of the Son's self-distinction from his Father. At the same time, the Father's deity is questioned and thus the Father shares the suffering of the Son in his "sym-pathy with the passion."[76]

Similarly to Moltmann, Pannenberg sees the cross as highlighting the role of the Spirit. For Pannenberg that comes to the fore in the act of the Spirit as the one who raises the Son from the dead (Rom. 1:4; 8:11; 1 Cor. 15:44ff.; 1 Tim. 3:16b), yet together with the Father (Acts 2:24 among others). "All three persons of the Trinity are at work in this event." Furthermore, the role of the Spirit as separate from and yet united with Father and Son is manifested in the glorifying of the Son. "By glorifying the Son, the Spirit also glorifies the Father and their indissoluble fellowship." As a consequence, here is then "a self-distinction which constitutes the Spirit a separate person from the Father and the Son and relates him to both."[77] While integrally related to the Son, the Spirit cannot be thought of as proceeding from the Son (*filioque*). "The Spirit proceeds only from the Father and is received by the Son." The fallacy of tradition is the look at the Trinitarian relations from the perspective of origin rather than reciprocity.[78]

In keeping with the principle of mutual self-distinction and dependency among Trinitarian members, Pannenberg critiques the idea of Father, Son, and Spirit as different modes of one divine subject and regards them rather as "living realizations of separate centers of action."[79] How this idea of separate consciousnesses can be reconciled with the unity of divine essence will be discussed in what follows.

If self-distinctions are the key to affirming the personhood of Father, Son, and Spirit in the one God,[80] it means also that "the relations between the persons are constitutive not merely for their distinctions but also for their deity."[81] This, however, does not mean that the monarchy of the Father is set aside. On the contrary:

74. Pannenberg, *Systematic Theology*, 2:1.
75. Ibid., 1:313.
76. Ibid., 1:314.
77. Ibid., 1:314–15 (all quotations in p. 315).
78. Ibid., 1:317–120 (quotation p. 317).
79. Ibid., 1:319.
80. Ibid., 1:320.
81. Ibid., 1:323; see also p. 329. Pannenberg acknowledges this insight by Robert W. Jenson, *The Triune Identity: God according to the Gospel* (Philadelphia: Fortress, 1982), 119.

"By their work the Son and Spirit serve the monarchy of the Father. Yet the Father does not have his kingdom or monarchy without the Son and Spirit, but only through them."[82] Nor does this mean that the subordination of the Son to his Father would imply ontological inferiority. By subjecting himself to the Father, the Son is "himself in eternity the locus of the monarchy of the Father" and so one with the Father and Spirit. The monarchy of the Father is not the presupposition but the result of the working together of three persons, and as such is then "the seal of their unity."[83]

The idea of self-distinction and resulting dependency among three persons leads Pannenberg to revisit traditional terminology as it relates to the coming of the Son and the Spirit. The Christian East has used the terms "generation" of the Son and "procession" of the Spirit; the West has used "procession" for both and made the distinction between the begetting of the Son and the breathing of the Spirit (John 20:22). "These processions in the eternal divine substance resulted in the persons of the Son and Spirit, who for their part are distinguished by relations (the Father actively begetting, the Son passively begotten, the Spirit passively breathed." Categorically tradition has thus separated the processions from all eternity from the sending of the Son and Spirit in time. Pannenberg finds this terminology both exegetically and theologically wanting and misleading because it does not adequately express the idea of mutuality and because it misses the point that biblical references to Jesus' begetting relate no less to the historical Son than statements about his sending; the same applies to the Spirit's breathing and the giving of the Spirit as gift.[84] Therefore, Pannenberg uses terms that suggest self-distinction and mutuality such as handing over, giving back, glorification, (voluntary) submission, and so forth.

THE UNITY OF GOD AS THE CHALLENGE TO CHRISTIAN THEOLOGY

As mentioned in the context of Moltmann's theology above, for advocates of the social analogy, the threeness is a given whereas the challenge is the establishment of the unity. This also applies to Pannenberg even though he is not a social Trinitarian. Methodologically Pannenberg begins with the idea of threeness rather than unity, and materially his starting point is the coming of the Son as explicated in biblical salvation history. Yet unlike Moltmann and many other social Trinitarians, Pannenberg's Trinitarian doctrine also has similarity to traditional approaches in that he affirms a single divine essence, as the title for chapter 6 on unity in *Systematic Theology*, volume 1, indicates: "The Unity and Attributes of the Divine Essence." Theologically it is also noteworthy that even when speak-

---

82. Pannenberg, *Systematic Theology,* 1:324.
83. Ibid., 1:325.
84. Ibid., 1:305–7 (quotation p. 305).

ing of self-distinction, the main way of affirming the separate personhoods of Father, Son, and Spirit, Pannenberg does not lose sight of the importance of unity, as shown by the subheading "Distinction and Unity of the Divine Persons."[85] Indeed, while threeness is the starting point for considering the Christian God, that does not compromise unity but rather helps to establish it: "For beyond the unity of God no more can be said about God. . . . Thus, the doctrine of the Trinity is in fact concrete monotheism in contrast to the notions of an abstract transcendence of the one God and abstract notions of a divine unity that leave no place for plurality."[86]

In a way that is similar to his view of the threeness, Pannenberg looks critically at tradition and finds many ways of affirming unity less than satisfactory.[87] He rejects the traditional way of establishing unity on the person of the Father as deity since it precludes mutuality and dependency.[88] The idea of God as the divine subject affirmed in various ways from Augustine to idealism to Barth is no more convincing for the simple reason that it truncates the principle of self-differentiation; one divine subject does not allow for the idea of divine persons as centers of consciousness and action nor does it link God to the economy of salvation in a proper way; thus a subtle modalism results, making God immune to world happenings.[89] Pannenberg is more sympathetic to the effort to base unity on perichoresis as Moltmann has done (and many have followed, such as Leonardo Boff and Millard J. Erickson, to be discussed). Yet, as noted in the context of Moltmann's theology, perichoresis presupposed another basis for unity; it merely manifests that unity. The starting point of perichoresis is trinity rather than unity.[90] Neither is the idea of establishing unity with the help of the Father's monarchy totally satisfactory. Pannenberg does speak of the Father's monarchy, as mentioned above, yet not as a presupposition but rather as the result of mutual activity in that the Son and Spirit serve the coming of God's rule.[91]

What is Pannenberg's own approach to establishing unity? Summarizing his complex and at times somewhat ambiguous discussion is challenging. Yet the outline is clear. Agreeing with tradition that the concept of "essence" is needed to affirm the unity of three persons, Pannenberg also revises this concept radically in order to move beyond the now-disputed substance ontology of the past. He conceives "the divine essence as the epitome of the personal relations among

85. Ibid., 1:300.
86. Ibid., 1:335–36.
87. For summary statements, see ibid., 1:334, 342. For a helpful short discussion, see Grenz, *Reason for Hope*, 52.
88. Pannenberg, *Systematic Theology*, 1:311–12, 314; see also p. 279.
89. Wolfhart Pannenberg, "Problems of a Trinitarian Doctrine of God," *Dialog* 26, no. 4 (Fall 1987): 251; See Pannenberg, *Systematic Theology*, 1:283–84, 287 for Augustine; 295–96 on Barth; and 357 for the importance of linking God's essence to the world.
90. Pannenberg, *Systematic Theology*, 1:334.
91. Ibid., 1:324–26 especially.

Father, Son, and Spirit."[92] The reason is simple: "We cannot connect with this any attempt to derive the trinitarian threeness from the unity of the divine essence. The task is simply to envision as such the unity of the divine life and work that is manifest in the mutual relations of Father, Son and Spirit. This requires a concept of essence that is not external to the category of relations."[93] Relationality not only helps move beyond the outdated substance ontology but also ties the discussion of the unity to the economy of salvation, including the coming of the kingdom. Therefore, the discussion of unity—as the heading for this section from Pannenberg illustrates—has to do also with attributes of God, which he classifies in two major categories, namely, infinity and love (based on the two biblical "definitions" of God, God as spirit and as love). Consequently, "discussion of the unity is a task for a doctrine of God's nature and attributes in the context of Christian theology" as it deals with all major topics from creation to Christology to ecclesiology to eschatology.[94]

"THE UNITY AND ATTRIBUTES OF THE DIVINE ESSENCE"[95]

In order to establish the link between God's essence, unity-in-threeness, and the economy of salvation, Pannenberg corrects the tradition's view according to which God's existence and essence can be gleaned from the work of creation whereas only revelation gives knowledge of the Trinity. Consequently, the unity became the main problem since the fourth century.[96] "In his estimation, the solution to this problem lies in viewing the divine attributes as arising out of the activity of God in the world, for God's essence (the divine "whatness") is bound up with God's existence (the divine "thereness"), and this existence is found only in the trinitarian persons."[97] To speak of the acts of God in the world and thus of God's essence from eternity to eternity, however, is not a function of analogical language (as in much of tradition) but of doxology. The reason for the need for doxological language has to do with Christian theology's insistence on God as incomprehensible.[98]

92. Ibid., 1:334. In order to establish a relational view of essence, Pannenberg appropriates critically and corrects the traditional relationship in Christian philosophy and theology, going back to the Middle Ages, of regarding God as currently existing being, which does not entail relationality. Ibid., 1:347–359, titled "The Distinction between God's Essence and Existence."
93. Pannenberg, *Systematic Theology,* 1:334–35, 366–67.
94. Ibid., 1:355.
95. The heading of this section is from chap. 6, ibid., 1:337.
96. Ibid., 1:341–42.
97. Grenz, *Rediscovering the Triune God,* 99.
98. This argumentation is developed in the first three sections of chap. 6 on unity in Pannenberg, *Systematic Theology,* vol. 1, chap. 6: §1, "The Majesty of God and the Task of Rational Discussion of Talk about God"; §2, "The Distinction between God's Essence and Existence"; and §3, "God's Essence and Attributes and the Link between Them in Action." For doxology, see Wolfhart Pannenberg, "Analogy and Doxology," in *Basic Questions in Theology,* 2 vols. (Philadelphia: Fortress, 1970), 1:211–38; for a brief statement, see Pannenberg, *Systematic Theology,* 1:55–56.

Correlating the idea of God's incomprehensibility with the infinite builds a bridge for Pannenberg to talk about "the infinite unity of his essence," which goes back to Gregory of Nyssa and was picked up by Duns Scotus. Descartes's development and application of this idea to the concept of God, however, is the philosophical basis for Pannenberg. While everything finite is limited by the infinite, infinity not only transcends but also embraces all that is finite (otherwise, infinity would not result).[99] At the same time Pannenberg is somewhat critical of the Cartesian idea according to which the insight of infinity already constitutes the knowledge of God; for Pannenberg that kind of "knowledge" is still confused and unthematized. As "incurably religious," the human person can grasp something of God, God's unthematized existence against the horizon of infinity, yet it is named the essence of the Christian God only by virtue of observing God's activities in the world. If God is the all-determining reality, God's presence is to be "felt" everywhere. Being relational in essence, God acts in the world as Father, Son, and Spirit—the "three forms of the existence of God"[100]—both being present and transcending the world. "The essence of things comes to manifestation in existence as a specific essence which is distinct from all others. It distinguishes itself from others by its attributes."[101]

The idea of infinity is described in the Bible as the idea of God as spirit and love. From the time of patristic theology, God as has been conceived of as reason and will, that is, mind. To Pannenberg the concept of "spirit" is superior.[102] Divine essence, thus, is understood by Pannenberg as the "incomprehensible field." According to him, "the presence of God's Spirit in his creation can be described as a field of creative presence, a comprehensive field of force that releases event after event into finite existence."[103] In this sense, God "is the 'field' in which creation and history exists."[104] This "field," spirit, is not only the impersonal presence of God but also the manifestation of the three Trinitarian persons. "The deity as field can find equal manifestation in all three persons."[105] The notion of Spirit theologically, thus, denotes the third person of the Trinity as well

99. Pannenberg, *Systematic Theology,* 1:349–51.

100. Ibid., 1:358–59.

101. Ibid., 1:359.

102. When the Fathers wanted to describe the infinite spiritual essence of God, they did so in terms of "reason" (or will) to escape the absurd implications of another option, namely, God as corporeal (thus including attributes such as divisibility, composition, extension, and so on) because of Stoic philosophy's idea of "spirit" (*pneuma*) as some type of fine matter. Today, those fears are no longer with us, and so—rather than viewing God as the highest reason, which takes us down a path alien to the biblical view of God that does not set "spirit" and "body" in such an antithesis—to speak of God as Spirit is both biblically and theologically more adequate. Furthermore, "spirit" in the Bible (as already shown) does not stand for reason but for the "source of life." Pannenberg, *Systematic Theology,* 1:370–74, especially. See further V.-M. Kärkkäinen, "'The Working of the Spirit of God in Creation and in the People of God': The Pneumatology of Wolfhart Pannenberg," *Pneuma* 26, no. 1 (Fall 2004): 17–35.

103. Pannenberg, *Systematic Theology,* 1:194.

104. Stanley J. Grenz and Greg Olson, *Twentieth Century Theology: God and the World in a Transitional Age* (Downers Grove, IL: InterVarsity Press, 1992), 194.

105. Pannenberg, *Systematic Theology,* 1:383.

as their shared divine life, their field. The idea of the divine life as a dynamic field sees the divine Spirit, who unites the three persons, as proceeding from the Father, received by the Son, and common to both, so that "precisely in this way he is the force field of their fellowship that is distinct from them both."[106] As a divine field, of course, the Spirit would be impersonal, a view totally alien to Christian theology.[107] It is also clear that the Spirit as person can be thought of only as a concrete form of the one deity like the Father and the Son.

Defining the divine essence in terms of relations, as mentioned, is a key insistence for Pannenberg. It allows the kind of reciprocal, mutually dependent understanding of relations between Father, Son, and Spirit that is, on the one hand, in keeping with his approach and affirming of God's relations with the world, and that is, on the other hand, the key to the principle of the unity of the immanent and economic Trinity.[108] In this understanding, "constitutive for each person of the Trinity are the other two persons and the relation to them. The world, in turn, arises not as a self-unfolding of the divine subject who makes the world but as God's free bringing forth of a world that differs from God out of the overflow of God's love. It is the product of the mutual activity of the Father, Son, and Spirit."[109]

Combining the idea of relationality of the essence and essence as infinite Spirit gives Pannenberg the needed resources to affirm the unity of the Godhead. These insights "now permit us . . . to understand the trinitarian persons, *without derivation* from a divine essence that differs from them, as centers of action of the one movement which embraces and permeates all of them—the movement of the divine Spirit who has his existence only in them."[110] Anticipating the charge that this perichoresis is only secondary, he continues: "The persons are not first constituted in their distinction, by derivation from the Father, and only then united in perichoresis and common action. As modes of being of the one divine life they are always permeated by its dynamic through their mutual relations."[111]

The common activity of three divine persons—against tradition's view[112]—is not enough to affirm unity. However, if activity is understood as "the external working of a will bringing forth works different itself [in which] the actor is 'with oneself' in the other," then, when applied metaphorically to God, the activity can be seen as the manifestation of the unity, in other words, unity between God's being *in se* and in the world. Related to this is another key insight of Pannenberg, namely, divine activity as self-realization. God's activity in the world in bringing the completion of creation manifests God's true nature.[113] Therefore, Pannen-

106. Ibid.
107. Ibid., 1:383–84.
108. Ibid., 1:367.
109. Grenz, *Reason for Hope*, 60.
110. Pannenberg, *Systematic Theology*, 1:385 (italics in the original).
111. Ibid.
112. See further ibid., 1:278.
113. Grenz, *Reason for Hope*, 61–62; Pannenberg, *Systematic Theology*, 1:385–88.

berg can hold on to the true threeness, yet claim the unity of God, because the subject who acts in the world is the eternal essence of God, something alongside—or "beyond"—the three persons, yet not a "fourth" something in addition to Father, Son, and Spirit.[114] This united work also brings the discussion to the kingdom of God as another "seal" of unity:

> The monarchy of the Father is God's absolute lordship. The Son serves it, and so does the glorifying of the Father and the Son by the Spirit. But the monarchy of the Father is mediated by the Son, who prepares the way for it by winning form for it in the life of creatures, and also by the Spirit, who enables creatures to honor God as their Creator by letting them share in the relation of the Son to the Father. *This is the action of the one God* by the Father, Son, and Spirit as it may be seen in light of the eschatological consummation of the kingdom of God in the world. Only herein is the one God the acting God as even before he is already the living God in the fellowship of Father, Son, and Spirit.[115]

By understanding the essence as infinite field—spirit—and in terms of relationality, Pannenberg can say without contradicting his former statement: "By the common action of Father, Son, and Spirit the future of God breaks into the present of creatures, into the world of creation, and on the basis of this divine action the attributes are predicated not merely of the trinitarian persons but also of the divine essence that is common to them all."[116]

This philosophically anchored concept of spirit as field is expressed in biblical teaching and made concrete in the second main nomenclature of God, namely, God as love (1 John 4:8).[117] "Finally, the statement that God is love will prove to be the concrete form of the divine essence that is initially described as Spirit and in terms of the concept of the Infinite."[118] Similarly to the spirit, love is "the one and only essence of God . . . has its existence in the Father, Son, and Holy Spirit . . . and . . . constitutes the unity of the one God in the communion of these three persons."[119] In keeping with the notion of love, each of the three persons achieve their selfhood "ec-statically," in relation to the two others, in the I-Thou relationship.[120]

Against tradition that considers love—as well as unity[121]—to be attributes, Pannenberg considers love the essence of God. Love and unity are related concepts; in

---

114. Pannenberg, *Systematic Theology,* 1:384, 389.
115. Ibid., 1:389 (italics mine); see also p. 325.
116. Pannenberg, *Systematic Theology,* 1:391.
117. For the connection between these concepts, see ibid., 1:395–96. For the discussion between love and trinity, see pp. 422–32.
118. Ibid., 1:396. Similarly, p. 427. In the delineation of attributes, the two categories are thus: The infinity of God: holiness, eternity, omnipotence, and omnipresence (§6) as well as the love of God: goodness, mercy, righteousness, faithfulness, patience, and wisdom.
119. Ibid., 1:428.
120. Ibid., 1:430.
121. Ibid., 1:442–44.

the work of love the unity of God finds its concrete form.[122] "Because God is love, having once created a world in his freedom, he finally does not have his own existence without this world, but over against it and in it in the process of its ongoing consummation."[123] In the final analysis, then, the establishment of divine unity is "bound up with the work of the three persons in the world (the economic Trinity), which work—and hence which unity—is completed only eschatologically and is linked to the relations found in the eternal life of the trinitarian persons (the immanent Trinity)."[124] Pannenberg summarizes:

> The thought of love makes it possible conceptually to link the unity of the divine essence with God's existence and qualities and hence to link the immanent Trinity and the economic Trinity in the distinctiveness of their structure and basis. This is because the thought of divine love shows itself to be of trinitarian structure, so that we can think of the trinitarian life of God as an unfolding of his love. It is also because the thought of love permits us to think of God's relation to the world as grounded in God.[125]

CRITICAL REFLECTIONS

The achievements of Pannenberg's ambitious and rigorous Trinitarian program are many and groundbreaking. First of all, more so than any other contemporary theologian, he has succeeded in making the Trinity not only the basis for the Christian doctrine of God—so that "the Trinity is not derived from God's essence; the Trinity is God's essence"[126]—but also of all of systematics.[127] This means, second, nothing else than turning upside down the classical Trinitarian canons: rather than beginning with one God, theology should begin with God as Trinity. Third, further developing Barth's groundbreaking idea of anchoring Trinity in revelation, he has made the doctrine arise out of salvation history as revealed in Scripture. Fourth, he has offered a dynamic revision of terminology in keeping with the idea of mutuality. Fifth, more strongly than anyone else, he has offered a proposal in which the two archenemies of Trinitarian theologies of the past and contemporary times—tritheism and unity on the one hand and subordinationism and modalism on the other hand—are claimed to be defeated. Finally, more vocally than anyone else, he has connected Trinitarian theology with the search for universal truth, public truth.

122. Ibid., 1:445.
123. Ibid., 1:447.
124. Grenz, *Rediscovering the Triune God*, 100; also see Pannenberg, *Systematic Theology*, 1:447.
125. Pannenberg, *Systematic Theology*, 1:447.
126. Richard Rice, "Wolfhart Pannenberg's Crowning Achievement: A Review of His *Systematic Theology*," *Andrews University Seminary Studies* 37, no. 1 (Spring 1998): 59.
127. See, e.g., Christoph Schwöbel, "Rational Theology in Trinitarian Perspective: Wolfhart Pannenberg's *Systematic Theology*," *Journal of Theological Studies*, n.s., 47, no. 2 (October 1996): 504; Rice, "Wolfhart Pannenberg's Crowning Achievement," 70.

At the same time, some of these praises can also be lifted up as challenges and invitations for further clarification: concerning method, namely, proceeding from threeness to unity because, so Pannenberg claims, that is the way revelation is open to questioning. Historically, the unity of God (Deut 6:4) was revealed first; threeness came only later in the New Testament. The idea of progressive revelation, beginning from the oneness and culminating in the threeness, would be in keeping with Pannenberg's insistence on the truth as historical, evolving. How would Pannenberg respond? He hasn't done so, but perhaps he would refer to the ontological priority of the future. It is from the future, from the coming of the Son and giving of the Spirit in anticipation of the coming end, that a specifically *Christian* doctrine of God can be formulated, rather than from a pre-Christian idea of one God.[128] With all due applause for Pannenberg's rigorous effort to argue for Christian truth in general and Trinitarian truth in particular with the help of rational means, it has also raised the question of an overemphasis on rationality.[129]

Pannenberg's idea of three divine persons as distinct centers of consciousness and action has naturally given rise to the charge of tritheism. Many believe that this idea in itself leads to tritheism.[130] Pannenberg is of course not tritheist.[131] On the other hand, it is true that his "idea of mutual reciprocity between the persons drives him *in the direction of tritheism.*"[132] Roger Olson speaks to the point when he says that the lack of clarity about whether the one God is Father or the three together or both may legitimately raise the question of tritheistic tendencies.[133] Even with these challenges, I do not see much danger of tritheism, even with the idea of distinct consciousnesses, because of Pannenberg's relentless insistence on the essence of God—unlike social analogy advocates—and his idea of God as spirit, as divine field.[134] This brings us to the discussion of the

---

128. See further Grenz, *Reason for Hope*, 69–70.

129. Few have gone as far as Paul D. Molnar, who makes the surprising charge that Pannenberg's unwavering accent on rationality and coherence of truth, rather than anchoring the truth in God, makes it "grounded in the *perception* of the coherence and unity of all that is true," and thus subjective. Paul D. Molnar, "Some Problems with Pannenberg's Solution to Barth's 'Faith Subjectivism,'" *Scottish Journal of Theology* 48 (1995): 322 (italics in original). J. A. Colombo similarly wonders if Pannenberg's heavy emphasis on the historicity becomes counterproductive. J. A. Colombo, *An Essay on Theology and History: Studies in Pannenberg, Metz, and the Frankfurt School* (Atlanta, GA: Scholars Press, 1990), 46.

130. See, e.g., John L. Gresham Jr., "The Social Model of the Trinity and Its Critics," *Scottish Journal of Theology* 46, no. 3 (1993): 330, 342; William Hill, *The Three-Personed God: Trinity as a Mystery of Salvation* (Washington, DC: Catholic University of America Press, 1982), 254.

131. Contra Henri Blocher, "Immanence and Transcendence in Trinitarian Theology," in *The Trinity in a Pluralistic Age: Theological Essays on Culture and Religion*, ed. Kevin J. Vanhoozer (Grand Rapids: Eerdmans, 1997), 107.

132. Robert E. Letham, *The Holy Trinity: In Scripture, History, Theology, and Worship* (Phillipsburg, NJ: P&R Publishing, 2004), 316 (italics mine).

133. Olson, "Pannenberg's Doctrine of the Trinity," 191, 195.

134. See here the helpful comment by Michael L. Chiavone, "The Unity of God as Understood by Four Twentieth-Century Trinitarian Theologians: Karl Rahner, Millard Erickson, John Zizioulas, and Wolfhart Pannenberg" (PhD diss., Southeastern Baptist Theological Seminary, Wake Forest, NC, 2005), 243.

ways Pannenberg argues for unity. A related question for Pannenberg has to do with his failure to clarify the claim that the God of Jesus is the Yahweh of the Old Testament.[135] What exactly was Jesus referring to when calling Yahweh his Father: the divine nature or the first person of the Trinity?[136]

Michael Chiavone has labeled Pannenberg's way of establishing the divine unity "the most nuanced" among the several leading theologians he studied.[137] Rightly it has been noted that Pannenberg's position hearkens back to the ancient idea of viewing the essence of God as a genuine *res* and the fundamental location of the divine unity.[138] Yet at the same time it has to be noticed that there is a lot of ambiguity and need for clarification, especially in Pannenberg's effort to establish this unity. In my mind the main question to Pannenberg is the plurality of ways he argues for unity. Since there are several of those—from divine essence to attributes to the idea of God as spirit to God as love to perichoresis to the kingdom of God!—the question naturally arises whether "Pannenberg's many descriptions of the divine essence can coherently and meaningfully refer to a single reality."[139] Problems or at least questions here are many. Even if love and spirit could be somehow regarded as synonymous, how could the third designation, God's rule or kingdom, be fitted in? Furthermore, isn't it the case that at least in some sense these three seem to be connected primarily with different Trinitarian persons: kingdom with the Father, and spirit and love with the Holy Spirit? What about the Son?[140] A comment from a sympathetic, knowledgeable commentator, Roger E. Olson, is illustrative: "His doctrine of the Trinity . . . seems to suffer from the same ambiguity that lies within his entire eschatological ontology."[141] Michael Chiavone's comment, in his recent dissertation on Pannenberg's understanding of unity, while somewhat exaggerated, illustrates frustration among commentators: he says that "the lack of clarity noted in many areas by many authors suggests that his position falls short of 'systematic description.' Without such a systematic description, it is difficult to offer more than a tentative evaluation of Pannenberg's understanding of Trinitarian unity, and even more difficult to heartily endorse it." Chiavone's conclusion is even more cynical; even if an overstatement, it calls for more clarification on Pannenberg's part:

> Pannenberg's understanding of the divine essence, the ground of the divine unity, appears to be fatally flawed. Because love, spirit, and rule are clearly

135. Pannenberg, *Systematic Theology*, 1:260.
136. George H. Tavard, A.A., review of *Systematic Theology*, vol. 1, *One in Christ* 28, no. 4 (1992): 390–91.
137. Chiavone, "Unity of God," 224.
138. Ibid., 244.
139. Ibid., 234.
140. See further ibid., 235–36.
141. Olson, "Pannenberg's Doctrine of the Trinity," 206. (The comment on eschatological ontology relates to the long-standing questioning and critiquing by many commentators as to what exactly is Pannenberg's view of the relationship between God's being and "becoming.") See also Rice, "Wolfhart Pannenberg's Crowning Achievement," 72.

different realities, actually identifying the divine essence with all three is impossible. If the identification is understood as predication, then God is not one in the manners which Pannenberg has suggested. If Pannenberg is using love, spirit, and rule loosely, then all his statements about the divine unity run the risk of becoming meaningless.[142]

In addition to the question of the unity, a major challenge to all writing about Trinitarian theologies in the wake of Rahner is the relationship between the economic and immanent Trinity, certainly for theologians such as Pannenberg and Moltmann who, following Barth, connect the divine life to (salvation) history and world events.[143] In line with Moltmann[144] and a host of other contemporary theologians, Pannenberg makes the Triune God stand in relation to and in some sense, at least, "dependent" on the history of the economy of salvation. As explained above, through the Son and Spirit the Father has made himself dependent upon the course of history.

Pannenberg is more nuanced about the way he relates the divine life to history than Moltmann and many others. Pannenberg negotiates with two extremes. Theological tradition has virtually made the relationship independent as a result of which the life of God *in se* broke loose from its historical moorings, untouched by the course of history. This has made Trinitarian theology one-sided and detached it from the biblical basis.[145]

Revision is needed. Yet Pannenberg is also critical of some contemporary revisions which for him seem to blur totally the distinction. He is critical of both process theology and Moltmann in this regard. While he is sympathetic to Moltmann's idea of the identity of the immanent and economic Trinity, Pannenberg finds problematic the absorption of the immanent Trinity in the economic.[146] Pannenberg rejects process theology's idea of a divine becoming in history if that means that the Triune God achieves reality only by virtue of eschatological consummation. Pannenberg's idea of the dependency of God on the world is not such that it makes God vulnerable, if not prisoner to, the unfolding of history; rather, it is "the dependence of the trinitarian persons upon one another as the kingdom is handed over and handed back in connection with the economy of salvation."[147] While—as said before—having created the world, God cannot be God without his kingdom and thus the consummation of salvation history, it is not that the consummation "brings about" the reality of God but rather that it "is only the locus of the decision that the trinitarian God is always the true God from eternity to eternity." The lordship and deity of God will be manifested at

142. Chiavone, "Unity of God," 240.

143. For a helpful, balanced discussion, see Grenz, *Reason for Hope*, 72–75.

144. For a brief comparison and contrast of Pannenberg and Moltmann, see Grenz, *Rediscovering the Triune God*, 102.

145. Pannenberg, *Systematic Theology*, 1:332–33.

146. As discussed in critical reflections on Moltmann's view; see Pannenberg, *Systematic Theology*, 1:330–31.

147. Pannenberg, *Systematic Theology*, 1:329; see also 331.

the end of history as God shows himself to be the one God he promised to be.[148] "The unity of God in the trinity of persons must also be the basis of the distinction and unity of the immanent Trinity and the economic Trinity."[149]

Clearly, Pannenberg takes Rahner's rule as the basis but expands and reformulates it in a significant way. Whereas for Rahner, the unity of the economic and immanent Trinity is a matter of soteriology and epistemology, as discussed in chapter 6, for Pannenberg that is not enough. For him the rule "means that the doctrine of the Trinity does not merely begin with the revelation of God in Jesus Christ and then work back to a trinity in the eternal essence of God, but that it must constantly link the trinity in the eternal essence of God to his historical revelation, since revelation cannot be viewed as extraneous to his deity."[150] This means that for Pannenberg the unity of the economic and immanent Trinity happens in relation to history and finds its culmination in the eschaton. Unlike the traditional view that external relationships of the Trinity (going out to creation and salvation history) are secondary to the inner-Trinitarian relations, Pannenberg's idea is that history is the arena in which the "handing over," "handing back," and "glorification" take place. As Powell succinctly puts it, "The Trinitarian persons are what they are because of their mutual relations in salvation history."[151] The coming to be of the lordship of the Triune God happens in history as the result of the ministry of the Son and Spirit. This comes to a climax in the eschaton.

So finally, the key to Pannenberg's negotiation of the immanent and economic Trinity lies in his foundational idea of the ontological priority of the future. It is here also that most critical questions have been raised. In relation to Pannenberg's view of revelation, we can say that the eschaton makes explicit what is implicit in revelation. It is anticipated proleptically at the resurrection of Jesus but will become manifested to all at the end. As said above, the "eschatological consummation is only the locus of the decision that the trinitarian God is always the true God from eternity from eternity."[152] In other words, the unity—but not total equation in terms of the immanent being subsumed under the economic—is being established retroactively from the perspective of the future.[153]

Now the question is, "Is a reading back of an eternal Trinity from the end constituted by the rule of God through Jesus and the Spirit in the world a valid

148. Ibid., 1:331–32 (quotation p. 331).

149. Ibid., 1:333.

150. Ibid., 1:328.

151. Samuel Powell, *The Trinity in German Thought* (Cambridge: Cambridge University Press, 2000), 238.

152. Pannenberg, *Systematic Theology,* 1:331.

153. It is a misreading of Pannenberg to say that "the immanent Trinity belongs to the future and is decided by the present, *rather than belonging to eternity and so transcending time*"; see Letham, *Holy Trinity,* 319 (emphasis mine). While the first part of the sentence is of course true, the latter part is not, if for no other reason than Pannenberg's understanding of eternity as embracing both time and that which transcends time (eternity).

approach to the immanent Trinity? It does unite the immanent and economic Trinity, but does it not at the same time make the rule of God in history in some measure constitutive of his being?"[154]

We can conclude that while there is unity between the immanent and economic Trinity, there is no subsuming one under the other[155] (as is the tendency in Moltmann's theology). Therefore, a charge such as that the reciprocity and mutual dependence is not *free* reciprocity, since it depends too much on the events in history, is mistaken in my opinion.[156] Pannenberg is fully aware of the danger of making the divine life the function of world events and is critical of views that do so, such as process theology.

Several key concepts that Pannenberg utilizes, especially "field," "infinity," and "self-distinction," have also come under critical scrutiny. It does not take too much thought to raise the critical question of the appropriateness of the field concept for theology.[157] While few would be ready to write off its use, it has met with mixed reaction from the critics. Experts in the sciences have doubted the adequacy of Pannenberg's interpretation of the meaning of "field" in contemporary physics.[158] Since I am not a scientist, I cannot comment on that charge and so leave it to specialists. More to my point is a related question: How adequate theologically is it to take a major concept from the sciences and use it to explain theological realities? One could also put the question like this: Is a concept borrowed from the physical sciences the most appropriate way to describe the essence of deity and the divine life force? A debated question among Pannenberg's critics is whether he really identifies the Spirit as a field or just uses the language analogically. I think Pannenberg is fussy about that.

154. John Thompson, *Modern Trinitarian Perspectives* (New York: Oxford University Press, 1994), 36.

155. Grenz, *Rediscovering the Triune God*, 106, agrees with this judgment. Even a conservative commentator such as Letham with grave concerns is willing in the end to acknowledge this. See Letham, *Holy Trinity*, 318.

156. Paul D. Molnar, *Divine Freedom and the Doctrine of the Immanent Trinity: In Dialogue with Karl Barth and Contemporary Theology* (Edinburgh: T & T Clark, 2002), 152.

157. With Pannenberg, several modern systematicians and pneumatologists have come to speak about the Spirit as field of force or force field, using a standard concept of modern physics: Michael Welker, *God the Spirit* (Minneapolis: Fortress, 1994); Bernd Jochen Hilberath, *Pneumatologie* (Düsseldorf: Patmos, 1994); even Karl Rahner in the 1970s had referred to the concept of "energy field" in his "Experience of Self," in *Theological Investigations*, vol.13, trans. David Bourke (New York: Seabury Press, 1975).

158. A persistent critic of Pannenberg in this respect is John Polkinghorne, "Wolfhart Pannenberg's Engagement with the Natural Sciences," *Zygon* 34, no. 1 (March 1999): 153–55; idem, "Fields and Theology: A Response to Wolfhart Pannenberg," *Zygon* 36, no. 4 (December 2001): 796–97. See the important comment by Mark William Worthing, *God, Creation, and Contemporary Physics* (Minneapolis: Augsburg Fortress, 1996), 124; I agree with his balanced judgment. After raising some critical issues, he concludes: "This does not imply that field theories are irrelevant for understanding God's sustaining presence in the world. In fact, Pannenberg is certainly correct in his assessment of their importance in this regard. Likewise, as models of the contingency of all matter they are very fruitful. Field theory certainly has value as a metaphor for God's continuing sustenance of the universe and may well influence the way in which theology confesses this continuing 'creative' presence of God. It would be a mistake, however, to build any part of our theology on a specific physical theory in such a way that the theory provides more than metaphors of meaning but becomes necessary for our theological formulations" (ibid.).

On the one hand, he seems not to make such an identification; instead, the Spirit is "a unique manifestation (singularity) of the field of the divine essentiality."[159] Yet one wonders if Pannenberg goes beyond the analogy, especially when he defines his doctrine of God as spirit with the help of the field concept. Even critics as sympathetic as Ted Peters, after acknowledging the advantages of the field concept for the doctrine of the Spirit in Pannenberg's theology (such as holism, Trinitarian approach, and avoidance of "body" language so prevalent in various current languages of creation), wonder if Pannenberg "rushes in where two-language angels have feared to tread." Peters's gravest concern is that Pannenberg not only uses the term analogically but indeed regards the Spirit as a field and thus brings himself to the "dangers of trying to float a theological assertion aboard a scientific ship" in the waters where "intellectual weather can change suddenly."[160]

A corollary question concerning the use of the field concept is this: How can one avoid making the Spirit impersonal? As a recent textbook summarizes, Pannenberg's view of God as spirit is "a God who is the whole that is greater than the sum of the world's parts but not a gracious, completely free and self-sufficient divine person."[161] Pannenberg is, of course, too good a theologian to ignore this obvious danger in his system, but it seems to me that he does not offer sufficiently clear argument to address it other than to insist that the Spirit his pneumatology speaks about may denote both the (impersonal) life force and the (personal) third person of the Trinity. My own proposal would be to pick up an idea that Pannenberg points toward but does not take further namely, the analogy between human communities ("common spirit") and divine life.[162] Wouldn't a human, interpersonal analogy be more appropriate for speaking about the divine life? That kind of exercise would also glean from the recent communion theologies in various nuances and tie with the social concept of love, otherwise embraced by Pannenberg. What I am saying here is not that we should leave behind the field language, since its potential for building bridges between science and the public sphere is undisputed; what I do insist on is that field language has to be seen as only one of the analogies for speaking of the Spirit.

The other two key concepts mentioned above, "infinity" and "self-distinction," have raised the question of the influence of Hegel on Pannenberg's theology. Some believe Pannenberg has baptized Hegelianism and thus idealism into his

159. Pannenberg, *Systematic Theology,* 2:83; cf. pp. 105, 109, 110. Elsewhere he speaks of the "field theories of science . . . as approximations to the metaphysical reality of the all-pervading spiritual field of God's creative presence in the universe" (Pannenberg, "The Doctrine of Creation and Modern Science," 47).

160. Ted Peters, "Pannenberg on Theology and Natural Science," in *Toward a Theology of Nature,* ed. T. Peters (Louisville, KY: Westminster John Knox Press, 1993), 114. Similarly, the scientist-theologian John Polkinghorne warns seriously about going beyond the analogical language (see further Worthing, *God, Creation, and Contemporary Physics,* 20). Cf. Colin Gunton, *The Triune Creator: A Historical and Systematic Study* (Grand Rapids: Eerdmans, 1998), 175.

161. Grenz and Olsen, *Twentieth Century Theology,* 199.

162. Pannenberg, *Systematic Theology,* 1:383.

systematic theology.[163] While there is no reason to deny the importance of some ideas of Hegel to Pannenberg's systematic reflection—which he himself freely acknowledges[164]—it is also a fact that he uses Hegelian resources critically and at times is critical of some ideas of Hegel. He is especially critical of Hegel's tendency to fuse God and history, rather than having them linked as Pannenberg himself wants to do.[165] I find it odd that merely raising the question of indebtedness to Hegelianism is seen by many commentators as a charge. Hegel is no more dangerous a dialogue partner to Christian theology than anyone else!

Apart from the Hegelian connections, the term "infinity" has been critiqued by Henri Blocher as an unfit term for the holiness of God because it is nonbiblical; in his mind "transcendence" and "otherness" are preferable.[166] I find this critique both misplaced and ironic. Neither is transcendence a biblical term, nor is the idea of transcendence or otherness lacking in Pannenberg's idea of holiness as infinity. Rather, in a way superior to traditional theology, the idea of infinity affirms the transcendence of God in a way that both embraces and transcends the concept.[167]

Regarding the theological *meaning* of self-distinction, Pannenberg has been invited to shed some more light on how exactly the self-distinction of the Son from the Father constitutes his sonship. In other words, how can the Son be God by rejecting and denying deity? "Is this simply God being God in two different ways? Or is it a pointer to two incompatible deities?"[168] It is easy to see why the self-distinction constitutes the humanity of the Son. Yet how it really translates into divinity calls for clarification.

Other challenges to Pannenberg's Trinitarian theology include his failure even to begin to tackle the issue of inclusivity with his insistence on Father as a legitimate name for the first person of the Trinity.[169] Especially by his American

163. For a helpful discussion, see Grenz, *Reason for Hope*, 72.

164. Wolfhart Pannenberg, "The God of History," *Cumberland Seminarian* 19 (Winter/Spring 1981): 34–35.

165. See further ibid., 34.

166. Blocher, "Immanence and Transcendence," 108–9.

167. I don't find the charge convincing that Pannenberg's use of the term "infinity" means establishing the universality of theological claims for truth based on reason in contrast to beginning with revelation. What Pannenberg is doing is looking for philosophical and other resources as tools for advancing systematic argumentation. Christoph Schwöbel, "Wolfhart Pannenberg," in *Modern Theologians: An Introduction to Christian Theology in the Twentieth Century*, ed. David F. Ford, 2 vols. (New York: Blackwell, 1989), 1:286–87.

168. Donald Macleod, "The Christology of Wolfhart Pannenberg," *Themelios* 25, no. 2 (February 2000): 36; so also Chiavone, "Unity of God," 254.

169. The brief discussion in Pannenberg, *Systematic Theology*, 1:260–62 (based on his earlier views presented in Wolfhart Pannenberg, *The Apostles' Creed in the Light of Today's Questions*, trans. Margaret Kohl [Philadelphia: Westminster Press, 1972], 31–33), is disappointing to say the least with his reluctance to dialogue with feminist concerns. Grenz wonders if this is because Pannenberg attempts to write for the long term rather than for the present situation (see Grenz, *Reason for Hope*, 71). If this is really the case, then for me Pannenberg is short-sighted: can we really believe that inclusivism is an idea likely to disappear in the future?

critics, Pannenberg has also been harshly critiqued for a total lack of dialogue with issues such as postmodernity and foundationalism[170]—vital issues for any (Trinitarian) theology claiming to set forth "universal" truth claims!—as well as theological voices outside Europe; not only non-Western and women's voices are lacking, but even theological contributions from the other side of the Atlantic are missing![171]

POSTSCRIPT AND PRELUDE: FROM BARTH TO PANNENBERG TO AMERICA AND BEYOND

The discussion of Pannenberg's Trinitarian theology provides a fitting ending to the consideration of some leading European contributions to contemporary Trinitarian theology as well as a prelude to American responses to and reflections on the Trinity. In Pannenberg, most of the key themes that have shaped Trinitarian theology on the Continent come to full fruition and are being discussed. When we bring Moltmann side by side with him, we can list the following leading themes present in European theologies of the Trinity. These will be picked up by North American respondents and negotiated in a new context:

1. There is an attempt to ground the Trinity in revelation and salvation history rather than abstract speculation.
2. Therefore, Rahner's rule—beginning with *oikonomia* to speak of *theologia*—has become a standard principle even when there is both disagreement about what that really means and more important whether the rule is about epistemology (order of knowing) or about ontology (order of being) or about both.
3. Consequently, Trinity is not only—and for some, such as LaCugna, even primarily—a statement about God's own life but also a statement about God sharing his life with us, God relating to us in salvation.
4. Not only the turn to revelation, but also the turn to history and the world, beginning with Barth and Rahner, has become one of the con-

---

170. Illustrative is here the critique by William C. Placher, "Revealed to Reason: Theology as 'Normal Science,'" *Christian Century*, February 1, 1992, p. 195: "He seems to live in a world where some significant paradigms can be assumed: a world where Western tradition as a whole remains essentially unproblematic, where people generally seem to know what counts as a reasoned argument, and where theologians know what counts as 'theological tradition.' One may envy that world or hate it, feel nostalgia for it, dream of restoring it or dismiss it as good riddance. But many of us trying to write theology in this country find it to be a world in which we do not live." On the lack of postmodern discussion, see also James H. Olthuis, "Symposium: IV. God as True Infinite: Concerns about Wolfhart Pannenberg's *Systematic Theology*, vol. 1," *Calvin Theological Journal* 27, no. 2 (November 1992): 319.

171. So, e.g., Francis Schüssler Fiorenza, review essay of *Systematic Theology*, vol. 1, in *Pro Ecclesia* 2, no. 2 (Spring 1993): 231-32. Brian J. Walsh, "Pannenberg's *Systematic Theology*, vol. 1: A Symposium," *Calvin Theological Journal* 27, no. 2 (November 1992): 306, calls it "contextless theology."

temporary canons of Trinitarian reflection. While pantheistic equation of the divine life with the world has been rejected, an agreement has emerged that intra-Trinitarian relations cannot be divorced from creation and salvation history. While Moltmann has emphasized the cross and Pannenberg the resurrection as the focus among historical events, they agree with the rest that Trinitarian theology apart from the world is a mistaken enterprise.

5. The turn to history has made reflection on the relationship between the economic and immanent Trinity a focal issue.

6. While the primacy of threeness is affirmed enthusiastically—by Moltmann because of his strong social analogy leanings, and by Pannenberg because he sees this in keeping with biblical revelation—there is an acknowledgment of the need to work toward establishing the unity. While Moltmann and Pannenberg work somewhat differently to accomplish this goal—and even if both of them have been critiqued by some for falling short of their goal—it is the unity, rather than the Trinity, that becomes the main task. Threeness becomes a given, unity a task. The unity of God and the relationship between the economic and immanent Trinity—related issues—are the defining issues in contemporary Trinitarian reflection.

7. Because of the centrality of these two questions, namely, the divine unity and the relationship between the economic and immanent Trinity, eschatology has risen to a new appreciation in Trinitarian theology. Reference to eschatology has been the way both Moltmann and Pannenberg, each in their own distinctive way, have attempted to negotiate the unity.

8. Because of the turn to social analogy under the leadership of Moltmann, the practical implications of Trinity are being discussed in a fresh way: what are the implications of the triune life to our view of community, humanity, and the world? Rahner started this move by linking Trinity to salvation history. Moltmann made it a leading theme in his "practically" oriented theology. In other words, for many—but not all, most prominently Pannenberg—Trinity has become a major tool of social and political criticism.

9. Finally, there is an acknowledgment of the need and call for widening the sphere of Trinitarian reflections beyond an academia that is narrow, European, and mostly male-dominated. Positively, this has been enthusiastically suggested by Moltmann, who has not only acknowledged his own limitations but also spoken of the importance of the worldwide fellowship of diversity and plurality. Negatively, Pannenberg's conscious limiting of Trinitarian reflections to European male theologians' ideas, past and present, is an occasion to work for inclusivity so that both men and women, Westerners and non-Westerners, rich and poor, privileged as well as underprivileged—all would be encouraged to give their own

testimonies and reflections. This is where we pick up the continuation of the Trinitarian story in the beginning of the third millennium, by first scrutinizing critically theological voices from North America and then from Asia, Africa, and Latin America.

B. North American Traditions: Dialogue with European Views

Chapter 10

The North American Context for Trinitarian Reflections

THE EMERGING WORLD THEOLOGICAL CENTER

Until recently, Europe was the center of the theological academy in terms of both higher education and publications. The situation is rapidly changing. Not only has the United States established itself as the center of global theological education, with students coming from all continents and many establishing their residence in North America, but that continent has also become the catalyst for the proliferation of theological literature. Part of this dramatic change has to do with linguistic factors: English has replaced German as the universal theological language. Currently all significant theological works written in German and other European languages are being translated into English. Nearly all theological conferences are conducted in or at least translated into English.

At the same time, speaking of "Western" theology still makes sense: Europe and North America share the same cultural and religious background. At present, several factors are shaping the thinking about God in North America; in my thinking, the following are the most formative theologically.[1]

---

1. See further Veli-Matti Kärkkäinen, *The Doctrine of God: A Global Introduction* (Grand Rapids: Baker Academic, 2004), 165–67, 239–40.

First, most theologians writing in North America are either trained in Europe or at least in European traditions. At the same time, because of the difference of cultural milieu, much of their theology involves going beyond the European heritage and asking questions relevant to the multicultural, multidenominational, and somewhat pluralist context of North America. Questions of equality and sexism, postmodernity, culture and cultural diversity are some of the most obvious issues on that side of the Atlantic Ocean. Not that these questions are not discussed in Europe, but in the North American context they create different questions and answers. North America has produced theological movements quite unique to that continent, such as process theology, radical orthodoxy, open theism, and the neoliberalism of Yale, to mention the best-known ones.

Second, North America's ecclesiastical scene differs remarkably from Europe in that the theological currents increasingly include not only evangelical churches with massive theological schools and growing theological productivity, but also various kinds of "Free Churches." In Europe, most churches are declining even if culturally they still occupy a significant role in the society, and outside the traditional churches, very little academic theology is produced. Not so in North America. Theological and ecclesiastical traditions that are almost unknown in European traditions are quite visible across the Atlantic. Fuller Theological Seminary, Pasadena, California, is a prime example of the kind of theological milieu totally unknown in Europe: as one of the world's largest theological seminaries, with several thousand students from all continents, its influence goes well beyond the evangelical movement that gave rise to its birth. Currently it is graduating more students with highest degrees in theology from mainline denominations such as the Presbyterian Church (U.S.A.) than any other American school while also training more students from evangelical, pentecostal, and independent churches than probably any other school in the whole world.

Third, North America provides fertile soil for the rise of contextual theologies for the simple reason of its multicultural population. What makes North America's multiculturalism distinctive is that it currently includes people from all continents and virtually all nations and languages. Thus, we have seen the rise of African American theologies and what can be called "immigrant" theologies: Asian American and Hispanic American. These are all huge populations in various parts of North America, with growing churches and emerging theological traditions. No wonder the North American theological academia is incorporating significant third-world voices in various forms. Women theologians—feminists, womanists (African American women), Latinas (women of Hispanic origin), and to a lesser degree women from Asian backgrounds[2]—have emerged and begun a creative and challenging theological movement. Among minority groups in many cultures, women's voices are particularly prominent.

As mentioned, the main dialogue partners for North American theologians have been European theologies. Therefore, this section on North American voices

---

2. For a survey of these views, see ibid., chap. 24.

has been labeled "Dialogue with European Views" of the Trinity. Before I introduce the main dialogue partners, I will offer a brief assessment of the contributions to Trinitarian thinking of North American contextual voices.

AFRICAN AMERICAN AND OTHER NORTH AMERICAN "CONTEXTUAL" THEOLOGIES ON THE TRINITY

Traditionally the major challenge to mainline North American theology has come from the significant minority population of black or African American people. In general, while African American theologians have contributed significantly to the doctrine of God—think of groundbreaking works such as James Cone's *God of the Oppressed* (1975)[3]—they have not felt the need to reflect on the Trinity, and at times they have been quite doubtful about the whole doctrine.[4] The widely used recent, brief manual on systematic theology from an African American perspective hardly mentions the term Trinity at all, even though there is a chapter on the doctrine of God.[5]

Yet there is much in the heritage and agenda of black theology that leans toward a relational and dynamic understanding of God, in other words, God as Trinity. Black theology's concept of God—in part owing to its African origins[6] and its social location among the oppressed minority people in the post-slavery New Continent—understands the divine-human relationship as dynamic and relational. Cone, in his *A Black Theology of Liberation* (1970),[7] does not begin the doctrine of God from Genesis 1–3 but from Exodus 1–3, where Israel, a minority people under oppression, cries out to God and God hears their cries. By delivering this people from Egyptian bondage, "God is revealed as the God of the oppressed." In this outlook, "the righteousness of God is not an abstract quality in the being of God, as with Greek philosophy. It is rather God's active involvement in history, making right what human beings have made wrong." In other words, the doctrine of God is a relational, dynamic concept. God is not only out there, but also involved with our history here.[8] Jesus' resurrection makes it evident that God's liberating work is not only for Israel, but for all who are enslaved.[9]

---

3. James Cone, *God of the Oppressed* (1975; reprint, Maryknoll, NY: Orbis Books, 1997). For African American views of God, including Cone's theology, see Kärkkäinen, *Doctrine of God*, 207–14.

4. Robert Hood, *Must God Remain Greek? Afro Cultures and God-Talk* (Minneapolis: Fortress, 1990), 109–10, 124.

5. James H. Evans Jr., *We Have Been Believers: An African-American Systematic Theology,* (Minneapolis: Fortress, 1992).

6. There is no scholarly consensus concerning the amount and nature of the African origins of African American theology. See further ibid., 56–57, with basic bibliographical guides.

7. In his preface to the 1986 edition, he mentions that if he were to write that book anew today, his approach to theology would be less systematic since there is no "abstract" revelation of human experiences; God meets us in the human situation, not as an idea or concept. James H. Cone, *A Black Theology of Liberation*, Twentieth Anniversary Edition (Maryknoll, NY: Orbis Books, 1990), xix.

8. Ibid., 2.

9. Ibid., 3.

Furthermore, for Cone and some other African American theologians, God is black.[10] The blackness of God is also the key to the doctrine of the Trinity in Cone's black theology:

> Taking seriously the Trinitarian view of the Godhead, black theology says that as Creator, God identified with oppressed Israel, participating in their bringing into being of this people; as Redeemer, God became the Oppressed One in order that all may be free from oppression; as Holy Spirit, God continues the work of liberation. The Holy Spirit is the Spirit of the Creator and the Redeemer at work in the forces of human liberation in our society today. In America, the Holy Spirit is black persons making decisions about their togetherness, which means making preparation for an encounter with whites.[11]

Another emerging theological voice in the North American context comes from Hispanic theologies. Rather than discussing those views in this section, I will speak of Hispanic views of the Trinity in the section on Latin American and Hispanic perspectives. It seems to me the U.S.-based Latino theologians' emerging work in theology in general and the doctrine of the Trinity in particular are so much connected with the general Latin American milieu that it is best to treat them there. While African American views do reflect some African influences, their relationship to Africa is far more distant not only in time but also thematically. When it comes to Native American theologies,[12] as far as I am aware of their writings, the Trinity has not been discussed in any significant way.

Several North American women theologians have contributed significantly to Trinitarian reflection. The interpretations of the Roman Catholic Elizabeth Johnson as a representative of feminist theologians and of Catherine Mowry LaCugna are discussed in detail in this section. Interpretations of the Trinity by other North American women theologians such as womanist (African American) and *mujeristas* (Hispanic) are yet to appear.[13]

"TWO MAKES THREE":[14] THE PROCESS VIEWS OF THE TRINITY

Undoubtedly, the most significant North American contribution to the doctrine of the Trinity apart from that of "standard theologians" discussed in this section comes from the process theology movement. Only reluctantly did I decide not to devote a separate chapter to process views of the Trinity; this was

10. Ibid., 63–64.
11. Ibid., 64.
12. For starters, see Kärkkäinen, *Doctrine of God*, chap. 22.
13. For North American feminist, womanist, and Latina views of God, see ibid., chap. 4.
14. The first part of the heading comes from Ted Peters, *God as Trinity: Relationality and Temporality in Divine Life* (Louisville, KY: Westminster John Knox Press, 1993), 114. Peters's is one of the rare contemporary surveys of Trinitarian doctrines to include a separate chapter on process theism.

mainly because the topic has not been studied in an intensive and systematic way among process theologians. However, a number of contributions come from that theological world, and it is only fair to give a brief presentation and assessment here.

One would assume that process theology with all its emphasis on relationality would be likely to develop a distinctive view of the Trinity.[15] That, however, has not been the case. In an important recent work titled *Trinity in Process* (1997) with an appropriate subtitle, *A Relational Theology of God*,[16] in which virtually all leading American process theologians reflect on the Trinity, the lead article by Marjorie Hewitt Suchocki elevates the Trinitarian vision as a paragon of human community in its relationality. Taking her cue from the *imago Dei*, she writes:

> If God is such that the deepest image of God in human society is attained not by an individual alone, not by societies made up of like-minded and like-looking individuals alone, but only through a society that becomes community through its embrace of irreducible differences, is there not a different force at work for peace in the world? Can we envision communities that not only embrace diversity within themselves, but that understand themselves to be but one irreducible community, whether religious or national, among valuable others? The model of a Trinitarian God, irreducibly diverse yet one, suggests a world community of irreducibly diverse communities. . . . The model of God as triune offers a new model for creating community in a world that too often answers difference with destruction in the name of homogenous unity.[17]

In her recent work, Suchocki has picked up the idea of diversity in the Godhead and applied it to other religions and to interfaith encounter.[18]

The basic challenge to process theology regarding the Trinity is of course obvious: theirs is a binitarian understanding of God involving the "primordial" and "contingent" aspects of God.[19] There are some thinkers such as John B. Cobb Jr. who argue that the binitarianism of process theology, which corresponds to the traditional economic and immanent Trinity distinction, is more important than Trinitarian doctrine even though it does not necessarily exclude a Trinity.[20] In his *Christ in a Pluralistic Age*, Cobb indeed equated the primordial nature with

16. Joseph A. Bracken, SJ, and Marjorie Hewitt Suchocki, eds., *Trinity in Process: A Relational Theology of God* (New York: Continuum, 1997).

17. Suchocki, "Introduction," in ibid., x–xi. The theologians represented in the book are John Cobb, David Ray Griffin, Philip Clayton, and Joseph A. Bracken, SJ, among others.

18. M. H. Suchocki, *Divinity and Diversity: A Christian Affirmation of Religious Pluralism* (Nashville: Abingdon Press, 2003).

19. For a brief exposition of main concepts and theologians, see Kärkkäinen, *Doctrine of God*, chap. 19. An accessible account and reflection on process theology's panentheistic vision, with some scattered notes on the Trinity, is offered by a leading contemporary theologian of the school, Philip Clayton, "God and World," in *The Cambridge Companion to Postmodern Theology*, ed. Kevin J. Vanhoozer (Cambridge: Cambridge University Press, 2003), 203–18.

20. John B. Cobb Jr., "The Relativization of the Trinity," in Bracken and Suchocki, *Trinity in Process*, 12.

Logos/Son and the consequent nature with the Spirit (or the kingdom of God), thus offering a binitarian view.

Yet some other process thinkers have been more inclined to develop a uniquely process understanding of the Trinity.[21] Some of their attempts to create a Trinitarian doctrine, however, seem to be so artificial and dubious in their correlation with biblical and Christian traditions[22] that it has prompted the Lutheran Ted Peters lament that "what we usually find are crude attempts at making the biblical symbols fit into already established metaphysical categories."[23] Some process theologians have admitted outright that "process theology is not interested in formulating distinctions within God for the sake of conforming with traditional Trinitarian notions."[24]

The pioneer among process theologians to begin to work toward a distinctive view of the Trinity was the British process thinker Norman Pittinger, who in 1977 published an important book titled *The Divine Triunity*.[25] Building on Whitehead's process philosophy, Pittinger attempted to produce a Trinitarian view of God negotiating the relatedness of a changing, and thus limited, God (since God is subject to the same metaphysical principles as all other entities) with the biblical notion of God as loving person, the "Cosmic Lover" who expresses himself in the world by God's "Self-Expressive Word"; God is also present in the world through God's "Responsive Agency." Other process theologians who have labored to combine process thought with Trinitarianism include Lewis S. Ford.[26] His proposal is based on the idea of "a single subjectivity as one actuality with three formally distinct natures." In that scheme, the Father is correlated with the

21. Roger E. Olson and Christopher A. Hall put it well: "The neo-liberal school of process theology at first attempted to develop a non-trinitarian, 'bi-polar' concept of God and then gradually began to attempt to discover some level of consistency between process theology and trinitarianism." Roger E. Olson and Christopher A. Hall, *The Trinity*, Guides to Theology (Grand Rapids: Eerdmans, 2002), 95–96.

22. See, e.g., Anthony Kelly, "Trinity and Process: Relevance of the Basic Christian Confession of God," *Theological Studies* 31 (Spring 1970): 393–414, in which he elaborates A. N. Whitehead's idea that there are some triadic patterns in God either in terms of the idea of "creative complex unity" being added to the standard process categories of primordial and consequent or, as Whitehead more often put it, "one," "many," and "creativity." In other words, each "process" is a result of "one" experiencing and influencing "other" as a result of which a new configuration, "creativity," emerges. Lewis S. Ford, "Process Trinitarianism," *Journal of the American Academy of Religion* 43, no. 2 (June 1975): 199–213, developed this idea.

23. Peters, *God as Trinity*, 115. He continues: "This renders almost laughable the frequent contention that somehow the Nicene theologians were guilty of capitulating to the metaphysics of their milieu, whereas contemporary neoclassical thinkers are innocent of such capitulation." For a dialogue between Peters and Cobb on the Trinity, see respectively: John B. Cobb Jr., *Christ in a Pluralistic Age* (Philadelphia: Westminster Press, 1975), 259–64; Peters, *God as Trinity*, 219; Cobb, "Response to Ted Peters," *Dialog* 30, no. 3 (1991): 243–44.

24. John B. Cobb Jr. and David Ray Griffin, *Process Theology: An Introductory Exposition* (Louisville, KY: Westminster John Knox Press, 1976), 110. I am indebted to Peters, *God as Trinity*, 115, for turning my attention to this reference.

25. Norman Pittinger, *The Divine Triunity* (Philadelphia: United Church Press, 1977). Schubert Ogden, "On the Trinity," *Theology* 83 (1980): 97–102, correlates "Son" with divine objectivity, "Spirit" with subjectivity, and "Father" with the inclusive essence of God.

26. Lewis S. Ford, *The Lure of God* (Philadelphia: Fortress Press, 1978), 99–112.

primordial envisagement, the Son/Logos with its outcome in the primordial nature, and the Spirit with the inverse or consequent nature.[27]

How well do these conceptions relate to a traditional understanding of God as three persons? Many commentators cast serious doubts about the capacity of this kind of approach to provide a basis for a truly *Trinitarian* understanding.[28]

In my estimation, one of the more promising process construals of the Trinity comes from the pen of the Jesuit Joseph A. Bracken, although he turns to many resources outside traditional process philosophy, in addition to Whitehead's imagery of a society (community) as a structured field of activity. He joins in the current communion theology combined with the idea of God as love (he also borrows key ideas from the philosopher Josiah Royce). He regards community as an "ontological reality in some sense superior to its person-members," indeed the "highest form of process, since it apparently constitutes the life of God,"[29] the three divine persons. The threeness is thus established in a way not typical of most other process views. But what about unity? Isn't Bracken's idea a suspect for tritheism? His response is similar to that of Moltmann: "Hence, even though each divine person has his own mind and will, they are of one mind and will in everything they say and do, both with respect to one another and in their relationships with human beings and the whole of creation."[30] Unlike imperfect human communities, Father, Son, and Holy Spirit "do achieve in fact total unanimity of mind and will. . . . They are, in other words, a perfect community."[31] As community, which is an ontological concept as much (or more) than that of "person," each divine person lives in an ongoing, deepening, self-giving love that is their common nature of the three.[32] Bracken's theology is still evolving and it is yet to be seen if he is able to convince theologians outside the process movement of the capacity of that movement to produce a Trinitarian vision compatible with biblical and systematic undergirdings.

DIALOGUE WITH EUROPEAN AND OTHER VOICES

Theologians selected as representatives for North American Trinitarian theology represent the wide theological and ecclesiastical diversity so prevalent in the New World. A fitting bridge between the theologies of the Old and New Continents

27. See also Paul S. Chung, *Martin Luther and Buddhism: Aesthetics of Suffering* (Eugene, OR: Wipf & Stock, 2002), 240–41.

28. A typical critique is that of Pittinger's proposal by Olson and Hall (*Trinity*, 103); who say that it is not able to go beyond modalism and suffers from its lack of the immanent Trinity.

29. Joseph A. Bracken, SJ, *The Triune Symbol: Persons, Process and Community* (Lanham, MD: University Press of America, 1985), 19, 20.

30. Ibid., 26.

31. Ibid., 24.

32. See further Joseph A. Bracken, "Panentheism from a Process Perspective," in Bracken and Suchocki, *Trinity in Process*, 95–113; idem, *Society and Spirit: A Trinitarian Cosmology* (Selinsgrove, PA: Susquehanna University Press/London and Toronto: Associated University Press, 1991), chap. 6, "The Triune God."

is the senior Lutheran scholar Robert W. Jenson, Wolfhart Pannenberg's student, formerly a teacher of theology in Europe and now one of the most respected living North American theologians. While fully in step with North American developments in theology, as the head of the prestigious Center for Theological Inquiry based in Princeton University, Jenson represents a true blending of the classical European theological heritage and a creative American constructive theology.

The late Catherine Mowry LaCugna, a Roman Catholic, is one of the few female theologians—not only in North America but also at the global level—who ever produced a full-scale monograph on the Trinity. While building on the work of the major Catholic theologian Austrian Karl Rahner, LaCugna also offers a highly creative dialogue with Eastern Orthodox and some Protestant voices. At the same time, LaCugna is known for her significant feminist contributions.

Another female theologian represented in this section is another Roman Catholic, Elizabeth Johnson, whose primary agenda is feminist. Johnson is also especially well suited for the North American section in dialogue with European views in that her monograph on the Trinity not only surveys critically and sympathetically the whole scope of Trinitarian history but also—unlike many of her female colleagues except for LaCugna—engages the whole spectrum of earlier and current Trinitarian thinkers mainly from European traditions.

The evangelical movement, whose theological contributions are almost nonexistent in Europe (with the exception of the British Isles with the rise to prominence of theologians from that tradition such as Alistair McGrath), represents a rapidly growing theological force not only in North America but also in the global English-speaking world. Millard J. Erickson is a leading thinker from that movement. While building widely on the contributions of historical and contemporary theologians, his social analogy, which gleans from Moltmann and Zizioulas among others, represents a new outlook from the more conservative theological milieu.

With the emergence of the question of the theology of religions—Christianity's relation to other religions and religious pluralism—several Christian theologians have labored in attempting to relate the most cardinal article of faith, Trinity, to other religions. Among those, a leading American constructive theologian is S. Mark Heim, another Protestant in this section. He links the key idea of diversity inherent in the Triune God with the diversity of the religious ends of religions. This linkage both critiques existing pluralistic approaches and attempts to ground a theologically adequate pluralistic approach that is still itself anchored in the foundations of Christian theology. Another pair of theologians writing together, namely, the senior scholar of religions Ninian Smart (Anglican) and his Eastern Orthodox student Steven Konstantine, offer yet another emerging way of relating the Trinity to religions, namely, by creatively working toward a religio-theological synthesis, not unlike Raimundo Panikkar's Asian-based interpretation to be studied in the Asian section. While religious studies are not unknown in Europe, in the United States they are a massive enterprise at all academic levels. Therefore, I saw fit to include this highly idiosyncratic interpretation of the Trinity at the juncture of various religions. I don't know any other major book on the

Trinity that discusses interpretations such as this. Even Heim's is not included in books on the Trinity, though he has discussed the topic since the mid-1990s.[33]

As Barth remarked about the doctrine of election—choosing one means opting out the rest—this discussion had to leave out theologians whose Trinitarian contributions are significant and would be worth studying. Another leading Lutheran scholar, Ted Peters, has been a formative figure in the renewal of the interest in the Trinity in North America. His relating of Trinity to history and time both reflects and expands a key trend in worldwide Trinitarian developments. As will be evident, I utilize his incisive remarks throughout the book as dialogue partners with selected theologians. The leading evangelical theologian from Canada, Clark Pinnock, was for a long time on my list to be included; his pneumatologically anchored social analogy would have made a fruitful addition. Yet I had to leave him out because of space limitations. As mentioned, none of the process theologians is included, with the exception of the brief critical survey of some of their contributions earlier in this chapter. Nevertheless, I have been able to include more North American voices than the six mentioned here—two Roman Catholics, two mainline Protestants, an Anglican as well as an Evangelical each; two women and four men—because in the sections on Asian and Latin American perspectives I have included two theologians who embody both Asian and Asian American (Raimundo Panikkar) and Latin American and Hispanic American (Justo González) theologies. Indeed, that is one of the unique features of the North American context: the emerging immigrant theologies provide a creative and challenging coming together of voices from Asia and Latin America in a North American setting.

---

33. I had planned to include a chapter on Smart and Konstantine in my *Trinity and Religious Pluralism: The Doctrine of the Trinity in Christian Theology of Religions* (Aldershot, UK: Ashgate, 2004) but could not do so because of space limitations.

Chapter 11

Robert Jenson

Triune Identity

"THE TRIUNE GOD-STORY"[1]

Through the Bible, this story is inescapably observable fact carried by three *dramatis dei personae* (divine characters in the drama). There is the God of Israel in person, whom Jesus distinctively addressed and referred to as "my Father," just so making himself out to be his distinctive Son. There is this Son, the protagonist of the Gospels, who according to the New Testament, appears also throughout the Old Testament in such figures as "the angel of the Lord" or "glory of the Lord" or the mysterious "servant" of Second Isaiah, or indeed, as Israel itself, the "Son" whom the Lord called from Egypt. . . . There is the Spirit of God, who is the agent of life and history throughout Scripture. The story of which these three are the *dramatis personae* is the story about the one and only God. It all comes together most stringently in the command of the risen Christ by which he launches the

---

1. The heading above is from Robert W. Jenson, "How Does Jesus Make a Difference? The Person and Work of Jesus Christ," in *Essentials of Christian Theology*, ed. William C. Placher (Louisville, KY: Westminster John Knox Press, 2003), 194. That chapter has an introduction by the editor and two essays, one by Jenson (pp. 191–205), another by Leanne Van Dyk (pp. 205–18), plus a bibliographical note (pp. 219–20).

church's mission. A formula specifying the three in their mutual relations, and so constituting a tight summary of the whole Bible's plot, is mandated as a personal name of the God to whom the mission brings hearers: They are to be baptized "into the name 'the Father, the Son, and the Holy Spirit.'"... The Bible surely tells its triune God-story as God's own. ... But it was a dogma of the pagan religion . . . that God can have no story because deity's defining character is sheer timelessness. . . . Confronted with the gospel, this culture therefore had to ask skeptically: Can God really be identified with one to whom things happen and who works at things, who even suffers birth and execution?[2]

This lengthy quotation from a recent writing of Robert W. Jenson, hailed as the most significant Trinitarian theologian of North America,[3] brings to focus all the major themes of his constructive proposal in which he builds on his mentor Karl Barth, gleans significantly from Rahner and Pannenberg, and creatively echoes and expands themes from other recent developments in Trinitarian theology such as the turn to history. Let me list these key themes and then elucidate and reflect critically on them in the rest of the chapter:

1. Trinity is the way to identify the God of the Bible among other gods. Indeed, the whole point of theology in general, not only the Trinitarian doctrine, is to help identify the true God.
2. Rather than on abstract speculation, the doctrine of the Trinity is based on the narrative of the Bible with two movements: the narrative of Israel as God's people and that of Jesus, who was raised from the dead. The Bible, in both the Old and New Testaments, has a "Trinitarian logic."[4]
3. In his desire to free Trinitarian theology from captivity to Hellenistic philosophy and "pagan religions," which only know a timeless eternity over temporal history, Jenson argues that history and time need to be incorporated into our understanding of the Triune God. "Eternity" in the Bible means the faithfulness of God to his promises rather than immunity to time.
4. Therefore, history becomes the locus for identifying God. The Yahweh of the Old Testament who called his people from Egypt is in the New Testament identified as the God who raised Jesus from the dead. Rather than speaking of God in terms of "substance," the proper way—the biblical way—is to speak of "becoming" and "event."

2. Ibid., 195–96.

3. R. Kendall Soulen, "YHWH the Triune God," *Modern Theology* 15, no. 1 (1999): 35, names Jenson "perhaps the major trinitarian theologian writing in English today." Earlier, Carl Braaten, "God and the Gospel: Pluralism and Apostasy in American Theology," *Lutheran Theological Journal* 25, no. 1 (1991): 47, had called Jenson the "first American theologian to write a systematic construction of the Trinity."

4. Robert W. Jenson, *Systematic Theology*, vol. 1, *The Triune God* (Oxford: Oxford University Press, 1997), 91.

5. The identity between the economic and immanent Trinity (Rahner) for Jenson is eschatological since (salvation) history is still unfolding. Yet, even with this eschatological outlook, there is strong insistence on the fact that the God identified *by* the events of the narrative of Israel and Christ is the God identified *with* these events. Otherwise, there would be a God "behind" or "beyond" history somewhere in the timeless eternity.

6. "Father, Son, and Spirit," rather than being a conventional way of naming God, a "nickname," is the proper name of the God of the Bible. It is the only, and as such irreplaceable, way to identify the *dramatis dei personae* (divine characters in the drama). This is the *Triune Identity*.

7. Because "Father [Son, and Spirit]" is a proper name, it cannot be replaced for the purpose of being politically correct—in this case, with regard to sexist charges, an insistence that has aroused a flood of criticism from both his own constituency and beyond.

While the Lutheran Jenson—for whom ecumenical concerns have become the leading theme in recent years[5]—has discussed the doctrine of the Trinity in various writings over the past twenty-five years of his prolific career, there are two major contributions.[6] The first is his monograph *The Triune Identity: God according to the Gospel* (1982),[7] and the second is the first volume of his theological magnum opus, the two-volume *Systematic Theology* (1997).[8] I will base my exposition on the *Triune Identity* for the simple reason that it is the major monograph by Jenson,[9] but I will take careful stock of changes and elaborations in the later major work.[10]

5. Ibid., 1:vii.

6. For the importance of the Trinity to Jenson's theology in general, see James J. Buckley, "Intimacy: The Character of Robert Jenson's Theology," in *Trinity, Time, and Church: A Response to the Theology of Robert W. Jenson,* ed. Colin Gunton (Grand Rapids: Eerdmans, 2000), 12.

7. Robert W. Jenson, *The Triune Identity: God according to the Gospel* (Philadelphia: Fortress, 1982). As a personal note, I am not quite sure what to think of the recurring claim by Jenson that the doctrine of the Trinity, rather than being a grand mystery, difficult to understand, is one of the claims by preachers that make sense to the congregations. At least his own book does not yield to an easy understanding. I would be interested in hearing what is the way this seasoned colleague translates the highly technical materials of his book into an easily digestible sermon or lesson!

8. For other discussions of the Trinity by Jenson, see "The Triune God," in *Christian Dogmatics,* ed. Carl E. Braaten and Robert W. Jenson, 2 vols. (Philadelphia: Fortress, 1984), 1:79–191; "The Logic of the Doctrine of the Trinity," *Dialog* 26, no. 4 (1987): 245–49; *Essays in Theology of Culture* (Grand Rapids: Eerdmans, 1995), 84–94, 190–201; "The Point of Trinitarian Theology," in *Trinitarian Theology Today,* ed. Christoph Schwöbel (Edinburgh: T & T Clark, 1995); 31–43; "How Does Jesus Make a Difference?" 191–205.

9. My approach is thus somewhat different in focus from a recent helpful discussion of Jenson's Trinitarian view by Stanley J. Grenz, *Rediscovering the Triune God: The Trinity in Contemporary Theology* (Minneapolis: Fortress, 2004), 106–16. Grenz builds his exposition on the first volume of Jenson's *Systematic Theology* and gives only passing references to Jenson's work *Triune Identity.* I believe our approaches are complementary, and neither one should claim to be the "canonical" one.

10. In the footnotes I will usually give the reference to *Triune Identity* first and then make reference, if available, to *Systematic Theology* (and other works of his). This of course applies to key ideas present throughout Jenson's career.

TRINITARIAN TRADITIONS IN NEED OF REVISION

Jenson is appreciative of tradition. At the same time, he is far from content with only repeating tradition in an uncritical way. He discerns several fallacies that have plagued Christian theology in general and Trinitarian theology in particular. In his own ambitious program he wants to combat these fallacies. His main concerns have to do with two issues deriving from Augustinian-Western thought, namely, an erroneous understanding of time (and eternity), with the corollary idea of history being excluded from divine life, and the idea of God as simple, which precludes genuine relationality and distinctions. A related error in the (Western) tradition is the underlying "substance ontology" that makes relationality secondary or marginal. His own temporal understanding of the Triune God—God as event—is meant to overcome the fallacies of this standard view.[11] In order to put Jenson's own proposal in perspective, let me unpack the meaning and his proposed revision of these fallacies as he sees them in the received tradition.[12]

While traditionally "modalism" denotes lack of real distinctions in the Trinity, Jenson adds an interesting twist to this heresy. He contends that beyond denying distinctions, modalism also fails by locating God above time.[13] If this is the fallacy of the tradition, "What would emerge if theologians were 'to reconceive the relationship between time and eternity so that what happens in the history of salvation becomes constitutive of the content of eternal life'?"[14] This is what

---

11. According to the interpretation of Ted Peters, "temporalization of the divine life is the means whereby Jenson overcomes the substantialist notion of God and affirms a relational understanding." Ted Peters, *God as Trinity: Relationality and Temporality in Divine Life* (Louisville, KY: Westminster John Knox Press, 1993), 130.

12. Jenson is also harshly critical of the famous Augustinian rule that while the inner works of the Trinity can be distinguished, the works of the Trinity *ad extra* are indivisible. Jenson's main concern is that that clause, rather than affirming the joint nature of all God's works, such as creation, is understood to mean "that the saving works are *indifferently* the work of each person and all" (Jenson, *Triune Identity*, 126). Jenson is not of course the only one to present a critique of the Augustinian rule. Rahner opposed it because in later tradition it was made to mean that any person of the Trinity could have been incarnated; see also Jenson, *Systematic Theology*, 1:11–12. Without being able to tackle their issues, let me just raise this simple question to Jenson: Why should we appropriate the rule in that way? It was hardly the way Augustine and the tradition used it. And as Pannenberg has shown, the rule was in effect well before Augustine; what Augustine did was to highlight the second part of the rule (the indivisibility of the outward works of the Trinity), echoing the teaching of the Cappadocians in the East. Wolfhart Pannenberg, *Systematic Theology*, trans. Geoffrey W. Bromiley, 3 vols. (Grand Rapids: Eerdmans, 1991–98), 2:3.

13. This he calls the "standard theory of the congregations." Jenson, *Triune Identity*, 65. In *Systematic Theology*, 1:95–96, he elaborates on the meaning of "modalism" in this respect. Jenson acknowledges (p. 100 n. 70) that in his earlier work, *Triune Identity*, 80–81, his discussion of Arianism was based on the older understanding (different from Hanson and other contemporary authors). Jenson also accuses the Apologists' *Logos* theology of the fallacy of subordinationism due to a mistaken understanding of the God-time relationship: While Father (the "God") could not relate to time, *Logos*, the Son, lower in the divine hierarchy, could. *Systematic Theology*, 1:97–98.

14. Question put to Jenson by Stanley J. Grenz, *The Social God and the Relational Self: A Trinitarian Theology of the Imago Dei* (Louisville, KY: Westminster John Knox Press, 2001), 41, quoting from Peters, *God as Trinity*, 102.

Jenson attempts to do, and he is following the groundbreaking move initiated by Barth and Rahner and later enthusiastically followed by Pannenberg and Moltmann, among others.[15] Alternatives are put dramatically: Religion is "either refuge from time [as in Hellenism] or confidence in it [as in biblical faith]."[16] These two are incompatible.[17]

Not only is time part of the divine life, but the related term "eternity" needs a revision, too. Here the important cue comes from the Old Testament understanding of the eternality of Yahweh. Yahweh's eternity means faithfulness through time (as in Ps. 119:89–90), Jenson surmises. The Hebrew term *emunah* (faithfulness) is the "reliability of a promise" of Yahweh. Unlike other gods, Yahweh is not immune to time; rather, Yahweh shows his faithfulness over the course of time. This is not a statement about ontological immutability as in classical theism but about continuity, faithfulness.[18]

In addition to timelessness, for Jenson the Augustinian-Western tradition has also replaced relationality with the simplicity of God, an idea based on substance ontology that does not allow for real distinctions.[19] Not surprisingly, Jenson embraces the theology of the Cappadocians as a corrective, the greatest contribution of which was to base the *hypostasis* of each Trinitarian member on their mutual relations. "God is the Father as the source of the Son's and the Spirit's Godhead; God is the Son as the recipient of the Father's Godhead; and God is the Spirit as the spirit of the Son's possession of the Father's Godhead."[20] Consequently, the understanding of God becomes relational; indeed, "the triune identities are *relations*."[21]

And—in keeping with the temporal orientation of Jenson's theology—it is important to note that this relationality is based on history and time.[22] The key problem in the traditional way of speaking of the Trinity is thus the naming of the Father as "God" as if Son and Spirit were not needed to consider God. In other words, the Father's relation to the Son and Spirit is not being taken as foundational for the identity of the Father. For Jenson, the whole Trinity—

15. Another prime American colleague of Jenson's is, of course, Ted Peters.

16. Jenson, *Triune Identity,* 4. On p. 25 he says the same.

17. For details, see ibid., 57–61 especially. In *Systematic Theology,* 1:94, he says: "Greece identified deity by metaphysical predicates. Basic among them is timelessness: immunity to time's contingencies and particularly to death, by which temporality is enforced."

18. Jenson, *Triune Identity,* 39–40; *Systematic Theology,* 1:46–50, 94–101. For a helpful brief explanation, see also Peters, *God as Trinity,* 129.

19. Tertullian, another key early Western theologian—despite the substance ontology (Jenson, *Triune Identity,* 74)—was able to avoid modalism with his idea of three *personae,* Father, Son, and Spirit being three mutually recognized proper names. Furthermore, Tertullian's Trinitarian view builds on biblical narrative such as the story of the baptism of Jesus, in which the three persons talk to each other; there is address and response. Most important, Jenson thinks that these relations of address and response establish the reality of relationships and community within God similarly to the relations of address and response among human individuals (p. 73).

20. Ibid., 106.

21. Ibid., 175 (italics in the original).

22. Ibid., 107 (italics in the original); so also in *Systematic Theology,* 1:105–7; see also Peters, *God as Trinity,* 133.

Father, Son, and Holy Spirit—is God.[23] Having discerned these foundational flaws in the tradition, Jenson puts forth his own constructive proposal.

THE CHARACTERS OF THE DRAMA OF GOD

"The doctrine of the Trinity comprises . . . the Christian faith's repertoire of ways of *identifying* its God, to say *which* of the many candidates for godhead we mean when we say, for example, 'God is loving' or 'Dear God, please . . .'"[24] This is an urgent task for the contemporary church, which finds itself in a pluralistic world. While Christian theology feels pressure to give up this task—as many pluralists have done—Jenson is not ready to go down that road. Furthermore, before we can say anything more about what God is like, we need to be able to define the identity.[25]

Jenson argues that "Father, Son, and Holy Spirit" is a proper name, something that has not been explicitly argued before.[26] This is in keeping with Jenson's understanding of the people of Israel's conceiving Yahweh as a proper name. The New Testament not only adopts the God of Israel but also makes a significant further identification by naming God as the one who raised Jesus from the dead.[27] "To the question 'Who is God?' the New Testament has one new descriptively identifying answer: 'Whoever raised Jesus from the dead.'"[28] Jenson takes pains in stressing the continuity between the two Testaments in identifying God first as the Yahweh who freed Israel from Egypt and as the God who raised Jesus from the dead.[29]

The historical precedent for expressing this for Jenson is the Cappadocians' use of the term *hypostasis*. Should we then continue using *hypostasis* language? Of course not, Jenson responds.[30] The contemporary term readily available is "identity." When applied to God-talk, it means that there are three identities in God—as the Cappadocians spoke of three *hypostaseis*. This means that "there are three discrete sets of names and descriptions, each sufficient to specify uniquely, yet all identifying the same reality"[31]—similar to the Cappadocians' idea of one *ousia*.

23. Jenson, *Triune Identity,* 51, 73.

24. Ibid., ix (italics in the original); see also p. 4; Jenson, *Systematic Theology*, vol. 1, chap. 3 especially. Methodologically Jenson seems to be following Pannenberg by discussing first Trinity (vol. 1 of his *Systematic Theology*) and only then the one God (*The Works of God*) in the second volume.

25. Jenson, *Triune Identity,* ix–xii. Therefore, Jenson argues, "not all addresses to the deity are equally true; . . . it is possible to be in simple error at the very base of religious life" (p. 168).

26. Ibid., xii: "But so far as I know, previous theology has not explicitly said that 'Father, Son, and Holy Spirit' is a proper name."

27. Ibid., 5–8; chap. 2, "Trinitarian Logic," unpacks the idea of the resurrection as the way the gospel identifies its God. Jenson, *Systematic Theology*, 1:4, 12, 42, 43–44, 49, 63, etc.; "to attend theologically to the Resurrection of Jesus is to attend to the triune God" (p. 13).

28. Jenson, *Systematic Theology*, 1:44.

29. Jenson, *Triune Identity,* 8; similarly Jenson, *Systematic Theology*, 1:43–44.

30. Jenson, *Triune Identity,* 108.

31. Ibid.

While in *Triune Identity* Jenson delves into complicated nomenclatures for
Father, Son, and Spirit, such as "Given" (Father),[32] "Present Possibility" (Jesus),[33]
and "Eschatological Outcome" (Spirit),[34] and speaks of God as "one event . . . with
three identities,"[35] in *Systematic Theology* he prefers to speak of the three as "*dramatis dei personae*, 'characters of the drama of God.'"[36]

Among the "agents" of the story of God, "the Son" comes to the fore first. The
Son is "another by and with whom God is identified, so that what he does to and
for this other he does to and for himself," in an analogy of parent and child,[37]
and in a way similar to the Yahweh-Israel relationship.[38] The primacy of Jesus as
the way of identifying God is based on the inclusion of time and history in the
divine life. Biblical faith—different from that of other religions—bases its identification on a historical event, thus making time and history belong to the life
of God.[39]

Yet another agent among the *dramatis dei personae* is the "Spirit of the Lord,"
the Lord's *breath (ruach)*, "the whirlwind of his *liveliness* that agitates whatever he
turns toward."[40] Distinctive to the New Testament description of the *persona* of
the Spirit is on the one hand the Spirit's integral relation to Jesus, the Messiah,
the bearer of the Spirit,[41] and on the other hand the Spirit's communal nature in
that, unlike the Old Testament manifestation on individual leaders, the Spirit will
be poured out on all flesh.[42]

And finally, the third agent of the drama is introduced:

32. Father is "Transcendence *given* to his [Jesus'] acts and sufferings, the Transcendence *over
against* whom he lives and to whom he is responsible—addressed in trust." The Father is not only the
one who raised Jesus from the dead but also "a *given* Transcendence to all that Jesus is and does." Jenson, *Triune Identity*, 24 (italics in the original).

33. In reference to biblical passages such as Matt. 28:18–20, Jenson reminds us of the fact that
everything Jesus has, even the power, is not his own but has been *given* to him (Jenson, *Triune Identity*, 30). If God is to be identified with Jesus, we can say that "God . . . is what happens with Jesus."
Now, the New Testament claims, this Jesus who identifies God not only died on the cross but was
risen, thus leaving death behind. This opens the future for us also: "God is what will *come* of Jesus
and us, together" (pp. 22, 23 respectively). In other words, Jesus is the "present Possibility of God's
reality for us"; his resurrection "is the event in which Jesus is future to himself and to us" (pp. 24,
23 respectively).

34. Spirit is the "eschatological outcome." In the Bible, the "Spirit" is God as the power of the
future, the bringer of the fulfillment of God's purposes. Thus, we can name the Spirit as the "Goal,"
the power of the eschaton. That Spirit is no one else than the Spirit of Jesus. Jenson, *Triune Identity*,
23–24.

35. Ibid., 114.

36. Jenson, *Systematic Theology*, 1:75. In his later work, Jenson is less concerned about resorting
to the language of "person," as the title of chap. 5 shows, "The Persons of God's Identity."

37. Ibid., 1:75–76; see also 77–86.

38. Ibid., vol. 1, chap. 4.

39. Jenson, *Triune Identity*, 22. In other words, there is no "getting to God past what happens
with Jesus in time" (p. 26).

40. Jenson, *Systematic Theology*, 1:86 (italics in the original).

41. Ibid., 1:88: "Jesus appears in the New Testament as a prophetic bearer of the Spirit. In all the
Gospels, his baptism is described as the descent of the Spirit."

42. Ibid., 1:87.

Not only the Son and the Spirit appear as *dramatis dei personae*; also the God whose Son and Spirit these are is identified as himself one *persona* of God, as the Father *of* the Son and sender *of* the Spirit. The God of Israel appears as himself one of the *persona dramatis* of the very God he is. That is the deepest mystery of his identity and the final necessity of the doctrine of God.[43]

DRAMATIC COHERENCE AND ANTICIPATION

In his systematic theology Jenson emphasizes narrative as the way to understanding the biblical revelation of God, although narrative was not absent in his earlier work.[44] Narrative is also key to understanding the meaning of the Trinitarian drama: "Since the biblical God can truly be identified by narrative, his hypostatic being, his self-identity, is constituted in *dramatic coherence*." This means that while the unfolding of narrative contains unexpected events and not all of them can be predicted, they still happen on account of each other, and so we can see "afterwards . . . it was just what had to happen."[45] In biblical revelation there are times when the Lord "explicitly puts his self-identity at narrative risk," as in Isaiah 40–45, where Yahweh's role as the ruler of history is at stake, or most importantly at the crucifixion, in which "the one called 'Father' here hands the one called 'Son' over to oppositional and deadly creatures."[46] In interpreting the meaning of these ambiguities and challenges to the task of discerning God's self-identity, Jenson walks the thin line of wanting to avoid both the dangers of considering them mere theatrical acts[47] and of leaving the self-identity question unanswered.[48] This brings the importance of the future into the picture: "Since the Lord's self-identity is constituted in dramatic coherence, it is established not from the beginning but from the end, not at birth but at death, not in *persistence* but in *anticipation*."[49] Anticipation means that the "future that moves a story must somehow be available within it if we are to live the story while it is still in progress."[50]

While he hardly mentions it, in principle Jenson affirms Rahner's rule of the identity between the immanent and economic Trinity because it highlights the importance of history as determining the Trinitarian identity. Yet in order to

---

43. Ibid., 1:89 (italics in original).
44. The programmatic statement is this: "The God to be interpreted in this work is the God identified by the biblical narrative." Ibid., 1:57. For the importance of narrative throughout Jenson's career, see Buckley, "Intimacy," 14.
45. Jenson, *Systematic Theology*, 1:64 (italics in the original).
46. Ibid., 1:65.
47. Jenson, *Triune Identity*, 4.
48. Jenson, *Systematic Theology*, 1:64, 65.
49. Ibid., 1:66 (italics in the original); see also Jenson, *Triune Identity*, 4.
50. Jenson, *Systematic Theology*, 1:67. Jenson (*Triune Identity*, 5) notes that "God," the Triune God of the Bible, is the "union" between past (memory) and future (anticipation), the future being open to new things.

protect the freedom of God, the immanent Trinity cannot be simply equated with the economic in the way Rahner did.[51] The union belongs to the future, to eschatology. Jenson's "rule" thus reads: "the identity of the 'economic' and 'immanent' Trinity is *eschatological*; . . . the 'immanent' Trinity is simply the eschatological reality of the 'economic.'"[52] That is the way to safeguard God's freedom.

If God's eternity means, as Jenson maintains, "'faithfulness' to the last future," then it means "the certainty of his triumph" as God who is Spirit.[53] Jenson believes that his proposal, better than traditional theology (especially in the West), is able to account for the genuine freedom of God. Freedom of God does not mean "the spurious freedom of unaffectedness" of a timeless God, but "openness to the future," in other words, "genuine freedom is Spirit."[54] "To be God is to be the power of the future to transcend what is," in other words, "unbounded futurity."[55]

What this means is that it is not the Father only as in traditional theology who is the "source" of the Trinity, but that Spirit and Son are constitutive in the Triune God. "The Spirit's witness to the Son and the Son's saving work are equally God-constituting." It is then herein that the personhood of God is located in Jenson's theology, in the "totality of God's self-constituting relations with the history of the world."[56] Here we encounter yet another important idea of Jenson's to be discussed before delving into critical reflections.

THE TRINITY AS PERSON

One of the groundbreaking contributions of Jenson's evolving thinking as presented in the first volume of his *Systematic Theology* relates to the continuing inquiry into the concept of "person" in relation to the Triune God. Jenson makes the bold suggestion that not only is Trinity itself a *personal* reality but that Trinity in itself is *person*. What is the reason for this unexpected move?[57] The starting point lies in his continuing struggle with defining the oneness of God in the Triune God. He works hard to go beyond the typical Eastern solution of locating unity in the monarchy of the Father, and the Western way of locating the unity in the simplicity of the divine essence. It is not that these views are so much

51. Jenson, *Triune Identity*, 139.
52. Ibid., 140 (italics in the original).
53. Ibid., 141. In *Systematic Theology*, 1:157, he puts it this way: "we have already many times noted and said where in fact the Spirit stands: at the End of All God's ways because he *is* the End of all God's ways" (italics in original).
54. Jenson, *Triune Identity*, 141.
55. Ibid., 167, 168, respectively.
56. Peters, *God as Trinity*, 134; see Jenson, *Triune Identity*, 142 especially.
57. The move is not unexpected in a general theological sense—the tradition has it that Father, Son, and Spirit have been named persons, i.e., *hypostaseis*—but it is unexpected for Jenson, especially in terms of his earlier views; he tended to be reserved about applying the concept of person to Trinitarian persons and preferred to speak of identity for that.

wrong as that they are limited. The strength of the Eastern view of unity is "the directness with which it can do this" by arguing that while the Father is without *archē* (source or origin), he is the *archē* of the Son and Spirit; the weakness of course is that it borders on Arianism and subordinationism by making the Father "higher." "The strength of the Western way of thinking is the simplicity with which it can say: therefore the *Trinity* is the one God"; the potential problem lies in distorting the biblical narrative, "telling us to read 'the Trinity' at places where we manifestly should see one of the three."[58]

In order to build on these views, especially on the one by the Christian East, and yet transcend their limitations, Jenson suggests that while there are three identities—Father, Son, and Spirit—in the Triune God, and each of them can be called "persons," the whole Trinity is also person. However, it is not possible to say that the Trinity is an identity since "the Triune God is always identified by reference to one or several of the three identities."[59] Two things follow: (1) that there is a distinction between "identity" and "person," against Western thought, in which a being with identity is a person; (2) that there is no reason to limit personhood to only one way of being; there is more than one way of being person. Apart from contemporary developments in linguistics and general postmodern deconstructive efforts to liberate "self . . . from a conceptual straitjacket,"[60] it is apparent that Father, Son, and Spirit "could not each be personal quite in the same way."[61] This can be seen most dramatically with regard to the Spirit: Spirit is inherently someone's spirit.[62] The key to being a person is address and response: "a person is one with whom other persons—the circularity is constitutive—can *converse*, whom they can *address*."[63] If so, even the Spirit can be conceived of as

58. Jenson, *Systematic Theology*, 1:116 (italics in original).

59. Ibid., 1:119.

60. Ibid., 1:121. To argue against the "apparent one-to-one correlation between identity and personality . . . imposed in Western conceptual tradition by the usual Western interpretation of the self," Jenson delves into dialogue with the structuralist theory of language of Ferdinand de Saussure, the poststructuralism of Jacques Derrida, and the phenomenology of Jean Paul Sartre, among others. In general, he greets the dissolution of self in much of postmodern thinking as a way of liberating Christian theology in reconsidering the distinction between identity and person. Ibid., 1:120–21.

61. Ibid., 1:121. Apart from *theo*-logical considerations, Jenson also supports the principle of "looseness in the connection between the identity and personality" with reference to the standard theological idea of the unity of Christ and the believer in salvation (Christ indwelling the believer) or the unity of humankind in original sin. Ibid., 119–20. The idea that "there may be *more than one way to be personal*, even to be 'a' person" also gets support from Jonathan Edwards's theology. Ibid., 120; italics in original. In n. 17 Jenson refers to his own study, *America's Theologian: A Recommendation of Jonathan Edwards* (New York: Oxford University Press, 1988), 53–64.

62. To support this Jenson gleans from the threefold definition of selfhood in Kant: (1) the focus of consciousness (what Kant called "the transcendental unity of apperception") that constitutes a consciousness as *a* consciousness; (2) "I" or "me," the diachronically identifiable individual (that makes it possible to identify the "I" that in this instance did this and in another something else, yet being the same "I"); (3) freedom, the mysterious relation between these two. Now Jenson contends that conceiving the Spirit as person (being someone's spirit) means that the Spirit's "I" and "focus of consciousness" are outside the Spirit, yet this does not make the personality of the Spirit null.

63. Jenson, *Systematic Theology*, 1:117 (italics in the original). "A person is one whom other persons may address in hope of response" (p. 121).

a person. Not only each person of the Trinity, but also the Trinity as a whole can be addressed as a community, Jenson claims.[64]

Jenson claims that distinguishing "identity" and "person" makes it possible to treat God as personal rather than as a "monadic entity, a self-possessed, closed unit"[65] (behind the threeness).

CRITICAL REFLECTIONS

I begin my critical reflections on Jenson's proposal—accurately described as "narrative, temporal, and eschatological"[66]—with a couple of comments regarding the handling of historical materials, for the simple reason that, as mentioned above, tradition plays a key role in his own constructive proposal. Jenson's *Triune Identity* appeared before the recent renewed interest in Augustine's view of the Trinity and as such reflects an earlier, somewhat outdated scholarly consensus.[67] Furthermore, as Pannenberg has noted, Jenson's treatment of the Cappadocians' Trinitarian doctrine is also biased in favor of a relational understanding.[68] His *Systematic Theology* basically echoes these views but is more moderate in its critique. Be that as it may, the value of Jenson's *theological* proposal cannot be assessed in terms of how accurately the historical notes reflect current scholarship. Even if the historical presentations are in need of correction, his theological proposal can stand on its own feet.

The application of Rahner's rule by Jenson has been the focus of debate with several critics.[69] I think Jenson has rightly identified the main potential problem

---

64. Ibid., 1:121–22.

65. Ibid., 1:123; see also pp. 116–17.

66. Grenz, *Rediscovering the Triune God*, 113.

67. Jenson's critique of Augustine sounds similar to that of Colin Gunton (yet is independent as far as I know).

68. Pannenberg, *Systematic Theology*, 1:323 n. 194; see also pp. 320–22 especially. In his *Systematic Theology* and elsewhere, Jenson, however, acknowledges the fact that in general the theology of the Christian East regards the Father as the source and principle of deity, thus undermining the Cappadocians' idea of relationality. In his critique of the Augustinian rule of the indivisibility of God's work *ad extra*, ironically Jenson seems to be unaware that it was the Cappadocians who had already used the rule before Augustine to establish the unity of Father, Son, and Spirit in terms of the unity of operation, as noted in the historical section. Jenson, *Systematic Theology*, 1:115–16. See further Pannenberg, *Systematic Theology*, 2:7; see also pp. 8–9. Regarding the rule of Augustine, I would also like to add that it simply is a mistake to assume (like Jenson) that the usage of this rule necessarily leads to understanding the outside works of God in creation and salvation "indifferently"; rather, it helps us emphasize the fact that while in their inner activities relative to one another distinctions apply, there is inseparable unity of the Trinitarian persons in their outward action. A case in point is Pannenberg's Trinitarian doctrine of the creation (2:20–35 especially): while affirming the unity of Father, Son, and Spirit in the act of creation, different "roles" come to the fore, for example, in terms of the Son representing independence (of creation from God) and the Spirit, unity; the goodness of the Father by which he gives and sustains creation is nothing else than the eternal love he shares with the Son from eternity.

69. See further Douglas Farrow, David Demson, and J. Augustine DiNoia, "Robert J. Jenson's *Systematic Theology*: Three Responses," *International Journal of Systematic Theology* 1, no. 1 (1999): 90 (Farrow's section).

in the original Rahnerian suggestion, namely, the question of God's freedom. Jenson claims to be able to get around that problem with reference to eschatology; thus his idea of the identity of the economic and immanent only at the eschaton. In this respect Jenson's proposal of course echoes strongly the turn to the eschatology of Moltmann[70] and shares the same problematic. For me, rather than resolving the question of God's freedom, Jenson borders on absorption of the immanent Trinity in the economic, ending up with a view that begins to resist the idea of freedom. While it is of course true that it is only in the eschaton that the "full deity" of God will be established (not in terms of a divine becoming in history as in process theology, but rather in terms of the demonstration of the Deity with the eschatological consummation of God's rule in the coming of God's kingdom), it is highly problematic to subsume the immanent into the economic Trinity. Wouldn't it be more correct to say that with the eschaton the economic Trinity reaches its completion in the immanent Trinity? While there is no full equation, there is integrity based on God's faithfulness. And then we should stop there. Speculation into the total identity of the immanent and economic Trinity on this side of the eschaton can only be that, speculation. Why should we reduce the immanent to the economic?[71] What are the gains? The eschatological turn in Moltmann and Jenson raises questions that make me cautious about going all the way with them.

The way Jenson utilizes Rahner's rule in his *Systematic Theology* (again, without reference to Rahner) has to do with his turn to narrative, and not only that, but also his strong insistence on the identification of God *by* and *with* the events narrated in Scripture about Israel and Jesus.[72] Positively, this means that *everything* we know of God from the biblical narrative can be trusted. There is no abstract metaphysical God "behind" or "beyond" the events narrated. Negatively, however, this rule begins to compromise the freedom of God, as noted by a number of critics.[73] My own corrective to Jenson would make reference to his key idea

70. While I acknowledge the teacher-student relationship, in contrast to Grenz (*Rediscovering the Triune God*, 114), I do not think that Jenson's proposal is also similar to Pannenberg's theology of the Trinity. As my discussion of Pannenberg here and in the chapter on his theology above suggests, in my reading Pannenberg has avoided collapsing the immanent Trinity into the economic.

71. When I say that at the eschaton the *economic* Trinity reaches its completion in the *immanent*, I am aware that when pressed this can be interpreted as implying that the economic Trinity lacks any *novum*. That is another danger to be avoided: historical events, especially the incarnation, cross, and resurrection, are something "new" in the divine life even though not something totally foreign. They are willed by God in his gracious freedom.

72. Indeed, Jenson claims that "the whole argument of the work depends" on this methodological argument (Jenson, *Systematic Theology*, 1:59).

73. Farrow, Demson, and DiNoia, "Robert Jenson's *Systematic Theology*," 103 (DiNoia's section): "Do the Father, Son and Holy Spirit enjoy a life independent of their engagement with us in creation and redemption?" In *Triune Identity*, where the narrative rule was not defined as consistently, Jenson seems to be able to address this question: "The legitimate theological reason for the 'immanent'/'economic' distinction is the freedom of God: it must be that God 'in himself' could have been the same God he is, and so triune, had there been no creation, or no saving of fallen creation, and so also not the Trinitarian history there has in fact been." Jenson, *Triune Identity*, 139. Some critics seem to go too far by blaming Hegelian influences to the point that history determines God's eternal being. See,

of God's faithfulness to his promises. Based on this faithfulness we can affirm an *integral* connection[74]—rather than full equation, eschatologically or in terms of the "narrative rule"—between the economic and immanent Trinity not only as an epistemological principle (meaning that our knowledge of God proceeds from the economy of salvation to the inner divine life) but also as a certainty that the works of God in salvation and creation reveal to us God's true being. It is possible to incorporate temporality in the divine life, as Jenson helpfully emphasizes, yet maintain the idea of God's freedom and grace (the latter because necessity does not follow; what arises out of necessity cannot be regarded as grace, to follow the ancient theological rule).

Jenson's bold suggestion that Trinity is person raises questions. The agenda behind this construal, namely, the avoidance of the idea of "the impersonal Trinity . . . [as] the 'deep' deity" that "compromise[s] the thoroughgoing personality of God as he appears in Scripture" is to be applauded.[75] Yet the way Jenson wants to avoid this danger is not fully satisfactory. I find Pannenberg's challenge most helpful.[76] Pannenberg maintains, unlike Jenson, that we must distinguish between the one divine essence and three persons who share the one and same eternal life. "If that distinction were not admitted, there would be no way to account for the Christian affirmation that the Father, the Son, and the Spirit—all three of them—are God, and only one God."[77] The one divine essence is no hidden or abstract God "behind" or "beyond" the Triune God but rather the "divine life they have in common." While it is true that apart from the interrelatedness of the three persons, the divine essence "would become a timeless abstraction,"[78] it doesn't have to be so necessarily. Positing the divine essence as

e.g., Paul D. Molnar, "Robert W. Jenson's *Systematic Theology*, Volume 1: *The Triune God*," *Scottish Journal of Theology* 52, no. 1 (1999): 120–24, 130. Along similar lines, yet in a less provocative way, see Jeremy Ive, "Robert W. Jenson's Theology of History," in *Trinity, Time, and Church: A Response to the Theology of Robert W. Jenson*, ed. Colin Gunton (Grand Rapids: Eerdmans, 2000), 157. In contemporary theology, reference to Hegel has become a mantra (often used in relation to Pannenberg's theology too) that can be called to aid whenever problems such as the ones related to Jenson's proposal arise.

74. Even though here I chose the weaker term "integral connection," I am also comfortable with continuing to use the term "identity" (of the economic and immanent Trinity) as long as it is not made an absolute rule but rather—as I indicated in the context of Rahner's theology—both an epistemological rule and a "pious guess" into the divine life based on God's faithfulness.

75. Jenson, *Systematic Theology*, 1:116–17.

76. I find it ironic that Jenson, in acknowledging Pannenberg's view as a major alternative to his own, wonders if Pannenberg's proposal owes more to philosophical idealism of nineteenth-century Germany than to the Bible. Jenson, *Systematic Theology*, 1:116 n. 4. The irony lies in that when constructing his own proposal (as noted above), Jenson depends heavily on contemporary philosophical resources! In my view, Jenson's claim that for Pannenberg "the appropriate ontological concept for the Trinity as such is that of an energetic 'field'" is only a half-truth. Of course, Pannenberg regards God as Spirit and defines Spirit as force field. Yet as the explanation below shows for Pannenberg, the one divine essence is the shared eternal life of the three persons.

77. Wolfhart Pannenberg, "Eternity, Time and the Trinitarian God," in *Trinity, Time, and Church: A Response to the Theology of Robert W. Jenson*, ed. Colin Gunton (Grand Rapids: Eerdmans, 2000), 69.

78. Ibid., 70.

"person" runs the risk of adding a "fourth person" to the notion of the Christian God. I agree with Pannenberg, and contra Jenson, that "in each of the three persons as well as in their interrelatedness the one God is personal and as such he is eternal life, in full and simultaneous procession of the wholeness of his life."[79]

Regarding Jenson's insistence that "Father, Son, and Holy Spirit" as proper name raises questions, it seems to me that while it is correct to say that both in the Bible and in the liturgical life of the church the usage of the name *resembles* the function of the proper name, to make it a rule is a conclusion less than warranted.[80] Jenson not only insists that Father, Son, and Spirit is the biblical way of naming God—a claim very few would want to contest—but that it is therefore normative for all times. His reasons for its normative and thus irreplaceable nature have to do with Christian life and theology. Following the biblical mandate, Christians are being baptized into the name of the Father, Son, and Holy Spirit. This refutes the idea that we first know about God and only afterward find a way to address him, Jenson argues. The opposite is the case: we do have access to the God of the Bible and have been baptized into the name of the Father, Son, and Holy Spirit. "Father" is not only—nor even primarily—"our Father" but the Father of the Son, Jesus. Similarly, "Spirit" does not denote any generic spirit but the Spirit of the Son and Father. Jenson puts this in perspective by speaking of "the Name as Doctrine."[81] This is based on the underlying theological rationale according to which the phrase "'Father, Son, and Holy Spirit' is simultaneously a very compressed telling of the total narrative by which Scripture identifies God and a personal name for the God as so specified." Therefore, "in it, the name and narrative description not only appear together . . . but are identical." From this he concludes that it is a "unique name" and "dogmatically mandated for that function by its constitutive place in the rite that establishes Christian identity."[82] I concur with another Lutheran, Ted Peters, that "to say that the Trinitarian formula is God's proper name is to say too much."[83] There are many reasons. First of all, there is no denying that in some sense the terms Father, Son, and Holy Spirit are metaphors regarding the Father-Son relationship: God is Father only analogically, not literally. Second, rather than being proper names, Father, Son, and

---

79. Ibid.

80. Even to call *Yahweh* in the Old Testament a proper name—rather than acknowledging its special meaning related to its function as self-revelation and as part of the covenant community's self-identification—invites the question, "Why make it a rule?" For a thoughtful reflection, see C. R. Seitz, "Handing Over the Name: Christian Reflection on the Divine Name YHWH," in *Trinity, Time, and Church: A Response to the Theology of Robert W. Jenson*, ed. Colin Gunton (Grand Rapids: Eerdmans, 2000), 23–41. See also the thoughtful comment by the NT scholar H. Conzelmann that Father acts "in the manner of a proper name" (he quotes here P. Bachmann). H. Conzelmann, *1 Corinthians*, Hermeneia (Philadelphia: Fortress Press, 1975), 144.

81. Jenson, *Triune Identity*, 16–17 ("The Name as Doctrine" is the subtitle for this section, [p. 16]); *Systematic Theology*, 1:46.

82. Jenson, *Systematic Theology*, 1:46.

83. Peters, *God as Trinity*, 53.

Spirit are titles. Titles cannot be arbitrarily changed, yet unlike proper names, they can be translated and are being translated with no one feeling a loss. There is a distinction between a proper name and a title. Third, the most reverend name for God, the Old Testament *Yhwh*, which was too holy to be pronounced and so a replacement had to be made, became "Lord" (*Kyrios* in Greek; *Adonai* in Hebrew). No one questions whether the designation "Lord" in the New Testament really refers to the same God as the OT *Yhwh*. Furthermore, other designations for this same God are employed in both Testaments. All of this convinces me that while Father, Son, and Spirit as the title of the Triune God is a specifically Christian name for God,[84] it cannot claim the status of a proper name. On the other hand, I am not willing to go as far as, for example, some feminists who would want to replace Father, Son, and Spirit with Creator, Redeemer, and Sanctifier. I have two reasons for rejecting this approach: Their proposed names are not personal, and more important, here names are replaced with terms designating function, and I think the functions are too vague and impersonal to identify the Christian God.[85]

Regarding the heated topic of inclusivity, Jenson of course rides against the tide during times when the social context cries for avoidance of sexist language. His proposal has been an object of critique in this respect.[86] While acknowledging the importance of dealing with the issue of sexism, for Jenson there is no way to replace the traditional language with a more "inclusive" one. The problem is twofold. On the one hand, proper names do not yield to changes. On the other hand, changing only one part of the proper-name formula, namely "Father," will not work since it is based on the filial relationship of Jesus to his Father and thus cannot be separated; furthermore, this being so, it makes the whole tripartite name "irremediably offensive."[87] However, Jenson contends that the biblical God is beyond sexual categories. The sexual distinctions of humanity do not define God. Jesus' addressing God by the name "Father" is unrelated to masculinity; it only denotes a filial relationship.[88] Jenson concludes:

> The assumption that it is a deprivation not to address God in one's very own gender is a case of humankind's general religious assumption of direct analogy from human perfections to divine qualities. In the faith of the

84. Ibid., 54.

85. My reasoning here is deeply indebted to ibid., 53–54.

86. The most vocal Lutheran critic has been Mary M. Sohlberg, who calls Jenson's view "authoritarian" in her "Concerning God's Proper Name: Comments on Robert Jenson's Discussion of the Masculinity of 'Father,'" *Dialog* 30, no. 4 (Autumn 1991): 32. A good overview of the responses in this respect to both *Triune Identity* and other writings published so far is offered by Ted Peters, "The Battle over Trinitarian Language," *Dialog* 30, no. 1 (Winter 1991): 44–49.

87. Jenson, *Triune Identity*, 13; for the Father-Son relationship, see also p. 107. Adopting a name like "parent" does not commend itself to Jenson since it is too general to be used in a filial address (p. 14).

88. Ibid., 15–16. Therefore, the term "mother" (alongside "father") would even more confuse the issue since that would make God inescapably sexual (p. 16).

Bible, this direct line is, for our salvation, broken. Indeed, Christianity's entire soteriological message can be put so: God's self-identification with the Crucified One frees us from having to find God by projection of our own perfections.[89]

It seems to me that both parties in the debate make a valid point, and it is yet to be seen if Jenson will be able to convince his detractors of the lack of sexism in his theological proposal. I will come back to the issue when looking at the feminist Trinitarian theology of Elizabeth Johnson.

As a minor note, let me mention that while reading Jenson is an enjoyable experience,[90] his prose is also quite idiosyncratic;[91] especially his earlier major work on the Trinity tends to develop terminology that is not only not very helpful but almost confusing. His latter work suffers less from those tendencies.

Another American theologian, the Roman Catholic Catherine Mowry LaCugna has made the Rahnerian idea of correlating the economic and immanent Trinity and the related ideas of the relation of divine life to history and salvation the main focus of her theology. While echoing many of the turns of Jenson—quite independently, it seems to me—she has also offered perhaps the most provocative and hotly debated proposal on the North American scene. LaCugna also speaks to the issue of inclusivity, yet her view has become the opposite of Jenson's and is closely linked with the opinions of her Catholic colleague Johnson.

89. Ibid., 16.
90. I am not quite sure what Philip Cary means when he says, "Reading Jenson is like no other experience in the world." Cary's review of *Systematic Theology*, vol. 1, *The Triune God*, by Robert W. Jenson, *Scottish Journal of Theology* 52, no. 1 (1999): 135.
91. Noted also by Grenz, *Rediscovering the Triune God*, 112.

Chapter 12

Catherine M. LaCugna
"God for Us"

THE DEFEAT OF THE DOCTRINE OF THE TRINITY

The reasons for the wide attention and debate caused by the Trinitarian proposal titled *God for Us* (1991)[1] of the late Roman Catholic Catherine Mowry LaCugna have to do on the one hand with her extraordinary capacity to bring together so many current developments in Trinitarian doctrine and on the other hand her bold suggestions to radically revise the received views. This Trinitarian theology is a brilliant incorporation of

> Zizioulas's dictum with Barth's focus on the revelational significance of the divine self-disclosure in Christ, Rahner's linking of the immanent Trinity with

---

1. Catherine Mowry LaCugna, *God for Us: The Trinity and Christian Life* (San Francisco: Harper-SanFrancisco, 1991). In addition to this book, LaCugna wrote a number of articles on the Trinity from the mid 1980s until her death in 1997. Those will be noted in the discussion even though her primary monograph naturally serves as the main source. A good synopsis of the main argumentation of *God for Us* can be found in Catherine Mowry LaCugna, "The Trinitarian Mystery of God," in *Systematic Theology: Roman Catholic Perspectives,* ed. Francis Schüssler Fiorenza and John P. Galvin, vol. 1 (Minneapolis: Fortress, 1991), 151–92.

the economic Trinity (albeit revised and reformulated as *theologia* and *oikonomia*), and the interest in viewing the divine life through the history of the Trinitarian persons evident in Pannenberg and Moltmann.[2]

Regarding the revisionist aspect of LaCugna's work, the most critical—and at the same time most hotly debated claim—is the hesitancy, if not refusal, to continue speaking of the immanent Trinity for the simple reason that the only thing we can know of the Triune God is based on the economy of salvation. The programmatic statement says it unambiguously: "Indeed, I argue that an ontological distinction between God *in se* and God *pro nobis* is, finally, inconsistent with biblical revelation, with early Christian creeds, and with Christian prayer and worship."[3] The theological method thus operates with the idea of linking closely theology proper (*theologia*) and soteriology (*oikonomia*). Therefore, there is only one Trinity, rather than two (immanent and economic). Closely related to this major turn in her proposal is the radically relational communion theology[4] as a way to banish substance-ontology once and for all from Christian theology and the insistence on the practicality of the doctrine of the Trinity instead of its past legacy as a speculative inquiry into the inner life of God. "The doctrine of the Trinity is ultimately a practical doctrine with radical consequences for Christian life" is the opening sentence of LaCugna's *God for Us*.[5]

To accomplish this ambitious program, LaCugna begins with a deconstructive and somewhat controversial reading of Trinitarian history.[6] The main critique against tradition is that with the disjoining of *oikonomia* and *theologia*, the focus changed to the inquiry into the "mystery of God" understood as *theologia*,[7] the end result being marginalization and finally defeat of the doctrine of the Trinity.[8] This, LaCugna contends, is different from the pre-Nicene understanding in which "economy" and "theology" belong together and describe the same reality, God.[9]

2. Stanley J. Grenz, *The Social God and the Relational Self: A Trinitarian Theology of the Imago Dei* (Louisville, KY: Westminster John Knox Press, 2001), 53; similarly also Stanley J. Grenz, *Rediscovering the Triune God: The Trinity in Contemporary Theology* (Minneapolis: Fortress, 2004), 148.

3. LaCugna, *God for Us*, 6.

4. Ibid., 1; so also p. 15.

5. Ibid., 1; so also p. 377. This is well illustrated in the title of one of her writings: Catherine Mowry LaCugna, "The Practical Trinity," *Christian Century* 109, no. 22 (July 15–22, 1992): 678–82.

6. Rightly Susan Wood remarks that LaCugna's work is both deconstructive and constructive. Susan Wood, Review Symposium of *God for Us*, *Horizons* 20–21 (1993–94): 127.

7. LaCugna, *God for Us*, 22–44.

8. See further the important article by Catherine Mowry LaCugna, "Philosophers and Theologians on the Trinity," *Modern Theology* 2, no. 3 (1986): 169–81. Typical of the older consensus, LaCugna mentions Schleiermacher as the culmination—or better: the low point—of the marginalization process. LaCugna, *God for Us*, 251. However, as mentioned in my historical section, not all agree today that the meager spaced allotted by Schleiermacher to the Trinity necessarily implies a lack of significance of the doctrine. See Grenz, *Rediscovering the Triune God*, 17–24. Illustrating his departure from the old consensus, Grenz titles the section in which Schleiermacher appears "The Stirring of Interest in Trinitarian Theology" (p. 16) in a chapter titled "The Eclipse of Trinitarian Theology"(chap. 1)!

9. LaCugna, *God for Us*, 30; see also pp. 41–42.

Why and when did this dramatic shift happen? LaCugna surmises it took place at Nicaea (325), when the orthodoxy responded to the challenge of Arianism. The core issue was the possibility—or as it was seen by the orthodoxy, the *impossibility*—of attributing suffering to deity.[10] In agreement with scholars such as R. P. Hanson,[11] LaCugna maintains that early theology prior to Nicaea in general subscribed to an "orthodox subordinationism," according to which Christ and Spirit are subordinate to the Father in the unfolding of salvation history as explicated in Scripture. This economic subordinationism, however, does not entail ontological subordinationism.[12] At the heart of Arianism was not only a statement about the inferior status of Son as "creature" in relation to the Father but also—in light of the worldview that underlined the transcendence of God, thus making God absolute and impassible—an ingenious way to deal with the seeming impossibility of ascribing suffering to God. If Son is "less than God," then it is possible to link suffering with this intermediary who is finite.[13] The results of the orthodox rebuttal of Arianism, however, were ironic. While insisting on the equal status of the incarnate Son with the Father, Christian theology of course held *oikonomia* and *theologia* together, but then the relegating of suffering only to the human nature of the Logos sundered the two, implying that in his inner life God cannot suffer.[14] "But this approach compromised the idea that in Christ, God as such is present."[15]

The subsequent development of Trinitarian history in LaCugna's reading is but consolidation of this dramatic separation between economy and *theologia*. The tradition has it that *oikonomia* deals with salvation (history) and *theologia* with the inner life of God. Not surprisingly—and echoing the judgment of theologians such as Colin Gunton—the two Latin theologians at the heart of LaCugna's critique are Augustine and Aquinas, the former because he turned the focus from salvation history to psychological analogies, among other faults, and the latter because in his theology the speculative, abstract approach finds its zenith.[16] A corollary error was the emergence of the divine substance or essence rather than person being conceived as the highest ontological principle.[17] With all her sympathies for the theology of the Christian East, especially that of the Cappadocians, quite surprisingly LaCugna maintains that it was not only Latin

10. Ibid., 42–43.

11. See R. P. Hanson, *The Search for the Christian Doctrine of God: The Arian Controversy 318–381* (Edinburgh: T & T Clark, 1988), xix, 64, among others.

12. LaCugna, *God for Us*, 24. LaCugna shows evidence that both Irenaeus and Tertullian advocated the view of orthodox subordinationism (pp. 26–29).

13. Ibid., 34–37.

14. Ibid., 35, 38.

15. Ibid., 42; for a summary statement, see p. 37.

16. For Augustine, see ibid., chap. 3, and for Aquinas, chap. 5; for a summary of the Trinitarian flaws of Aquinas, see p. 145.

17. Ibid., 101. This, however, is not only the tendency in the Christian West; even in the Eastern tradition, especially in Gregory of Palamas, who helped to ratify the *essence* and *energies* separation (received from the Cappadocians and other early theologians) into a dogmatic statement, the idea that "the *ousia* of God exists trihypostatically" was blurred (p. 192).

theology that separated economy from theology, but also the East.[18] The Christian East helped the separation of theology and economy especially by their distinction between divine *ousia*, God in God's inaccessible divine nature, and *energies*, what God is toward us.[19]

While it is nothing new to say that in the West the Trinity waned after the patristic developments, it is something new to hear LaCugna argue that the same happened also in the Christian East, traditionally considered the bastion of this doctrine:

> In scholastic theology, the doctrine of the Trinity was identified as the science of God's inner relatedness. The result of this was a one-sided theology of God that had little to do with the economy of Christ and the Spirit, with the themes of Incarnation and grace, and therefore little to do with the Christian life. Greek medieval theology took refuge in an exaggerated agnosticism that relegated the trinitarian persons to a region far beyond our capacity to experience or understand. Hence the defeat of the doctrine of the Trinity.[20]

THEOLOGIA AS OIKONOMIA

A key claim for LaCugna is that the purpose of the doctrine of the Trinity is not— as is the case in her reading of tradition[21]—the inner life of God but rather the *relationship* between economy and the inner life of God:

> The doctrine of the Trinity is the attempt to understand the eternal mystery of God on the basis of what is revealed about God in the economy of redemption. Theology of God is at the same time theology of Christ and Spirit. The economy of salvation is the basis, the context, and the final criterion for every statement about God. Trinitarian doctrine focuses on the relationship between *oikonomia* and *theologia* or . . . the "economic" Trinity and "immanent" Trinity.[22]

Two important implications follow. First, the only way for humans to know anything about God is to ascend from the economy of salvation to God's own life. We ascend from the works of God to the life of God.[23] Having said that, an important qualification is in order, lest LaCugna's proposal be misunderstood: economy of salvation is not only the beginning but also the *end* of our knowledge of

19. Ibid., 39. This distinction of course means that "'theology' in the proper sense is the doctrine of God considered in Godself." Ibid. So also p. 210. The subsequent chapters in the first (historical) part of LaCugna's *God for Us* trace the implications of this dramatic change for Trinitarian doctrine. For Gregory Palamas and his contribution to the separation, see chap. 6.
20. Ibid., 210.
21. Ibid., 2; so also p. 210.
22. Ibid., 22.
23. Ibid., 1.

God.[24] To repeat one of the key arguments of LaCugna: there are not "two" trinities, but only one. So, in the final analysis, when theological knowledge ascends from the economy, it will never reach anything else than "economy";[25] there is no "hidden God,"[26] no *theologia* apart from *oikonomia*.[27] "*Oikonomia* and *theologia* are two aspects of the *one* self-communication of God."[28] Consequently, LaCugna insists on the "identity of the economic and immanent Trinity," which for her "means that what God has revealed and given in Christ and the Spirit *is* the reality of God as God is from all eternity." Therefore, if there is any distinction allowed between the economic and immanent, it is "strictly conceptual."[29]

Because of the identity between the economic and immanent Trinity, LaCugna prefers a dynamic, chiastic model of the Trinity as against the typical derivative approaches. In that model there is one ecstatic movement of God outward

> by which all things originate from God through Christ in the power of the Holy Spirit, and all things are brought into union with God and returned to God. There is neither an economic nor an immanent Trinity; there is only the *oikonomia* that is the concrete realization of the mystery of *theologia* in time, space, history, and personality. In this framework, the doctrine of the Trinity encompasses much more than the immanent Trinity, envisioned in static ahistorical and transeconomic terms; the subject matter of the Christian theology of God is the one dynamic movement of God, *a Patre ad Patrem*. There is no reason to stop at any one point along the curve, no reason to single out one point as if it could be fixed or frozen in time.[30]

Second, the "life of God—precisely because God is triune—does not belong to God alone. . . . Divine life is therefore also *our* life. The heart of the Christian life is to be united with the God of Jesus Christ by means of communion with one another."[31] Traditionally union with God has been expressed with the Eastern Orthodox concept of *theōsis*, an idea heartily embraced by this Roman Catholic theologian.[32]

Building on the theology of Rahner, LaCugna reminds us that the only basis for the knowledge of the Triune God is God's free self-revelation: "*Theological* statements are possible not because we have some independent insight into God, or can speak from the standpoint of God, but because God has freely revealed

24. Ibid., 321.
25. Ibid., 1.
26. Ibid., 322.
27. Ibid., 381: "The doctrine of the Trinity remains *derivative*, derived from the economy" (italics in original).
28. Ibid., 13 (italics in original), so also p. 319.
29. Ibid., 212; also p. 231. Or to put it in another way: "Yet, the distinction is not ontological" (ibid.).
30. Ibid., 223.
31. Ibid., 1.
32. Ibid., 3, 10, etc.

and communicated God's *self,* God's personal existence, God's infinite mystery."[33] This is a highly pregnant statement: God's self-revelation is more than revelation *about* God; it is God's *self*-offering.[34] Yet when she speaks of the self-revelation of God in terms of God revealing God's infinite mystery, it does not mean that from economy we can ascend to something beyond economy, to a God apart from economy. "Theology is inseparable from soteriology, and vice versa."[35] Is this, then, an exercise in reducing theology into soteriology? LaCugna responds no. The doctrine of the Trinity cannot be understood merely as functional, as merely our experience of God. While Trinitarian theology is that, "it is also a statement, however partial, about the mystery of God's eternal being." What is needed here is balance:

> A theology built entirely around *theologia* produces a nonexperiential, nonsoteriological, nonchristological, nonpneumatological metaphysics of the divine nature. A theology built entirely around *oikonomia* results in a skepticism about whether how God saves through Christ in the power of the Holy Spirit is essentially related to who or what God is. The unity of *theologia* and *oikonomia* shows that the fundamental issue in Trinitarian theology is not the inner workings of the "immanent" Trinity, but *the question of how the Trinitarian pattern of salvation history is to be correlated with the eternal being of God.*[36]

"THE TRIUMPH OF RELATIONALITY"[37]

Drawing from various sources such as the personalist philosophy of John MacMurray, the Eastern Orthodox communion theology of John Zizioulas, the Latin American liberationist John Boff, feminist theologies, and some contemporary ethical theologies,[38] LaCugna develops a thoroughgoing Trinitarian "theology of relationship" in which "the 'essence' of God is relational, other-ward, [such] that God exists as diverse persons united in a communion of freedom, love, and

33. Ibid., 3 (italics in the original), also p. 210. A careful dialogue with Rahner and his axiom can be found in Catherine Mowry LaCugna, "Re-Conceiving the Trinity as the Mystery of Salvation," *Scottish Journal of Theology* 38 (1985): 1–23.

34. Speaking of early Christian theology, the statement of which she affirms as lasting, LaCugna writes: "At the heart of the Christian doctrine of God were two affirmations: God has given Godself to us in Jesus Christ and the Spirit, and this self-revelation or self-communication is nothing less than what God is as God" (*God for Us,* 209).

35. Ibid., 211; also LaCugna, "The Practical Trinity," 681.

36. LaCugna, *God for Us,* 4 (italics in the original).

37. Heading taken from the title of chap. 4 in Grenz, *Rediscovering the Triune God,* in which he discusses John Zizioulas and Leonardo Boff in addition to LaCugna.

38. All of these approaches are discussed in LaCugna, *God for Us,* 255–88. While she was willing to "learn a great deal from cultural, anthropological, philosophical, and psychological approaches to personhood, [she believed] the doctrine of the Trinity ultimately must measure its reflections on personhood by the revelation of the divine personhood in the face of Christ and the activity of the Holy Spirit" (pp. 292–93).

knowledge." In other words, hers is "an ontology of relation," based on the idea of personhood as communion, as in-relation-to the Other(s).[39] While the Cappadocians were the trailblazers for communion theology with their idea of "*relation* or *person* (*hypostaseis*) as the mode of God's *ousia*,"[40] perhaps surprisingly LaCugna maintains that it was not only the Christian East but also the West that affirms communion as the nature of ultimate reality, provided that, in the ascendancy of scholastic theology, communion was most often related with the inner life of God over against Greek theology's relating it with salvation.[41] With Zizioulas, LaCugna argues that personhood—and thus relationality—is not an addition to being but the very mode of existence, first of God and then by derivation of human beings.[42] In other words, "personhood [is] constitutive of being,"[43] or "*personhood is the meaning of being*."[44] Methodologically this fits in the "from below" approach of LaCugna: since God is relational, it means that access to God is only through relationality; there is no access to "God's being in-itself or by-itself."[45]

An important corollary to the idea of God existing in relations is that the ultimate goal of the doctrine of the Trinity is "not to produce a theory of God's self-relatedness" (immanent Trinity) but rather to say something about the encounter between God and the world including us (economic Trinity). If this is taken seriously, it means that theological talk about God becomes dynamic rather than static and self-sufficient.[46]

Before looking at several important implications of casting the doctrine of the Triune God into a solely personal mode, let me register the somewhat surprising—and at the same time quite brilliant—way that LaCugna moves beyond the ancient problem of where to locate the "person" of God, in the one nature or the three *hypostases*. While these are not the only two options (think of Robert W. Jenson's idea of the whole Trinity being "person"), these are the two standard routes. LaCugna in a way dismisses the whole question as long as God's personhood is being affirmed![47]

Relational ontology for LaCugna is the key to considering the topic of the "attributes" of God that in traditional theology follows the topic of the one God, before discussing the Triune God. This is a reversal of classical theism with its

39. Ibid., 243; so also p. 383, and LaCugna, "Philosophers and Theologians on the Trinity," 177.

40. LaCugna, *God for Us*, 243.

41. Ibid., 249. Later, however, LaCugna has qualified this affirmation by saying, "Theologians trained in the categories of Latin theology have only scarcely begun to realize the vast implications of this ontology of personhood." LaCugna, Author's Response in Review Symposium, *Horizons* 20–21 (1993–94): 138.

42. LaCugna, *God for Us*, 244–46.

43. Ibid., 245.

44. Ibid., 248 (italics in original). On pp. 288–93, LaCugna elaborates on the meaning of looking at persons as communion, and on pp. 293–300 she considers communion theology from the perspective of Christology and pneumatology.

45. Ibid., 246.

46. Ibid., 320.

47. Ibid., 305.

preoccupation with Greek philosophy, operating with terms such as the incomprehensibility, immutability, and simplicity of God. The difficulty in relating suffering to God for traditional theology, with its doctrine of immutability (no change in God) and impassibility (no suffering in God)—the roots of which are also part of the Arian controversy as discussed above—can be overcome, so LaCugna believes, with her way of linking attributes to communion. Immutability in this new outlook means that if personhood is essential to being, God's and ours, then God is "*immutably personal.* God cannot be anything but personal." And consequently, "[o]nce the personal history of Jesus, including his death, is made central to the theology of God, then we must conclude that God suffers in Christ."[48] Similarly, the ancient attribute of incomprehensibility from a communion perspective does not mean so much that we do not know God (even though that is also true) but that God is incomprehensible because God is personal. Personhood means something indefinable, unique, and ineffable.[49]

The idea of personhood as communion also speaks to the practical aspects of the doctrine of the Trinity, a key insistence in LaCugna's theology.[50] While not "pragmatic" in the sense of being able to directly furnish solutions to the problems of humans and society, it guides Christian life in keeping with what they believe about God, who is personal, ecstatic, and fecund love:

> God, too, lives from and for another: God the Father gives birth to the Son, breathes forth the Spirit, elects the creature from before all time. Living from others and for others is the path of glory in which we and God exist together. . . . Orthopraxis requires that we exercise the modes of relationship that serve the truth of God's economy: words, actions, and attitudes that serve the *reign of God.* This rule is opposite of tyranny and arbitrariness. God's rule is accomplished by saving and healing love, by conversion of the heart, through the forgiveness of sins. God's household is administered (economized) by the power of the Holy Spirit, who rules through justice, peace, charity, love, joy, moderation, kindness, generosity, freedom, compassion, reconciliation, holiness, humility, wisdom, truthfulness, and the gifts of prophecy, healing, discernment of spirits, speaking in tongues, interpretation of tongues.[51]

Against Zizioulas and his tradition, from which she otherwise borrows so much in terms of communion theology, LaCugna speaks against monarchy based on the idea of one ruler and for shared rule. Her view of Trinity speaks for the primacy of communion among equals against imperial rule. A Trinitarian theology of God as explicated above presents a powerful critique against political[52] and

48. Ibid., 300–301 (301; italics in original)
49. Ibid., 302.
50. Ibid., 410; see also LaCugna, "Re-Conceiving the Trinity," 16–17.
51. LaCugna, *God for Us*, 383–84 (italics in original).
52. Ibid., 390–400.

ecclesial[53] as well as sexist[54] abuses and misuses of power, generating from non-Trinitarian theologies of God.

TRINITARIAN THEOLOGY AS DOXOLOGY

With Pannenberg and Moltmann on the one hand and the whole Eastern tradition, including Zizioulas, on the other hand, LaCugna comes to the conclusion that the proper mode of doing theology is doxology and adoration. Her main reasons for highlighting the importance of doxology, however, are somewhat different from (if not opposite to) her Protestant counterparts. In this respect, her view is close to that of the Christian East while also borrowing from Aquinas and others. LaCugna refers to the universally[55] shared idea that personhood is both ineffable and incomprehensible.[56] Human talk about God can never exhaust God, nor can the "mystery of God who is alive and . . . has ongoing relationship with creation and persons . . . be frozen or fixed in time." Therefore, God remains "the incomprehensible Origin of everything that is."[57] The only appropriate response, thus, is adoration and worship. This is not to undermine the importance of rational talk, but rather to seek a balance between apophatic (negative) and kataphatic (positive) approaches.[58] In that sense, "Theology is as much knowing and unknowing" in its attempt to say something about the person of God, which by definition is ineffable,[59] and which—unlike any other objects of human inquiry—is "subject."[60] The balance for LaCugna can only be found in the balanced blending of kataphatic and apophatic approaches in doxology, adoration of the Triune God.[61]

In the doxological mode, the doctrine of the Trinity is more like a signpost or an icon than a fixed doctrine.[62] This is not, however, to introduce the distinction between the economic and immanent Trinity as if there were a "hidden God (*deus absconditus*) behind the God of revelation history." Nor is it to say that God in God's eternal mystery would be anything other than what God reveals Godself to be.[63]

---

53. Ibid., 401–10.

54. Catherine Mowry LaCugna, "God in Communion with Us—The Trinity," in *Freeing Theology: The Essentials of Theology in Feminist Perspective*, ed. Catherine Mowry LaCugna (San Francisco: HarperSanFrancisco, 1993), 83–114.

55. LaCugna, *God for Us*, 325.

56. Ibid., 323.

57. Ibid., 321.

58. Ibid., 333. Greek tradition favors the method of apophasis when speaking of the limitations of human language with regard to God, whereas the favored Latin method is that of analogy (p. 325). See also LaCugna, "Re-conceiving the Trinity," 19–21.

59. LaCugna, *God for Us*, 333–34 (333).

60. Ibid., 332.

61. Ibid., 361. In "Re-conceiving the Trinity," 21–22, she speaks of a "contemplative" style of theology.

62. LaCugna, *God for Us*, 321–22.

63. Ibid., 322.

What the doxological nature of theology wishes to say is that the one self-revelation of God in salvation history "by no means diminishes the Absolute Mystery of God." One way theology speaks of this mystery is with the pair of terms "transcendence" and "immanence." The term "immanence," however, does not denote the "economic" any more than the term "transcendence" denotes the "immanent" Trinity. Thinking that they did would mean considering God apart from God's relationship to us, thus violating LaCugna's basic methodological axiom. Rather, "God is transcendent because God's nearness to us in history does not exhaust the ineffable mystery of God." Therefore, both transcendence and immanence can be predicated of both economy and theology.[64]

Here we come to the brilliant observation of LaCugna that predicating the identity of the *oikonomia* and *theologia* means that the economy of salvation ("economic Trinity") is no less a mystery than the eternal mystery of God ("immanent Trinity").[65]

CRITICAL REFLECTIONS

By far the most substantial challenge posed by LaCugna's constructive Trinitarian proposal has to do with her recasting of the relation between economy and *theologia* and her refusal to continue talk about the immanent Trinity.[66] Although LaCugna claims that this is "one step toward greater precision,"[67] I believe with many that the lack of clarity in LaCugna's proposal concerning this foundational question is instead a source of much controversy.[68] As mentioned, for LaCugna the distinction between the immanent and economic Trinity is "strictly conceptual"[69] "because if the distinction is ontological, then *theologia* is separated from *oikonomia*." If the distinction is merely epistemological, then it means that economy is the gateway to theology.[70] But is it a contradiction when on the next page LaCugna approvingly cites Piet Schoonenberg, who claims with Rahner that "there can not be strict identity between the economic and immanent Trinity"?[71] The context for the latter statement explains what LaCugna means, and therefore this statement (at least) is not a denial of her affirmation of the identity. If there is strict identity, it

64. Ibid.
65. Ibid. This is illustrated in the title of one of her important articles, "Re-Conceiving the Trinity."
66. Grenz, *Rediscovering the Triune God*, 159.
67. LaCugna, "Author's Response," 139.
68. Even a critic as friendly and nuanced as Stanley J. Grenz cannot help but conclude that "LaCugna's attempt to provide an alternative conceptual scheme to this reigning but, in her estimation, problematic language [concerning the traditional economic-immanent distinction] comprises perhaps the most difficult and most readily misunderstood aspect of her proposal." *Rediscovering the Triune God*, 153.
69. LaCugna, *God for Us*, 212.
70. Ibid., 217.
71. Ibid., 218.

would mean that one could begin at the either end, either from God or economy. But LaCugna—as well as Rahner, of course—takes it as an axiom that one can only begin with the economy. So it seems to me that *epistemologically* speaking, in terms of the method of theology, the identity has to be qualified in a way that does not frustrate the economy as the starting point.[72]

Things get more complicated when we inquire into the *ontological* equation of the two identities. Remarking that Rahner's approach to Trinitarian theology can be called "from below," analogously to Christology, in that it begins with the economy of salvation, she adds: "This does not mean that the Trinity exists only in our experience."[73] Does this mean what it says at face value, that there is an immanent Trinity beyond the economic? Or does it say less, just the fact that there is Trinity beyond our experience but that Trinity is only "economic"? It seems to me it is clear that these kinds of statements only speak to the issue of the epistemological starting point. There are, however, other statements that seem to go beyond epistemology to ontology. LaCugna listens carefully to several Catholic theologians[74] who have qualified Rahner's axiom and argued that some kind of asymmetry needs to be posited lest God's freedom be compromised. One of the ways this asymmetry is affirmed is the way Yves Congar speaks of the fact that while there is only one Trinity, "'this [self-communication] takes place in a mode that is not connatural with the being of the divine Persons.' The mode of the economy is condescension, *kenōsis*. Thus there remains a certain degree of disparity between what God is *in se*, and what God is able to be *ad extra*."[75] As a result of this and related considerations, LaCugna concludes: "The incomprehensible and ineffable mystery of God is not diminished by God's self-expression in the history of salvation. Nonetheless, because of the unity of *theologia* and *oikonomia*, the specific details of God's self-revelation in Christ and the Spirit reveal God's nature."[76] The same is affirmed in another statement: "As for the nature of this unity [between the immanent and economic Trinity], there cannot be a strict identity, either epistemological or ontological, between God and God for us. Transposed into the language of Orthodox theology, there is an essential unity though not strict identity between divine essence and divine energies."[77]

72. Ibid.

73. Ibid., 216.

74. Piet Schoonenberg, Walter Kasper, and Yves Congar.

75. LaCugna, *God for Us*, 219, quotation within the quotation from Yves Congar, *I Believe in the Holy Spirit*, trans. David Smith, 3 vols. (New York: Seabury Press, 1983), 3:15.

76. LaCugna, *God for Us*, 221. Many have wondered whether LaCugna's proposal compromises God's freedom to the point of taking Trinitarian theology in the direction of pantheism. This concern occupies the minds of both persistent critics of LaCugna such as Paul D. Molnar ("Toward Contemporary Doctrine of the Immanent Trinity: Karl Barth and the Present Discussion," *Scottish Journal of Theology* 49 [1996]: 314–15), as well as the minds of theologians otherwise quite favorable to her such as Joseph Bracken, review of *God for Us*, *Theological Studies* 53 (1992): 559–60; and J. A. DiNoia, review of *God for Us*, *Modern Theology* 9 (1993): 215–16. Mark Samuel Medley, *Imago Trinitatis: Toward a Relational Understanding of Being Human* (Ann Arbor, MI: UMI Dissertation Series, 1995), 146, completely dismisses the whole criticism against LaCugna with regard to this point.

77. LaCugna, *God for Us*, 221; similarly, p. 321. The last statement—with reference to Ortho-

So there are statements such as these that seem to support the conclusion that, despite her insistence on the primacy of the economic identity, LaCugna still considers talk about the immanent Trinity legitimate. Other statements and qualifications elsewhere in her monograph, however, seem to belie this conclusion. With all the ambiguity surrounding her views about the legitimacy of the distinction between the economic and immanent Trinity and the corollary question of the nature of the immanent Trinity, it seems to me the evidence points toward her denial of both of these. Take, for example, the following important quotation. While the first part of the statement at first seems to support the idea of the distinction, the rest of the quotation clearly speaks for its rejection. Commenting on both Western and Eastern traditions' views of affirming the ineffability of God, she writes:

> This is not to say that we do not know God. If God is truly *self*-communicating, then we do know the essence (personal existence) of God: we know God as God truly is, in the mediation of God's self-revelation in Christ and the Spirit. The immanent Trinity is not transhistorical, transempirical, or transeconomic. Nor is the immanent Trinity a "more real" God—more real because the mode of discourse used to describe it is ontological. Rather, to speak about God in immanent Trinitarian terms is nothing more than to speak about God's life with us in the economy of Christ and the Spirit.[78]

This judgment (namely, that LaCugna at the end of the day seems to be virtually denying the existence of and therefore the possibility of talking about the immanent Trinity) is perfectly in keeping with her radical revision of the terms "economic" and "immanent" Trinity itself. LaCugna argues that *oikonomia*, rather than being the Trinity *ad extra*, is the overall saving plan of God from creation to consummation, whereas *theologia*, rather than being God *in se*, only denotes the mystery of God.[79] But what is the "mystery of God"? Is that something "beyond" what we experience in salvation? No, LaCugna responds. And this seems to me to settle the question: For LaCugna, there is no "immanent" Trinity apart from the economic: "the mystery of God is the mystery of God with us."[80] The same is also affirmed in the statement that "[t]he sphere of God's being-in-relation is the economy of creation and redemption in which the *totality of God's life is given*."[81] A further support for my judgment—shared by many[82]—comes from the observation

---

dox theology—however, sounds odd since LaCugna elsewhere, as noted, opposes Orthodoxy's separation of two identities (that it calls essence and energies)!

78. LaCugna, *God for Us*, 229 (italics in original).

79. Ibid., 223.

80. Ibid., 223–24.

81. Ibid., 246 (italics mine). It is only in light of LaCugna's revised understanding of *oikonomia* and *theologia* that some of her statements that could be read in support of the need to continue maintaining the distinction between two identities should be read: "God's presence to us does not exhaust without remainder the absolute mystery of God" (p. 228), or, "It would be more accurate to say that an immanent theology of God is an inexact effort to say something about God *as God is revealed in the economy of salvation history*" (p. 230, italics in original).

82. Even critics as careful and nuanced as Stanley J. Grenz (*The Social God*, 55) and Ted Peters (*God as Trinity: Relationality and Temporality in Divine Life* [Louisville, KY: Westminster John Knox

of Ben Leslie. After a careful review of all LaCugna's main writings on the topic of the Trinity, he concludes that that there is a development in her thought from guarded caution to outright rejection of speaking of the immanent Trinity.[83] There are unambiguous statements to that effect. Again, building on her revised understanding of the terms, she says "*Theologia* is what is given in *oikonomia* and *oikonomia* expresses *theologia*," and therefore, "*an 'immanent' Trinitarian theology of God is nothing more than a theology of the economy of salvation.*"[84] This is as clear a rebuttal of the concept of "immanent" Trinity as can be.[85] There is also what LaCugna adds as a "practical" reason for not equating the immanent Trinity with God's inner life, and that has to do with one of the basic axioms of this Catholic theologian, namely, that "*Trinitarian life is also our life.*"[86]

The few concessions LaCugna seems to make in favor of continuing the distinction do not in my mind affect the basic judgment above; rather, these concessions add confusion. The statement that the distinction (immanent-economic and essence-energies) is "useful to the extent that it enables the theologian to say that God truly *is* what God has shown Godself to be"[87] is nothing other than a reaffirmation of her methodological starting point (in keeping with Rahner's rule). Another concession makes sense but sounds ironic. LaCugna admits that the distinction could be justified for those who want to continue using the terms economic and immanent Trinity in that it "*may be* a legitimate enterprise for a purely speculative theology"; however, a word of warning is issued here: that may easily lead and has often led to leaving the economy behind.[88] Yet another concession in support of continuing the distinction leaves me wondering what exactly LaCugna means. With reference to her foundational idea of God as person, that is, as communion, she argues that the economic and immanent Trinity distinction is a way

---

Press, 1993], 143) have come to this conclusion. Not all agree with this judgment. Medley (*Imago Trinitatis*, 146) argues that to assume that LaCugna has given up the whole notion of the immanent Trinity "is to miss her point entirely." Unfortunately, it is less than clear how Medley supports so categorical an opinion.

83. Ben Leslie, "Does God Have a Life? Barth and LaCugna on the Immanent Trinity," *Perspectives in Religious Studies* 24, no. 4 (Winter 1997): 384. In that sense methodologically I don't find persuasive Grenz's judgment that LaCugna's 1985 article "Re-conceiving the Trinity as the Mystery of Salvation" is the convincing proof of her rejection of immanent Trinity, even though I of course agree with Grenz's opinion materially (Grenz, *Reconsidering the Triune God*, 161). Taking my clue from Leslie's careful observation, I have tried to support my view by looking at LaCugna's views in her major monograph (written several years later than the above-mentioned article).

84. LaCugna, *God for Us*, 224 (italics in the original).

85. Ibid., 225, repeats it.

86. Ibid., 228. In a somewhat confusing way—to make sure that her argument is heard—LaCugna twists the whole meaning of the technical term "immanent" by saying that "an immanent theology of the Trinity is thus ineluctably a theology of the 'internal' structure of the economy of redemption" (p. 224).

87. Ibid., 225.

88. Ibid., 227 (italics in original). I assume this is the meaning of another statement that is quite ambiguous in light of her overall theology: "Still, inquiry into the immanent ground of the missions of Son and Spirit remains a legitimate theological enterprise *provided* this inquiry is understood properly and modestly, that is, as reflection on God's self-disclosure in the person of Christ and the activity of the Holy Spirit" (pp. 231–32).

to affirm that God is personal and thus free, and that "God cannot be reduced to human history or perception." She explains this further: "The mystery of *theologia* exceeds or transcends what can be expressed in *oikonomia*, just as our own personhood exceeds any one self-expression or even a lifetime of self-expression."[89] While the latter part of the sentence is of course affirmed by all, I don't understand why LaCugna would need any economic-immanent distinction to safeguard this view (even though it makes sense in that for her *theologia* does not mean speculation into the inner life of God but rather the mystery of God as coming to expression in salvation history). Wouldn't just the universally agreed-upon idea of personhood as something ineffable better serve LaCugna's own purposes?—as she has indeed done.[90]

In sum, it seems to me the end result of LaCugna's program is the collapse of the immanent Trinity into the economic.[91] Why is this of such importance? The reason is simply that "[w]ithout a notion of the immanent Trinity, the claim that in the *oikonomia* we encounter God as God really lacks sufficient ground."[92] If the question of the immanent Trinity—or however one may want to put it if the term itself is problematic—is left open, one could also put the question in this way: "On what basis then can a theology claim authenticity for itself that does not ground itself in its own truth?"[93] It seems to me that for LaCugna it is the *experience* (of salvation) that serves as the ground. Many have voiced criticism against such a shaky foundation.[94] That criticism cannot be easily dismissed. Again, it would be another issue if experience would be seen as the *methodological* starting point for the knowledge of God (as Rahner maintains) rather than the end and maybe substance of the doctrine of the Trinity.

Other questions and challenges to LaCugna's proposal include the question raised against the accuracy of her reading of Trinitarian traditions. It is doubtful whether the claim for a pre-Nicene economic focus (to the exclusion of the *theological* in the traditional sense of the word) is historically accurate. It has been noted that theologians such as Tertullian did not dismiss the inquiry into the inner life of God.[95] It seems very likely that LaCugna reads early history with an agenda to make her point.

---

89. Ibid., 304.

90. Ibid., 323.

91. In addition to Grenz and Peters, cited above, other theologians agree with this final conclusion. See, e.g., Thomas Weinandy, "The Immanent and Economic Trinity," *The Thomist* 57 (1993): 61.

92. Leslie, "Does God Have a Life?" 394 (I have amended the text for English grammar; the original has the word "is" before "lacks sufficient ground"). Leslie himself, in contrast to me, holds the opinion that while LaCugna gives the impression that it is not justifiable to talk about God's inner life, this is not meant to be understood as total denial of the concept of the immanent Trinity. Rather, Leslie argues, "[w]hat she surrenders is the possibility that one may speak of God *in se* in abstraction from revelation" (ibid.). Even Leslie admits that his conclusion gives rise to other problems in LaCugna, for example, concerning the denial of the "hidden God" behind economy. Surely, if one continues to speak of the immanent Trinity, some type of "hidden God" needs to be posited!

93. Leslie, "Does God Have a Life?" 394.

94. Especially Molnar, "Toward Contemporary Doctrine," 319.

95. Leslie, "Does God Have a Life?" 385 n. 32, with reference to other scholars; David S. Cunningham, *These Three Are One: The Practice of Trinitarian Theology* (Cambridge: Blackwell, 1998), 37; Grenz, *Rediscovering the Triune God*, 159.

The critique against LaCugna's preferred way of understanding salvation as *theōsis* in my understanding is not a problem nor weakness but rather a way to connect Trinity to salvation in a more integral way.[96] Deification, as is well known, is not only the way the Christian East conceives salvation but also one of the most ancient soteriological concepts.[97]

The Catholic Susan Wood makes a remark concerning the relationship between doxology, liturgy, and Scripture in LaCugna. While beginning with economy, Wood argues that LaCugna still operates within "the conceptual framework of a specific philosophical system rather than beginning with a study of the relationship between Father, Son, and Spirit as expressed in Scripture."[98] It seems to me that Wood's criticism is basically correct. Like Barth and unlike Pannenberg, LaCugna at best builds on a formal principle arising out of—or at least in keeping with—the biblical text but hardly builds on a careful reading of salvation history as presented in Scripture.

While the relational ontology and thus the idea of person as communion is one of the undisputed convictions of the contemporary Trinitarian renaissance, a question has been raised about whether LaCugna's interpretation takes too far the basing of God's relationality, the ecstatic nature of God, on the economy of salvation. Certainly God is relational—if we take seriously the distinction of Son and Spirit from the Father and from each other; yet, when pressed, doesn't this sound like God is in "need [of] our existence in order to be"? We need to turn the tables and affirm rather that "God's interpersonal being *pro nobis* is rooted in God's interpersonal being *in se.*"[99] It is one thing to say that we know of God's *inner* relationality via *oikonomia* and another to imply that *oikonomia* is the basis for the intradivine relationality.

Another concern regarding the focus on personhood arises from the obvious observation that while LaCugna is seemingly successful in moving beyond the typical impasse of locating the term "person" either in the unity of God or the threeness, she fails in establishing the personhood of the Son and Spirit. Clearly, she focuses almost exclusively on the personhood of Father and the whole Trinity even though she claims that her doxological communion theology "forces the Christian doctrine of God to remain *christological* and *pneumatological.*"[100]

---

96. For a typical Western misunderstanding, see the critique of LaCugna's soteriology by Millard J. Erickson, *God in Three Persons: A Contemporary Interpretation of the Trinity* (Grand Rapids: Baker Books, 1995), 308: "She [LaCugna] speaks of the 'deified human being.' This, however, seems to confuse the relationship of salvation with ontology, so that we are not only related to God but joined with him metaphysically."

97. See further Veli-Matti Kärkkäinen, *One with God: Salvation as Deification and Justification* (Collegeville, MN: Liturgical Press, 2004).

98. Wood, Review Symposium, 129.

99. See Barbara A. Finan, Review Symposium, *Horizons* 20-21 (1993-94): 135.

100. LaCugna, *God for Us*, 362–64 (362). The charge of lack of attention to the personhood of Christ and the Spirit has been voiced by Robrecht Michiel, review of *God for Us*, *Louvain Studies* 20, no. 1 (Spring 1995): 91. In LaCugna's defense, however, we should refer to the discussion of some aspects of the personhood of the Spirit and Son in LaCugna, *God for Us*, 292–300.

The charge of modalism raised by some sounds strange regarding a Trinitarian theology so distinctively relational, and thus beginning from the three separate *hypostaseis*.[101]

While LaCugna's theology claims to be inclusive not only for doctrinal but also for spiritual and political/social implications, ironically it also tends to become reductionistic because of its radical "God for us" orientation. As Mark Samuel Medley insightfully puts it:

> LaCugna reduces "all of reality" to persons and God. The self-communication of God is incomplete if the focus is primarily on *pro nobis*—for humans. The triune self-communication is also for the entire cosmos. Her reflection on the Trinity is thus limited to the degree that she focuses exclusively on human redemption to the diminishment of a cosmocentric focus.[102]

I started this chapter by noticing that one of the reasons for the great interest in the Trinitarian theology of this late Catholic theologian is her extraordinary capacity to integrate various strands of traditional and contemporary Trinitarian insights. At the same time she is a crucial bridge between Trinitarian theologians coming from various quarters of the theological world. Even theologians as distant from Roman Catholicism as the evangelical Millard J. Erickson, to be studied after Elizabeth Johnson, echo many insights popularized and recast by LaCugna such as relationality, communion, and the primacy of the *three* in one. The Trinitarian theology of another Roman Catholic theologian, Johnson, is a fitting counterpart to that of LaCugna. On the one hand, they hold a lot in common, such as great respect for tradition even when tradition is critiqued, approach "from below," communion theology, and especially the shared concern for feminist issues and inclusivity. On the other hand, in many ways these two American Catholic theologians also advocate quite different agendas: while advocating a "from below" approach, their methodology differs significantly; the way they attempt to resolve the thorny question of the relationship between the economic and immanent Trinity comes to radically different conclusions, and so on.

101. Molnar, "Toward a Contemporary Doctrine," 320.
102. Medley, *Imago Trinitatis*, 73 n. 89.

Chapter 13

Elizabeth Johnson

*A Feminist Interpretation
of the Triune Symbol*

TRINITY AND THE FEMALE CONSCIOUSNESS

"Even with all their diversity, feminist, womanist, and *mujerista* theologies have one thing in common: they make the liberation of women central to the theological task."[1] While united in the central task of liberation,[2] women's voices in theology no longer form a united front but rather display the kind of variety that can be expected of any theology in the beginning of the third millennium. Therefore, to speak of "feminist" theology in generic terms is quite misleading. The term "feminist" refers to white women's approaches, while "womanist" applies to African American and *mujerista* to Latina women.[3] The proliferation of views is enhanced by the emergence of women's voices from Africa, Latin America, and

1. Mary McClintock Fulkerson, "Feminist Theology," in *The Cambridge Companion to Postmodern Theology*, ed. Kevin J. Vanhoozer (Cambridge: Cambridge University Press, 2003), 109.
2. To do justice to the diversity of women's approaches in various locations, even the idea of liberation needs to be expressed in a most open-ended way.
3. For an introduction to the views of God among these three women's theologies, see Veli-Matti Kärkkäinen, *The Doctrine of God: A Global Introduction* (Grand Rapids: Baker Academic, 2004), chap. 24, "Feminist, Womanist, and Latina Theologies."

Asia.[4] In this discussion feminist—that is, the voices of white women—are studied for the simple reason that other women's voices on the topic of the Trinity are not yet widely available.

Traditional God-talk in general[5] and Trinitarian discourse in particular[6] are on a collision course with feminist consciousness. Catherine Mowry LaCugna, who represents a moderate feminist stance, put it succinctly:

> There is far from a consensus on whether God's name as Father, Son, and Holy Spirit is revealed and cannot be changed, or whether it can be changed, on what basis, in what contexts, or by whom. Baptism into the triune name of God presents a special problem, because some churches will not recognize the validity of another church's baptism, if there is any deviation from the formula given in Matthew 28:19.[7]

It all boils down to the question of whether Trinitarian language as employed in Christian theology is sexist, and if it is, what to do about that.[8] Theologians have understandably responded in more than one way. At one extreme are those who call for an immediate moratorium on Father-Son language.[9] Let this be called the substitution argument. Being metaphors, "Father" and "Son" can be exchanged for more appropriate ones.[10] The other extreme, critical of the appeal to the metaphorical nature of God-talk, we may call the nonsubstitution argument: for those theologians, Trinitarian names are proper names and can never

---

4. For an introduction to these women's theologies of God, see ibid., 261–63, 277–78, 296–98 respectively.

5. Among others, Mary Daly, *Beyond God the Father: Toward a Philosophy of Women's Liberation* (Boston: Beacon Press, 1973); Elisabeth Schüssler Fiorenza, *In Memory of Her: A Feminist Theological Reconstruction of Christian Origins* (New York: Crossroad, 1983); Anne E. Carr, *Transforming Grace: Christian Tradition and Women's Experience* (San Francisco: Harper & Row, 1988); Anna Case-Winters, *God's Power: Traditional Understandings and Contemporary Challenges* (Louisville, KY: Westminster John Knox Press, 1990).

6. Ruth Duck, *Gender and the Name of God: The Trinitarian Baptismal Formula* (New York: Pilgrim Press, 1991); Gail Ramshaw, *God beyond Gender: Feminist Christian God-Language* (Minneapolis: Fortress, 1995); Marjorie Suchocki, "The Unmale God: Reconsidering the Trinity," *Quarterly Review* 3 (1983): 34–49; Patricia Wilson-Kastner, "The Trinity," in *Faith, Feminism, and the Christ* (Philadelphia: Fortress, 1983), 121–37; Barbara Brown Zikmund, "The Trinity and Women's Experience," *Christian Century* 104 (April 15, 1987), 354–56; Rebecca Oxford Carpenter, "Gender and Trinity," *Theology Today* 41 (1984): 7–25.

7. Catherine Mowry LaCugna, "God in Communion with Us," in *Freeing Theology: The Essentials of Theology in Feminist Perspective*, ed. C. M. LaCugna (New York: HarperSanFrancisco, 1993), 99.

8. A thoughtful biblical look that enhances reflection on this issue is offered by Gerald O'Collins, *The Tripersonal God: Understanding and Interpreting the Trinity* (Mahwah, NJ: Paulist Press, 1999), 184–88.

9. Mary Daly, "After the Death of God the Father," in *Womanspirit Rising: A Feminist Reader in Religion*, ed. Carol P. Christ and Judith Plaskow (San Francisco: Harper & Row, 1979), 52–63; Naomi R. Goldenberg, *Changing of the Gods: Feminism and the End of Traditional Religions* (Boston: Beacon Press, 1979).

10. The best-known attempt to develop a metaphorical theology that would make it possible to pile up names of God to find balance is offered by Sallie McFague, *Models of God: Theology for an Ecological, Nuclear Age* (London: SCM Press, 1987).

be replaced. In the middle are those who, while accepting the metaphorical nature of God-language, are not ready to replace Father, Son, and Spirit with terms that are socially less offending. The mediating position argues that even though the original way of addressing God in Christian theology has been patriarchal and oppressive, a proper interpretation can help redeem its sexist nature.[11]

The substitution position considers traditional Trinitarian language not only sexist but also as supporting oppressive structures.[12] To heal this problem, they say, we must take seriously the metaphorical nature of God-talk.[13] If God is mysterious unknown, as even classical theology maintains, it is very hard to point to a specific "name" of God, at least in the sense of a fixed "proper" name.[14] At best, names for God are analogical and thus only approximate their object. As Ted Peters describes this view (which is not his own view): "To speak of God as Father, as has been the Christian custom, is to describe God in terms of a human father. It would be idolatrous, however, to speak of God *literally* as our Father. This would deify human maleness."[15] A whole new repertoire of descriptions of God are then available such as Source, Word, and Spirit; Creator, Liberator, and Comforter; Creator, Redeemer, and Sanctifier; God, Christ, and Spirit; Parent, Child, and Paraclete; Mother, Daughter, and Spirit; Mother, Lover, and Friend; Father, Child, and Mother.[16] The goddess-language has also been employed by some theologians.[17] The point is that a gender-free way of addressing the Triune God would avoid the problems related to traditional discourse.[18] Women theologians

11. I follow here the helpful discussion in Ted Peters, *God as Trinity: Relationality and Temporality in Divine Life* (Louisville, KY: Westminster John Knox Press, 1993), 46–55. Yet my typology differs slightly from his in that I discern only three main positions; Peters makes a distinction between two mediating positions.

12. These feminist theologians are not content with "correcting" Christian discourse about God but want to "reformulate" it in order to "emancipate" and "transform" the world. Rebecca S. Chopp, *The Power to Speak: Feminism, Language, God* (New York: Crossroad, 1991), 21.

13. There is of course a host of theologians who advocate the metaphorical nature of theological language in general and God-talk in particular, and not all those approaches agree in all details; for the purposes of this discussion, I will not go into details. John Hick is an example of those who for the sake of Christian theology of religions have argued for an extremely metaphorical nature of all religious talk. In women's theology, as mentioned above, Sallie McFague has been the leading voice with her idea of a metaphorical theology.

14. For the significance of "name" in religious and theological studies, see among others F. M. Denny, "Names and Naming," in *Encyclopedia of Religion*, ed. M. Eliade, vol. 10 (New York: Macmillan, 1987), 300–307; H. Wettstein, "Causal Theory of Proper Names," in *The Cambridge Dictionary of Philosophy*, ed. R. Audi (Cambridge: Cambridge University Press, 1995), 109–10.

15. Peters, *God as Trinity*, 47.

16. See further O'Collins, *Tripersonal God*, 184.

17. Rosemary Radford Ruether, *Sexism and God-Talk: Toward a Feminist Theology* (Boston: Beacon Press, 1983); Carol P. Christ, "Why Women Need the Goddess: Phenomenological, Psychological, and Political Reflections," in *Womanspirit Rising: A Feminist Reader in Religion*, ed. Carol P. Christ and Judith Plaskow (San Francisco: Harper & Row, 1979), 273–87.

18. According to Roberta C. Bondi, we should not be bound to the sexist and thus oppressive formulation of the creeds, in this case the Nicene creed. It is a metaphorical way of speaking of God and thus exchangeable for a less offensive one. Roberta C. Bondi, "Some Issues Relevant to a Modern Interpretation of the Language of the Nicene Creed, with Special Reference to Sexist Language," *Union Seminary Quarterly Review* 40, no. 3 (1985): 21–30. A rebuttal is offered by Deborah Malacky

remind us that metaphors used of God are not neutral; there is an agenda behind each metaphor employed.[19]

The mediating position is in the business of trying to redeem the sexist and patriarchal nature of Christian Trinitarian discourse without replacing Father, Son, and Spirit by other names. Having acknowledged the oppressive nature of the language, this approach takes comfort in the leading principle of relationality in ancient and contemporary Trinitarian theology. Rightly understood, "Trinity is more supportive of feminist values than is a strict monotheism" since it is about persons in communion and relationships.[20] It is also noted that Christian tradition does not ascribe maleness to the divine and thus does not necessarily contribute to oppression.[21]

The nonsubstitutionalist position rejects any attempt to replace Father, Son, and Spirit with other terms. As discussed above, Robert W. Jenson argues that traditional Trinitarian names form the proper name of God. Proper names are irreplaceable. According to Wolfhart Pannenberg, while the term "Father" is undoubtedly related to the patriarchal constitution of the Israelite family, it has absolutely nothing to do with sexuality; one indication of that is that at times, though not often, the Old Testament can refer to God using mother imagery. God transcends all sexual differences. The sociological starting point of Father language in the Bible, time-bound as it is, "does not justify the demand for a revision of the concept of God as Father because there have now been changes in the family structure and the social order." The reason is that "[o]n the lips of Jesus, 'Father' became a proper name for God" and thus "ceased to be simply one designation among others."[22] The conclusion, Pannenberg argues, is that we cannot eliminate God as the heavenly Father from the message of Jesus.[23] The evangelical theologian Donald Bloesch concurs. According to him "resymbolization" of the biblical talk about God means replacing "real knowledge" of the eternal God with metaphorical or symbolic language. The end result is the transformation of the term "God": "the debate over sexist language is ultimately a debate concerning the nature of God."[24] A leading North American anti-feminist female theologian, Elizabeth Achtmeier, is also critical of changing the traditional way of addressing God since in her estimation inclusion of feminine imagery would frustrate the Bible's attempt for the

Belonick, "Revelation and Metaphors: The Significance of the Trinitarian Names, Father, Son and Holy Spirit," *Union Seminary Quarterly Review* 40, no. 3 (1985): 31–42.

19. Janet Martin Sockice, *Metaphor and Religious Language* (Oxford: Clarendon Press, 1985), 62–63: "The implications of one metaphor are very different from those of another. . . . Metaphor is not a neutral or ornamental aspect of speech."

20. Wilson-Kastner, *Faith, Feminism, and the Christ*, 122.

21. Belonick, "Revelation and Metaphors."

22. Wolfhart Pannenberg, *Systematic Theology*, trans. Geoffrey W. Bromiley, 3 vols. (Grand Rapids: Eerdmans, 1991–98), 1:262.

23. Ibid., 1:263.

24. Donald Bloesch, *Is the Bible Sexist? Beyond Feminism and Patriarchalism* (Westchester, IL: Crossway Books, 1982), 66. See also D. Bloesch, *The Battle for the Trinity: The Debate over Inclusive God-Language* (Ann Arbor, MI: Vine Books, 1985), 1, 11–12, 62–63 especially.

Creator not to be identified with the creation. For her, not only goddess language but any kind of feminine expressions related to God-talk introduce the danger of pantheism.[25]

In order to continue discussion and reach some preliminary conclusions, the bulk of this chapter is devoted to a critical dialogue with the work of a leading feminist, white theologian, the Catholic Elizabeth Johnson, particularly her creative re-casting of the Trinitarian doctrine. Focusing on a careful exposition and assessment of her theology, I would like to avoid too generic a discussion and make the topic more concrete. Selecting Johnson as my main dialogue partner was not a difficult choice for many reasons. In several contemporary studies purporting to present a representative Trinitarian theology produced by a female theologian, Elizabeth Johnson is a household name.[26] Her main monograph on the topic, *She Who Is: The Mystery of God in Feminist Theological Discourse* (1993), has received outstanding reviews and has been hailed as a groundbreaking feminist contribution to thought concerning the Trinity.[27] Furthermore, what makes Johnson's feminist discussion of the Trinity extraordinarily valuable is her deep and wide knowledge of and dialogue with Christian tradition. She is widely critical of many aspects of tradition, but her superb command of biblical and historical sources is unsurpassed. While focusing on *She Who Is*, I will take into consideration Johnson's writings on Christology, pneumatology, ecology, Mariology, and ecclesiology, insofar as they pertain to the topic under discussion.[28]

THE HOLY MYSTERY—BEYOND ALL IMAGINING

For Elizabeth Johnson's *She Who Is: The Mystery of God in Feminist Theological Discourse*, "[n]ormative speech about God in metaphors that are exclusively, literally, and patriarchally male is the real-life context for this study."[29] The reason

25. Elizabeth Achtmeier, "Exchanging God for 'No Gods': A Discussion of Female Language for God," in *Speaking the Christian God: The Holy Trinity and the Challenge of Feminism*, ed. Alvin F. Kimel Jr. (Grand Rapids: Eerdmans, 1992), 8; idem, *Nature, God, and Pulpit* (Grand Rapids: Eerdmans, 1992), 108–9.

26. For example Stanley J. Grenz, *Rediscovering the Triune God: The Trinity in Contemporary Theology* (Minneapolis: Fortress, 2004), 164–81; William J. La Due, *The Trinity Guide to the Trinity* (Harrisburg, PA: Trinity Press International, 2003), 168–73.

27. Mary McClintock Fulkerson, review of Elizabeth Johnson, *She Who Is*, in *Religious Studies Review* 21 (January 1995); Review Symposium of *She Who Is*, *Horizons* 20, no. 2 (Fall 1993).

28. Elizabeth Johnson, *Consider Jesus: Waves of Renewal in Christology* (New York: Crossroad, 1990); "God Poured Out: Recovering the Holy Spirit," *Praying* 60 (May–June 1994): 4–8, 41; *Women, Earth, and Creator Spirit* (New York: Paulist Press, 1993); "Heaven and Earth Are Filled with Your Glory: Atheism and Ecological Spirituality," in *Finding God in All Things: Essays in Honor of Michael J. Buckley*, SJ, ed. Michael J. Himes and Stephen J. Pope (New York: Crossroad, 1986), 84–101; "The Marian Tradition and the Reality of Women," *Horizons* 12, no. 1 (1985): 116–35; "The Symbolic Character of Theological Statements about Mary," *Journal of Ecumenical Studies* 22, no. 2 (Spring 1985): 312–35; "Mary and the Female Face of God," *Theological Studies* 50 (1989): 500–526; *Friends of God and Prophets: A Feminist Theological Reading of the Communion of Saints* (New York: Continuum, 1999).

29. Elizabeth Johnson, *She Who Is: The Mystery of God in Feminist Theological Discourse* (New York: Crossroad, 1993), 44.

for her attention to the nature of God-speech is simply that the "symbol of God functions."[30] The way we speak of God dramatically shapes our view of God and therefore, in the estimation of this Catholic theologian, the ecclesial language in liturgy, prayer, and catechesis suggests that "God is male, or at least more like a man than a woman, or at least more fittingly addressed as male than as female."[31] The root cause for these unfortunate effects is literal-mindedness that also leads to exclusivity and thus patriarchalism. The option is not the denial of the legitimacy of male symbols but rather balancing them with female ones. Female images are needed to both challenge and correct the prevailing structures of patriarchalism.[32] This is of course the main agenda for feminist theology, which is a form of liberation theology and thus represents "discourses of emancipatory transformation."[33] Analogous to other women's studies, feminist theology exposes the dangers of sexism, searches for alternative symbols of God, and by doing so attempts to reconstruct theological discourse.[34] Two dangers are to be avoided: reverse sexism that simply replaces one from of domination (male) for another, female domination, and sameness that levels out differences between sexes.[35] Aware of the need to speak from the perspective of the world's women in various contexts, Johnson limits her discussion to feminist perspectives.[36]

The foundational point in Johnson's insistence on the necessity of female symbols/metaphors of God lies in the mysterious nature of God. "The holy mystery of God is beyond all imagining," a truth not foreign to classical theology.[37]

The mystery and thus incomprehensibility of God make it not only possible but also mandatory to use various kinds of symbols of God, including those that are nonpersonal or suprapersonal in nature. Talk about God is historically open-ended since the reality of God as mystery is beyond human imagination and can never be contained by any single symbol.[38] That divine discourse is mysterious is not to say that it is not historical and thus context-bound at the same time. Indeed, it is "always and only mediated through an experience that is specifically historical, the changing history of women's self-appraisal and self-naming."[39]

Women's theologies have toyed with several strategies in trying to find the most satisfactory and balanced way of addressing the Mystery. Adding feminine qualities to God, who is still predominantly imagined as male, or discerning feminine

---

30. Ibid., 4, 5.
31. Ibid., 5, 36–37.
32. Ibid., 33; see also pp. 4–5.
33. Ibid., 5, see also pp. 8– 9, 17, 31.
34. Ibid., 29–30; see also pp. 22–28 for an extended discussion of analysis of sexism.
35. Ibid., 32.
36. Ibid., 10.
37. Ibid., 45. Here Johnson refers to Aquinas, *De Potentia* (Westminster, MD: Newman Press, 1952), q. 7, a. 5: "Since our mind is not proportionate to the divine substance, that which is the substance of God remains beyond our intellect and so is unknown to us."
38. Johnson, *She Who Is*, 7, 44–45; for the importance of *image* and imagination in God-talk, see further pp. 46–47.
39. Ibid., 77.

dimensions in God, most often in the Holy Spirit, are approaches that seem marginal to Johnson, though not without worth. Hers is "speech about God in which the fullness of female humanity as well as of male humanity and cosmic reality may serve as divine symbol, in equivalent ways."[40] Programmatic to her feminist Trinitarian theology is the attempt to find and employ divine symbols that encompass the whole of humanity and the created world:

> The mystery of God is properly understood as neither male nor female but transcends both in an unimaginable way. But insofar as God creates both male and female in the divine image and is the source of the perfections of both, either can equally well be used as metaphor to point to divine mystery. Both in fact are needed for less inadequate speech about God, in whose image the human race is created. This "clue" for speaking of God in the image of male and female has the advantage of making clear at the outset that women enjoy the dignity of being made in God's image and are therefore capable as women of representing God. Simultaneously, it relativizes undue emphasis on any one image, since pressing the multiplicity of imagery shows the partiality of images of one sex alone. The incomprehensible mystery of God is brought to light and deepened in our consciousness through imaging of male and female, beyond any person we know.[41]

SEARCHING FOR RESOURCES
IN THE CHRISTIAN TRADITION

One of the unique features of Johnson's feminist Trinitarian theology is its deep and learned dialogue with Christian tradition, both biblical and historical-theological. Unlike many of her female colleagues, Johnson is not ready to dismiss tradition and its often exclusive use of male symbols in relation to God. She acknowledges the fact that theological tradition is profoundly ambiguous, yet—analogous to her church's current approach to other religions—she wants to affirm whatever good there is in tradition and revise that which needs revision.[42]

For this theologian, while biblical terminology is normative, it is not necessary to restrict our speech about God to the mere repeating of biblical names as long as we follow the sense of Scripture.[43] At the same time, she works hard to

40. Ibid., 47; see also pp. 47–56.
41. Ibid., 55.
42. Ibid., 9. However, she wonders whether sticking to the term "God" rather than "God/ess" (Rosemary Radford Ruether) or something similar, may be an interim strategy (p. 43). Anyway, the revisionist task calls at times for "a strong critique against traditional speech about God" because that is "both humanly oppressive and religiously idolatrous" (p. 18); for the idolatrous nature of male-oriented speech for God, see also p. 39. Like most contemporary writers, Johnson targets her criticism against classical theism and its speech about God as the Supreme Being quite distant from the world and its happenings (pp. 19–22). For current critique against classical theism, see further Kärkkäinen, *Doctrine of God*, 10–12, 53–59.
43. Johnson, *She Who Is*, 7.

uncover resources in the biblical trajectories that would help to balance the male-dominant discourse. Three biblical symbols of God are highlighted as the basic structure for her Trinitarian theology, namely, Spirit/Shekinah, Wisdom/Sophia, and Mother. Even though these symbols are typically enmeshed in an androcentric framework in the biblical record, they can also be used to construct a more egalitarian way of speaking of Deity.[44]

When speaking of God's transcendent creative presence and activity in the world, the terms "Spirit"—along with "wisdom" and "word"—are used. "Spirit" "points to the livingness of God who creates, sustains, and guides all things and cannot be confined."[45] For Johnson, imagery that accrues around the Spirit seems to be close to realities and activities familiar to women such as birth, healing, teaching, and inspiration. "Whether hovering like a nesting mother bird over the egg of primordial chaos in the beginning (Gen. 1:2), or sheltering those in difficulty under the protective shadows of her wings (Pss.17:8; 36:7; 57:1; 61:4; 91:1; Isa. 31:5), or bearing the enslaved up on her great wings toward freedom (Exod. 19:4; Deut. 32:11–12), the divine Spirit's activity is evoked with allusion to femaleness."[46] In the New Testament, the Spirit is spoken of in connection with the ministry and resurrection of Jesus and the growth of the community.[47] In the Jewish traditions during the intertestamental period the symbol of *Shekinah*, the glory of God (from the Hebrew term "to dwell") is used often in place of Spirit.[48]

Along with the Spirit, the symbol of Wisdom is used widely in the biblical trajectory to speak of the mystery of God, not only in the so-called Wisdom literature but also beyond. Both Spirit (*ruach*) and Wisdom (*khokmah*) are "symbols of God's energy involved in universal cosmic quickening, inspiring the prophetic word of justice . . . [and] renewing the earth and human heart."[49] Especially in the Wisdom literature, *khokmah* is a highly developed personification of God's presence, and Johnson finds its use in the Bible suggestive of many female traits such as "casting her as sister, mother, female beloved, chef and hostess, preacher, judge, liberator, establisher of justice, and a myriad of other female roles."[50] While there is no consensus among the commentators as to whether Sophia (the Greek term for Wisdom) is best depicted as a male or female symbol, Johnson finds credible the option holding that Sophia is a female personification of God.[51] Along with other titles, Divine Sophia was

44. Ibid., 82.
45. Ibid., 83.
46. Ibid.
47. Ibid., 83–84.
48. Ibid., 85.
49. Ibid., 94.
50. Ibid., 87.
51. Ibid., 91. With reference to female theologians such as Elisabeth Schüssler Fiorenza, Johnson argues that Jewish wisdom writers—unlike the classical prophetic traditions—were not afraid of employing the goddess traditions of the surrounding cultures to bring home the idea of a female side of God (p. 93).

picked up by the Christian church as a way to speak of Jesus. Jewish traditions knew of Sophia having been sent by God to a specific time and context. At times, Jesus is depicted as the Wisdom of God, often with cosmic connotations and as being the agent of creation.[52]

Yet another constellation of biblical symbols revolves around the imagery of motherhood: bearing, birthing, nursing, laboring, midwifery, rearing, and so forth. God's loving passion and care is at times compared to a woman's (Isa. 49:15; 63:13, among others).[53]

These resources serve Johnson's program well: "Discourse about holy mystery in the symbols of spirit, *Sophia*, and mother provides glimpses of an alternative to dominant patriarchal language about God"; especially considering that these texts arise out of cultural contexts that were highly sexist and patriarchal.[54]

Subsequent Christian tradition has been slow to employ these symbols in the service of speech about God. Yet there are key potential resources in Christian theology that could have been helpful in finding a more balanced way and that now are in need of rediscovery. The most fruitful of such resources for Johnson are these three: divine incomprehensibility, the principle of analogy, and the use of many names for God. Christian theology has never claimed to be able to comprehend God in any exhaustive way. Even when apophatic theology has not been followed as a methodological principle, reservation and humility have described theological talk. For feminist theology, Johnson contends, this is an important clue: patriarchal and sexist language about God can never be considered as final and ultimate. It can only say so much about the mystery of God. Other approaches are needed to complement it.[55]

Furthermore, if God is basically incomprehensible, no literal descriptions can be invoked. Christian theology has always acknowledged this and therefore resorted to analogical speech about God. Analogies taken from the creaturely world are able to say something—but not everything—about God. "The understanding that all speech about God is analogical assumes a strongly critical function when the androcentric character of traditional speech is faced with the question of naming God arising from women's experience today."[56]

If God is incomprehensible and can only be addressed with the help of analogy, it follows that a proliferation of names is needed to say even a little about the divine. This, again, has been the approach of Christian theology based on the biblical precedent.[57] Why not, then, add a few more that are helpful for women?

52. Ibid., 95; see further pp. 94–100.
53. Ibid., 100–101.
54. Ibid., 103.
55. Ibid., 104–12.
56. Ibid., 113–17 (117).
57. Ibid., 117–20.

A TRINITARIAN THEOLOGY "FROM BELOW"

These resources are employed by Elizabeth Johnson in her construal of a Trinitarian theology that does not begin from the abstract concept of Deity in general but rather from the experience of Spirit as a gateway to Trinity. "A theology of the Triune God that sets out from the experience of Spirit" seems to be consonant with women's experience as well as the human experience of salvation. Before there is experience of God in incarnation, God-made-flesh, God's presence in the world is encountered in Spirit.[58] Highlighting the primacy of the Spirit in the experience of the Trinity is appropriate also because Christian theology has tended to forget the Spirit.[59]

Before looking in more detail at her Trinitarian theology from below, a further note on her method is in order. Johnson, like so many others, takes Rahner's rule as the basic methodological orientation. This rule assures us that there are not two Gods, one we encounter and another in God's own inner life. While acknowledging that many question the latter part of the formula—that the immanent Trinity is the economic Trinity—Johnson is not too concerned about that since her overall theology of God insists on the inability of any human discourse to exhaust the mystery of God. No literalism here; humans can only speak allusively of incomprehensible mystery.[60]

The "first" member of the Trinity, then, is Spirit-Sophia, the presence and absence of the living God occurring through the mediation of history in a variety of ways and happenings. Not only some but *all* experience can potentially mediate God's Spirit; there is no exclusive zone. Therefore, in a qualified sense, the "historical world becomes a sacrament of divine presence and activity"; through the natural world, on the level of the personal and interpersonal experience, as well as "the level of the macro systems that structure human beings as groups, profoundly affecting consciousness and patterns of relationships, experience of the Spirit is also mediated."[61] Various kinds of activities can be attributed to the Spirit such as creating, indwelling, sustaining, resisting, re-creating, challenging, guiding, liberating, and completing. These activities and many others draw attention to the affinity of such language with feminist values, Johnson notes.[62] While insisting on a holistic economy of God with the world, these various Spirit activities can be summarized under broad categories: vivifying, renewing and empowering, gracing—the explicitly religious sphere as distinct (but not separate) from those mentioned above, which encompass the widest possible realms. When speaking of "religious," Johnson notes that "[n]othing explicitly

---

58. Ibid., 122–23 (122); see also pp. 197–201 for the importance of deriving the doctrine of the Trinity from experience (of salvation).

59. Ibid., 128–31.

60. Ibid., 197–205. Importantly, the section in which she discusses Rahner's rule is titled "Freeing the Symbol from Literalness" (p. 197).

61. Ibid., 124–26 (126).

62. Ibid., 133.

religious has been singled out as the field of her play, although the flourishing of the earth, of social structures, and of every person's life is of immeasurable religious significance." Yet there are functions of the Spirit that are distinctively religious, relating to the role of Spirit in the life of Jesus and the community founded by the Messiah.[63]

In her attempt to rediscover potential resources in the Christian tradition, Johnson points to metaphors widely used in theology that could be employed in a nonsexist discourse, such as Augustine's favorite terms for the Spirit, namely, love and gift. More explicitly feminine and personalist symbols related to Spirit-Sophia are known to the Christian tradition, such as friend and sister, as well as, of course, mother and grandmother.[64] What unites these impersonal and personal metaphors is relationality, a key value not only in contemporary Trinitarian theology in general but in Johnson's view in particular.[65]

Johnson is well aware of the critique expressed by theologians, including some leading feminists such as Sallie McFague, against the use of the term "Spirit" (of God). It has been said to be personally amorphous and vacant in what it evokes; it has been used to denote the immanence of God to the neglect of transcendence; it can be used as a way to affirm the body-spirit dualism of the Western world, and so forth. Acknowledging these dangers, Johnson argues for the appropriateness of this metaphor in its capacity to embrace both "God's indwelling nearness, . . . the living God at her closest to the world, pervading the whole and each creature," and yet her transcendence: "She is in the world but not bound by it."[66]

The way Spirit-Sophia as divine love, gift, and friend becomes manifest in our world is "in a concrete gestalt, the loving, gifting, and befriending first-century Jewish carpenter turned prophet." This is the essence of the Christian confession of Jesus being Christ, the Anointed with the Spirit.[67] This inclusive picture of Jesus-Sophia, however, has been distorted in Christian theology, having been immersed in an exclusively androcentric tradition that has resulted in a patriarchal image of God and an androcentric anthropology.[68] There is a fallacy in Christian thinking "that collapses the totality of the Christ into the bodily form of Jesus." Christian theology, however, has considered Christ inclusive even though Jesus of Nazareth as a particular person was a man; this comes to expression for example in the idea of the church being the body of Christ or all Christians, men and women, participating in the death and resurrection of Christ.[69] "To make of the maleness of Jesus Christ a Christological principle is to deny the universality of salvation."[70]

63. Ibid., 133–41 (139).
64. Ibid., 144–46.
65. Ibid., 143; so also p. 148.
66. Ibid., 147, 131–33.
67. Ibid., 150.
68. Ibid., 152–53.
69. Ibid., 71–72.
70. Ibid., 73. For the importance of the Christian identity in participation in "the whole Christ," who in the Spirit transcends the limitations of social, cultural, and historical strictures, see pp. 161–64.

Rediscovering a holistic, inclusive view of Christ and human beings means celebrating one human nature, yet one that is multidimensional, in an interdependence of multiple differences, neither "a binary view of two forever predetermined male and female natures, nor abbreviation to a single ideal, but a diversity of ways of being human: a multipolar set of combinations of essential human elements, of which sexuality is but one."[71] In a brilliant sentence Johnson turns the maleness of Jesus into constructive critique against patriarchalism and exclusion: "The heart of the problem is not that Jesus was a man but that more men are not like Jesus, insofar as patriarchy defines their self-identity and relationships."[72]

The actions attributed to the "second member" of the Trinity, Jesus-Sophia, include preaching, ingathering, confronting, as well as dying and rising. In all of these activities, Jesus-Sophia is also linked with the female figure of personified Wisdom. Wisdom categories by their own force help expand the traditionally too-limited view of Christ to encompass cosmic dimensions including "belief towards a global, ecumenical perspective respectful of other religious paths." Sophia also bespeaks justice and peace having incarnated and thus identified with suffering humanity.[73]

Mother-Sophia is Johnson's preferred term for what in traditional theology is named Father. There is a Trinitarian movement from below here:

> The story of Jesus reprised in history through the power of the Spirit manifests the character of God's absolute mystery as one of graciousness and compassion, bent especially upon the hurt, captive, and lost. This but intensifies the mystery, turning it into the absolute mystery of love. Without origin, without sources, without beginning, what people call God generates everything and seeks its flourishing. From this unoriginate radiance stream forth all the little lights and the power to resist the night.[74]

Johnson reminds us that in the parent-child analogy, the metaphor of mother is appropriate for God since motherhood suggests birth, nourishing and growth, and rearing, including cosmic and creational dimensions in the coming into existence of all creation.[75] Mother language in relation to God brings home these key biblical and Christian elements of our faith. Mothering also includes the task of establishing the "mercy of justice." That there has been an eclipse of mother language is strong impetus for theologians to rediscover it along with—and not in exclusion of—the father metaphor.[76]

---

71. Ibid., 155.
72. Ibid., 161.
73. Ibid., 165–67 (166).
74. Ibid., 170.
75. In her *Women, Earth, and Creator Spirit*, Johnson has developed a pneumatological-Trinitarian approach to ecological theology, again beginning from the Spirit, "from below." For an informed discussion, see Patricia A. Fox, *God as Communion: John Zizioulas, Elizabeth Johnson, and the Retrieval of the Symbol of the Triune God* (Collegeville, MN: Liturgical Press, 2001), 169–79.
76. Johnson, *She Who Is*, 170–85; for "mercy of justice," see pp. 181–85.

TRINITY AS AN INCLUSIVE COMMUNITY

Elizabeth Johnson shares the contemporary theological conviction of Trinity as communion:

> The mutual coinherence, the dancing around together of Spirit, Wisdom and Mother; or of mutual Love, Love from Love, and unoriginate Love; or of the three divine persons—this defines who God is as God. There is no divine nature as a fourth thing that grounds divine unity in difference apart from relationality. Rather, being in communion constitutes God's very essence.[77]

At the heart of Johnson's communion theology is the insistence on the Trinity as a dynamic, lively symbol; this is brought home by her "from below" method, which resists the sterile, abstract, speculative way of the past.[78] This model attempts to replace the derivationist, subordinationist, and hierarchical ways of conceiving the Triune God with a relational, equalitarian, and inclusive way, one that is "a relational pattern of mutual giving and receiving."[79]

For Johnson, "The symbol of the triune God is the specific Christian shape of monotheism."[80] It speaks of one God who is not a solitary God but a communion of love.[81] She is speaking of this symbol and all the *hypostaseis* (persons) of the Trinity both in male and female metaphors to make the language—and thus faith—inclusive; at the same time, she acknowledges that this is not to deny the fact that divine *hypostaseis* also transcend the categories of male and female. Speaking analogically—since literalism is to be avoided—there is however enough overlap for us to be able to say *something* of the Triune God.

When *something* is to be said of the symbol of the Triune God, what are the essential values? Johnson summarizes them under these rubrics as they derive from her experience-based method from below. First, this symbol speaks for mutual relation. It can be spoken of, for example, with the help of the metaphor of friendship, which is the "most free, the least possessive, the most mutual of relationships, able to cross social barriers in genuine reciprocal regard."[82] Second, the symbol of the Triune God speaks for radical equality. Quoting another

---

77. Ibid., 227. Cf. the title of the book that studies the Trinitarian theologies of John Zizioulas and E. Johnson, *God as Communion,* by Patricia Fox. For Johnson, one of the resources for advancing feminist Trinitarian theology is to dialogue with theologies from other contexts with concerns similar to those of women such as the theology of J. Moltmann, Latin American liberation theologies (L. Boff), some process theologians (Norman Pittenger), the Indian American Catholic theologian of religions R. Panikkar, and many others. Johnson, *She Who Is,* 205–11.

78. Johnson, *She Who Is,* 192.
79. Ibid., 194–97 (196).
80. See further ibid., 211.
81. Ibid., 222.
82. Ibid., 216–18 (217).

feminist theologian, Rosemary Radford Ruether, Johnson defines authentic relationship as "not a relation between two half selves, but between whole persons, when suppression and projection cease to distort the encounter."[83] The Christian symbol of the Trinity for Johnson bespeaks a community of equals, patterns of differentiation that are nonhierarchical.[84] Third, the symbol of the Trinity speaks for community in diversity, in classical theology expressed with the term perichoresis, a picture of an eternal divine round dance.[85]

This loving communion, the one relational God, while being utterly transcendent in that no finite category may limit her, is also intimately related to everything that exists; this symbol is a profound expression of solidarity with the world. The Triune God constantly sustains life and resists destructive powers of nonbeing and violence.[86] God is thus in the world, but so is also the world in God. Johnson negotiates her way between classical theism's strong emphasis on the transcendence of God and thus separation from the world and pantheism's equation of God and world. Panentheism or dialectical theism is her favorite term for the mediating position.[87]

From her panentheistic view of the God-world relationship, Johnson draws implications for her anthropology and cosmology. Like Moltmann in his version of panentheism, Johnson is fond of the kabbalistic notion of self-limitation of God in the act of creation to make room for the other, and she links it with the idea of *kenōsis*. This is another demonstration of God's free, loving self-giving. There is no reason why this should be expressed only in male metaphors; motherly categories obviously seem to fit it better. The panentheistic vision of the mutual indwelling of God and world can also be linked with the metaphor of friendship, which has a natural affinity with women's experience of closeness and sharing.[88]

Finally, at the end of her study of Trinitarian theology from women's perspective, Johnson comes to suggest the divine name that is part of her book title, SHE WHO IS. This is an inclusive rendering of the ancient translation of YHWE as revealed in Exodus 3:14, "I am who I am," often called HE WHO IS, as in Aquinas's theology. Johnson says that linguistically SHE WHO IS is possible; so is it theologically and spiritually:

> In a word, SHE WHO IS discloses in an elusive female metaphor the mystery of Sophia-God as sheer, exuberant, relational aliveness in the midst of the history of suffering, inexhaustible source of new being in situations of

---

83. Ibid., 218, quoting from Rosemary Radford Ruether, *New Woman, New Earth: Sexist Ideologies and Human Liberation* (New York: Seabury Press, 1975), 26.

84. Johnson, *She Who Is*, 219.

85. Ibid., 220.

86. Ibid., 228–30; see also pp. 246–72 for an important elaboration on the theme of suffering and the passionate God.

87. Ibid., 231.

88. Ibid., 233–36.

death and destruction, ground of hope for the whole created universe, to practical and critical effect.[89]

CRITICAL REFLECTIONS

Where does Johnson's feminist Trinitarian theology locate itself in the threefold typology presented in the beginning of this chapter? While it shares much of the substitution approach's critique of the sexism and patriarchalism of traditional theology and suggests a new terminology to address the Christian God, it also majors in much of the agenda of the mediating position, namely, that Christian God-speech can be redeemed to be inclusive and equalitarian. Her book *She Who Is* lays out a profound attempt to find resources in the Christian tradition on the one hand and critique the mistaken ways of addressing the divine on the other hand. As mentioned, unlike many colleagues, Johnson does not spare any effort to establish the validity of speaking of God in an alternative way, both biblically and in terms of the history of theology. Many feminist colleagues of hers, those in the substitution camp, reject outright the aberrant tradition, as they see it, and look for resources for alternative God-speech outside of or on the margins of the Christian tradition.

How does Johnson's method fare in light of her own methodological definition? I think there is some discrepancy between what she explicitly states as her methodological choice and what she is doing in her main monograph. When weighing three different strategies to redeem God-talk by women theologians—that of giving feminine qualities to God (still imagined mainly in terms of male images), that of uncovering a feminine dimension in God, most often in the Spirit, and that of equivalent male and female images of God—she categorically opts for the last one.[90] Much of her theological work itself, however, operates with all these three strategies while the equivalent speech is her ultimate goal. My understanding is that the first and second options are but some of the many strategies to reach equivalent terminology. Quite rightly Johnson, however, points to the weaknesses of both the first and second strategy. In my mind, the attempt to uncover a feminine dimension in God is helpful, as such, but its most serious flaw is that when it focuses on the Holy Spirit, it becomes counterproductive by suggesting that Spirit is (only) feminine, and is "weak" and "soft."[91] Focusing on the whole Trinity's capacity to encompass the feminine dimension—along with the masculine—is indeed the basic agenda for Johnson. I wish she had been more explicit about these methodological nuances.

Having equivalent terminology as the main goal is to be applauded. Johnson succeeds in offering an alternative way of addressing the divine that is still firmly

89. Ibid., 243; see also pp. 241–45.
90. Ibid., 47–57.
91. This is rightly noticed by Johnson and many other feminists; ibid., 51.

and deeply anchored in Christian tradition. So far so good. However, I would like to challenge her in what I see as her main agenda, namely, *equivalent* symbols of God. While her Trinitarian theology is a tribute to the validity of female-laden ways of addressing God, she is much less successful in validating the traditional Father-Son-Spirit language. A counterquestion is of course raised immediately: Why should that be expected of a theologian who works hard to rehabilitate the legitimacy of female talk about God? For the simple reason that—to repeat myself—rather than trying to replace traditional God-talk, she is offering an alternative to be used along with the traditional language, the implication being that both men and women use both traditional and this alternative discourse. If so, Johnson should be more self-critical of the potential weaknesses of her own approach and more appreciative of the nonsexist nature of Father-Son-Spirit language.

With her creative proposal—addressing the Triune God as Spirit-Sophia, Jesus-Sophia, and Mother-Sophia—Johnson is able to avoid many of the potential weaknesses of feminist proposals that are often impersonal (for example, Creator-Redeemer-Sanctifier or Parent-Child-Paraclete, among others), implicitly Arian or otherwise subordinationist (for example, Creator-Christ-Spirit, suggesting that only the "first" person of the Trinity is truly divine, being the source), or crypto-modalist (for example, Creator-Liberator-Comforter, implying that one nonpersonal God employs several functions).[92] At the same time, one wonders, Why attach the term "Sophia" to all of the three Trinitarian members? Doesn't that confuse rather than clarify Johnson's program? On the one hand, there is a mixing of both personal and nonpersonal terms for one "person" such as Mother. Second, as Johnson herself acknowledges, the wisdom tradition in general has been conceived in Christian tradition in terms of male images even when the Old Testament/biblical allusions to the female dimension have been rightly acknowledged.[93] Wouldn't the nomenclature "Spirit-Jesus-Mother" serve her purposes in a more unambiguous way? And perhaps instead of the name "Jesus," which denotes a particular, historical figure, the term "Christ" would better serve her purposes.

Johnson's Catholic colleague Gerald O'Collins notes that while there is no reason in the contemporary context to exclude alternative ways of addressing the Triune God, we should not ignore the fact that there are compelling reasons to retain the traditional way as valid. O'Collins mentions the theology of religions argument: The names "Father," "Son," and "Holy Spirit" are the distinctively and uniquely Christian way of identifying the God of the Bible. Second, that naming has been the principal—yet never exclusive—way for all Christians at all times to identify their God.[94] I would add one more weighty reason for maintaining the traditional way of addressing God (but not, I repeat, exclusively),

---

92. Some of the examples taken from O'Collins, *Tripersonal God*, 189.
93. See Johnson, *She Who Is*, 90–91 especially.
94. O'Collins, *Tripersonal God*, 190.

namely, that the Trinitarian formula "Father, Son, and Holy Spirit" is a datum of Christian revelation. With theologians such as Wolfhart Pannenberg and Ted Peters I affirm that both the necessity and the content of Trinitarian doctrine is based on biblical salvation history.[95] Therefore, the Trinitarian formula Father, Son, and Holy Spirit is irreplaceable, yet not exclusive as long as other ways of addressing our Christian God are neither seen as a replacement for the biblical formula nor are so far divorced from the biblical datum that the discernment of the biblical God among the gods of the religions is at stake. Thus Peters's critique does not in my understanding apply to proposals such as that of Johnson: "To bypass the biblical terms in favor of some substitutes is to identify with a God other than that of Jesus Christ."[96] If "bypassing" here means leaving behind or rejecting, I agree with Peters. If it means finding alternative ways, then I disagree with him. Everything about Johnson's proposal tells me that she is working hard to anchor her alternative way of addressing the Triune God in the Bible, and that therefore there is no danger of confusing that God with other gods. In sum: while I consider Johnson's alternative way of addressing the Triune God as Christian and valid,[97] it does not commend itself to me as the best alternative for various reasons, nor does it acknowledge the primacy of the traditional Trinitarian formula.

Moving from terminological considerations (which of course lie at the heart of feminist theologies in general and Johnson's in particular) to other issues in her Trinitarian theology, I find Stanley J. Grenz's assessment both enlightening and helpful:

> Johnson's contribution to the renaissance of trinitarian theology lies above all in the attempt to foster a return of the immanent Trinity endemic to her recasting of the triune God according to the female image of Sophia. As several observers point out, Johnson does not march in lockstep with those who claim that proceeding "from below" leads inevitably to the conclusion that talk about the inner being of God is inappropriate or impossible. On the contrary, she takes pains to point out that speaking about the immanent triune God remains possible, even though language for God is always analogical, symbolic, and inadequate.[98]

Unlike her Catholic feminist colleague Catherine Mowry LaCugna and a number of other female and male theologians, Johnson holds on to the postulate of an immanent Trinity. As discussed above, she affirms Rahner's rule and claims to be able to avoid the restriction of God's freedom by her passionate presenta-

---

95. Peters, *God as Trinity*, 54; for Pannenberg, see chap. 10.
96. Ibid., 54.
97. Cf. the assessment by Janice Daurio, review of *She Who Is*, New Oxford Review 61 (April 1994): 28: "This is not the book feminists who are faithfully Christian have been waiting for."
98. Grenz, *Rediscovering The Triune God*, 180. Appropriately, Grenz titles chap. 5, in which he discusses Johnson's Trinitarian theology, along with Hans Urs von Balthasar and Thomas F. Torrance, as "The Return of the Immanent Trinity."

tion of the inadequacy of human language to contain very much of the Mystery of God. Taking note of the reluctance of many theologians to posit an immanent Trinity, especially since the advent of postmodernity, Johnson responds that "we would lose a great deal if we ceased speaking altogether of the immanent triune God." Carefully sticking to her rule of the symbolic and analogical nature of human speech about God, she continues: "For this language is not a literal description of the inner being of God who is in any event beyond human understanding." With these linguistic reservations, she argues that human speech, however, is "language which affirms that what is experienced in Christian faith really is of God." To put it differently, this Catholic theologian assures us that the God we meet in Jesus Christ "does not wear a mask"; rather, "the threefold relatedness to us suggests that a certain corresponding threefoldness characterizes God's own true being."[99] In other words, in a careful, balanced way Johnson on the one hand avoids the pitfall of collapsing the immanent Trinity into the economic, as is often the case when the starting point is "from below," and on the other hand, the danger of limiting God's freedom by speaking of "correspondence" rather than exact identity between immanent and economic Trinity.

Why is it, then, that several commentators such as Paul D. Molnar have wondered if Johnson denies altogether the immanent Trinity?[100] Even those who generally affirm her proposal, such as Stanley Grenz, have wondered if Johnson is fuzzy about this issue.[101] In my estimation the reason lies in readers' neglecting the context of some passages that seem to suggest doubt about the immanent Trinity. When Johnson notes that "the Trinity is a legitimate but secondary concept that synthesizes the concrete experience of salvation in a 'short formula,'"[102] she is of course not denying the immanent Trinity but rather making a statement affirmed by most about the nature of theology. A stronger candidate for denying the immanent Trinity, however, is her saying that "the symbol of the Trinity is not a blueprint of the inner workings of the godhead" and that "[i]n no sense is it a literal description of God's being *in se*," but rather as the outcome of theological reflection, "it is a symbol that indirectly points to God's relationality."[103] Commentators, however, have neglected the context of these statements and the discussions, in light of which they have to be interpreted. Johnson is critiquing not only the attempt of classical theology to start "from above" in a speculative and abstract inquiry into the inner life of God but also its taking theological statements (about God) in too literal a sense. With her conclusion of this discussion, Johnson clearly reveals that her intention is not so much to cast doubt on the possibility of our knowing something of the inner life of God as it is to warn against literal-mindedness: "Negating the literalness of this symbol enriches

99. All the quotations are from Johnson, *She Who Is*, 200.
100. Paul D. Molnar, *Divine Freedom and the Doctrine of the Immanent Trinity: In Dialogue with Karl Barth and Contemporary Theology* (Edinburgh: T & T Clark, 2002), 23–24.
101. Grenz, *Rediscovering the Triune God*, 181.
102. See Johnson, *She Who Is*, 198.
103. See ibid., 204.

understanding, loosening the hold of particular philosophical interpretations and setting our minds in the direction of holy mystery. . . . The triune God is not simply unknown, but positively known to be unknown and unknowable—which is a dear and profound knowledge."[104]

Having argued that Johnson is able to hold on to the immanent Trinity even though her method is from below, one has to ask at the same time if her starting point from below, from the experience (of salvation) is a legitimate way of doing Trinitarian theology. I strongly disagree with the appraisal that Johnson has simply "exchange[d] the revelation of God for the experience of women and thus collapse[d] theology into anthropology."[105] This charge assumes that traditional theology does not have any "agenda" but rather is interest-free, and that the experience of salvation as a human category in principle would be antagonistic to the revelation of God. That kind of dualism is hardly supportive of theological projects in general, much less any kind of "contextual approach" in particular. (It also neglects the fact that even traditional theology is context- and tradition-laden.) I agree that there are feminist and other liberation theologians who border on subsuming theology into anthropology; Elizabeth Johnson's study *She Who Is* hardly fits in that genre, even though it takes women's experience seriously. My own critical question concerning her choice to take women's experience as the starting point lies elsewhere. While I submit that her starting with experience (the way she proceeds in her book) is not theologically truncated, I wonder if she is critical enough of her own starting point, namely, women's experience.[106] To acknowledge the fact that women have been misused and abused at the hands of classical theologians is not to say that any kind of replacement of male experience for female is theologically adequate. Adding some self-criticism of women's perspective might also help make her theology more equivalent in being open to acknowledging more values in the traditional way of addressing Trinity.

One commentator has surmised that Johnson's Trinitarian proposal lacks adequate pneumatological grounding because it "rests on a Christological presupposition."[107] This complaint is surprising and in my estimation misleading for two reasons. First, the whole method of Johnson's "from below" proceeds from the Spirit, who is the contact point between the divine and the world. This fact alone would make her theology of the Trinity integrally pneumatological. Second, I see it as a great asset that Johnson's pneumatology is informed and mutually dependent on Christology because it is a tendency in feminist and

104. See ibid., 205. With the last statement, Johnson masterfully pushes aside the criticism against apophatic theology which maintains that we cannot know anything much about God. The counterquestion is naturally, How do you know that you do not know much about God? Apophaticism of course entails knowledge (as Johnson says, knowledge of the unknowability of God, which is a grand theological truth!).

105. Molnar, *Divine Freedom*, 10.

106. See the helpful discussion in John Carmody, Review Symposium of *She Who Is*, *Horizons* 20-21 (1993-94): 336.

107. Charles Marsh, "Two Models of Trinitarian Theology: A Way beyond the Impasse?" *Perspectives in Religious Studies* 21 (Spring 1994): 62.

other women's theologies to buy too easily into the kind of pluralistic or polytheistic approach in which the Spirit is "freed" from the contours of a healthy Trinitarian framework. The result is a "theology" of the Holy Spirit so generic that it is not distinctively Christian (nor often representative of any other religion, but instead a kind of synthesis of religious and cultural views). I believe it is the careful reading of the New Testament Gospels, amply cited in the book, that has helped Johnson develop a Spirit-Christology or christological pneumatology.

Having discussed three mainstream American theologians, one Protestant and two Roman Catholic, I next turn to a dialogue partner who comes from a very different constituency, representing the theologically more conservative, yet rapidly growing segment of Christianity. Too often the views of the so-called evangelical movement are excluded either because they are not known well enough or because there is prejudice among mainline theologians against their perceived conservative mind-set. Any inclusive and representative look at the contemporary theological scene of North America that dismisses that theological world, however, does so only to its own detriment.

Chapter 14

Millard J. Erickson

An "Evangelical" Doctrine of the Trinity

THE LACUNA OF TRINITARIAN THEOLOGIES
AMONG EVANGELICALS

In recent decades the term "evangelical" in North American parlance (and by extension in the wider English-speaking world, including the British Isles) has become a technical term referring to a conservative segment of Christian churches who want to hold on to the biblical authority and classical Christianity as explicated in the ancient creeds and the Protestant Reformation.[1] This is, of course, a significant departure from its original meaning in which "evangelical" denoted Protestant theology as opposed to Catholic theology; thus, for example, the "Evangelical Lutheran Church" or "evangelical theological faculty." While

1. See further Derek J. Tidball, *Who Are the Evangelicals? Tracing the Roots of Today's Movement* (London: Marshall Pickering, 1994). For a helpful current discussion of the historical background, subgroups, and salient doctrinal and spiritual features, see further Gerald R. McDermott, *Can Evangelicals Learn from World Religions? Jesus, Revelation and Religious Tradition* (Downers Grove, IL: Inter-Varsity Press, 2000), 25–34. For the religious and theological significance of evangelicalism, see Alister McGrath, *Evangelicalism and the Future of Christianity* (Downers Grove, IL: InterVarsity Press, 1995).

critical of "liberal theology," the evangelical movement, which is transdenominational and global,[2] representing not only all sorts of Protestants from Lutherans to Presbyterians to Baptists to Pentecostals but also Anglicans,[3] has distanced itself from the more reactionary fundamentalism (even though most fundamentalists claim themselves to be the "true" evangelicals).[4] In this book the term "evangelical" follows the established English-speaking world's usage, especially that of North America.

In general, evangelicals have not contributed significantly to constructive Trinitarian theology, perhaps because it has not been an issue of contention between conservatives and liberals. Widely used theological manuals among evangelicals such as the Reformed Luis Berkhof's *Systematic Theology*[5] follow Western theology and traditional Protestant orthodoxy both methodologically and materially.

In recent years few evangelical theologians have started constructive work in the area of the Trinity. Among that few, the most noted is the Baptist theologian Millard J. Erickson with his 1995 title *God in Three Persons*,[6] to which I turn momentarily. While Erickson represents the more conservative side of evangelicalism, a "left-wing" segment of the movement known as open theism[7] has also shown interest in the Trinity in its attempt to revise classical theism. Gregory Boyd's dissertation, titled *Trinity and Process*,[8] carries on an appreciative and critical dialogue with Charles Hartshorne's process theology, and Clark Pinnock, the leading open theist, has worked in several writings toward a communal social analogy of the Trinity.[9] Recently, a massive study titled *The Holy Trinity: In Scripture, History, Theology, and Worship* has been launched by the conservative (Orthodox) Presbyterian theologian and priest Robert Letham.[10] This is the most thorough up-to-date evangelical scrutiny of all main Trinitarian issues with a view

2. The growth of the evangelical movement in the two-thirds world (illustrated by the 160 million members of the World Evangelical Alliance, the majority of whom come from outside the U.S.A.) will significantly affect the future of theology. However, at the moment we do not see contributions on the Trinity by those theologians.
3. Recently a new term, "Evangelical Catholics," has been coined to refer to Catholics with evangelical viewpoints.
4. On the evangelicals' relation to fundamentalism, see further McDermott, *Can Evangelicals Learn from World Religions?* 34–37, and on evangelicals' relation to Protestant orthodoxy, liberalism, and postliberalism, see pp. 37–39.
5. Luis Berkhof, *Systematic Theology* (Grand Rapids: Eerdmans, 1941).
6. Millard J. Erickson, *God in Three Persons: A Contemporary Interpretation of the Trinity* (Grand Rapids: Baker Books, 1995)
7. See further Veli-Matti Kärkkäinen, *The Doctrine of God: A Global Introduction* (Grand Rapids: Baker Academic, 2004), chap. 20.
8. Gregory Boyd, *Trinity and Process: A Critical Evaluation and Reconstruction of Hartshorne's Di-Polar Theism Towards a Trinitarian Metaphysics* (New York: Peter Lang, 1992).
9. Clark Pinnock, *Flame of Love: A Theology of the Holy Spirit* (Downers Grove, IL: InterVarsity Press, 1996), chap. 1. In his subsequent monograph *Most Moved Mover: A Theology of God's Openness* (Grand Rapids: Baker Academic, 2001), Pinnock has continued and expanded this constructive work.
10. Robert Letham, *The Holy Trinity: In Scripture, History, Theology, and Worship* (Phillipsburg, NJ: P&R Publishing, 2004).

to their relevancy for liturgy and spirituality. However, Letham's own proposal is limited mainly to consideration of some issues[11] rather than offering a whole doctrine of the Trinity. So far theologically and ecumenically the most promising evangelical Trinitarian proposal, in critical dialogue with voices from all Christian traditions, has come from the pen of the late Stanley J. Grenz. His productive life, however, came to a sudden end; the six-volume systematic theology, based on a Trinitarian vision, never saw daylight.[12] Another leading North American constructive evangelical theologian, the Reformed Donald Bloesch, has produced an important Trinitarian proposal as part of his seven-volume Foundations in Christian Theology series, a tribute to the long and productive life of this professor emeritus.[13] The reason I chose Erickson over Bloesch is that Erickson's Trinitarian proposal—even though his theology is more conservative than that of Bloesch, who in general dialogues widely with voices from all theological persuasions—connects more clearly with many of the key issues of contemporary Trinitarian dialogue at the ecumenical and international level.

Typical of older approaches, Millard Erickson's massive *Christian Theology*,[14] by far the most widely used doctrinal manual in the U.S. evangelical schools during the past two decades, follows the standard Western approach. Having first discussed the attributes of God,[15] the unity of God is presented next and then the Trinity.[16] Even God's immanence and transcendence are discussed prior to Trinity![17] Clearly, unity is primary; Trinity is affirmed but more or less as an afterthought, as the order of the topics also clearly illustrates.

A significant shift occurs in his major monograph *God in Three Persons*. Now this Baptist theologian is offering a social analogy with emphasis on the threeness of the Christian God. Rightly, this work has been hailed as a landmark of evangelical theology of the Trinity.[18] Yet what is astonishing about the next major monograph is that in his *God the Father Almighty: A Contemporary Exploration of the Divine Attributes* (1998), Erickson is totally silent about the Trinity.[19] The implications of the social doctrine of the Trinity are not carried over

11. Such as incarnation and the question of person, ibid., chaps. 17, 20 respectively.

12. The first installment in the six-volume Matrix of Christian Theology Series is Stanley J. Grenz, *The Social God and Relational Self: A Trinitarian Theology of the Imago Dei* (Louisville, KY: Westminster John Knox Press, 2001).

13. Donald G. Bloesch, *God the Almighty: Power, Wisdom, Holiness, Love* (Downers Grove, IL: InterVarsity Press, 1995).

14. Millard J. Erickson, *Christian Theology*, three volumes in one (Grand Rapids: Baker Academic, 1987).

15. Ibid., chaps. 12, 13.

16. Ibid., chap. 15. On p. 337 Erickson summarizes "essential elements of a doctrine of the Trinity": "We begin with the unity of God. . . . God is one, not several." In keeping with the emphasis on the oneness of God, Erickson favors typical Western analogies such as the psychological ones (pp. 338–42) going back to Augustine.

17. Ibid., chap. 14.

18. James Leo Garrett Jr., review of *God in Three Persons: A Contemporary Interpretation of the Doctrine of the Trinity*, by Millard Erickson, *Southwestern Journal of Theology* 40, no. 3 (1998): 78.

19. Only one reference to the Trinity can be found, on p. 230, in reference to Christology!

to considering the themes of unity and the attributes of God. In that sense Erickson continues the basic methodology adopted in his earlier works, following the traditional Western view. The following discussion is based on his monograph on the Trinity.[20]

THE COMMUNION OF THREE PERSONS

The following statement from the conclusion of *God in Three Persons* summarizes and encapsulates Erickson's main approach:

> The Trinity is a communion of three persons, three centers of consciousness, who exist and always have existed in union with one another and in dependence on one another. Each is dependent for his life on each of the others. They share their lives, having such a close relationship that each is conscious of what the other is conscious of. They have never had any prior independent existence, and will not and cannot have any such now or in the future. Each is essential to the life of each of the others, and to the life of the Trinity. They are bound to one another in love, *agapē* love, which therefore unites them in the closest and most intimate of relationships. This unselfish, *agapē* love makes each more concerned for the other than for himself. There is therefore a mutual submission of each to each of the others and a mutual glorifying of one another. There is complete equality of the three. There has been, to be sure, temporary subordination of one member of the Trinity to the other, but this is functional rather than essential. At the same time, this unity and equality do not require identity of function. There are certain roles that distinctively belong primarily to one, although all participate in the function of each.[21]

Clearly, the view of the Trinity by Erickson echoes the rise to prominence of communion theology in current theology in which Trinity is seen as a divine society of equals.[22] From Pannenberg, Erickson borrows the idea that all Trinitarian members have their own center of consciousness as well as the idea of mutual dependency. He makes it clear that his own approach "tends to emphasize the uniqueness and distinctness of the three persons more than do some theologies."[23]

---

20. A popular companion to his major monograph is Millard Erickson, *Making Sense of the Trinity: Three Crucial Questions* (Grand Rapids: Baker Books, 2000). I refer to that nonscholarly work only if it adds a different perspective or clarifies what the monograph is saying.

21. Erickson, *God in Three Persons*, 331.

22. Michael L. Chiavone ("The Unity of God as Understood by Four Twentieth-Century Trinitarian Theologians: Karl Rahner, Millard Erickson, John Zizioulas, and Wolfhart Pannenberg" [PhD diss., Southeastern Baptist Theological Seminary, Wake Forest, NC, 2005], 110–11) shows convincingly that Erickson's social analogy parallels quite well that of Leonard Hodgson, one of the twentieth-century pioneers of social Trinity as expressed in his *The Doctrine of the Trinity: Croall Lectures, 1942–1943* (London: Nisbet, 1943; reprint, 1951). Hodgson spoke of the unity of God in terms of "organic unity" or "internally constitutive unity," (pp. 90, 108). While Erickson does not use these terms, his approach indeed parallels that of Hodgson.

23. Erickson, *God in Three Persons*, 226.

While not mentioned explicitly in this quotation, the ancient idea of perichoresis and its contemporary application by theologians such as Moltmann best illustrates Erickson's attempt to speak to the mutual interpenetration of Father, Son, and Spirit. While insisting on the full equality of Trinitarian Persons—and thus going against the Eastern Church's view of the monarchy of the Father—interestingly enough, Erickson approves the patristic and subsequent idea of functional, but not ontological, subordination of Spirit and Son. What is curiously missing in Erickson's proposal, which in so many ways relates to contemporary Trinitarian developments, is the relation of divine life to history and time. Furthermore, while mentioning Rahner's rule, Erickson does not seem overly concerned about the issue of the immanent-economic Trinity. Like any subscriber to the social analogy, Erickson is more successful in establishing the threeness than the unity of the Godhead.

Building on his earlier major study on Christology,[24] Erickson makes considerations of the reliability of biblical traditions about Christ and other christological themes occupy an important place in his proposal, as do the logical problems facing the doctrine of the Trinity.

BIBLICAL AND METAPHYSICAL CONTOURS

Erickson mainly employs two kinds of resources on the way to constructing a social analogy of the Trinity, namely, biblical study and what he calls metaphysical considerations. He also offers a brief, quite selective, survey of tradition[25] and considers logical problems in reference to the intelligibility and coherence of statements about Trinity.[26]

Erickson's approach to the Trinity's biblical basis differs from both some mainline theologians' approaches such as those of Barth and Pannenberg on the one hand, and the traditional way of reading Trinity into passages such as the "we" saying of Genesis 1:26–27 on the other. He acknowledges the changed situation in exegesis that does not allow us necessarily to see Trinity in passages such as Isa-

---

24. M. J. Erickson, *The Word Made Flesh: A Contemporary Incarnational Christology* (Grand Rapids: Baker Books, 1991).

25. Chaps. 1, 2, and 3 in Erickson, *God in Three Persons*, survey historical developments until the end of the fourth century. Later developments are not systematically traced. Erickson makes it clear (p. 9) that he is not intending to offer a complete history of the doctrine. A good example of a conspicuous lack is Augustine. Whatever the reason for those kinds of lacunae (Garrett, review of *God in Three Persons*, 79, surmises that it is perhaps due to the very different nature of Erickson's own view), it sounds strange, to say the least, to offer a patristic survey of the doctrine of the Trinity—especially in light of the fact that Erickson emphasizes the importance of the fourth century (p. 75)—and ignore the Bishop of Hippo!

26. Erickson, *God in Three Persons*, 130–38, 239–70. The latter part, however, which occupies one whole chapter (11), seems to go well beyond "logical" problems, as stated in the former section. Indeed, that is the only place where Erickson deals with, for example, Rahner's view of the identity between the economic and immanent Trinity (pp. 243–49).

iah 6:3 with its triad of "holy."[27] In contrast to Barth, who based the doctrine on the formal principle of Scripture, and to Pannenberg, for whom the unfolding of the biblical salvation history is the basis for this doctrine, Erickson follows the path taken by many today, namely, acknowledging the lack of explicit teaching on the Trinity, yet looking for "indications of complexity or the composite character of God in the Old Testament"[28] as well as more developed ways the New Testament speaks of the relationships between Father, Son, and Spirit, especially the incarnation.[29]

In his discussion of the Old Testament perspectives, Erickson makes two significant contributions, the importance of which have not been employed in Trinitarian considerations as they should be. Both of them point to social analogy. The first has to do with the Hebrew concept of extended personality. In that view "the individual is never to be thought of merely as an isolated unit. Rather, he [sic] lives in constant reaction toward others—both those with whom he is close-knit within the sphere of his [sic] social unit as an extended or larger self and those who fall outside this sphere."[30] The second one is a corollary idea, namely, that "the Hebrew conception of God included the idea of a unity that had an extension beyond itself,"[31] which helps negotiate the ancient philosophical problem central to Trinity—the issue of one and many in a way that is elastic and fluid.[32] The New Testament section offers few surprises; the Gospel of John occupies in this discussion a proportionately large part.[33]

Regarding the metaphysical basis of the doctrine of the Trinity, Erickson, with the rest of contemporary theologians, acknowledges the problematic nature of maintaining the dualistic substance ontology of classical theism owing to Greek philosophy.[34] Against classical liberalism and much of twentieth-century philosophy, Erickson agrees with process theology's insistence on the necessity of metaphysics in the Christian doctrine of God and reality, yet strongly disapproves of the process view of God.[35]

In Erickson's own metaphysical view, three claims tower above all else and shape critically his view of the Trinity. First, he maintains that "the spiritual is most real" and that "[t]herefore, there is one eternal, uncreated reality, God" because the Bible teaches God is spirit, not matter (John 4:24).[36] Second, this

---

27. Ibid., 97–98. Erickson also dialogues with scholars that think Trinity cannot be found in the Bible in any sense (pp. 98–108). His dialogue partner is Cyril C. Richardson, *The Doctrine of the Trinity* (Nashville: Abingdon Press, 1958).
28. Erickson, *God in Three Persons*, 159.
29. Ibid., 175.
30. Ibid., 164.
31. Ibid., 166.
32. Ibid., 171. Here Erickson builds on the important work of Aubrey R. Johnson, *The One and Many in the Israelite Conception of God* (Cardiff: University of Wales Press, 1961), among others.
33. Out of two chapters (8 and 9) in Erickson, *God in Three Persons*, the latter chapter is totally devoted to the Fourth Gospel.
34. Ibid., 115.
35. Ibid., 122–30, 212–14.
36. Ibid., 219.

Baptist theologian argues that the universe is personal. What he means by this ambiguous statement is not that there are not impersonal segments of reality; "it is rather to deny the ultimacy of the impersonal."[37] Third, reality appears to Erickson as primarily social. This goes back to the idea of the "supreme being," God, not wanting to remain solitary but creating the world external to himself and reaching out in loving relationship to it. "This means that the most powerful binding force in the universe is love."[38]

THE DISTINCTNESS AMONG TRINITARIAN PERSONS

In keeping with the textbook wisdom, Erickson claims that there are two main approaches in Christian history to the relationship between the oneness and threeness. The Greek approach took the monarchy of the Father as the basis and from there worked back to threeness, taking personhood (*hypostaseis*) as primary,[39] while the Latin approach built on divine substance as the starting point in its fear of reigning polytheisms.[40] Erickson claims to propose a third alternative, going back to the Cappadocians, that "emphasizes the three persons intimately linked to another by perichoresis."[41] The following quotation accurately describes Erickson's approach. Utilizing a favorite idea of his, Erickson refers to God as "organism"; that idea speaks of God[42]

> less as a unity, in the sense of simplicity, than as a union, involving three persons, Father, Son, and Holy Spirit. Without each of these, God would not be. Each is essential to the life of the whole. God could not exist simply as Father, or as Son, or as Holy Spirit. Nor could he exist as Father, or as Father and Spirit, or as Son and Spirit, without the third of these persons in that given case. further none of these could exist without being part of the Trinity. There would be no basis of life, apart from this union. Thus, in speaking of union, there should be no inference combining that which antecedently existed, prior to coming together. None has the power of life within itself alone. Each can only exist as part of the Triune God.

While of course affirming the oneness of God, as will be evident in what follows, Erickson resists the idea of an antecedent "substance" in God prior to the

---

37. Ibid., 220.
38. Ibid., 220–21 (221).
39. Ibid., 230, 291. What is confusing is that when Erickson begins to explicate the meaning of the Greek approach, he takes two Roman Catholic theologians, Rahner and LaCugna, as the main representatives! (pp. 291–99).
40. Ibid., 230, 291. Regarding the Latin approach, Erickson chooses three theologians as main proponents: Benjamin B. Warfield, the liberationist Leonardo Boff, and Pannenberg. By any account, these three form a very mixed bag, and neither Pannenberg nor Boff can be regarded in any way as a typical proponent of the alleged "Western" approach, usually attributed to Augustine (whom Erickson does not mention in this connection at all!).
41. Ibid., 230.
42. Ibid., 264.

threeness; this of course fits in his nonsubstantialist ontology and relational approach to reality and God. In the grammar of Christian theology, the meaning of the word "is" in the sentence "Father is God" or "Son is God" or "Spirit is God" is that of predication or attribution. The meaning of those statements, rather than saying literally that Father is God, is to say Father is divine and Spirit is divine, respectively.[43]

In keeping with this approach and in line with theologians such as Moltmann and Leonardo Boff, Erickson conceives of Trinity as society. Divine society can also be called a "complex of persons" united with love as the binding relationship of each of the persons to each of the others. Being love means that God is more than one person. Multiplicity follows since love entails more than one person.[44]

But why three persons rather than two? Erickson responds that for the love to be genuine and overcome narcissistic self-love, three are required. Two persons may simply reciprocate love but not be able to share that love with anyone else. "With three persons, there must be a greater quality of selflessness, of genuine *agapē*. Thus the Trinity founded upon love is a demonstration of the full nature of *agapē*."[45]

Erickson strengthens the idea of threeness in the Godhead by borrowing a key idea from Pannenberg, that of self-distinction. According to Pannenberg, Jesus as the obedient Son distinguishes himself from the Father by submitting to his authority and by serving the lordship of the Father. This, for Erickson, speaks for the distinctness of personhood or of consciousness of the Son from the Father. "The Son is only Son because of his distinction from the Father." Similarly, again based on Pannenberg's ideas, the handing over of the kingdom to the Son and then the Son's handing it back to the Father not only speak for distinction but also for dependence. The Father's fatherhood and lordship over his kingdom is predicated by the Son's obedience. Uniqueness and distinctness, Erickson argues, is indeed something innate to being a person.[46]

THE PERICHORETIC UNITY OF GOD

For any advocate of social Trinity, as mentioned, threeness is much easier to establish than unity. How does Erickson support his basic contention that the "Trinity is three persons so closely bound together that they are actually one"?[47]

---

43. Ibid., 265–66. The other two options, inappropriate to theological grammar in this context, are the "is" of identity (as in "The author of this book is Veli-Matti Kärkkäinen") or that of inclusion (as in "This car is blue") (pp. 264–65).

44. Erickson, *God in Three Persons*, 221.

45. Ibid., 221–22 (222).

46. Ibid., 226–27 (227). Erickson, *God the Father Almighty*, 231, in keeping with this program, calls for a revision of old substance metaphysics; see also Erickson, *Word Made Flesh*, 525–26, 529.

47. Erickson, *God in Three Persons*, 221.

Erickson is well aware of the danger of tritheism and works hard in establishing unity.[48] His main resources come from the consideration of God as love on the one hand, and the principle of interrelatedness or interpenetration in the God-head on the other hand.

God is love. Love entails sharing. Therefore there is multiplicity in the God-head, Erickson has established so far. For him, however, love not only establishes the principle of distinct persons; it also serves to establish unity. The key to that task is the distinction between divine and human love. If the divine society suffered from the limitations of human love, tritheism would result. The correspondence, however, between human and divine love is only partial. Divine love's difference from human love speaks for the unity. There are several limitations in human love that cannot be attributed to the Triune God as loving society. Humans are limited by physical bodies, they share differing experiences of life, and they are often plagued by preoccupation with oneself, one's own needs. None of these characterize God. God is not a bodily being. Even incarnation, Erickson says, represented a temporary self-imposed voluntary limitation such as ignorance of the day of the return of the Son of Man (Matt. 24:36). The limitations of differing experiences are overcome by sharing the consciousness of each of the others. Each person in the Godhead "thinks the others' thoughts, or at least is conscious of those thoughts," and therefore there are, strictly speaking, no separating experiences. Even when the incarnated Son has experiences not shared by others such as temptation, Father and Son "have experienced Christ experiencing temptation." Therefore, there are no experiences that are not understood by other divine members. And if God is love, there is no preoccupation with one's self, nor any selfishness.[49]

While Erickson, as noted, argues for separate consciousnesses in the divine society, he also qualifies this principle of threeness by linking the three consciousnesses into each other. Being a community, Trinitarian persons have direct access to the consciousness of the others. "As one thinks or experiences, the others are also directly aware of this. They think the other's thoughts, feel the other's feelings. It is an extreme, perhaps we might say, infinite case of the type of empathy sometimes experienced by two human persons."[50] Consequently, the goals, intentions, and values are shared by all three.[51]

Traditionally, this unity-in-diversity, this mutual interpenetration, has been expressed with the help of the term "perichoresis." So, for Erickson, perichoresis speaks both for threeness and unity of three-in-oneness. The concept goes back to Pseudo-Dionysius and especially John of Damascus and has been recently

48. Under the subheading "Perichoresis as the Guard against Tritheism," Erickson writes: "There is a danger of falling into tritheism. The guarantee against that, which would be three separate, distinct, and independent individuals, is in the closeness and interaction among them." Erickson, *God in Three Persons*, 228.
49. Ibid., 222–24 (224).
50. Ibid., 225.
51. Ibid., 226.

employed by Moltmann in particular.[52] Regarding the use by John Damascene, Erickson argues that its goal was to establish the unity in the Triune God.[53] As Erickson rightly notes, the Latin rendering of the term has two related meanings, both of which are relevant to Trinitarian expression: *circuminsessio* (to be seated in) conveys the more static conception of being located within one another, whereas *circumincessio*, a more dynamic concept, literally means the permeation or interpenetration. "Together, these ideas found in *perichoresis*, mean both permanence of location with respect to another and ongoing interchange of sharing."[54]

Erickson sees the principle of perichoresis supported by Scripture, especially in the union of the incarnate Son with the Father as taught especially in the Gospel of John. For Erickson, incarnation "gives the most complete revelation both into the nature of . . . [triune] relationships during the time of that earthly existence and also in the eternal interaction of the three."[55]

Earlier I noted that for Erickson distinctness belongs to the notion of "person." The same term, however, also speaks for unity. Building on the reflection of Boff,[56] he discerns different meanings of the term "person," such as that of an existing subject distinct from others, which affirms plurality but frustrates unity and therefore is not satisfactory. In keeping with the social analogy, Erickson prefers the idea of "person" as "a being-for, a knot of relationships, an identity formed and completed on the basis of relationships with others." He thus sees the orientation toward others included in the notion of personhood.[57]

Erickson employs several analogies to illustrate the threeness in one and oneness in three such as human organisms consisting of the heart, brain, and lungs in which each organ is distinct yet not separable; organs are dependent for their existence on the shared life. Each organ supplies life for the others. Siamese twins formed by virtue of a single fertilized egg provide another analogy; unable to function separately, they are "conjoined" and may even share some vital organs, such as the heart, the life source. The third one is a perfectly married couple. The point of these analogies is this: "The Father, Son, and Holy Spirit are so

---

52. Ibid., 229, cites Jürgen Moltmann, *The Trinity and the Kingdom: The Doctrine of God* (San Francisco: Harper & Row, 1981), 174, who speaks of the "circulatory character of the eternal life," in which "an eternal life process takes place in the triune God through the exchange of energies."

53. Erickson (*God in Three Persons*, 229) quotes from John of Damascus, *Exposition of the Orthodox Faith* 1.8: "The subsistences dwell and are established firmly in one another. For they are inseparable and cannot part from one another, but keep to their separate courses within one another, without coalescing or mingling, but cleaving to one another. For the Son is in the Father and the Spirit: and the Spirit in the Father and the Son: and the Father in the Son and the Spirit, but there is no coalescence or commingling or confusion."

54. Erickson, *God in Three Persons*, 230.

55. Ibid., 230–31 (230).

56. Ibid., 232 refers to Leonardo Boff, *Trinity and Society*, trans. Paul Burns (Maryknoll, NY: Orbis Books, 1998), 87–89 (Erickson gives here a slightly inaccurate page reference, limiting the reference to pp. 88–89 even though he cites verbatim also from p. 87).

57. Erickson, *God in Three Persons*, 232–33 (233), quotation from Boff, *Trinity and Society*, 89 (the quotation both in Erickson and Boff employs emphases that I have omitted for the sake of clarity).

intimately interlinked and intertwined that they are unable to live apart from one another. Each supplies life to the others. What they do, although it may be primarily the work of one of them, is done together."[58] The last statement points to the fact that the perichoretic unity can also be discerned in the works of God, creation, redemption, and sanctification. While creation can be attributed to Father, redemption to Son, and sanctification to Spirit, these works are interrelated.[59]

Unlike most other contemporary theologians of the Trinity, Erickson works hard to combat the typical objection concerning the contradictory nature of affirming oneness in three and vice versa.[60] He maintains that while Trinity is a "mystery," it is not necessarily a "contradiction. Mystery is "an apparent contradiction which there is good reason to believe." It is rational to believe in mystery when there is sufficient reason to believe that its alleged contradictory nature is just that, alleged, not real; belief is even more rational when there are compelling theological reasons to believe that mysterious doctrine,[61] granted that Trinitarian discourse represents what is sometimes called "logically odd language."[62]

EQUALITY IN THE DIVINE SOCIETY

One of the key ideas in Erickson's Trinitarian proposal is the equality of Father, Son, and Spirit. The Father is not seen as the source (*archē*), and there is no monarchy, as in much of traditional theology and still in the Eastern tradition. The notion of subordination in the Godhead needs to be dismissed. While Erickson affirms the begottenness of the Son from the Father and procession of the Spirit, for him these are no situations of causation or subordination. The three divine persons are not of course identical or interchangeable, but neither is there any inequality.[63]

In the final analysis, Erickson believes that Scripture teaches neither subordination nor derivation of one person from the other. What about those passages in the Bible that clearly refer to the begottenness of the Son (John 1:14, 18; 3:16,

---

58. Erickson, *God in Three Persons*, 234–35.

59. Ibid., 235–37. While not elaborating on that, Erickson also notes that the traditional categories of immanence and transcendence can also be expressed with the help of the Trinitarian perichoretic union (pp. 237–38). Oddly enough, however, in his subsequent monograph *God as Father*, where Erickson devotes a whole chapter (chap. 11) to this topic, Trinitarian considerations are totally absent!

60. Erickson, *God in Three Persons*; chap. 11 is titled "The Logical Structure of the Doctrine of the Trinity." Here, interestingly enough, Erickson discusses philosophical approaches to Trinity such as that of William Power or relative identity theory (which he applies to Trinity) as well as the approaches of theologians such as Rahner and LaCugna. His own approach owes much to Stephen T. Davis.

61. Erickson, *God in Three* Persons, 256–57 (257), building on the ideas of Stephen T. Davis, *Logic and the Nature of God* (Grand Rapids: Eerdmans, 1983), 141–43 especially.

62. Erickson, *God in Three Persons*, 270. Good examples are to say of the Trinity, "They is one" or "He are three," both examples employed by Erickson (ibid.).

63. Ibid., 294–95.

18; Heb. 11:7; 1 John 4:9)? Erickson surmises that these passages refer only to the economic Trinity, not to the life of God *in se*.[64] This is supported by the insight that there is a variation of the terminology in Scripture regarding the relations among the Three, including the order in which the names appear; Father is not always necessarily the first. Erickson also wonders if the term "Son"—which to us seems to imply inferiority—means rather equality and likeness at the same time.[65] In keeping with the principle of radical equality, Erickson is not willing to talk about the Father as the source of deity when it comes to the immanent Trinity: "Rather than one member of the Trinity being the source of the other's being, and thus superior to them, we would contend that each of the three is eternally derived from each of the others, and all three are eternally equal."[66] Consequently, rather than the term "God" being equivalent to "Father," it is the Trinity that is to be called God. As noted above, other uses of "God" are predicables (meaning "Father is divine" and so on).[67]

THE IMPLICATIONS OF THE TRINITY FOR HUMAN RELATIONSHIPS AND SOCIETY

Erickson is aware of female theologians and other liberationists who have accused the traditional doctrine of the Trinity for its neglect of the issue of inclusivism. While critical of what he calls feminist theologies' "Objection to the Universality of Trinitarian Christianity,"[68] Erickson also maintains that there are resources in traditional Trinitarian teaching to encompass more inclusively all kinds of people. The way forward, however, is not what he calls an attempt by some feminist theologians, such as Sallie McFague, to "desex" the persons of the Trinity since that smacks of losing the Trinity "in the older ontological sense." In that theology, Erickson argues, there is only the economic Trinity but not the immanent.[69] If that appears to be too harsh a statement, feminist theology has at least produced a depersonalized view of God. In addition to those two problems, in feminist theologies there can also be an all-too-wide inclusivism: "Some types of language not only do not include enough about God; they also do not exclude enough." This is where goddess language and doctrinal laxity, allowing modalism, for example, find their ways into theological language when instead of Father, Son, and Spirit the terms Creator, Redeemer, and Sanctifier are being

---

64. Ibid., 289–99.
65. Ibid., 299; Erickson builds here on the work of Benjamin B. Warfield, "The Biblical Doctrine of the Trinity," in *Biblical and Theological Studies*, ed. Samuel G. Craig (Philadelphia: P&R Publishing, 1952), 50–55 especially.
66. Erickson, *Making Sense of the Trinity*, 90.
67. Erickson, *God in Three Persons*, 265–66.
68. Subheading in ibid., 139. On pp. 139–50 Erickson discusses critically the proposals of various feminist theologians such as Sallie McFague and their attempts to revise traditional Trinitarian language.
69. Erickson, *God in Three Persons*, 271–75 (275).

adopted. For these reasons, Erickson rejects the substitution of traditional Trinitarian language with nongendered language.[70]

Agreeing with most, Erickson argues that God is neither male nor female and that therefore gender, in the strict sense, does not apply to God. God encompasses both feminine and masculine and goes beyond them. This insight is also a reminder to traditional theology to not limit God-talk solely to male images. At the same time, those dangers of patriarchal language, drawn from human society rather than divine revelation, need to be exposed. "The Triune God is . . . the God of all people."[71]

That God is the God of all people does not mean for Erickson giving up talk about God as Lord, as many feminist theologians and others such as Moltmann have done. For Erickson, becoming Christian means surrendering to the lordship of the Triune God.[72]

On the one hand Erickson affirms full equality in the Trinity and, on the other hand he affirms the lordship of God in relation to humanity and the world. What are the implications of this equation for our relationships and society? He maintains that tritheism leans toward individualism with its idea of three relatively independent persons, whereas monotheistic monarchial views support one authority. Erickson's view is a communal understanding of God that stresses relationality and interaction. This, however, does not lead to individualism since the divine relationships are based on self-sacrificial and self-giving love. Out of this emerges the idea of mutual submission rather than selfishness. This informs our views of how to live family life, share with others in need, carry on church life and even interchurch relationships. In addition to these spheres of life, personal piety and devotion should also be informed by the social analogy of God.[73]

CRITICAL REFLECTIONS

Unlike other contemporary theologians discussed in this book, Erickson's Trinitarian proposal has not elicited much response. To my knowledge, there are only two major reviews of his monograph on the Trinity.[74] In addition to those, a recent doctoral dissertation discusses Erickson's Trinitarian views—along with those of Pannenberg, Zizioulas, and Rahner—regarding their capacity to establish the unity of God.[75]

70. Ibid., 275–78 (277); for goddess-language, see pp. 144–45.
71. Ibid., 278–82 (282).
72. Ibid., 282.
73. Ibid., 329–39.
74. Garrett, review of *God in Three Persons*; Jonathan P. Case, review of *God in Three Persons: A Contemporary Interpretation of the Doctrine of the Trinity*, by Millard J. Erickson, *Dialog* 35, no. 3 (Summer 1996): 234–37. Even the recent books on the Trinity written by a conservative evangelical ignore Erickson. See, e.g., the new massive monograph produced by a conservative evangelical, Letham, *Holy Trinity*.
75. Chiavone, "Unity of God."

Before I deal with the most obvious challenge to Erickson's Trinitarian vision—the establishment of divine unity in a radical social analogy—let me begin with remarks on his handling of Trinitarian traditions and his theological method. Above I mentioned that his reading of history is selective, indeed very selective. I do not find that necessarily a weakness as long as it is neither one-sided nor flawed. Dismissing theologians such as Augustine, however, creates a major gap, especially for a study that focuses on patristic developments in history and makes the explicit claim that the fourth-century developments are most significant![76] Along with selectivity, there are some choices that sound eccentric at their best and erroneous at their worst, such as naming Roman Catholic Rahner and LaCugna as main proponents of the Greek or Eastern approach.[77] Apart from the designation itself (Greek or Eastern), Rahner and LaCugna form an odd marriage! Of course these two Western theologians do have much in common, but the differences for Erickson's purposes are striking: Rahner emphasizes the unity and is very reserved about person-language, whereas LaCugna claims to build on the Cappadocians' social analogy and pushes the distinctness of personhood language. In this, LaCugna represents much of Erickson's agenda, whereas Rahner does not.[78] No more convincing is the presentation of the Western or Latin traditions, especially because again there are apples and oranges in the same basket: B. B. Warfield with a rather typical Western view, and Social Trinitarians such as Boff and Moltmann, along with Pannenberg; the last three mentioned all represent Trinitarian views very critical of the typical "Western" view with its alleged emphasis on the oneness. Indeed, except for Warfield, all three "Western" representatives would be much closer to many Greek/Eastern emphases with the idea of beginning with three and emphasizing the distinctive *hypostaseis* (the only main deviation from the standard Eastern view is the reluctance to make the Father the source of the Deity). To further complicate this model, Erickson names the Cappadocians as the third party even though theologians such as Moltmann and Boff claim to build on them as well as LaCugna![79] I also wonder if it is true that the emergence of the Cappadocians' approach "was in large part a means of countering the tritheism into which some tended to fall."[80] In my understanding it was rather the opposite: the Cappadocians wanted to emphasize the threeness of the Christian Godhead to the point that soon their own proposal was suspected of falling into tritheism; it was out of this struggle that the Cappadocians felt the need to defend their proposal against polytheistic charges.

76. Erickson, *God in Three Persons*, 75.

77. Ibid., 291–99.

78. As accurately noted by Chiavone, "Unity of God," 107: "Erickson's position falls at the opposite end of the spectrum from that of Rahner. While Rahner makes repeated reference [*sic*] to the singular essence of God, Erickson avoids any reference to a singular essence when presenting his understanding of the trinitarian unity. Erickson replaces Rahner's singular personality and consciousness with an understanding of 'three persons, three centers of consciousness.'" Regarding the quoted phrase, Chiavone cites Erickson, *God in Three Persons*, 331.

79. Erickson, *God in Three Persons*, 230.

80. Ibid., 230.

Another remark concerning the handling of historical materials relates to the fact that Erickson claims to build on John of Damascus's use of perichoresis in his argument for the unity of God. According to Erickson, in contrast to the typical Eastern way of affirming divine unity in terms of the Father being the source, the Damascene elucidates the Cappadocians' view by establishing the unity on the basis of mutual penetration, the shared life of God.[81] For John of Damascus, however, as mentioned in the chapter on Moltmann—unlike Erickson—perichoresis is not the means of affirming unity, but rather unity is the presupposition for perichoresis. Unity for John is established by the idea of the Father as the source of the Spirit and Son.[82] Now this is not necessarily a charge against the use of perichoresis as a means of establishing unity (to which I return in what follows) but rather a note about the inaccuracy in handling historical materials. The principle of perichoresis, apart from its use by John of Damascus in history, on its own may or may not be able to accomplish the task to which Erickson sets it.

Erickson's method—while he never explicates it—appears to be a method "from below." However, it is not a "from below" method in the same sense as that of liberationist theologians—whether the feminist Elizabeth Johnson or the Latin American Leonardo Boff, to be discussed later—building from a particular experience of oppressed or suppressed people. Erickson's is from below in terms of shaping the idea of God based on the structures of human reality. His analogies, drawn mainly from human organisms and family structures, begin from world experience and work back to God.[83] These analogies for Erickson seem to be more than just analogies: they function as methodological guides in his establishment of both unity and Trinity. Regarding the role of Scripture in Erickson's project, above I mentioned that Erickson, in his use of the Bible—occupying a significant portion of his Trinity monograph (over fifty pages with numerous biblical references and quotations)—is different from both Barth and Pannenberg.

---

81. Ibid., 229–30.

82. Wolfhart Pannenberg, *Systematic Theology*, trans. Geoffrey W. Bromiley, 3 vols. (Grand Rapids: Eerdmans, 1991–98), 1:334; this is argued in more detail in Chiavone, "Unity of God," 125–27. The structure of John Damascene's discussion confirms this judgment. He begins the treatment of Trinity with the oneness of God and then proceeds from there to considering Trinity, thus—ironically—anticipating the standard Western tradition.

83. Noted accurately by Chiavone, "Unity of God," 121: "There is nothing in Erickson's description of the divine unity which is not an amplified part of human existence. Christians share lives and love sacrificially. Organs depend upon one another, as do equal co-owners of a business. These examples, taken to whatever degree, seem too mundane to adequately characterize the unity of God." However, I think Chiavone is somewhat unnuanced when later (p. 145) he insists that for Erickson "the unity of God is univocally like the unity of believers, or a married couple, differing only in its infinite intensity." Erickson's way of putting it is a bit milder: "Not that these latter relationships (taken from the human sphere) are by any means of the same degree as the relationship of the Father and Son to one another, but there must *at least be some univocal* element present, for such an analogy even to be suggested." Erickson, *God in Three Persons*, 227–28 (italics mine). This statement by Erickson, however, calls for some clarification when he says that an "analogy" needs to posit some "univocal" element. Is this a new category in addition to the three standard ones (univocal, equivocal, and analogical), namely, a "semi-univocal analogy"?

For Barth, the formal principle of revelation drawn from scriptural materials is the key whereas for Pannenberg, who uses many fewer biblical references than Erickson (or Barth, for that matter), the unfolding of the structure of salvation history, the coming of the Son to serve the coming of the kingdom of the Father in the power and unity of the Spirit, is the foundation. For Erickson, the face value of biblical statements about the unity and plurality give the raw materials for developing a social analogy explicated and argued "from below," beginning from the created order.

A related methodological remark has to do with Erickson's claim that the subordination at the economic level cannot be read back into the immanent Trinity.[84] Apart from one's view of this particular issue, this contention raises a bigger methodological issue: should we ascend from the economic Trinity to immanent Trinity as Rahner and many others claim, or should we not? If we cannot or should not, we would not have any reliable way of establishing the deity of the Son and by extension the deity of the Spirit—unless we do it on the basis of the face value of biblical statements. This, however, is extremely problematic for theologians and can hardly convince many outside of the most conservative wing of the theological guild. While Erickson is not quite clear about the use of this foundational rule, it seems to me—in his opposing all kinds of notions of subordinationism in the life of God—he ends up arguing against the principle of the economic Trinity being a reliable guide to the inner life of God. This position resorts to speculative doctrine of the Trinity, characteristic of Erickson.[85] Even with the proviso that Rahner's rule cannot be taken as an absolute identification of the economic and immanent Trinity (to preserve the freedom of God), it is also problematic to go with Erickson's view. It implies that he has another way of knowing about the life of God, apart from the pattern of salvation history as it unfolds in Scripture. The deity of the Son, as Pannenberg argues, is a result of the reading of salvation history: the Son who comes to serve the coming of his Father's kingdom is shown to be the eternal counterpart of the Father from all eternity.

Returning to Erickson's means of avoiding subordinationism in the immanent Trinity, indeed, it seems to me Erickson's own theology has resources to combat subordinationism that he is not utilizing: the principle of mutual dependence (as Pannenberg emphasizes). But rather than saying that what happens at the economic level is not indicative of the divine life *in se*, Erickson should say instead that the mutuality of Father and Son with each other and by extension the Spirit as the third member, as discerned on the basis of salvation history, clearly indicates that the kind of subordinationism that posits the Father one-sidedly as the source or relegates Son and Spirit to a lesser role cannot be substantiated. Even then—I personally argue—scriptural testimony seems to indicate some kind of

---

84. See also Erickson, *Making Sense of the Trinity*, 86.
85. A representative example can be found in Erickson, *God in Three Persons*, 307.

priority of the Father, but not the kind of priority that violates the principle of mutual interdependence.[86]

Arguing, as Erickson does, that the titles "Father," "Son," and "Holy Spirit" are purely economic and not eternal[87] leads to the very danger that Rahner warns us against, namely, the medieval speculation that any of the three persons could have been incarnated. But that would run against Erickson's idea of the primacy of Trinitarian *hypostaseis*. The Son—in the biblical salvation history—would not be the Son apart from incarnation. Father or Spirit could never become incarnate if we base our Trinitarian doctrine on the biblical salvation history.

There is also a problematic statement in Erickson about the relationship between the economic and immanent Trinity, one that runs against all other interpretations that I am aware of: "There is a rather obvious sense in which we can say that the immanent Trinity and the economic Trinity are the same. That would be the metaphysical identity, whereby there are not two different Trinities. The epistemological identity is something quite different, however. While the economic Trinity is certainly part of the immanent Trinity epistemologically, it does not exhaust it."[88] Erickson claims this is a "preferable alternative" to Rahner and LaCugna and is supported by Warfield, Boff, and Pannenberg.[89] For most theologians, Erickson's statement is far from being as "obvious" as he himself claims; it raises all kinds of problems. What is the meaning of "metaphysical" identity? Does that mean the equation of the economic with the immanent (or vice versa)? If so, then Erickson is agreeing with LaCugna and against Pannenberg, the opposite of what he is saying himself. But if so, then the first statement of the quotation is contradicting the last one, which says that epistemologically they are not identical. How could they possibly be different "epistemologically" if "metaphysically" they are not? The only option then would be that the economic Trinity is not necessarily a reliable guide to the immanent, a position Erickson, as mentioned above, at times seems to be supporting. Most theologians, apart from LaCugna (and possibly Moltmann, but for different reasons), are saying that while Rahner's rule can be affirmed *epistemologically*, it cannot necessarily be affirmed in terms of the absolute identity of the economic and immanent Trinity. This does not mean, however, as Erickson assumes, that there are "two" Trinities; no theologian argues for that. Rather, it means that while economy is the only reliable way to know something of the inner life of God, God *in se* is always beyond any human conception. What we can know of God— even if analogically—is reliable if it is based on the revelation as offered to us in

---

86. Erickson rightly says that rather than one member of the Trinity being the source of the others, and thus superior to them, each of the three is eternally derived from each of the others and therefore are eternally equal. Erickson, *Making Sense of the Trinity*, 90. But again, this statement is derived from salvation history, from the coming of the Son to serve the Father's kingdom, thus showing us that the Son has been the counterpart of the Father from all eternity.

87. Cf. Erickson, *Christian Theology*, 362–63.

88. Erickson, *God in Three Persons*, 309.

89. Ibid.

Scripture, but it is even at its best partial and can never exhaust God, who is beyond human capacities of knowing. I think that is also what Erickson means, yet the way he puts it theologically adds to the confusion.

As mentioned, there are two main ways Erickson attempts to establish the unity of God: mutual dependence and interpenetration as well as love. Chiavone raises a crucial issue when he claims that while Erickson insists on the interdependence and mutual penetration, he fails to argue why that is necessary and what it is exactly. The only way Erickson seems to express perichoresis as the basis of unity is the shared experiences.[90] "The guarantee against [tritheism] . . . which would be three separate, distinct, and independent individuals, is in the closeness and interaction among them that we have described."[91] The analogies employed are drawn from human organism and family life and are just that, analogies; they can hardly establish the theological truth. Chiavone scrutinizes each of the three main analogies and finds them wanting: the analogy of organs supports the idea of one presenting only part of the whole, thus implying interdependence foreign to Trinity; the analogy of Siamese twins supports the idea of a shared dependence met by a single source (the heart in this case), not applicable to Erickson's view of Trinity, which resists the idea of any Trinitarian member as source; and the analogy of the perfectly married couple supports the idea of the interdependence of multiple things that together possess something impossible for them to have separately, an idea difficult to apply to Father, Son, and Spirit, who are each full deity.[92]

Regarding the ability of the idea of love to establish unity, one needs to make the obvious remark that usually in the Christian tradition love has been used to justify plurality in the Godhead, an idea that Erickson himself of course supports. It is not self-evident at all how love would imply unity. Erickson claims that the three together, as God, "constitute a new entity, a single being, which is more than the sum of the parts."[93] But can this statement, taken from an analogy of human organism—heart, lung, brain as diverse entities—establish the needed unity for three equal persons?[94] And this argument leans toward the idea of three plus one in the Godhead: Father, Son, Spirit, and the "being." Not only is this not an orthodox idea, but it is also hostile to Erickson's radically nonsubstantialist, relational ontology. Chiavone's conclusion regarding the lack of clarity and persuasion in Erickson's attempt to establish the unity of God seems well taken: "Thus the primary theological objection to Erickson's understanding of divine unity is that it is too weak, that it risks tritheism. Many would raise such an objection against any theology which posits three centers of consciousness."[95] Pannenberg, as an advocate of distinct consciousnesses in the Triune God, is able to avoid

---

90. Chiavone, "Unity of God," 132.
91. Erickson, *God in Three Persons*, 228.
92. Chiavone, "Unity of God," 132–34.
93. Erickson, *God in Three Persons*, 269.
94. See further Chiavone, "Unity of God," 134–36.
95. Ibid., 142. I have corrected the original text, which read as follows: "Thus the primary theological objection to Erickson's understanding of divine unity is that it is too weak, that it is risks tritheism."

that trap by radically defining God as Spirit, a dynamic divine force field. Erickson's way of resorting to the traditional idea of Spirit understood as mind/reason would not be as successful in that task, and after all, while advocating the idea of God as Spirit, Erickson does not call on that resource to help defend unity. Erickson's insistence on the shared life, shared experiences, shared love as the guarantor for unity smacks of what Alvin Plantinga, another social analogy advocate, calls "congregational theory of trinity membership."[96] It speaks of closeness and mutuality but can hardly establish the unity called for by radical monotheism.

Chiavone claims that one of the weaknesses of Erickson's equalitarian position is its inability to avoid conflicts in decision making even for a perfectly good God. The three persons in God have separate consciousnesses, yet think the thoughts of all and make decisions jointly.[97] According to Chiavone: "if God is at all free, there are certain areas in which God could have done otherwise than he in fact has done. Unfortunately, an egalitarian system has no means of resolving conflict, and perfect goodness does not preclude the possibility of conflict. Nor can a voting system work, for an almighty being has infinite choices."[98] I find Chiavone's criticism misguided, and it is based on abstract speculation. Erickson makes it clear that while the three have separate consciousnesses, they are bound to each other in unselfish love; there is a mutual submission of each to each of the others, and the thoughts of all are shared by others. While philosophical theology speculates on the possibility of conflict in the divine society, a Trinitarian doctrine ascending from the economy of salvation as explicated in Scripture has no place for that speculation. There is absolutely nothing in the Christian account of God that would raise that kind of question. Chiavone also fails to note that if egalitarianism is replaced by the primacy of the Father as the "commander-in-chief"[99] the whole biblical idea of mutual submission and obedience is truncated.

Concerning what Erickson calls the "metaphysical basis" of his proposal, two issues call for further clarification: his idea of reality as personal and the way he defines God as Spirit. To begin with, I am not quite sure what it means to call the universe "personal." The whole complexity of the history and meaning of the term "person" in itself should warn us against such an application. Calling God "personal" is a challenge big enough, especially when we speak of Trinity with three "persons." I understand what Erickson is after in his insistence on the idea of the universe as personal: he resists the idea of ultimate reality being "impersonal" (as

---

96. Alvin J. Plantinga, "Social Trinity and Tritheism," in *Trinity, Incarnation, and Atonement: Philosophical and Theological Essays*, ed. Ronald J. Feenstra and Cornelius Plantinga Jr., Library of Religious Philosophy 1 (Notre Dame, IN: University of Notre Dame Press, 1989), 28. I am indebted to Chiavone, "Unity of God," 143, for this reference.

97. For a summary statement, see Erickson, *God in Three Persons*, 310.

98. Chiavone, "Unity of God," 129.

99. Ibid., 131. But no social Trinitarian to my knowledge argues univocally from the human to divine society; rather, as does Erickson, they hasten to remind us of the limitations of analogies drawn from the human sphere.

in Platonic idealism) or great mind (as in eighteenth- and nineteenth-century German idealism). But that can be best—and a lot more easily—ascertained by insisting on God as "personal."

Borrowing from Pannenberg and others, Erickson—in my mind, rightly—speaks of God as Spirit. However, the way he supports and elaborates this issue calls for revision. On the one hand, it strikes me as odd that Erickson still operates with the outdated spirit-versus-matter distinction. As Pannenberg and others have shown, contemporary physics understands even "matter" in a quite "spiritual" way, namely, as movements and forces. This idea has certain parallels with the biblical idea of the Spirit of God as the life principle.[100] Even more important to my point here, it is a mistake to identify Spirit—as Erickson does, God as Spirit—with mind.[101] This is the way patristic theology defined the spiritual nature of God because the Fathers were tied to the ontology of their times. They had to define spirit in terms of reason (or will) to escape the absurd implications of another option, namely, God as corporeal (thus including attributes such as divisibility, composition, extension, and so on) because of Stoic philosophy's idea of "spirit" (*pneuma*) as some type of fine matter. Today, those fears are of course no longer with us and therefore, instead of opting for the idea of Spirit as mind/reason (or will), the biblical idea of Spirit as the principle of life should be invoked.[102]

One of the key ideas for the social Trinity in Erickson is the idea of self-distinction among Trinitarian persons. Here Erickson borrows from Pannenberg, who has made this a leading theme in his theology of the Trinity. Contrary to Pannenberg and the ideas Erickson borrows from this German theologian, however, Erickson at times resorts to the traditional way of arguing for "limitations" of the incarnated Christ in a manner that is neither helpful nor, strictly speaking, dogmatically correct. Jesus' ignorance of the day of his return Erickson explains in terms of a temporary humiliation of the Son.[103] The problem with this explanation is that—against the canons of orthodox Christianity—it blurs the idea of incarnation as a union of divine and human natures (implying that as "human" Jesus did not have access to omnipotence); furthermore, with regard to Pannenberg's idea of self-distinction, it ignores the leading idea that precisely as the obedient Son who voluntarily laid down his life in the service of his Father and the coming of his kingdom, Jesus shows himself to be the Son. This is not a matter of a temporary resort to semi-human existence by a concealed deity, but rather a manifestation of the true divinity and humanity of the incarnated Son in real distinction from and dependence on the Father. The reason I am measuring the validity of Erickson's proposal in light of Pannenberg's view is that it is from him

---

100. See, e.g., Pannenberg, *Systematic Theology*, 2:79-82.

101. Here Erickson (*God in Three Persons*, 219) quotes with approval from Carl F. Henry, *God, Revelation, and Authority* (Waco, TX: Word Books, 1982), 5:105.

102. See further Pannenberg, *Systematic Theology*, 1:370-74 especially.

103. Erickson, *God in Three Persons*, 223.

that Erickson borrows the key idea of self-distinction. But having done so, Erickson does not follow that idea consistently.

Similarly to many social Trinitarians, Erickson argues not only for the two persons in the Godhead, the Lover and Beloved, but for three. Erickson's defense of three persons as a requirement for the intelligibility of the idea of God as love is no more convincing than that of Richard of St. Victor (whom Erickson never mentions in his Trinity book). Erickson's insistence on the need for the third party as the recipient and instigator of love shared makes the point that *more* than two are needed but fails to make the point that *no more* than three can be imagined for that kind of love. It amazes me that with all the energy devoted to the consideration of the "logical structure" of the doctrine of the Trinity (about forty pages, almost as much as his biblical discussion!), Erickson seems to be totally unaware of this challenge. Yet it has plagued the social analogy since medieval times and has never been satisfactorily resolved. What it shows is that correlating the biblical idea of God as Love—which is based on the concrete view of Father, Son, and Spirit as sharing love with each other and sharing that with the created world—with the *formal* argument of the social analogy can only be done at best *analogically*. The idea of Victor and his followers is like a parable: it makes the main point and nothing else. That, however, is not acknowledged by Erickson even though it should be of great interest to all social Trinitarians.

My final remark has to do with Erickson's comment about an ancient soteriological concept employed by Trinitarian theologians such as LaCugna, namely, *theōsis:* "She [LaCugna] speaks of the 'deified human being.' This, however, seems to confuse the relationship of salvation with ontology, so that we are not only related to God but joined with him metaphysically."[104] Erickson's remark reflects an ignorance and misconception of this view of salvation, unfortunately typical of much Western and evangelical theology.

To complete the North American section, two distinctively different theologians will be discussed next, both of whom have a common agenda in that they purport to expand Trinitarian discourse for interfaith dialogue.

---

104. Ibid., 308. See further Veli-Matti Kärkkäinen, *One with God: Salvation as Deification and Justification* (Collegeville, MN: Liturgical Press, 2004).

Chapter 15

S. Mark Heim

A Trinitarian Theology
of "Religious Ends"

"SALVATIONS: A MORE PLURALISTIC HYPOTHESIS"[1]

The Trinitarian proposal of S. Mark Heim evades typical categorizations in that, on the one hand it looks quite traditional in elevating the Trinity as a major theological topic, and on the other hand, while critical of existing pluralistic theologies of religions, it attempts to advance a radically pluralistic view of religious ends based on the idea of the diversity in the Godhead. In some respects, Heim's vision works with some of those also in the proposal of Smart and Konstantine (to be examined next), yet it explicitly anchors itself in the mainstream Christian tradition. Heim's Trinitarian theology of religions also has commonalities with that of the Indian American Raimundo Panikkar (to be studied in chap. 23).

Heim began to develop his Trinitarian theology of religions in the 1995 work titled, significantly, *Salvations*. The recent title *The Depth of the Riches: A*

---

1. The heading above is from the title for chap. 5 (p. 129) in S. Mark Heim, *Salvations: Truth and Difference in Religions* (Maryknoll, NY: Orbis Books, 1995).

Trinitarian Theology of Religious Ends (2001)[2] represents a full-blown vision of the Trinity as the guarantor of more than one goal for the followers of religions, including Christians for whom communion with God is the highest aim.

The reason for Heim's criticism concerning (other) pluralistic theologies lies in their denial of real differences among religions. The pluralisms of John Hick,[3] Paul F. Knitter,[4] as well as Wilfred Cantwell Smith all assume an underlying common foundation of a "world religion," an idea unacceptable to Heim[5] (as well as to Panikkar, as will be seen). One of the problems of this "rough parity" kind of pluralistic ethos is that it negates the legitimate particulars of existing religions.[6] In line with the critique expressed by Gavin D'Costa—but independently from him—Heim judges existing pluralisms to be self-contradictory and no different from inclusivistic attitudes.[7]

The key idea in Heim's Trinitarian understanding of the theology of religions is simple and straightforward: "One set of religious ends may be valid for a given goal, and thus final for that end, while different ways are valid for other ends."[8] A twofold affirmation is included in this programmatic statement: not only that differences among religions are real but that those differences should be honored and made an asset rather than an obstacle.[9] This means that *moksha* or nirvana of Buddhist religion is not only a legitimate end for Buddhists, but that it takes Buddhism as a particular religion to make those ends possible. The same applies to salvation as communion with God as promised for Christians.[10] Consequently, as Heim himself notes, the title of his earlier book needs to be taken seriously: *Salvations* conveys the possibility of more than one type of salvation.[11]

---

2. S. Mark Heim, *The Depth of the Riches: A Trinitarian Theology of Religious Ends* (Grand Rapids: Eerdmans, 2001).

3. For a brief introduction to and a critical dialogue with Hick, see Veli-Matti Kärkkäinen, *Trinity and Religious Pluralism: The Doctrine of the Trinity in Christian Theology of Religions* (Aldershot, UK: Ashgate, 2004), chap. 7.

4. For a brief introduction to Knitter's pluralistic theology, see Veli-Matti Kärkkäinen, *An Introduction to the Theology of Religions: Biblical, Historical, and Contemporary Perspectives* (Downers Grove, IL: InterVarsity Press, 2003), chap. 35.

5. Heim, *Salvations*, part 1, offers a critical dialogue with these theologians and their pluralisms.

6. Ibid., p. 3.

7. Ibid., 101–3. The term "inclusivism" in Christian theology of religions means an approach that regards Jesus Christ as constitutive for salvation yet acknowledges the possibility of—and in the case of the post-conciliar Roman Catholic doctrine even takes for granted—salvation apart from conscious knowledge and acknowledgment of Jesus as Savior. Inclusivisms thus assign (the possibility of) salvation to Christ and not to other religions; one should say that people in other religions can be saved despite their religions (and because of Christ). Pluralisms, of course, not only acknowledge that but usually also argue for the salvific value of religions on a more or less equal basis.

8. Ibid., p. 3.

9. See also ibid., p. 7.

10. Heim, *Depth of the Riches*, 31.

11. Heim, *Salvations*, 6. Heim calls his version of Trinitarian pluralism "orientational pluralism," based on some leading ideas of Nicholas Rescher's *The Strife of Systems* (Pittsburgh: Pittsburgh University Press, 1985). See further Kärkkäinen, *Trinity and Religious Pluralism*, chap. 9.

Before delving into the implications of this bold program concerning religious ends, let us inquire into the "basis" of Heim's Trinitarian doctrine and see how it compares to that of other contemporary theologians.

INCARNATION AND COMMUNION

Two key affirmations seem to be of crucial importance for the way Heim builds his Trinitarian doctrine. The first has to do with the role of Jesus Christ, especially his incarnation. The second concerns the biblical basis of his view of the Trinity.

When it comes to the place of Jesus Christ in Heim's view of the Trinity in general and in his theology of religions in particular, there seems to be a tension. On the one hand, in line with other pluralists, Heim does not make Jesus Christ the "exclusive" way of salvation; on the other hand, unlike most pluralists, he makes Jesus (at least for Christians) constitutive for salvation and eschews talk about multiple "incarnations." This is how he puts it:

> The Trinity teaches us that Jesus Christ cannot be an exhaustive or exclusive source for knowledge of God nor the exhaustive and exclusive act of God to save us. Yet the Trinity is unavoidably Christocentric in a least two senses. It is Christocentric in the empirical sense that the doctrine, the representation of God's triune nature, arose historically from faith in Jesus Christ. And it is so in the systematic sense that the personal character of God requires particularity as its deepest mode of revelation.[12]

While Christ is not exclusive in the sense of traditional Christian doctrine, neither is he the kind of "obstacle" to a more open-minded relation to the Other that pluralistic theologies typically deem Jesus Christ to be. The key lies in the Christian doctrine of the incarnation. For Heim, based on the salvation history in the Bible, the incarnation testifies to the fact that in Jesus the internal relations that constitute God's divinity (the Trinitarian relations) and the external relations between God and humans (the creator-creature relations) participate in each other.[13] On the basis of the incarnation Christians know about the coming together of Trinitarian relations *ad intra* and *ad extra*. Yet for Heim, "God's living presence in the world has a complex variety" and therefore there is no need to "limit the going out of God into creation to just one instance."[14] What Heim is trying to affirm here is that the incarnation matters—it is an "embodiment" of the ontological relationality in the Triune God. Since he bases his theology of religions on his theology of the Trinity, in contrast to many pluralistic theologies, we should not look for other incarnations—in order to qualify the particularity of the Jesus-event—but we should rather maintain the possibility and actuality

12. Heim, *Depth of the Riches*, 134.
13. Ibid., 130–31.
14. Ibid., 133.

of God's saving presence in the world in other forms. What those other forms are, Heim does not tell us, and that is a question that naturally arises in the mind of the readers.

Concerning the second key issue, namely, the role of the biblical salvation history vis-à-vis a more generic kind of approach to Trinity, Heim focuses on the former (while Panikkar and Smart and Konstantine, to be discussed below, argue for the Trinitarian structure of not only religions but the whole of reality, apart from the Bible). For Heim, the centrality of the Trinity is not based on some general religious or philosophical idea but rather on the particularity of the biblical salvation history. It is only on the basis of the biblical salvation history that Christians can say that in "the incarnation God forms an irrevocable relation with a human being at the deepest possible level," and that the communion with God in which Jesus participated in the incarnation as a human being is now a continuing possibility for us through a universalized relation with Christ.[15]

Consequently, Heim wholeheartedly affirms the key insight of communion theology according to which relationality in the Godhead speaks for communion. Yet he takes communion theology to a new level in his insistence that relationality not only speaks to the community of the three but also to the real diversity: "In articulating Trinity as the character of ultimate being, Christians affirm an ontology in which the differences of the persons are basic and integral. There is no being without both difference and communion."[16] The implications of Heim's communion theology, which points out the differences, carry over to the doctrine of salvation in terms of affirming a diversity of religious ends. Heim's take is clearly different from (even) contemporary communion theologians and social Trinitarianists. While for others such as Moltmann, the Trinitarian issue requiring attention is the need to establish unity in the midst of diversity, Heim takes as his main challenge not only affirming diversity, but making it a key theological program.

FROM THE DIVERSITY IN THE GODHEAD TO DIVERSITY IN ENDS

If relationality in the Godhead speaks for communion—yet communion in diversity—then it also follows that salvation means varying degrees of being in communion with God or being related to God.[17] Salvation simply means being in relation. The following quotation from Heim's mature Trinitarian approach is a helpful guide to the key ideas in his program:[18]

---

15. Ibid., 56–57.
16. Ibid., 175.
17. Ibid., chap. 2.
18. Ibid., 3; see also p. 12.

We can . . . see the connection between the Trinity and varied religious aims. The actual ends that various religious traditions offer as alternative human fulfillments diverge because they realize different relations with God. It is God's reality as Trinity that generates the multiplicity of dimensions that allow for that variety of relations. God's threefoldness means that salvation necessarily is a characteristic communion in diversity. It also permits human responses to God to limit themselves within the terms of one dimension. Trinity requires that salvation be communion. It makes possible, but not necessary, the realization of religious ends other than salvation.[19]

The implications of this approach are staggering: "The 'one way' to salvation and the 'many ways' to religious ends are alike rooted in the Trinity."[20] Whether one looks for communion with God (as in the Christian religion) or dissolution into the divine (as in the mainstream Hinduistic religion[s]), these goals are "grounded in God, in the coexisting relations in God's own nature."[21]

What about the differences among religions, which Heim affirms? How do the differences in how people in various religions are related to God play into the differences in the religious ends? Here Heim introduces an idea of a "hierarchy" of religious ends, an idea that helps him differentiate ends but is also problematic in the sense that hierarchy implies there are "higher" and "lower" ends. That kind of grading, however, can only be done from a particular perspective: what seems to be a "higher" end for, say, Christians might not appear as high to the devout Hindu. Therefore, I have suggested that perhaps a term like "taxonomy" would be more appropriate for his purposes.[22]

Heim argues that the whole Trinity is related to all religions, but diversity within the Trinity makes it possible to envision varying faiths' ends.[23] Heim lays out four main categories regarding religious ends: salvation as communion, religious ends of other religions, human destinies that are not religious ends at all (instances of human beings clinging to created reality in place of God), and negation of creation itself leading to annihilation.[24] The main criterion for grading different levels is the intensity of communion with the Triune God. For our purposes, there is no need to go into the details.[25]

What about biblical and historical support of Heim's view? In contrast to most pluralists, such as Panikkar and Smart and Konstantine, Heim works hard to

19. Ibid., 180.
20. Ibid., 209.
21. Ibid., 179.
22. Kärkkäinen, *Trinity and Religious Pluralism*, 150.
23. Here Heim is echoing the approach taken by Smart and Konstantine, even though Heim differs from them in several significant points. See further Heim, *Depth of the Riches*, 164–65.
24. Ibid., 272–73. This is a somewhat difference taxonomy from his earlier work in which he lists three ends: lostness, penultimate religious fulfillment, and communion with the triune God (*Salvations*, 165).
25. For details, see Kärkkäinen, *Trinity and Religious Pluralism*, 138–40. Suffice it to say here that there is a movement from the "impersonal identity" to real communion, perichoresis, a mutual indwelling of human and divine.

anchor his theological vision in the biblical data. On the basis of extensive biblical investigation, Heim concludes—quite surprisingly—that the traditional view according to which there are two opposite ends, heaven and hell, seems to be the mainstream biblical view, even though this observation needs to be balanced by the arguments deriving from church history that seem to give some hope to those who have never heard the gospel (such as "pagan saints" or Jews). One of the more creative parts of the inquiry into the history of Christian theology is Heim's extensive dialogue with Dante's *Divine Comedy*, which—in his reading—speaks not only for two destinies (heaven and hell) but also for the presence of God in both destinies. Indeed, he concludes by saying that "the *Comedy* in fact presents us with a variety of ultimate ends. There is great diversity within hell, purgatory, and paradise."[26] Heim's vision of religious ends, again quite surprisingly, is open to the possibility of loss based on the freedom given by the Creator to his creatures. This possibility derives from the God's "withdrawal" from humans in creation to provide the space for self-existence and self-determination.[27]

What about the implications of this variety of ends for the eschatological victory of God? Here again we can register another brilliant move in Heim's theological vision. Rather than trying to offer a defense of God's omnipotence against the charge that God's victory is in danger of being compromised because of failure to reach the goal of the unity of all humanity under one God—a problem which is of course just as acute in traditional theologies that assign people to hell or annihilation—Heim makes this another major theological asset. He dubs it the principle of eschatological plenitude.[28]

Setting aside the option of universalism, which Heim agrees in principle would be the most logical solution to the problem of God's final victory being compromised—but one that has not met with much approval in Christian theology—Heim argues that his vision is in keeping with the traditional Christian eschatological vision based on the ancient idea of "plenitude."[29] The principle of plenitude means simply that God's infinite nature entails the proliferation of the greatest variety of types (but of course not number) of beings. This is the standard understanding in historical theology. Heim adds another significant twist here by naming it the "theological principle of plenitude." Based on his communion theology and the centrality of relationality, he contends that plenitude is a qualitative description of the divine life as triune; a personal communion-in-difference is better than a pure divine substance. This divine fullness is expressed in all God's creation, with humans created with freedom and thus capable of choosing whether they desire communion or not. God's purpose for creation allows that variety to work itself out in different ways. All this variety goes back to diver-

---

26. Heim, *Depth of the Riches*, 117.

27. Ibid., 182.

28. The discussion can be found in Heim, *Salvations*, 163–71; *Depth of the Riches*, chap. 7.

29. Heim also offers a number of supporting arguments in favor of this argumentation in *Depth of the Riches*, 246–48.

sity in the Godhead: the "alternatives to salvation are in fact constituents of salvation, standing alongside each other. These ends are not evil or empty. They could not be real unless they were relations to God."[30] So, based on the plenitude within the Trinity, Heim presents a vision in which there is a plenitude of communion within salvation, but also a plenitude of religious ends alongside it.

CRITICAL REFLECTIONS

Given that Heim's purpose is to develop a pluralistic view of religious ends based on the diversity of the Godhead, my critical reflections on some key issues in Heim's Trinitarian theology must be formed with his purpose in mind. At the same time, I am not here attempting to offer an assessment of this Trinitarian theology of religions as a whole (which I have done elsewhere[31]). There is no doubt that Heim has significantly advanced the flourishing Trinitarian discourse in general and theology of religions in particular by making Trinity a major theological asset. This is a needed corrective to so much of the pluralistic ethos, which does everything to shy away from this crucial Christian doctrine. Heim's proposal, however, raises serious theological questions that call for much further work in order to persuade many.

In my reading of his works, Heim fails to deal with the question of the unity in the Godhead; it seems to me that he takes it almost as a given. In fact, the way he approaches the unity is noteworthy. He speaks of God's personal reality as complex; in a sense, God is "made up" of personal communion-in-difference. However, how this accounts for the unity is not pursued by Heim. In defense of Heim, we have to keep in mind the fact that he is neither trying to develop a full-blown Trinitarian doctrine nor a theology of religions, but rather setting forth a bold proposal as to how these two could come together. Therefore, expecting him to tackle the issue of unity to any great extent is perhaps to ask for too much. Yet the question of the unity cannot be put aside in a theology that makes the diversity a key issue. Therefore, it is left as an open question to which Heim will hopefully return in future work.

One way to highlight the importance of tackling the question of the unity is to ask, To what extent can Heim's vision be considered to be in keeping with the classical canons of Christian theology? This question is legitimate because Heim often makes the claim that his theological program is a faithful, albeit creative, interpretation of biblical and historical theology. As Heim himself notes, the main impetus for the rise of the doctrine of the Trinity in early Christian theology was to secure the closest possible union between Yahweh of the Old Testament and Jesus Christ.[32] Not only that, but the Trinity was also needed to negotiate the apparent tension

---

30. Ibid., 255.
31. Kärkkäinen, *Trinity and Religious Pluralism*, chap. 9.
32. Heim, *Depth of the Riches*, 131.

between the transcendence of God and the historical particularity of the incarnated Son as the very revelation of God. So the original purpose of the doctrine of the Trinity was not so much to affirm diversity in God as it was to affirm belief in one God. In that sense, the way Heim works toward his theology of the Trinity is exactly the opposite. That in itself is of course not a problem, but unless the unity is secured, I fear that making the diversity the main theological asset is suspect.

The question of the unity aside, the main critical question—again, in need of much more elaboration—is, So what? Granted that there is diversity in the Godhead—and all Trinitarian doctrines affirm it—one needs to ask about the implications for our theology. The foundational problem in Heim's theology can be expressed simply: To make a jump from the principle of the diversity in the Godhead to the diversity in the religious ends willed by the Triune God is both unwarranted and logically less than convincing. Logically the claim may or may not be true; biblically and theologically I fear it is not a legitimate move. Indeed, to me it seems to speak against the very idea of communion: in the biblical vision, the purpose of humanity, created in the image of God, is to (re)turn to eternal communion with the Triune God. Even when that does not happen, Christian theology affirms that it is not because God has not willed it but rather because God honors the freedom given to humanity. To allow the possibility of lack of communion (as with the doctrine of hell or annihilation) is radically different from making the failure to reach that communion a theological program. Heim's use of the Trinitarian doctrine seems to conflict with the biblical vision of the gathering of all people in the New Jerusalem under one God (Rev. 21–22). In fact, Heim does not try very hard to establish his case biblically; rather, he focuses his scrutiny of the biblical materials on supporting the idea that the traditional teaching is not as clear as often thought—which I do not think is a much-contested claim. Ironically, it takes another pluralist, the Catholic Paul F. Knitter, to bring to light the problem I am trying to highlight here:

> Christians have always taken for granted, and still do, that because there is one God, there is one final destination. Heim's efforts to draw out the possibility of many salvations from the Christian doctrine of the Trinity go only half-circle. Yes, Christian belief in three divine persons does mean that diversity is alive and well and a permanent part of the very nature of God; and this could well mean, as Heim concludes, that it is alive and well and enduring among the religions. But that's only the first half of the circle of Christian belief in God as triune; the other half swings back to oneness: the three divine persons, Christians also affirm, have something in common that enables them to relate to each other, enhance each other, achieve ever greater unity among themselves. Heim does not seem to apply this part of the Trinitarian cycle to the world religions: as diverse as they are, as incommensurable as their differences may seem, they also, like the persons of the Trinity, have something in common that enables them to transcend their differences without doing away with them.[33]

33. Paul F. Knitter, *Introducing Theologies of Religions* (Maryknoll, NY: Orbis Books, 2002), 231.

A quick look at the history of theology tells us that with all the debates concerning the religious ends, the route taken by Heim has hardly been appealing. Even an extensive appeal to Dante's *Comedy* is questionable. Not only does it fail to represent mainline Christian theology (being a highly speculative work of art), but also it does not necessarily support Heim's idea of the presence of God in hell as anything desirable but rather as punitive.

The final question has to do with what kind of pluralism, if any, Heim's Trinitarian vision is championing. He makes the bold claim of being "more" authentically pluralistic.[34] Yet the fact that Heim does not give religions—Christianity included—the right to issue universal claims regarding the key issue in religions, namely, salvation, is hardly in keeping with a more pluralistic ethos. Most, if not all, religions would disagree with Heim's vision, not only because other religions do not like one particular religion to tell others how their vision of salvation is related to the Christian God, but also because religions usually distinguish between "right" and "wrong" religious ends. It is not good news to the Hindu or Buddhist to be told that their nirvana is an end willed by the Christian God and that it is "lower" than communion with the Triune God. How pluralistic is such a claim? With other pluralists, Heim seems to be guilty of the very attitude he critiques in others, namely, dubbing the idea of a rough parity "wrong" and the idea of differences "right." It is not too far from the typical "imperialistic" hetero-interpretation of other religions.

A related problem is that Heim takes the Christian God for granted in his theology of religions by linking the salvation in all religions to the Triune God of the Bible. While this is axiomatic to Christianity, it certainly is not to other religions, and it thus prevents his theology from being pluralistic. Buddhists would strongly oppose the idea that the validity of nirvana for the Buddhist end is based on the Triune God.[35] This kind of reading of other religions doesn't fare much better than Rahner's idea of "anonymous Christian." Further consideration of this issue would take us to the highly disputed question concerning a unified concept of God among world religions (or lack thereof). This issue cannot of course be dealt with here. But it needs to be raised if an explicitly Christian doctrine of the Trinity is invoked as a major asset to pluralism.

My final conclusion—based on an earlier more extensive study— is that

> Heim's proposal is not pluralistic but inclusivist, even if very novel; to be pluralistic in light of Heim's desire to hold on to varying ends, his trinitarianism should leave behind the particularity of the *Christian* trinitarianism. Either way, his trinitarian pluralism fails. The implications for interfaith dialogue are less than satisfactory.[36]

---

34. Heim, *Salvations*, title for chap. 5 (p. 129).
35. See Heim, *Depth of the Riches*, 179 especially.
36. Kärkkäinen, *Trinity and Religious Pluralism*, 151.

The implications for interfaith dialogue are equally meager if not counterproductive. Why should one bother dialoguing if there is no common destiny? Why not let religions hold on to their own varying visions of the end?

As mentioned in the introduction, one of the distinctive features of the present book is an attempt to register and critically engage the current interest in Trinitarian theology to link the discourse to interfaith encounter. Heim and the scholar-pair of Smart and Konstantine, to be discussed next, both share this agenda. At the same time their entry point to the theology of religions discourse is somewhat different. S. Mark Heim, a theologian, looks at the *theology* of the religion and its relation to Trinity from the perspective of Christian tradition. Ninian Smart and Steven Konstantine, scholars of religious studies, take their point of departure from the theology of *religions* by blending, in a creative way, insights from Christian faith and other faiths.

Chapter 16

Ninian Smart
and Steven Konstantine

*The Divine Threefoldness
in the Christian Neo-Transcendentalistic
Vision of Love*

TOWARD A WORLD THEOLOGY[1]

For students of religions and religious studies, Ninian Smart, along with other celebrities in the field such as Wilfred Smith, is a household name.[2] What makes his recent book *Christian Systematic Theology in a World Context* (written in collaboration with his student Steven Konstantine)[3] groundbreaking is that Smart enters, as the title indicates, the field of Christian systematic theology in a way that has not been typical of his work, with the exception of the 1979 title *In Search of Christianity.*[4] The purpose of Smart and Konstantine (hereafter, S&K)

---

1. The heading above is from Wilfred C. Smith, *Toward a World Theology* (Philadelphia: Westminster Press, 1981).

2. A prolific writer, Ninian Smart has established an enviable publishing record; see among others: *World Religions: A Dialogue* (Baltimore: Penguin Books, 1966); *Philosophers and Religious Truth* (New York: Macmillan, 1968); *The Phenomenon of Religion* (New York: Herder & Herder, 1973); *The Philosophy of Religion* (New York: Oxford University Press, 1979); *The Religious Experience of Mankind*, 4th ed. (New York: Scribner's Sons, 1991).

3. Ninian Smart and Steven Konstantine, *Christian Systematic Theology in a World Context* (Minneapolis: Fortress, 1991).

4. Ninian Smart, *In Search of Christianity* (New York: Harper & Row, 1979).

is to set forth a "vision," *darśana*, for "modern, liberal, scientifically-minded citizens of a plural world," in close correlation with the study of religions. This vision is based on the underlying idea of the social Trinity, which sees God as love.[5] "From our perspective," S&K say, "Christianity is a social Trinitarian vision of the Divine Reality and a lifestyle based on that vision."[6]

While attentive to the contributions and insights of other religions and worldviews, S&K do not regard religions as one; all religions do not have the same "deep structure" (in contrast, for example, to John Hick and many other pluralists). Smart, an Anglican, and Konstantine, an Eastern Orthodox, hold on to a more nuanced and dynamic view of the interrelationship among religions:

> The Divine *Īśvara* we follow is Lord of Compassion, is the Great Ultimate, is Kwoth, and shows forth the love which bodhisattvas display. But while we see echoes of our faith in the world's religions and great and meaningful overlaps, we do not hold that all religions are one, or that we are in orbit round the same Sun. We do not follow Radhakrishnan or Aldous Huxley or John Hick. But we take with utmost seriousness the existence of and challenge of all worldviews. . . . From a Christian perspective we can say that God put other faiths there to keep us honest. We can all be friendly critics of one another.[7]

In addition to social Trinity, another key nomenclature for the theological vision of S&K is the idea of neo-transcendentalism, which sees the world from a transcendent perspective and thus resists the reductive tendency in much of religious studies.[8] Epistemologically, they advance the combination of "soft non-relativism with possible inner certitude."[9] This simply means that while there is no way to "prove" one's worldview, one can still assume some kind of relationship between statements made and reality. While public certainty is impossible, personal conviction of the "truth" and power of one's vision is attainable.

THE EMERGENCE OF THE TRINITARIAN VISION IN THE EXPERIENCE AND LITURGY OF THE EARLY CHURCH

"The historical and experiential basis of the doctrine of the Trinity, as it later became clarified, lies in the important events of the life of Jesus and of the early Christian community." Jesus' own religious experience, especially—or to be more precise, the way it was conceived of by his followers—laid the foundation for the

5. Smart and Konstantine, *Christian Systematic Theology*, 17, 10.
6. Ibid., 194.
7. Ibid., 10–11.
8. Ibid., 21–22, 114–20.
9. Ibid., 22; on p. 88 they use the terms "soft epistemology" and "non-relativism" to describe their approach. For the relationship between public and private certitude, see also pp. 93–95.

Trinitarian vision.[10] Laying aside the tricky historical questions concerning the historical accuracy of the Gospel narratives, especially regarding the resurrection, S&K maintain there is enough supporting evidence for the view "that the early followers of Jesus experienced, through exterior and interior visions, the living reality of Christ."[11] Jesus was experienced as "divine savior in these numinous experiences" by his followers after his death and resurrection. This was the way to affirm Jesus' divinity:

> Salvation could only be accomplished by God, and it is for this reason that we here stress [that] he is *divine* savior. This saving was seen as due to his death and self-sacrifice on the cross, liberating human beings from their alienation from God and therefore from death. His resurrection was a visible sign of this victory. . . . [T]his vision of Christ was expressed through worship. It thus appears that from very early times, Christians experienced Christ as divine and yet as a distinct entity from his heavenly Father.[12]

If this experience of Jesus as divine accounts for the distinction between Father and Son, what about the Spirit? For S&K, the outpouring of Pentecost explains the role of the Spirit in the Trinitarian vision. Already in the spiritual life of the historical Jesus, the Spirit was instrumental in prophetic and devotional dimensions. At Pentecost, the emerging Christian community felt that the promise of Jesus to give the Spirit to help them be connected with the Father was fulfilled. The Spirit thus is the bond of love, the bond of communion. Beyond that, other aspects of spiritual life were attributed to the Spirit in the experience of the early community, such as sanctification and charismatic gifts. The result was that "[f]rom all these experiences there emerged in the consciousness of Christians a conviction that the Spirit was somehow a personal living entity distinct from the living Son, and guiding them individually from within. They worshipped this entity . . . together with the Father and Son."[13]

Two factors were critical in shaping the Trinitarian doctrine. Liturgy and worship is one of them: "Worship is a more important index of who is 'god' than just doctrines, which it precedes." Out of the liturgical experience arose the idea that the Spirit, rather than just being an energy or force, was a center of consciousness, a personal "he" rather than "it."[14] The other factor has to do with salvation, especially in the Christian East. Christ had to be divine to be able to save us and also human in order for his identification with human beings to be

10. Ibid., 149.
11. Ibid., 153. S&K are not necessarily denying the "physicalist" understanding of resurrection (meaning that it was a historical event) but rather argue that that is a nonissue. Their vision, in which public certitude is not the goal, can embrace both "conservative" approaches (with their physicalist understanding) and "liberal" approaches (with their mythical-experiential view), they believe (see p. 154 especially).
12. Ibid., 155 (italics in the original). The *that* in brackets replaces a typo, *the,* in the original.
13. Ibid., 155–57 (quotation on p. 157).
14. Ibid., 157.

real. Philosophical and apologetic reasons, while not totally missing, were less important than liturgical and soteriological reasons, S&K argue.[15]

While not rational in the first place, the understanding of the Trinity of course had to be expressed in conceptual terms. This fact, however, brought about certain difficulties in the classical formulations. According to S&K, the challenges have to do mostly with limitations of a particular culture and language, in this case Greek, to communicate vision in ways adequate to later times and other contexts. Difficulties also stem from the "impersonal and static" flavor of classical theistic formulations, especially in the substantial understanding of God (as is evident in the widespread use of the terms *ousia* and substance to denote the Godhead).[16]

In order to do justice to the earlier, dynamic way of approaching the topic of Trinitarian vision and also to combat the difficulties in the classical formulations, S&K propose a highly creative picture of the Trinity.

THE DIVINE THREEFOLDNESS AND UNITY OF DIVINE LIFE

In order to substitute for the "abstract, static and impersonal category of the divine substance" an approach that is more dynamic and personal, S&K suggest speaking of "divine life" common to all three identities.[17] Gleaning especially from the work of Leonard Hodgson,[18] S&K contend that divine life should be conceived of in terms of organic unity, which includes plurality. As with life in general, the higher level the organism, the more complex the unity becomes. That this analogy does not lead to tritheism is supported by the notion that speaking of divine life means speaking of life in the intensity of the infinite, which exceeds anything we know. Quoting from Hodgson, S&K affirm: "The divine unity is a dynamic unity actively unifying in the one divine life the lives of the three divine persons."[19]

This means there are three "identities," persons in the Godhead, even though there is one united divine life. Drawing from the work of another twentieth-century theologian, the Sri Lankan Lynn de Silva,[20] S&K amplify the primarily biological analogy of divine life with an orientation that moves toward a more (inter)personal arena. S&K envision each of the divine identities as "selfless

15. Ibid., 160–62, 193–94.

16. Ibid., 165–67.

17. Ibid., 168.

18. Leonardo Hodgson, *The Doctrine of the Trinity* (New York: Scribner's Sons, 1944).

19. Ibid., 95, quoted in Smart and Konstantine, *Christian Systematic Theology*, 168.

20. Lynn de Silva, *The Problem of Self in Buddhism and Christianity* (Colombo, Sri Lanka: Study Centre for Religion and Society, 1975), develops the notion of *anattá-pneuma*. The Theravada Buddhist term *anattá* means "non-self-centered," and *pneuma*, "spirit," is here interpreted as self-conscious personal life. Consequently, *anattá-pneuma* denotes "non-egocentric mutuality" or (with John Hick) "mutually open [i.e., not-self-centered] center of consciousness."

spirit," which means that they do not "exist over against the others as self-enclosed centers of consciousness, as with human persons, . . . but rather each dwells in the others through a kind of inter-permeation." This can be expressed more technically in this way: "The consciousnesses are fused but not confused." This is the ancient notion of perichoresis, mutual interpenetration.[21]

Perhaps unexpectedly, S&K connect this idea of divine life also with Augustine's idea of the Spirit as *vinculum amoris,* the bond of love between Father and Son. This is to express the biblical idea of God being love; with reference to biblical teaching (Rom. 5:5; 1 John 4:7–19), Augustine gathered the idea that the Spirit is love poured out into our hearts. From this S&K conclude that "the very nature of the divine life is a process of self-giving love." Out of love, Father eternally engenders Son, the second divine identity, who in turn communicates back the divine life through a responsive love that results in the coming to existence of the Spirit, "as blissful love."[22] The idea of God as love thus conceived has parallels in other religions such as the formula *sat-cit-ānanda* (being, consciousness, and bliss) of the Advaita Vedanta tradition. Yet there are also differences: the Vedantic notion views Brahma, the ultimate entity, as single and undivided, while Trinity speaks for differences in unity. The same applies to other parallels such as another familiar Hindu vision of three deities, *Brahma, Shiva, Vishnu.* While these are three deities, in Advaita Vedanta teaching they are rather understood as three different modes of divine operation; in the final analysis there is, however, only ultimate oneness of everything, a nonduality that is impersonal. Even more important—which will become evident in what follows—the Christian Trinitarian vision in the interpretation of S&K is able to synthesize both personal and nonpersonal aspects at the one level; in Hindu traditions, in general the "personal" belongs to a lower level, thus leading to a two-level understanding foreign to the Christian vision.[23]

Before delving into the question of how Christian Trinitarian vision as presented by S&K is able to embrace both personal and impersonal aspects, let us note that, again quite unexpectedly, S&K end up affirming two classical Trinitarian rules that usually do not go together. On the one hand, they affirm the Western, Augustinian idea of the *filioque,* that both the Father and Son together are the source of the identity of the Spirit, as the previous explanation of God as love implies. On the other hand, they also affirm the typical Eastern idea of the Father as the ultimate source of the divinity. This means that Father is "self-possessed"; having his identity in the Father alone, the Son receives his identity from the Father, and the Spirit from both together. What about the identity of the Spirit? Can we say the Spirit is more than a relation (bond of love)? S&K believe that since the "Spirit's identity is the expression of a process of mutual self-giving love and communication of divine life between the Father and the Son," a "personal" identity follows.[24]

21. Smart and Konstantine, *Christian Systematic Theology,* 169.
22. Ibid., 170.
23. Ibid., 170–71, 176.
24. Ibid., 171–72 (quotation on p. 72).

THREE ASPECTS OF THE TRINITY

Now we are in a position to describe in more detail the way S&K paint the picture of the Trinity in their neo-transcendental vision. The following quotation summarizes it:

> As well as being conscious of themselves as divine identities the Persons possess together a common divine consciousness though which they are aware of sharing the divine life and love and in which they act together in perfect harmony. . . . Through the common divine consciousness the identities form a communal or corporate self, an I within the We.[25]
>
> We can make a distinction too between the non-relational and the relational aspects of the Trinity. There is, first, the infinity of the divine life as it circulates through the selfless spirits. This is the non-relational aspect. Then, second, there is the plurality of the three Persons. Third, there is the communal life—the shared ego of the three. These last two aspects are relational (the first to one another, the second towards creatures).

Two significant distinctions are made in this statement. The first distinction has to do with three different yet related aspects of the Trinity: (1) The infinity of the divine life (such as the circulation of blood in a living organism) speaks for the unity and oneness in the Trinity. This dynamic understanding of the unity is meant to replace the typical "substance" ontology of much of classical theology.[26] This bottom aspect, as it were, of divine life, relates on the one hand to impersonal descriptions in the religions such as Tao, *Dharmakāya,* or Emptiness, and on the other hand to notions of nonduality, timelessness, unity with the divinity, "liberation and penetration through the illusion of the world."[27]

(2) The plurality of the three persons in relation represent three different centers of consciousness, an idea often (mis)understood to denote tritheism; as explained above, for S&K the existence of three consciousnesses does not lead to tritheism since there is the unity of the divine life. This aspect is the heart of the social analogy. The way S&K speak of this relates to the analogy of two people, close to each other, together sharing a joint work such as creating a garden.[28] There is harmony as a result.

(3) The common will or common consciousness, the "collective I," reflects the kind of unity of purpose taught by the classical Augustinian rule of the works of the Trinity *ad extra* being undivided.

The second distinction relates to one of the key ideas in S&K's *darśana,* namely, the capacity of the Christian vision of the Trinity to encompass both personal and impersonal aspects. The "base" level (1), the infinity of the divine life,

25. Ibid., 173–74.
26. See further ibid., 168.
27. Ibid., 174–75.
28. Ibid., 174.

represents impersonality and nonrelationality. The two other aspects (2 and 3) are personal, the second being interpersonal in the analogy of a human community, and the third one internal, "an integrative unity . . . in the individual's personal consciousness."[29]

The personal and relational nature of the Christian Trinity means relation to history: "This threefoldness becomes manifest to Christians through history, insofar as the Jewish people and the early Christians had encounters, so they considered, with a divine Creator, and then with Jesus Christ and with the Spirit, from Pentecost onwards." The transcendent must happen in history, through historical events; in other words, "the Divine occurs as transcendent in the midst of history."[30] Therefore, as mentioned above, S&K speak boldly of the physical embodiment of Christ, which makes him different—notwithstanding many similarities—from the multiplicity of *boddhisattvas* and other religious figures.[31]

In their Trinitarian *darśana*, however, S&K are not content to stay only on the economic level but also want to penetrate into the inner structure of the Trinity, in classical terminology, the immanent Trinity. The great potential of the Christian Trinity lies in its capacity to hold on to both immanent and economic, relational and nonrelational, personal and impersonal aspects—thus reflecting the highly complex and inclusive nature of divine life with the end result that "we can embrace the phenomenology of religious experience worldwide and so give an account of other religious traditions which sees them too as containing apprehensions of the same Transcendent."[32]

THE TRINITY AMONG THE RELIGIONS

As mentioned above, the capacity of the Christian Trinity to encompass both personal and impersonal dimensions makes it different among other Trinitarian-type visions among religions. Unlike many Christian theologians, S&K emphasize that there is no way to prove the superiority of their vision—or any other vision, for that matter; nevertheless, they insist that their Christian *darśana* "of the divine Threefoldness diverges from other threefoldnesses in the history of religions."[33] For example, regarding Hinduism, S&K respect the "social multiplicity of the Gods" in that religious view, but also note that it is a polytheistic vision while theirs is monotheistic.[34]

So what S&K are saying is that on the one hand Christian theology should pay close attention to religions and religious phenomenology to learn from them.

29. As paraphrased by S. Mark Heim, *The Depth of the Riches: A Trinitarian Theology of Religious Ends* (Grand Rapids / Cambridge: Eerdmans, 2001), 157.

30. Smart and Konstantine, *Christian Systematic Theology*, 177.

31. Ibid., 255–59 especially.

32. Ibid., 177–78.

33. Ibid., 176.

34. Ibid., 192–93.

With Raimundo Panikkar (whose ideas will be studied in what follows), S&K firmly believe that there is a kind of Trinitarian (sub)structure to religions. On the other hand, the acknowledgment of the phenomenon of threefoldness, in contrast to typical pluralists (such as J. Hick) does not lead S&K to equate the Trinitarian visions of religions but—perhaps—rather to place them alongside each other, learning from each other, critiquing each other in a friendly spirit, and contributing to common vision.

CRITICAL REFLECTIONS

The pluralistically oriented Trinitarian vision of S&K succeeds in avoiding two key pitfalls—as I see them—of "typical"[35] pluralistic theologies, namely, the idea of a "rough parity" among religions and the tendency to shy away from elevating any proposal as superior. S&K set forth their own Trinitarian vision among religions firmly believing that this Christian *darśana* of the divine threefoldness, while related to other religions, is both different and may have explanatory power superior to others.

Yet another significant difference from many pluralistic approaches is the desire of S&K on the one hand to anchor their vision in the revelation of the Christian Bible, especially the Gospel traditions, and on the other hand to insist on the "physicality" of Christ in contrast to salvific figures of other religions. The latter insistence, however, also raises my first question, which relates to the role of Christology in their theology, a question always pertinent to any Christian Trinitarian vision.[36]

The question has two facets. First, how can one insist on the "physicality" and thus the difference of Jesus among savior figures if at the same time one basically dismisses the question of historicity as S&K do in their study of the biblical traditions? In other words, how can one, for example, set aside the question of the factuality/historicity of the resurrection, and yet claim that the doctrine of the Trinity is based on the biblical salvation history? Second, consequently, is it appropriate to build the emergence of the doctrine of Trinity on the "experience" of the early community as well as the liturgy that quickly developed? These

---

35. I am aware of the plurality of pluralistic theologies! In other words, there are various "tribes" of pluralistic theologies in relation to (other) religions, as I have tried to show in my study: Veli-Matti Kärkkäinen, *Trinity and Religious Pluralism: The Doctrine of the Trinity in Christian Theology of Religions* (Aldershot, UK: Ashgate, 2004), part 3 of which discusses the pluralistic proposals of John Hick, Raimundo Panikkar, and S. Mark Heim. Yet amid the plurality there are also some common features to which I refer here under the somewhat ambiguous notion of "typical."

36. Cf. the incisive comment of Craig Evans ("Jesus' Self-Designation 'the Son of Man' and the Recognition of His Divinity," in *The Trinity*, ed. Stephen T. Davis, Daniel Kendall, and Gerald O'Collins [Oxford: Oxford University Press, 2001], 29): "Apart from the divine identity of Jesus as the Son there could not be a Trinity—at least not in the traditional Christian sense. The concept of Trinity expresses the idea that the three Persons that make it up are fully divine: God the Father, God the Son, and God the Holy Spirit."

are both major methodological issues widely dealt with in both systematic and biblical studies.

These two questions of course belong together, and they presuppose—or mutually determine—each other. So we need to ask the critical question: How viable is it to build the doctrine of the Trinity on the "experience" of the early church? Isn't that yet another resort to the now discredited attempt of classical liberalism to find a "foundation" in religious experience? It is of course true that the experience of the early church, embedded in its liturgy and spirituality, was a vehicle from which Trinitarian doctrine emerged. Then the question becomes, How can we know that this experience corresponds in any way to the logic of salvation history in the coming of Jesus of Nazareth and his claim to a unique relationship with the Father? Doesn't it make a world of difference whether or not the early church's claim, especially of the rising from the dead of Jesus of Nazareth, happened? In other words, the issue involves how to deal with conflicting truth claims between religions if the historical question is put aside at the outset.[37] As long as S&K fail to address these foundational methodological questions, the distinctively *Christian* contribution of their proposal is hard to assess. While dogmatism is not a virtue in a postmodern era, I don't find the insistence of S&K very appealing either, namely, that the best one can aim for is a personal or inner certitude rather than any kind of public validity.[38] Easy solutions are not available. I am not naively assuming that hard work alone will bring about "evidence." What I am critiquing is the approach that makes the impossibility of any kind of public validity a theological theme and virtue.

In addition to these weighty methodological questions, I have several theological questions that relate to details of their Trinitarian formulation. Not all are convinced that the use of biological analogies to describe the "essence" of divine life is any more personal than the substance ontology of the past. True, the biological analogy as used by S&K may be less "abstract" and "static," but it is hardly less impersonal.[39] I am not saying we should go back to substance ontology, but simply noting that their alternative hardly delivers what they promise.[40]

A related question refers to the view of the Spirit as the bond of love (borrowed from Augustine).[41] One of the most commonly expressed criticisms against the Augustinian idea of the Spirit as love is that it tends to blur the meaning of the personality of the Spirit.[42] S&K's attempts to overcome the weakness as explained above hardly clarify the issue. But why resort to this image of the

---

37. See further Wolfhart Pannenberg, "Religious Pluralism and Conflicting Truth Claims: The Problem of a Theology of the World Religions," in *Christian Uniqueness Reconsidered: The Myth of a Pluralistic Theology of Religions*, ed. G. D'Costa (Maryknoll, NY: Orbis Books, 1990), 96–106.
38. See further Smart and Konstantine, *Christian Systematic Theology*, 22, 88, 93–95 especially.
39. Ibid., 168.
40. For S&K's explanation, see especially ibid., 172.
41. Ibid., 170.
42. See, e.g., Veli-Matti Kärkkäinen, *Pneumatology: The Holy Spirit in Ecumenical, International, and Contextual Perspective* (Grand Rapids: Baker Academic, 2002), 18.

Spirit in the first place? I don't easily see why it serves the purposes of S&K's social analogy. The way they speak of the Spirit as "co-beloved blissful love"[43] is hardly best expressed by the Augustinian terminology.

Two more issues, the idea of the Father as the source of the divinity and the affirmation of the *filioque* clause (that the Spirit proceeds from both the Father and Son), have an obvious yet ironic connection with the Eastern Orthodox background of Steven Konstantine: Orthodox theology insists on the first and bluntly rejects the second! First the question of the Father as the ultimate source of the divinity: I have a hard time seeing how this idea serves S&K's vision, which is thoroughly social Trinitarian. It is a commonplace among social analogists to critique Eastern theology for making the Father the source, thus implying a lack of equality among the three Trinitarian members.[44] However, S&K reject any notion of inequality among the three. One could also ask how this view relates to the understanding of the divine life as perichoresis, mutual indwelling. If—as S&K insist[45]—both Spirit and Son receive their identity from the Father, how can there be a genuine perichoresis?[46] In my opinion, it would much better serve the Social Trinity of S&K to reject the idea of the primacy of the Father.

What about the *filioque*? This is for me one of the biggest surprises in S&K's understanding of the divine threefoldness. Of course their affirming *filioque* is the result of utilizing the Augustinian idea of the Spirit as the bond of love. My reading of S&K's vision[47] makes it vulnerable to the standard critique by Orthodox theologians of the subordination of the Spirit in the Trinity and the resulting implications for spiritual life.[48]

My final query has to do with the meaning of the term "identity" in S&K's Trinitarian vision. S&K freely use the term but do not explain the distinctive meaning they attach to the term, even though in recent Trinitarian discourse "identity" has become one of the key terms—with various meanings as our discussion has shown (Barth, Rahner, Jenson, among others). No more clear is the meaning of the term "person," which occasionally emerges in the discussion. Despite their creative efforts to synthesize concepts from both world religions and the Christian Trinitarian tradition, both of these terms need a more careful analysis to make the vision of S&K more compelling.

43. Smart and Konstantine, *Christian Systematic Theology*, 171.

44. Pannenberg rejects the idea since it opposes the principle of mutual dependence of Trinitarian members for their divinity; Moltmann rejects it since it introduces the idea of hierarchy into the life of the Trinity; and so forth.

45. Smart and Konstantine, *Christian Systematic Theology*, 172.

46. Eastern theology affirms the idea of Father as the source *and* perichoresis. So S&K's choice rests on a venerable tradition in Christian theology. Yet these ideas point in different directions.

47. See especially the way they set forth the genesis of the Spirit from the Son and the Father, in Smart and Konstantine, *Christian Systematic Theology*, 171–72.

48. For this see, e.g., Kärkkäinen, *Pneumatology*.

PART FOUR
CONTEMPORARY
TRINITARIAN VIEWS
Non-Western Views

Chapter 17

Introduction

Trinitarian Reflections
in the World Context

ENCOUNTERING THE OTHER AND THE DIFFERENT
AS A THEOLOGICAL CHALLENGE

A landmark volume written by two leading Roman Catholic missiologists in the United States, titled *Constants in Contexts,*[1] accurately illustrates the need for Christian theology to negotiate the *constant* features of core Christian doctrine such as the Trinity in ever-changing, diverse, and often perplexing *contexts*. Christian theology has tried more than one way to "accommodate" to the cultural challenge; some of the approaches have been less than successful.[2] While the issue in

---

1. Stephen B. Bevans and Roger P. Schroeder, *Constants in Context: A Theology of Mission for Today* (Maryknoll, NY: Orbis Books, 2004).
2. Hans Frei, in his posthumous work *Types of Christian Theology,* classified contemporary theologies on a continuum of five approaches. The first approach starts at one end with those that are totally ignorant of the context and build solely on Christian tradition (Barth being a prime example of this in my mind, even though some would put him in the second category). Those at the opposite end take the surrounding context so seriously that little of the distinctive Christian message is left. In the latter, elements in the Christian tradition are used only if they fit in the context (death-of-God theologies, for example). Among several in-between options, the second approach takes Christian tradition as the

itself is extremely complex, I believe the wise counsel from Miroslav Volf, who himself comes from the war-stricken Balkans and has developed a politically sensitive social Trinity to help negotiate our fear of and rejection of the other, is worth hearing:

> Christian difference is always a complex and flexible network of small and large refusals, divergences, subversions, and more or less radical alternative proposals, surrounded by the acceptance of many cultural givens. There is no single correct way to relate to a given culture as a whole, or even to its dominant thrust; there are only numerous ways of accepting, transforming, or replacing various aspects of a given culture from within.[3]

In his attempt to develop a global Pentecostal theology in critical dialogue with mainline theologies as well as with the changing cultural and religious contexts of the third millennium, the Malaysian Chinese American theologian Amos Yong discounts any attempts to find a "rigidly defined theological methodology that will enable us to engage culture without getting our gospel hands dirty." That kind of attempt is doomed to fail since gospel and culture, rather than being two separate things, are intertwined: "the gospel always comes in cultural dress." The way forward is to acknowledge the fact that our "theologies are multiperspectival, multidisciplinary, and multicultural."[4] Multiperspectivalism, Yong reminds us, means "taking seriously the insights of all voices, especially those previously marginalized from the theological conversation—for instance, women, the poor, the differently abled or disabled, perhaps even the heretics!"[5] At its best, the way of doing theology in the current context is a dialogue between contexts, viewpoints, and perspectives that both challenge and enrich each other:

---

norm, yet still tries to make it understandable to the surrounding culture. Perhaps right-wing evangelicalism falls in this category. Tillich may be an ideal example of the middle or third position, in which correlation between culture and Christianity is the aim. The fourth option takes a particular philosophy or worldview as its primary guide and interprets Christian faith in that light while still wanting to hold on to Christian faith as much as possible. Process theology comes immediately to mind as a candidate here. Hans Frei, *Types of Christian Theology*, ed. George Hunsinger and William C. Placher (New Haven, CT: Yale University Press, 1992). This scheme is used, for example, in David F. Ford, "Introduction to Modern Christian Theology," in *The Modern Theologians: An Introduction to Christian Theology in the Twentieth Century*, ed. David F. Ford, 2nd ed. (Cambridge, MA: Blackwell, 1997), 1–15. For the relevance and limitation of Frei's typology, see Stanley J. Grenz, *Theology for the Community of God* (Grand Rapids, MI: Eerdmans, 1994), 19–20.

3. Miroslav Volf, "When Gospel and Culture Intersect: Notes on the Nature of Christian Difference," in *Pentecostalism in Context: Essays in Honor of William W. Menzies*, ed. Wonsuk Ma and Robert P. Menzies (Sheffield, UK: Sheffield Academic Press, 1997), 233. According to Volf, liberal accommodationism, postliberal traditionalism, or sectarian retreat are all unsatisfactory ways of addressing the cultural challenge (pp. 233–36).

4. Amos Yong, *The Spirit Poured Out on All Flesh: Pentecostalism and the Possibility of Global Theology* (Grand Rapids: Baker Academic, 2005), 239–40.

5. Ibid., 240.

The surprise of our generation has been that the younger churches have provided insights into the meaning of the gospel and the mission of the church that the older churches sorely needed. From Asia, Africa, and Latin America, as well as from ethnic minorities in North America and in other places, and from women all over the world, have come stunning visions of the meaning of the gospel, and a number of theologians in the traditional centers of theological learning have seen the value of these insights. The dialogue that has resulted means that theology will never be the same again.[6]

"MACROREFORMATION"[7]

When speaking of the challenge of culture and diversity, we are no longer talking about a luxury that Christian theology may or may not take into consideration. Diversity and plurality are givens in the beginning of the third millennium—or to be more precise, while they have always been with us, at this point in history the *acknowledgment* of diversity and plurality is a given. There is no way of going back, nor should we try. Plurality and diversity can also be(come) an asset to Christian theological reflection.

Demographic shift in itself has turned the tables.[8] The statistics are staggering: by 2050, only about one-fifth of the world's three billion Christians will be non-Hispanic whites. Thus, terms have emerged such as "the Third Church" on the analogy of the Third World.[9] A transformation of the Christian church is advancing so rapidly that even specialists have a hard time keeping track of it. According to Philip Jenkins's *The New Christendom*, the most recent attempt to take stock of the changes, the typical Christian in the first decades of the third millennium is a non-white, non-affluent, non-Northern person, more often female. "If we want to visualize a 'typical' contemporary Christian, we should think of a woman living in a village in Nigeria or in a Brazilian *favela*."[10] Or as the Kenyan theologian John Mbiti has put it, "the centers of the church's universality [are] no longer in Geneva, Rome, Athens, Paris, London, New York, but Kinshasa, Buenos Aires, Addis Ababa and Manila."[11] The Hispanic scholar Justo L. González speaks of the "Reformation of the Twentieth Century."[12] Jenkins

---

6. Justo L. González, *Mañana: Christian Theology from a Hispanic Perspective* (Nashville: Abingdon Press, 1990), 49.

7. This term was coined by González (ibid.). He refers to radical changes taking place in world Christianity as it is shifting from the North to the South.

8. For a current, short statement, see John Parratt, "Introduction," in *An Introduction to Third World Theologies*, ed. John Parratt (Cambridge: Cambridge University Press, 2004), 1.

9. Walbert Buhlmann, *The Coming of the Third Church* (Slough, UK: St. Paul, 1976).

10. Philip Jenkins, *The Next Christendom: The Coming of Global Christianity* (Oxford: Oxford University Press, 2001), 2.

11. Quoted in Kwame Bediako, *Christianity in Africa* (Edinburgh: University Press / Maryknoll, NY: Orbis Books, 1995), 154.

12. González, *Mañana*, 48.

calls this phenomenon "Christianity literally 'going south,'"[13] and as such it is "one of the transforming moments in the history of religion—not only of Christianity—worldwide.[14]

Take Africa, for example, currently the "most Christian" continent. Andrew Walls, the leading scholar on African Christianity, argues that a distinctively new tradition—"a new church"—is in fact arising in Africa, the center of the rapid growth of world Christianity: besides Catholicism, Protestantism, and Orthodoxy, it represents a fourth major force combining elements of all of those older traditions, of new Pentecostal/charismatic spiritualities, and of emerging independent, often locally colored beliefs and practices. Walls points to this as "the standard Christianity of the present age."[15]

Radical implications follow from these shifts. Jung Young Lee, the theologian from Korea whose Trinitarian theology will be discussed in chapter 22, reminds us that due to the dramatic demographic shift, "Christianity is no longer exclusively identified as a Western religion. In fact, Christianity is already not only a world religion but a world Christianity. Thus Christianity cannot be understood exclusively from a Western perspective." Consequently, theological education needs to be shaped to reflect the nature of Christian theology as a "world theology."[16]

As a result of this "macroreformation," theology in the third millennium will be done collectively in the world community, negotiating differences and seeking new ways of framing questions and answers. As González puts it:

> One characteristic of our macroreformation is that voices are being heard from quarters that have not been the traditional centers of theological inquiry, and from people who have not been among the traditional theological leaders. When mission theoreticians in the past decades spoke of the "three self" as a goal for younger churches, they included self-support, self-government, and self-propagation. They did not envision self-interpretation or self-theologizing. They expected theology to continue being what it was, for the meaning of the gospel was fully understood by the sending churches, and all that the younger ones had to do was continue proclaiming the same message. At best, these younger churches were to recast the message in terms of their own culture.[17]

---

13. This is the basic thesis of Jenkins, *Next Christendom;* see, e.g., p. 3; he explains his choice of "North"-"South" as the dominant pattern, especially in chap. 1; that chapter also includes good bibliographical references. The basic statistical source is David B. Barrett, George T. Kurian, and Todd M. Johnson, *World Christian Encyclopedia,* 2nd ed. (New York: Oxford University Press, 2001); for global statistics, see pp. 12–15 especially.

14. Jenkins, *Next Christendom,* 1.

15. Christopher Fyfe and Andrew Walls, eds., *Christianity in Africa in the 1990s* (Edinburgh: Centre of African Studies, University of Edinburgh, 1996), 3. See also, Andrew Walls, *The Missionary Movement in Christian History* (Maryknoll, NY: Orbis Books, 1996).

16. Jung Young Lee, *The Trinity in Asian Perspective* (Nashville: Abingdon, 1996), 11.

17. González, *Mañana,* 49. So also Veli-Matti Kärkkäinen, *Pneumatology: The Holy Spirit in Ecumenical, International, and Contextual Perspective* (Grand Rapids, MI: Baker Academic, 2002), 147: "In our contemporary world theology now has the burden of showing its culture sensitivity. Theology can no longer be the privilege of one people group. Instead, it must be context specific as it addresses God's world in specific situations and in response to varying needs and challenges."

Yet, as John Parratt notes in an introduction to a recent compilation of essays on multicultural theologies, in view of the radical "'moving of the centre' of the Christian faith it is remarkable that so little attention has been paid to the phenomenon of 'Third World theologies' in the theological discourse of Europe and North America."[18]

TRINITARIAN THEOLOGY IN A PARTICULAR CONTEXT

By definition any particular theology is tied to its own context. In his *The Trinity and the Kingdom,* Jürgen Moltmann recognizes the conditions and limitations of his own position as a European male theologian. However, he has worked hard to initiate a genuine dialogue based on fellowship and freedom, which are "the human components for knowledge of the truth, the truth of God." Therefore, his theology doesn't necessarily have to be Eurocentric nor androcentric. Doing theology in this new context "means a critical dissolution of naive, self-centered thinking." The ideal here is nothing less than a "free community of men and women, without privilege and without discrimination, . . . the earthly body of truth."[19]

The truth of theological testimonies can be viewed, according to Moltmann, both in light of their particularity and their universality.[20] One of the fallacies of traditional Western philosophy and theology is the confusion of the universal with the dominant. This marginalizes theologies from other contexts, as Justo González argues:

> North American male theology is taken to be basic, normative, universal theology, to which then women, other minorities, and people from the younger churches may add their footnotes. What is said in Manila is very relevant for the Philippines. What is said in Tübingen, Oxford or Yale is relevant for the entire church. White theologians do general theology; black theologians do black theology. Male theologians do general theology; female theologians do theology determined by their sex. Such a notion of "universality" based on the present unjust distribution of power is unacceptable to the new theology. If the nature of truth is . . . both in its historical concreteness and in its connection with orthopraxis, it follows that every valid theology must acknowledge its particularity and its connection with the struggles and the vested interests in which it is involved. A theology that refuses to do this and that leaps to facile claims of universal validity will have no place in the postreformation church of the twenty-first century.[21]

18. Parratt, "Introduction," p. 2. He illustrates this point with reference to two contemporary widely used readers in theology that contain less than half-a-dozen contributions from third-world theologians between them: *The Christian Theology Reader,* ed. Alister McGrath, 2nd ed. (London: Blackwell, 2001), and *The Practice of Theology,* ed. Colin Gunton (London: SPCK, 2001).

19. Jürgen Moltmann, *The Trinity and the Kingdom: The Doctrine of God* (San Francisco: Harper & Row, 1981), xii–xiii.

20. Ibid., xv.

21. González, *Mañana,* 52.

Acknowledging the particularity and thus "contextuality" of each position gives a fairer picture of tradition.[22] It is not the case that contextuality is a new phenomenon as if theologies in the past had been done from a "neutral" place. No doctrine of God and Trinity, as our historical and contemporary survey has so far shown, operates in or arises from a vacuum. While talk about "contextual theologies" is a quite recent phenomenon, Christian theology has always been contextual. No other kind of theology ever existed. What has changed is that in contemporary theology there is more willingness and readiness to acknowledge the necessarily contextual and tradition-laden nature of all theological work, that of the past as well as the present. To take the most obvious examples, all the classical creeds from the fourth-century Nicene onward, in which faith in the Triune God has been cast mainly in Greek metaphysical categories, are highly contextualized forms of presenting Christian faith. All of these—and many others could be added—are examples of how the context of Christian theology both shapes and inspires talk about God and related topics. This in itself is, of course, no limitation to theology; it is a wonderful asset, a means of making sense of God-talk. However, the challenge is to honestly and openly face the reluctance that Christian theology has shown—and still shows in a more subtle, unacknowledged way (when theological studies are carried on as if Western theology is *the* Christian theology)—to expose the limitations of its mainly white Western interpretations.

What is the significance of all these developments for the doctrine of the Trinity? To begin with, Jung Young Lee illustrates the need for a genuinely cross-cultural interaction in contemporary theology:

> An Asian perspective complements a Western or an American perspective because Christianity belongs to both Asia and the West simultaneously. If Christianity is a Western religion only, non-Western perspectives on Christianity should be regarded as subsidiaries to the Western perspective. Even today [in 1999] many traditional theologians view most Third World theologies, including liberation and indigenous theologies, as subsidiaries of traditional Western theologies. As long as Third World theologies continue to attempt to validate their work according to the views of Western theologies, they will continue to be supplementary to Western theologies. . . . My work intends not to supplement the traditional idea of the Trinity but to complement it by presenting a new interpretation of the Trinity from an Asian perspective.[23]

This does not of course mean that tradition is to be dismissed. Contemporary interpretations dialogue with tradition in the context of contemporary cul-

---

22. A helpful *theological* orientation to contextual theologies is Robert J. Schreiter, *Constructing Local Theologies* (Maryknoll, NY: Orbis Books, 1985). While there is no want of books on contextual theologizing from missiological perspectives, their contribution to systematic theology is often quite limited due to the lack of a genuinely theological outlook in favor of anthropological, sociological, and linguistic emphases.

23. Lee, *Trinity in Asian Perspective,* 12.

ture and philosophy. What is happening currently with the emergence of a global theological guild from Africa, Asia, and Latin America is a culturally and religiously sensitive response to the two millennia of Christian tradition. This dialogue happens in the intersection of many diverse influences, not only Christian tradition in general and local culture, philosophy, and religions, but also to a large extent between these and the particular Christian tradition inherited by Asians, Africans, and Latin Americans from their Western counterparts. My remarks in my book *The Doctrine of God: A Global Introduction* regarding the view of God in general also applies to the doctrine of the Trinity in particular:

> The Christianity received in the southern hemisphere is a Christianity mainly, if not exclusively, exported by Western missionaries, who have usually been quite conservative. The doctrine of God as taught in Two-thirds World Bible colleges, many theological seminaries, and predominantly in the churches owes much more to Augustine and Aquinas than to secular theologies of the West. Thus, theologically, Two-thirds World churches—just think of the rise of the church of China with adherents numbering tens of millions—partially live in the "pre-Enlightenment" era; by this comment, unlike many of my Western colleagues, I am not suggesting "primitive."[24]

The voices we hear in the Western academy—and read in the books published in the West—usually come from those third-world scholars who have been trained in Western academies (and often move to teach there). I am not saying that those are not authentic African, Asian, and Latin American voices; rather, they represent only a voice, and certainly not the majority, of the grassroots Christianity.[25] But this same principle applies to a large extent to Western theologians: what most European Christians believed about God in the first half of the twentieth century was neither Barthian nor Tillichian, but something between and beyond. Or, to speak of the North American context,

24. Veli-Matti Kärkkäinen, *The Doctrine of God: A Global Introduction* (Grand Rapids, MI: Baker Academic, 2004), 243.

25. Jenkins, *Next Christendom*, 6–8, argues that the "new Christianity" in the southern hemisphere, rather than being "fervently liberal, activist, and even revolutionary" as liberal, secularly oriented Western academicians have predicted since the 1960s, churches and theologies in the southern hemisphere seem to be conservative and traditionalist. Most of these churches read the Bible literally, take the "supernatural" as "natural," and look upon God as the one who intervenes. Most of them perceive reality as consisting of God and his opponents—Satan and demonic forces. Classic Christian practices, which liberal Christians are ashamed of even mentioning after Bultmann's demythologization program, such as dreams, visions, prophecies, and all kinds of miracles, especially healings, are everyday phenomena for the majority of African, Asian, and Latin American Christians and for Pentecostals and charismatics even in the West. This is also a major challenge to established theological academia in the West, which still tends to operate under the old paradigm. Few are as courageous as Harvey Cox—the writer of *Secular City* in the 1960s—who took up the challenge of discovering the transformation of Christianity as a result of Pentecostalism's dramatic growth all over the world, especially in Africa and Latin America. Harvey Cox, *Fire from Heaven: The Rise of Pentecostal Spirituality and the Reshaping of Religion in the Twenty-First Century* (Reading, MA: Addison-Wesley, 1995).

neither the process view of God nor open theism is the norm for the church folk, even though these views reflect something crucial about the current trends.

My own interpretations of the perspectives on and contributions to Trinity arising from Latin America, Asia, and Africa—the last major part of the book— are no less immune to limitations and particularity than anyone else's. My exposition and critical analysis betray the context of a white European male theologian. I hope to be able to offer an outsider's sympathetic listening to local voices as expressed by some representative theologians. There is danger of oversimplifying, misinterpretation, and ignorance. Even for areas that I myself know to some extent—because I have lived and worked in Asia for several years and am fluent in one of the major languages—personal experience is very limited. For the benefit of the reader without knowledge of or firsthand experience of these major areas, I provide a brief introduction to the context and background out of which those particular Trinitarian theologies arise even when I acknowledge that there, if anywhere, the danger of oversimplification is almost unavoidable.[26]

26. That I have not provided contextual and background information for European theologies does not mean that they are less "contextual"; the reason for the choice is purely practical. With very few exceptions, all readers of this book, whether professional theologians, ministers, students, or laypersons, are either educated in Europe or in an educational environment that owes to the West. Furthermore, as mentioned, non-Western Trinitarian perspectives are responses to or in dialogue with the Christian tradition as developed in the West (whereas most contemporary Western Trinitarian theologies bluntly dismiss their non-Western counterparts).

A. The Trinity in Latin American and Hispanic Perspectives

Chapter 18

The Latin American
and Hispanic Context
for Trinitarian Reflections

THE EMERGING LIBERATION CONSCIOUSNESS

Speaking of his own frustration as a *Mexicano* Catholic student of theology living
in the then predominantly white United States, as well as of that of many of his
colleagues from outside the majority population, Virgilio P. Elizondo confesses:

> We shared the scandal, the outrage, and the anger at our respective churches,
> which are often concerned with great buildings, well-planned worship serv-
> ices, orthodox theologies, and appropriate liturgical songs but have no
> knowledge of the suffering of the millions of Lazaruses all around them. We
> shared the frustration with schools of theology and theologies, whether lib-
> eral or conservative, Protestant or Catholic, fundamentalist or mainline,
> who ignore the needs of the poor and dispossessed of this world and con-
> tinue to read Scripture and the Christian tradition from within the perspec-
> tive of the rich, the nicely installed, and the powerful of the world.
> Theologies, churches, and preaching seem more concerned with helping
> people feel good about being in this world with all its hedonistic tendencies
> than with calling individuals and nations to a true conversion to the way of
> Jesus of Nazareth. There seemed to be more concern with the Christ of
> Glory who could justify the glories of the United States way of life than with

Jesus of Nazareth who lived and died as a scandal to all the respectable, religious, and fine people of *this world!* The churches have often presented the Glory of Christ more in terms of the glories and glitter of this sinful world, thus preventing the true light of the Glory of Christ from illuminating the darkness of our present society.[1]

Yet as Elizondo forcefully argues, it is this Mestizo[2] tradition that can enrich the Protestant and Catholic traditions in the West: "because it is the Christian religious expression of the millions of poor, oppressed, and marginated peoples of the Americas, it has within it the potential of redeeming the Christian religious expression of Europe and the United States. It is the Christian poor of today's world that will bring salvation to the Christians of the rich nations of the world, who because of the material wealth of their own nations are too blind to see the truth of the gospel."[3] This reflects "the growing self-consciousness of many who were mostly silent until recent times."[4]

Silence and neglect have been the lot of too many Latin American people in general and Christians in particular, both those in various South American countries as well as those—Hispanic or Latino Christians—who have immigrated to the United States, where they have already become a rapidly growing subculture. The often-quoted story behind the popular cult of Guadalupe illustrates the neglect of the first people of South America over against the conquerors.[5] The Virgin appeared to Juan Diego, a poor and unlearned Indian, and gave him certain instructions to be handed over to the bishop of Mexico. The bishop, of course, did not want to listen to the man until he was forced to do so by a miracle that assured him that the Virgin had really manifested herself to the poor man. "Thus the Virgin of Guadalupe became a symbol of the affirmation of the Indian over against the Spanish, of the unlearned over against the learned, or the oppressed over against the oppressor."[6]

1. Virgilio P. Elizondo, foreword to *Mañana: Christian Theology from a Hispanic Perspective*, by Justo L. González (Nashville: Abingdon Press, 1990), 10–11 (italics in the original).

2. North Americans of Hispanic/Latino origin—most of whom are *mestizos*, persons of mixed race—are often looked down on by the dominant white population in North America for not being American enough and by South Americans and Mexicans for not being true Latino/as. See further Virgilio P. Elizondo, *Christianity and Culture* (Huntington, IN: Our Sunday Visitor, 1975); *Galilean Journey: The Mexican-American Promise* (Maryknoll, NY: Orbis Books, 1983). Hispanic/Latino theology in North America shares with other immigrant theologies the struggle of marginalization and identity formation. Even though Hispanics/Latinos are not newcomers to North America—as González (*Mañana*, 31) pointedly remarks, the Anglo-American, not the Hispanic American, is the newcomer—and as a significant minority population Anglo-Americans also represent a growing Christian presence, they have had to struggle to establish their own identity over against Latin American theology in general and liberation theology in particular.

3. Elizondo, foreword to *Mañana*, 13–14.

4. González, *Mañana*, 47.

5. A helpful current account of historical developments and their relation to faith and theology in Latin America, beginning with the first major invasion at the end of the fifteenth century, can be found in Jose Miquez Bonino, "Latin America," in *An Introduction to Third World Theologies*, ed. John Parratt (Cambridge: Cambridge University Press, 2004), 16–43.

6. As told in González, *Mañana*, 61.

While generalizations are just that, generalizations, there is much truth in the saying that whereas in Africa theology begins with a shout of joy, in Latin America theological reflection starts from a cry of despair. One could also say that while African theologians are drawn to issues of culture and identity, many Latin American theologians wrestle with social and political issues.[7] Of course, the theme of identity is not irrelevant to the Latin context either in light of the hundreds of years of subjugation of native peoples, which has obliterated or torn apart whole peoples and societies.

The theme of liberation, as is routinely mentioned, is the driving force in much of Latin American liberation theology, including the immigrant theologies written by Hispanic theologians in the United States. A number of factors have contributed to the rise of the theme of liberation as the key to theology and God-talk in Latin America. On the negative side, those factors include massive poverty and injustice, the present context of which grows out of the "modern" history of Latin America, a history that, since the "discovery of the New World," has been marked by oppression and colonization and perhaps even more importantly by "anthropological poverty,"[8] meaning that alien languages, mainly Spanish or Portuguese, were imposed on the "natives," or for immigrants, English, and their own cultures were denigrated. On the positive side, the emergence of liberation theologies owes to the development of liberation consciousness by the Roman Catholic Church, still the main Christian family on the South American continent[9]—and to a growing extent to many Protestant churches, too, since the 1950s—at first inspired by some political theologians in Europe.[10] Some liberationists, but not all, were also

7. See further William Dyrness, *Learning about Theology from the Third World* (Grand Rapids: Zondervan, 1990), 71–72.

8. Term coined by John Parratt, "Introduction," in *Introduction to Third World Theologies*, 5. While Parratt does not apply this concept specifically to the Latin American context alone, peoples from that area are of course a prime example. As a result of the anthropological poverty, the leading historian of liberation theology, Enrique Dussel, insightfully remarks, Latin Americans have always been outsiders to writing their own history; others have written it for them. Enrique Dussel, *The History of the Church in Latin America: An Interpretation* (San Antonio, TX: Mexican-American Cultural Center, 1974), 3; see also Dyrness, *Learning about Theology from the Third World*, 75.

9. The Roman Catholic Church, still the main Christian force on the South American continent, since the transformative effect of Vatican II (1962–65), has actively, yet self-critically, empowered liberation efforts. Since the time of Vatican II, liberation theologians of the Roman Catholic Church— followed by many in the Protestant churches as well—have come to see Christ as identified with the poor and oppressed and have focused on the self-understanding of the church "from underneath." For an overview, see, e.g., M. D. Chenu, "Vatican II and the Church of the Poor," in *The Poor and the Church*, ed. Norbert Greinacher and Alois Muller, Concilium 104 (New York: Seabury Press, 1977), 56–61. The so-called CELAM, the Second Conference of Latin American Bishops at Medellín, Colombia (1968), meeting in the presence of Pope Paul VI, is usually taken as the historical milestone in the Catholic church's new awareness of social justice and liberation. That meeting of the bishops placed efforts toward justice and peace as one of its main foci. *The Church in the Present-Day Transformation of Latin America in the Light of the Council: Second General Conference of Latin American Bishops, Medellín, August 26–September 6, 1968*, vol. 2, *Conclusions* (Washington, DC: National Conference of Catholic Bishops, 1968), chaps. 1, 14, 15 especially.

10. Rebecca S. Chopp, "Latin American Liberation Theology," in *The Modern Theologians: An Introduction to Christian Theology in the Twentieth Century*, ed. David F. Ford, 2nd ed. (Cambridge, MA: Blackwell, 1997), 410–11.

inspired by several Marxist ideas and the tools of social analysis.[11] Ronaldo Muñoz, a Chilean theologian who lives and works in the working-class barrio of Santiago, insightfully remarks that much of Latin American theological reflection oscillates and negotiates between two reductionist approaches to God: that which resorts to a kind of Platonic-mystical stamp that relates God only to the salvation of the individual after death, or the "utopistic" Marxist interpretation in which salvation comes as a result of collective efforts.[12]

THE FACE OF GOD IN THE POOR

Latin American bishops who met in Puebla in 1979 made a significant theological-methodological observation by identifying the poor as the locus of God's revelation. They pronounced that the proper subjects of liberation theology are

> the faces of young children, struck down by poverty before they are born; ... the faces of indigenous peoples, ... living marginalized lives in inhuman situations; ... the faces of the peasants; as a special group they live in exile almost everywhere on our continent; ... the faces of marginalized and over-crowded urban dwellers, whose lack of material goods is matched by the ostentatious display of wealth by other segments of society.[13]

This human reality—what it is to be the poor, the despised, the marginalized—is understood as the "praxis" of theology.[14] The term has three interrelated meanings. First, human beings are constituted through political-historical reality. Second, praxis means that human reality is intersubjective, "that human beings are not first ahistorical 'I's that express their unique essences in relations to others through language, but that all subjectivity arises out of intersubjective relations between human beings." Third, praxis means that humans must and can intentionally create history, "transforming and shaping reality for the improvement of human flourishing."[15]

The "preferential option for the poor" is not only a practical result of all theology; poverty, suffering, and death also form the right methodological guide to discerning God and doing theology. "From the experience of death of the poor,

---

11. See further Enrique D. Dussel, "Theology of Liberation and Marxism," in *Mysterium Liberationis: Fundamental Concepts of Liberation Theology,* ed. Ignacio Ellacuria, SJ, and Jon Sobrino, SJ (Maryknoll, NY: Orbis Books/San Francisco: CollinsDove, 1993), 85–103. Liberation theologians who have not resorted to Marxist resources are, e.g., Leonardo Boff in Latin America and Justo L. González in the U.S.A.

12. Ronaldo Muñoz, *The God of Christians* (Maryknoll, NY: Orbis Books, 1990), 8.

13. John Eagleson and Philip Scharper, eds., *Pueblo and Beyond: Documentation and Commentary* (Maryknoll, NY: Orbis Books, 1979), 32–39.

14. Cf. Chopp, "Latin American Liberation Theology," 413.

15. Ibid., 412. See also Pablo Richard, "Theology in the Theology of Liberation," in *Mysterium Liberationis,* ed. Ignacio Ellacuria, SJ, and Jon Sobrino, SJ (Maryknoll, NY: Orbis Books/San Francisco: CollinsDove, 1993), 150–51.

a God who liberates and gives life is nevertheless affirmed." He is a God who manifests himself in weakness, yet overcoming death.[16] "God is God who saves us not through his domination but through his suffering. . . . And it is thus that the cross acquires its tremendous revelatory potential with respect to God's weakness as an expression of his love for a world come of age."[17]

THEOLOGY IN A CRITICAL MODE

Luis Segundo, a senior liberation theologian, recalls a story that prompted him to the path of liberation theology: A Latin American is escorting a visiting bishop around the city of Rio de Janeiro in Brazil. Having seen all the glamour of the world-class city, they finally come to the hillsides encircling the city famous for *favelas* (slums). Astonished by what he sees, the bishop reminds his guide of the fact that this should be a Christian country and that they have inhabited this land for over five hundred years. Then he asks the pointed question, "Is this what you mean by Christianity?"[18] For Segundo, the main agenda of liberation theology as well as theological reflection in general in the Latin American context is an attempt to address this question.

Critical analysis of not only theological ideas but also the political and socioeconomic implications of theology lies at the heart of liberation theologies.[19] Segundo, among others, has made the notion of "critical" one of the building blocks of his theology and God-talk. He presents his methodological starting point in the famous idea of a "hermeneutical circle":[20]

1. Our way of experiencing reality leads to ideological suspicion.
2. The next step is the application of our ideological suspicion to the whole ideological superstructure in general and to theology in particular.
3. A new way of experiencing theological reality leads to the exegetical suspicion, namely, that the prevailing interpretation of the Bible has not taken important pieces of data into account.
4. The final result is a new hermeneutic, a new way of interpreting the Scripture with the new elements at our disposal.

16. Gustavo Gutiérrez, *The God of Life* (Maryknoll, NY: Orbis Books, 1991), xiii–xiv.
17. Gustavo Gutiérrez, *Essential Writings,* ed. James B. Nickoloff (Minneapolis: Fortress, 1996), 39.
18. Quoted in Alfred T. Hennelly, *Liberation Theologies: The Global Pursuit of Justice* (Mystic, CT: Twenty-Third Publications, 1995), 26.
19. Segundo refers to "ideological suspicion" or a "hermeneutics of suspicion"—terms now widely used in liberation discourse—as a means of exposing those latent assumptions and interpretations that guide our theology and view of God. According to him, traditional Western theology is a textbook example of a theology adapted to the particular ideological interests of the dominant social classes. That theology is not ideology-free; no theology is. Thus, it can never hide behind the label of "an academic discipline in the security of some chamber immune to the risks of the liberation struggle." Juan Luis Segundo, *Our Idea of God* (Maryknoll, NY: Orbis Books, 1973), 27.
20. Juan Luis Segundo, *The Liberation of Theology* (Maryknoll, NY: Orbis Books, 1976), 9.

This hermeneutical circle—or perhaps, spiral—"keeps on moving on to an ever more authentic truth that is to be translated into ever more liberative praxis."[21] This methodology is not a secondary issue to Segundo. He makes the famous statement: "The one and only thing that can maintain the liberative character of any theology is not its content but its methodology."[22] The doctrine of God is the main target of Segundo's ideological criticism. He maintains that the typical Christian conception of God is that God is more interested in timeless values than in efforts to solve historical problems in this world. This is the heritage of classical theism and the traditional approach to theology.[23] That conception is foreign to the biblical teaching about God. The biblical God shows himself to be "the God of life," as highlighted by the title of a book by Gustavo Gutiérrez.[24]

GOD *AS* SOCIETY—GOD AND SOCIETY

In contrast to the European and North American societies—but like most societies in Africa and Asia—Latin American societies value community and communalism. Justo González claims that this is one of the most radical differences between the typical Western and Hispanic theological approaches:

> The best theology is a communal enterprise. This is a contribution that Hispanics can bring to theology. Western theology—especially that which takes place in academic circles—has long suffered from an exaggerated individualism. Theologians, like medieval knights, joust with one another, while their peers cheer from the stands where they occupy places of honor and the plebes look at the contest from a distance—if they look at all. The methodology of a Hispanic "Fuenteovejuna"[25] theology will contrast with this. Our is not a tradition that values individualism, as does that of the North Atlantic. . . . Coming out of that tradition, our theology will result

---

21. Ibid., 97.

22. Ibid., 39–40. Echoing the approach currently known as the sociology of knowledge, Segundo engages in a critical scrutiny of existing theologies. This is most appropriately called ideology critique. See further Juan Luis Segundo, *Faith and Ideologies* (Maryknoll, NY: Orbis Books, 1982). For an introduction to the doctrine of God and Trinity in Segundo, see Veli-Matti Kärkkäinen, *The Doctrine of God: A Global Introduction* (Grand Rapids: Baker Academic, 2004), 267–71.

23. Segundo (*Liberation of Theology*, 43) makes our view of God the criterion of true theology: "One person pictures a God who allows dehumanization whereas another person rejects such a God and believes only in a God who unceasingly fights against such things. Now those two gods cannot be the same one. So a common faith does not exist within the church. The only thing shared in common is the formula used to express the faith. And since the formula does not really identify anything, are we not justified in calling it a *hollow* formula vis-à-vis the decisive options of history."

24. The basic thesis of that book, a biblical study on the doctrine of God, is this: "our starting point is our faith: we believe in the God of life. We aim to think through this faith by going ever deeper into the content of biblical revelation. And we do this while taking into account the way in which the poor feel God. Faith and reflection on God feed each other." Gutiérrez, *God of Life*, xvii.

25. Based on the play by Lope de Vega, *Fuenteovejuna*, emphasizing the importance of the unity of the people and community.

from a constant dialogue among the entire community. . . . It will not be a theology of theologians but a theology of the believing and practicing community.[26]

Illustrative of the communal nature of the Hispanic method in theology is the lack of the term "privacy," so dearly embraced by typical Westerners.[27] Consequently, a number of Latin American and Hispanic theologians make a connection between God as a society of persons—a communion of three persons—and our view of human society. Certainly the two theologians I have chosen to discuss in more detail, Leonardo Boff and Justo L. González, make this one of their key themes. Before both of these, Juan Luis Segundo, as one of the first liberationists, emphasized the idea of God as equal society. For Segundo, God is a society of persons, encountered only within the history of this world. What the doctrine of the Trinity is trying to say is how God is related to history and humanity. In Segundo's terminology, the Father is "God before us"; the Son, "God with us"; and the Spirit, "God within us." Thus, in Segundo's view, the biblical portrayal of God is tied to history, salvation history.[28] On the basis of how God was perceived to relate to history and humanity, there arose, from the soil of Jewish monotheism, a view of the Trinitarian God as a society of persons, unified for the sake of the common goal, yet with distinctive "persons."[29] "In other words, the unity and plurality revealed a God who was a cooperative effort (love) to transform (save) history."[30]

True, this picture of God as society faded into the background over the course of history. Unlike many, Segundo does not believe it was mainly because of the changing mind-set from Hebraic modes of thought to Greco-Roman. He assumes that a deeper reason lies beneath this crucial shift, one that has to do with the Western cultural emphasis on the "private," also illustrated in the way capitalistic economy is set up, to protect the individual's rights. Thus, God was looked to as the "private" par excellence. This, in turn, is nothing other than "shift[ing] onto God the features wherewith the individual feels he can find self-fulfillment in a society based on domination."[31]

This "monotheistic" notion tends to "end up by denying God-with-us in history" and focus on the "God of reason" or the divine nature.[32] But that kind of God, unlike the Father of Jesus Christ, has very little to do with the world and human beings. Liberation theology emphasizes that we encounter God in history, and thus, "humanity [is the] temple of God." The active presence of God

26. González, Mañana, 29–30.
27. Ibid., 30.
28. Ibid., 21–31, 37–42.
29. Ibid., 66.
30. Stanley David Slade, "The Theological Method of Juan Luis Segundo" (PhD thesis, Fuller Theological Seminary, School of Theology, Pasadena, CA, 1979), 358.
31. Ibid., 68.
32. Ibid., 101.

in the midst of the people is part of the oldest and most enduring biblical promises, Gutiérrez maintains.[33] The prophets extended the concept of the presence of God so that it was not limited to the temple since "God dwells everywhere." This is the biblical idea of transcendence and universality. While not limiting that principle, the incarnation of God in Jesus brought the biblical promises of the presence of God to fulfillment.[34]

Some Latina women, both in South America and in the United States, are beginning to bring their own contribution to theological reflection in general and Trinitarian thought and praxis in particular.[35] For Latina women, the Trinity is about the mystery of the communion of the three divine persons. To say that God is Father, Son, and Spirit does not have to do with God being male. Thus, God the Father can also be called Mother, or Maternal Father or Paternal Mother. Some Hispanic women wonder if the term *rakhamin* (womb), whose usage has biblical precedent, could be used to speak of the love of God. "This divine female womb, pregnant with gestation and birth, identified with the Father, appears also in the incarnate Son." With regard to the Spirit, Maria Clara Bingemer offers this image: "The Spirit is sent like a loving mother to console the children left orphaned by Jesus' departure (John 14:18, 26) and to teach them patiently to pronounce the Father's name, Abba (Rom. 8:15)."[36]

It is out of this soil that Trinitarian reflection by two representative theologians from this part of the world emerges: Leonardo Boff, a former Catholic priest from Brazil, and Justo L. González, a Methodist theologian born in Cuba, based in the United States. Having two theologians, one a Catholic from South America and another a Protestant from the U.S.A., speak to Hispanic perspectives is an attempt to illustrate the unique feature of theological reflection among Latin American–origin Christians both in terms of two locations and two main Christian traditions. At the same time, I am well aware of the grave limitations of my discussion of Latin American and Hispanic context(s) and theology(ies). I have not mentioned a crucial factor that plays in to the piety and folk Christianity of the Latin Americans, namely, folk religions.[37] Furthermore, I have neglected the transforming significance of the rapidly

33. Gustavo Gutiérrez, *A Theology of Liberation: History, Politics, and Salvation*, rev. ed. with a new introduction by the author (Maryknoll, NY: Orbis Books, 1988), 106–7; biblical passages he refers to are Exod. 29:45–46 and Ezek. 37:27–28, among others. Note that chap. 4 is appropriately titled "Encountering God in History."

34. Ibid., 108.

35. See Maria Clara Bingemer, "Reflections on the Trinity," in *Through Her Eyes: Women's Theology from Latin America*, ed. Eliza Tamez (Maryknoll, NY: Orbis Books, 1989), 81–95.

36. Maria Clara Bingemer, "Women in the Future of the Theology of Liberation," in *Feminist Theology from the Third World*, ed. Ursula King (Maryknoll, NY: Orbis Books, 1994), 315.

37. My colleague at Fuller Theological Seminary, Juan Martínez, in a discussion related to a common project (*Global Dictionary of Theology*, ed. William Dyrness and Veli-Matti Kärkkäinen [with a team of associate editors, among which Juan also serves] [Downers Grove, IL: InterVarsity Press, 2007, forthcoming]), once made a remark that in order to find representative folk Catholicism, one does not need to travel to Guatemala (where he has taught for a number of years) but just drive to East Los Angeles and visit local Catholic communities.

growing Pentecostal and charismatic movements to all Hispanic Christian communities, including the Roman Catholic Church. Latin American and Hispanic Pentecostals have not produced much academic theology in general and Trinitarian reflection in particular, so at the moment the only thing we can do is explicitly acknowledge their presence.[38]

38. A uniquely helpful discussion of the role of Pentecostalism in shaping the mosaic of Christian churches in Latin America as well as of the related issue, the uneasy relationship between mainline churches and (American originated) evangelical newcomers, can be found in Bonino, "Latin America," 35–39.

Chapter 19

Leonardo Boff

Trinity as a Society of Equals

LIBERATION THEOLOGY "FROM ABOVE"

Leonardo Boff, a foremost Latin American liberationist who is a Roman Catholic theologian and former Franciscan from Brazil—a background similar to that of Catherine Mowry LaCugna—gathers together several key developments in contemporary theology and revamps them into a unique Trinitarian vision. As Ted Peters rightly notes, Boff is a culmination in the development of the "notion of interpersonal personhood" as a way of appropriating Trinity, different from Barth and Rahner but owing to Moltmann (as well as Zizioulas, whom Boff does not mention) and reflected in contemporaries such as Pannenberg and LaCugna, among others.[1] From Barth and Rahner, his mentor, Boff takes the idea of the importance of history. From Moltmann, Boff also borrows another key idea, namely, the replacement of a "monotheism" that supports hierarchy and domination with loving communion and the idea of Trinity as an "open society."

---

1. Ted Peters, *God as Trinity: Relationality and Temporality in Divine Life* (Louisville, KY: Westminster John Knox Press, 1993), 82, 36–37.

Boff's Trinitarian vision is outlined and defended in his landmark work *Trinity and Society*.[2] It is not at all a typical liberationist's book. First of all, it is intended for the whole church rather than for those who are primarily interested in the theme of liberation or in Latin America.[3] Second, rather than focusing on social and political issues, it is a wide-ranging classical study of biblical,[4] historical,[5] systematic, and pastoral aspects of the Trinity. In the words of a reviewer: "It is not just a promotion of liberation theology, but a generally informative and enlightening historical introduction to the doctrine of the Trinity."[6] As such, it also promotes a social and political agenda, yet it is based on and draws from the bulk of the presentation, which focuses on the theology of the Trinity. Third, the study makes a conscious effort to anchor its work firmly not only in Christian tradition[7] but also in Roman Catholic doctrinal pronouncements.[8]

Another feature that makes Boff's work distinctive among liberation theologies is the starting point of doing theology. While liberationists typically argue for a "method from below"—the social context and experience[9] (of the oppressed or marginalized)—Boff makes a case for beginning "from above," even when the goal is to develop a socially and politically relevant liberation program: "The Trinity is not something thought out to explain human problems. It is the revelation of God as God is, as Father, Son, and Holy Spirit."[10] Rather than praxis being the matrix out of which the communal social Trinity arises, there is a correlation between divine and human society: "Human society is a pointer on the road to the mystery of the Trinity, while the mystery of the Trinity, as we know it from revelation, is a pointer toward social life and its

---

2. Leonardo Boff, *Trinity and Society*, trans. Paul Burns (Maryknoll, NY: Orbis Books, 1998). A popular, shorter version is *Holy Trinity: Perfect Community*, trans. Phillip Berryman (Maryknoll., NY: Orbis Books, 2000). I will only refer to the latter book where it departs from or adds to the former one. Boff has published several other works, but for some reason Trinitarian discussions do not appear there. The two most important works (both of them such that they could have invited Trinitarian reflections) are *Passion of Christ, Passion of the World: The Facts, Their Interpretation, and Their Meaning Yesterday and Today*, trans. Robert R. Barr (Maryknoll, NY: Orbis Books, 1987); and *Ecclesiogenesis: The Base Communities Reinvent the Church*, trans. Robert R. Barr (Maryknoll, NY: Orbis Books, 1986).

3. Boff, *Trinity and Society*, v, as mentioned in the preface to the "Theology and Liberation Series," of which that book is the first installment.

4. Ibid., chap. 2.

5. Ibid., chap. 3 especially.

6. John W. Cooper, review of *Trinity and Society*, *Calvin Theological Journal* 26 (April 1991): 170. Another indication of the rich and variegated discussion of the Trinity in Boff is the use of imagery as a supplement to discursive rational talk (*Trinity and Society*, chap. 5).

7. A telling example of Boff's desire to first develop what he explicitly calls "Trinitarian orthodoxy" is the list of seven propositions, clearly an affirmation of classical Trinitarian canons, in *Trinity and Society*, 97–99.

8. Ibid., chap. 4.

9. From another viewpoint, experience is of course primary. Doctrine and theology as the second-order "devout reasoning" is a human attempt to make sense of the encounter with the Mystery. "In the first place came the original experience" (ibid., 1). "Trinitarian doctrine is the systematic working out by human intelligence of the trans-subjective reality of the Trinity" (ibid., 25).

10. Ibid., 3. In this Boff follows his own methodological precept: "At the root of all great human problems there always lies a theological issue." Boff, *Holy Trinity*, xi.

archetype. Human society holds a *vestigium Trinitatis* since the Trinity is 'the divine society.'"[11] In keeping with this methodological insight is the observation that there is also a mutual relationship between our way of understanding Trinity and the social context out of which this understanding emerges.[12] As will become evident, Boff has listened carefully to contemporary voices that need to inform our view of the Trinity, such as emphasis on subjectivity, personality, participation, and community.[13] Trinity is good news especially for those who are oppressed and yearn for liberation.[14]

In keeping with his "from above" approach, Boff firmly believes that not only is there correspondence between the divine society and human society but that the former is the blueprint for structuring the latter. "The community of the Father, Son, and Holy Spirit becomes the prototype of the human community dreamed of by those who wish to improve society." As such the divine society serves "as a source of inspiration, as a utopian goal . . . [for] the oppressed in their quest and struggle for integral liberation."[15] So strong is Boff's belief in the archetypal nature of the Trinity as a guide to the right structuring and living out of human community that he dares to call that kind of community the "sacrament of the Trinity."[16]

Other methodological guidelines for Boff are the following: In line with his mentor Rahner and the contemporary consensus, he acknowledges the economic Trinity as the proper starting point of the knowledge of God.[17] Furthermore, he acknowledges the importance of the social, relational notion of personhood,[18] which leads to the primacy of communion and community rather than individuality. In this new understanding, society is more than the sum total of individuals that comprise it; society "has its own being woven out of the threads of relationships among individuals, functions, and institutions."[19] Yet another methodological guide—owing to Moltmann—is what he calls "the trans-sexist theology of the Maternal Father and the Paternal Mother" as a critique against patriarchal and sexist views.[20]

These reflections on Boff's theological method in constructing a liberationist theology of the Trinity are at the same time a preview of the main themes he discusses.

---

11. Boff, *Trinity and Society*, 119.

12. Ibid., 112: "In retelling the mystery of the triune God we cannot leave out the contributions of modern culture, which directly affect our understanding of culture."

13. Ibid., 112–13.

14. Ibid., 6.

15. Ibid., 6–7. So also p. 11, among others.

16. Ibid., 13.

17. Ibid., 115.

18. Against many interpreters but in line with current Augustinian studies, Boff contends that Augustine picks up the relational idea of the personhood from the Cappadocians and further develops it, making relationality and communion primary. Ibid., 54–55.

19. Ibid., 118–20 (119). Boff acknowledges here his indebtedness to Moltmann (119).

20. Ibid., 120–22.

"IN THE BEGINNING IS COMMUNION"[21]

A crucial insight for Boff is that in Christian theology God and the world do not represent two different realities; they are intertwined.[22] An older static conception of reality is giving way to a more dynamic one in which "categories such as history, process, freedom, and so on, then dynamism, interplay of relationships, and dialectics of mutual inclusiveness make their appearance." In that kind of worldview, the world poses itself as the "receptacle of God's self-communication" and "begins to belong to the history of the triune God."[23] Communion, thus, is a basic category of existence.[24] Consequently, with Zizioulas (while not mentioning him), Boff affirms communion as the way of being. "The Christian God is always trinitarian."[25]

Misunderstandings abound in theology that have grave implications for communal distortions. Overemphasis on the Father to the neglect of the communion with the Son and Spirit leads to oppression. Overemphasis on the Son without proper relation to the Father and Spirit leads to self-sufficiency and authoritarianism. Fixation on the Spirit to the exclusion of Father and Son may end up with anarchism and lack of concern for others.[26]

In keeping with the communitarian and communal outlook, the term "person" must be conceived in a relational way. This is a corrective to earlier ways of seeing personhood either in terms of "an existing subject (subsistant) distinct from others," which borders on either modalism or tritheism, or in terms of "a subsistent relationship or the individual and incommunicable subsistence of a rational nature that, while acknowledging distinctions and relationships among the Three, however, does not make true communion possible because of its idea of incommunicability (of each in the act of communicating."[27] The contemporary notion of personhood in terms of being-in-relationship is about being oriented toward the other, reciprocity, and mutuality. In this outlook, "a person is a subject existing as a centre of autonomy, gifted with consciousness and freedom."[28] This can also be expressed with the help of a litany according to which God is "absolute openness, supreme presence, total immediacy, eternal transcendence and infinite communion."[29] Persons "face each other," share the life of one with the others, without boundaries, in immediacy.[30]

---

21. The section heading here is taken from the chapter title in ibid., 9.
22. There is an interesting discussion under the subheading "The Influence of the Holy Spirit on Processes of Change" (ibid., 191–96).
23. Ibid., 112–13.
24. Ibid., 139: "The ultimate basis of reality is not to be found in the solitude of One but in the co-existence and communion of Three."
25. Ibid., 189.
26. Ibid., 15.
27. Ibid., 87–89.
28. Ibid., 115, 129–31.
29. Ibid., 131.
30. Ibid., 128–29.

Communion is the paradigm for structuring human societies. As paradigm, the Trinity has both a critical and a constructive role. Our way of building community is based on either one of these alternatives: "a-Trinitarian" monotheism, based on the worldview that takes unity and identity as its starting point, that resists difference and otherness; or Trinitarianism, with its idea of communion as a way to affirm both unity and diversity, difference.[31] Trinity resists individuality, isolationism, use of privileges without consideration of others, and similar abuses of power so prevalent in our society. Trinity also critiques political and economic systems, both the capitalist model where the property-owning class takes advantage and the socialist model that has a hard time affirming differences between persons. Against capitalism, Boff argues for Trinity-like communion that does not know dominion but rather mutual acceptance and giving, a society built on fellowship, equality, and generosity; against socialism, he speaks for the embrace of the Other: "The greatness of trinitarian communion . . . consists precisely in its being a communion of three different beings. In it, mutual acceptance of differences is the vehicle for the plural unity of the three divine Persons."[32] The same applies to the structuring of church life, including ecumenism.[33]

Similarly to Moltmann, Boff resists all notions of the use of power in the Godhead. When speaking of the kingdom of God, he argues that this is not about ruling in the normal sense of the word: "it means the inauguration of goodness and mercy, the renunciation of privilege in favour of service; it implies the exaltation of the humble and the restoration of violated rights."[34]

UNITY AS PERICHORESIS

For Boff, threeness is primary.[35] Three is first, then follows unity.[36] God as the "primary Reality is not undifferentiated eternal Life, but eternal Life gushing out as Father, Son and Holy Spirit. They are three Livings."[37] Therefore, as for any advocate of the social Trinity, establishing the unity is the main challenge. Boff recognizes the danger of tritheism[38] and attempts to present an alternative to the traditional way of establishing the unity of God. The Christian East bases unity on the primacy of the Father; Father communicates divinity to Son and Spirit. The Latin church anchors unity in the shared spiritual nature. In contemporary theology, both Barth and Rahner, in their own distinctive ways, still built on the primacy of the oneness rather than threeness.[39] With Molt-

31. Ibid., 139–40, among others.
32. Ibid., 149–51 (150).
33. Ibid., 152–54.
34. Ibid., 167.
35. Ibid., 146, among others.
36. E.g., ibid., 123.
37. Ibid., 7.
38. Ibid., 5, 139, among others.
39. Ibid., 137.

mann, Boff seeks to guarantee oneness with the help of the ancient idea of *peri-chōrēsis*. This is the key concept of Boff since "the eternal relationships bringing about, realizing, the interpenetration and co-inherence of the divine Three, . . . properly speaking, *constitute the trinity and unity* of God."[40] This means that the unity of God is to be found in "Father, Son and Holy Spirit in eternal correlation, interpenetration, love and communion, which make them one sole God."[41] This interpenetration is simultaneous and eternal.[42] The perichoretic communion means that "the permanent interpenetration, the eternal co-relatedness, the self-surrender of each Person to the others form the trinitarian union, the union of Persons."[43]

Perichoresis correlates with the relational and communal understanding of personhood. "The essential characteristic of each Person is to be *for* the others, *through* the others, *with* the others and *in* the others. They do not exist in themselves for themselves: the 'in themselves' *is* 'for the others.'"[44] Unity is based on communion. Communion represents unity: "Diversity-in-communion is the source-reality in God, whose unity can only be the union of this personal diversity. The divine unity is the actualization of the process of one Person communing with the others, of one Living sharing in the lives of the others."[45] Another way of saying this is that death, in contrast, marks the breaking of all relations, thus solitude. Therefore, living is synonymous with communing, being with others. Father, Son, and Spirit are always in the presence of one another.[46]

For Boff, the centrality of the model of perichoresis is not primarily based on the interest in contemporary theology and secular thought in the concept nor even on its honorary pedigree in the (Eastern) Christian tradition, but in the first place on its biblical basis. Perichoresis and communion are but another way of saying that God is love.[47] Boff argues that the New Testament presents the actions and life of Father, Son, and Spirit as

> three Subjects who engage in mutual dialogue, love one another and are intimately related. . . . The everlasting love that pervades them and forms them unites them in a current of life so infinite and complex as to constitute the unity between them. Unity in the Trinity . . . is always a union of Persons; it is not something that comes after them, but is simultaneous with them. Since they are always one *with* the others and *in* the others. The Persons are

40. Ibid., 128 (italics mine). So also p. 147 and 173, among others. Boff acknowledges the fact that this concept has not been at the center of Trinitarian discourse in the past. In his attempt to establish unity, it is "put at the centre of the mystery" (128) and "expresses the union better than any other formula"; indeed, that model "seems to be the most adequate way" (p. 137).
41. Ibid., 3.
42. Ibid., 4–6, 23, 144, 146.
43. Ibid., 4–5 (5); so also p. 128, among others.
44. Ibid., 127–28 (italics in the original); so also pp. 133, 135.
45. Ibid., 128.
46. Ibid., 128, 133.
47. Ibid., 145.

not the product of the relation of their nature to itself, but are at the origin
of the divine nature, being co-eternal and co-equal.[48]

The idea of perichoresis is the main way for Boff to defend the oneness of the
God who exists as three. What about the three distinct consciousnesses? How can
that be reconciled with the unity of the Godhead? Here Boff enters into somewhat
abstract and speculative discussions of what it means for God to be life.[49] In order
to combat the danger of tritheism from this perspective, he argues that the talk
about separate consciousnesses needs to be qualified by the idea of the Three as subjects rather than objects, as "a spiritual entity," completely open to one another.
This means that in the final analysis, there "are then one consciousness and three
conscious subjects."[50] I will come back to this notion in my critical reflections.

OPEN TRINITY

With Moltmann, Boff emphasizes that Trinity is an alternative to either
monotheism,[51] which speaks for the solitude of One, and polytheism, the idea
of the plurality of gods. Trinity speaks for both unity and diversity. "In our experience of the Mystery there is indeed diversity (Father, Son and Holy Spirit) and
at the same time unity in this diversity, through the communion of the different
Persons by which each is in the others, with the others, through the others and
for the others." That God is three means avoiding solitude, separation, and exclusion. In this outlook, the Father represents "identity," the Son "difference of identity," and Spirit "difference of difference." Threeness rather than biunity helps
avoid a "narcissistic contemplation" because threeness is about openness and
communion.[52] The final result is an "open Trinity" that "includes other differences" and finally makes it possible for the creation to enter into communion
with the divine."[53] The inclusiveness of the perichoretic Trinity embraces all people and history. This is what Boff sees in biblical passages such as John 17:21.
"This Trinitarian unity is integrating and inclusive."[54]

While borrowing from Moltmann the key idea of an open Trinity, Boff also
revises it significantly. In his ecclesiological manifesto, *Ecclesiogenesis*, Boff speaks
strongly for upholding the rights of women and against their oppression.[55] There
he does not develop a Trinitarian basis for his inclusivity; this he does in *Trinity*

48. Ibid., 138–39 (italics in the original).
49. Ibid., 124–28.
50. Ibid., 115.
51. For the critique of monotheism and its implications for community, see ibid., 16–23. Similarly to Moltmann, Boff argues that a-Trinitarian monotheism generates totalitarianism, patriarchalism, and paternalism in the society and church.
52. Ibid., 2–3 (3); see also p. 194.
53. Ibid., 3.
54. Ibid., 148; see also p. 147.
55. Boff, *Ecclesiogenesis*, 76–98.

and Society. Against the monotheistic idea of the universal fatherhood of God embracing all people on the basis of creation, Boff sets forth a Trinitarian understanding of the fatherhood based on God as person. With the same love with which Father begets the Son, he gives birth to all creatures through his Son. The divine "circle of love" is not closed but rather "opens out to the universe of creation."[56] All human beings thus share in the sonship of Christ.[57] Fatherhood also means maternity that derives from the eternal begetting of the Son in which all creatures are held in love and communion. Consequently, human beings are not outside the Trinity but included in divine Trinitarian life.[58] Even creation as a whole exists in the Trinity and is a "receptacle capable of holding the manifestation of the Trinity."[59] Boff therefore feels comfortable in calling creation the body of the Trinity.[60]

Another way the openness of the Trinity comes to the fore in Boff's theology is the existence of both maternal and paternal features in God. God is both "Father" and "Mother"; both metaphors are needed to adequately describe God. Indeed, he uses the expression "Maternal Father and Paternal Mother"[61] as well as, speaking of Jesus, "sisterly Son or brotherly Daughter."[62] This corresponds to humanity created in the image of God. Femininity is a basic constituent of the human being. Christologically this means that there is a feminine dimension to Jesus as Son even though he is male, not only externally, as it were, but rather "hypostatically taken on by the eternal Son."[63] While feminine and maternal features are present in all Three, it is in the person of the Holy Spirit that the feminine and maternal dimensions come to full fruition.[64]

THE SPIRIT IN THE TRINITY—AND IN THE LIFE OF THE VIRGIN MARY

Leonardo Boff is a Catholic theologian. According to *Lumen gentium*, the ecclesiological document of Vatican II, Mary has received a special standing among women being *theotokos*, the mother of God,[65] yet her status is below her Son, the Savior.[66] The official magisterial teaching leaves it here and does not engage in

---

56. Boff, *Trinity and Society*, 173, 220–22.
57. Ibid., 187.
58. Ibid., 168–70, 224.
59. Ibid., 227. The title of chap. 14 is "Forever and Ever: The Trinity in Creation and Creation in the Trinity," and the last phrase echoes the title of Moltmann's work on creation.
60. Subheading in Boff, *Trinity and Society*, 230.
61. Subheading in ibid., 170.
62. Ibid., 185,
63. Ibid., 182–83 (183). Similarly to the Father, the Son is also beyond gender even when embracing both masculine and feminine perfections (p. 185).
64. Ibid., 196–98, surveys biblical, including apocryphal, and patristic materials, typically employed by feminist writers, demonstrating the femininity of the Spirit.
65. *Lumen gentium*, # 53, 66, among others.
66. Ibid., # 60, among others.

speculation concerning the Spirit's role in Mary's life (other than affirming the biblical statement of the conception of Jesus by the Spirit) or the Spirit's role with the person of Christ. Boff takes up that task and offers innovative and controversial suggestions. The route to that proposal goes via the negotiation of the role of the Spirit in the Trinity and the corollary ancient issue of *filioque* in relation to the Virgin Mary. Regarding this unexpected turn, we need to ask first whether Boff supports the *filioque* clause. Basically he does, as is clearly shown by statements such as this one that refers to the Father "as the first Person of the Trinity, the Father who begets the Son and who together with (and through) the Son breathes out the Spirit."[67] Yet, as with so many other topics, he recasts it in a unique way. In his effort to find what he calls a "trinitarian balance," Boff suggests—based on his leading idea of perichoresis and thus the consubstantiality and coeternity of the Spirit—we should speak both of *filioque* and *spirituque*:

> The meaning of these two formulas is that each Person has to be contemplated simultaneously in its relationships with the other two. So the Son through his begetting receives the Holy Spirit from the Father and is then, in his being, eternally inseparable from the Holy Spirit; the Son, then, is begotten *ex Patre Spirituque*. In the same way, the Spirit proceeds from the Father and rests on the Son; this is what corresponds to *per Filium* and *ex Patre Filioque*. In all the interpersonal relationships within the Trinity, there is always an *and* and a *through*. The Father begets the Son with the participation of the Holy Spirit and breathes out the Spirit with the participation of the Son. Even the Father's unbornness involves the participation of the Son and the Holy Spirit, who witness to it by the fact of deriving from the Father as their only source.[68]

What are the implications of the *Spirituque* clause, the idea that in some sense the Son proceeds from the Spirit? Here we come to the crux of Boff's innovative proposal. Boff finds in biblical statements such as Luke 1:35 concerning the coming upon Mary of the Spirit the idea of "a personal (hypostatic) self-communication to the Virgin Mary," or as he also puts it: "I would say that the Holy Spirit, coming down on Mary, 'pneumatized' her, taking on human form in her, in the same manner as the Son who, in a personal and unmistakable manner, set up his tent amongst us in the figure of Jesus of Nazareth (cf. John 1:18)." To make his point, Boff adds that the presence of the Spirit in Mary's life was "intensified . . . in such a real and identifiable way as to be personally present in her in the same way as the Son was incarnate in

---

67. Boff, *Trinity and Society*, 164; so also pp. 172, 173, among others. Stanley Grenz rightly notes that Boff's Trinitarian proposal is decidedly Western and as such supports the *filioque* view. Stanley J. Grenz, *Rediscovering the Triune God: The Trinity in Contemporary Theology* (Minneapolis: Fortress, 2004), 124.

68. Boff, *Trinity and Society*, 204–5 (205); for the discussion of *filioque* in a wider context, see also pp. 198–207.

Jesus." This means nothing less than that "God . . . dwells in her and makes her a true and living temple."[69]

There is an important corollary to his proposal that amplifies Boff's idea of the Trinity as open and inclusive of all humanity. Corresponding to the divinization of maleness by the Son in the incarnation, there is the divinization of femaleness in Mary. As such Jesus and Mary represent the whole of humanity and anticipate the full divinization of humanity in the eschatological coming of the kingdom.[70] From Mary, the "central source . . . the presence of the Spirit would flood out over all the just, especially women; over the church, . . . over humanity," which culminates in liberation in the communion of the Trinity.[71]

"THE IMMANENT TRINITY, IN ITSELF"[72]

Karl Rahner is the other main theological mentor of Boff. From his Catholic teacher Boff adopts the rule of the identity between the economic and immanent Trinity but handles this rule with great care. He affirms the first part, namely, that the economic Trinity is the immanent Trinity. While ontologically the God experienced in history is identical to God in his own life,[73] epistemologically the experience of God in history, especially the incarnation, brings something different.[74] While affirming the first part of Rahner's rule—differently from his mentor Moltmann as well as the Catholic LaCugna but in keeping with his own "from above" approach—Boff insists that Christian theology should speak boldly about the immanent Trinity.

The economic Trinity faithfully and accurately reflects the immanent Trinity but does not subsume it. "But the Trinity as absolute and sacramental mystery is much more than what is manifested. . . . What the Trinity is in itself is beyond our reach, hidden in unfathomable mystery, mystery that . . . will always escape us in full, since the Trinity is a mystery in itself and not only for human beings." This means, in other words, "the economic Trinity is the immanent Trinity, but not the whole of the immanent Trinity."[75] This non-identity of the economic Trinity with the immanent Trinity, however, must not be read in terms of excluding history from the divine life: "All that happens to the divine Persons in history is taken on by them: they take on human littleness, the form of a servant in Mary's case, hunger, thirst, joy, friendship and love." Indeed, the very contradiction of

---

69. Ibid., 210–11; so also p. 215.
70. Ibid., 211. Already in the incarnation of the Son, femaleness was "implicitly" divinized, Boff surmises (ibid.).
71. Ibid., 212.
72. The heading above is from part of the chapter title in ibid., 213 (chap. 12).
73. Ibid., 214.
74. Ibid., 9–10.
75. Ibid., 215.

this assumption of history and sinfulness is what "makes the Son and Holy Spirit reveal what they are in the immanent Trinity."[76]

While insisting on the necessity of affirming the immanent Trinity, Boff is also conscious of the limits of human language in speaking of divine life *in se*. He joins the long list of Christian theologians from the past and present—for example, another liberationist, the Catholic feminist theologian Elizabeth Johnson—to speak of God as "the ineffable Mystery." Therefore, the "words hide more than they reveal," even when it is understood that only analogical and indicative language can be used of God.[77] Ultimately, only doxology is the appropriate vehicle for humanity to address God, not to the exclusion of rational talk, but rather, having finished the analytic work, as a fitting end to all talk about God.[78]

CRITICAL REFLECTIONS

Boff is a liberation theologian. Therefore, the adequacy of his proposal should first and primarily be assessed against the liberationist framework and agenda. As mentioned, typically liberation theologies take for granted the "from below" approach. While for some commentators Boff's method is similar to his counterparts,[79] in my reading this Roman Catholic Brazilian succeeds in combining the "from above" with "from below" approach in a way few theologians have done. There is no question about his agenda, namely, to bring the Trinity to bear on social realities—whether "secular" or ecclesiastical—yet the way he does it is to work hard with the classical doctrine of the Trinity as based on Christian Scriptures and tradition, including his own church's magisterial pronouncements, and then proceed to addressing social and political issues. The structure and contents of *Trinity and Society* embody this method: most of the discussion is devoted to a careful, balanced *theological* analysis and reflection, yet all the time making connections between theology and praxis. At no point is Boff uncritically willing to let Trinity become but one "tool" to help fix social problems, the solutions of which are based on nontheological foundations.[80]

---

76. Ibid., 215–16.
77. Ibid., 7; the latter quotation is a subheading on p. 7.
78. Ibid., 7–8, 217–18,
79. Peters (*God as Trinity*, 111) says that Boff claims to make society his starting point for Trinitarian reflection.
80. My assessment here is the opposite of that of Peters who, on the contrary, considers the duality in Boff's theology a grave weakness. He writes in *God as Trinity*, 112–13: "This is indicative of the wider problem that characterizes Boff's whole approach to the Trinity. On the one hand, he claims to make social community his starting point, which would eventually lead to a social doctrine of the Trinity similar to that of Moltmann. On the other hand, Boff holds so tenaciously to the classical—even monarchian—formula that he risks falling into traditional subordinationism; and he tries to save himself by ascribing all the difficulties to the eternal mystery of the Trinity." As said above, I do not think Boff takes social reality as the starting point. In what follows I will come back to the question of whether there is monarchy/authority in Boff's Trinitarian view. Cooper, review of *Trinity and Society*, 171, basically agrees with my assessment.

The strength of Boff's Trinitarian liberationist proposal rests on the consistent theological ramifications and in-formation of the sociopolitical program. As the above discussion shows, he firmly believes that the way to reform human societies and way of life is to keep the loving, equalitarian communion as the paradigm.[81] So far so good. Ironically, this is also the vulnerability and potential weakness of his program. Can one really read from the divine life precepts for structuring human society? Is the Trinity meant to serve in that capacity?[82] Of course there is correspondence between the human and divine communities, if for no other reason than because humanity exists as *imago Dei*. Yet this correspondence, even at its best, is partial and fragmentary.[83] Isn't Boff too naive not only about the amount of correspondence but also about the capacity of any human society to reflect the divine life? While general principles certainly can be deduced from the divine to human sphere, any specific applications concerning, for example, the structuring of society, such as whether it should be capitalist or socialist, go well beyond the contours of Trinitarian discourse. All in all, Boff's effort to draw lessons from divine society for restructuring human societies share the potential and weaknesses of other like-minded theologians such as Moltmann.

A related issue—still at the heart of any liberation theology—is the question of whether Boff in the final analysis is able to present a truly equalitarian view of the Trinity, as he claims. Ted Peters does not believe he is successful in this: "Although Boff wants to work with a correlation between a divine society and a human society on a nonhierarchical basis, the divine society of which he speaks is in fact a monarchy."[84] It seems to me Boff is less than consistent about this issue. Boff contends that the perichoretic communion excludes the idea of the monarchy of the Father.[85] However, there are features in his theology that at least imply notions of monarchy and thus the authority of the Father, as well as subordinationism, all of which are in tension with equalitarianism. Affirming the Irenaean idea of the Spirit and Son as two hands is of course a subordinationist idea.[86] While

81. For appreciative comments, see Todd H. Speidell, "A Trinitarian Ontology of Persons in Society," *Scottish Journal of Theology* 47, no. 3 (1994): 289–91.

82. Many commentators have raised these questions. See, e.g., Grenz, *Rediscovering the Triune God*, 130–31; David S. Cunningham, *These Three Are One* (Malden, MA: Blackwell, 1998), 51–53 especially.

83. See the helpful discussion of the limitations of the correspondence in Miroslav Volf, "'The Trinity Is Our Social Program': The Doctrine of the Trinity and the Shape of Social Engagement," *Modern Theology* 14, no. 3 (1998): 403–23.

84. Peters, *God as Trinity*, 114. Ironically, while I find Peters's critique of Boff here helpful (albeit overstated), I do not agree with the grounds he presents for his opinion, one of which is that "because this monarchy is shrouded in eternal mystery apart from the time in which we live, no genuine correlation with human society can be made" (p. 114; this sentence immediately follows the citation above). It is true that Boff warns us of the limitations of human language when speaking of God and that at the end of the theological analysis one must acknowledge the mystery of the Trinity. At no point, however, does Boff make this an excuse for not being able to find correlation between the divine and human society. On the contrary, as mentioned above, he seems to be too excited about drawing lessons from the divine life.

85. Boff, *Trinity and Society*, 145.

86. Ibid., 26–28.

at times Boff seems to be speaking of mutuality and mutual dependence of the Three because communal relations are eternal,[87] basically he considers the Father the source of the Son and Spirit in that the Father, following classical traditions, is unoriginated while the Son and Spirit proceed or derive from the Father.[88] Then there are also ambiguous remarks, for example, that according to the Bible there is an order in the relationships, the Father being the first.[89] Traditionally, the taxis (order) has been interpreted in terms of the monarchy of the Father.[90] Boff leaves it open (other than claiming that taxis is not about causality[91]). In sum, Boff's proposal calls for further clarification.

A related question has to do with Boff's somewhat unnuanced view of power. With Moltmann, Boff seems to be reluctant to assign any kind of (coercive) power to either Trinity in general or any of the Trinitarian members in particular. When speaking of the kingdom of God, he argues that this is not about ruling in the normal sense of the word: "it means the inauguration of goodness and mercy, the renunciation of privilege in favour of service; it implies the exaltation of the humble and the restoration of violated rights."[92] The statement evokes questions such as whether this is a biblical view, and even more, whether this is a logically and practically consistent opinion. Boff works hard in trying to anchor his Trinitarian doctrine not only in the church's tradition but also in the scriptural witness. Therefore, it is appropriate to make the obvious remark that one can hardly do away with the notions of power and majesty—at times quite harsh—and the coercive use of power in the biblical description of God. Concerning the consistency—or lack thereof—of this position, how is it possible to establish justice in a fallen world without any kind of use of power? Is it possible to restore the rights of those oppressed or violated without touching the structures—power structures—of any society? Even relegating the establishment of justice and equality to the eschaton—an option that is not appealing, of course, to the liberationists—would call for the use of power unless one naively believes that the world is going to improve on its own and culminate in peace and harmony. Again, this is a weakness that Boff shares with his Protestant mentor Moltmann.

Boff's innovative view of sexual inclusivity in the divine life—another liberationist feature in his Trinitarian vision—calls both for affirmation and a critical remark. Differently from most (feminist) liberationists, Boff assigns feminine features to all three Trinitarian members rather than just to the Spirit, the typical candidate. This helps avoid the trap of reducing femininity to something "weaker" and as such only pertaining to the Spirit who in Christian tradition is usually depicted as counterpart to the "stronger" Father (and Son). Applying both

---

87. Ibid., 83, 146, among others.
88. So also Peters, *God as Trinity*, 113.
89. Boff, *Trinity and Society*, 140.
90. Peters, *God as Trinity*, 113, concludes that the classical "position, of course, makes the Father the monarch and risks subordinationism within a divine hierarchy."
91. Boff, *Trinity and Society*, 140.
92. Ibid., 167.

feminine and masculine features to Father, Son, and Spirit helps envision a more inclusive and balanced view of humanity. At the same time, there is a more sublime way Boff still continues the tradition of viewing the female as something "weaker." He argues that femininity is a basic constituent in every human being—which means characteristics such as tenderness, care, mercy, sensitivity, among others.[93] While few object to this, isn't it also counterproductive, as many feminists are saying? It makes women the "weaker" sex on the one hand, and on the other hand reduces the picture of maleness to something lacking in these features (both of which are ideas contrary to the agenda of Boff's inclusive view of humanity and sexuality). I also agree with Ted Peters that there is a need for Boff to clarify his somewhat self-contradictory position according to which the Triune God is beyond sex and yet capable of serving as a paradigm for both maleness and femaleness on the human level. It seems the first statement implies that sexuality and sexual distinctions pertain only to the created order and not to the divine.[94]

This discussion takes me to the most problematic issue in Boff's doctrine of the Trinity, namely, *spirituque* and his Mariology. My criticism of his view of Mary does not arise from parochial—in this case non-Catholic—reservations about the high status of Mary in piety and theology but rather from theological consistency.[95] As a Catholic theologian, Boff is more than welcome to reflect on the role of the Blessed Virgin in the divine economy. The way he does so, however, is for me neither convincing nor theologically helpful. Boff is well aware of the fact that his idea of the *spirituque* and especially the speculation into Mariology goes beyond the magisterial teaching; his is a *theologoumenon*, a pious theological opinion.[96] Very problematic is Boff's view of "a kind of incarnation of the Spirit in Mary."[97] Not only does it go beyond scriptural teaching and church tradition, including the tradition of Boff's own church, but the idea also fails theologically. Christologically it smacks of adoptionism,[98] and in terms of Mariology, it makes the Virgin something between divinity and humanity unknown to Christian tradition.

Moving from specifically liberationist concerns to a more general theological assessment, one has to address the question of whether Boff is successful in defending the unity of God, being a staunch advocate of social analogy. Commentators' opinions vary from those who accuse him of tritheism[99] to those

93. Ibid., 182.
94. Peters, *God as Trinity*, 112.
95. For an extended discussion of the theme, see Leonardo Boff, *The Maternal Face of God: The Feminine and Its Religious Expressions*, trans. Robert R. Barr and John W. Diercksmeier (San Francisco: Harper & Row, 1987).
96. Boff, *Trinity and Society*, 211.
97. So Grenz, *Rediscovering the Triune God*, 128.
98. So also ibid., 129–30.
99. Charles Talbert, review of *Trinity and Society*, by Leonardo Boff, *Perspectives in Religious Studies* 17 (Summer 1990): 192. One of the more striking—and in my understanding mistaken—remarks on Boff's use of *perichōrēsis* is Talbert's claim that for Boff "the divine unity is unity of action not of being. In our culture, his model for God is the corporate board: multiple individuals who are one in all action and communication. It is difficult to see how this can escape the charge of Tritheism." Ibid.

who applaud Boff's capacity to do even better than other social Trinitarians in defending the oneness.[100] My own assessment is twofold. On the one hand I consider it a bit problematic that theologians who base their defense of the unity of God in the ancient concept of *perichōrēsis*—in addition to Boff, theologians such as Moltmann and Erickson—seem to be unaware of the historical setting of the concept as advocated by John of Damascus and other early theologians. As mentioned in the discussion of Erickson's use of this concept, for the Damascene perichoresis was not the means of affirming unity but rather unity was the presupposition for perichoresis; unity for John was established by the idea of Father as the source of the Spirit and Son.[101] Now that is not a problem in itself; later theology has every right to both revise the meaning of ancient concepts as well as put them to a new use. By doing so, however, one would expect theologians to reflect on the ramifications and potential weaknesses of a recasting. That is absent in Boff (as well as in Moltmann and Erickson). On the other hand I applaud the continuing and sustained efforts of Boff to avoid tritheism. In my opinion it is not fair to charge Boff with tritheism. Making him tritheist would likely make theologically suspect a whole host of both traditional and contemporary advocates of various types of social Trinity, beginning with the Cappadocians. While not guilty of the charge of tritheism, Boff's way of defending the unity on the basis of perichoresis has a couple of weaknesses (in addition to the one mentioned above). First, going back to his desire to guarantee the scriptural basis of his theology, I am much more doubtful than Boff himself concerning the clarity of the New Testament's support of perichoresis. Boff claims that the perichoretic idea arises out of the way the New Testament speaks of the "three Subjects who engage in mutual dialogue, love one another and are intimately related."[102] It is one thing to say that perichoresis as a theological abstraction is compatible with the economic narrative of the New Testament; it is another thing to claim scriptural basis for the idea. Second, while I find Boff's use of *perichōrēsis* helpful theologically in defending both plurality and unity in the Godhead, I find his talk about "one consciousness and three conscious subjects"[103] ambiguous and confusing. For an advocate of social analogy, avoiding talk about three distinct consciousnesses sounds like an overreaction (since after all, this is analogical talk and only a way to affirm the distinctness of three persons). Then the remark of "three conscious subjects" (yet one consciousness) adds to the confusion. I do not understand what a conscious subject is without a distinct consciousness.[104]

100. Shirley C. Guthrie, review of *Trinity and Society*, by Leonardo Boff, *Theology Today* 46 (1989): 206.

101. Wolfhart Pannenberg, *Systematic Theology*, trans. Geoffrey W. Bromiley, 3 vols. (Grand Rapids: Eerdmans, 1991–98), 1:334.

102. Boff, *Trinity and Society*, 138.

103. Ibid., 115.

104. It doesn't clarify the issue at all that Boff contains a quite speculative and abstract discussion of life under the subheading "God Is Eternal Living" (*Trinity and Society*, 124-28).

Regarding Boff's view of the relationship between the economic and imma-nent Trinity, in my assessment his insistence on holding on to the immanent Trin-ity is to be commended. Ted Peters is right in remarking that whereas Boff starts out in the same direction as Moltmann, Boff does not go so far, being unwilling to do away with the immanent Trinity.[105] This is a corrective to both those who stress "experience" (a danger with some feminists and other liberationists) or his-tory and relationality (Moltmann) or the economy (LaCugna) to the point that all we can say of God is the God-for-us. By upholding the difference between the immanent and economic Trinity, Boff is nevertheless not making the Trinity a matter of speculation apart from the economy of salvation, spirituality, or social realities—the usual suspects in the minds of those who want to subsume the immanent into the economic.

105. Peters, *God as Trinity*, 111.

Chapter 20

Justo L. González

God Who Is a Minority

THEOLOGY FROM A MINORITY PERSPECTIVE

The Cuban-born historian and theologian Justo L. González is a household name for theology students because he has written several widely used textbooks in historical theology and on various topics of theology. For this leading Hispanic theologian in the United States, no theology worth its name can be neutral.[1] God has an agenda, and so does the Bible, the divine revelation: the Bible presents a non-innocent history, non-idealized, even scandalous in its authenticity.[2] True

---

1. Justo L. González begins the first chapter in *Mañana: Christian Theology from a Hispanic Perspective* (Nashville: Abingdon Press, 1990), 21, with these words: "What follows is not an unbiased theological treatise. It does not even seek to be unbiased. On the contrary, the author is convinced that every theological perspective, no matter how seemingly objective, betrays a bias of which the theologian is not usually aware."

2. Ibid., 75–78. This is echoed by many Latin American liberationists, such as Gutiérrez, according to whom the "whole Bible, from the story of Cain and Abel onward, is marked by God's love and predilection for the weak and abused of human history." Gustavo Gutiérrez, *A Theology of Liberation: History, Politics, and Salvation,* rev. ed. with a new introduction by the author (Maryknoll, NY: Orbis Books, 1988), 240.

theology is biased toward God's agenda, with love and care for God's creation and especially those who are weak and powerless: "God has certain purposes for creation and is moving the world and humankind toward the fulfillment of those purposes. This means that, in a sense, God is biased against anything that stands in the way of those goals, and in favor of all that aids them."[3]

The biased nature of the Bible is accentuated by its "preferential option for the poor,"[4] a model to be followed when "[r]eading the Bible in Spanish."[5] González himself experienced a twofold marginalization, first as a minority-group Christian in Latin America, growing up Protestant in a predominantly Catholic culture—yet, as a Protestant theologian, González fully embraces his Catholic background as a Hispano[6]—and later as an immigrant theologian in North America. He belongs to the people in exile, "by the waters of Babylon."[7] It is out of this "border experience" that his *Mañana* interpretation of God emerged.[8]

Thus, the task of theology is not to produce some sort of neutral, "and therefore inane," interpretation of the nature of God and the universe, but rather to discover the purposes of God.[9] The way God is presented in the Bible implies a "political agenda"; God is not interested primarily in "spiritual salvation," but in life here and now.[10] Being political, Scripture deals with issues of power and the lack thereof. Therefore, the right hermeneutical questions are, "Who in this text is in power? Who is powerless? What is the nature of their relationship? Whose side does God take?"[11] This kind of Bible reading does not have as its main goal the right hermeneutics, but seeks rather to allow "it to interpret us and our situation."[12]

Christian theology has had a hard time, however, recognizing its links with political, socioeconomic, racial, and other power issues:

---

3. González, *Mañana*, 21–22.

4. See also Virgilio Elizondo, foreword to González, *Mañana*, 18; and Gustavo Gutiérrez, "Option for the Poor," in *Mysterium Liberationis: Fundamental Concepts of Liberation Theology*, ed. Ignacio Ellacuria, SJ, and Jon Sobrino, SJ (Maryknoll, NY: Orbis Books / San Francisco: CollinsDove, 1993), 241–44.

5. "Reading the Bible in Spanish" is the title of chapter 5 in González, *Mañana*.

6. See further ibid., 55–66; for new horizons in Latino ecumenism, see pp. 73–74 especially. Elizondo speaks of the new ecumenism: "But for the most part Hispanic Protestants have not yet discovered and reclaimed as their own the marvelous aspects of our Iberoamerican Catholic heritage that they left behind in becoming Protestants. It is precisely this aspect that I admire so much about Justo! He is so comfortable celebrating our common Iberoamerican religious heritage." Elizondo, foreword to *Mañana*, 13.

7. See further ibid., 41–42.

8. See further Virgilio Elizondo, *Christianity and Culture* (Huntington, IN: Our Sunday Visitor, 1975); *Galilean Journey: The Mexican-American Promise* (Maryknoll, NY: Orbis Books, 1983).

9. González, *Mañana*, 22. He also remarks: "But if there is one thing that can be said with absolute certainty about the God of Scripture, it is that God cannot be known through rational objectivity" (p. 21).

10. Ibid., 83–85, quotations on p. 84.

11. González, *Mañana*, 85. See further Justo L. González and Catherine Gunsalus González, *Liberation Preaching: The Pulpit and the Oppressed* (Nashville: Abingdon Press, 1980), 69–93.

12. González, *Mañana*, 86.

When Christians, in their eagerness to communicate their faith to the Greco-Roman world, began interpreting their God in Platonic terms, what they introduced into theology was not a sociopolitically neutral idea. What they introduced was an aristocratic idea of God, one which from that point on would serve to support the privilege of the higher classes by sacralizing changelessness as a divine characteristic. Yahweh, whose mighty arm intervened in history in behalf of the oppressed slaves in Egypt and of widows, orphans, and aliens, was set aside in favor of the Supreme Being, the Impassible One, who saw neither the suffering of the children in exile nor the injustices of human societies, and who certainly did not intervene in behalf of the poor and the oppressed.[13]

A "biased" theology, theology in behalf of the poor and oppressed, by its very nature challenges the old concept of "truth." Older theology operated with the "'Eleatic-Platonic' understanding of truth as that which is changeless and universal, and then has sought such truths in the Bible. The new reformation believes that our understanding of the nature of truth must be such that the particular man Jesus, at a particular time and place, can say, 'I am the truth.' Biblical truth . . . is concrete, historical truth." This is about ortho-*praxis*, living the truth, as much as ortho-*doxy*, right knowledge.[14] González thus invites his Hispanic Christian colleagues to lay aside useless speculations about the Trinity and instead concentrate on the application of the Trinitarian shape of life to everyday living. At the same time, Hispanics have the potential of helping their white brothers and sisters to learn the same lesson.[15] Another methodological difference from the traditional way of doing theology relates to the categories of universal and particular. The long tradition of Western philosophy and theology, according to González, confuses dominant with the universal; therefore "contextual" theologies, such as the one represented by Hispanics, are considered little more than a footnote to established canons.[16]

My discussion of González's doctrine of the Trinity is based on his doctrinal manual titled *Mañana: Christian Theology from a Hispanic Perspective*, a misleadingly simple and straightforward book that, however, has as its backbone a wide reading of Christian history, a passionate liberationist agenda, and a wealth of creative, often challenging insights. Unlike typical presentations of systematic theology, the author devotes about one-third of the book to the presentation of the social context of Hispanic Christianity and special features of Latinos. The order of the topics follows the typical systematic sequence, beginning with one God and then proceeding to Trinity, anthropology, Christology, and ecclesiology. While following the typical sequence, González shapes the discussion in a way that is innovative and fresh.

13. Ibid., 89.
14. Ibid., 50. "To believe the truth means to live in the truth, and this means to be in love and justice with our neighbors, both near and far" (ibid.).
15. Ibid., 115.
16. Ibid., 52.

"LET THE DEAD GODS BURY THEIR DEAD"[17]

ne discussion of one God that precedes Trinity in González's presentation of
ispanic theology differs significantly from typical scholastic ones. He pursues
ro goals: first, to critique the various forms of idolatry—the attempt to rely on
ead gods"—and the subtle, and at times less subtle, ways the dynamic biblical
ew of God was baptized into the canons of Greco-Roman and later Western
tegories.

Whereas apologetics begins with an attempt to prove the existence of God,
onzález not only dismisses this task as impossible—"Any God whose existence
n be proved is an idol"[18]—but also makes his main task the discernment of the
dical difference between the God of the Bible and idols of various types. "Some
ıds are better dead than alive."[19]

That idols are made by humans does not mean, therefore, that we should try
get rid of anthropomorphic language when speaking of God. Limited anthro-
ımorphic terminology is the only language available to us. Even analogical lan-
ıage is anthropomorphic. Take for example the terms used of God's attributes,
ınipotent, omnipresent, omniscient, and so on. What happens here is an exag-
rating of human characteristics deemed desirable. The necessity of anthropo-
ırphic God-talk, rather than being an obstacle, is rather the function of divine
velation. God, who wanted to reveal himself to us, used terms and categories
ıderstandable to humans. Indeed, it belongs to the very heart of Christian the-
ogy to affirm anthropomorphic language, which reflects incarnation, God
coming human. A further reason for the anthropomorphic language is the cre-
ion of humanity in the *imago Dei*.[20]

17. The section heading above is from the title of chap. 6 in ibid., p. 89.
18. Ibid., 90. Here he echoes the concerns of Segundo, who brings ideological criticism into a
l theological analysis. He seriously doubts if the traditional discussions of the existence and attri-
tes of God have any meaning for modern believers other than "specialists and 'snobs.'" Segundo
o faults the death-of-God theologies for worrying about God's existence rather than trying to find
appropriate way to speak of the God to oppressed people. Juan Luis Segundo, *Our Idea of God* (Mary-
oll, NY: Orbis Books, 1973), 4.
19. González, *Mañana*, 89. In many respects, González's analysis reflects the insightful ideas of
naldo Muñoz, a Chilean theologian who lives and works in the working-class barrio of Santiago.
ıñoz has widely analyzed "the uses of God-talk" as well as the role of "idols" in relation to power
d powerlessness. The privileged minorities use the name of God as they fight with all the weapons
power and technology to defend their property and rights. The underprivileged minorities use the
me of God in a totally different context; they try to live human lives in inhuman conditions and
uggle just to survive. Within these same impoverished majorities, most resign themselves to their
stitution in the name of God, though a growing number of people are awakening to a struggle for
eration. Those who are mainly politically oriented use the name of God to call for social reconcil-
ion. For some, the most important thing about the doctrine of God is orthodoxy and right belief,
d they try to convert and proselytize others to their own particular understanding, and so forth.
naldo Muñoz, *The God of Christians* (Maryknoll, NY: Orbis Books, 1990).
20. González, *Mañana*, 90–92. At times Christian theology has resorted to apophatic language
d defined God in terms of negatives, thus the idea of God as *im*passible or *in*finite. But the
ophatic cannot be the only way of speaking; to say what God is not like presupposes at least some
owledge of what he is (p. 91).

The guide to the right way of speaking of God is to follow the Bible's way of speaking of God. Biblical discourse of God serves as the critic of many established canons of traditional theology of God. The Bible never attempts to speak of God in Godself, but rather in relation to us. God is not depicted in Scripture as "the unmoved mover" of Aristotle or of Thomism, nor as the "pure actuality" of classical theism. When the Bible speaks of God, it speaks of creation and redemption, God for us. Nor does the Bible describe God as impassible. On the contrary, there are repeated references to divine anger, love, and even repentance.[21]

Ironically, the God of the Bible is both an active participant in the affairs of the world, such as calling out a nation and leading them to a land, and also the object, even the victim of history. "God does not rule the world with an iron fist, as Pharaoh ruled over Egypt or Pinochet ruled Chile." God does not destroy all opposition "with a bolt from heaven," nor is the opposition something God has created—"like the military dictator who sets up an opposition party in order to claim that his rule is democratic." Does this view compromise the power of God? No, says González. "The Crucified is also the Risen One, who shall come again in glory to judge the quick and the dead. What it denies is an easy jump from creation to resurrection, with no cross." The cross is indispensable; it is "the supreme instance of the manner in which God's power operates."[22]

Some may claim that this view denies God's omnipotence. González responds that Scripture nowhere claims God to be omnipotent in the sense of being able to do "whatever strikes the divine fancy."[23] That kind of notion is rather a human invention, characteristic of an idol rather than of the biblical God.[24] Even in the creeds' naming of God the "Father Almighty," the term *pantokrator* is not an abstract philosophical statement about some real or imagined power to do any and all things, but rather an affirmation of the extension of God's rule over all creation, everywhere. The same principle applies to other attributes of God such as infinity. Again, rather than an abstract principle of "endlessness"—the final meaning of which is of course beyond any human imagination—this is a reminder to us that God's care and love never come to an end. God is the same yesterday, today, and tomorrow. The biblical way of affirming all of this and much of what classical theology attempted to describe with the terminology of the attributes is to say that God is the living God. This God is different from idols that are dead and deserve to die.[25]

The basic problem of Christian theology of God is not that early theologians made great efforts in relating biblical teaching about God to existing cultural patterns and thought-forms, but rather that eventually the philosophical canons of Hellenism took over the dynamic biblical narrative. Soon Greek philosophy

21. Ibid., 92.
22. Ibid., 93.
23. Ibid.
24. Ibid., 93–94.
25. Ibid., 94–95.

became the norm to judge the appropriateness of biblical talk about God, and biblical discourse was deemed at times both "rude" and less sophisticated.[26] Linked with this development was the inability of Christian theology to see the connection between the philosophically shaped view of God and the interests of ruling classes. The trick about these interests is that for the most part they are subtle and unacknowledged. Take for example the attribute of immutability. The idea of the changelessness of God as the supreme perfection supports the status quo and preserves the existing structure of society.[27] This takes us to the heart of González's politically sensitive reading of the history of theology. A God that is omnipotent, impassible, and divorced from the happenings of the world clearly helped support earthly powers in both the ecclesiastical and political realms. The Yahweh of the Old Testament who freed slaves from oppression and led them to the Land of Promise was replaced by "the Supreme Being, the Impassible One," who is unmoved by human suffering and the injustices of human societies, who remains detached from the needs of the poor and the oppressed. Indeed, he argues that the whole history of the doctrine of the Trinity could—and should—be studied from the perspective of power play and the defense of the status quo in favor of the rulers.[28]

POLITICAL AND SOCIOECONOMIC IMPLICATIONS OF EARLY TRINITARIAN DEBATES

One of the most distinctive features of González's *Mañana: Christian Theology from a Hispanic Perspective* is his critical reading of the socioeconomic and political implications of the way Christian theology came to express faith in "The One Who Lives as Three" (the title of chapter 7). In keeping with his politically and socially sensitive reading of Trinitarian history, González recasts the typical terminology of the "economic" Trinity to denote socioeconomic consequences of the Trinity. For him, that is what makes the doctrine of the Trinity meaningful and significant.[29]

---

26. A related problem is that when God was defined in terms of being impassible, immutable, infinite, and so forth, it meant defining God in terms of negating all human limitations. This widened the gap between the divine and human to the point that it could hardly be bridged. Now, in the incarnation, this gap was bridged, an idea quite impossible for Hellenistic thought. See Ibid., 145–46.

27. Ibid., 96–98. Speaking of the introduction of Platonic philosophy as the framework for expressing the theology of God in Christian theology meant nothing other than "an aristocratic idea of God, one which from that point on would serve to support the privilege of the higher classes by sacralizing changelessness as a divine characteristic" (p. 98). On the implications of the classical doctrine of God with the attributes of omnipresence, omnipotence, and omniscience to giant institutions in our time such as transnational corporations, see further in ibid., p. 99.

28. Ibid., 98. Neither is idolatry free from power implications: "Idols have a socioeconomic function" (p. 99).

29. Ibid., 111–12. Basically, he is willing to dismiss the whole debate about the economic and immanent Trinity per se: "the debate seems pointless, for we have no way of knowing how God is in Godself, and therefore to speak of an 'essential' Trinity, apart from God's revelation and relations with the world, is nonsense" (p. 112).

The basic dilemma of the orthodox doctrine of the Trinity in González's view was the idea of God as the absolute immutable. That kind of view led to the problem of how such a God can relate to the world of transitory experience. The *Logos* doctrine of the apologists was one such attempt to find a mediator.[30]

Arianism was also a way to negotiate this problem. What is highly ironic about Arianism, which of course was soon deemed heretical, is that according to González it emerges out of the same framework as *Logos* theology in its attempt to negotiate the impasse of early Christian theology, based on Greek philosophy, to relate the immutable God to the mutable world. Consequently, in González's reading of this debate, Arianism was not an attempt to reaffirm Jewish monotheism in light of the claim of the deity of Jesus. Rather, both parties, Arians versus Athanasius with other orthodox, were tackling the same issue of immutability, foreign to the biblical view but necessitated by the canons of Hellenistic philosophy. Arius's problem was this: if the intermediary was God, that would also make God mutable if for no other reason than because of the incarnation. Introducing the idea of change in turn would destroy the idea of God as the Supreme Being. The political implication would be that eventually this would make Christian doctrine less suitable in service of Constantinian politics and its desire to maintain the status quo.[31]

Yet with all the political and ecclesiastical power struggles as well as its theological inconsistency[32]—maybe ironically exactly because of this inconsistency—Nicaea also helped Christian theology not to lose all of its connections with the biblical idea of the Triune God. Granted this happened perhaps unwittingly, González argues that linking the One who "came for us and for our salvation . . . in the form of man and suffered" with "true God from true God, . . . of one substance with the Father" resisted the ontologist and static notion of God in Greek thought. Even when the Greek notions became dominant in Christian theology, their implications were not carried to their ultimate consequences. As a result, "the gospel of the minority God was preserved even as enormous forces were reshaping the very notion of God" so it would be better suited to serve the new Christendom sharing in the powerful status of the state.[33]

Regarding other political overtones of Nicaea—besides the obvious irony that it was the emperor who presided and guided the deliberations at Nicaea—it was no wonder that soon after the council, Constantine began to have second thoughts about its decisions. The theological inconsistency of Nicaea seemed to

30. Ibid., 103.

31. Ibid., 103–9.

32. González insightfully notes that in a true sense Arianism was more consistent than the Nicene position in insisting on a mediator who was mutable yet preexistent, a creature who had become incarnate in Jesus. There were other reasons, however, that forced orthodoxy to reject Arianism, especially coming from the doctrine of salvation (Athanasius): if the Word made incarnate is less than God, we owe our salvation to a being less than God. A related reason for the rejection was that the incarnation of God made it possible for a transcendent God to communicate directly with the world he had created, an idea impossible for Arianism (ibid., 107).

33. Ibid., 106–7. At times he uses the term "Constantinization" of God, which is the extreme form of Hellenism (p. 139).

compromise the exaltation of the supreme changeless God, an idea linked with the semi-divine status of the emperor as God's champion: "If a carpenter condemned to death as an outlaw, someone who had nowhere to lay his head, was declared to be 'very God of very God,' such a declaration would put in doubt the very view of God and of hierarchy on which imperial power rested."[34]

González considers it significant that it was not Arianism but rather patripassianism that appealed to the masses. Patripassianism, the modalistic idea that God in fact suffered in the Son, showed

> clearly that God was one of their number. God was not like the emperor and his nobles, who had an easy life in their lofty positions. God had toiled and suffered even as they must toil and suffer every day. On this point, it would seem that the Patripassianist had an insight into the nature of the biblical God that the more powerful leaders of the church had begun to lose.[35]

Even though González regards the rejection of patripassianism a right choice, the underlying motifs behind its appeal, namely, asserting the suffering God, must not be ignored. Theologically, the modalistic idea behind patripassianism does not do justice to the biblical salvation history, and it makes the incarnation only a passing moment. Christian theology, with the doctrine of the ascension, makes humanity a permanent quality of the Godhead. Furthermore, the orthodox rejection of modalism maintains "the dialectic of power and powerlessness, of suffering and hope," which "makes the suffering of Christ a sign of hope . . . [in that] even in the midst of his suffering, next to him stands a Father who is to raise him from the dead."[36]

González summarizes the implications of these early theological disputes:

> The triumph over Arianism ensured that even amid the majority church of the Middle Ages and of modern times, the voice could be heard of the minority God who was made flesh in a humble carpenter belonging to an oppressed nation. The victory over Patripassianism assured Christians of all ages that suffering, oppressions, and despair do not have the last word, for behind the suffering Son and suffering humankind stands the One who vindicates the Son and all those who, like him, suffer oppression and injustice; that at the right hand of the throne of glory stands the Lamb of God, in representation of all those who are like lambs taken to the slaughter. But the profound insight of this Nicene faith was often overshadowed by the fact that Christians had now become a powerful body and would soon be literally a majority.[37]

---

34. Ibid., 105–6, 108 (108).
35. Ibid., 109.
36. Ibid., 109–10 (109).
37. Ibid., 110. Other heretical views having to do with Christology that had great appeal to the masses were Gnosticism and docetism. Many oppressed felt, in the spirit of gnostic dualism that undermines the value of material and bodily existence, that salvation is a happy exit from the struggles of life into the "spiritual" life beyond. Docetism also fits this kind of thinking: whatever happens in human existence—suffering, death, and the like—is not real. These ideas understandably appealed

This identification with the powers that be has now become such that while there is separation between the church and state in terms of legislation, the church is still part of the unjust power structures of the society. For many Hispanics this has meant a retreat from the Christian faith. It is only by replacing faith in the "prime unmoved mover" who sacralizes power with faith in the living God of the Bible and the Crucified One who is of one substance with the Father, that liberation can be found again. "It is a faith in the God who is a minority and who therefore speaks Spanish . . . not in the sense of speaking this language in preference to others but in the biblical sense that the oppressed who speak Spanish—like those who speak black English—are given special hearing."[38]

COMMONALITY IN THE TRIUNE GOD AS THE PATTERN

One of the ways González speaks of his own theological method is through "*Fuenteovejuna* theology," in keeping with the wider Latin American context, which is a call for a community-based approach. This theology, whose name comes from Lope de Vega's play *Fuenteovejuna*, speaks for an unwavering sense of community and unity of the people. It represents a departure from the traditional Western individualistic way of doing theology: "If theology is the task of the church, and the church is by definition a community, there should be no such thing as an individual theology. The best theology is a communal enterprise."[39] The Bible in its original setting was meant to be read in the community rather than studied in privacy.[40]

The communal approach to the study of Trinity is in keeping with the life of the Trinity, which is about commonality: "The doctrine of the Trinity, once cleared of the stale metaphysical language in which it has been couched, affirms belief in a God whose essence is sharing." This is what the Bible means with the idea of God as love.[41] It is here that González finds the basic guide for sharing, including sharing of material goods. He finds a precedent for this in the writings of the fathers such as Ambrose, Jerome, and the Cappadocians, all of

---

to the Christians, who still existed as a minority and who were taught to believe in the Immutable One (pp. 140–43). González also offers a fascinating analysis of the ways Apollinarianism could be used by the ruling classes as a way to make their point, namely, that the human mind is not in need of salvation; the problem lies in our bodily nature. Those who controlled society could thus regard themselves intellectually superior and the "mind" of the society—the societal structures set up by those in power—not in need of redemption. The problem is then found among those who take care of physical tasks in the society (pp. 147–48).

38. Ibid., 110–11. In Peru, González guesses, God speaks Quechua rather than Spanish, the language of a significant minority on the borders and margins of the society (p. 111).

39. Ibid., 29.

40. Ibid., 85.

41. Ibid., 115. So also Gustavo Gutiérrez, "Theology and Spirituality in a Latin American Context," *Harvard Divinity Bulletin* 14 (June–August 1984): 4.

whom support the idea of sharing based on the principle of commonality in the Triune God.[42]

> The commonality that exists within the Trinity is the pattern and goal of creation and is therefore the example that those who believe in the Trinity are called to follow. . . . If the Trinity is the doctrine of a God whose very life is a life of sharing, its clear consequence is that those who claim belief in such a God must live a similar life. And it is true that from a very early date the doctrine of the Trinity was developed in terms of sharing.[43]

He argues that sharing is built into the doctrine of the Trinity from the beginning. Tertullian's Trinitarian formula, "one substance and three persons," argues that the oneness of the Three is based on their sharing of a common substance. Tertullian offered illustrations taken from the sharing of a common possession.[44] Tertullian also introduced the term *oikonomia* into (Latin) Trinitarian discourse, the original meaning of which has to do with administration and management. In sum, González understands Tertullian to mean that "the One God exists according to an inner order, and that this order is best understood in terms of the sharing of a *substantia*—which in the legal terminology of that time could mean 'property'—by three persons."[45] Again, the socioeconomic and political implications of sharing should not be ignored.

For González, imitating the life of sharing becomes the way to identify whether our claims to serve the biblical God are true or not: "for if God is love, life without love is life without God; and if this is a sharing love, such as we see in the Trinity, then life without sharing is life without God; and if this sharing is such that in God the three persons are equal in power, then life without such power sharing is life without God."[46]

Another way of speaking of communality as the central feature of the Triune God is to use the term "God is being-for-others." Jesus was entirely for others; he lived and died for others. Calling God by this name is but paraphrasing the biblical idea of God as love.[47] By derivation, since humans are created in the image of God, their life is also meant to be a "being for others."[48] God's loving being-for-others means also being judge of everything that resists the principles of equality and justice. God judges those who oppress the widow, the poor, and the alien; hence God's preferential option for the poor.[49]

42. González, *Mañana*, 112–13, with quotations from these Fathers.
43. Ibid., 113, 114.
44. Ibid., 114 with reference to Tertullian, *Against Praxeas* 4.
45. González, *Mañana*, 114.
46. Ibid., 115.
47. Ibid., 151–53.
48. Ibid., 131–33.
49. Ibid., 153.

CRITICAL REFLECTIONS

As with assessing Boff, the Trinitarian reflection of González should first and fore-most be assessed against his stated purpose, that is, to contribute to a Hispanic perspective on theology in general and on the Trinity in particular. Yet there are two main differences between these two Hispanic writers. Boff sets for himself the task of producing a monograph, a full study of the Trinity, whereas González's Trinitarian reflections are part of an outline of a Hispanic theology written in a style between strictly academic and popular. Furthermore, while both writers are committed to the idea of liberation, for Boff—living and ministering in Latin America—liberation *theology* is a self-defined context. González's book con-tributes significantly to liberationism but is not necessarily contained by that framework. Being a part of a larger whole rather than a monograph and having been written in the form of an "experiment" by a "[s]cholar trained in traditional theology,"[50] the occasional nature of *Mañana* should be acknowledged.

Since González is a renowned church historian and historian of theology, his main contribution to the doctrine of the Trinity, in my reading, has to do with his innovative way of not only interpreting tradition but also casting it in a new framework, namely, the sociopolitical context. *Mañana*'s discussion of the his-tory of ideas is full of creative and brilliant insights, such as viewing Arianism in the context of the debate about changelessness rather than monotheism (a grow-ing consensus among recent scholars), seeing Nicaea in terms of both affirming and challenging the older view of God as an "immutable tyrant," unpacking the sociopolitical appeals of heresies such as patripassianism, and so forth.

At the same time—and exactly because history is González's area of special-ization—it is not only legitimate but also necessary to scrutinize the theolog-ical consistency of his reading of Trinitarian history. Unfortunately, this part of *Mañana* has not received appropriate attention among reviewers.[51] It seems to me that González too easily succumbs to a biased reading of the history of tradition to support his main agenda. This happens in two complementary ways, on the one hand making some ideas and concepts of the Trinity fit into his main argument, and on the other hand dismissing other aspects of history with a pen stroke. Let me illustrate the first tendency. In order to help make a stronger case for the claim of the primacy of communality in the Triune God and of sharing among human beings as the proper response consequently, González argues that Tertullian's formula, "one essence and three persons," emphasized *sharing* (of divinity) as the key value, and furthermore that the North African theologian's adoption of the term *oikonomia* was perfectly fit-

50. Orlando O. Espin, review of *Mañana: Christian Theology from a Hispanic Perspective, Missi-ology* 19 (October 1991): 483; see also p. 484.

51. Routinely the commentators who have reviewed *Mañana* mention the innovative reading of the history of Trinity and Christology, but none of them enters into any kind of theological assessment.

ting in that its original meaning has to do with administration and management. In other words, this Hispanic historian sees in the early development of Trinitarian canons by Tertullian a conscious politico-economical slant. This, however, is a claim that other commentators have not discerned, and Tertullian himself—apart from some illustrative purposes that González himself notes[52]—seems not to be burdened by this agenda. An example of the somewhat unfair and unfounded dismissal of classical theistic traditions is the expression about the tradition's intention of "sacralizing changelessness" of God in support of the status quo. The issue is not the harshness of his critique of tradition so much as whether methodologically and materially the main thesis of González can be substantiated, namely, that the classical substantialist-immutabilist understanding of the Triune God was *consciously* used by Christians and rulers of the Christendom-dominated states to uphold their own rights and privileges in putting down the masses. It is one thing to say that the *effects* of certain types of Trinitarian understandings—absolutist, hierarchical, "monotheistic" (Moltmann, Boff), and the like—turn out to support power structures, civil as well as ecclesiastical. It is another thing to say—as González insists time after time—that a certain type of Trinitarian view was *upheld* in order to maintain the elite status of the rulers.

One of the marked differences between the liberationist approaches of Boff and González is that while Boff works hard not only in retrieving the benefits of tradition but also in constructing a doctrine of the Trinity in keeping with classical orthodoxy,[53] González seems quite cynical about the value of tradition's "interpretations that see it [Trinity] in purely speculative or metaphysical terms"[54] and urges his fellow Hispanics to concentrate on the practical implications of the doctrine. González is not only dismissive but unnuanced here—just think of the diversity of classical traditions of the doctrine of God from Eastern Orthodoxy's apophatic approach to the medieval mystics' visions to Luther's theology of the cross (Joachim Fiore among others), and so forth.[55]

González, with his practical orientation, says the whole debate about the economic and immanent "seems pointless, for we have no way of knowing how God is in Godself, and therefore to speak of an 'essential' Trinity, apart from God's revelation and relations with the world, is nonsense."[56] For most contemporary theologians, including many Liberationists, this distinction is crucial and

---

52. González, *Mañana*, 114, with reference to Tertullian, *Against Praxeas* 4.
53. Leonardo Boff's whole book *Trinity and Society* (trans. Paul Burns [Maryknoll, NY: Orbis Books, 1998]) is a testimony to this attempt, with summaries such as "Seven Propositions of Trinitarian Orthodoxy" (pp. 97–99), and the summary statements at the end (pp. 232–37) make this effort a mark of the monograph.
54. González, *Mañana*, 115.
55. For the diversity and plurality of traditions of God, see Veli-Matti Kärkkäinen, *The Doctrine of God: A Global Introduction* (Grand Rapids: Baker Academic, 2004), part 2.
56. González, *Mañana*, 112. His claim that the Bible never attempts to speak of God in Godself (p. 92) is hardly true even when one admits that the Bible's main approach to speaking of God is economic.

worth debating.[57] The debate is not to circumvent the discussion of practical—social and political—implications of the Trinity, as González seems to assume,[58] but rather the contrary: to find a proper theological basis for such a project. Apart from practical implications, there is in my understanding a necessity to continue to speak of the immanent Trinity, if not for other reasons, then to safeguard God's absolute freedom.

It seems to me, then, that this Hispanic theologian adopts the "from below" method in a way that is open to both theological and ideological questions. Theologically, he ends up dismissing all talk about God *in se*. Ideologically, he rejects the classical tradition's bias toward power structures and replaces that with an agenda for not only a certain segment of humanity (Hispanics) but more important, a specific agenda (liberation). The question arises as to whether González's approach and the classical or "mainline" are complementary, even while mutually critical, or exclusive of each other. It seems to me that González really considers them complementary, yet the way the book expresses itself implies that the Hellenistic takeover of biblical Christianity should be replaced by a Hispanic takeover of classical theism.

My somewhat critical comments on González's Trinitarian reflections are not meant to downplay the superb contributions his work makes as the first outline of a Hispanic (American-based Latino) systematic theology. I have touched on issues the author claims to be central to his presentation, and I applaud González for adding a new perspective on the history and significance of the central church doctrine.

57. A confusing way to describe the economic Trinity is to call it "nonessential" Trinity (González, *Mañana*, 114). I am not quite sure what is meant by this concept here: whether it means something like "not important" or just distinctive from "essential," i.e., not immanent trinity.
58. Ibid., 112.

B. The Trinity in Asian Perspectives

Chapter 21

The Asian Context
for Trinitarian Reflections

GOD IS RICE[1]

According to the Korean-born theologian Jung Young Lee, whose creative Trinitarian reflections from an Asian perspective will be studied in what follows, the "cultural and historical context of the West is so very distinct from that of the East that they seem opposite to each other." However, he adds, "their difference should be regarded not as a source of conflict but as a basis for mutual fulfillment. Their contextual difference will enrich a holistic understanding of the Christian faith."[2] Lee's own biography is typical of so many non-Western theologians. Having conducted his theological studies in the West by focusing on Euro-American male theologians' writings, only slowly did he begin to reclaim his own Asian tradition. In the course of two decades of teaching Asian religions and philosophy in the United States, he not only became an expert in that area but also was able to attempt a fruitful dialogue between traditional Western and his own Korean Chinese East Asian background.[3]

It is appropriate to begin the introduction to the Asian context of Trinitarian theology with a reference to a particular biography since narrative and (personal)

---

1. The heading above comes from Masao Takenaka, *God Is Rice: Asian Cultures and Christian Faith* (Geneva: World Council of Churches, 1986).
2. Jung Young Lee, *The Trinity in Asian Perspective* (Nashville: Abingdon Press, 1996), 17.
3. Ibid., 21–23.

story—along with poems, myths, and folklore—are preferred vehicles of communication of religion and theology in Asia. In the words of David Ng of China, "One's life story becomes a lifestory, a way of relating the events to providence."[4] Not inappropriately, then, a book compiled by Asian and Asian American theologians on theological method is titled *Journeys at the Margin: Toward an Autobiographical Theology in Asian-American Perspective.*[5] Masao Takenaka of Japan paints a delightful picture of doing theology in a mood compatible with ancient cultures of his own context, so different from typical modern Western discursive analysis. In his book *God Is Rice,* he calls this an "Ah-hah!" method, a dynamic way of doing theology much closer to the Bible, in which people did not come to know God by discussion or argument but by experiencing him. We "must awaken in ourselves the appreciation of the living reality who is God. In the Bible we have many surprising acknowledgements. . . . 'Ah-hah!' In this way, God is working in our world, in a way I did not know."[6] This is an alternative to the typical Western approach based on analysis and debate, which he calls "Ya-ya" method.[7]

But what is Asia? What is the role of Christianity in that continent? Asia is huge both geographically and in population. "Asia" is a generic concept—so typical of the Enlightenment mentality's universalizing tendency in Western discourse! While Christianity has not made inroads evenly into that part of the world[8]—the continent inhabited by more than one-half of the world's population—it is not appropriate to undermine the significance of the Christian faith there. After all, it claims an ancient pedigree, given the presence of the Christian church from missionary work of the apostle Thomas in the Middle East and the western and southern coast of India, and the vital Catholic missionary influence after the discovery of the sea route to India and the rest of Asia in the later Middle Ages, and the modern missionary movement of European (and later American) origins, which has been mainly Protestant.[9]

---

4. David Ng, "A Path of Concentric Circles: Toward an Autobiographical Theology of Community," in *Journeys at the Margin: Toward an Autobiographical Theology in American-Asian Perspective,* ed. Peter C. Phan and Jung Young Lee (Collegeville, MN: Liturgical Press, 1999), 82. So also Paul F. Knitter, *No Other Names? A Critical Survey of Christian Attitudes Toward the World Religions* (Maryknoll, NY: Orbis Books, 1985): xiii: "All theology, we are told, is rooted in biography." The first major monograph on the topic of biographical theology was offered by the late James McClendon Jr., *Biography as Theology: How Life Stories Can Remake Today's Theology* (Nashville: Abingdon Press, 1974). For important methodological considerations from an Asian perspective, see also Anselm K. Min, "From Autobiography to Fellowship of Others: Reflections on Doing Ethnic Theology Today," in *Journeys at the Margin,* ed. Phan and Lee.

5. Peter C. Phan and Jung Young Lee, eds., *Journeys at the Margin: Toward an Autobiographical Theology in American-Asian Perspective* (Collegeville, MN: Liturgical Press, 1999).

6. Takenaka, *God Is Rice,* 9.

7. Ibid., 8.

8. Statistically, the number of Christians in Asia ranges from less than 1 percent (Japan, Thailand, among others) to a few percent at most, with the exception of the predominantly Roman Catholic Philippines (about 85 percent Christian) and more recently South Korea (less than a third Christian) and China (estimations vary widely from 50 million to 70 million or so).

9. See further George Gispert-Sauch, SJ, "Asian Theology," in *The Modern Theologians: An Introduction to Christian Theology in the Twentieth Century,* ed. David F. Ford, 2nd ed. (Cambridge, MA: Blackwell, 1997), 455.

How do we approach Asia theologically? What classifications or typologies might offer some help without hopelessly oversimplifying the complexity? In terms of theological centers, the following scheme is one way to describe this huge area.[10] On the forefront of Asian theological reflection have been India and Sri Lanka, with a strong Hindu influence. Theologians such as Raimundo Panikkar, Swami Abhishiktananda, M. M. Thomas, Stanley J. Samartha, and Aloysius Pieris are well-known figures in the wider international theological academia. A rising center of theological thinking is Korea, with its phenomenal church growth. A strong proliferation of Korean theology ranges from fairly conserva- tive evangelical theology that cuts across denominational boundaries to a more liberal strand of Asian pluralism and Minjung theology. In another cluster of Asian countries, Buddhism has played a major role: China, Taiwan, Thailand, and Japan. The Japanese theologian Kosuke Koyama, who spent several years as a missionary-theologian in Thailand, is well known among his peers, as is also the Taiwanese-born Choan-Seng Song. Like so many of their counterparts, both of these Asian theologians currently teach in the United States and contribute to the emerging Asian-American theological guild. The predominantly Catholic Philippines stands in its own category, as does Indonesia, which is strongly influ- enced by Islam but also in some areas by Hinduism and Buddhism.

For the purposes of this book I have worked with an even rougher and more inclusive typology of Asian theology, sampling two theologians who represent in my view the two key centers of theological conversation, namely, India and East Asia (China, Japan, Korea): the Indian-born Raimundo Panikkar and the Korean-born Jung Young Lee, who employs extensively Chinese traditions.[11] Both theologians are also representative in that, while firmly anchored in Asian soil, they both live in the West (U.S.A.) and thus engage in an extensive theolog- ical dialogue. Panikkar is Roman Catholic and Lee is Protestant (United Methodist), reflecting the Christian makeup of their continent.

PLURALISM AND POVERTY AS THE CONTEXT
FOR GOD-TALK

Asian Christian theology is still emerging and distinguishing itself in various Asian forms after a long hegemony of Western influence;[12] understandably Asian theologians have leveled various criticisms concerning the limitations of tradi- tional and Western theology, especially when it comes to the doctrine of God.[13]

---

10. I am making use of and adapting the classification by Gispert-Sauch, "Asian Theology," 456.
11. My choice matches the approach of a recent major text edited by John Parratt, *An Introduc- tion to Third World Theologies* (Cambridge: Cambridge University Press, 2004), which divides the presentation of Asian theologies into two camps: India and East Asia.
12. A helpful discussion is offered by Merrill Morse, *Kosuke Koyama: A Model for Intercultural Theology* (Frankfurt am Main: Peter Lang, 1991), chap. 5.
13. Tissa Balasuriya of Sri Lanka laments that Western theology for Asians is ethnocentric, eccle- siocentric, clerical, patriarchal, pro-capitalist, devoid of socioeconomic analysis, and nonpractical.

To borrow the title of a book by the Taiwanese Choan-Seng Song,[14] how would a "theology from the womb of Asia" look? What are its sources? What are the defining features? The words of the Sri Lankan Roman Catholic liberationist Aloysius Pieris are often quoted to set the stage for theologizing in that continent: "The Asian context can be described as a blend of a profound religiosity (which is perhaps Asia's greatest wealth) and an overwhelming poverty."[15] Asian religiousness is rich and variegated and touches all aspects of life. In contrast to the Western modernist dualism between the sacred and secular, for most Asians not only is religion an irreducible part of all life, but it also undergirds beliefs, decisions, and behavior of everyday life. With all the rapid developments in technology and education, Hinduism, Buddhism, Confucianism, and a host of other religions, most of them manifested in forms that used to be called "animistic" (having to do with spirits), still permeate all of life. As in Africa, religion is visible and part of everyday life. Thus, talk about God/gods can be carried on everywhere, from the street markets to luxurious hotels to desperate slums to exotic restaurants.[16]

The challenge of pluralism is nowhere stronger than in Asia. It shapes Asian Christianity, Christian theology, and reflection on God in a significant way. In any Asian country, Christians live in a minority position. This fact has implications for Asian theologies when compared to European and U.S. theologies, which are often written from the standpoint of Christianity being a major force in the society. The thrust of Asian theology is to inquire into the identity of Christianity vis-à-vis other religious confessions. Kosuke Koyama aptly notes the various forces that shape Asian Christianity as Asians are addressing the question of Jesus of Nazareth: "But who do you say that I am?" (Matt. 16:15):

> This question comes to Asian Christians, who live in a world of great religious traditions, modernization impacts, ideologies of the left and right, international conflicts, hunger, poverty, militarism, and racism. Within these confusing and brutal realities of history the question comes to them.

Asian liberation theologians, with the leadership of Aloysius Pieris, another Sri Lankan, have complained about the lack of relevance of Western approaches to the social and political context of Asia. Choan-Seng Song faults Western theology for rationalism and lack of imagination. Jung Young Lee similarly decries the Western approach for being captive to Aristotelian logic of the excluded middle, which is in opposition to an inclusive *yin-yang* thinking of Asia. See further Tissa Balasuriya, "Toward the Liberation of Theology in Asia," in *Asia's Struggle for Full Humanity: Toward a Relevant Theology,* ed. Virginia Fabella (Maryknoll, NY: Orbis Books 1980); Tissa Balasuriya, *Planetary Theology* (Maryknoll, NY: Orbis Books, 1984), 2–10 especially; Aloysius Pieris, *An Asian Theology of Liberation* (Maryknoll, NY: Orbis Books, 1988), 81–83 especially; Choan-Seng Song, *Third-Eye Theology: Theology in Formation in Asian Settings,* rev. ed. (Maryknoll, NY: Orbis Books, 1991), 19–23; Jung Young Lee, *Marginality: The Key to Multicultural Theology* (Minneapolis: Fortress, 1995), 64–70; Lee, *Trinity in Asian Perspective,* chaps. 2 and 3.

14. Choan-Seng Song, *Theology from the Womb of Asia* (Maryknoll, NY: Orbis Books, 1986).
15. Aloysius Pieris, "Western Christianity and Asian Buddhism," in *Dialogue* 7 (May–August 1980): 61–62.
16. For the significance of the encounter with other religions to emerging Christian theology in Asia, see further Morse, *Kosuke Koyama,* 100–102.

Here the depth of soul of the East is challenged to engage in a serious dialogue with the Word of God. Jesus refuses to be treated superficially.[17]

A number of Asian theologians have focused their theological work in general and the doctrine of God on the challenge of pluralism. For example, Samartha of India has labored to develop a theocentric Christology in which Christ is seen as *a* way to the Father but not exclusively.[18] Panikkar is a leading theologian of religions, as will be seen in the discussion on his Trinitarian doctrine.

Poverty and injustice are not peculiar to the Asian continent: Latin Americans and Africans, among others, suffer from similar exploitation. Yet the amount of poverty—if for no other reason than the huge population—in the East is overwhelming and breathtaking. Most Asian countries are poor, with the exception of Japan, Taiwan, and South Korea. From the Western viewpoint, it is painful to acknowledge the fact that one—if not *the*—major reason for poverty in too many Asian countries is the tragic history of colonialization. This historical fact should make Western preachers of Christ aware of the difficulty with which many Asians hear their message, the message of the former masters. For many Asian Christian theologians, then, struggle for liberation and justice are key themes.

One of the most noted of those champions is M. M. Thomas, a layperson of the Mar Thoma Church of South India who also held a leadership role in the World Council of Churches. His gateway to theology was the emergence of political and social consciousness, coming as he was from Marxist philosophy. The title of his main book, *Salvation and Humanization,* reveals the central orientation of his thinking. For Thomas, the validity of Christian theology is based less on its doctrinal orthodoxy than on its contribution to the human quest for a better quality of life and for social justice. Aloysius Pieris of Sri Lanka, among others, has joined in this fight against poverty and oppression. In his Christology, this Roman Catholic theologian links Asia's poverty and spirituality to Jesus' "double baptism" in "the Jordan of Asian religions and the Calvary of Asian poverty." This is Jesus' immersion in the Asian context and life. Jesus pointed to the ascetic John as the archetype of the true spirituality of the kingdom of God and denounced the striving for the accumulation of wealth and trust in mammon. Jesus' radical social program, in Pieris's analysis, led him finally to the cross, executed by the power elite. The powerful crucified him at "a cross that the money-polluted religiosity of his day planted on Calvary with the aid of a colonial power (Luke 23:1–23). This is where the journey, begun at Jordan, ended."[19]

17. Kosuke Koyama, "Foreword by an Asian Theologian," in *Asian Christian Theology: Emerging Themes,* ed. Douglas J. Elwood (Philadelphia: Westminster Press, 1980), 14.

18. See, among others, Stanley J. Samartha, *One Christ—Many Religions: Toward a Revised Christology* (Maryknoll, NY: Orbis Books, 1991). For a wider sampling of Asian theologians in conversation with the challenge of pluralism, see Veli-Matti Kärkkäinen, *An Introduction to the Theology of Religions: Biblical, Historical, and Contemporary Perspectives* (Downers Grove, IL: InterVarsity Press, 2003), chaps. 28, 33, 34.

19. Aloysius Pieris, *Asian Theology of Liberation,* 49.

YIN-YANG AND ADVAITA THEOLOGY

The sources of Asian theology in general and specifically the doctrine of God, thus, while anchored of course in Christian Scripture and traditions,[20] relate to the realities of Asian life described above. The billions of Asian people themselves with their daily "stories of joy and suffering, hope and despair, love and hatred, freedom and oppression" form one of the sources. According to the Vietnamese Peter C. Phan, this collective memory includes the women's stories, voicing women's marginalization and oppression that is often even greater than that of men. Furthermore, the sacred texts and ethical and spiritual practices of Asian religion and philosophy serve as sources, as the Trinitarian theologies of Panikkar and Lee illustrate.[21] Yet another distinctive feature of Asian theological (re)sources, already alluded to, is the rich tradition of cultural tools such as myths, folklore, symbols, poetry, stories, songs, visual art, and dance.[22] In that kind of environment, in addition to and sometimes in preference over discursive analysis, theology embraces other methods, especially narrative and storytelling. For Choan-Seng Song,

> theology is like storytelling. The story unfolds itself as you tell it. It moves in all directions. It may even stray into byways. But this is the excitement of telling stories. A story grows and expands. It leads to new terrains and depicts new scenes. If this is what our storytelling is like, how much more so is God's storytelling! The story of creation—who are we to define it and restrict it—God's activity in the world—how are we to predict it and dictate it? God's ultimate goal for humanity and for the entire creation—how on earth are we to set a time-frame to it?[23]

In his delightful classic work *Waterbuffalo Theology*, the Japanese Kosuke Koyama, who has worked in Thailand, speaks of the need for a narrative, concrete approach to divinity among Thai farmers. They are not concerned about metaphysical problems related to God, but are interested in hearing that the "monsoon rain cannot make God wet! God is the Lord of monsoon rain. He sends his monsoon for his purpose."[24] Koyama wondered what would happen if, instead of dry philosophical categories of the West totally unrelated to the Asian context, we used kitchen imagery such as "pepper" and "salt."[25] Koyama also reminds us in *Three*

---

20. Peter C. Phan, "Introduction: An Asian-American Theology: Believing and Thinking at the Boundaries," in Phan and Lee, *Journeys at the Margin*, xv (italics in the text). See further R. S. Sugirtharajah, ed., *Voices from the Margin: Interpreting the Bible in the Third World* (Maryknoll, NY: Orbis Books, 1991).

21. See further Peter C. Phan, "The Christ of Asia: An Essay on Jesus and the Eldest Son and Ancestor," *Missionalia* 45 (1996): 25–55.

22. Phan, introduction to *Journeys at the Margin*, xii–xviii, quotation on p. xvi; I have modified Phan's categorization.

23. Choan-Seng Song, "Five Stages Toward Christian Theology in the Multicultural World," in *Journeys at the Margin*, ed. Phan and Lee, 2. See also Choan-Seng Song, *The Believing Heart: An Invitation to Story Theology* (Minneapolis: Fortress, 1999).

24. Kosuke Koyama, *Waterbuffalo Theology* (Maryknoll, NY: Orbis Books, 1974), 41.

25. Ibid., 79–83.

Mile an Hour God that God is in no hurry, that God is better suited for the Thai context with the mentality of *maiphenrai* (meaning something like "It does not matter" or "It is okay").[26]

One of crucial differences between Western and Eastern thinking relates to the starting point. Both Panikkar and Lee, among others, remind us of the fact that while Western thinking approaches reality in general and the doctrine of God in particular from an anthropocentric perspective, Asians begin with the cosmic. In the words of Lee, who speaks specifically from the East Asian context (China, Japan, Korea) but whose reflections relate inclusively to the Asian way of thinking: "While the West is interested in an anthropocentric approach to cosmology, East Asia is more interested in a cosmocentric approach to anthropology. In East Asia, anthropology is a part of cosmology; a human being is regarded as a microcosm of the cosmos."[27] Consequently, Lee uses the term "anthropocosmology,"[28] terminology reminiscent of Panikkar's "cosmotheandric" principle, to be studied in what follows.

Western thinking is founded on the dualistic principle of the excluded middle. A sentence can be only true or false, not both-and. The Asian way of thinking resists that kind of either/or distinction. It is expressed in various ways; the two terms that are best known outside of Asia are "*yin-yang*" and "advaita." These two concepts play a crucial role in the Trinitarian theologies of the two authors selected as representatives for this study: Lee builds his vision of the Trinity on *yin-yang,* and Panikkar's "cosmotheandric" Trinitarian vision is based on the concept of advaita.[29] The pair *yin-yang* includes contradictions and opposites, yet inclusions; it is "both-and" rather than "either-or."[30] The (Hindu) notion of advaita means "nonduality" (literally, not-two). Applied to the Trinity it means, in the words of Panikkar, that there "are not two realities: God and man (or the world), as outright atheists and outright theists are dialectically driven to maintain. Reality is theandric; it is our way of looking that causes reality to appear to us sometimes under one aspect and sometimes under another because our vision shares in both."[31] Applied to the ancient

26. Kosuke Koyama, *Three Mile an Hour God: Biblical Reflections* (Maryknoll, NY: Orbis Books, 1979).

27. Lee, *Trinity in Asian Perspective,* 18; see also p. 21.

28. Ibid.

29. And by many other well-known Asian theologians such as Stanley J. Samartha, "The Cross and the Rainbow: Christ in a Multireligious Culture," in *Asian Faces of Jesus,* ed. R. S. Sugirtharajah (Maryknoll, NY: Orbis Books, 1995), 110–11. See further Kim, "India," 49–50, 61, 66.

30. Jung Young Lee, *The Theology of Change: A Christian Concept of God in an Eastern Perspective* (Maryknoll, NY: Orbis Books, 1979), 3–9; idem, *Patterns of Inner Process* (Secaucus, NJ: Citadel Press, 1976), 193–205, chap. 2 (explaining the basis of *yin-yang* in *I Ching,* the foundational Chinese text); Lee, *Trinity in Asian Perspective,* chap. 2.

31. Raimundo Panikkar, *The Trinity and the Religious Experience of Man: Icon-Person-Mystery* (Maryknoll, NY: Orbis Books/London: Darton, Longman & Todd, 1973), 75. So crucial is the concept of advaita in Panikkar that a recent commentator, Everett H. Cousins, has coined the term "advaitic Trinitarianism"; see his "Panikkar's Advaitic Trinitarianism," in *The Intercultural Challenge of Raimon Panikkar,* ed. Josef Prabhu (Maryknoll, NY: Orbis Books, 1996), 119–301; for a helpful explanation of the term "advaitic," see especially p. 120.

problem of unity and diversity in the Trinitarian God, the advaitic principle implies that Father and Son are not two, but they are not one either; the Spirit unites and distinguishes them.[32] Related to this both/and view of reality is the cyclical world-view instead of the linear Western understanding.

Other unique ways of describing the mode of theology in Asia, closely linked with *yin-yang* and advaita, among others, is C. S. Song's *Third-Eye Theology*.[33] "Third-eye" refers to the Buddhist master who opens our eyes to see areas previously unknown. The goal of that kind of authentic Asian theology is "the freedom to encounter Jesus the savior in the depth of the spirituality that sustains Asians in their long march of suffering and hope."[34]

Panikkar and Lee are by no means the only Christian theologians from Asia who have turned their attention to the topic of Trinity through the lens of the culture and thought patterns of their own milieu. An important contribution is offered by the Japanese theologian Nozomu Miyahira in his *Towards a Theology of the Concord of God: A Japanese Perspective on the Trinity*.[35] Building on the Japanese idea of "concord" and "betweenness," deriving from the ancient rice culture and its cooperation and sense of communalism, Miyahira utilizes creatively biblical, historical, and systematic materials and attempts to offer a corrective to Western Trinitarian theologies that arise out of particular philosophical and cultural influences such as Tertullian's Stoic, Augustine's Platonic, and Barth's Hegelian background. He wants to make a shift from the Western "Three Persons in One Substance" to "The Triune God: Three Betweennesses in One Concord."[36]

Both Raimundo Panikkar of India and Jung Young Lee of Korea have carried out most of their productive academic life—and are residing—in the United States. While the American scene for some time has been the locus for emerging "contextual" theologies such as African American/black or Hispanic theologies, Asian American theological reflection is quite novel.[37] Yet the Asian Americans form a rapidly developing immigrant community with a highly active church life and steady growth of ministerial students studying in a variety of divinity

---

32. Panikkar, *Trinity and the Religious Experience*, 62.

33. Song, *Third-Eye Theology*.

34. Song, *Theology from the Womb of Asia*, 3.

35. Nozomu Miyahira, *Towards a Theology of the Concord of God: A Japanese Perspective on the Trinity* (Exeter, UK: Paternoster, 2000).

36. Ibid., part 1 and part 2, respectively.

37. That Asian American theology is less known even in academic circles than African American and Hispanic American is well illustrated by the fact that even the most recent version of the widely used globally representative textbook *The Modern Theologians: An Introduction to Christian Theology in the Twentieth Century* (ed. David F. Ford, 2nd ed. [Cambridge, MA: Blackwell, 1997]) does not include a section on this North American perspective even though African, Hispanic, and Native American voices are given a fair treatment. For a comparison of African, Hispanic, and Asian American theologies, see Peter C. Phan, "Contemporary Theology and Inculturation in the United States," in *The Multicultural Church: A New Landscape in the U.S. Church*, ed. William Cenkner (New York: Paulist Press, 1996), 109–30, 176–92. According to Phan, there are a number of reasons for this lack, such as the short time that Asians have been in the United States and their general lack of interest in academic disciplines other than the empirical and scientific. Phan, introduction to *Journeys at the Margin*, xii.

schools. Since about the 1970s influential Asian American voices such as Choan-Sen Song (Taiwan), Jung Young Lee (North Korea), Peter C. Phan (Vietnam), Anselm Kyongsuk Min (South Korea), Andrew Sung Park (South Korea; originally, North Korea), Paul M. Nagano (Japan), and David Ng (China) have offered suggestions as to the development of an Asian theology in the North American context.[38]

Jung Young Lee argues that marginality is the key to multicultural theology, as in the title of one of his works. His theology takes seriously both the Asian origin of Asian American theology and its marginal status in the North American context. It is not purely Asian nor purely American, but both. Almost without exception all Asian American theologians until now have received their education in the West and thus are quite familiar with the Western tradition; ironically, many of them have devoted less time to their Asian roots. As Jung Young Lee argues, being an immigrant means being "in-between."[39] To Americans, they are outsiders; to Asians back in their homelands, they are Americanized; and when they themselves go back to Asia, it is a "foreign home."[40] Yet, at the same time Lee argues that because of the interrelatedness of Asia and America, interpretations of Christian faith coming from both contexts are needed. "If the Asian culture has become a part of American life, and if theology and life are inseparable, then Christian theology in America without an Asian perspective is incomplete."[41] Thus, being "in-between"—what Phan calls being "betwixt and between"[42]—and at the margins, is not altogether negative; it is also an asset.

38. For the background of these peoples in the U.S.A., see Lee, *Marginality*, 7–27.
39. Jung Young Lee, "A Life In-Between: A Korean-American Journey," in Phan and Lee, *Journeys at the Margin*, 23–39.
40. For vivid illustrations of this dilemma, see Julia Ching, "The House of Self," in Phan and Lee, *Journeys at the Margin*, 41–62.
41. Lee, *Trinity in Asian Perspective*, 12.
42. Peter C. Phan, "Betwixt and Between: Doing Theology with Memory and Imagination," in Phan and Lee, *Journeys at the Margin*, 113–33.

Chapter 22

Jung Young Lee

Trinity as an Embrace of Yin-Yang

THE THEOLOGY OF CHANGE[1]

"There appears to be . . . a correlation between the *yin-yang* way of thinking and the divine symbols of the Trinity. The Creator (of the Father) is correlated with the change, the Word (of the Son) with *yang*, and the Spirit (of the Holy Spirit) with *yin*. Can this correlation," asks the Korean-born Asian American theologian Jung Young Lee, "explain the heart of Christian paradoxes: 'the threeness in one and oneness in three'?"[2] To explore this exciting line of questioning, Lee offers first a revisionist understanding of God as change as a corrective to both classical theism and as a further development of process thought.[3] Lee is optimistic

---

1. The heading above comes from the book title by Jung Young Lee, *The Theology of Change: A Christian Concept of God in an Eastern Perspective* (Maryknoll, NY: Orbis Books, 1979).

2. Jung Young Lee, *The Trinity in Asian Perspective* (Nashville: Abingdon Press, 1996), 13.

3. Among other writings of this author on the topic, see Jung Young Lee, *God Suffers for Us: A Systematic Inquiry into a Concept of Divine Passibility* (The Hague: Martinus Nijhoff, 1974); idem, *Embracing Change: Postmodern Interpretations of the I Ching from a Christian Perspective* (London and Toronto: Associated University Presses, 1994); idem, "Can God Be Change Itself?" *Journal of Ecumenical Studies* 10, no. 4 (1973): 751–70.

about the prospects of this kind of revisionist Trinitarian doctrine since in his reading of the signs of the times there is a convergence between the West and the East on the horizon. Once separate from each other intellectually, there is a rapprochement as the West is becoming more sensitive to the "internal process of self-realization,"[4] reflected even in a nonstatic, dynamic scientific worldview.[5] Lee's main Trinitarian monograph is appropriately titled *The Trinity in Asian Perspective*; he has dealt with Trinity in several other writings too.[6]

The basic ideas of the revised understanding of God can be summarized as follows:

> The theology of change . . . presupposes a radical shift in our way of thinking and in our understanding of God. It is based not on the substance of being but on the process of change, and change becomes the fundamental category of theological expression. This shift away from the substance of being to the process of change is based on a metaphysical principle expressed in the *I Ching*. That principle is typically East Asian, but it is also compatible with our contemporary, relativistic worldview.[7]

As mentioned, the proposed theology of change is based on the East Asian way of thinking as expressed first and definitively in the Chinese classic *I Ching*.[8] For Asians, "[r]eality is not a state of being but is always in the process of becoming,"[9] as expressed in the relation of sun and moon in never-ending change.[10]

In the older "theology of substance,"[11] being takes precedence and change is viewed as a function of being. In Lee's "theology of change," it is change that is primary, and it is indeed "the very source of becoming, the reality of being."[12] Lee appreciates the efforts of process theology to move from the substance-based view of reality to a reality in process. It is an attempt to conceive of God in terms of relativistic and organic categories. Process theology, however, falls short of the

---

4. Lee, *Theology of Change*, 1. "The contemporary trend in Western intellectual life can be understood as the transition from the external to the internal process of self-realization." Jung Young Lee, *Patterns of Inner Process: The Rediscovery of Jesus' Teachings in the I Ching and Preston Harold* (Secaucus, NJ: Citadel Press, 1976), 11.

5. Lee, *Patterns of Inner Process*, 12; Lee, *Theology of Change*, 22–23, among others. So also Wilfred Smith, *The Faith of Other Men* (New York: New American Library, 1963), 67, who already in the 1960s claimed that the emerging scientific worldview in the West is approaching that of the *I Ching*.

6. The basic outline is already presented in Lee, *Theology of Change*. See also Jung Young Lee, "Trinity: Toward an Indigenous Asian Perspective," *The Drew Gateway* 59 (Spring 1990): 71–84.

7. Lee, *Theology of Change*, 120.

8. For a basic introduction to the *I Ching*, see Lee, *Patterns of Inner Process*, chap. 2; Lee, *Theology of Change*, 1–9; Lee, *The Trinity in Asian Perspective*, 24–34. For more extensive discussion, see two earlier monographs: Jung Young Lee, *The Principle of Changes: Understanding the I Ching* (New Hyde Park, NY: University Books, 1971); idem, *The I Ching and Modern Man: Essays on Metaphysical Implications of Change* (Secaucus, NJ: University Books, 1975).

9. Lee, *Patterns of Inner Process*, 15.

10. Lee, *Theology of Change*, 3, 5.

11. At times Lee also calls the older substance theology the "theology of the absolute," in contrast to the "theology of process" and the "theology of change." Lee, *Theology of Change*, 19, among others.

12. Lee, *Theology of Change*, 120.

Eastern view, not only because of a different worldview—the Eastern view is cyclical while process thought operates with the linear view of the West—but also because for that movement "process," which presupposes creativity, is primary, whereas for Eastern thought the ultimate reality is "change."[13] "According to the *I Ching*, then, it is change, not process, that is the ultimate, noncontingent reality."[14] Yet another critical difference has to do with logic. In keeping with the Asian mind-set, Lee wants to replace the Aristotelian either/or logic still present in the context of process thought by a dynamic, inclusive "both-and" logic.[15]

The implication of this revisionist theology is simple and profound: if change is the ultimate reality, then it means that God is to be understood as change itself. How does this accord with the traditional Christian understanding of God as immutable? Lee goes back to the biblical record, where the key passage is Exodus 3:14, naming God as *Yahweh*.[16] "This God is a reality without attributes and can be described only by his is-ness. The Judeo-Christian God's nonsymbolic nature is identical with Brahman, nirvana, and *tao*. Since ultimate reality, whether called YHWH, Brahman, nirvana, or *tao*, is beyond human qualifications, 'isness itself' is its only possible definition."[17] The best way to name this "is-ness," unlike classical theism's idea of God as "being itself" and in keeping with the openness of the Exodus passage's approach, is to express it in terms of change. This is similar to the Asian way of identifying Tao with the ultimate reality, that is, change.[18] "God as change itself is the source of every creative becoming."[19] Does this, however, mean that the immutability of God is compromised? Lee's nondualistic worldview allows speaking of "'Change itself' as changeless." The changelessness of God in the Bible does not mean stasis but rather consistency and steadfastness,[20] an idea similar to Robert W. Jenson's emphasis on Yahweh as faithful.

13. Paul S. Chung partially disagrees with Lee's critique of process thought. Chung believes that process theology's relational theory of God is not necessarily "caught in 'either-or thinking'" but stands in dynamic relationality between God and the world on the basis of a primordial nature and subsequent nature." Paul S. Chung, *Martin Luther and Buddhism: Aesthetics of Suffering* (Eugene, OR: Wipf & Stock, 2002), 236 n. 153.

14. Lee, *Theology of Change*, 13–15 (15).

15. Ibid., 16–18. "The God who transcends the Aristotelian "either-or" is not only the "becoming" God but also the "being" God. He is *both* process *and* state, *both* organic *and* inorganic, *both* creative *and* destructive, and *both* generation *and* degeneration. This principle—the inclusive 'this as well as that' or 'both-and'—underlines the theology of change and differentiates it from process theology" (p. 18; italics in the original).

16. For the complicated and debated understanding of this nomenclature, see further Veli-Matti Kärkkäinen, *The Doctrine of God: A Global Introduction* (Grand Rapids: Baker Academic, 2004), 19–21.

17. Lee, *Theology of Change*, 42; for the argumentation, see chap. 2.

18. E.g., Lee, *Trinity in Asian Perspective*, 23, among others.

19. Lee, *Theology of Change*, 41–43 (43).

20. Ibid., 43–44.

YIN-YANG AS THE PRINCIPLE OF REALITY

The priority of change comes to expression in the "interplay of *yin-yang* [that] is the mechanism of change."[21] The cosmology of East Asian people is encapsulated in the bipolarity of nature, which operates cyclically in terms of growth and decline, or the waxing and waning of the moon. Everything in the world has its opposite. The opposites are necessary and also complementary. Thus, the organizing principle of the cosmos is *yin* and *yang*.

> Yang is the essence of heaven, while yin is that of the earth. Yang moves upward, and yin moves downward. Yang is the masculine principle, while yin is the feminine principle. Yang is positive, yin is negative; yang is activity, and yin is quiescence; yang is motion, and yin is rest; yang is life, but yin is death.[22]

Although *yin* and *yang* are opposite in character, they are united together. *Yin* is not only *yin* but also *yang*; *yang* is not only *yang* but *yin* as well.[23] Regarding the doctrine of God, a good illustration is God's transcendence and immanence. God cannot be "either-or" but is "both-and."[24] Because of the principle of inclusivity, Lee argues that conceiving of God as both personal and impersonal is possible. He claims that whereas in the Judeo-Christian tradition God is commonly thought of as a personal God, both personal and impersonal elements need to be included in order to embrace the mystery of God. Being person—"God who bears the nature of a person"—God is both male and female. There is no reason to choose either-or. God is both the negation and affirmation of both genders.[25]

What is highly significant for Trinitarian theology is that *yin* and *yang* are relational symbols rather than ontic or substantive symbols like those of classical theism of the West. Day is day because it is brighter than night; night is night because it is darker. But day can be day only in relation to night and vice versa. Husband is *yang* in relation to his wife, but *yin* in relation to his father. It is thus relationship that determines if something is *yin* or *yang*.[26] Thus, relationship is a priori to an entity;[27] "relationship takes precedence over substance or entity,"[28] yet relationality does not negate substances but rather makes them

---

21. Ibid., 5. According to Lee (ibid.,1–2), *yin-yang* "represents the primordial ethos and thinking of most Asian peoples." For the history of *yin-yang* thinking in East Asian civilizations, see Lee, *Trinity in Asian Perspective*, 35–49. Lee summarizes the significance of *yin-yang* (p. 49): "Ying-Yang symbolic thinking is so deeply rooted in the minds of traditional East Asian people that it is difficult to understand the civilization of East Asia without considering the symbols of yin and yang."

22. Lee, *Trinity in Asian Perspective*, 25; so also Lee, *Theology of Change*, 4–5, among others.

23. See further Lee, *Patterns of Inner Process*.

24. Lee, *Theology of Change*, 49.

25. Ibid., 50–51. For *yin-yang* as the embrace of male and female, see chap. 16.

26. Lee, *Trinity in Asian Perspective*, 29–32 especially.

27. Ibid., 53; see also p. 52.

28. Ibid., 30; see also p. 32.

derivative from relations.[29] Neither *yin*, nor *yang* can be absolute. For example, one increases, the other decreases, as the interrelation between light and darkness in relation to day and night illustrates. What makes things good is the balance and harmony between these opposites.[30] One of the important implications of the relationality of everything is that the *yin* and *yang* principle is based on both/and rather than either/or logic.[31]

A DISTINCTIVELY ASIAN WAY OF DOING TRINITARIAN THEOLOGY

According to Jung Young Lee, Western and Asian ways of doing theology are different not only in terminology and topics but also in the underlying thought forms and approach to reality. The distinctively East Asian way of looking at reality is based on the inclusive *yin-yang* approach.[32] Therefore, a distinctively Asian interpretation of Trinitarian theology is needed. His own proposal is one of the many Asian interpretations[33] and is meant to complement rather than replace Western doctrines.[34] Lee considers his own task as revisionist and complementary, rather than critical.[35] It is not only from an Asian—to be more precise *East* Asian (Chinese, Japanese, Korean)—perspective that Lee's constructive proposal emerges, but also, and in the first place, out of his own life narrative.[36]

Approaching the doctrine of the Trinity from the perspective and thought patterns of Asia, the method is thus inductive. In order for the *yin-yang* interpretation of the Trinity to make sense, Asian cultural, philosophical, and religious resources are employed. With many other Asian theologians (Panikkar among others), Lee discerns triune patterns in Asian religions. One of these is the Buddhist idea of the *Trikaya* (three bodies): the *Dharmakaya*, the body of *dharma* (law); the *Nirmanakaya*, the historical manifestation of Buddha (Siddhārtha Gautama); and the *Sambhoyakaya*, "the body of bliss." Many have seen here a parallel to the Father, Son, and Spirit respectively.[37] While not beginning with

29. Ibid., 54.

30. Ibid., 31.

31. Ibid., 32–35.

32. Lee has developed theological implications also in his "The Yin-Yang Way of Thinking: A Possible Method for Ecumenical Theology," *International Review of Mission* 51, no. 239 (1971): 363–70.

33. Lee, *Trinity in Asian Perspective*, 17.

34. Ibid., 12. If the Western understanding cannot replace the Eastern, neither can the Eastern replace the Western since both of them come out of a particular context and only make sense for those sharing that framework (pp. 14–15). Unlike many critics of Western views, Lee affirms the legitimacy of the substance-based doctrine of the Trinity in early Christian theology as it emerged from—and made sense in—a particular context (p. 16).

35. Lee, *Trinity in Asian Perspective*, 67.

36. Ibid., 23; see also 21–24, 67.

37. Ibid., 68. He gives reference to Roger Corless and Paul F. Knitter, eds., *Buddhist Emptiness and Christian Trinity: Essays and Explorations* (New York: Paulist Press, 1990). With reference to the "Chinese Trinity" or "Asian Trinity," that is, heaven as the Father, earth as the mother, and humanity as their children, including other creatures as companions, Lee offers another parallel: "That is, to me, the very

special revelation, one needs, however, to acknowledge the lack of any perfect equation between Asian and biblical symbols. Asian resources cannot replace the symbols employed by Christian theology, but rather complement and enrich existing interpretations of the Trinity.[38] At the same time, Lee makes an effort to employ "the standard traditional and contemporary tenets of Christian thought" rather than ignoring them.[39]

Another central methodological thought for Lee—with many other contemporary theologians—is the acknowledgment of God as an unknown mystery, unknowable to us in any direct way. God transcends our knowing and cannot be categorized in our finite expressions. Echoing the teaching of *Tao Te Ching*, he says, "Name that can be named is not the real Name."[40] Creatures can never describe in any exhaustive way who the Creator is. To be more precise, theology represents a limited human understanding of God, the symbolic expression of God; God in himself is not identical with this symbolic human talk. Thus, Lee argues, theology always begins with human experience rather than with a propositional statement.[41]

Clearly, *yin-yang* thinking comes close to Zizioulas's idea of communion as the primary manner of existence over substance. I have not seen this connection made in literature, but it offers a fascinating topic for further thinking about God and the Trinity.

If the *yin-yang* includes contradictions and opposites, yet inclusions, it is "both-and" rather than "either-or." Lee takes the example of the transcendence of God. When God is named transcendent—even in classical theism—it is understood that God is immanent as well.[42] Whereas in the West it is taken for granted that "an intelligent man must choose: *either* this *or* that,"[43] the Asian mind-set holds together both "either-or" and "both-and" at the same time. This is related to the fact that *yin-yang* symbolic thinking is based on the idea that change is the foundation of all existence.[44]

---

nature of the Christian idea of *oikoumenē*, the household of God. Moreover, using familial symbols to personify the cosmos is very close to the Christian idea of the Trinity: the Father, the Holy Spirit, and the Son. The Father is closely related with the heavenly realm, and, therefore, is called the heavenly Father. The Holy Spirit is closely related with the earth as the sustainer and with feminine orientation, and, therefore, is the symbol of mother. The Son is closely identified with children or people, who are products of the father and mother. This is one of the paradigms most useful in relating an Asian trinitarian perspective to the Christian concept of the Trinity." Lee, *Trinity in Asian Perspective*, 64.

38. Lee, *Trinity in Asian Perspective*, 68–69.

39. Lee, *Theology of Change*, 8.

40. Ibid., 13. See also *Tao Te Ching: A New English Version*, ed. Stephen Mitchell (New York: Harper & Row, 1988); chap. 1 says, "The tao that can be told is not the eternal Tao. The name that can be named is not the eternal name." Lee, however, does not intend to identify the Tao with the Christian idea of God.

41. Lee, *Trinity in Asian Perspective*, 13; see also p. 50.

42. Ibid., 33–34.

43. Smith, *Faith of Other Men*, 72 (italics in the original).

44. See further Lee, *Trinity in Asian Perspective*, 53–54 especially.

WHAT IS "TRINITARIAN"
ABOUT THE *YIN-YANG* PRINCIPLE?[45]

One of the many common features between the Korean Jung Young Lee and the Indian Raimundo Panikkar is the affirmation of the Trinitarian principle in religions beyond Christianity.[46] Lee posits the Trinitarian structure in, for example, Chinese religions such as in *Tao Te Ching* (chap. 42): "The Tao gives birth to one. One gives birth to two. Two gives birth to three. Three gives birth to all things."[47] More important, again similarly to Panikkar, Lee sees Trinitarian structure in all of reality.[48] Both theologians see in Asian thinking and thought patterns something that more or less directly relates to the Trinitarian understanding of God even when there is not full equation. For Panikkar, that "something" is named the "cosmotheandric" principle, which for him can be equated with Trinitarianism. For Lee, the *yin-yang* logic in itself is Trinitarian when viewed from the perspective of Christian theology.[49]

Several key elements in the *yin-yang* principle fill the requirements for speaking of the Trinity and indeed make it superior to the existing Western logic. These are its symbolic nature first, its relativity second, and third, the idea of change as primary. Before unpacking these features, let me add that for Lee the root problem in traditional Trinitarian theology is the either-or logic of the West.[50] His theology is a remedy to that. *Yin* and *yang* are not entities in themselves but rather symbols that point to something. This means that, strictly speaking, *yin* is not female or earth or darkness—any more than *yang* is male or heaven or light; rather, they represent or symbolize these elements. This corresponds to the symbolic nature of God-talk. Symbolic language is inclusive and holistic and resists the absolutizing tendency. Furthermore, relationality takes precedence over substance, yet without negating substance because it is the by-product of relationality. What *yin* and *yang* are has to do with relation to each other. They are both opposites and complementary. Finally and most important, there is the primacy of change. "Yin and yang symbols are the manifestations of a process of change. Change is the ultimate reality in *yin-yang* symbolic activities. Thus change itself is unknowable. Change that manifests itself in the world is known though yin and yang symbolic activities."[51] Change is the Ultimate Reality, the God.

When applied to the interpretation of the Christian doctrine of the Trinity, the

45. The question in the heading above (paraphrased differently) is raised in ibid., 51.
46. Interestingly, Lee never refers to Panikkar in his main Trinitarian monograph. I have not done a thorough search of Panikkar's Trinitarian writings to see if he ever mentions Lee; in my recollection, there are no references.
47. Cited in Lee, *Trinity in Asian Perspective*, 62.
48. Ibid., 63.
49. E.g., ibid.
50. Lee, *Theology of Change*, 112–13.
51. Lee, *Trinity in Asian Perspective*, 51–54 (53).

result is a uniquely Asian conception. The inclusive nature of *yin-yang* interpretation helps us better understand the meaning of "in" in the Johannine Jesus' saying: "Believe me that I am in the Father and the Father is in me" (John 14:11). Whereas for the dualistic, either-or logic of Aristotelian-Western reasoning the "in" becomes an insurmountable problem,[52] for Asian thought it makes sense.

> When two (or yin and yang) include and are included in each other, they create a Trinitarian relationship. Since yin and yang are relational symbols, yin cannot exist without yang or yang without yin. Moreover, yin and yang are related to each other because they include each other. This inclusiveness can be simply symbolized by the preposition "in," the inner connecting principle of yin and yang. . . . The Father and the Son are one in their "inness," but also at the same time, they are three because "in" represents the Spirit, the inner connecting principle which cannot exist by itself. In the inclusive relationship, two relational symbols such as yin and yang are trinitarian because of "in," which not only unites them but also completes them.[53]

Yin-yang symbolic thinking's Trinitarian explanatory power also comes to the fore in statements such as the following: "The Father and I are one" (John 10:30), again a problem for dualistic Western thinking. *Yin* and *yang* cannot exist without each other because relationality takes precedence over individuality, and because the principle is based on both/and rather than either/or logic. Indeed, this "and" signifies a Trinitarian statement: there is interdependence and union. With regard to Trinity, the two, Father and Son, are one because of "and." There is unity and diversity.[54]

What about the Spirit? How is the *yin-yang* able to explain the third member of the Trinity? Lee responds that again the solution is in the both-and thinking. "The 'and' is not only a linking principle in both-and thinking but also the principle that is *between* two. When 'two' exist, what is not two is the third, which exists between them." In Western either-or logic the middle is excluded, whereas in Asian thinking the middle represents the connecting element between the two, thus the Third.[55]

Lee summarizes the connection between *yin-yang* symbolic thinking and Christian Trinitarian thinking:

> Two (both), therefore, are three because of the third or the between-ness. Yin is yang because it includes yang, just as yang includes yin. Thus yin and yang (two) are one, and one is two. They are also three because they contain the one that connects them. Thus, in yin-yang symbolic thinking, one is in three and three are in one because of two. Without two, trinitarian thinking is not possible, for the Trinity is the completion of two. The

52. Ibid., 59–60.
53. Ibid., 58.
54. Ibid., 59.
55. Ibid., 60–61.

difficulty the early church fathers had in dealing with the divine Trinity was, then, due to their failure to know that two-ness is essential for understanding the relationship between one and three.[56]

In this framework, as mentioned, Father is understood as change, the ultimate reality. "Yin and yang are symbols of a process of change, which is characteristically different from the static and substantial ontology of Greek philosophy."

SON, SPIRIT, AND FATHER IN AN ASIAN PERSPECTIVE

Traditionally, Trinitarian talk has started with the Father; this order is evident, for example, in the ancient creeds. Some theologians have recently suggested we should rather begin with the Spirit. The feminist Elizabeth Johnson supports that order since for her the Spirit is the first contact point between the Triune God and the world. Lee offers an interesting proposal in that his approach is Son-driven: "I will begin with God the Son because the dual nature of Christ is a key to understanding the divine Trinity. Moreover, God the Son represents the fulfillment of the trinitarian principle though the incarnation."[57] The Son is the way to know the Father, and therefore the inductive method, ascending from the Father's historical manifestation in the world in the Son, is a method preferred over the traditional deductive one.[58]

Lee's foundational principle of *yin-yang* provides a superb way for Asian Christology to explain the mystery of Christ's two natures: "The relationship between Christ's divinity and humanity is the relationship between *yin* and *yang*. Just as *yang* cannot exist without *yin* nor *yin* without *yang*, the humanity of Jesus cannot exist without the divinity of Christ nor the divinity of Christ without the humanity of Jesus."[59]

Applying the *yin-yang* symbolism which is cosmo-anthropological (rather than only anthropological as in the West) to the doctrine of the incarnation helps link it with creation, Lee argues. "The incarnation of God in human form must therefore be considered as part of the cosmic process."[60] The *yin-yang* symbolism also helps negotiate the mystery of fullness and emptying evident in passages such as the Philippians 2 hymn, to which Lee finds parallels in Taoist philosophy.[61] Similarly, this approach helps make sense of the maleness and femininity as well as the individuality and community of the Son.[62] Lee also applies this inclusive

---

56. Ibid., 61–62.
57. Ibid., 19. The methodological choice is also illustrated in the order of discussion: chap. 4 on Son, chap. 5 on Spirit, and chap. 6 on Father.
58. Ibid., 70.
59. Lee, *Theology of Change*, 98.
60. Lee, *Trinity in Asian Perspective*, 71–72 (72).
61. Ibid., 73–74.
62. Ibid., 78–82.

Asian way of thinking to the mystery of death and resurrection, a profound dialectic of death and life, life and death.[63] The undergirding principle behind all these reflections is the replacement of an "either-or" duality with a "both-and" inclusivity and the idea of *yin* and *yang* as both limiting and complementing each other, opposing as well as embracing each other. The notions of singularity and plurality provide a good example. While Christ is an individual (individuality), Christ is also community (plurality), rather than either one or the other.

What about the relation of the Son to the Father? Here Lee makes a surprising move. For him the main mistake of early Christian orthodoxy lies in its insistence on the coequality (expressed in the *homoousion* doctrine) of the Son with the Father. Building on the Christology of Emil Brunner, whose views have been suspected of subordinationism, if not Arianism, Lee surmises that nowhere does the New Testament claim the identity of the Son with the Father. The Johannine Jesus' saying that "I and the Father are one" (10:30) should not be read as meaning "I am the Father and the Father is I." Rather, Christ "is only what is manifested of God." Identifying the Father with the Son means for Lee identifying "the creator with the revealer, the Christ," which means nothing less than "deny[ing] the inexhaustible nature of the divine creativity. God as creator is more than what is manifested, and his mystery is not and will not be exhausted. He is more than the One revealed in Christ. God as creator is active where Christ is not." Consequently, "Christ is subordinate to the creator, and his work as savior and redeemer is one part of the work of God as creator."[64] This is to correct a fatal mistake in traditional theology and Christology, namely, the subsuming of creation into redemption[65] or devoting more attention to the Son than the Father.[66] For Lee, creation is the primary act of God; he understands creation as the process of ordering the existing creation (cf. Gen. 1:2). Lee sees Christ's salvific role as fighting heavenly powers and cosmic powers to bring about order. Clearly then, Christ's role as redeemer is subordinate to the Father's as creator; the hierarchical family order—which is honored in the Confucian tradition, expecting the obedience of the Son to the Father—also speaks for the subordinationist view.[67]

The *yin-yang* symbolism also makes talk about divine suffering inevitable. The mutuality and interdependency of this symbolism excludes the idea of the immunity of one member of the Trinity (Father) to the experiences of the other (Son). Therefore, Lee is not critical of patripassianism, the idea of God suffering, which was deemed heretical. The denial of patripassianism for Lee is a

63. Ibid., 82–87.
64. Lee, *Theology of Change*, 88; also Lee, *Trinity in Asian Perspective*, 88.
65. Lee, *Theology of Change*, 86–87, claims that in Christian theology the saving work has been "attributed exclusively to the Christ and the creative work to the Father. Almost all past theology disjoins the doctrine of salvation from that of creation, giving the impression that the creation was a discrete event occurring prior to salvation." So also Lee, *Trinity in Asian Perspective*, 86–87, among others.
66. Also Lee, *Trinity in Asian Perspective*, 87–88, among others.
67. Ibid., 88–89.

result of the Greek concept of *apatheia* (impassibility). Echoing Moltmann (but not mentioning him), Lee offers a corrective: "The loving God who is active in history is neither immutable nor impassible. God is a living and dynamic God who suffers for the sake of all children." Similarly, the Spirit suffers when the Son and Father suffer.[68]

The clue to the basic meaning of the Spirit in the Trinity comes from the biblical idea of *ruach* as the "wind" and "breath," parallel to the Sanskrit word *prāṇa*, which in the older Vedic literature denotes "the breath of life." The twofold biblical meaning of *ruach* is a pointer for Lee to the twofold understanding of God as Spirit both in terms of a personal and impersonal nature. As wind, Spirit represents the nonpersonal; as the breath of his creatures, the personal.[69] The same principle comes to the fore in another East Asian concept related to the Spirit, namely, ch'i. According to Lee—even though he doesn't explain it fully—in this concept, categories of personal and impersonal are resolved and transcended. The basic meaning of ch'i is the vital, creative energy, the essence of all life and all existence, similar to the Hebrew concept of *ruach*.[70]

While the Father represents masculinity, the Spirit represents femininity. The Spirit represents *yin*, receptiveness, anonymity, quiescence, and femininity.[71] The symbol of ch'i is connected with the maternal principle as well as the earth, corresponding to the Father, the symbol of heaven. A number of images and metaphors can be used of this maternal spirit, the protector and sustainer of the earth, such as weaving clothes, water, a wagon that moves a community, and so forth.[72] In the biblical traditions, the Spirit also represents transformation, such as new birth, as well as the mysterious, miraculous, and ecstatic.[73]

Even though in Trinitarian discourse the Father appears only after the Son and Spirit, the Father is the preeminent member of the Trinity. Why? Because it belongs to the nature of fatherhood that the Father is preeminent; it is a relational statement: as the Father of the Son, Father is first.[74] What about the Father's relation to the Spirit, the Mother? Lee struggles here between the Western idea of equality and his own Asian background, especially Confucianism, in which male (and thus husband) is superior to female (wife). Reluctantly, he opts for the Asian hierarchical notion and makes analogically the Father superior to the Mother/Spirit in the Trinity.[75] Father is the masculine member of the Trinity.[76]

---

68. Ibid., 91–94 (92). For an extended discussion of the Trinity in relation to suffering, see Lee, *God Suffers for Us*, chap. 3 especially. Yet the whole book consists of rebutting arguments against and offering arguments for divine passibility (against the impassibility view of classical theism).

69. Lee, *Theology of Change*, 103–4; Lee, *Trinity in Asian Perspective*, 96–97.

70. Lee, *Trinity in Asian Perspective*, 95–98.

71. Lee, *Theology of Change*, 110.

72. Lee, *Trinity in Asian Perspective*, 102–11.

73. Ibid., 111–22.

74. Ibid., 124–26.

75. Ibid., 127–30. Lee notes that in some East Asian traditions, especially in Taoism and Shamanism, mother is preeminent (p. 127). However, as a general rule, Father is preeminent.

76. Lee, *Trinity in Asian Perspective*, 136–40.

Father as the representative of heaven represents the highest moral and spiritual principles for the people of East Asia, such as origination, success, and correctness.[77]

IMAGINING THE ORDERS OF THE TRINITY

As mentioned, Lee offers a distinctive proposal as to the order of the Trinitarian members, beginning with the Son rather than with the Father as in tradition. Continuing his Trinitarian reflections from an Asian perspective, his book *Trinity in Asian Perspective* also offers an interesting re-imagination of all various possibilities available.[78] This is not meant to be a dogmatic treatise but rather a creative imagining based on familial Asian resources:

1. The Father, the Spirit, the Son: This order is distinctly Asian, based as it is on the "Asian trinity," heaven (Father), earth (Spirit, mother), and Son. It has parallels in various Asian religious images, too,[79] and it corresponds to the cosmic order, the background to the *yin-yang* symbolism.

2. The Father, the Son, the Spirit: This is the traditional Christian order of the Trinity as illustrated for example in the creeds. For Lee, this focuses on salvation and redemption, the Son being sent by the Father. Being patriarchal, it is also widely embraced by Asians.

3. The Spirit, the Father, the Son: While foreign to both biblical and Christian traditions, this is an image dear to those Asians who have lived in a family where the Mother was preeminent. It corresponds to the Taoist tradition in which mother is the most important member of the family.

4. The Spirit, the Son, the Father: As in the previous model, the Spirit, Mother, is preeminent, but the Son has taken the place of the Father as the second member. This is a fully matriarchal scheme, with mother being superior both to her husband and son. While foreign to Asians (except for Shamanism, the "religion of women," as it is called in Korea), it relates to some aspects of contemporary Western life in which youthfulness and young age are preferred over age and in which family structures are more fluid.

5. The Son, the Father, the Spirit: This model goes against the East Asian family concept and Confucian traditions by having the Son over the Father. At times, it may happen that the Son claims his independence from the father and mother. In other parts of Asia where Buddhism is

77. Ibid., 131–36.
78. Ibid., chap. 7.
79. See ibid., 153.

the dominant religion, this scheme may make sense because in India, the cradle of Buddhism, the Father renounces himself (by leaving home and becoming a monk) once the Son marries and has his own family.[80]

6. The Son, the Spirit, the Father: This is Lee's own conception. While he holds the Father as preeminent, this order "represents the existential situation of human experience."[81] The way to know Father is through the historical embodiment of God, in Jesus.

As said, this thought experiment is but an imagining of various orders in the Trinity based on human experience, especially in family life, and as such it only indirectly relates to the inner relations in the Trinity. However, there should be some kind of analogical relationship between God and human family life, and therefore utilizing familial concepts from one's own context is legitimate.[82]

A REVISION OF RAHNER'S RULE

That Lee wants to revise Rahner's rule on the basis of his understanding of reality based on *yin-yang* symbolic thinking comes as no surprise. While in principle he affirms that the economic Trinity is the immanent Trinity and vice versa, the rule has to be qualified. The economic Trinity is not identical to the immanent Trinity. He illustrates this from his own life experience. His own life and his life with his family are his life. In this respect he can say that "my own life is my life with my family." However, his own life without his family is not identical to his life with his family. "My life with my family, which corresponds to the economic Trinity, involves a new dimension of relationship with the 'other.' This relationship with others makes my life outside the family (or without the 'other'), which corresponds to the immanent Trinity." The conclusion is that if God's presence in the world is completely unaffected by the world, it is possible to conceive that the economic Trinity is the immanent Trinity and vice versa. However, this kind of "immutable and impassible God is unthinkable if God is love."[83]

There is a better way to express the relationship between the economic and immanent Trinity. Just as *yin* and *yang* always coexist without losing their distinctive identities, the economic Trinity and the immanent Trinity always coexist, but they are different. Lee puts Rahner's rule in this way: "The immanent Trinity is *in* the economic Trinity and the economic Trinity is *in* the immanent Trinity." In other words, following *yin* and *yang*, the immanent and economic Trinity are inclusive of each other but different. In this inclusive rather than identical rela-

80. See ibid., 170.
81. Ibid., 172.
82. Ibid., 175–76.
83. Ibid., 67.

tionship, the immanent Trinity is not free of the world—everything that happens in the world is part of God's "experience"—nor can the economic Trinity exclude the life of God.[84]

CRITICAL REFLECTIONS

In his preface to *The Trinity in Asian Perspective*, Lee gives counsel to his critics:

> Let me remind you that this book is written from an Asian perspective to a Western audience. Therefore, I expect that some Western readers will disagree with me in many issues that arise out of contextual differences. I will notify you from time to time that I use the Eastern paradigm to understand the Trinity, so that you should not judge me based on Western categories. As I said, what I attempt to do in this book is not to criticize or to replace the traditional Western view but to present an alternative view of the Trinity from the Asian perspective.[85]

Lee also mentions that he has tried to cite works by Western theologians as little as possible and has spent more time in reflection than in the library.[86] The preface raises several questions and, like any statement in the book, is open to critical reflections. In light of the fact that the book is meant for Western readers, denying the right of Westerners to engage in a critical dialogue sounds odd at best and patronizing at its worst. Why then has the author any right to critique the Western tradition from an Eastern perspective? What kind of dialogue is it when one party has the right to speak and critique the other, whereas the other does not? And being a Western reader, how else could I critique the proposal than from my own Western perspective? At times his prose is quite difficult to follow, and I wonder if the reference to either the *yin-yang* or (as his Asian colleague Panikkar sometimes does) to advaitic thinking is an appropriate excuse. Let me take an example: "The changelessness of God does not negate his essential nature as change but affirms the unceasingness of his changing. It is the constancy of change that makes changelessness possible, and therefore the element of changelessness is found within the change itself."[87]

Lee's method is from below,[88] from an East Asian perspective, using its cultural, religious, and philosophical resources. As such it is not only a legitimate but also a badly needed enterprise. His desire to present *an* Asian perspective is highly commendable. It adds to the diversity of emerging Asian theologies of the Trinity. Being a from-below method, it is also quite speculative and abstract.

---

84. Ibid., 67–68.
85. Ibid., 20.
86. Ibid., 12.
87. Ibid., 43.
88. Lee's method can also be called "inductive" as in Chung, *Martin Luther and Buddhism*, 237.

Even when based on East Asian resources, the author utilizes them in a highly creative way, constantly looking for correlations between the East and West. In that sense, it goes against many contemporary (Western) Trinitarian theologies that claim to be based on concrete history, be it salvation history as a principle or more directly based on a biblical text. Lee's approach is at times quite speculative and abstract.[89]

What is the relation of Lee's proposal to Christian *tradition?* He himself is somewhat ambiguous about the matter. On the one hand Lee says he has not made an effort to write either a critical study of received traditions nor occupy himself with (Western) literature dealing with tradition and contemporary theology. On the other hand he claims that he does not leave behind Christian tradition. I think this ambiguity is quite indicative of the way he presents his Asian interpretation. Clearly, he is well read in Christian traditions, both biblical and historical. Biblical materials do not play a central role in his theological construction,[90] yet occasionally he backs up his discussion with biblical references. Regarding the history of Christian reflection on the Trinity, it seems to me Lee picks and chooses. He avoids mentioning theologians by name, even the most prominent, and the only thing he does with tradition is to revisit briefly some of the creedal formulations or what he thinks are the established views.

One could easily find in Christian tradition, historical and contemporary, a lot of resources that would have helped Lee to make his case stronger and perhaps more understandable and appealing to the Western audience.[91] It is here where I want to add few comments. While Lee claims not to take up the critical task of looking at the failures and mistakes of Trinitarian theology in Christian tradition, he is doing that and at times in a way that calls for a counter-critical note. Let me take few examples. Few Christian theologians would agree with Lee's view that "in Judeo-Christian tradition God is never called *she*" and that therefore gender is a part of the Christian concept of God.[92] Nor is it true that Christian theology has excluded impersonal elements from God.[93] At times Lee borrows a concept from Christian tradition and uses it at its face value, totally neglecting the checkered history behind the term. The most striking example is the term "person";[94] Lee assumes that all agree on its meaning. On the other hand some of Lee's "discover-

---

89. Noted by commentators such as Julie Green, review of *The Trinity in Asian Perspective*, by J. Y. Lee, *Scottish Bulletin of Evangelical Theology* 17 (Spring 1999): 67.

90. Similarly ibid.

91. See also the incisive comments in Roderick T. Leupp, review of *The Trinity in Asian Perspective*, by J. Y. Lee, *Christian Century* 115 (March 1998): 266.

92. Lee, *Theology of Change*, 50.

93. Other examples of inaccurate sweeping statements regarding historical views in Christian theology could be added, such as the following. It is not true, as Lee (*Theology of Change*, 67) claims, that the importance of the Creator God has been ignored in Christian theology nor that salvific work has been "attributed exclusively" to Christ and creation to the Father (ibid., 86–87). A critical note can also be added to the claim that the Christian tradition has affirmed the theology of God as the "Unmoved Mover" (ibid., 30). Many have, but by no means has it been an uncontested view.

94. See Lee, *Theology of Change*, 50.

ies" do not seem particularly distinct to Asian theology, for example, the insistence that God embraces both maleness and femaleness.

Having said this, I also have to add a qualifying statement to my own criticism on Lee's handling of Trinitarian traditions. As Wai-Ching Angela Wong mentions in her review of *The Trinity in Asian Perspective*, Lee distinguishes himself among Asian writers in two ways. First, he presents his own views as complementary to rather than competing with Western interpretations, and second, he is not declaring his distaste for Western theology in the way many of his colleagues continue doing.[95]

Regarding tradition, Lee's relation to the *filioque* view is interesting. On the one hand he seems not to be scared of defining Trinitarian relations in a way that affirms the derivation of the Spirit from the Father and Son, yet in his imagining of various orders in the Trinity, the order that supports the *filioque* (number two in the list) is only one of the options and thus not normative.[96]

Regarding his relation to Asian traditions, some commentators have wondered if he fails to be critical of his own context and thus is in danger of uncritically subsuming Trinity into an Asian framework.[97] Shouldn't the Christian doctrine also serve a critical function, say, in relation to patriarchal cultures?[98] To the last point, I will come back momentarily.

This observation brings me to the somewhat related point of whether it is legitimate or desirable to try to affirm the existence of Trinitarian structure in religions, and even more in all of life, as Lee does. According to Lee, "The triune God is not unique to Christianity."[99] This says much more—and in my view something very different from—other sayings of Lee, namely, that he seeks only to express Trinitarian doctrine, the core of Christian faith, with the help of Asian concepts and resources.[100] Lee is ambiguous here to say the least. W.-C. Angela Wong raises significant questions to this effect, saying that Lee's effort to derive from the East Asian context the doctrine of the Trinity is "as interesting as it is questionable":

> His conclusion that "life is none other than trinitarian"[101] makes one wonder if any significance remains with the specific use of he term. While it is

95. Wai-Ching Angela Wong, review of *The Trinity in Asian Perspective*, by J. Y. Lee, *The Journal of Religion* 79, no. 2 (1999): 322–23. Another commentator disagrees and claims that Lee's proposal is plagued by the dichotomization of the "East" and "West." Kereon Gopf, review of *The Trinity in Asian Perspective*, by J. Y. Lee, *Journal of Ecumenical Studies* 34 (Fall 1997): 578.

96. The flexibility shown in Lee's theology regarding the *filioque* is appreciated by another Asian theologian, Amos Yong, *The Spirit Poured Out on All Flesh: Pentecostalism and the Possibility of Global Theology* (Grand Rapids: Baker Academic, 2005), 222.

97. See Gavin D'Costa, review of *The Trinity in Asian Perspective*, by J. Y. Lee, *Anglican Theological Review* 80, no. 4 (1998): 631.

98. Surely, many theologians concerned about women's issues will be put off by the uncritical baptizing of patriarchal Asian views into Trinitarian theology. See further Peter C. Phan, review of *The Trinity in Asian Perspective*, by J. Y. Lee, *Theological Studies* 59, no. 1 (1998): 151.

99. Lee, "Trinity: Toward an Indigenous Asian Perspective," 81.

100. Lee, *Trinity in Asian Perspective*, 15.

101. Ibid., 180.

an important endeavor for one to make sense of the doctrine of the divine Trinity in the modern context of East Asia, the attempt to convert a specific theological formulation first conceived by the early churches of the West into an interpretation of contemporary Asian thought and practice is rather suspicious. Is this an attempt mainly to defend a Christian doctrine for the sake of upholding the universality if not superiority of Christianity? Is it justified to blanket East Asia's variegated and sometimes conflicting strands of thought and life by a theological term that is entirely foreign to the culture itself? And what is achieved when such a doctrine is said to be found already everywhere in the culture and beliefs of the peoples of East Asia?[102]

All of this raises the all-important methodological question: Why focus on similarities between Christian traditions and Eastern ones but totally neglect differences?[103] Isn't that unfair to both parties? This question is all-important since in my view the attempt to build a *Christian* doctrine of the Trinity out of the Asian principle of *yin-yang* faces significant and critical challenges. Let me take up the most obvious: The symbolism of *yin-yang*—at least at the outset—represents a binitarian rather than Trinitarian structure. Consequently, Lee's attempt shares the same problem as that of process theology, namely, how "two makes three"—to use the pointed expression of Ted Peters.[104] Another Asian theologian, native Korean Paul S. Chung, who is appreciative of many aspects of Lee's Trinitarian thinking, believes the *yin-yang* is problematic since it tends to be modalistic. Chung notes that Lee cannot avoid modalism in identifying the Father (as Change) with Tao while at times also making the same identification with the Son. The end result is of course patripassianism.[105] Chung thus concludes: "Therefore, the inseparability and mutual inclusiveness of yin-yang dialectics is not able to distinguish God in the Trinity as divine Persons."[106]

Yet another challenge to the application of the symbolism of *yin-yang* in my view has to do with the difficulty in assigning any kind of personal nature to the "members" of Lee's trinity. To begin, How would we consider the Father as "Change" as personal in any way that is even distantly like "fatherhood"? This is indicative of a larger problem in Lee's theology regarding the personal nature of the Triune God. Let me take two examples. Speaking of Christ's salvific role, Lee writes in a way that smacks of a nonpersonal view of God, leading to an exhortation that is hardly appealing: "Salvation, then, means to follow the way of change without nostalgia. When Jesus said, 'I am the Way,' he was referring to the way of change. By calling us to him, Jesus calls us to be one with the change, which is the source of all changes."[107] Another example has to do with

---

102. Wong, review of *The Trinity in Asian Perspective*, 323.

103. So also ibid., 323.

104. Ted Peters, *God as Trinity: Relationality and Temporality in Divine Life* (Louisville, KY: Westminster John Knox Press, 1993), 114.

105. Chung, *Martin Luther and Buddhism*, 237. For an example of identifying the *Tao* with the Son, see Lee, *Trinity in Asian Perspective*, 73.

106. Chung, *Martin Luther and Buddhism*, 237–38.

107. Lee, *Theology of Change*, 93.

the way Lee purports to assign both personal and impersonal features to God as Spirit: he names the Spirit as "wind" and "breath" and claims that the former denotes the impersonal and the latter personal characteristics.[108] Even with qualifications, namely, that the Hebrew idea of *ruach* has the basic meaning of "breath of life," the nomenclature "breath" hardly sounds personal; especially in light of the fact that in the OT *ruach* is the life principle of all life, whether human or animal. Nor to a Western reader (for whom the book is intended) does the Asian concept of ch'i sound any more personal. A more promising way to establish the personal nature of the Spirit is the reference to "the Advocate"; it is, however, only a passing mention.[109]

Lee emphasizes the symbolic nature of the doctrine of the Trinity since God *in se* is unknowable and beyond finite human categories. He claims that therefore "we must not speak of God, which is a mystery to us," but rather "speak of our own (limited) understanding of God." The God we speak of is not identical with Godself. "Since the divine reality transcends our knowing, that which we know of this reality is always symbolic." Rather than the divine reality, the point in our speaking of the divine is about "its meaning in our lives." Any statement about God is then nothing other than "a symbolic statement about its meaning."[110] Now, what are we to make of all of this? Is this about the distinction between the immanent and economic Trinity? Or is this a nonrealistic understanding of religious language in the sense that the "object" it speaks of does not exist in "reality" but is rather an experience of religious consciousness? Lee is not quite clear about that. He rather confuses the issue by the following explanation:

> Because the divine symbol is that which not only points to but also participates in the divine reality itself, theology as a symbolic statement of the divine is meaningful. It is not a mere human imagining of the divine but a meaningful correlation of human imagination with a human experience of the divine. Experience of the divine provides the meaning of the symbol of the divine, which in turn upholds the significance of experience. Thus theology as a symbolic quest of divine reality begins with human experience rather than with a propositional statement.[111]

In my reading, he nevertheless ends up affirming the reality of God, even when unknown. While we experience the divine through experiencing God's presence in our lives—and as such need to make a distinction between our experience of God and God *in se*—"divine reality itself must be the same forever."[112] So far so good. Yet this statement also raises two questions. First, how does one know the divine reality stays the same forever once one has vehemently denied any direct

108. Ibid., 103–4.
109. Lee, *Trinity in Asian Perspective*, 95.
110. Ibid., 13.
111. Ibid., 13.
112. Ibid., 13–14.

access to the knowledge of God? Is the statement based solely on the received revelation? In Lee's view, I think that is the case.[113] The second question, more substantial, is whether the Triune God is something "beyond" time and history in a way that makes the Deity almost the kind of "God of classical theism," unmoved by anything that happens in the world, which is strongly criticized by Lee. Everything in Lee's theology speaks against it; yet it is curious that he affirms a statement like that.

Lee's Christology also raises critical questions. Christology is a crucial aspect of his Trinitarian thinking in that he begins with the Son, in contrast to tradition, which assigns the first place to the Father, or to some feminists who begin with the Spirit.[114] It raises the eyebrows of many that Lee considers the *homoousion* doctrine as erroneous. His way of supporting this view is not convincing either, based as it is on a questionable reading of the Johannine statements regarding the union between Father and Son. The saying "I and the Father are one" (John 10:30) is not to be read, as Lee surmises, as a modalistic affirmation in terms of "I am the Father and the Father is I," but rather as implying what the *homoousios* statement is saying—that Father and Son are of the same essence. Putting God as "Creator" over against Christ, the Revealed One[115] opens Lee's views to the Arian type of heresies universally rejected by Christian tradition.

As mentioned above, Lee oscillates between affirming an inclusive view of the Trinity, which then would support an equalitarian and inclusive view of humanity, including female-male relations, and on the other hand his Asian-inherited patriarchal view. It seems the *yin-yang* symbolism of inclusivity fails here: "Even in the yin-yang relationship, yang is always placed before yin in East Asian life. The *Book of Change*, for example, begins with the great yang or *chi'en* rather than the great yin or *k'un*. . . . In this respect, it has been part of East Asian thinking that yang is more prominent than yin, even though there have been various attempts to equalize it."[116]

Another procedure that raises critical questions in the minds of many theologians who advocate sexual inclusivism is Lee's way of naming Son as *yang* and Spirit as *yin*. This is exactly the kind of identification feminist theologians have

---

113. My assumption is based on statements such as the following: "It is the basic assumption here that the divine Trinity is a Christian concept of God implicit in scripture, even though the assumption can be debated by scholars. Because I believe that the divine Trinity is the core of the Christian faith, it is important for me to provide a new meaning to it through an alternative interpretation based on an East Asian Context." Lee, *Trinity in Asian Perspective*, 15.

114. Chung (Martin Luther and Buddhism, 238) claims that Lee's starting point is not christological but rather Trinity-centric because of *yin-yang*. While Chung is basically correct, I would also like to add—with reference to the very same passage in Lee (*Trinity in Asian Perspective*, 149) that Chung also cites ("The centrality of the Father is marginalized through the Spirit and is recentered in the Son. Just as the cell divides itself to create a new cell, recentering is needed in the process of creativity and change.")—that the starting point is not absolutely changed. This also comes to the fore in his imagining six different patterns of the order in the Trinity.

115. Lee, *Theology of Change*, 88.

116. Lee, *Trinity in Asian Perspective*, 129.

vehemently opposed because it reinforces the idea of maleness as something "strong" while the female is "weak." How can there be a transcending of the sexes when the Spirit is tied to the feminine and maternity and the Father is the masculine member of the Trinity? What Lee has done is to exclude the Spirit.[117] Is that really an inclusive theology, a theology of God who transcends sexes?

My last remark on Lee's Asian contextual Trinitarian theology has to do with eschatology, a topic Lee does not discuss much. He nevertheless makes some occasional parallels between the cyclical Eastern view and Judeo-Christian theology of the end. I can go a long way with Lee. For example, he quite rightly argues that neither for the East nor for biblical eschatology is the eschaton the end of all or the end of the old.[118] The new creation in biblical theology is the bringing to culmination and fulfillment of the (old) creation even when a radical transformation and judgment is in view. Yet I would like Lee to shed more light on the compatibility, if any, between the cyclical view of history that he affirms as part of the Asian worldview and the Judeo-Christian linear view of history. The doctrine of the Trinity as the structuring principle of Christian theology from creation to salvation to consummation is integrally related to the understanding of the coming of God's kingdom as the fulfillment of God's creative and saving purposes.

Lee's Asian colleague Raimundo Panikkar of India has presented a highly creative and widely debated cosmotheandric interpretation of Trinity, to which I turn next. While echoing many of the same concerns and insights, as noted in the introductory section to Asian theology, it also exhibits a number of unique features.

---

117. So also Wong, review of *The Trinity in Asian Perspective*, 323-24.
118. Lee, *Theology of Change*, 96; see also pp. 128-30.

Chapter 23

Raimundo Panikkar

A Cosmotheandric Mystery of the Trinity

THE COSMOTHEANDRIC STRUCTURE OF REALITY

If Karl Barth deserves the honor of being the one who stirred up the general interest in the Trinity in contemporary theology, Raimundo Panikkar should be commended for his pioneering role in relating the Trinity to other religions. Indeed, he was the first one to see the significance of this distinctive Christian doctrine for how Christianity relates to other religions. Radically different from typical pluralists who tend to see Trinity as a major obstacle to establishing relations to other faiths, Panikkar made this doctrine a major asset of his theology in general and the theology of religions in particular.[1]

The other commonality with Barth relates to the extreme challenge of expositing and evaluating Panikkar's views on any topic, the Trinity certainly, that being the major structuring principle of his thought. The reasons for this challenge are

---

1. "He is the 'exception that proves the rule, a pluralist who *does* invoke the Trinity and who believes it to be at the heart of all human religions.'" Kevin J. Vanhoozer, *The Trinity in a Pluralistic Age: Theological Essays on Culture and Religion* (Grand Rapids: Eerdmans, 1997), 58, italics in the text.

many, including the fact that he is one of the most prolific writers among contemporary students of religion and theology. Furthermore, his writing career
encompasses so many different areas—he holds doctorates in three fields!—from
theology to religion to philosophy to culture to science, to mention the most typical ones. The fact that he is multilingual and draws on many cultures of the East
and West and the learning of these cultures does not make the task easier. The
often quoted autobiographical comment according to which he "left" Europe as
a Christian, "found" himself as a Hindu, and "returned" as a Buddhist, fittingly
illustrates his diverse background and the varied orientations he utilizes.[2] A
Catholic priest and theologian, born to a Spanish Roman Catholic mother and
a Hindu father, Panikkar places himself at the confluence of the four rivers:
Hindu, Christian, Buddhist, and secular.[3]

The underlying notion of Panikkar's theological vision in general and Trinitarian understanding in particular is presented in his neologism "cosmotheandrism." The term is created from two terms meaning "God" and "human
person,"[4] combined with the term referring to the cosmos. Whatever else "cosmotheandrism" means, it has reference to the coming together of God, humanity, and the world. Panikkar gives this definition: "The cosmotheandric principle
could be stated by saying that the divine, the human and the earthly—however
we may prefer to call them—are the three irreducible dimensions which constitute the real, i.e., any reality inasmuch as it is real."[5] Or, "There is no God without Man and the World. There is no Man without God and the World. There is
no World without God and Man."[6] In other words, in Panikkar's vision the cosmotheandric principle expresses the fundamental structure of reality in terms of
the intimate interaction of God, humankind, and the world or cosmos. There is
no hierarchy, no dualism; one of the three does not dominate or take precedence.

A key insight for Panikkar is that Trinity, while a distinctively Christian way
of speaking of cosmotheandrism, is not an exclusively Christian reality. "It simply is an unwarranted overstatement to affirm that the trinitarian concept of the
Ultimate, and with it the whole of reality, is an exclusive Christian insight of

2. Raimundo Panikkar, *The Intrareligious Dialogue* (New York: Paulist Press, 1978), 2.

3. Raimundo Panikkar, *The Unknown Christ of Hinduism* (London: Darton, Longman & Todd,
1964), 30. A fine, up-to-date discussion by a number of leading scholars from various persuasions
concerning Panikkar's thought is Joseph Prabhu, ed., *The Intercultural Challenge of Raimon Panikkar*
(Maryknoll, NY: Orbis Books, 1996).

4. The term has roots especially in Eastern theology (Dionysius the Areopagite and Maximus the
Confessor). It was related to the two "energies" in the person of Jesus Christ in his saving work; deity
and humanity are joined together in his person.

5. Raimundo Panikkar, *The Cosmotheandric Experience: Emerging Religious Consciousness*, edited,
with introduction, by Scott Eastham (Maryknoll, NY: Orbis Books, 1993), ix. Elsewhere he puts it this
way: "There is a kind of perichoresis, 'dwelling within one another,' of these three dimensions of Reality, the Divine, the Human and the Cosmic—the I, the you and the it." R. Panikkar, "The Myth of
Pluralism: The Tower of Babel—A Meditation on Non-Violence," *Cross Currents* 29, no. 2 (1979): 214.

6. Kajsa Ahlstrand, *Fundamental Openness: An Enquiry into Raimundo Panikkar's Theological Vision
and Its Presuppositions*, Studia Missionalia Upsaliensia 57 (Uppsala: Uppsala University, 1993), 134.

revelation."[7] Indeed, the Trinity is hardly understood by Christianity, and therefore a real appreciation of its meaning and significance requires constant interaction with other religions. Christianity can learn from others, but it also has a significant role to play in leading "to the plenitude and hence to the conversion of all religions."[8] In the final analysis, the end of this process (and the goal of Christianity) is "humanity's common good." Christianity "simply incarnates the primordial and original traditions of humankind."[9]

Before entering the exposition and evaluation of his Trinitarian doctrine, it is helpful to note that in his Christology Panikkar has a strong pluralistic bent. Especially in his significantly revised version of *The Unknown Christ of Hinduism* in 1981, he moved definitely toward a pluralistic version of Christology. In that book he rejects all notions of Christianity's superiority over or fulfillment of other religions by arguing that the world and our subjective experience of the world have radically changed since the Christian doctrine concerning Christ was first formulated. Panikkar's revised Christology also builds on the cosmotheandric principle: "Christ is . . . a living symbol for the totality of reality: human, divine, cosmic."[10] As such, Christ represents an intimate and complete unity between the divine and the human. The meaning of the confession "Christ is God the Son, the Logos" is that Christ is both symbol and substance of this nondualistic unity between God and humanity.

A methodological note is also needed to gain a proper perspective on Panikkar's highly distinctive theology of the Trinity. This can be best expressed with the term coined by Everett Cousins, "advaitic Trinitarianism."[11] The Hindu term "advaita" means "nonduality" (literally, not two). This notion, of course, belongs together with theandric nondualism. According to Panikkar, there "are not two realities: God and man (or the world). . . . Reality is theandric; it is our way of looking that causes reality to appear to us sometimes under one aspect and sometimes under another because our vision shares in both."[12] Applied to the ancient problem of unity and diversity in the Trinitarian God, the advaitic principle implies that Father and Son are not two, but they are not one either; it is the Spirit who unites and distinguishes them.[13]

7. Raimundo Panikkar, *The Trinity and the Religious Experience of Man: Icon-Person-Mystery* (Maryknoll, NY: Orbis Books / London: Darton, Longman & Todd, 1973), viii.

8. Ibid., 4.

9. Raimundo Panikkar, "The Jordan, the Tiber and the Ganges: Three Kairological Moments of Christic Self-consciousness," in *The Myth of Christian Uniqueness: Toward a Pluralistic Theology of Religions,* ed. John Hick and Paul F. Knitter (Maryknoll, NY: Orbis Books, 1987), 102.

10. Raimundo Panikkar, *The Unknown Christ of Hinduism,* rev. ed. (London: Darton, Longman & Todd, 1981), 27. All subsequent references to this book cite the 1981 edition unless otherwise indicated.

11. Everett H. Cousins, "Panikkar's Advaitic Trinitarianism," in *The Intercultural Challenge of Raimon Panikkar,* ed. Josef Prabhu (Maryknoll, NY: Orbis Books, 1996), 119–301; for the term "advaitic," see especially p. 120.

12. Panikkar, *Trinity and the Religious Experience,* 75.

13. Ibid., 62.

FATHER, SON, AND SPIRIT
IN AN "ADVAITIC TRINITARIANISM"

For Panikkar, not only is the Trinity an indispensable heritage of Christianity not to be relegated to the margins for the sake of interfaith dialogue, but it is even more: a concept that can be found in all religions, though taking various forms. Trinity is not a specifically Christian idea; rather, Trinity is "the junction where the authentic spiritual dimensions of all religions meet."[14]

In his small yet important book *The Trinity and the Religious Experience of Man* (1973) Panikkar develops his Trinitarian theology on the basis of his cosmotheandric vision. He regards the term "Trinitarian" as synonymous with [cosmo]theandric.[15] The reason Trinitarian—cosmotheandric—language is appropriate even in a nonexclusive theology of religions is that it genuinely reflects the structure of reality. The doctrine of the Trinity is not a forced concept. Rather, Panikkar speaks of "the intuition of the threefold structure of reality, of the triadic oneness existing on all levels of consciousness and of reality, of the Trinity." In other words, "the Trinity is the acme of a truth that permeates all realms of being and consciousness."[16]

Panikkar's cosmotheandric Trinitarian vision goes beyond the contours of classical Christian theology, yet builds on it creatively by utilizing some key insights from Asian spiritualities. This becomes clear when he attributes new meanings to the members of the Trinity. For Panikkar, the Father is "Nothing." What can be said about the Father is "nothing"; this is the apophatic way, the way to approach the Absolute without name.[17] There is no "Father" in himself; the "being of the Father" is "the Son." In the incarnation, *kenōsis,* the Father gives himself totally to the Son. Thus the Son is "God."[18]

Panikkar believes this understanding is the needed bridge between Christianity and Buddhism as well as advaitic Hinduism. What kenosis (self-emptying) is for Christianity, nirvana and *sunyata* are for these two other religions. "God is total Silence. This is affirmed by all the world religions. One is led towards the Absolute and in the end one finds nothing, because there *is* nothing, not even Being."[19]

"It is the Son of God who is, and so is God," Panikkar affirms.[20] In that sense the Son is the only "person" of the Trinity. For this statement to make sense, Panikkar notes that the term "person," when used of the internal life of the Trinity, is an equivocal term that has different meanings in each case. Since the "Father" is a different kind of "person" compared to the "Son," and the "Spirit"

14. Ibid., 42.
15. Ibid., 71.
16. Ibid., xi.
17. Ibid., 46.
18. Ibid., 45–47.
19. Ibid., 52.
20. Ibid., 51.

differs in nature from both, it is not advisable to use the same term, "person," for these different meanings.[21] That qualified sense makes it understandable when Panikkar says that there is in fact "no God" in Christian theology in the generic sense of the term. There is only "the God of Jesus Christ"; thus, the God of theism is always the "Son," the only one with whom human beings can establish a relationship.[22]

What about the Spirit? The Spirit is "immanence." To make more concrete the meaning of the Spirit as immanence is challenging (acknowledged in all theologies, for that matter): "Immanence is incapable of revealing itself, for that would be a contradiction of terms; an immanence which needs to manifest itself, is no longer immanent." Panikkar uses images, and paints pictures to say something more about the Spirit: The Father is the source of the river, the Son the river that flows from the source, and the Spirit the ocean in which the river ends.[23]

This is the basic shape of the Trinitarian doctrine in Panikkar. Recognizing that for him Trinitarianism is not only a doctrine but also an underlying structure of all reality, including religions, it is no wonder that he goes beyond the mere exposition of how Father, Son, and Spirit can be understood. One of Panikkar's most distinctive contributions to the Christian theology of religions is the way he speaks of three different, and yet complementary spiritualities among world religions. Each of these three spiritualities has its distinctive orientation, based on some aspects of the Trinitarian vision.[24]

TRINITY AND RELIGIONS

It has already become clear that Panikkar envisions a coming together of world religions. Yet his pluralistic vision, based on the doctrine of the Trinity, is radically different from the typical pluralistic idea of a "rough parity" among religions. Trinity speaks for diversity, not for uniformity or denial of differences.[25] "The mystery of the Trinity is the ultimate foundation for pluralism."[26] And "In the Trinity a true encounter of religions takes place, which results, not in a vague fusion or mutual dilution, but in an authentic enhancement of all the religious and even cultural elements that are contained in each."[27] Instead of pluralism,

---

21. See further ibid., 51–52.

22. Ibid., 52.

23. Ibid., 63.

24. Space does not allow an exposition here. Interested readers can find the basic outline in ibid., chap. 1; see also Veli-Matti Kärkkäinen, *Trinity and Religious Pluralism: The Doctrine of the Trinity in the Christian Theology of Religions* (Aldershot, UK: Ashgate, 2004), chap. 8.

25. As A. S. Raj (*A New Hermeneutic of Reality: Raimon Panikkar's Cosmotheandric Vision* [Bern: Peter Lang, 1998], 39) puts it, "In the pluralistic approach of Panikkar, differences between cultures and religions are neither absolutized nor ignored but they are transformed into creative polarities."

26. Panikkar, "The Jordan, the Tiber and the Ganges," 110.

27. Panikkar, *Trinity and the Religious Experience*, 42.

Panikkar prefers the term "parallelism": all religions run parallel to meet only in the Ultimate, at the end of time.[28]

Furthermore, for Panikkar, the Christian understanding of the Trinity is in need of deepening from other religions; at the same time, Christianity also contributes to a fuller understanding of that vision among other religions. Exclusivism is avoided by maintaining that Christianity, along with other religions, can never absolutize its current historical understanding. Panikkar firmly maintains that religions need each other and are mutually dependent.[29] His cosmotheandric vision sees the need to affirm diversity and posit mutuality on the basis of Trinitarian relations. All attempts toward universalization, so prevalent in Western culture as he sees it, are anathema to Panikkar.[30]

One term Panikkar uses to speak of the diversity and complementarity is "perichoresis." For Panikkar, the idea of perichoresis implies the mutual conditioning and transformation of religions in their diversity on the way to convergence.[31] Another implication of the perichoresis concept is that plurality as such is not a problem, but rather an asset. The goal of pluralistic theologies is not to water down or dismiss plurality but to enhance it. Therefore dialogue matters; through interaction religions condition and enrich each other. Each religion comes out of the encounter with a deeper sense of its own identity, yet with the awareness of needing the others.

Finally, in a very bold move, Panikkar places the world's religious traditions interior to the Godhead and depicts them as pluralistic self-revelations of divinity. "The Trinitarian life is one of pluralism in oneness, or distinction in unity, that is constantly replenishing itself."[32]

CRITICAL REFLECTIONS

Panikkar's significance for the development of Christian Trinitarian thinking cannot be underestimated even if it also faces great challenges. In my understanding, the main contribution is elevating the doctrine of the Trinity to a central place not only in Christian theology in general but in the theology of religions in particular. This is a healthy, badly needed corrective in the midst of so much cheap talk about the irrelevance and problematic nature of this crucial Christian

---

28. See further Panikkar, *Intrareligious Dialogue.*
29. See further Ahlstrand, *Fundamental Openness,* 184.
30. See further B. J. Lanzetta, "The Mystical Basis of Panikkar's Thought," in Prabhu, *Intercultural Challenge of Raimon Panikkar,* 97.
31. I agree with Ahlstrand (*Fundamental Openness,* 184) that this is not what the term "perichoresis" means in Christian Trinitarian or christological discourse, and so Panikkar uses the term idiosyncratically. Terminology aside, the idea itself is something worth entertaining since it takes seriously the historical form and developments of religions in God's economy, an idea not far from Pannenberg (even though Pannenberg does not affirm pluralism in the way Panikkar does).
32. Lanzetta, "Mystical Basis," 95.

doctrine. With his bold move, Panikkar has offered a major critique of pluralism. The implications of his Trinitarian doctrine, especially the insistence on diversity-in-unity, is another major asset. Furthermore, the fact that he has been able not only to "contextualize" the doctrine but also to relate it to his own Asian context and religiosity is an admirable achievement.

Another asset of Panikkar's Trinitarian theology is that he genuinely wrestles with the ancient problem of one-and-many. Here the Asian advaitic thinking, an affirmation of nondualism, is of help. Panikkar is hardly able to solve the problem that has plagued philosophy from of old, but he sheds some light on the topic. Both Trinitarian doctrine and advaita do desire to go beyond both monism and dualism. The Father and the Son are not two, but they are not one either: it is the Spirit who unites and distinguishes them.[33] Even with my reservations about the usefulness of the advaitic principle, I still believe the ancient question of one-and-many needs constant attention, especially when considering the relation of the Trinity to the church.

What are the challenges for Panikkar's Trinitarianism? Elsewhere I have provided a more comprehensive assessment of Panikkar's Trinitarian doctrine, from the perspective of the Christian theology of religions.[34] I therefore limit my critical comments here to some key aspects of his vision of the Trinity.

The first comment has to do with his Christology, a topic critical to any Trinitarian doctrine, but especially for Panikkar's to whom the Son is the "real" God after the kenosis of the Father. While there is not necessarily a compelling reason to make a total identification between Jesus and Christ, neither is it possible to make the kind of separation that Panikkar's 1981 edition of the *Unknown Christ of Hinduism* posits. The approach of the first edition (1964) is healthier theologically in that it leans toward a dialogue but still holds on to the uniqueness of Jesus when defining Christ, while not totally exhausting all that Christ is. The main problem with his later approach is that he expands the Christic principle—as he calls it—beyond the figure of Jesus of Nazareth, which has serious implications for the doctrine of the Trinity. According to Christian theology, one does not have access to Christ, at least in the biblical-historical sense, apart from the person of Jesus of Nazareth. And while it is of course possible to "expand the Christic principle," do we still have the Christian Trinity when historical and theological criteria are left behind? Panikkar's Christology and thus Trinitarianism seems to share the typical weaknesses of "theocentric" approaches to the theology of religions, according to which the significance of Jesus is to be diminished in favor of the concept of God. This move, however, while typical of pluralistic approaches, works against the Trinitarian idea of equality, unity-in-diversity of three divine persons. Holding on to the Trinitarian doctrine (even in Panikkar's unique way) seems very problematic if the Christic principle is divorced from history and salvation history. Especially in light of the fact that in Panikkar's Trinitarian doctrine the Son is the whole focus of deity, his pluralistically constructed Christology creates internal contradiction. Sometimes Panikkar seems to support his Christology with reference to the "mystical" or "Mystery," or to the idea of advaitism or nonduality, but the concrete meaning intended by this kind of appeal is vague.

Regarding the foundational question as to whether Panikkar's revised vision of cosmotheandrism really represents a Christian doctrine of the Trinity, one needs to tackle the question he puts to himself: "Why do I persist, in still speaking of the Trinity when, on the one hand, the idea that I give of it goes beyond the traditional idea by Christianity?"[35] Without really giving substantial answers, he lets it suffice to insist on the continuity with Christian tradition.[36] His version of Trinitarianism, however, certainly elicits serious questions.

Panikkar's interpretation of the Johannine saying that no one comes to the Father except through the Son (John 14:6)[37] seems to go beyond any exegetical warrants. He reads this verse as meaning that only the Son exists. In contrast to his interpretation, Christian theology has understood from this saying not that the Father does not exist, but that the only way to know the Father is through the Son sent by his Father. Panikkar's motive here is to relate the Father of Christianity to the Godhead in the Buddhist concept of nirvana and *sunyata*[38]—but I fear that he is mispresenting both Buddhist and Christian sources. Let me quote my assessment from elsewhere:

> Whatever similarities there might be with the basically a-theistic, nonpersonalist Buddhist notion of *nirvana,* in my opinion, no amount of stretching of the meaning of the concepts could make it compatible with the personalist, theistic notion of the Father in Christian faith. This is to confuse the way we talk about God (in apophatic terms) with how God exists (if in Buddhism there is any kind of concept of the divinity). Rather than trying to connect Buddhism and Christianity with the help of this most suspect twisting of terms, Panikkar should rather be faithful to his foundational idea of radical differences between religions and their concepts of the divine. So I think Panikkar has committed the most typical sin of pluralism (of which he is often critical), namely, dismissing the real differences among religions and their conceptions by assuming a similarity behind the terminology. A strong case could be made for the claim that the conceptions of the divine in Buddhism and Christianity are incompatible; that should be taken as an issue to deal with in the interfaith dialogue rather than positing a superficial similarity. I am not saying that bridges could not be built between the trinitarian conception of the deity in Christianity

---

35. Panikkar, *Trinity and the Religious Experience,* 43.
36. See the serious reservations expressed by Ahlstrand, *Fundamental Openness,* 152–56 especially.
37. Panikkar, *Trinity and the Religious Experience,* 47.
38. Ibid.

and Buddhism; what I am saying is that Panikkar's version does not appeal to me, neither from the Christian nor from the Buddhist perspective.[39]

Equally problematic is Panikkar's interpretation of the role and meaning of the Son in his Trinitarian vision. In Christian tradition the Son is not the focus. Thus, ironically, Panikkar's version of Trinitarianism is too "christocentric": in the biblical canon, especially in the Gospel of John, it is made clear that even the Son's equality to the Father never implies taking the place of the Father. On the contrary, as Pannenberg and others have shown, the point of the New Testament incipient references to the subsequently formulated Trinitarian understanding of God is to emphasize the voluntary submission of the Son to the lordship of the Father.

I could also name other problems and challenges in Panikkar's theology, especially one having to do with the question of the truth. While I think it is appropriate for him as a theologian drawing from Asian wells to utilize the thought forms available in those cultures, I also fear that his quite uncritical use of the advaitic principle becomes problematic. It seems to me that an advaitic principle is called forth whenever serious logical or other intellectual problems are encountered. Resorting to either the advaitic or mystical principle can become an exercise in avoiding the core problem. G. J. Larson, in a recent appraisal of Panikkar's pluralism, puts this basic problem in perspective by saying that Panikkar's "notion of pluralism becomes unintelligible in a two-valued (truth-falsehood) logic, inasmuch as the principle of the excluded middle is violated," and therefore, "the notion of pluralism so formulated is as self-defeating as any formulation of relativism and as tripped up by the problem of self-referentiality as any formulation of universalism or absolutism."[40] Panikkar acknowledges this dilemma by saying, "We cannot, by definition, logically overcome a pluralistic situation without breaking the very principle of noncontradiction and denying our own set of codes: intellectual, moral, esthetic and so forth".[41] Any kind of universal theory, in Panikkar's opinion, denies pluralism; he opts for the latter.[42] But, of course, Panikkar's own notion of pluralism cannot be a universal theory, and therefore truth itself is pluralistic.[43] Panikkar, however, no more than any other relativistically oriented thinker, cannot live up to his philosophical claims to

---

39. Kärkkäinen, *Trinity and Religious Pluralism*, 138. I also fear that Panikkar's claim to apophaticism is forced: what Eastern Christianity (and some strands of Western Christianity) have meant with apophaticism is not the virtual "non-existence" of the Father but rather the principle of negativity regarding statements about divinity; this apophatic principle applies as much to the Son and the Spirit as to the Father.

40. G. Larson, "Contra Pluralism," in Prabhu, *Intercultural Challenge of Raimon Panikkar*, 72.

41. R. Panikkar, "Invisible Harmony: A Universal Theory of Religion or a Cosmic Confidence in Reality?" in *Toward a Universal Theory of Religion*, ed. L. Swidler (Maryknoll, NY: Orbis Books, 1987), 118–53 (125).

42. Ibid., 132.

43. See Larson, "Contra Pluralism," 77.

relativism. His position, like that of many other pluralists, makes certain propositional claims and thus requires a propositional network and operates with truth-falsehood logic.[44] I think Panikkar confuses rather than clarifies the truth issue by his statement that "to understand is to be convinced," as the title of one of his essays puts it.[45] What Panikkar means by this is that rather than positing common, taken-for-granted criteria of meaning and validity on the "religious" plane, understanding what a statement means is the same as acknowledging its truth. If so, one cannot really understand the views of another if one does not share them. But how do we then assess the truthfulness (in any traditional sense of the term) of religious statements?[46]

One more question that I want to present to Panikkar concerns his understanding of the nature of salvation and the religious ends in religions. Panikkar postulates a coming convergence of religions: Does that mean envisioning one single end for all? Or different goals for different religions? A related question, one that Panikkar has not really dealt with much in his writings, is the question of the relation of the Trinity to existing religions of the world.[47]

44. See further ibid., 81.

45. R. Panikkar, "Verstehen als Uberzeugtsein," in *Neue Anthropologie,* ed. H.-G. Gadamer and P. Vogler, Philosophische Anthropologie 7 (Stuttgart: Thieme, 1975), 134.

46. For an incisive assessment of Panikkar's view of truth, see D. J. Krieger, "Methodological Foundations for Interreligious Dialogue," in Prabhu, *Intercultural Challenge of Raimon Panikkar,* 201–3.

47. Everett Cousins ("Panikkar's Advaitic Trinitarianism," 128–29), based on personal conversations with Panikkar in the 1960s, outlines the relationship in this way: Buddhism is the religion of the silence of the Father; Judaism, Christianity, and Islam, religions of the revelation of the Son; and Hinduism, the religion of the unity of the Spirit. Does this vision, then, entail a common goal for all? If so, how is the unity of the Triune God to be maintained? According to classical Trinitarian canons, *ad extra* Trinitarian persons always work together: positing different ends for the religion of the Father from that of the Son or Spirit would compromise the very basics of Trinitarianism, an issue I have also raised regarding Heim's proposal.

C. The Trinity in African Perspectives

Chapter 24

The African Context
for Trinitarian Reflections

FEATURES OF THE AFRICAN WORLDVIEW

Even though Andrew Walls has recently claimed that "anyone who wishes to undertake serious study of Christianity these days needs to know something about Africa,"[1] systematic theological reflection on God has not paid much attention to how African theologies and spiritualities have challenged classical theism and contemporary God-talk.[2] John Pobee has argued: "If there is to be a serious and deep communication and rooting of the gospel of Christ, the African stamp will have to replace the European stamp."[3]

Can anything general be said concerning the "African worldview" as background to God-talk in the midst of literally thousands of ethnic groups and languages? Understandably, scholarly assessments vary. Yet it is reasonable to assume

1. Andrew Walls, "Eusebius Tries Again," *International Bulletin of Missionary Research* 24, no. 3 (2000): 105.
2. See further Kwesi Dickson, "African Theology: Origin, Methodology and Content," *Journal of Religious Thought* [Washington] 30, no. 2 (1975): 37.
3. John Pobee, *Toward an African Theology* (Nashville: Abingdon Press, 1979), 17.

some basic orientations are shared by most African cultures, which have shaped and been shaped by traditional religions, and in turn have shaped their Christian interpretations of God. Features routinely assigned to the African context include these elements:[4]

- In Africa religion permeates all of life. In the words of John Mbiti, "There is no formal distinction between the sacred and the secular" or between "the spiritual and material areas of life."[5]
- The search for harmony and well-being is based on the order of creation secured by God and the ancestors. Harmony is affirmed even when facing life's fears and problems.
- The reality of spirits is affirmed all over in Africa. The visible world is "enveloped in the invisible spirit world."[6]
- Life and world, including humanity,[7] are governed by God, the ancestors, and (other) spirits. In Mbiti's study of over three hundred peoples in Africa, all had some notion of God as the supreme being.[8]
- Ancestors are regarded as real powers, created by God to mediate his power. The veneration and worship of ancestors does not compromise the basically monotheistic orientation of most African religions.
- A "this-worldly" orientation is one of the best-known features of African religions. This does not exclude the other-worldly reality; rather, reli-

---

4. Veli-Matti Kärkkäinen, *The Doctrine of God: A Global Introduction* (Grand Rapids: Baker Academic, 2004), 245–46. For a concise survey, see William Dyrness, *Learning about Theology from the Third World* (Grand Rapids: Zondervan, 1990), 43–52. Charles Nyamiti, *African Tradition and the Christian God*, Spearhead 49 (Eldoret, Kenya: Gaba Publications, 1978), 44, summarizes in four statements: (1) dynamism and vitalism; (2) solidarity, totality, and participation; (3) the sacred; and (4) anthropocentrism.

5. John S. Mbiti, *African Religions and Philosophy* (London: Heinemann, 1969), 2. Similarly, Gerhardus Cornelis Oosthuizen, "The Place of Traditional Religion in Contemporary South Africa," in *African Traditional Religion in Contemporary Society*, ed. Jacob K. Olupona (New York: Paragon House, 1991), 40–41. Derek B. Mutungu has argued that on the basis of their alternative worldview, Africans see spiritual and physical beings as real entities that interact with each other in time and space. These African Christians reject both the secularist worldview as well as missionaries' Western conceptions of reality and spirit. Orthodoxy has left Christians helpless in real life, and so an alternative pneumatology is needed that can relate to needs other than the spiritual alone. Derek B. Mutungu, "A Response to M. L. Daneel," in *All Together in One Place: Theological Papers from the Brighton Conference on World Evangelization*, ed. H. D. Hunter and P. D. Hocken (Sheffield: Sheffield Academic Press, 1993), 96–126, 127–31.

6. Tokunboh Adeyemo, "Unapproachable God: The High God of African Traditional Religion," in *The Global God: Multicultural Evangelical Views of God*, ed. Aida Besançon Spencer and William David Spencer (Grand Rapids: Baker Books, 1998), 130–31.

7. The Bantu concept *ubuntu* or *ubuntunse* describes what it means to be human. At first it was applied only to black people; after the advent of the Westerners, it now applies to all humanity. See further Joe M. Kapolyo, *The Human Condition: Christian Perspectives through African Eyes* (Downers Grove, IL: InterVarsity Press, 2005), 35–40; for traditional African anthropology from a Christian perspective, see also chap. 4.

8. Dyrness, *Learning about Theology from the Third World*, 44; Mbiti, *African Religions and Philosophy*, 29.

gions are brought to bear on this life and these particular people.[9] An African understanding of "salvation" thus encompasses the visible and invisible worlds.[10]

- Communality and participation are key values in all African cultures.[11] "Communality, relationality, and fundamental interconnection underlie the African mode of seeing and being in the world."[12]
- Life is gift from God.[13] Life is therefore sacred. Yet there is no separation between the "secular" and sacred as is typical of the West.[14]
- Holistic in its approach, the African conception of life does not make distinctions but regards all life as constituting an undivided entity, whether social, psychological, or spiritual. Physical life is not something to be abhorred but something to be celebrated and honored. Physical life can be considered a dimension of religious faith and patrimony.

While understanding traditional African cultural and religious beliefs and customs is necessary for appropriating theology from an African perspective, it is also true that "[t]he intellectual and cultural atmosphere of today's Africa is marked by an encounter with Western influence."[15] As a result,

African traditional cultural patterns are challenged and Africans have to determine which of the new influences are desirable, and in which form, while attempting to preserve their African identities. However, traditional cultures themselves also need to be re-evaluated in the light of modern needs. . . . African theology in the written academic form is one way of answering the call and clarifying the situation."[16]

According to Bénézet Bujo, with all the positive developments in African theology, there is also a danger: the tendency of theology to dwell exclusively on the African cultural heritage:

It is of course true that this heritage must be one aspect of a genuinely African theology, and that any attempt to incarnate the Christian message

9. See further Cyril C. Okorocha, "Religious Conversion in Africa: Its Missiological Implications," *Mission Studies* 9.2:18 (1992): 168–81.
10. See further Cyril Okorocha, "The Meaning of Salvation: An African Perspective," in *Emerging Voices in Global Christian Theology,* ed. William A. Dyrness (Grand Rapids: Zondervan, 1994), 59–92.
11. See further Kapolyo, *Human Condition,* 40–44.
12. A. Okechukwu Ogbonnaya, *On Communitarian Divinity: An African Interpretation of the Trinity* (St. Paul: Paragon House, 1998), 1.
13. See further Diane Stinton, "Africa, East and West," in *An Introduction to Third World Theologies,* ed. John Parratt (Cambridge: Cambridge University Press, 2004), 120–21.
14. Mbiti, *African Religions and Philosophy,* 2.
15. Mika Vähäkangas, *In Search of Foundations for African Catholicism: Charles Nyamiti's Theological Method* (Leiden/Boston/Köln: Brill, 1999), 1.
16. Ibid.

in African culture must take it into account. However, while this tendency speaks of understanding the faith, . . . it ignores the contemporary African context. One must therefore ask whether such a theology can speak seriously of either understanding the faith or of incarnating the message of Christ today.[17]

Many African Christologies, says J. Onaiyekan, "are so concerned with the past cultures of Africa that they become irrelevant to our contemporary African needs and concerns." Consequently, it "is possible to end up in a sort of exotic archaeological theology, which may perhaps fascinate foreigners, but has nothing relevant to say to the day-to-day life of our Christians."[18]

A critical factor of the African religious context is the tension between the persistent and growing influence of traditional religious beliefs and the conservative, often fundamentalist version of Christianity brought by Western missionaries.[19]

A COMMUNAL LIFE

All observers of the African context agree that community, communalism, and participation are key features of those cultures.[20] John Pobee reinterprets the famous saying of Descartes: "Whereas Descartes spoke for Western man when he said, 'Cogito ergo sum,'—I think, therefore I exist—Akan man's ontology is 'Cognatus ergo sum'—I am related by blood, therefore I exist, or I exist because I belong to a family."[21] This reminds us of Mbiti's statement: "I am because we are, and since we are, therefore I am."[22]

So deep is the sense of the community in the African context that the theologian A. Okechukwu Ogbonnaya, whose Trinitarian theology will be studied in chapter 26, can say, "My belief in African community was formed—long before I heard the word 'theology'—by a communal experience of belonging among my people and various African peoples."[23] For Africans, unlike those in the West and many other cultures, the sense of community is all-embracing; to quote again

---

17. Bénézet Bujo, African Theology in Its Social Context (Maryknoll, NY: Orbis Books, 1992), 15.

18. John Onaiyekan, "Christological Trends in Contemporary African Theology," in Constructive Christian Theology in the Worldwide Church, ed. William R. Barr (Grand Rapids: Eerdmans, 1997), 366.

19. See further Dickson, "African Theology," 34–45; and John Parratt, Reinventing Christianity: African Theology Today (Grand Rapids: Eerdmans/Trenton, NJ: Africa World Press, 1995), chap. 1. The harshest pronouncement of the irrelevancy of traditional Christian theology to the African context has come from F. Eboussi Bolanga; see his Christianity without Fetishes (Maryknoll, NY: Orbis Books, 1984); "The African Search for Identity," in The Churches of Africa: Future Prospects, ed. C. Geffre and B. Luneau (New York: Seabury Press, 1977), 26–34.

20. Among others, see Pobee, Toward an African Theology, chap. 3; Stinton, "Africa, East and West," 129–32.

21. Pobee, Toward an African Theology, 49.

22. Mbiti, African Religions and Philosophy, 106.

23. Ogbonnaya, On Communitarian Divinity, vii.

from Ogbonnaya, it includes "the ancestors, spirits, and other beings within both my immediate cosmos and beyond. I was taught that I was connected with all and the All was connected to me."[24] Ogbonnaya takes as an example the Igbos of West Africa, to whom community exists as a spiritual bond uniting people in ways that extend beyond distance or even death.[25] In that sense, the idea of leaving one's community does not make sense to Africans since community cannot be broken or destroyed by anything.[26] While community is an idea not unknown elsewhere, what makes the African understanding of it so distinctive is the fact that it not only transcends the limits of close family ties but also time and eternity. Consequently, for Africans, the community consists of "many individuals in one spiritual bond."[27] An outsider may gain the impression that the African ethos is so communal that the individuality of the person is negated. This is not so. According to Ogbannaya, the conception of the community among Africans has the capacity of holding together the individual and the community.[28] This is an idea to which we will return when looking at Ogbonnaya's theology of the Trinity.

There is an interesting dynamic here. Even though for Africans the face-to-face encounter is, as Ogbonnaya says, a "fundamental philosophical assumption," the existence of community depends on more than just physical face-to-face contact. It is about spiritual ties to the community.[29]

"SHADE-TREE THEOLOGY"

The leading scholar of the history of Christianity in Africa, Andrew Walls, speaks of a "new church" arising in Africa. According to him, the African church represents a fourth dimension of Christianity along with Catholicism, Protestantism, and Orthodoxy. Its uniqueness lies in its capacity to combine elements of all of those older traditions, new pentecostal/charismatic spiritualities, and emerging independent, often locally colored beliefs and practices. Walls points to this as "the standard Christianity of the present age."[30] Speaking of the importance of academic theology for interpreting the ever-changing African situation, Vähäkangas makes an important note: "The major part of African theology, however, takes place outside of lecture-halls and libraries, in

24. Ibid.
25. Ibid., 4.
26. Ibid., 8.
27. Josiah Royce, *The Problem of Christianity* (Chicago: University of Chicago Press, 1968), 133, as quoted in Ogbonnaya, *On Communitarian Divinity*, 4.
28. Ogbonnaya, *On Communitarian Divinity*, 10.
29. Ibid., 7.
30. Christopher Fyfe and Andrew Walls, eds., *Christianity in Africa in the 1990s* (Edinburgh: Centre of African Studies, University of Edinburgh, 1996), 3. See also Andrew Walls, *The Missionary Movement in Christian History* (Maryknoll, NY: Orbis Books, 1996).

the life of the Christian communities, a growing number of which are so-called African Independent Churches (AICs)."[31] This is especially true in light of not only the AICs but also Pentecostal/charismatic movements.[32] The AIC and Pentecostal/charismatic churches have numerically far outstripped their mother churches.[33]

In light of the dramatic growth and proliferation of the Christian church on that continent, what is the state of theological reflection? John Mbiti's lament in the beginning of the 1970s that the Christian church in Africa is "without theology, without theologians, and without theological concern"[34] is no longer valid. What complicates and makes more challenging any study of African conceptions of God is that much of the theology is in oral, nonwritten form. Africans are not less "theological" about their faith in God than others;[35] they employ different forms of theologizing—as do, for example, many Asians—than formal academic treatises.[36] Cameroonian theologian Jean-March Ela calls the theological mode of many Africans "shade-tree theology," which is done in villages and cities, in the midst of people and their struggles. Shade-tree theology is done within the community.[37] For many African theologians, affirming the unique context, method, and issues of Africa is the important step on the way to freeing African theology from "the North Atlantic Captivity of the Church."[38]

When speaking of the nature of the theological reflection in the African context,[39] Ogbonnaya offers a highly interesting approach. He says that for him theology is "divination." By that he means that theology is "divining our way through the various experiences of the world with which we are privileged to have." Like the diviners of old whom Ogbonnaya calls "apprentices in the world," his own Trinitarian theology is an exercise in trying to "divine a way of thinking and talking about the Divine."[40]

31. Vähäkangas, *In Search of Foundations for African Catholicism*, 1.

32. W. J. Hollenweger, foreword to *African Initiatives in Christianity: The Growth, Gifts and Diversities of Indigenous African Churches—A Challenge to the Ecumenical Movement*, ed. John M. Pobee and Gabriel Ositelu II (Geneva: WCC Publications, 1998).

33. An up-to-date introduction to the AICs is provided by Allan H. Anderson, *African Reformation: African Initiated Christianity in the Twentieth Century* (Trenton, NJ: Africa World Press, 2000).

34. John Mbiti, "Some African Concepts of Christology," in *Christ and the Younger Churches*, ed. Georg F. Vicedom (London: SPCK, 1972), 51.

35. Kwesi Dickson, *Theology in Africa* (London: Darton, Longman & Todd, 1984), 13.

36. For methodological approaches in current African theology and biblical scholarship, see Chris Ukachukwu Manus, "Methodological Approaches in Contemporary African Biblical Scholarship: The Case of West Africa," in *African Theology Today*, ed. Emmanuel Katongole (Scranton, PA: University of Scranton Press, 2002), chap. 1.

37. Jean-Marc Ela, *African Cry* (Maryknoll, NY: Orbis Books, 1986), vi.

38. John Pobee, "Jesus Christ—The Life of the World: An African Perspective," *Ministerial Formation* 21 (1983): 5.

39. For helpful sources, see Parratt, *Reinventing Christianity*; Stinton, "Africa, East and West," chap. 5.

40. Ogbonnaya, *On Communitarian Divinity*, vii.

Related to the approach of "divination"—which of course is more engaging and dynamic than the typical Euro-American analytic, discursive method—is the acknowledgment of the interconnectedness of everything, including thinking and reflection. "Thinking in this context is synthetic rather than analytically oriented, which implies that everything is interdependent and in the end has religious value."[41]

Of course, as one could guess, the problem for the rise of a distinctively African theology has been the Western claim that theological understanding is not significantly affected by the particular context.[42] Nowadays hardly any theologian (even in the West) maintains that opinion, yet the emergence of a genuinely African theology is still to come. African theology is routinely divided into two categories: "African" and "black" theology. The latter usually denotes black liberation theologies, especially from the South African context; the former refers to African theology in general. As long as this division is understood as a pedagogical and heuristic device more than an absolute divider, it is helpful. Yet it has to be noted that there are "liberation theologies" that are not South African, and several "African" theologians have been politically active.[43] According to Bénézet Bujo, African theology is by nature "liberation theology," since the idea of liberation is inherent in the concept of life in Africa. This is accentuated by the this-worldly orientation of the African mentality, focusing on the now rather than the future. "Though God is present implicitly in every situation, the African outlook is essentially anthropocentric."[44]

South Africa has become the center of liberation theologies in Africa, understandably, in light of the history of apartheid.[45] Allan Boesak popularized the term "black consciousness," which, though echoing concerns similar to those of American black theology under Cone, has distinctive elements too.[46] For Boesak, as for other black theologians, theology is about liberation. "Black Theology believes that liberation is not only 'part of' the gospel or 'consistent with' the gospel; it is the content and framework of the gospel of Jesus Christ."[47]

41. Royce, *Problem of Christianity*, 40.

42. See further Ogbonnaya, *On Communitarian Divinity*, 9–10.

43. See further Parratt, *Reinventing Christianity*, 25–28. See also Alfred T. Hennelly, *Liberation Theologies: The Global Pursuit of Justice* (Mystic, CT: Twenty-Third Publications, 1995), 160–94, which discusses Bénézet Bujo; and see Deane William Ferm, *Third World Liberation Theologies: An Introductory Survey* (Maryknoll, NY: Orbis Books, 1986), chap. 3, which lists more than ten names under the category "African liberation theology," most of them from outside of South Africa.

44. For details, see Parratt, *Reinventing Christianity*, 122–25.

45. Oddly, the widely acclaimed recent major survey, Hennelly's *Liberation Theologies*, when introducing liberation theologies in Africa almost totally ignores South African contributions, with the exception of a brief discussion of John de Gruchy, whose name does not appear in the outline (in contrast to Bénézet Bujo and Mercy Amba Oduyoye as main representatives of the continent).

46. See further Basil Moore, "What Is Black Theology?" in *The Challenge of Black Theology in South Africa*, ed. Basil Moore (Atlanta: John Knox Press, 1974), 1–10.

47. Allan Boesak, *Farewell to Innocence: A Socio-Ethical Study on Black Theology and Black Power* (Maryknoll, NY: Orbis Books, 1977), 9.

THE PLACE OF THE TRINITY IN AFRICAN THEOLOGIES

It is routinely noted that Christology stands at the heart of Christian theology in Africa. Other topics widely discussed are ecclesiology and pneumatology. One would assume that Trinity would fare well in the African milieu, if for no other reason than the key role played by communality and communion in African cultures and religions. Add to this the central role of intermediaries, both ancestors and spiritual beings, and one could imagine a revival of interest in the Trinity.[48] That, however, has not been the case. On the contrary, with some exceptions such as Charles Nyamiti (to be discussed in what follows), the doctrine has been marginalized, even eschewed. This lacuna has many causes: for instance, as a doctrine based on Hellenistic metaphysics, it is very difficult to understand[49] (an idea hardly unknown elsewhere!); it uses the non-African term "person"[50]; and it has a nonpractical nature,[51] among other issues.

African theology, however, needs to continue work on the Trinity, if for no other reason than that "It is not possible to maintain that there would be a genuine African Christology if the doctrine of the Trinity is inherited from the West without original African reflection."[52]

Most African Trinitarian reflections represent the social analogy in one form or another.[53] This is understandable in light of the primacy of communion in general and family community in particular. Family for Africans, of course, means extended family, consisting of both the living and the dead, as well as the spiritual world, an idea closely related to the African concept of the church. Thus, ecclesiology has been an impetus for Trinitarian theology in Africa.[54] Closely related to the family imagery, yet more extensive, is the widely used concept of *ujamaa* (literally, familyhood) originating in the political thinking of Julius Nyerere, which has been linked with Trinity.[55]

---

48. See Stinton, "Africa, East and West," 125–28, for "theologies of mediation," which discusses the role of ancestors and other mediaries in Africa from a Christian perspective.

49. Gabriel Setiloane, "Where Are We in African Theology?" in *African Theology en Route: Papers from the Pan-African Conference of Third World Theologians, December 17–23, 1977, Accra, Ghana*, ed. Kofi Appiah-Kubi and Sergio Torres (Maryknoll, NY: Orbis Books, 1979), 64–65.

50. Jesse N. K. Mugambi, *African Heritage and Contemporary Christianity* (Nairobi: Longman Kenya, 1989), 75.

51. Cristopher Mwoleka, "Trinity and Community," *African Ecclesiastical Review* 17, no. 4 (1975): 203: "It is a pity that many people find it very difficult to understand what this mystery is all about. Many Christians do now know what to do with it except that it must be believed." See further Mika Vähäkangas, "African Approaches to the Trinity," *African Theological Journal* 23, no. 2 (2000): 33–34. (This article can also be found in *African Theology Today*, ed. Emmanuel Katongole [Scranton, PA: University of Scranton Press, 2002], 69–84.) I am indebted to his discussion for some of the references.

52. Vähäkangas, "African Approaches to the Trinity," 34.

53. See, e.g., Mercy Amba Oduyoye, *Hearing and Knowing: Theological Reflections on Christianity in Africa* (Maryknoll, NY: Orbis Books, 1986), chap. 11, "Trinity and Communion."

54. See further Vähäkangas, "African Approaches to the Trinity," 37–39. He mentions that Nyamiti's "family-trinitology is . . . a kind of a 'side-product' of his family ecclesiology" (pp. 38–39). See also Charles Nyamiti, "The Trinity as Source and Soul of African Family Ecclesiology," *African Christian Studies* 15, no. 1 (1999): 34–39.

55. See, e.g., Camillus Lyimo, "An Ujamaa Theology," in *African Christian Spirituality*, ed.

Not only are there several African cultural features that point to the possibility of a specifically Christian interpretation of the Trinity in that context; there is also a rich and variegated *theological* heritage with a long history of African conceptions of the divine. The disputed and widely debated question is the continuity—or lack thereof—between the specifically Christian understanding of God and African views of God. Opinions differ radically, and the topic is far from being settled.[56]

On the way "toward an African theology"—to borrow the title of a book by a leading African theologian, John Pobee—when "the African stamp will . . . replace the European stamp,"[57] one wonders if the doctrine of the Trinity is a viable starting point. In order to address that question, we will study the theologies of the Trinity contributed by two African theologians, the Roman Catholic Charles Nyamiti and the Methodist A. O. Ogbonnaya. Representing Roman Catholic and Protestant traditions, these two theologians give a fair snapshot of African ecumenical and theological diversity.

Aylward Shorter (Maryknoll, NY: Orbis Books, 1980), 128; Mwoleka, "Trinity and Community," 203–5.

56. For basic bibliographical references, see Kärkkäinen, *Doctrine of God*, 247–49.

57. John Pobee, *Toward an African Theology*, 17. See also Dickson, *Theology in Africa*.

Chapter 25

C. Nyamiti

Trinitarian Processions
as Ancestral Relationships

ANCESTRY AS A THEOLOGICAL THEME
IN AFRICAN THEOLOGIES

While the theme of ancestry is not by any means limited to emerging African theologies—as examples from Asia and elsewhere testify[1]—if anything is distinctive to the African context, it is the use of ancestors as a theological resource: "In many African societies ancestral veneration is one of the central and basic traditional and even contemporary forms of cult."[2] A number of African theologians

---

1. See, e.g., Jung Young Lee, ed., *Ancestor Worship and Christianity in Korea*, Studies in Asian Thought and Religion 8 (Lewiston, NY: Mellen Press, 1988). It is interesting, however, that the doctrine of the Trinity is not employed in that book, not even in the chapter "Ancestor Worship from a Theological Perspective," by Jung Young Lee (pp. 83–91).

2. Charles Nyamiti, "African Ancestral Veneration and Its Relevance to the African Churches," *African Christian Studies* [Nairobi] 9, no. 3 (1993): 14, cited in Mika Vähäkangas, *In Search of Foundations for African Catholicism: Charles Nyamiti's Theological Method* (Leiden: Brill, 1999), 171 n. 106. For an interesting account of "ancestral hermeneutics" in the African context, see Gerald West, "Negotiating with 'the White Man's Book': Early Foundations for Liberation Hermeneutics in Southern Africa," in *African Theology Today*, ed. Emmanuel Katongole (Scranton, PA: University of Scranton Press, 2002), 35–38.

have tried their hand at this theme.[3] Among them, the Roman Catholic theologian Charles Nyamiti is undoubtedly the most prominent.[4] His widely acclaimed work *Christ as Our Ancestor* (1984) established his fame in this respect even though he has widely discussed the theme from the beginning of his theological career. One of his earlier works, *African Tradition and the Christian God* (1978), also focused on the role of ancestors in the Gikuyu context in Kenya and beyond. Furthermore, he has written extensively on method in theology and the need to develop African theology.[5]

Kwesi Dickson, among others, has emphasized the importance of the role of ancestors in representing the sense of community and the "concept of corporate personality," a theme that is also part of the Israelite faith in the Old Testament.[6] The ancestors, as well as those not yet born, are regarded as part of the community, and by their presence they express the solidarity of the community. The spirits of the ancestors use their power for the well-being of the community; this is consistent with the fact that not all dead become ancestors. Ancestors are primarily those who have lived a good, virtuous life or served as the leaders of the community. Ancestors are certainly lower in status than God, but higher than humans.[7] They are called upon at the important moments of life.[8]

Another African theologian, Bénézet Bujo, builds his Christology on the idea of ancestors. He maintains that in Africa the *gesta* (manifestations) of ancestors are constantly reenacted through ritual. This enables an African to recall these *gesta* and conform one's conduct to them. This is the starting point for Bujo's reflection on the mystery of Christ, whom he considers a proto-ancestor, the unique ancestor, the source of life and highest model of ancestorship.[9] According to Bujo, the idea of Jesus as the ancestor is no superficial concession to the existing cultural need. It is no cheap technique of contextualization for making Christ relevant to Africans but rather a legitimate way to bring home the central

3. Kwame Bediako, *Jesus in African Culture: A Ghanaian Perspective* (Accra: Asempa Publishers, 1990); idem, *Christianity in Africa: The Renewal of a Non-Western Religion* (Edinburgh: Edinburgh University Press/Maryknoll, NY: Orbis Books, 1995), 84–86; F. Kabasele, "Christ as Ancestor and Elder Brother," in *Faces of Jesus in Africa*, ed. Robert J. Schreiter (Maryknoll, NY: Orbis Books, 1991), 116–27. For a helpful overview and assessment, see Mika Vähäkangas, "Trinitarian Processions as Ancestral Relationships in Charles Nyamiti's Theology: A European Lutheran Critique," *Revue Africaine de Théologie* 21 (1997): 61–75.
4. For the significance of Nyamiti to African theology, see Vähäkangas, *In Search of Foundations for African Catholicism*, 2.
5. Charles Nyamiti, *The Scope of African Theology* (Eldoret, Kenya: Gaba Publications, 1973).
6. Kwesi Dickson, *Theology in Africa* (London: Darton, Longman & Todd, 1984), 170; see also pp. 172–74.
7. Peter Fulljames, *God and Creation in Intercultural Perspective: Dialogue between the Theologies of Barth, Dickson, Pobee, Nyamiti, and Pannenberg* (Frankfurt am Main/New York: Peter Lang, 1993), 47.
8. Dickson, *Theology in Africa*, 69.
9. Bénézet Bujo, *African Theology in Its Social Context* (Maryknoll, NY: Orbis Books, 1992), 79. For the ancestral theme, see pp. 79–121 especially. See also Bénézet Bujo, "The Two Sources of Life: The Eucharist and the Cult of Ancestors in Africa," in *African Christian Studies* 4, no. 1 (1998): 23–27. For an overview and exposition, see Veli-Matti Kärkkäinen, *Christology: A Global Introduction* (Grand Rapids: Baker Academic, 2003), chap. 28.

idea of Word becoming flesh (John 1:14).[10] Ancestorship, consequently, is also a legitimate way of describing the Trinity in the African context: "The Father has the fullness of eternal life and begets the Son. They live for each other in a total and vital union, mutually reinforcing their common life. The vital power goes out from the Father to beget the Son and finally returns to the Father." This vital union that produces the interaction between Father and Son is nothing other than the Holy Spirit, the bond between the Father and the Son.[11]

In addition to the theme of communion (and related topics such as family), the ancestor theme reflects a number of key issues in African theology.[12] One of the pioneers in the field, a Franciscan missionary in the Belgian Congo, Placide Temples, contended that the importance of "life force" is so central to the African worldview that for the African "to be" is the same as "to have life force." Ancestors are often considered to be the first ones to whom God communicated the divine "vital force."[13] Relationality is another key aspect in the ancestral theme, an idea that has been developed into the notion of "vital participation"; this certainly has obvious links with Trinity.[14]

SYSTEMATIC THEOLOGY FOR THE AFRICAN CONTEXT

What makes Nyamiti's approach to African theology unique is that he calls for a more systematic approach to the doctrine of God and other Christian doctrines.[15] While acknowledging the presence of African theology in prayers, hymns, and other forms of spirituality, he argues that theologians need to move beyond these toward building a systematic theology from an African perspective[16] because Africa is rapidly moving from its "traditional mode of life to the technological and scientific age."[17] Nyamiti notes that Christian theology has always tended to be systematic and to make use of existing philosophical and other means for presenting a coherent account of its beliefs. Another reason he calls for a more systematic approach is that he proposes an interaction between

---

10. Bujo, *African Theology in Its Social Context*, 83.

11. Ibid., 86.

12. See further Mika Vähäkangas, "African Approaches to the Trinity," *Africa Theological Journal* 23, no. 2 (2000): 45–50.

13. Bujo, *African Theology in Its Social Context*, 57; Kabasele, "Christ as Ancestor and Elder Brother," 120–26.

14. Vähäkangas, "African Approaches to the Trinity," 47–48, attributes the genesis of this idea to Vincent Mulago, building on the work of Placide Temples. Mulago, however, has not yet made the explicit connection with Trinity. Vital force as a resource for Trinitarian thought has been subsequently employed by several African theologians, including Nyamiti.

15. For a comprehensive study of Nyamiti's theological method, see Vähäkangas, *In Search of Foundations for African Catholicism*.

16. See further ibid., 45–51 especially.

17. John Pobee, "Approaches to African Theology," in *The Emergent Gospel*, ed. Sergio Torres and Virginia Fabella (Maryknoll, NY: Orbis Books, 1979), 35.

the African cultural context and the tradition of the Catholic Church and its interpretation of the biblical message. Of course, many have criticized him for suggesting that Africans use categories from non-African cultures,[18] but he responds by saying that the systematization of the Christian doctrine in the African context has to be done critically and with necessary modifications.[19]

In his attempt to build a genuinely *systematic* approach to African theology, Nyamiti is not oblivious to the need to address social and political issues such as racism and oppression. Yet he issues a warning about the danger of building one's theology on a particular case. He is concerned that these and related problems remain linked to the root problem of sin and alienation from God.[20]

Nyamiti is also open to the possibility of developing an African philosophy as a tool for elucidating Christian faith—something like the use of Aristotelianism in the medieval era—in the African context.[21] This task would require both affirmation of those traits that are in harmony with Christian faith and a critical scrutiny of ones that are not. This is what Christian theology has always done, Nyamiti argues.[22]

AN ANCESTRAL VIEW OF THE TRINITY

While Nyamiti is best known for his application of the ancestral theme to the Trinity, his use of that African cultural theme is not limited to Trinity. He uses the category of ancestor in three interrelated ways:

- God as ancestor[23]
- Christ as ancestor[24] or "brother ancestor"[25]
- the "communion of saints" as ancestors[26]

What is the significance of the ancestor theme for the African context? Nyamiti summarizes it in five perspectives:[27]

---

18. For a moderate, constructive dialogue with Nyamiti, see Bujo, *African Theology in Its Social Context,* 56.
19. Nyamiti, *The Scope of African Theology,* 33; see further Fulljames, *God and Creation in Intercultural Perspective,* 98–99.
20. Charles Nyamiti, *African Tradition and Christian God* (Eldoret, Kenya: Gaba Publications, 1978), 26–43; Pobee, "Approaches to African Theology," 42–44.
21. Pobee, "Approaches to African Theology," 35.
22. Ibid., 38.
23. Nyamiti, *African Tradition and the Christian God,* chap. 8.
24. Charles Nyamiti, *Christ as Our Ancestor* (Gweru, Zimbabwe: Mambo Press, 1984).
25. This usage comes occasionally in Nyamiti, *African Tradition and the Christian God.*
26. See, e.g., Charles Nyamiti, "Uganda Martyrs: Ancestors of All Mankind," *African Christian Studies* 2, no. 1 (1986): 37–60.
27. Charles Nyamiti, "The Trinity from an African Ancestral Perspective," *African Christian Studies* 12, no. 4 (1996): 41.

- kinship between the dead and living kin
- sacred status, usually acquired through death
- mediation between human beings and God
- exemplarity of behavior in community
- the right to regular communication with the living through prayer and rituals

All of these traits are more or less relational. Only the sacred status could be understood predominantly as essential (even though it does not totally exclude the idea of relationality). An important characteristic of the sacred status of the ancestor is the possession of "superhuman vital force" deriving from the special proximity to the Supreme Being. That gives the ancestor the right to be a mediator. Also important here is the understanding that as the progenitor of the living, the ancestor is considered the "source of life" for the living.[28]

Now with regard to the doctrine of God, for Nyamiti, all of these qualities, with the exception of mediation, can be found in God, yet only analogously since there are also differences.[29] At the heart of Nyamiti's doctrine of God is the claim that ancestral relations exist within the Godhead, in the immanent Trinity.[30] All the good features of human ancestry can be found in God in a perfected nature. Indeed, "the category 'ancestor' is a pure perfection" in the Triune God, human ancestry being but "a faint and imperfect replica of divine ancestorship."[31]

Consequently, for Nyamiti this parallelism between human and divine ancestry, even when analogous, as mentioned, is more than an illustration or metaphor. He seems to claim that ancestry belongs to the essence of the Godhead[32] when he says, "The particular relationship between an ancestor and his or her offspring is not a matter of pure convention. It is based on the natural constitution of man."[33] This point can also be inferred from his Christology: if Christ is essentially an ancestor, subscribing to orthodox Trinitarian canons (*homoousios*) necessitates concluding that the whole Trinity is ancestral. This of course means that it is not only applicable to the African context but is a universal truth.[34]

One of the reasons the ancestor theme is an appropriate and fitting way of constructing the Christian view of the Triune God is the emphasis on commun-

28. Ibid.; for the linkage to the Bantu worldview, see Vähäkangas, "African Approaches to the Trinity," 43.

29. For similarities and differences between the divine and human ancestry, see Nyamiti, "Trinity from an African Ancestral Perspective," 46–48.

30. Nyamiti, *African Tradition and the Christian God,* 48–49.

31. Ibid., 48.

32. See further Vähäkangas, "African Approaches to the Trinity," 43.

33. Nyamiti, *African Tradition and the Christian God,* 45: See also Nyamiti, *Christ as Our Ancestor,* 17.

34. Nyamiti, "Trinity from an African Ancestral Perspective," 42–43.

ion. For Nyamiti, the Trinity "reveals God as essentially communicative. . . . He is the *immanently communicating and communicated independent Vital Force.*"[35] In God, there is "unbounded sharing . . . in perfect harmony and absolute one- ness among the divine Persons."[36] Along with communion, the idea of partic- ipation is also a key to Nyamiti's understanding of the Trinity. The Trinity is where Africans find the fulfillment of their yearning: "The African unquench- able search for participation in power, life, holiness and solidarity is, in fact, a quest for the triune God, that is, the vision of God as he is, for in him alone is the total and perfect participation for which we long."[37] In traditional theol- ogy the inner-Trinitarian relationships are conceived in terms of opposition. For this Catholic theologian, the African notion of personality is based on par- ticipation and sharing. This echoes the views of contemporary personalist philosophies with their idea of the "I" being constituted by the "thou."[38] Finally, the fact that ancestorship represents holiness—ancestors by definition are holy—is conducive to this particular way of understanding Trinity: the Father "is the Ancestor of His Son because He is the Father and also because He is holy."[39]

ANCESTRAL RELATIONS AS TRINITARIAN PROCESSIONS

In this scheme, then, the Trinity appears as follows: the Father is the Ancestor, the Son is the Descendant, and the Spirit is the Oblation:

> God is ancestor because he not only generates the Son but is also the Proto- type of the Son and because there exists between him and the Son an inti- mate relationship of sacred communication of nature and love through the Holy Spirit. . . . The Descendancy of the Son is related to the Father and the Holy Spirit—to the Father as proceeding from him, to the Spirit because it is in him and through him that the Descendant communicates mystically in love with the Ancestor, and thus fulfils his "ancestral" duties. The *ultimate* basis of Descendancy is generation and the sanctity of the Father. . . . The title which the Father has for sacred communication with his Son demands the presence of the Holy Spirit, through whom this loving and mutual com- munication takes place. . . . Both the Ancestor and the Descendant com- municate with one another in and through the Spirit, and seen from this perspective, the Spirit appears as the *expression* of their mutual love—in as much as this love is expressed by the mutual giving to each other of the divine Gift, that is, the Holy Spirit.[40]

35. Nyamiti, *African Tradition and the Christian God,* 62 (italics in the original).
36. Ibid., 64.
37. Ibid., 64.
38. Ibid., 63. Nyamiti further notes that the traditional understanding that bases relationships in the Trinity on their opposition is not a wrong idea as much as it is in need of qualification by the idea of participation (ibid.).
39. Nyamiti, "Trinity from an African Ancestral Perspective," 50.
40. Nyamiti, *African Tradition and the Christian God,* 48–49 (italics in original).

Nyamiti's view of the Spirit is based on the duty of the descendant to offer a sacred rite to the ancestor. Out of this emerges an Augustinian-type idea of the Spirit as the mutual love of Father and Spirit. As such, it also supports *filioque*.[41]

This Catholic African theologian considers the ancestral way of defining the Trinity as superior to—even if not replacing—the typical Father-Son-Spirit scheme in that it shows the intrinsic link between the Father and Son in relation to the Spirit. Apart from the ancestorship, "the Holy Spirit appears as a 'stranger' to the Father and the Son and, as it were, extraneous to their relationship." In the African ancestral conception, however, "an ancestor is *essentially* entitled to the sacred communication with his descendant." Since this communication in the Godhead can only happen through the Holy Spirit, the Spirit belongs necessarily to the Trinity.[42] An important corollary is that ancestorship and descendancy are in Nyamiti's opinion more closely related to love than what is true of the Father-Son relation. This has significant implications for us. "Through our descendancy in Christ, we are more closely related to God's love than through our divine sonship." This is mutual love, not only received love: descendants owe love to our Father, who is also our Ancestor in Christ.[43]

Nyamiti applies the ancestor theme to Christ based on his role as the mediator between God and humanity. Christ as "Brother Ancestor" is the means by which God communicates with humanity. Within the Trinity there is an eternal ancestral relationship between the Father and Son, who are therefore described as "Ancestor" and "Descendant." The Holy Spirit as part of the Trinity is introduced here: "The Ancestor and the Descendant communicate with one another in and through the Spirit, and seen from this perspective, the Spirit appears to be the expression of their mutual love—in as much as love is expressed by the mutual giving to each other of the divine gift, that is, the Holy Spirit." Thus, according to Nyamiti, the Holy Spirit is needed to secure the sacred communication between Ancestor and Descendent: "Since in God, this sacred communication can only be made through the Holy Spirit, divine ancestorship and descendancy demand by their very nature the presence of the Holy Spirit."[44]

For Nyamiti, Christ's redemptive activity can only be understood in terms of the incarnation of one who is in eternal relationship with the Father, the Parent-Ancestor. He thus understands redemption as the bridging of the gap between God and humanity caused by sin.[45] Such an understanding is appropriate in that there are stories in many African societies of God withdrawing to heaven after his friendship with humans was broken. Nyamiti also notes that his view of incarnation is close to that of the Greek fathers, for whom "Christ saved the totality of mankind by assuming human nature and uniting it . . . to God."[46]

---

41. Ibid., 49.
42. Ibid. (italics in the original).
43. Ibid., 50.
44. Ibid., 49.
45. Nyamiti, *Christ as Our Ancestor,* 74–76.
46. Ibid., 73.

What about the death of Jesus? Nyamiti echoes Moltmann's idea that the death had to do primarily with inner-Trinitarian relations. Thus, "the crucifixion of the Son is the sacred communication and ritual self-giving of the Descendent to his divine Ancestor, whereas the glorification of the Son by the Father through the Spirit is the divine ancestral answer."[47]

CRITICAL REFLECTIONS

Christian theology as represented by missionaries and those Africans building on that influence in the mainstream has either totally rejected or at least downplayed the significance of ancestorship to Christian theology in general and Christology and theology proper in particular.[48] The Roman Catholic Nyamiti offers a creative and unapologetic response by building his whole Trinitarian doctrine on several themes drawn from the ancestral world of Africa.

Nyamiti's method of doing Trinitarian theology is from below: he looks at the meaning of ancestorship in the African worldview and out of that constructs a particular doctrine of the Trinity. Yet as Mika Vähäkangas rightly notes,[49] at the same time Nyamiti's method is also from above since he does not intend to replace the received Catholic doctrine of the Trinity based on revelation and Scripture, but rather wants to develop it further. More important,

> Nyamiti does not mean by this a translation of Western theological and philosophical categories to the language of African ancestral relations. Such a translation would be illegitimate for him. Rather, he considers his work to be authentic theological elaboration based on the principle of analogy. This means that speech about ancestorship is not merely figurative speech, i.e., metaphor, but that there really exists ancestorship in the Trinity. One can discern in Nyamiti's writings that he considers the analogy he builds to be of proper proportionality."[50]

This judgment is confirmed by the many ways—some of them noted above—with which Nyamiti wants to validate his emphasis on the idea of ancestorship belonging to the Triune God. One of them begins with the idea of perfection. Ancestorship represents perfection; only in God can this perfection be found in an absolute way.[51]

Indeed, Nyamiti believes that the ancestral way of constructing the classical doctrine is superior to the classical ways, for several reasons, such as these:

47. Ibid., 46.
48. See Vähäkangas, "Trinitarian Processions as Ancestral Relationships," 65,
49. Also noted by Vähäkangas, ibid., 64.
50. Ibid., 62.
51. Ibid., 63.

1. The ancestral way of viewing the Trinity highlights the importance of communion and participation unlike any other view.
2. The Holy Spirit is seen as integral or internal rather than "external" to the Trinity.
3. The holiness of the Father is an integral part of his being.
4. Ancestors being the models of exemplary conduct illustrates perfectly the Son's role as the perfect image of his Father, in obedience and humility.[52]

Consequently, Nyamiti's doctrine of the Trinity should be evaluated in light of its capacity to represent key ideas in the classical theology of Trinity on the one hand and essential ancestral themes on the other hand. As mentioned, these are the two key values Nyamiti purports to cherish. Let me ask first how appropriately this ancestral construction of Trinity echoes the African understanding of ancestorship. It goes without saying that I am doing this assessment as an outsider to that culture. Yet, if it is true, as Nyamiti claims, that his African interpretation is universal in some sense, then people from other cultures should have the right to test that claim.

Several commentators have noticed problems related to the way Nyamiti selectively appropriates the term *ancestor* in his Trinitarian theology.[53] At the outset, Nyamiti excludes mediation from consideration since it is not applicable to the Trinity and he claims that it is not an essential feature. That is not the only characteristic in need of qualification: kinship needs to encompass also a non-consanguineous type in order to make any sense with regard to the Trinity. And even the sacred status of the ancestor, gained through death, needs radical revision. In sum, only two of his five key elements remain intact, namely, exemplary conduct and right to sacred communication.[54] Vähäkangas's conclusion echoes that of many commentators:

> It is doubtful whether these two are enough for defining ancestorship. Should ancestrality serve as a proper locus of theology, it should be properly defined so that its essential elements would be logically and systematically determined and analyzed. In this way they may be used for qualifying or disqualifying phenomena as ancestral. This would be the methodological prerequisite for the academic usage of ancestorship as a theological point of departure.[55]

One can of course dismiss this criticism and assess the value of Nyamiti's view of the Trinity apart from its capacity to faithfully reflect its alleged African

52. See further Nyamiti, "Trinity from an African Ancestral Perspective," 51–52. Vähäkangas compiles a somewhat similar list with some different nuances ("Trinitarian Processions as Ancestral Relationships," 64).

53. For a helpful bibliographical guide, see Vähäkangas, "Trinitarian Processions as Ancestral Relationships," 66 n. 30.

54. My critique in this paragraph is based on the careful discussion in ibid., 67.

55. Ibid. See also Vähäkangas, *In Search of Foundations for African Catholicism*, 214.

ancestorship themes. The problem, however, is then twofold. First, the basic intention of Nyamiti is being frustrated: his explicit aim is to develop an *African* interpretation of the Trinity. Second, while interesting for speculative purposes, most theologians and layfolk would probably not be too excited about taking seriously an African interpretation of the Trinity that is deemed to be quite distant from its African context, and that thus ends up being just an individual theologian's mental construct. Furthermore, arguing that, because of the difference between the divine and human realities, the human concepts of ancestorship by definition need qualification is not very convincing. The challenge is to show which features in the Trinity are essential to ancestorship and which are not.

Vähäkangas takes up two more challenges to Nyamiti's use of the ancestral theme in his Trinitarian doctrine. First, with regard to Christ's role, it is not enough to assert that he is Descendant; he is also (our) Ancestor at the same time. This means that the concept of ancestorship in this regard entails two levels, Christ being both Ancestor and Descendant. However, this is a feature totally unknown to any African culture. Second, concerning the grounds for the Oblation having to be mutual: this idea, in order to be convincing, calls for further elucidation. In African cultures, it is a one-way street, the descendant offering oblation to the ancestor, the latter being merely the receiver. Of course there is communion between the two, but not in terms of the ritual offering being mutually offered, as Nyamiti's line of thinking claims.[56]

Now, what is Nyamiti's response to these kinds of challenges? While he has not dealt with them in any comprehensive way, neither is he unaware of them. His response is that none of these is necessarily a threat to his view since *"African theology is not African social (or cultural) anthropology."*[57] While Nyamiti's response needs further elucidation concerning the limits of the freedom of theologians to claim a particular interpretation of Christian doctrine based on the central cultural features of their context, in the main one has to acknowledge the force of his reasoning. Therefore, regarding the cultural appropriateness of Nyamiti's proposal, I agree with the conclusion of Vähäkangas: while there are limits to Nyamiti's way of handling the ancestral theme, these limitations should not necessarily make us reject the theological construction. All theological constructions are limited.[58]

Concerning the *theological* value of Nyamiti's proposal, in light of traditional and contemporary Christian views, one has to question first its compatibility with the biblical data. It doesn't take too much thinking to note that the ancestral cult may be in conflict with explicit biblical commands to not consult the deceased (Lev. 19:31; Deut. 18:11; 1 Sam. 28). In light of the fact that Nyamiti subscribes to the Bible's supreme authority[59] and to church tradition,

---

56. Vähäkangas, "Trinitarian Processions as Ancestral Relationships," 68.
57. Nyamiti, "Trinity from an African Ancestral Perspective," 42 (italics in the original); see also p. 45.
58. Vähäkangas, "Trinitarian Processions as Ancestral Relationships," 68.
59. Nyamiti, *African Theology: Its Nature, Problems and Methods* (Kampala: Gaba Publications, 1971), 27.

it is amazing that Nyamiti has nowhere dealt with this issue. So we don't have any way of knowing how he would negotiate his way here; an obvious argument from silence is that he doesn't see a problem here.

Nyamiti seems to support a hierarchical view of the Trinity, which would as a result subject him to the charge of subordinationism.[60] This comes from the idea of the Father being the generator and "prototype" of the Son. Nyamiti is himself aware of the danger of subordinationism in his theology, but thinks he can avoid it by holding on to the divinity of Christ.[61] Few will be satisfied with that answer; throughout Christian history the danger of subordinationism has been lurking in Trinitarian views that have affirmed the deity of the Son. Nyamiti's enthusiastic emphasis on participation and communion might offer resources for tackling the issue of hierarchy. However, he has not delved into that issue in any systematic way.

Two problems arise regarding the Holy Spirit in the Trinity. First, Nyamiti supports the *filioque* clause: the Holy Spirit is "produced" by both the Father and Son.[62] Apart from the fact that—with many contemporary theologians—I regard the *filioque* clause as problematic and thus in need of revision, regarding Nyamiti I see it particularly disturbing that based on his ancestral construction, it seems that the Spirit should come only from the Son, the Father being rather the receiver of the Spirit. It is the Son who gives the Oblation, the shared gift. Now that would turn upside down one of the most typical ways that ecumenical theologies attempt to qualify the *filioque* addition to the creed (in order to make it more balanced as well as acceptable to the East), namely, speaking of the Spirit as proceeding from the Father and resting on or received by the Son. Second, in the Christian understanding the Spirit is the Spirit of love (both with regard to inner-Trinitarian relations and the relation between God and us), whereas in ancestral beliefs of Africa the relationship between the ancestor and human beings is either ambivalent or based on fear. Therefore, in this regard there is a real incompatibility between the ancestral relation and the Christian understanding of the Trinity.[63] Nyamiti's response that fear indeed belongs to the biblical understanding of the divine-human relationship[64] is hardly convincing. The fear spoken of in the ancestral context has to do with negative fear because of lack of trust, whereas in the biblical context fear shows respect and gives honor to the Almighty God and arises out of childlike trust and awe.

As for any social analogy advocate, for Nyamiti the question of the unity of God is a pressing issue. How is Nyamiti's social model of the Trinity able to defend the unity? His response builds on the centrality of the idea of commun-

60. For a careful discussion of hierarchy in an African ancestral view and theology, see Vähäkangas, *In Search of Foundations for African Catholicism*, 227–35.

61. Nyamiti, *Christ as Our Ancestor*, 20.

62. Nyamiti, *African Tradition and the Christian God*, 49.

63. See further Vähäkangas, "Trinitarian Processions as Ancestral Relationships," 79–80.

64. Nyamiti, "Trinity from an African Ancestral Perspective," 68.

ion and participation—a route taken by many Western theologians as well. Indeed, Nyamiti regards the *African* approach to communion as superior in defending the unity when compared to typical Western notions: "In the Trinity, participation implies the communication of the one single divine life and power among the three Persons. This in no way implies having a *part* of the divine life or power: the Father shares his *entire* being with the Son and the Spirit. Here the African sense of participation is closer to the truth than is the Western 'pars capere,' to have a part." As a result, the divine Persons are "one and identical in life, nature and power."[65] Nyamiti's approach to unity shares the strengths and weaknesses of views of social Trinitarians such as Moltmann and Erickson, who resort to the concept of perichoresis. While I appreciate the desire to acknowledge and resist the danger of tritheism, I am also left wondering why it is that mere *sharing* (in this case of life and power) necessarily entails absolute unity. Communion implies just that—com-union—but not necessarily union.

Other challenges to Nyamiti's proposal include the somewhat uncritical affirmation of the values related to traditional African ancestor worship, such as the supremacy of the male and its use as a vehicle of political ascendancy. These features hardly leave room for the kind of efforts for liberation that arise out of the gospel message.[66] Other differences between core theological convictions of the Christian doctrine of the Trinity and African ancestral beliefs include self-sacrifice. The self-sacrifice of Christ as superior to human beings' self-sacrifice contradicts the pattern of ancestral cults in Africa.[67]

Despite the problems and unanswered questions, Nyamiti must be credited with creating an ingenious theory on the Trinity, connecting the central elements of traditional Augustinian-influenced Roman Catholic teaching to an African theory of ancestral relations. The greatest merit of this construction is that it succeeds in describing the intrinsic unity of the two Trinitarian processions. As such it serves at least as a complement to the traditional theological formulations on the Trinity. This speculation on the immanent Trinity is Nyamiti's greatest contribution in the field of African theology considering the contents of doctrinal discussion.[68]

---

65. Nyamiti, *African Tradition and Christian God*, 62 (italics in the original). Another way of putting it is this: "This perfect oneness or totality of sacred life and power is the consequence and goal of the divine communication, as well as the overflow of the fecundity of the divine life energy" (ibid.).

66. So also Vähäkangas, "Trinitarian Processions as Ancestral Relationships," 73. He gives a reference to A. Shorter, who discusses the obstacles to liberationism in African ancestral beliefs in "Obstacles to Liberation in Africa [*sic*] Religious Tradition," in *Towards African Christian Liberation*, ed. L. Namwera et al. (Nairobi: St. Paul Publications, 1990), 18.

67. Vähäkangas, "Trinitarian Processions as Ancestral Relationships," 73.

68. Vähäkangas, *In Search of Foundations for African Catholicism*, 187.

Chapter 26

A. O. Ogbonnaya
Trinity as Communitarian Divinity

AN AFRICAN INTERPRETATION OF THE TRINITY

What makes A. Okechukwu Ogbonnaya's book *On Communitarian Divinity: An African Interpretation of the Trinity* (1994)[1] exciting is not only that it is a genuine attempt to construct a Trinitarian doctrine from the perspective of the African culture and its focus on the community, but also that it uses as a major source an ancient African theologian, Tertullian. Yet the challenge of the book is that, having laid out the program and presented in great detail the doctrine of the Trinity in Tertullian from the perspective of African communalism, it stops right where one would expect it to reap a harvest. Within the confines of only ninety pages,[2] one can hardly develop a Trinitarian doctrine as a whole (even though there is a parallel in the book (almost a booklet) of Rahner's *The Trinity*; yet Rahner has ample opportunities elsewhere to comment on the Trinity, unlike

---

1. A. Okechukwu Ogbonnaya, *On Communitarian Divinity: An African Interpretation of the Trinity* (New York: Paragon House, 1994).
2. In addition, the book contains a helpful bibliography.

Ogbonnaya). This means that one's expectations should be quite modest as we engage first in the exposition of this distinctively African understanding of Trinity and then in critical reflections.

This is the way Ogbonnaya introduces his study:

> This book explores, from an African communal worldview, the idea of the Trinity as found in the work of Tertullian. The examination of the concept of the Divine in its African context is meant to propose a new way of seeing and speaking about the Divine. An African worldview is brought to bear upon Tertullian's historical formulation of the Trinity.[3]

Ogbonnaya's study, consequently, is meant to offer, not a generic African approach to the Trinity, but rather a focused exploration of the relevance of an ancient (North) African theologian, Tertullian. Even Tertullian's whole theology of the Trinity is not meant to be examined but rather those aspects that have bearing on the communal nature of the African worldview, as explained above.

The choice of Tertullian as an African theologian is of course a brilliant move. Tertullian is routinely taken as the architect of the Western understanding of the Trinity. That he is indeed. This North African lawyer,[4] well-educated in Scripture and the classical arts, including Stoic philosophy, is the architect of Latin theology; he coined key terms such as *trinitas* and *persona* in reference to the doctrine of the Trinity.

Likewise, the choice of the community as the mode of doing Trinitarian theology is most appropriate for a contemporary theologian wanting to say something relevant in the African context. Indeed, Ogbonnaya's goal is ambitious. He wants to call into question the traditional talk about the Divine and "join the ranks of those who are calling for a new way to envision and speak of the Divine,"[5] in line with a communal way of thinking and living.

Ogbonnaya's main thesis is bold and subject to debate:

> Tertullian's historical-critical situation allowed him to develop a particular conception of the Divine as community—one which enhances ontological equality, personal distinctiveness within the Divine, and a functional subordination among the persons of the Trinity that is temporal rather than ontological. . . . Tertullian's concept of Divinity holds in dynamic interplay the idea of ontological equality, personal distinction, and functional-temporal subordination.[6]

---

3. Ogbonnaya, *On Communitarian Divinity*, ix.
4. Historians debate whether Tertullian was a lawyer, but this is not a problem for this book. A helpful introduction to Tertullian's doctrine of God is Richard A. Norris, *God and the World in Early Christian Theology: A Study in Justin Martyr, Irenaeus, Tertullian, and Origen* (New York: Seabury Press, 1965), chap. 4.
5. Ogbonnaya, *On Communitarian Divinity*, ix.
6. Ibid., xiii.

The implications of this loaded statement are to be examined in what follows. At this point, let us take his thesis at face value.

The most controversial part of Ogbonnaya's argument is that not only is the communality the underlying principle of the Christian God, but that, indeed, this communality means also the community of gods. With this twist he enters the complicated discussion of the original nature of African religion either as monotheistic or polytheistic.

"COMMUNALITY IS THE ESSENCE OF THE GODS"[7]

The reason Ogbonnaya enters the discussion of the mono- or polytheistic nature of African religion has to do with the ancient discussion of the one and the many. The question, so widely debated both in Western philosophy and, for example, in Asian religions, in the African context has to do with overcoming two extremes, what he calls "monotheism" or "separatist polytheism." Monotheism means here the conception of the Divine as an absolute, singular, personalistic God, and "separatist" polytheism refers to an understanding of "many gods with completely separate natures, unconnected and not intrinsically related."[8]

Ogbonnaya's own preference is for a third option, since polytheism has become a pejorative term that fails to take into account the interrelationality of the gods. His own view builds on the idea of the *community of gods*, which is neither monotheism nor polytheism. Ogbonnaya finds fault in the interpretations of his fellow African scholars who argue for the ultimately monotheistic nature of the African "High God" tradition since it ignores both the communality of the African worldview and the idea of the presence of kinship through progeny among the gods. "The One in African thought should be understood in terms of communal oneness."[9] He also argues that separatist polytheism is being resisted, at least by those African scholars who emphasize the relationality among gods as the distinctive idea of African religions.[10] The idea of gods as community is explained in these terms: "Divine Communalism is the position that Divine is a community of gods who are fundamentally related to one another and ontologically equal while at the same time distinct from one another by their personhood and functions."[11]

---

7. The heading above is from Edmund Ilogu, *Christianity and Igbo Culture* (New York: JOK Press, 1974), 201, as quoted in Ogbonnaya, *On Communitarian Divinity*, 13, in a preface to chap. 2. "Divine Communalism is the position that the Divine is a community of gods who are fundamentally related to one another and ontologically equal while at the same time distinct from one another by their personhood and functions." Ibid., 23; on monotheistic and polytheistic options, see 14–23.

8. Ogbonnaya, *On Communitarian Divinity*, 13. For the debate between monotheistic and polytheistic interpretations, see further Veli-Matti Kärkkäinen, *The Doctrine of God in Global Context: Biblical, Historical, and Contemporary Perspectives* (Grand Rapids: Baker Academics, 2004), 60–61.

9. Ogbonnaya, *On Communitarian Divinity*, 14–21 (quotation on p. 25).

10. Ibid., 21–23.

11. Ibid., 23.

The way Ogbonnaya now attempts to negotiate the problem of one and many follows the logic of one person as representative of many other persons. As senseless as it is to claim that because one man is a village head, there can be only one real man, so it is senseless to claim that only one (person) can be divine. "Manyness is not in opposition to the concept of oneness, but is inclusive of all of the gods," if, as Ogbonnaya claims, a god is a divine person but as divine person is not the whole Divinity.[12] As a concrete example, Ogbonnaya refers to the Dinka tribe in southern Sudan, to whom the idea of one supreme force, *Nhialic,* does not hinder the acknowledgment of other divine personifications, gods related to one another.[13] Ogbonnaya's interpretation is that *Nhialic* might be the general term for the divine nature as shared by other gods (Deng, Garang, Macardit, and Abuk).[14] In other words, the gods seem to be connected with each other by their common nature, derived "from the all-pervasive force that is their common substance."[15] This conception, of courses, raises the question of whether this idea of a "High God" being the "source" of the shared nature of gods means hierarchy—like the Christian tradition of viewing the Father as the "source," rather than as ontological equality. We will come back to this question.

TERTULLIAN'S COMMUNAL VIEW OF THE TRINITY

According to Ogbonnaya, three streams of influences come together in Tertullian's Trinitarian doctrine, namely, the African traditions, coming especially from ancient Egypt;[16] Stoic philosophy; and biblical revelation. The latter two have been routinely mentioned, but the first one has hardly received attention.[17]

On scriptural bases such as the "Let us . . ." sayings of Genesis 1:26 and 11:7, Tertullian maintained the idea of plurality in God.[18] For Tertullian biblical sayings such as "Behold, man is become like one of Us" (Gen. 3:22)[19] speak for the plurality in the one God.[20] In contrast to the Jewish interpreters, he speculated

---

12. Ibid., 24.
13. See R. Godfrey Leinhardt, *Divinity and Experience: The Religion of the Dinka People* (Oxford: Clarendon Press, 1960).
14. Here Ogbonnaya (*On Communitarian Divinity,* 25) gives references in support of his view from Leinhardt, *Divinity and Experience,* 57.
15. Ogbonnaya, *On Communitarian Divinity,* 26.
16. Chapter 3 in *On Communitarian Divinity* contains an extended study on the conception of the Divine in ancient Egypt as a background. The conclusion is that in terms of communality and relationality, two principles are emphasized. On the one hand the individuality of the gods implied freedom and creativity. On the other hand, while acknowledging the unique individuality of the gods, the commonality was emphasized rather than what separated them. Ibid., 47.
17. Ibid., 51–52.
18. Tertullian, *Against Praxeas* 12 (p. 606). In this chapter I am following Ogbonnaya in using Tertullian, *Adversus Praxeas,* trans. Peter Holmes, in *Ante-Nicene Fathers: Translations of the Writings of the Fathers Down to A.D. 325,* vol. 3 (reprint, Grand Rapids: Eerdmans, 1951).
19. In this chapter I am following Ogbonnaya's paraphrasing of the biblical text.
20. Tertullian, *Against Praxeas* 12, referred to in Ogbonnaya, *On Communitarian Divinity,* 55.

that God had "his son close at his side as a second Person" and "the third Person also, the Spirit."[21] For Ogbonnaya, these scriptural passages speak of the unity of the Trinity in terms of the "community of persons within the Divine One."[22] Tertullian, in other words, spoke of the Christian God as "Divine One and Many."[23]

In Ogbonnaya's reading of Tertullian, his main concepts, such as *monarchia*, *disposition*, and *oikonomia*—are metaphors related to the social sphere and imply communality.[24] When interpreting *monarchia*, Tertullian emphasizes that it does not denote singular monotheism but rather stands for a "fundamental relational base on which a kingdom is founded." According to Ogbonnaya, the kingdom for Tertullian is ruled not by one single individual but by a community of persons.[25] Yet the textual example Ogbonnaya quotes[26] as a support does not seem to say this exactly, but instead says that it is possible for a ruler, monarchy, to have a son or to administer his own monarchy with the help of agents. Ogbonnaya is more accurate in his interpretation of Tertullian when he says that for Tertullian "communal relation affects his understanding of rulership." The North African theologian writes:

> No dominion so belongs to one only, as his own, or is in such a sense singular, or is in such a sense a monarchy, as not also to be administered through other persons most closely connected with it and whom it has also provided as officials to itself.[27]

Pressing this idea of the monarchy as communion, Ogbonnaya interprets Tertullian as arguing that the monarchy does not belong to only the ruler but to all members of the family, including the minors. This is a highly significant argument for Ogbonnaya in that it means the rejection of an "atomistic separation of the members of the Divine community" in the thinking of Tertullian.[28] The idea of the interconnectedness of the Trinitarian members, instead of separationism, is evident in Tertullian's analogies from nature (roots-branch-fruit; source-river-rivulet; sun-ray-tip), Ogbonnaya argues.[29]

According to Ogbonnaya, "Tertullian marked a move from a mainly cosmological trinitarian language to ontological considerations of the inner relation of the life

21. Tertullian, *Against Praxeas* 7, quoted in Ogbonnaya, *On Communitarian Divinity*, 55.
22. Ogbonnaya, *On Communitarian Divinity*, 55.
23. Ibid., 57.
24. For an extended discussion of these metaphors, see ibid., 64–69 especially.
25. Ibid., 65.
26. "I am not sure that (monarchia) has another meaning than a single and individual rule but for all that, this monarchy does not, because it is the government of one, preclude him whose government it is, either from having a son or from having made himself actually a son to himself, or from ministering his own monarchy by whatever agents he will." Tertullian, *Against Praxeas* 3, as quoted in Ogbonnaya, *On Communitarian Divinity*, 65.
27. Tertullian, *Against Praxeas* 3, as quoted in Ogbonnaya, *On Communitarian Divinity*, 65-66.
28. Ogbonnaya, *On Communitarian Divinity*, 66.
29. Ibid., 63; see also pp. 61–64.

of God as a community."[30] On the other hand, the notion of the Trinity in Tertullian is connected to salvific economy.[31] Furthermore, Ogbonnaya claims that for Tertullian, "work, the persons, and the revelation of the Divine community through incarnation finds [sic] its raison d'être in symbolic, communal, mutual relationships of the gods (persons) within the Divine, both in terms of ontology and function."[32]

The way Ogbonnaya paraphrases Tertullian's understanding of the Trinity as One and Many sounds similar to most interpretations of Tertullian and hardly adds to it anything significantly "African":

> Tertullian's doctrine of the Trinity, which I call *the Divine community*, derives from the fact that a second person within Divinity is considered not only Divine, but also a deity in the full sense of the word, though not absolutely identical with the other deities within that community. . . . This someone, this second or third or other, is seen as an intrinsic part of the definition of the Divine communion. Yet, this same one is spoken of as begotten Son. By placing this principle in the center of the Divine communal self-definition, Tertullian essentially makes equality of nature a criterion if not a necessity.[33]

It seems to me that this is exactly what Christian Orthodoxy has insisted against Arians and others who have wanted to make the Son "less god" than the Father. Therefore, one can hardly see established here a distinctively "new" interpretation of an "ontological equality."

CRITICAL REFLECTIONS

Ogbonnaya's creative Trinitarian proposal has not elicited many theological responses. David Tonghou Ngong argues that Ogbonnaya's Trinitarian theology from an African perspective has two main merits: the emphasis on the communitarian nature of the Christian God and the inclusion of Egypt and its religions in an African consideration of theology.[34] The emphasis on a communitarian view of the Trinity is a helpful corrective to the "static and hierarchic paradigms dominant in Western theology."[35] The study's main limitations as a representative of *African* theologies has been noted by some commentators: emphasis on one theologian in the distant past can hardly speak to African theology in any comprehensive way.[36]

---

30. Ibid., 58.
31. Ibid., 59.
32. Ibid.
33. Ibid., 60 (italics in the original).
34. David Tonghou Ngong, review of *On Communitarian Divinity: An African Interpretation of the Trinity, Review and Expositor* 100, no. 4 (2003): 730–32.
35. Akintunde E. Akinade, review of *On Communitarian Divinity: An African Interpretation of the Trinity, Missiology* 24 (October 1996): 539.
36. See Bengt Hoffman, review of *On Communitarian Divinity: An African Interpretation of the Trinity, Journal of Ecumenical Studies* 33 (Spring 1996): 264.

Consideration of Ogbonnaya's proposal concerning an African interpretation of the Trinity, it seems to me, should proceed at two interrelated, yet distinct levels. On the one hand we need to examine whether his interpretation of Tertullian as an advocate of a communal, equalitarian understanding of the Trinity is in keeping with historical materials. Second, apart from that, we need to assess the potential contributions of this African reading of the Trinity from a communal perspective.[37] Since I am not an expert in the history of theology, I leave the first question mainly to my colleagues in the history department and will concentrate on the second one: How viable is the interpretation of the Trinity Ogbonnaya offers here?

Nevertheless, I would like to begin by discussing one historical question here, that is, with Ogbonnaya's quite novel revisiting of the ancient *homoousion/ homoiousion* debate caused by Arianism. What is unclear to me is Ogbonnaya's thesis that the Orthodox party advocated "an eternal ontological hierarchy" by arguing for an eternal generation, and thus it was no better than the Arian party according to which the "substance of one particular member was inferior to the other members of the Divine community."[38] I don't quite see why the Orthodox stance necessarily supports the hierarchical notion as such. The idea of generation, both in the East and West, has certainly been interpreted as meaning the monarchy of the Father as the "source" of the Godhead. Yet to maintain that the idea of eternal generation "generated" an ontological hierarchy seems unwarranted. However, one has to agree with Ogbonnaya's argument that regarding the equality he champions, along with many other contemporary theologians (such as Moltmann and Pannenberg, even though quite differently), the issue was not resolved by the Arian debate. Both parties built on a hierarchical notion: Arians in maintaining the inferiority of the Son, and their Orthodox opponents by interpreting the Father-Son relationship as that of the "source" and "derivation."

One of the main theses of the book is that Tertullian—against the more traditional interpretation in Christian theology—is a champion of an equalitarian view of the Trinity. Ogbonnaya contends that Tertullian's emphasis on communality and equality "was eclipsed . . . by the debates that ensued after his death, which fostered concepts of ontological hierarchy instead of equality."[39] What are we to make of this judgment? Ogbonnaya's contention will be left open until two

---

37. Here I see a parallel between Ogbonnaya's project and that of Miroslav Volf, who advocates a Trinitarian communion ecclesiology in dialogue with John Zizioulas, among others. While Volf agrees with the quite negative judgment of Zizioulas's critics as to the historical misinterpretation of patristic materials, Volf is still ready to take the communion ecclesiology of Zizioulas as a helpful starting point for his own Free Church–oriented doctrine of the church.

38. Ogbonnaya, *On Communitarian Divinity*, xiii. Ogbonnaya maintains that Arius based his idea of the inferiority of the Son on the statement from Tertullian's *Against Praxeas* "There was a time when the Son was not." Usually this declaration is taken as a quotation from Arius rather than an affirmation presented by Tertullian. Ibid.

39. Ogbonnaya, *On Communitarian Divinity*, xiii.

questions are addressed. First, if no historical evidence is shown as to how this "eclipse" took place, it can only be assumed. Second, Ogbonnaya's thesis itself, namely, that Tertullian himself (in contrast to his followers) advocated an idea of "ontological" equality, calls for critical scrutiny.

Ogbonnaya is too good a theologian to ignore the charge of subordination-ism routinely leveled against Tertullian.[40] Despite the claim that he believes he can offer a new perspective on this issue, his reasoning is hardly convincing or groundbreaking. Ogbonnaya contends that that while there is functional subor-dination, it does not compromise the ontological equality. The ontological is the function of shared substance; the concept of functional subordination is an "inherent part of community."[41] Ogbonnaya is convinced that the "idea of com-mon Divine substance helps Tertullian avoid an ontological subordination."[42] Yet the way this helps is not explained in his book. Sharing in the same divine sub-stance does not make Tertullian's view of the Trinity equalitarian, as Ogbonnaya argues (any more than is the case with, say, Irenaeus, who speaks of the Son and Spirit as the "two hands of God," thus subordinating them to the Father). Rather, the contrary is the case: *Even though* Father, Son, and Spirit share in the same sub-stance, there is subordinationism in that the Father is the ruler, albeit the One who allows his rulership be shared by other members. Ogbonnaya's own com-ment elsewhere seems to confirm my suspicion. Having referred to the saying by Tertullian that the Son and Spirit are understood as "instruments of God's might and . . . the power and entire system of the monarchy,"[43] Ogbonnaya then has-tens to add that because the Son and Spirit share in the substance of the Father, this does not mean subordinationism; rather, there is here a "plurality of rulers" or "authoritative functions" among the Trinitarian members sharing "similar sub-stance and, hence, power."[44] Again, this is nothing more than an affirmation by Ogbonnaya; he does not present the logic behind this reasoning, and it therefore calls for more elucidation to be convincing.

However, at the very end Ogbonnaya opens up a question that could have been critical in his discussion of the problem of subordination. He mentions that the concept of the Divine community as developed in the African worldview, on the one hand affirms individuality of the person, and on the other hand assigns different roles such as son and daughter vis-à-vis mother and father to a "temporal-functional" phenomenon.

A father is not a father always. The idea of Spiritual pre-existence in a State of Spiritual equality-de-ontologizes [*sic*] the concept of father or mother. In African world then there is a sense in which that one who [*sic;* "is"?] child

40. Ibid., 65.
41. Ibid., 63–64 (quotations on p. 64). On p. 85 he calls this subordination at the "historical-temporal-functional" level, while they are equal at the "natural, substantial, or ontological" level.
42. Ibid., 71.
43. Tertullian, *Against Praxeas,* as quoted in Ogbonnaya, *On Communitarian Divinity,* 66.
44. Ogbonnaya, *On Communitarian Divinity,* 66–67 (quotation on p. 67).

today in the future becomes parent of that one who is parent today. . . . One is not ontological [*sic;* "ly"] inferior just because one is child-son, daughter of [*sic;* should be "or"?] grand child [*sic*].[45]

Leaving aside the problem that arises with the idea of the father not being a father always (contra tradition, going back to Athanasius, who insisted the opposite in his defense of the deity of the Son), it would be profitable to pursue this whole line of reasoning—affirming the individuality of the person and also assigning different roles to a "temporal-functional" phenomenon—and to explore whether that could open up new vistas for dealing with the economic-immanent dynamic in relation to the issue of subordinationism.

Approaching the issue of subordinationism, not from the perspective of Christian theology as above, but rather from the point of view of African religions, one cannot but wonder if the concept of the "High God" and other gods/divinities—so enthusiastically embraced by Ogbonnaya as a way of relating the diversity in the Trinity to African culture—would speak to hierarchy rather than equality. At least, one needs to ask for more clarification on this issue.

Theologically, the most serious query in my reading of Ogbonnaya's *On Communitarian Divinity* has to do with the wisdom of applying the polytheistic concept of "gods" to Tertullian's view of the Christian God. For example, speaking of Tertullian's idea of the Father before creation existing alone and having "reason" within himself, Ogbonnaya paraphrases this in terms of speaking of "gods."[46] This is a problematic usage of language and less than helpful. The idea of the Trinity in Christian theology does not speak for a plurality of gods but rather for the relationality within the one Triune God. Even pluralistic Christian theologians such as Heim and Panikkar do not claim that the Christian God consists of "gods." Ogbonnaya further confuses rather than clarifies this issue by arguing that Tertullian's view of the Trinity is more "pluralistic" than that of other theologians. Yet he rightly refers to Tertullian's rebuttal of the charge of tritheism[47] and thus of pluralism. This self-defense by Tertullian alone makes Ogbonnaya's claim about the pluralistic nature of his theology self-contradictory. The meaning of "pluralism" in Ogbonnaya's thinking thus calls for more clarification. All in all, it would be more helpful to talk about the "communitarian divinity" (singular) rather than "community of gods" (plural) when speaking of the Christian God.

Regarding the meaning of the term "Trinity," Ogbonnaya contends that Tertullian operated both in immanent and economic terms. He mentions that Tertullian, as the first one to apply the term "Trinity" to the Christian God, referred

---

45. Ibid., 85–86. This passage is indicative of the criticism of Ngong regarding the numerous grammatical errors throughout this work and the need for a revised edition. Ngong, review of *On Communitarian Divinity*, 732.

46. Ogbonnaya, *On Communitarian Divinity*, 70–71. On p. 70 he for example writes, "The gods are no longer alone as community in time and space."

47. Tertullian, *Against Praxeas*, 1, referred to in Ogbonnaya, *On Communitarian Divinity*, 83.

not only to the economic but also to the immanent Trinity.[48] I am not saying Tertullian did not do so, but I am asking, What is the textual ground for claiming he did so? Ogbonnaya refers here to the manifold linguistic forms of Tertullian's Trinitarian discourse, well-known among students of this African theologian, such as images from nature, society, and family.[49] Yet these hardly address the question above; as illustrations at best, they reflect the way God's threeness is revealed to us in the economy of salvation.

Other related terminological questions arise from of Ogbonnaya's proposal. He makes the claim that Tertullian initiated a move away from "cosmological" to "ontological" language; yet he also mentions that Tertullian advocates economic talk about the Trinity. Two problems emerge. First, who are the theologians who spoke in "cosmological" terms, and second, what is the content and meaning of this way of speaking? What is the "cosmological" Trinitarian language referred to by Ogbonnaya? Moreover, this purported move toward ontological speculation into the inner life of God goes in a different direction than a focus on the economy of salvation. Ogbonnaya does not offer help here.

Another related terminological issue is the frequent reference to the concept of "substance." In Christian theology, that term is usually reserved for classical theism's[50] emphasis on God's unity as distinct from (but not opposite to) the more socially oriented relational understanding of the Trinity. As our discussion of Pannenberg's and Moltmann's theology, among others, showed in the social Trinity model—to which Ogbonnaya's view definitely belongs—the term "substance" is highly problematic. Perhaps Ogbonnaya is using the term more loosely, in its everyday meaning, rather than in its technical theological meaning.

As mentioned, Ogbonnaya's study is a first exploration into the form of Tertullian's view of the Trinity in an African perspective. As such it is a sketch and calls for more work.[51] One of the theologically most pregnant statements appears toward the end of the book, when Ogbonnaya makes a parallel between the biblical statement about God as Spirit, affirmed by Tertullian, and the idea in the African worldview of the Spirit as the basis of all that there is, "including the gods." This would come close to Tertullian's (and many other Christian theologians') idea of the Spirit as the "substance which is common to all the members of the divine community."[52] In addition, the related idea that the Spirit has the capacity for interpenetration connects with the relationality in the Triune God.[53]

48. Ogbonnaya, *On Communitarian Divinity*, 71.

49. Ibid., 59.

50. For discussion about the meaning of classical theism, see Veli-Matti Kärkkäinen, *The Doctrine of God in Global Perspective: Biblical, Historical, and Contemporary Perspectives* (Grand Rapids: Baker Academic, 2004), chap. 3 especially.

51. One of the obvious weaknesses of the book is its unusually bad grammar and at times unpolished language. This is also noted by reviewers such as Ngong, review of *On Communitarian Divinity*, 732.

52. Tertullian, *Against Praxeas* 5, referred to in Ogbonnaya, On Communitarian Divinity, 71.

53. Ogbonnaya, *On Communitarian Divinity*, 71–72.

How these ideas would correlate with the idea of the God as Spirit in Christian theology in general and in theologies such as that of Pannenberg in particular would make an exciting further study.

My final comment has to do with the overall approach of Ogbonnaya. While I have applauded his creative study in considering the ancient theology of the North African Tertullian in relation to even more ancient Egyptian and other African views of God, I also wonder—and this question has been raised especially with my African students—if it would be much more relevant to tap into more recent resources in the African worldview, culture, and religiosity. Isn't it also a fact that Egypt is quite a marginal culture for Africa in general and certainly to the contemporary African way of life? Communality, the main virtue Ogbonnaya finds in Tertullian and in ancient African religions, both monotheistic and polytheistic, can be found everywhere in Africa apart from these quite distant sources.

PART FIVE
TOWARD A RENEWED
TRINITARIAN THEOLOGY
IN THE WORLD CONTEXT

Chapter 27

An Assessment and Agenda

"THE HOLY TRINITY: THE STATE OF THE QUESTION"[1]

Rather than trying to summarize the innumerable insights and lessons of the long and winding story of Trinitarian theology in biblical, historical, and contemporary settings, my aim in this final chapter is to take a bird's-eye view and distill the key contributions emerging from this discussion. Even here I take the liberty of being selective and discussing those perspectives that I see as groundbreaking and critical for the continuing global conversation. In addition to registering those contributions, I will also continue the dialogue by suggesting some further tasks and pointing to some challenges as well as possible directions the discourse may take in the near future. In other words, this final chapter represents one theologian's assessment of the key contributions and insights emerging out of a wide global conversation.

---

1. The heading above is from Gerald O'Collins, SJ, "The State of the Question," in *The Trinity*, ed. Stephen T. Davis, Daniel Kendall, SJ, and Gerald O'Collins, SJ (Oxford: Oxford University Press, 1999), 1.

It might be beneficial to list those key contributions:

- Trinity as the structure of theology
- Trinity revealed in the biblical narrative
- Trinity as communion
- Trinity and Christology
- Economic and immanent Trinity
- Threeness and oneness
- Trinity and the question of identity
- Trinity as social critic
- Trinity in a particular context
- Renaming the Triune God

This is not in any way a comprehensive or final list of topics. Postmodernity reminds us constantly that rather than trying to be comprehensive ("universal"), a particular and perspectival approach is preferred ("Small is beautiful"). One of the purposes of this chapter is to encourage continuing reflection on the topic of the Trinity and so invite theologians from various contexts to join the conversation.

"THE TRINITY: THEOLOGY'S STRUCTURAL MOTIF"[2]

The discussion of Trinitarian developments in this book confirms the observation of Stanley J. Grenz that "the rebirth of trinitarian theology must be presented as one of the most far-reaching theological developments of the century."[3] The reverberations of the Trinitarian renaissance at the end of the second millennium heralded by the landmark work of Claude Welch, *In This Name: The Doctrine of the Trinity in Contemporary Theology* (1952),[4] are felt all over, from theology to liturgy to social issues such as community and equality to Christianity's relation to other religions. The preceding pages stand as a testimony to that claim.

These developments have meant nothing less than the rise of the Trinity into the very center of Christian faith and piety. Once a revered, yet largely neglected dogma or at best "of edificatory value to those who already believe,"[5] there is a growing consensus that the Trinity is both a profound confession of faith at the heart of Christianity and a guide to and the structure of all genuine Christian expressions of faith. To quote the programmatic words of Colin Gunton:

2. The heading above is from Stanley J. Grenz and John R. Franke, *Beyond Foundationalism: Shaping Theology in a Postmodern Context* (London/Louisville, KY: Westminster John Knox Press, 2001), 166 (for chap. 6).

3. Stanley J. Grenz, *Rediscovering the Triune God: The Trinity in Contemporary Theology* (Minneapolis: Fortress, 2004), 1.

4. Claude Welch, *In This Name: The Doctrine of the Trinity in Contemporary Theology* (New York: Scribner's Sons, 1952).

5. Colin Gunton, *The Promise of Trinitarian Theology*, 2nd ed. (Edinburgh: T & T Clark, 1997), 7.

"Because the theology of the Trinity has so much to teach about the nature of our world and life within it, it could be the centre of Christianity's appeal to the unbeliever,"[6] as well as, of course, the believer!

From the very beginning of the theological enterprise in the early Christian community, the Trinity has served as the basis for structuring theology. Ancient creeds follow Trinitarian patterns, from the Father as Creator to the Son as Redeemer to the Spirit as Sanctifier. Even where a more "monotheistic" mind-set was at times blurring the significance of the Trinity as a specifically *Christian* approach to religion and the world, a Trinitarian substructure behind Christian theology and liturgy, especially some prayers, kept the church from neglecting this most cardinal truth of ours.

While Karl Rahner set the direction for much of the renewal of contemporary Trinitarian reflection, he himself failed to structure his own theology in a Trinitarian way. Barth was more successful, but his placing of the doctrine in the prolegomena is not totally satisfactory since Trinity cannot be just assumed in post-Enlightenment theology and in a religiously pluralistic environment. The starting point for the legitimacy of the Trinity needs to be won with the help of rational argumentation. Therefore, Pannenberg's approach, while not without its challenges (to be noted in what follows), is methodologically more satisfactory. He argues that while Trinity is not just a chapter in Christian dogmatics but rather an overarching structure, it cannot be taken fideistically. Instead, it needs to be related to the religiosity of the human person created in the image of God and to the history of religions as well as the Christian doctrine of revelation.

Asian theologians Raimundo Panikkar and Jung Young Lee have argued that Trinity is not only a structuring principle of *Christian* faith and Christian theology but also of reality itself. As long as that is understood as a distinctively *Christian* claim, one can hardly contest it. If the God of the Bible is the creator of all reality and the human being has been created in the image of the Triune God, then it is inevitable that imprints of the Trinity can be found in the created reality. However, to impose the Trinitarian structure on other religions—whether one calls it the cosmotheandric or *yin-yang* principle—hardly wins the favor of many followers of other religions. It still demands careful consideration of the alleged similarities between various religions' capacity to embrace Trinitarian faith, a topic to which I will return.

SALVATION HISTORY AND BIBLICAL NARRATIVE

The doctrine of the Trinity is not the product of philosophically speculative theology gone awry, but the outworking of communal Christian reflection on the concrete narratives of Scripture, which call for coherent explanation. For

6. Ibid.

this reason, the centrality of the Trinity in giving shape to theology is likewise demanded by these narratives, which witness to the revelation of God in Christ. The biblical narrative leads to the conclusion that the affirmation of God as the Triune One lies at the very heart of the Christian faith and is its distinctive conception of God. Therefore, insofar as the theological enterprise is embedded methodologically in the biblical narratives, a truly Christian theology must be Trinitarian in structure, and in this way theology becomes the study of the God of the Bible, who is the Triune One.[7]

For a long time it seemed that the focus on the Trinity would not only help make Christian faith more abstract by divorcing it from history but also make it oblivious of narrative. The doctrine of the Trinity would be just that, *doctrine*, whereas narrative and story would be the form of biblical revelation. Currents in Trinitarian theology have helped us avoid both pitfalls. Rather than being grounded on abstract speculation, the Trinity is anchored firmly in salvation history, the economy of God. And rather than relying on philosophical and speculative formal statements, the doctrine of the Trinity is based on the revelatory narrative of the Bible. Therefore, Pannenberg's critique of tradition, including Barth's conscious effort to avoid tradition's tendency to separate this doctrine from the biblical revelation, is basically correct. Trinity is not based on a formal, logical inference but on the unfolding of the biblical narrative, at the center of which stands the coming of the Son to inaugurate the kingdom of the Father in the power of the Spirit.

Yet at the same time one needs to remind Pannenberg of the obvious fact that if we follow the unfolding of the biblical narrative, the revelation of one God is introduced first and only then comes the revelation of the one God as three. Even when Pannenberg's counterargument about the primacy of the future, based on the proleptic confirmatory significance of Jesus' resurrection, is acknowledged, in my opinion there is nothing wrong in Christian theology's making the one God the first chapter and then moving to consideration of the three. The only potential danger in that order is that it may push the doctrine of the Trinity into the margin—as it has done since the Middle Ages.

Another Lutheran, Jenson, has been one of the key voices reminding us of the significance of the narrative. The unfolding of the Trinitarian narrative in the biblical revelation is a drama of God. Like any genuine drama, it has elements of surprise; nevertheless—as Jenson helpfully reminds us—this real drama, being the drama of God, is not likely to be frustrated in its final result. While the final manifestation of the identity of the biblical God is yet to be seen in the eschaton, we know enough to trust that this God is in control of the twists and turns in the dramatic story.

7. Grenz and Franke, *Beyond Foundationalism*, 177.

"FROM THE ONE SUBJECT TO THE THREE PERSONS"[8]: THE RISE OF COMMUNION THEOLOGY

If there is one crucial development concerning the Trinity on which almost all Christian theologians are currently in agreement, it is the rise to prominence of the understanding of God as communion. As both the historical and contemporary discussion above clearly showed, there has been a definite shift in Christian theology from considering the God of the Bible as one subject to seeing God as Father, Son, and Spirit, an eternal communion of love. Barth and Rahner paved the way, and the Orthodox John Zizioulas, as well as a number of Western theologians such as Jürgen Moltmann, Wolfhart Pannenberg, Elizabeth Johnson, Catherine Mowry LaCugna, Leonardo Boff, and Millard J. Erickson, developed it further.

The idea of God as communion indicates simply the biblical notion of God as love, who shares and is related. Relationality between Father, Son, and Spirit and by extension between the Triune God and the world, rather than the idea of the one God as self-contained monad, is indeed a biblical and theologically correct way of speaking of the Christian God. The implications of this relational communion theology have been applied with enthusiasm to other theological and spiritual topics such as theological anthropology, Christology, prayer, and other religions, to name just a few.

The move to relationality is also in keeping with the dynamic understanding of reality and the human being as well as human community in late modernity. Speaking of postmodern insight for Trinitarian thought, Cunningham mentions relationality as first (along with embodiment and rhetoric).[9] The concepts of isolation, individualism, and independence are children of modernity. Over against the typical modernist bias to classify and categorize everything into distinct units (only think of the methods of the natural sciences), postmodernity speaks of relationality, interdependence, becoming, emerging, and so on. In this changing intellectual atmosphere, the value of communion theology is being appreciated in a new way:

> To speak of "Father" or "Son" is not to speak of an individual who is potentially isolated from other individuals; rather, the two terms specify *relations* that depend absolutely on *each other* for their meaning. There can be no child without a parent, but neither can there be a parent without a child: the two terms are tied together into a knot of mutual causation and interdependence.[10]

---

8. The first part of the heading above is from Stanley J. Grenz, *The Social God and Relational Self: A Trinitarian Theology of the Imago Dei* (Louisville, KY: Westminster John Knox Press, 2001), 23 (chap. 1).

9. David S. Cunningham, "The Trinity," in *The Cambridge Companion to Postmodern Theology,* ed. Kevin J. Vanhoozer (Cambridge: Cambridge University Press, 2003), 187.

10. Ibid., 189.

While hardly a uniquely postmodern idea, the mutual *relationship* between Father and Son—an insight emphasized by Athanasius of old—is but one example of the thoroughly relational nature of God as communion. "In sum, then, postmodernism's emphasis on complex relationality . . . has made it easier for theologians to think through the fundamentally relational nature of God that is inscribed in the doctrine of the Trinity. In the process, ancient claims about the Trinity's co-equality, co-eternity, and mutual reciprocity are being recovered and reendowed with a fullness of meaning and significance that had been largely obscured in the modern era."[11]

Along with relationality, postmodernism affirms difference and thus offers another corrective to modernity, with its love of universal claims. Communion theology, much more than a "monotheistic" view of God, makes room for and celebrates diversity and difference. Father, Son, and Spirit, while one (Deut. 6:4), speak for diversity (1 Cor. 12:4–6).

Ironically, the celebration of difference helps Christian theology to highlight the importance of particularity. The "universal" claims of the gospel revealing the Creator God who is Redeemer of the world in the power of the Spirit are anchored not in a "natural theology" but rather in a particular story of the Man of Nazareth, his death, glorious resurrection, and ascension to the right hand of the Father; the subsequent pouring out of the Spirit; and the formation of a community of God made of diverse communities.[12]

Considering the God of the Bible as loving communion also helps Christian theology to move beyond the mistaken idea of God as one who is simple, unchangeable, and incapable of suffering. Love participates. Love relates. Love shares joys and sorrows. Love is concerned. This is the portrait of the God in the Bible: the Father who seeks the lost, the Son who gives up his life, the Spirit who groans within the believers and in creation. Moltmann's and others' critique of the passionless God of classical theism is indeed in need of radical revision. Going back to the dynamic biblical testimonies about God is the first step in that revisionary work.[13]

CHRIST IN THE TRINITY

David S. Cunningham, writing on the Trinity from a decisively postmodern perspective, makes the simple yet profound statement that what is distinctive about Christians and their belief in the Trinity is that

> unlike the adherents of other faiths, Christians believe that God has entered fully and directly into the created order, and has become *concretely embodied*

---

11. Ibid., 190.
12. See also ibid., 190.
13. For beginners, see Veli-Matti Kärkkäinen, *The Doctrine of God: A Global Introduction* (Grand Rapids: Baker Academic, 2004), part 1.

in the world, in two ways: God became incarnate in the womb of a Jewish woman named Mary; she gave birth in Palestine some two thousand years ago, and her child was named Jesus. In addition, God has also been poured out on the world, into the communities of the believers known as Israel and the church; this concrete embodiment of God is called the Holy Spirit.[14]

Out of this Cunningham draws the all-important theological conclusion: "These two concrete manifestations of God are considered sufficiently different from the One who forever dwells in "light inaccessible" that the designation "monotheism" may simply be inadequate as a description of the Christian faith. For Christians, the one God is also three.[15]

Embodiment brings incarnation, and thus Christology stands at the center of Trinitarian theology. In mapping out the contemporary scene of international and ecumenical reflection on the Trinity, the Roman Catholic Gerald O'Collins, SJ, makes this pointed statement: "In the 'bad old days' one could write a christological study and largely leave out the Trinity, and—vice versa—one could write a trinitarian study that made little or no reference to Jesus of Nazareth. Among other defects, such non-trinitarian christologies normally ignored the eschatological character of Christian faith: that final return of all people and things to the Father through the mission of the Son and the Spirit."[16]

Both Moltmann and Pannenberg, in their own respective ways, have helped contemporary theology return Christology to the center of Trinitarian theology. What Moltmann did was to take the cross, the unity-in-diversity—the Father giving over, the Son submitting to, and the Spirit emerging out—as the basis of Trinitarian theology. Pannenberg looked at not only the cross and resurrection but also the whole history of Jesus of Nazareth, yet from the perspective of his resurrection, as the starting point and foundation of the Trinity. Further reflection is needed to clarify some details. Both agree that without Christ there is no Trinity, and vice versa: no Trinity without Christology. Consequently, the question of Christology, especially an affirmation of Christ's divinity in any traditional sense, becomes a major challenge to religious pluralists and others who have so radically revised Christology that it has placed itself outside the Christian canons: "Apart from the divine identity of Jesus as the Son there could not be a Trinity— at least not in the traditional Christian sense. The concept of Trinity expresses the idea that the three Persons that make it up are fully divine: God the Father, God the Son, and God the Holy Spirit."[17]

In light of the centrality and indispensable nature of history to Christology and thus to the Trinity, I find the approaches of theologians such as Panikkar and Ninian Smart and Steven Konstantine to be unsatisfactory. The dismissal of the

14. Cunningham, "The Trinity," 186.
15. Ibid.
16. O'Collins, "State of the Question," 3.
17. Craig C. Evans, "Jesus' Self-designation 'the Son of Man' and the Recognition of His Divinity," in Davis, Kendall, and O'Collins, Trinity, 29.

need to pursue the historical basis for christological statements undermines the uniqueness of Christian claims about Christ and the Trinity. By saying this, I am not necessarily determining in what way the uniqueness is best expressed; there is obviously more than one way. That discussion should be left to the theology of religions; yet that discourse is being frustrated when Christian theology too easily leaves behind the rigors of historical-critical inquiry.[18]

While I find Cunningham's above-quoted reference to the Holy Spirit's "embodiment" in the people of God, both Israel and the church, idiosyncratic, I also agree that traditional theology has not highlighted the importance of the Holy Spirit to Christology and Trinity in the way it should.[19] The slow acknowledgment of the importance of the Spirit to the Trinity is in keeping with the way the *doctrine* of the Trinity took shape. As the historical investigation revealed, for some time the relation of the Son to the Father preoccupied early theologians. Yet with the Eastern Fathers (the three Cappadocians and Athanasius), the divinity of the Spirit was established. Only much later was the integral relationship between the Spirit and Christ acknowledged, and here again the Eastern theologians were on the forefront: Zizioulas, building on the work of Lossky and other theologians in the East, spoke of the importance of the Spirit to the history and meaning of Christ. All this is needed to construe a fully biblical and theological interpretation of the Trinity.

THE ECONOMIC AND IMMANENT TRINITY

Rahner's rule puts it succinctly: we ascend from the economy to theology. We know God from God's works—adapting the famous christological rule of Philipp Melanchthon: "To know Christ is to know his benefits." This is yet another needed check and balance for Christian theology, lest it become carried away by a constant tendency toward speculation and abstract philosophical fantasies. Observing the deeds of God in reverence and humility—staying close to the worshiping church in its joy and sorrow, victory and humiliation—is a proper way to learn more about the theology of the Trinity.

All contemporary theologians agree that economy/history is the proper—and indeed, the only—place to begin the knowledge of God. It is also the end of the knowledge of God in the sense that going anywhere else may lead us into idolatry at its worst or fanciful and wishful dreaming at its best. Yet here the roads diverge. Not all contemporary theologians are willing to speak of the "Trinity and the eternal 'history' of God."[20] There are some who consider his-

---

18. See further Veli-Matti Kärkkäinen, *Trinity and Religious Pluralism: The Doctrine of the Trinity in Christian Theology of Religions* (Aldershot, UK: Ashgate, 2004), 169–73, and more widely, 164–84.

19. O'Collins, "State of the Question," 4.

20. Adapted from a heading in Grenz and Franke, *Beyond Foundationalism*, 174.

tory as the end in a more limited sense, meaning that the history of the world is the only thing we can speak of when we speak of the Triune God. While theologians who approach this conclusion—both LaCugna and Moltmann—are getting quite ambiguous when asserting this view, there is a tendency to stop at the border of history and not say much, if anything, about the divine life itself. Could we—and more importantly, should we—say anything about the eternal "history" of God? Even with all our human limitations and potential errors, I think we should. If Trinitarian theologians shy away from that reverent enterprise, who will do it? Biblical writers—against the prejudices of some contemporary interpreters—did say something about the inner life of the Deity. They didn't dwell on it, nor were they anything like systematic about it. Yet speak they had to:

> The biblical narrative speaks of three historical encounters with God: with the one God of Israel, with Jesus the incarnate Son, and with the Spirit as the manifestation of the ongoing presence and guidance of God in the community and in the world. While the constitutive narratives of the Christian tradition bear witness to the engagement of God with the world, they also point beyond this encounter to the eternal divine life. In addition to acting in the history of the world, the biblical materials view God as having a "history.". . . In other words, God has an internal "history" (the inner divine life) as well as an external history (God's actions and engagement with the world). The narratives of scripture invite theologians to take account of both the internal and external aspects of God's life and to think through the details and the implications of this history.[21]

There are some contemporary theologians such as the feminist Johnson who begin the Trinitarian theology "from below," yet ascend from there "to above." Another liberationist, Boff, follows the same route. Pannenberg does the same even though for different reasons. In my opinion, that is the way to go. A parallel from Christology is helpful here: with all the significance of beginning with the "from below" method, a distinctively *Christian* theology of Christ can never stop at the border of history. If it does, it is neither historical nor Christian. It is nonhistorical in the sense that it has capitulated to the strictures of the modernist worldview, which hinders many theologians and especially biblical scholars from opening up to the possibility of the transcendence. In doing so, theology becomes reductionistic and violates in principle the nature of the object of its study. It is non-Christian in the sense that—unlike Pannenberg, who is a stalwart defender of historical-critical methodology—it offers a general history-of-religions interpretation of the Christ event rather than a theological interpretation of the meaning of the Christ story for Christianity and therefore also for the rest of the world (if the biblical God is, as Christianity claims, the Creator of all). Barth was right when insisting—against the long tradition of classical liberalism

---

21. Ibid., 175.

and the Enlightenment—that "trinitarian theology is the story of God and God's actions in the world, which finds its ultimate center in Christ."[22]

At the same time we must acknowledge that theologians such as Moltmann and LaCugna need a reminder from Pannenberg not to conflate the immanent Trinity with the economic Trinity. Older theology certainly missed much by making the opposite error of speaking about the immanent Trinity rather independently from the economic Trinity. While Rahner's rule is a helpful methodological guide, like any theological rule it needs to be handled with care. If the immanent Trinity is indeed being incorporated into the economic in the way some of these theologians are doing, it puts the freedom of God and of God's grace in danger of being compromised. Merely mentioning that danger and yet dismissing it is not a theologically satisfactory response.

Why should Christian theology fail by stopping at the border of history or subsuming the immanent Trinity into the economic? There are no compelling biblical or theological reasons for doing so, but there are compelling reasons to avoid those errors and still follow the rule of Rahner, taking it as predominantly epistemological. Otherwise, we let abstract and fancy speculation in the back door while the front door has been closed to older theology's tendency in that direction. If we subsume the immanent Trinity into the economic, we claim to know more about the inner life of God than we indeed do. The economy is a faithful way—indeed the only way—to know the Triune God, Father, Son, and Spirit. Being faithful, however, is not synonymous with being complete or comprehensive. By ascending from the economy to theology, we can only know so much. There is still mystery. There is still the unknown, as the apophatic tradition, both Eastern and Western, has always emphasized. Call it doxology or call it silence; I am not so concerned about that. What I am concerned about is the danger of the economy being lifted up to the place where it indeed is everything that we can say of God. By definition, the transcendent God can never be confined to immanent categories. LaCugna's and Moltmann's legitimate concerns about the abuses of the idea of a "God behind the God" can be addressed otherwise. Correcting errors of abuse doesn't have to lead to the other extreme.

When Grenz finishes his critical survey of and dialogue with leading contemporary Trinitarian theologians in the West, he sums up the economic-immanent issue succinctly:

> As the preceding story indicates, the golden thread that weaves its way throughout a century of trinitarian theological renewal is the question as to how theology can conceptualize the relationship between God-in-eternity and God-in-salvation in a manner that both takes seriously the importance of the latter to the former and avoids collapsing the former into the latter or compromising the freedom of the eternal God. If the twentieth-century

22. Ibid., with reference to David Ford, *Barth and God's Story* (Frankfurt am Main: Peter Lang, 1985).

conversation reached any point of consensus regarding this issue, it is that any helpful explication of the doctrine of the Trinity must give epistemological priority to the presence of the trinitarian members in the divine economy but reserve ontological primacy for the dynamic of the relationality within the triune life.[23]

THREENESS AND ONENESS

The long narrative of Trinitarian theology as presented in this book has shown it to be a central topic that has both shaped the discussion of and presented constant challenges to Christian theology. The question of the relationship between the immanent and economic Trinity has certainly become a burning issue. While the contours of the discussion are clearly marked, much work is needed to clarify this issue. Another obvious issue, which goes farther back in Christian tradition, is the relationship between the unity and diversity, the one and many, the threeness and oneness. In other words, how do we reconcile the Shema of Israel, which speaks for strict unity, with the shape and content of the Trinitarian salvation history as revealed—and taken for granted—in the Second Testament?

From the beginning of history, two dangers or heresies have helped to frame the issue. Modalistic options have focused so much on the unity that no real place has been left for threeness. From Sabellius's explicit modalism to Barth's (and, at least in Moltmann's opinion, also Rahner's) *alleged* modalism, debates have continued. Tritheism has been considered a more radical danger, and few, if any (in Moltmann's opinion, none) have fallen into that temptation, even though at times concerns about it have been raised, from the Cappadocians to Moltmann to Erickson to Boff, and so on.

In my opinion, real modalists are few, if any, in contemporary theology. The charge of Barth's (and Rahner's) alleged modalism is not to be taken literally, yet it contains a kernel of truth. As long as the starting point for considering the Christian God is so much based on the idea of the one subject or the one Godhead that Trinity becomes an optional appendix, modalistic dangers lurk behind. In the current theological climate that is no longer a danger. What about tritheism? I agree with Moltmann that no Christian theologian has ever been a true believer in three gods. Yet I also acknowledge that the rise to prominence of the social analogy on the one hand, and the sometimes quite harsh critique of earlier Western (Augustinian-Thomistic) oneness-oriented approaches on the other hand—both have made tritheism a danger to be acknowledged. Therefore I would call for a much more sophisticated analysis of the relation of threeness to unity than has been done. Just invoking the principle of perichoresis can hardly establish it; perichoresis as the hoped-for guarantor of unity has almost become a mantra (Moltmann, Boff, LaCugna, Erickson). Pannenberg's prolonged efforts

---

23. Grenz, *Rediscovering the Triune God,* 222.

to secure unity should be acknowledged, yet his lack of clarity also calls for a more precise formulation of the idea.

Pannenberg's approach gives some important clues. His willingness to speak of the divine essence is to be welcomed, especially coming from the theologian who both methodologically and materially gives precedence to threeness. The weakness of typical social-analogy advocates is that they are not able to reconcile the priority of threeness with the talk about one essence. The danger in that talk is obvious: it may easily lead to the idea of 1 [essence] + 3 (persons) = 4, but it doesn't have to. Another important clue is Pannenberg's relating of the unity to the attributes of God. This is a superb approach from the perspective of both considering attributes (an enterprise that often becomes abstract and unrelated to the Trinity) and regarding the question of the unity. The task of investigating how the issue of attributes—that is, how God relates to the world—is connected with the biblical idea of God as love and as spirit is a task still awaiting resolution. A corollary task is to clarify the relationship between these two main designations of God in the biblical account, namely, God as love and as spirit. While there is nothing wrong with trying to do that by using philosophical concepts, the way Pannenberg has done it in relation to the Cartesian concept of infinity is not the final word, though it has advanced the discussion.

For those non-Western theologians who opt for the social analogy, the question of the unity and threeness is a burning issue as well, as my dialogue with the African Charles Nyamiti, among others, has illustrated.

THE IDENTITY OF THE BIBLICAL GOD

Karl Barth made the programmatic statement that "doctrine of the Trinity is what basically distinguishes the Christian doctrine of God as Christian, and therefore what already distinguishes the Christian concept of revelation as Christian, in contrast to all other possible doctrines of God or concepts of revelation."[24] Barth failed to follow that lead further, though it has been picked up by others, especially Robert W. Jenson. He has spoken untiringly of the irreplaceable role of the Trinity as the criterion for distinguishing between the God of the Bible and the gods of religions.

> By its very definition, theology—the teaching about God—has as its central interest the divine reality, together with God's actions in creation. The chief inquiry for any theology, therefore, is the question of the identity of God. The Christian answer to the question "Who is God?" ultimately leads to the doctrine of the Trinity. The one God, Christians assert, is triune—

---

24. Karl Barth, *Church Dogmatics*, ed. G. W. Bromiley and T. F. Torrance (Edinburgh: T & T Clark, 1956), I/1:301. Likewise, A. W. Argyle notes that God is not specifically "named" in the NT; A. W. Argyle, *God in the New Testament* (Philadelphia: J. B. Lippincott, 1965), 9.

Father, Son, and Spirit, to cite the traditional designations for the Trinitarian persons—and consequently the confession of the triune God is the sine qua non of the Christian faith.[25]

Now that the question of the theology of religions—the relation of Christian faith to other faiths—is becoming a key concern for theologians, the implications of the identity question appear in an even more challenging light. The question of the relationship between the identity of God and the Trinity vis-à-vis the gods of religions is a complex and multifaceted issue. So far I have not seen it framed in a way that would help us move beyond the impasse.[26] I see at least three interrelated perspectives as critical in the conversation. First is the failure of those pluralistic theologians who for the sake of dialogue and tolerance make every effort to dilute the uniqueness of the Trinity in relation to other religions. Raimundo Panikkar, with all his theological sensitivities, tends to move to this direction; the same can be said of Ninian Smart and Steven Konstantine. The Roman Catholic theologian of religions Gavin D'Costa has offered a powerful critique against those failing attempts.[27]

Second, while resisting the naive attempts of modernist pluralisms to hide the uniqueness of the Trinity, one should also be careful not to cut off bridges. By making the Trinity an insurmountable obstacle to dialogue, Christian theology of religions only frustrates its own possibilities for dialogue. The attempt to build bridges and find commonalities is a lasting value in the Trinitarian theologies of Panikkar and Lee among others. Even where Panikkar's efforts seem to go beyond the contours of a specifically Christian theology of religions, his untiring desire to find Trinitarian structure in religions and in the whole of reality is a welcome effort. If the Triune God of the Bible—as all Christians agree—is the Creator of all reality, then the absence of any kind of "Trinitarian clues" would be unthinkable.

Third, in keeping with the second statement—and following in the footsteps of Pannenberg—Christian theology and philosophy have to resist the temptation to leave behind the *task* of correlating the uniquely Christian conception of God with the idea of God in philosophical theology. The first pages of the Hebrew Bible carry an everlasting reminder of the general idea of God (*Elohim*) and a uniquely Judeo-Christian covenant God (*Yahweh*). While many of the attempts of the philosophical theology of the past appear to be unsatisfactory, the task per se should not be dismissed. This task will protect against the widespread post-Enlightenment attempt to reduce the concept of God into the interiority of the

---

25. Grenz and Franke, *Beyond Foundationalism*, 169–70.
26. See further Kärkkäinen, *Trinity and Religious Pluralism*.
27. Gavin D'Costa, *The Meeting of Religions and the Trinity* (Maryknoll, NY: Orbis Books, 2000). D'Costa also speaks of failing attempts by some theologians of other religions, such as those coming from neo-Hinduism or Tibetan Buddhism, to deliver on their promises of tolerance and openness even though their views appear to be "pluralistic" and so in keeping with the ideal of modernity as exemplified most radically in the theology of John Hick. See further discussion of and dialogue with D'Costa's Trinitarian theology of religions in Kärkkäinen, *Trinity and Religious Pluralism*, chap. 4.

believing person, as happened most radically in classical liberalism. No wonder the Trinity lost its significance at the center of Christian faith and theology, as Schleiermacher's example illustrates. While Pannenberg might be overly optimistic about the capacity of Christian theology to rehabilitate the Trinity as "public truth" for a postmodern world, that enterprise in a more modest form is, in my own opinion, an indispensable task for a genuinely Christian understanding of the Trinity.[28]

THE TRINITY AS A SOCIOPOLITICAL CRITIQUE

Once a pious and mysterious doctrine, yet one unrelated to Christian life and the forming of community, Trinity has now become a main critical and constructive asset in many theologies at the end of the second millennium. God as loving, equal communion is indeed a paradigm for the right ordering of human societies, both religious and "secular." If God is the Creator of all reality, God's truth can never be confined to the religious sphere. It may take more sophistication than the Christian church has often had to infiltrate sociopolitical communities with the wisdom of the Triune God, yet in principle the critique coming from Moltmann, Boff, LaCugna, and others is a needed "practical" implication of this core doctrine.

So far, so good. However, there are also qualifications and challenges to the idea, widely embraced in contemporary theology, that "the Trinity is our social program."[29] Apart from the obvious differences—for example, the divine community is eternal, the human is not; the divine community may embody a full perichoresis, humans cannot[30]—there is the issue of the incapacity of a fallen, fragile, broken humanity to reflect the perfection of the Triune God. So the claims need to be modest and tentative. Even more important, those who are most vocal about the crucial role of the Trinity as social critic are also most radically opposed to all notions of power and hierarchy. Yet one can hardly contest the fact that the biblical God is presented not only as loving Father, a "persuader" of process theology, but also as omnipotent, powerful God. So the dialogue between those who argue for the legitimacy of hierarchy in the Trinity (Zizioulas) and those who absolutely oppose it (Moltmann, LaCugna, and perhaps Boff) needs to continue. Pannenberg affirms the monarchy of the Father, yet not subordinationism. Negatively, all these agree—and that should be affirmed—that subordinationism should be avoided. Yet how to negotiate a positive convergence is yet to be seen.

---

28. When speaking of Schleiermacher in the historical section, I acknowledged the fact that some of the newest studies (Stanley J. Grenz, among others) have helped reconsider the scholarly consensus according to which the Trinity was only a short appendix to Schleiermacher's *Christian Faith*. Even then my comment above stands on its own feet. Whatever Trinity meant to Schleiermacher and classical liberalism, it was not a public statement about the uniqueness of the Christian God.

29. As in the title by Miroslav Volf, "'The Trinity Is Our Social Program': The Doctrine of the Trinity and the Shape of Social Engagement," *Modern Theology* 14, no. 3 (July 1998): 403–23.

30. For a helpful discussion, see Volf, "Trinity Is Our Social Program."

We must also note that the biblical writers were no more likely than later Christians to connect the value of the Trinity with its "practical" meaning. While it is not a mistaken effort to reap the practical harvest of theology, we should oppose the growing tendency in Christian theology to assess the value of doctrines solely with regard to their practical relevance. While I agree with Colin Gunton and John Zizioulas that the Trinity has indeed everything to do with our world and our lives,[31] even apart from that it is a doctrine given to the Christian church to know and distinguish its God among the powers of the world.

THE TRINITY IN VARIOUS CONTEXTS

One of the main aims of this book is to argue for the importance of relating theology to a particular context. Christians read the *text* in—or literally with (*con*)— the *context*. The emerging non-Western theologies of the Trinity need to be both affirmed and given a fair hearing. Even where I have criticized aspects of the attempts by African, Asian, and Latin American theologians, I am enthusiastically affirming their efforts.

Like Trinitarian theologies developed in the West (including the Christian East), these new "contextual" theologies engage critically—and at times not so critically (again, similar to Western theologies)—their environment, culture, thought patterns, and religious heritage. This can only help continuing Trinitarian reflection. No theology has ever been done in a vacuum. The more faithful we can be to our location, the better we are able to serve our people in their need to have the Word incarnated in their own lives.

At the same time, I discern some challenges and weaknesses in these first-generation attempts at reading the Trinitarian doctrine in a non-Western environment. Some contextual attempts seem to show little concern for the value of Christian tradition, assuming that by definition something that has been believed by the Christian church so far is either oppressive and harmful or at least foreign or irrelevant to the context. At times an outside reader gets the impression that what these new Trinitarian theologies are producing is something new and unheard of. In most cases, though, it is not. Christian theologians have always struggled with relating their faith and theological reflection with the context.

For the "contextual" interpretations to develop and contribute more widely to the global conversation, a self-critical ethos is needed. On the one hand, there needs to be a more critical look at the context out of which and in correlation

---

31. John Zizioulas, "The Doctrine of God the Trinity Today: Suggestions for an Ecumenical Study," in *The Forgotten Trinity* vol. 3, *A Selection of Papers Presented to the British Council of Churches Study Commission on Trinitarian Doctrine Today*, ed. Alasdair I. C. Heron (London: British Council of Churches/CCBI, 1991), 19; Colin E. Gunton, *The One, the Three, and the Many: God, Creation and the Culture of Modernity*, Bampton Lectures for 1992 (Cambridge: Cambridge University Press, 1993), 149.

with which the Trinitarian reflection is carried on. When reading both Western contextual approaches such as feminist and other women's views or non-Western approaches, be they African, Asian, or Latin American, including various liberationist agendas, I do not see the kind of critical analysis of the limitations and problems of their own contexts that I see in their often one-sided critique of tradition. We badly need a critique of the Christian tradition's ways of constructing the doctrine of the Trinity. Those arose out of particular (Western, male-oriented) contexts. A similar kind of self-critical attitude is to be expected from those contemporary theologians who glean from the surrounding religious, cultural, and other resources in their particular location. In addition, one needs to be more critical about the resources in some approaches such as process theology or the *yin-yang* principle concerning their distinctively *Trinitarian* potential.

RENAMING THE TRIUNE GOD

With the rise of women's consciousness, a wide acknowledgment of the limitations of traditional ways of addressing the Triune God has emerged. While I argued above that the acknowledgment of the limits of tradition does not persuade me to replace Father, Son, and Spirit with other terms for speaking of God, I am also of the opinion that complementary ways are needed. The alternative ways of addressing God so far have not yet won a wide following for several reasons, such as that many of them are nonpersonal in nature or they are mainly functional. Both men and women need to collaborate in finding more appropriate names that are complementary, especially ones in keeping with tradition. Here I find the work of the feminist Elizabeth Johnson a good model.

However, it is not only women's consciousness that calls for investigating new ways of addressing the Christian God. This need also arises from the rapidly widening theological reflection from other liberationist agendas as well as among theologians from Asia, Africa, Latin America, and other cultures. Take ancestor-terminology as an example. What if African and Asian theologians would collaborate and find more appropriate and theologically suitable ways of utilizing this basic cultural element? Or what would come about if a more inclusive international team of theologians—men and women, Northerners and Southerners, representing a variety of theological and confessional persuasions were to join forces?

What needs to be said of new cultural expressions and their need to find appropriate ways of addressing God? I am thinking here, for example, of the so-called emerging church—or as it has also been called most recently, the "fresh expressions of the church." That new generation of the West is creating not only their own music and way of life, but also highly contextual ways of worshiping the one God. How would emerging global Christian theology of the Trinity speak to that new generation?

Or, to widen the context, what about African Independent Churches (AICs) with their highly contextualized spirituality and faith expressions, at times bordering on syncretism? How would they best name the Triune God?

Naming goes beyond formalities. Naming means doing theology; it is a creative and constructive task. To this creative task, as well as to the ever widening *global* conversation about various facets of the doctrine and spirituality of the Trinity—the heart of which is the myriad of *local* conversations—theologians and Christians from various quarters are being invited.

Index of Authors

Index of Subjects

Advaita, Advaitic, 249, 313–14, 328–39, 342, 344
African American theology(ies), 155–56
African Independent Churches (AICs), 354
ancestors, ancestry
 Christ as proto-ancestor, 359, 367
 Brother Ancestor, Parent Ancestor, 364
 significance in African life, 350, 353, 359, 362, 365
 as theological resource, 358, 361
 and Trinitarian persons, 359–60, 362–67
Apologists, 22, 24, 29–30
apophatic, 88–90, 186, 212n104, 339, 392
Arius, Arian(s), Arianism, 21, 27, 31–35, 58, 180, 185, 298–99, 302, 334, 375–76
asymmetry in divine relations. *See* hierarchy
Athanasian rule, 26, 60
attributes of God, 139n18
 abstraction vs. God's activity in world, 295n18, 296–97
 approach to topic, 184–85
 manifesting God's unity or essence, 136–39, 394

begetting of the Son, 31–32, 34, 134, 224–25. *See also* Son: as a creature; Son: preexistence
binitarian(ism)
 move from to Trinity, 9, 11–12, 14–15, 22
 of process theology, 157–58
 of *yin-yang* theology, 332
black consciousness, 355
both-and thinking, 313, 318–21, 323, 325
Buddhism/ist, 320, 327–28, 339, 343–44

change
 in God. *See* history; immutability of God
 theology of, 317–18, 322, 324
Christology
 as basis for doctrine of Trinity, 9–10, 101, 103, 129, 212–13, 237, 252, 389
 separation of Jesus and Christ, 342–44
Christomonism, 57n90
classical theism/theology
 affirmed, 99, 334
 drawn upon, 207, 303
 critique/corrective, 102, 211, 219, 248, 250, 272, 296–97, 304, 316, 318–19, 365–66
 reversed, 140, 184
communion
 ontological, 90–93, 95, 97
 theology, 39, 44, 93, 99, 146, 159, 179, 183–85, 206, 217, 238, 273, 276–79, 371–77, 387–88
 See also social analogy; social trinitarianism
community
 definitive for Trinity, 63, 114, 206
 of gods, 372–75, 378
 importance of, 159, 352–53
 inclusive, 157, 206–7, 278
 theology done in, 272–73, 300, 354, 371
 See also society
Constantinople, First Council of (381), 37, 40–41
consubstantiality, 40, 58
 of Son, 22, 34
 of Spirit, 35–37, 284
contextual theology
 development and methods, 257–59, 294, 307–9, 312–14, 320, 329, 355, 360–61, 365–68, 370–72, 375, 380, 397–98

8485533R0

Made in the USA
Lexington, KY
04 February 2011